Learn As You Go

Cue Cards

1. Press F1 or click the Help button.
2. Click the Cue Cards button.

Help/Glossary

1. Click the Search button.
2. Type a word, phrase, or glossary.
3. Choose Show Topics.
4. Choose a topic, then click Go To.

Close Cue Card/Help

- Double-click the Control-menu box.

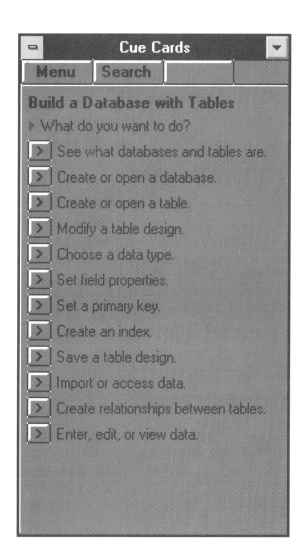

Cue Cards

| Menu | Search | | |

Build a Database with Tables

▶ What do you want to do?

- > See what databases and tables are.
- > Create or open a database.
- > Create or open a table.
- > Modify a table design.
- > Choose a data type.
- > Set field properties.
- > Set a primary key.
- > Create an index.
- > Save a table design.
- > Import or access data.
- > Create relationships between tables.
- > Enter, edit, or view data.

Computer users are not all alike.
Neither are SYBEX books.

We know our customers have a variety of needs. They've told us so. And because we've listened, we've developed several distinct types of books to meet the needs of each of our customers. What are you looking for in computer help?

If you're looking for the basics, try the **ABC's** series. You'll find short, unintimidating tutorials and helpful illustrations. For a more visual approach, select **Teach Yourself,** featuring screen-by-screen illustrations of how to use your latest software purchase.

Mastering and **Understanding** titles offer you a step-by-step introduction, plus an in-depth examination of intermediate-level features, to use as you progress.

Our **Up & Running** series is designed for computer-literate consumers who want a no-nonsense overview of new programs. Just 20 basic lessons, and you're on your way.

We also publish two types of reference books. Our **Instant References** provide quick access to each of a program's commands and functions. SYBEX **Encyclopedias** and **Desktop References** provide a *comprehensive reference* and explanation of all of the commands, features, and functions of the subject software.

Sometimes a subject requires a special treatment that our standard series don't provide. So you'll find we have titles like **Advanced Techniques, Handbooks, Tips & Tricks,** and others that are specifically tailored to satisfy a unique need.

We carefully select our authors for their in-depth understanding of the software they're writing about, as well as their ability to write clearly and communicate effectively. Each manuscript is thoroughly reviewed by our technical staff to ensure its complete accuracy. Our production department makes sure it's easy to use. All of this adds up to the highest quality books available, consistently appearing on best-seller charts worldwide.

You'll find SYBEX publishes a variety of books on every popular software package. Looking for computer help? Help Yourself to SYBEX.

For a complete catalog of our publications:

SYBEX Inc.
2021 Challenger Drive, Alameda, CA 94501
Tel: (510) 523-8233/(800) 227-2346 Telex: 336311
Fax: (510) 523-2373

SYBEX is committed to using natural resources wisely to preserve and improve our environment. As a leader in the computer book publishing industry, we are aware that over 40% of America's solid waste is paper. This is why we have been printing the text of books like this one on recycled paper since 1982.

This year our use of recycled paper will result in the saving of more than 15,300 trees. We will lower air pollution effluents by 54,000 pounds, save 6,300,000 gallons of water, and reduce landfill by 2,700 cubic yards.

In choosing a SYBEX book you are not only making a choice for the best in skills and information, you are also choosing to enhance the quality of life for all of us.

Understanding
Microsoft Access

Understanding
Microsoft® Access

ALAN SIMPSON

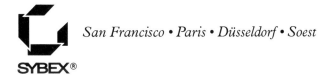

San Francisco • Paris • Düsseldorf • Soest

SYBEX®

ACQUISITIONS EDITOR: Dianne King
DEVELOPMENTAL EDITOR: David Peal
EDITORS: Doug Robert and Richard Mills
TECHNICAL EDITORS: Mark D. Hall, John H. Maurer, and Dan Tauber
BOOK DESIGNER: Suzanne Albertson
SCREEN GRAPHICS: Aldo Bermudez
ELECTRONIC PAGE LAYOUT: Deborah Maizels
PRODUCTION COORDINATOR/PROOFREADER: Catherine Mahoney
INDEXER: Matthew Spence
COVER DESIGNER: Archer Design
COVER PHOTOGRAPHER: Michael Lamotte
PHOTO ART DIRECTION: Ingalls + Associates
Screen reproductions produced with Collage Plus.

Collage Plus is a trademark of Inner Media Inc.

SYBEX is a registered trademark of SYBEX Inc.

TRADEMARKS: SYBEX has attempted throughout this book to distinguish proprietary trademarks from descriptive terms by following the capitalization style used by the manufacturer.

SYBEX is not affiliated with any manufacturer.

Every effort has been made to supply complete and accurate information. However, SYBEX assumes no responsibility for its use, nor for any infringement of the intellectual property rights of third parties which would result from such use.

Library of Congress Card Number: 92-62327
ISBN: 0-7821-1168-8

Manufactured in the United States of America
10 9 8 7 6

To Susan, Ashley, and Alec

ACKNOWLEDGMENTS

LIKE I always say, every book is a team project and this one is no exception. Many thanks to the folks at SYBEX who presented me with the opportunity to write this book. And for their patience in seeing it through.

Many thanks to SYBEX's editorial and production teams for their much needed, and much appreciated, support: David Peal, developmental editor; Doug Robert and Richard Mills, editors; Mark Hall, technical editor; Suzanne Albertson, book designer; Deborah Maizels, electronic page layout; Catherine Mahoney, proofreader; and Aldo Bermudez in screen production. Thanks also to Abby Azrael, Michelle Nance, John H. Maurer, and Dan Tauber for their extra help in getting chapters into production when things were running late.

Many thanks to other writers who contributed material to this book: Elizabeth Olson (Chapters 4 and 19, and the glossary), Kelly Gillespie (Chapters 14 and 18), and David Rhoades (Chapter 20 and Appendix A).

Thanks to Martha Mellor, and all the gang at Waterside Productions, for their support and management.

And of course, thanks to Ashley, Susan, and Alec for their patience and support through Daddy's long bouts with keyboard and mouse.

*C*ontents
AT A GLANCE

CONTENTS

PART TWO   MANAGING DATA

PART FIVE   SPECIAL TOPICS

INTRODUCTION

THIS MIGHT sound more like the start of a TV commercial than a computer book, but all I can think of to say right off the bat is, "Wow—what a program!" Microsoft has outdone themselves on this one. And aptly named the product as well. I personally don't know of any program that provides so much, well, *access* to so much data.

I'm not just talking about data stored in an Access database either. I'm talking about text, pictures, sounds—all kinds of data from all kinds of applications. And not just the stuff that's on your hard disk, but data from remote computers as well.

If you're a Windows power user who is looking for *more* power, you've come to the right place. Whether you're just looking for better, easier ways to "get at" information, or are looking for a means of developing your own full-blown custom Windows applications, you'll very likely find all the tools you need in Microsoft Access.

But I'm getting ahead of myself here. Surely those of you who are new to the database management game are already wondering what on earth I'm talking about. Don't worry, in Chapter 1 I'll contain my enthusiasm and give you a more detailed description of what database management is all about.

Who This Book Is For

Like Access, this book is geared toward experienced Windows users. That's not to say that you need to be a Windows genius to use Access. But, if you're just now making the transition from DOS to Windows, or just getting started with computers, you'll surely want to get your Windows "basic skills" down pat before you start using Access.

You can learn those skills from the *Getting Started* manual that came with your Windows (not Access) program. Or check out a book that's geared toward developing those skills, such as *The ABC's of Windows 3.1,* written by Alan R. Neibauer, also published by SYBEX.

New to Database Management?

In this book, I'll only assume that you know how to use Windows. It's not necessary to know anything about database management or programming to use this book. As far as database management goes, we'll start at square one in Chapter 1. As for programming—don't worry about it. Programming is definitely in the "not required" category when it comes to using Microsoft Access.

If you're new to database management, you may also skip the jargon-filled section that follows, and go straight to the "Learning the Ropes" section after that.

Experienced Database Whiz?

For those of you who are experienced DBMS whizzes and want to talk shop, here's a thumbnail sketch of what's new and not so new in Access. First, Access, like most database management systems, is based on the relational model, where data is stored in normalized tables. Therefore, your database design and querying skills will carry over quite nicely to Access.

But beyond that, you're likely to find the object-oriented nature of Access to be completely new turf. Just getting the hang of designing forms and reports takes some time and practice.

As an experienced developer, you may be accustomed to working in an environment where you write code to handle much of the "action" in an application. In Access, you'll surely find yourself writing much less code, and spending much more time creating forms, and developing macros that are triggered by events on those forms. In fact, unless your application is very specialized, you may find that you've finished creating an application without writing any code at all!

A word of advice to experienced programmers—don't "skip the interface" and launch right into Access Basic. Even though Access Basic includes all the BASIC constructs (even that dreadful GOTO command), the entire language has been revamped to manage Access objects. Therefore, little of the language will make sense until after you've learned about Access objects and the general interface for creating those objects, i.e., the stuff that's in *this* book.

Learning the Ropes

Database management is not quite like other applications that you may already be familiar with. In most applications, you tend to work with one "object" at a time, such as one spreadsheet, or one document.

In a database, you work with a variety of objects: tables, queries, forms, reports, and macros for the most part. These are all interdependent, and you need to learn about them in a certain order. For example, it doesn't make any sense to try to create a nicely printed invoice, form letter, or other *report* until you've learned how to create a table to store the text and data that's to be printed on that report.

Many people don't have the time (or the patience) for this kind of "linear learning." Unfortunately, there's really no way around it in databases. But on the bright side, Microsoft has come up with a tool to help make it all a little easier. It's called *Cue Cards*, sort of an online coach that helps you learn as you work. Once you've learned to start Microsoft Access, you can look inside the front cover of this book, and toward the end of Chapter 4, for more information on using the Cue Cards.

Features of This Book

This book offers several features to help you learn, and to find information when you need it, including:

- *Access in an Evening* (Chapter 2) takes you through a hands-on guided tour of Access, so you can get a feel for how to work the program in just a few short lessons.

- *Endpapers:* Look inside the front and back covers for quick reference to techniques and tools in Microsoft Access.

- *Notes, Tips, and Cautions* provide good ideas, shortcuts, references to related topics, and warnings that point out when you might want to think twice before clicking that mouse!

- *Fast Track* speed notes at the beginning of each chapter summarize important topics and techniques, and point you to the appropriate pages for more information.

- *Boldface text* helps you to find at a glance the name of the dialog box being discussed or the name of another program relevant to the procedure at hand. In step-by-step sections, I've also indicated by means of boldface any text that you are expected to type.

You'll also find references to Access's online help sprinkled throughout the book. You might think this lazy on my part, but I assure you, laziness is not the motivation. Rather, it's to your advantage to get into the habit of pressing F1, or clicking that Help button, whenever a question arises. More often than not, you'll find that the information that appears on the screen is just what you're looking for.

Undocumented Features, Workarounds, Etc.

Late-breaking news, undocumented features, and installation tips and workarounds are included in the *readme.txt* file that came with your Microsoft Access program. You can open that file using Windows Notepad or any other text editor.

I've also included some of that information in this book. For instance, the undocumented *Database Analyzer* is presented in Chapter 18. But for the real nitty-gritty stuff, like getting around problems in using Access with a third-party memory manager, your best resource for up-to-date information is either the readme file, Microsoft, or that third-party manufacturer.

About the Latest Update

Information about Version 1.1, which included a few bug fixes and addressed problems some users were having with the original release of the program, may be found in Appendix B at the back of the book.

PART ONE

Getting Started

What Can Access Do for Me?

fast TRACK

A form is   10

much like a fill-in-the-blank printed form, used for entering information into a table.

A query is   12

a means of asking questions about your data, or of looking up specific information, or of isolating groups or categories of information.

A relational database management system   14

—like Microsoft Access—has a major advantage over other types of applications, in that it lets you separate data into separate tables based on specific subjects, and then "mix and match" that information in any format you wish.

MICROSOFT Access is a powerful and yet remarkably easy to use computer program, or *application*, designed to help you store and manage information. It's a very flexible tool that can help you take control of virtually any kind of information. For instance, Access can help you to:

- Manage mailing lists and telephone directories

- Manage customer, sales lead, and membership information

- Handle bookkeeping and accounting information including general ledger, accounts payable, and accounts receivable

- Manage and fulfill orders, control and maintain inventory

- Manage a personal or professional library of information, including pictures, photos, sounds, and animation sequences

- Build and keep track of schedules, such as students in classes or goals in a project

- Store and analyze statistical and research data

What Is Microsoft Access?

You may already be familiar with word processing, spreadsheets, or other kinds of applications. Microsoft Access falls into a different category, sometimes called "database programs." More specifically, Access is a *relational database management system*. To understand what that means, let's break that lengthy description down into its parts.

A *database* is a collection of information, or *data*. You've probably worked with a "paper database" before—a file cabinet, a Rolodex file, or a shoebox full of index cards.

A database management system (abbreviated DBMS) is a tool designed to help you manage the information in a database. For instance, Microsoft Access can help you to add new information as it becomes available, update the information as needed, quickly alphabetize and categorize the information, compute instant totals, subtotals, averages, and other calculations, and print the information in a wide variety of formats. And perhaps most importantly, Access can help you find exactly the information you need, when you need it.

The term *relational* refers to how Access "expects" the data you're managing to be organized. A relation, as it's called in mathematics, is simply a *table* of information that's neatly organized into rows and columns. You've undoubtedly seen countless everyday examples of information organized in table format. Price lists, order forms, phone number listings, and airline schedules are just a few examples of information that's often organized into tabular format so that you can easily look up whatever information you need.

A relational database management system is one that is specifically designed to manage information that's organized into one or more tables. The requirement of having the data organized in a table format might sound like a heavy restriction, particularly if the information you want to manage *isn't* in a tabular format at the moment. But as you'll see, just about any kind of information can be organized to fit nicely into one or more tables. And don't worry—you don't need to know *anything* about mathematical relations to use Access effectively!

What Is a Table?

A table is simply a collection of information that's neatly organized into rows and columns. But before we go any further on that, we need to clear up a couple of buzzwords: In database management terminology, we refer to each row in a table as a *record,* and each column as a *field.*

For example, Figure 1.1 shows a small table of names and phone numbers with the terms field and record illustrated. The field names at the top of the table briefly describe what information is in each field, e.g., Last Name, First Name, and Phone number.

As you can see, except for the buzzwords, the Access table is just like the tables you see in everyday life. It has rows and columns, and the field names act as column headings to describe what's in each column.

What if the data you want to store *isn't* already stored in that tabular format? In that case, you do need to think about how you will organize that information into one or more tables. We'll get into that topic in depth in Chapters 3 and 4, but perhaps a simple example will help illustrate.

Suppose you want to take all the information from your Rolodex and put it into an Access table. Looking at a single index card, as in Figure 1.2, might not give you any immediate clues about how you might store this information in a table.

But if you don't think so much about the specific information on this one card, and instead think about the *types* of information on this card, you're well on your way to putting that information into a table format. The types

FIGURE 1.1

A tiny sample table of names and phone numbers, illustrating the terms *record, field,* and *field names*

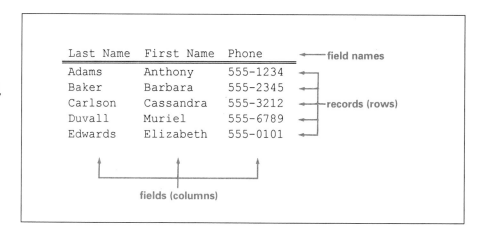

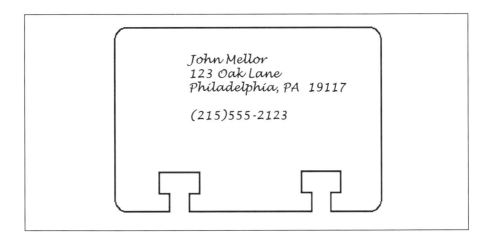

of information on this card include a name, a street address, a city, state, zip code, and phone number. If you look at other cards in the Rolodex, each of those would probably contain the exact same types of information.

The types of information that each card contains define the fields in the table. After you create a table with those fields, you'll find that you can type the specific information from each Rolodex card into a separate record. Hence, your Rolodex file might end up looking like the Access table shown in Figure 1.3, which currently has information from eight Rolodex cards stored in it.

The point is, even if the information you want to manage *isn't* organized in tabular format right now, you'll almost certainly be able to get it into that format without any trouble.

Last Name	First Name	Address	City	State	Zip Code	Phone
Mellor	John	123 Oak Lane	Philadelphia	PA	19117	(215)555-2123
Kenney	David	P.O. Box 123	Los Angeles	CA	92323	(213)555-2121
Mohr	Richard	47 Rainbow Dr.	Jefferson	SD	57083	(123)-555-9867
Jones	Janet	911 Carrera Way	Roswell	NM	88201	(432)555-9584
Schumack	Susan	65 Overton Hwy	Holland	MI	49423	(323)555-4938
Watson	Wilbur	Box 113	Bangor	ME	01876	(493)555-4039
Zeepers	Zeke	1417 Crest Dr.	Chicago	IL	60606	(434)555-3049
Ramirez	Raul	8018 Mill St.	Marlow	NH	03456	(515)555-5049

Table: Names and Addresses

Record: 9

Printing, Viewing, and Finding Information

Storing information in a table is, of course, only a small part of the overall picture. You also want to be able to view that information on the screen, print it in whatever format suits your fancy, and find the exact information you need when you need it. Most of all, you want this all to be as quick and easy as possible.

To help with these tasks, Access lets you create *reports*, *forms*, *queries*, and *macros*, all of which you can store in your database along with your tables.

What Is a Report?

A report is simply data that is printed out or displayed on the screen. There's virtually no limit to the ways in which you can organize information into a report. You can print simple lists, form letters, mailing labels, invoices, reports with totals and subtotals, …whatever you need.

Just to give you a couple of examples, Figure 1.4 shows some mailing labels printed from a table of names and addresses. Figure 1.5 shows a personalized form letter printed by Access.

N O T E   You'll learn how to design and create reports in Chapter 12.

What Is a Form?

With a "paper database," the term *form* refers to a "fill-in-the-blank" sheet of paper with a separate "field" for each item of data. With a computerized database, form means essentially the same thing, except that it appears on the screen. As with a paper form, you can enter and edit data

FIGURE 1.4

Data from a table printed onto mailing labels

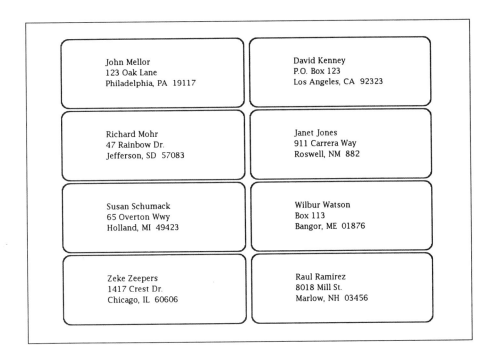

directly on the on-screen form. You can create forms to your liking, even make them look exactly like printed forms that you might already be using. For example, Figure 1.6 shows a form for entering and editing names and addresses on the screen.

Figure 1.7 shows a fancier example with a custom form that a bird-watcher might create to store and manage information about birds, including photos and recorded sounds.

NOTE Sounds can only be played on a computer that has a sound card installed. Double-clicking the sound icon plays the sound.

FIGURE 1.5

A sample form letter for a single record in a table

Orchid Jungle

1074 Ocean Breeze Way
Malibu, CA 91234
☎ (800) 555-1234

December 1, 1992

John Mellor
123 Oak Lane
Philadelphia, PA 19117

Welcome aboard!

Here is our latest catalog of vibrant, exciting orchids. Here you'll find flowers for every orchid enthusiast, from the beginning hobbyist to the serious collector. We have orchids that bloom in every season, so you need never be left without a flowering plant.

So why not browse through our catalog, and give us a call when you're ready to place an order. Our sales representative will gladly help you pick the best plants for your new, or established collection.

Thanks again,

Wilma Dendrobium

Wilma Dendrobium
President

What Is a Query?

A *query* is basically a question—a means of finding or isolating specific types of records in one or more tables. For example, with a query you could:

- Quickly locate the name and address of a particular person in a table

- Print letters and labels for individuals in a particular city, state, or zip code region

- If your table contains information about an inventory, print a "reorder report" for only those items that need to be reordered

FIGURE 1.6

An example of a
form for entering
and editing data one
record at a time. You
can develop forms to
resemble the paper
forms that your
information may
currently be stored on.

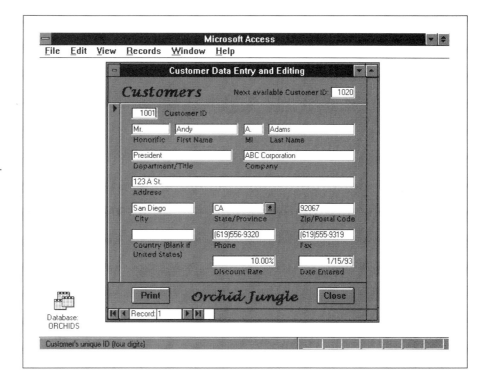

- If your table contains sales information, print a summary of all sales, subtotaled by product or date

- If your table contains account information, print different reminder letters for customers whose accounts are 30 days overdue, 60 days overdue, or 90 days overdue

N O T E   You'll learn how to query your tables in Chapter 7.

What Is a Macro?

A *macro* is a means of automating some task. For instance, suppose that it normally takes you 15 or 20 steps to print invoices and envelopes at the

FIGURE 1.7

A custom form
displaying data
from one record in
a bird-watcher's
database. Here the
table includes a photo
and recorded sound.

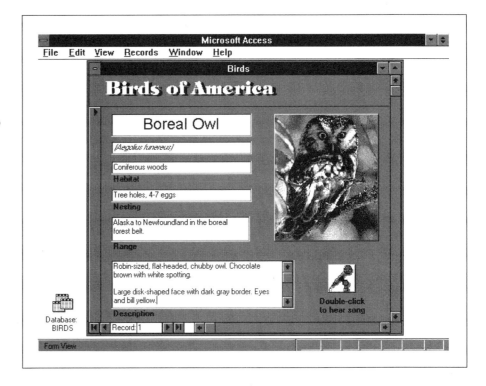

end of each month. With a macro, you could reduce that to one simple button click! In fact, you could probably develop a collection of macros to automate most of the jobs typically entailed in managing your database—all without any programming.

Managing Multiple Tables

If you've ever used a word processing application or spreadsheet, you may be thinking that you can do just about anything we've described so far with one of those programs. However, a relational database management system offers a couple of unique capabilities that are not easily duplicated by word processors or spreadsheets. One is the ability to create custom applications, as described in the next section. Another is the ability to manage separate but related tables of information.

Let's say you want to manage an entire mail-order business, keeping track of orders, products, and customer accounts. There's really no convenient way to combine that information into a single table. Instead, you'd need several tables. For instance, you might create a table to store information about products, as in Figure 1.8.

A second table could contain information about customers or accounts, as in Figure 1.9. (Additional information, such as street address, city, state, and zip code, is currently scrolled off the screen.)

Finally, a third table could keep track of orders. In the example shown in Figure 1.10, each record defines who placed the order (via the Customer ID number), what was ordered (via the Product ID), the quantity ordered, and the date that each order was placed.

FIGURE 1.8

A sample table containing information about the current inventory (products)

Table: Products

Product ID	Product Description	Selling Price	Units in Stock	Category ID
MO-100	Margo	$18.00	120	MOTH
MO-101	Playtime	$18.00	88	MOTH
MO-102	Goliath	$49.50	54	MOTH
MO-103	Dark Delight	$20.00	154	MOTH
MO-104	Peppermint Pleasure	$16.00	254	MOTH
PA-100	Midnight Giant	$28.50	54	PANSY
PA-101	Independence Day	$15.00	132	PANSY
PA-102	Piccadilly	$26.50	76	PANSY
PA-103	Blue Boy	$17.00	197	PANSY
PA-104	Goodnews	$17.50	32	PANSY
PR-100	Majestic	$40.00	100	PROM
PR-101	Pink Sensation	$25.00	67	PROM
PR-102	Breaker's Reach	$35.00	0	PROM
PR-103	Rolling Thunder	$32.50	65	PROM
PR-104	Polar Haze	$40.00	132	PROM
PR-105	Memory Lane	$32.50	298	PROM
PR-106	Jeweler's Art	$34.50	265	PROM

Record: 1

FIGURE 1.9

Sample table of customers, where each customer is assigned a unique customer number (or account number)

Customer ID	Mr/Mrs	First Name	MI	Last Name	Department/Title	Compan
1001	Mr.	Andy	A.	Adams	President	ABC Corporatio
1002	Miss	Marie	M.	Miller	Software Consultant	
1003	Dr.	Robert	K.	Baker	Radiology Dep't	St. Elsewhere H
1004	Nr.	Andy	R.	Zorro		
1005	Mr.	Robert	J.	Miller	Botanist	Evergreen Nurs
1006	Miss	Maria	A.	Adams	Author	
1007	Mr.	John	J.	Newell	President	Newell Constru
1008	Dr.	Susita	M.	Schumack	Neurosurgeon	Reese Clinic
1009	Mr.	Richard	R.	Rosiello	President	Rickdontic Lab
1010	Mr.	John	Q.	Smith		
1011	Dr.	Mary	K.	Smith	Graduate School of Business	Cal State L.A.
1012	Mr.	Frank	R.	Watson	Greenskeeper	Whispering Pal

Table: Customers
Record: 13

FIGURE 1.10

A sample table containing information about orders. The Customer ID and Product ID fields indicate who placed the order, and what was ordered.

Customer ID	Order Date	Product ID	Qty	Unit Price
1001	1/15/93	MO-100	1	$18.00
1001	1/15/93	MO-101	1	$18.00
1001	1/15/93	PA-100	2	$28.50
1001	1/15/93	PR-106	2	$34.50
1004	1/17/93	MO-100	1	$18.00
1004	1/17/93	MO-104	2	$16.00
1004	1/17/93	PA-101	1	$15.00
1008	1/16/93	MO-104	1	$16.00
1008	1/16/93	PR-100	2	$40.00
1008	1/16/93	PR-105	1	$32.50
			0	$0.00

Table: Order Detail
Record: 11

Breaking the information into separate tables makes it easy to manage the information independently. For instance, you can work just with customer information and not have to be concerned about products or orders.

Moreover, because Access is a relational database management system, it is easy to combine information from separate tables as needed. This gives you total flexibility in managing your information. For instance, even though in the examples above we've divided information about customers, orders, and products into multiple tables, we can still easily manage the information as a whole when needed, as though it were all in one table. For instance, even with the data split up into several tables, you could still:

- Print invoices (like Figure 1.11), receipts, and packing slips for current orders by combining information from the Customers, Products, and Orders tables.

FIGURE 1.11

Even though information about customers, products, and stock is stored in separate tables, you can combine information from these separate tables as needed. In this example, an invoice includes information from all three tables.

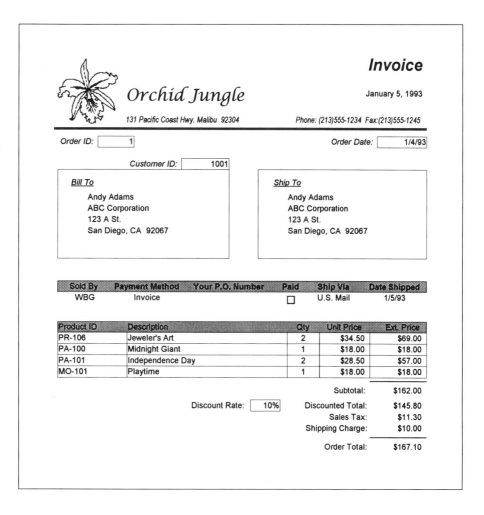

Invoice

Orchid Jungle

January 5, 1993

131 Pacific Coast Hwy. Malibu 92304   Phone: (213)555-1234 Fax:(213)555-1245

Order ID: 1   Order Date: 1/4/93

Customer ID: 1001

Bill To

Andy Adams
ABC Corporation
123 A St.
San Diego, CA 92067

Ship To

Andy Adams
ABC Corporation
123 A St.
San Diego, CA 92067

Sold By	Payment Method	Your P.O. Number	Paid	Ship Via	Date Shipped
WBG	Invoice		☐	U.S. Mail	1/5/93

Product ID	Description	Qty	Unit Price	Ext. Price
PR-106	Jeweler's Art	2	$34.50	$69.00
PA-100	Midnight Giant	1	$18.00	$18.00
PA-101	Independence Day	2	$28.50	$57.00
MO-101	Playtime	1	$18.00	$18.00

Subtotal: $162.00

Discount Rate: 10%

Discounted Total: $145.80
Sales Tax: $11.30
Shipping Charge: $10.00

Order Total: $167.10

• Create a custom data-entry form for entering new orders into Access, like the example shown in Figure 1.12.

• As orders are fulfilled, automatically subtract the quantity of each item shipped from the Products table, so you can get accurate up-to-date information about your inventory.

• Automatically use the Orders table to verify that there are enough items in stock to fulfill the order, and if not, place the order in a Backorder table, to be fulfilled when the stock is replenished.

FIGURE 1.12

You can also create a custom form on the screen to combine information from several tables. Here's a form for entering orders.

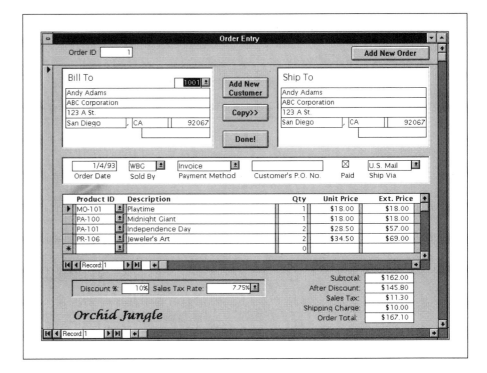

Building Applications

A second big advantage that a database offers over other types of applications is the ability to create *applications*. An application lets you automate virtually all the tasks involved in managing a database, reducing even complex tasks to simple mouse clicks.

One of the real advantages of custom applications is that they can make it easy for employees to manage a database even if they have virtually no knowledge of tables, forms, and reports. For example, Figure 1.13 shows the opening screen for a custom application designed to allow staff members to easily keep track of customers, products, and orders just by clicking the right buttons.

FIGURE 1.13

The sample opening screen for a custom application designed to help the user manage a customer database. The user of this application need only choose options from this screen, and doesn't really need to know anything about database management or even about Access.

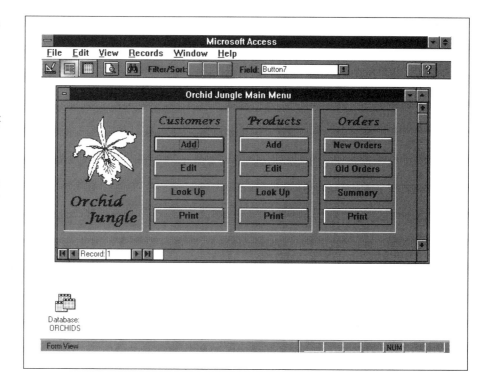

Access provides two tools for creating applications:

- **macros,** which we briefly described earlier, let nonprogrammers create powerful and sophisticated applications. There is no programming involved.

- **Access Basic,** a powerful, built-in programming language, is for programmers and power users who want total control over their applications.

Getting Your Feet Wet

In summary, suffice it to say that Access lets you manage whatever information you need to manage, in whatever manner you wish. In fact, the name *Access* comes from what this program does best: it gives you complete access to whatever information you've stored on disk!

The first step to doing anything in Access is, of course, to get a feel for the way it works. So in the next chapter, I'll take you on a quick tour of Access, and show you how to get around and get things done in just a few brief lessons. After you complete the lessons, you'll have a good feel for how Access works, and you'll be ready to dive into the more detailed information that starts in Chapter 3.

Access in an Evening:
Five Easy Lessons

fast TRACK

To add new data to a table   36

> Type the contents of the current field, then press Tab or → to move to the next field, or click the next field you want to put data into.

To close the current table   41

> and also save its current contents, choose File ➤ Close, or double-click the table's Control-menu box.

To create a new query   42

> to isolate certain fields and records, and/or to sort the data into some meaningful order, first choose the Query object button, then choose the New button. Choose the table(s) to include, then specify fields to view and/or fields to sort on. Optionally, you can also specify query criteria for isolating specific records.

To create a new form or report   48

> use the same basic technique you use for creating tables and queries. That is, choose the type of object you want to create using the object buttons in the database window. Then click the New button, and select from the options that follow. You can use the optional Wizards to help you create forms and reports.

To close and save any object   52

> choose File ➤ Close or double-click the object's Control-menu box.

THE FIRST step to learning any new program is simply to learn your way around, kind of like learning the major highways in a new neighborhood before you go exploring the side streets. This chapter takes you on a guided tour of Access's "major highways," to get you up to speed in a jiffy. First you'll learn how to create a database, and then you'll add some objects to it—a table, a query, a form, and a report.

Before You Start the Lessons

Before you begin these lessons, you should have already installed Access on your computer. If you haven't done this yet, turn now to Appendix A.

Also, you should already have your Windows basic skills down pat—including using a mouse, sizing, moving, opening, and closing windows, using dialog boxes, and so forth. If you're new to Windows, your best bet might be to spend *this* evening learning those Windows basic skills. You can use the Windows *Getting Started* manual or some other tutorial, such as my own *Windows Running Start* book (also published by SYBEX) to do so. Or, for a quick crash course, you can follow the Windows tutorial by choosing Help ➤ Windows Tutorial from the Windows 3.1 Program Manager menu bar.

Starting Microsoft Access

Step One, of course, is learning how to start Access. Here's how:

Microsoft
Access

1. Starting from the Windows Program Manager, double-click the Microsoft Access group icon (shown at left) to open that window.

2. Double-click the Microsoft Access application icon to start Access.

You'll probably see the *Welcome to Microsoft Access* screen, which offers some handy ways to get started. (This screen is optional, and you won't see it if somebody before you has disabled it.) Feel free to explore those options if you wish. But if you're ready to get started with these lessons now, just click the Close button near the bottom of this screen. You'll want to start these lessons from a clean Access desktop, as shown in Figure 2.1. Like most Windows applications, the Access desktop includes a menu bar, tool bar, status bar, title bar, Control-menu box, and buttons for sizing the window.

FIGURE 2.1

The Access desktop

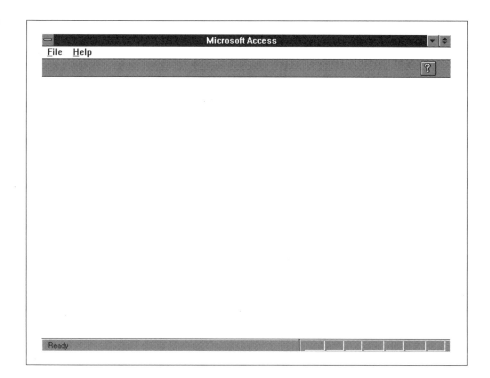

Following Our Menu Sequences

Throughout this book, we'll display a series of menu selections in an abbreviated format, as shown below:

Choose File ➤ Open Database

This simple format means "choose File from the menu bar, then choose Open Database from the pull-down menu." You can use any of the standard Windows techniques to choose the menu commands—by clicking commands with the mouse, or by pressing Alt plus the underlined shortcut key (we'll use a different font for that key instead of an underline), or by using the arrow and ↵ keys.

Exiting Microsoft Access

If at any time you want to stop one of the following lessons, make sure you exit Access before turning off your computer, to ensure that any work in progress is saved. To exit Access:

* Choose File ➤ Exit.

You'll be given the chance to save any unsaved work before being returned to the Windows Program Manager. If you're not prompted to save anything, rest assured that the work you've been doing will be saved automatically.

Lesson 1: Creating a Database and Table

A *database* is a collection of all the *objects,* including tables, forms, and reports, that make up a collection of information. Your first step in using

Access will always be either to open an existing database or to create a new one.

Creating a Database

In this lesson we'll start by creating a new database named *Lessons.* Assuming you've already started Access, as described above, here are the steps to follow:

1. Choose File ➤ New Database.
2. Type the name of the database, in this case lessons, in the File Name text box.
3. Choose OK (or press ↵).

You'll see an empty **Database:** window, as in Figure 2.2. The menu bar and tool bar also change to present some new options. The database window includes *object buttons* and *command buttons.* As you'll see soon, the database window will also list the names of any new objects you create.

N O T E   If the tool bar doesn't appear on your screen, choose View ➤ Options. Then choose the General category, click the *Show Tool Bar* option, and use the drop-down list button to select *Yes.* Then choose OK.

Creating a Table

The first object you'll probably want to create after creating a new database will be a table to store information in. In these lessons we'll create and use a simple table of names and addresses. Here's how to get started:

1. Click the Table object button, just to make sure it's selected.
2. Click the New button near the top of the database window.

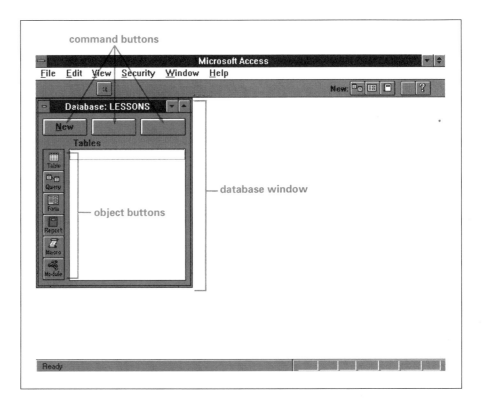

You'll be taken to the Table window, in Design View, where you can list the names, data types, and optional descriptions of fields you want to store in a table. Figure 2.3 shows how this window looks at first.

Defining the Fields

To define the structure of the table, you just need to type a field name for each field, then choose a data type. You can, optionally, enter a description of the field. Follow these steps to create the first field for the current table:

1. Type Last Name, then press Tab or click in the Data Type column just to the right of the current column.

FIGURE 2.3

The Table view
window, in Design
View. Here you tell
Access the name and
data type of each field
you want to include in
the table.

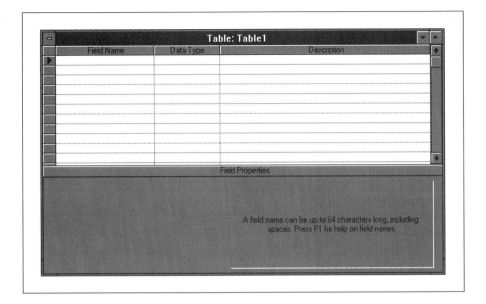

2. When the highlight gets to the Data Type column, a drop-down-list button appears. You can click that button to view available data types, as shown below.

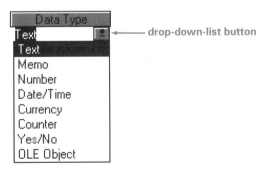

drop-down-list button

3. For this first field, choose *Text*.

4. Press Tab, or click in the Description column of this same row.

5. Type in the optional description, such as Type the person's surname as shown at the top of Figure 2.4. This description will appear at the bottom of the screen later when you start using the table.

6. Press Tab to move to the next row.

Following those same basic steps, you should be able to fill in the rest of the table structure as shown in Figure 2.4. Notice that we've used the Text data type for every field *except* the last field, Date Entered. Be sure to choose Date/Time when you're defining that field in your table.

NOTE Chapter 4 will discuss all of the available data types in detail.

If you make a mistake and need to make corrections, you can do any of the following:

• Click wherever you need to make a change, then type your changes. (Use the Backspace and Delete keys if necessary to delete characters.)

• If you need to delete a row, click the row you want to delete and choose Edit ➤ Delete Row.

FIGURE 2.4

Our sample names and addresses table structure in Design View

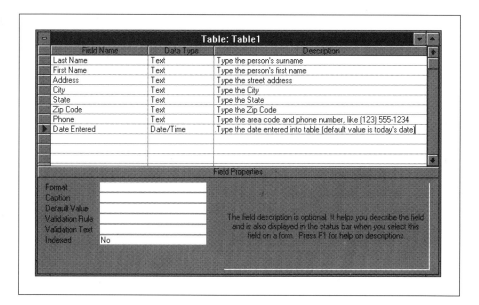

- To insert a row, move to the place where you want to insert a row, then choose Edit ➤ Insert Row.
- To undo your most recent change, choose Edit ➤ Undo, or press Ctrl+Z.

NOTE   For simplicity, our current table design is geared toward addresses within the United States. Chapter 4 shows an example of a table that can handle international names and addresses.

Changing a Field's Properties

In addition to giving each field a name, data, type, and optional description, you can assign certain *properties* to each field. In this sample table we'll assign a *default value* property to the Date Entered field. As you'll see later, this default property will be entered into the field automatically when you're entering new records, but you can change the default if you want.

To assign the current date as the default property for the Date Entered field:

1. Click anywhere in the row in which the Date Entered field appears (for example, click on the field name Date Entered). A triangular symbol appears to the left, indicating that this is the currently selected field.

2. Click in the text box next to Default Value in the lower pane (Field Properties) of the Table window.

3. Type =Date() into that text box, as shown in Figure 2.5. Be sure to include the open and closed parentheses, and don't type any blank spaces.

FIGURE 2.5

We've set the default value property for the Date Entered field to =Date( ) here. Notice the triangular symbol next to the Date Entered field, indicating that this is the field you're assigning a property to.

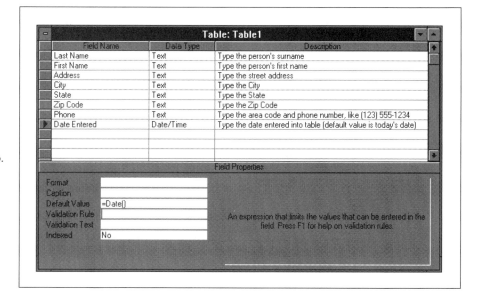

Saving the Table Structure

Once you've finished defining the table structure, you can save and close it:

1. Choose File ➤ Close. You'll see a dialog box asking if you want to save your changes to the table.

2. Choose Yes.

3. In the **Save As** dialog box that appears, type in a new name for the table, such as Names and Addresses.

4. Choose OK or press ↵.

5. Next you'll see this dialog box:

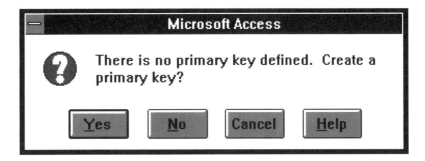

6. We'll discuss the role played by the primary key in Chapter 4. For now, just choose Yes to have Access create a primary key for you. The name of your new table appears in the database window.

You'll learn more about designing and creating tables, field properties, and the role of the primary key in Chapters 3 and 4.

Taking a Break

If you want to take a break at any time during these lessons, you can exit Access using File ➤ Exit. Then when you're ready to resume the lessons, just restart Access from the Windows Program Manager, then reopen the Lessons database by choosing File ➤ Open Database, and double-click on the *lessons.mdb* file name.

Lesson 2: Adding and Editing Data

Once you've created a table structure, you can open the table and start adding data.

Opening the Table

To open the **Names and Addresses** table:

1. If necessary, click the Table object button in the database window.

2. Click on the *Names and Addresses* table name, then click on the Open button.

TIP

In Step 2, you can also just double-click the name of the table you want to open.

When you first open the new table, you'll see the table in *datasheet view*—that is, with the field names across the top of the table, and a blank record beneath the field names, as in Figure 2.6. Some fields might also be scrolled off the screen, but they will scroll into view as you add data to the table.

You'll also notice a new field, named *ID* in this example, with *(Counter)* beneath it. This is the "primary key" field that Access created automatically. As you add new records to the table, (Counter) will change to a number that's increased by one for each record you add.

Entering Data

Entering data into a table is simply a matter of typing it in, then pressing Tab (or →), or clicking the next field to move to that field. If you have a Rolodex or little black book of names and addresses that you use regularly,

FIGURE 2.6

The new, empty Names and Addresses table open in Datasheet View. Access added the ID field as a primary key.

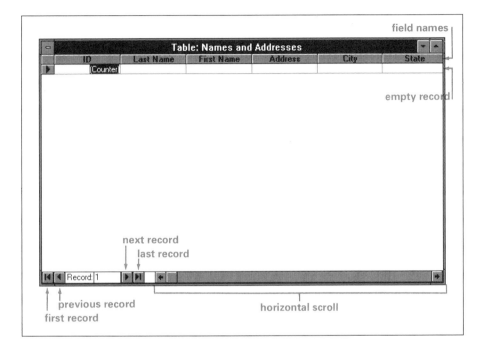

you might want to grab it now to find some names and addresses to include in your new table. Optionally, you can just enter some fictitious names and addresses. Either way, follow these general steps to add data to the table:

1. Press Tab, ↵ or →, or click on the empty Last Name field to move the highlight to that field. (You cannot enter anything into the ID field.)

2. Type a person's last name, such as Smith, or perhaps one of the last names from your Rolodex or little black book.

3. Press Tab, or →, or click the next field to move on.

4. Type a person's first name, then press Tab, or →, or click the next field to move to it.

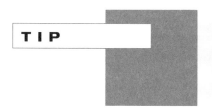

T I P

As you move from field to field, the description that you assigned to the field when designing the table appears in the status bar near the lower left corner of the screen.

5. Repeat this general process, filling in each field with some information of your choosing, until you get to the Date Entered field.

6. When you get to the Date Entered field, notice that the current system date is already entered for you. That's because we made the current date the default value for this field. To keep that default value, you can just press Tab to move on. Or, you can type in a new date, if you wish, and then press Tab.

When you've completed the above steps, you will have filled in one complete record, and the focus moves to a new blank record (except for the *(Counter)* indicator). Try adding five or ten records on your own now. Here are some basic guidelines to help you out:

* Be sure to take a look at the screen to make sure the focus is in the correct column before you type in data. For instance, you don't want to type a person's first name into the Last Name field, or a zip code into the City field.

* You needn't worry about typing names and addresses in alphabetical (or any other) order, since you can instantly resort the records however you want later.

* You needn't do anything to save a record after typing it in. Access saves each record as soon as you've finished typing it.

* If the data you enter into a field is wider than the field, the field's contents will appear to be "cut off." However, all the data you type will still be in the field. You can verify this by widening the field if necessary.

TIP

As you'll learn in Chapter 5, you can widen or narrow a field by dragging the bar that is to the right of the field name.

- If you want to copy the data from the previous record into the field you're about to type data into, press Ctrl+' (Ctrl with an apostrophe). You can think of this key as *Ctrl+ditto* since it copies data from directly above into the current field.

- As soon as you start typing in a new record, a pencil icon appears at the far left of the current record, and Access adds yet another new blank record, marked with an asterisk, beneath the current record. For now, you can just ignore that extra blank record below the record you're entering.

- If you make mistakes, you can correct them now or later using techniques described under "Editing Data" below.

Try entering anywhere from five to ten records on your own now, so you'll have some sample data to work with. Figure 2.7 shows some sample data entered into the table on a high resolution (1024×768) screen, so you can see all the data I'll be using in upcoming lessons. But again, feel free to use names and addresses instead.

FIGURE 2.7

Some sample data entered into the Names and Addresses table, shown here on a high-resolution (1024×768) monitor

ID	Last Name	First Name	Address	City	State	Zip Code	Phone	Date Entered
1	Smith	Michael	123 A St.	San Diego	CA	92067	(619)555-1234	9/6/92
2	Adams	Andrea	P.O. Box 3211	Jefferson	SD	57038	(515)555-2354	9/6/92
3	Smith	Zeke	12 Whispering Oak	Bothell	WA	98011	(212)555-9302	9/6/92
4	Baker	Barbara	65 Rainbow Dr.	Roswell	NM	88201	(313)555-8491	9/6/92
5	Williams	Vanna	71 Delaware Ave.	Herndon	VA	22071-1234	(414)555-0493	9/6/92
6	Smith	Ann	2210 Elm St.	Marlow	NH	03456	(616)555-9483	9/6/92
7	Lopez	Lucinda	22 Overton Hwy.	Holland	MI	49423	(717)555-4039	9/6/92
8	Zastrow	Michelle	P.O. Box 44	Bangor	ME	01876	(111)555-1039	9/6/92
9	Peterson	Brooke	61 Wander Dr.	La Jolla	CA	92037	(619)555-6758	9/6/92
10	Groth	George	911 Portia Way	Wyandotte	OK	74370	(919)555-2032	9/6/92
(Counter)								

Table: Names and Addresses

Record: 11

Editing Data

You can easily change any of the data in your table at any time using any of the techniques described below:

- To move to an item of data you want to change, click on it directly or use the Tab, Shift+Tab, ←, →, ↑, or ↓ keys to move the focus to the item you want to change. (You can also press Home to move to the first field, or End to move to the last field.)

NOTE The arrow and other special keys on the numeric keypad work only when the Num Lock key is off.

- You can also use the scroll bar and buttons at the bottom of the **Table:** window to move through fields and records (as illustrated in Figure 2.7).

- If you use the keyboard to move to a field, the entire field's contents are selected (highlighted) when you first get to the field. Anything you type will instantly *replace* the current contents of the field. If you want to *change*, rather than replace, the field's current contents, click wherever you want to make a change, or press F2 and use the ← and → keys to move the blinking insertion point within the field.

TIP Pressing F2 toggles between the insertion point and a fully selected field.

- You can use the Backspace and Delete keys to delete text.

- Any new text you type into a field will be *inserted,* unless you first switch to Overwrite mode. Pressing the Insert (Ins) key toggles between Insert and Overwrite modes. The "OVR" indicator appears near the lower right corner of the screen when you're in Overwrite mode. That indicator is empty when you're in Insert mode.

- To undo any changes that you've just made to a field or record, press Escape (Esc).

- You cannot change the contents of the ID field.

Printing the Data

To print a copy of the entire table:

1. Choose File ➤ Print.

2. Choose the OK button from the **Print** dialog box that appears.

The resulting printout is an exact copy of the table that appears on your screen, with fields spread across several pages if necessary. We'll discuss techniques for printing more refined reports in Lesson 5.

Closing a Table and Saving Your Work

When you've finished entering (and perhaps editing), your sample data, you can save your work and close the table by following this one step:

- Choose File ➤ Close, or double-click the Control-menu box to the left of the **Table: Names and Addresses** title.

You'll be returned to the **Database:** window, where only the name of the table you just closed appears in the window. You can reopen the table at any time by double-clicking its name.

Lesson 3: Sorting and Querying a Table

A *query* is a database object that offers several capabilities. In this lesson, we'll discuss the three most often used ones, which allow you to:

- Choose specific fields to view (or all fields)
- Choose specific records to view (such as CA residents only, or addresses within a certain zip code range)
- Choose a sort order for displaying records, such as alphabetically by name, or zip code order for bulk mailing

TIP   As you'll learn in Chapters 7 and 8, you can also use queries to simultaneously change several records, as well as to combine data from multiple tables.

Let's create a query now that displays an alphabetized list of names with phone numbers.

Creating a Query

To create a query, starting from the **Lessons** database window:

1. Click the Query object button. (No queries are listed in the window, because we haven't saved any yet.)
2. Click the New button at the top of the database window.
3. In the **Add Table** dialog box that appears, click the Add button to choose *Names and Addresses* as the table to query.
4. Click the Close button to leave the Add Table dialog box.

At this point you should see the **Select Query:** dialog box as shown in Figure 2.8.

Choosing Fields to View

The first step to using a query is to tell Access which fields you're interested in viewing. In this example, we'll view just the Last Name, First Name, and Phone fields. Follow these steps:

1.   Click the drop-down list button next to Field: in the query form, then click on *Last Name* in the list that appears. The selected field name appears in the box.

2.   Press Tab to move to the next column.

3.   In this second column, click the drop-down list button again, and this time click on the *First Name* field.

4.   Again, press Tab to move to the next column.

5.   Click the drop-down list button again, but this time scroll down to the Phone field name using the ↓ key or scroll bar at the right edge of the list, then click on the Phone field name.

FIGURE 2.8

A Query window with the Names and Addresses table chosen as the table to query

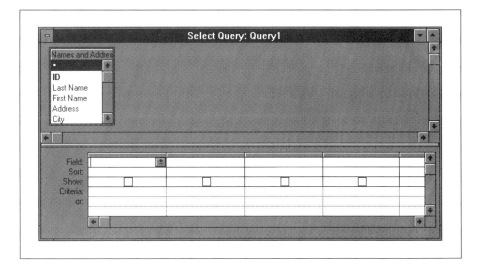

The lower portion of your query window should now look something like this:

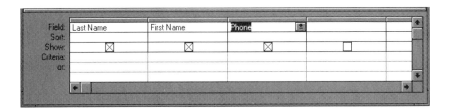

Choosing a Sort Order

Next we'll tell Access that we want the resulting records alphabetized by last and first name. Here's how:

1. Click the empty column just to the right of Sort: under Last Name.

2. Click the drop-down list button that appears, then choose *Ascending*.

3. Press Tab to move to the next column (under First Name), and again click the drop-down list button and choose *Ascending*.

Notice that we've asked Access to sort on two different fields, Last Name and First Name. Because the Last Name field is to the left of the First Name field, records will actually be alphabetized by last name, and the First Name field will act as a tie-breaker for records with identical last names in them. For instance, if there's an Ann Smith and a Michael Smith in the table, Ann Smith will be listed before Michael Smith, just as in the phone book.

Choosing Records to View

Now let's say that rather than viewing everyone's name and phone number, you just want to look up the phone number for someone with the last name Smith. In that case, you need to enter a query criterion in the Last

Name field that tells Access to display only records with Smith in that field. Here's how:

1. Click in the column next to Criteria: under Last Name.

2. Type in the last name you want to search for (Smith in this example, but if you didn't put any Smiths in your table, type a last name that you know does exist in the table).

Figure 2.9 shows how the bottom part of your query window should look now, though of course yours may have some name other than Smith under the Last Name field name.

FIGURE 2.9

An alphabetized query to display only records with Smith in the Last name field

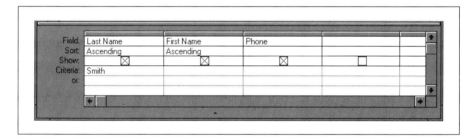

Performing the Query

To perform the query,

1. Choose View ➤ Datasheet from the menu bar, or click the Datasheet button (shown at left) in the tool bar.

2. The query window is replaced with something called a *dynaset* (explained below) that displays only the requested fields and records.

Figure 2.10 shows an example using our sample data. Yours, of course, will show data from your particular table. The dynaset will be empty if no records in your table match the query criterion you entered in the query window.

FIGURE 2.10

The results of a
query are displayed in
a *dynaset*.

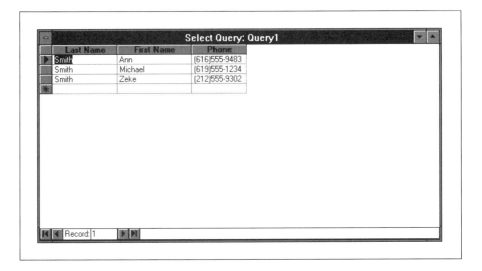

The term *dynaset* refers to the fact that what's shown is a *dynamic subset* of records. It's a subset because this table shows only the fields and records that you specified in the query window. It's dynamic because it's "live data." That means if you happen to make any changes to the set of records currently displayed on the screen, those changes will automatically be carried over to the original table.

Changing a Query

Now let's suppose that you want to change this query and view all the records in the table, but still only the Last Name, First Name, and Phone fields from those records, and still in alphabetical order. You can easily switch back to the query window and remove the query criterion by following these steps:

1. Choose View ➤ Query Design, or click the Design View button (shown at left).

2. Delete "Smith" (or whatever name you entered as the query criterion) either by using the Backspace key or by dragging the mouse pointer through "Smith" and pressing the Delete (Del) key. Be sure to delete the quotation marks as well as the name.

NOTE   Access automatically added the quotation marks surrounding your query criterion just before you performed the query.

3. To perform the query again with the query criterion removed, click the Datasheet button on the tool bar, or choose View ➤ Datasheet again.

This time, all the records are displayed, as shown in Figure 2.11.

FIGURE 2.11

Running the modified query displays the Last Name, First Name, and Phone fields for all the records in the table, alphabetized by last and first name.

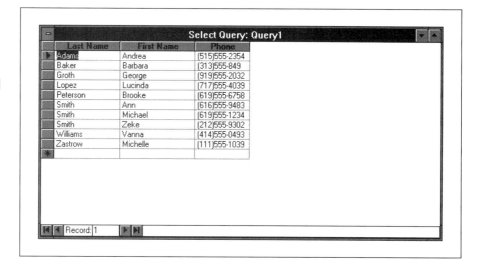

Last Name	First Name	Phone
Adams	Andrea	(515)555-2354
Baker	Barbara	(313)555-849
Groth	George	(919)555-2032
Lopez	Lucinda	(717)555-4039
Peterson	Brooke	(619)555-6758
Smith	Ann	(616)555-9483
Smith	Michael	(619)555-1234
Smith	Zeke	(212)555-9302
Williams	Vanna	(414)555-0493
Zastrow	Michelle	(111)555-1039

Select Query: Query1

Record: 1

Printing the Results of the Query

To print a copy of the current dynaset, use the same technique you use to print the full table. That is, choose File ➤ Print, then choose the OK button from the **Print** dialog box.

Saving a Query

If you plan on using a query often, you can save some time by saving the query. That way, you won't have to recreate the query from scratch in the future. To save (and close) the current query:

1. Choose File ➤ Close, or double-click the Control-menu box at the upper left corner of the dynaset. You'll see a prompt asking if you want to save the query.

2. Choose Yes to save this query.

3. Type in the name All Phone Numbers as a good description of this query, then choose OK.

The name of the query appears in the database window. You'll see a handy use of this saved query in Lesson 5, but for now keep in mind that each time you use this saved query, it will always reflect the current data in the table. So even if you add, change, or delete records in the table, there's no need to recreate the query.

N O T E   Although the Names and Addresses table seems to have disappeared, it's simply not visible at the moment because the Query object button is selected, rather than the Table object button. Clicking the Table object button will display the table name.

Lesson 4: Creating a Form

The datasheet view that you used earlier to enter and edit records is just one way to view your data. You can also view just one record at a time

using a *form*. In this lesson you'll learn to create a form the easy way—
by using the "FormWizard." To get started:

1. In the database window for the Lessons database, click the
   Form button. (No form names appear, because you haven't
   created any yet.)

2. Click the New button. You'll see this dialog box:

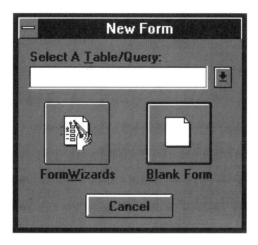

3. Click the drop-down list button next to the text box, then click on
   Names and Addresses (the second item in the list) as the table to
   build the form for.

4. Click the FormWizards button. You'll see the first FormWizard
   screen (Figure 2.12).

5. For this sample form, choose *Single-column* by clicking that option
   and then clicking the OK button.

6. Next you need to tell the Wizard which fields to include on the
   form. In this example, you can just click the button with the >>
   symbol. This selects all the field names.

7. Click the Next> button.

8. You'll see the next FormWizard screen (Figure 2.13), which lets
   you choose the kind of look you want to give the form.

FIGURE 2.12

The FormWizard screen lets you choose a basic style for your form.

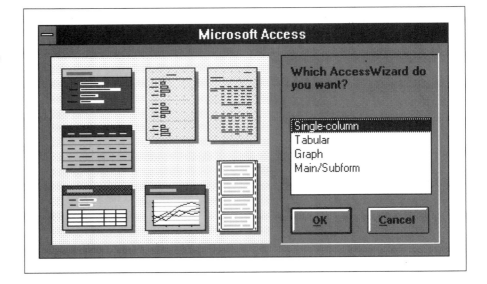

FIGURE 2.13

This FormWizard screen lets you chose a particular appearance for your form.

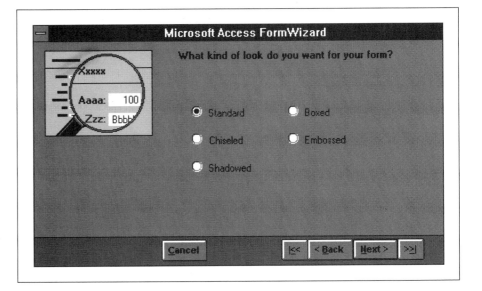

9. You can click any option you want to get an idea of how the form will look. An example appears under the magnifying glass to the left of the options.

10. For this example, choose *Embossed*, then click the Next> button.

11. In the next dialog box, just click the Open button to keep the suggested form title.

Access creates the form, then displays it on the screen for you as in Figure 2.14. Notice how the form shows all the fields for a single record, unlike the datasheet view, which shows several records but only as many fields as will fit across the screen.

The form window, like the datasheet view, has a scroll bar for scrolling left and right as well as the various buttons for moving up and down through records. In the form view, you can use the ↑, ↓, Tab, and Shift+Tab keys to move from field to field. You can press PgUp and PgDn to move through records.

FIGURE 2.14

A sample form, with an embossed look, created by a FormWizard.

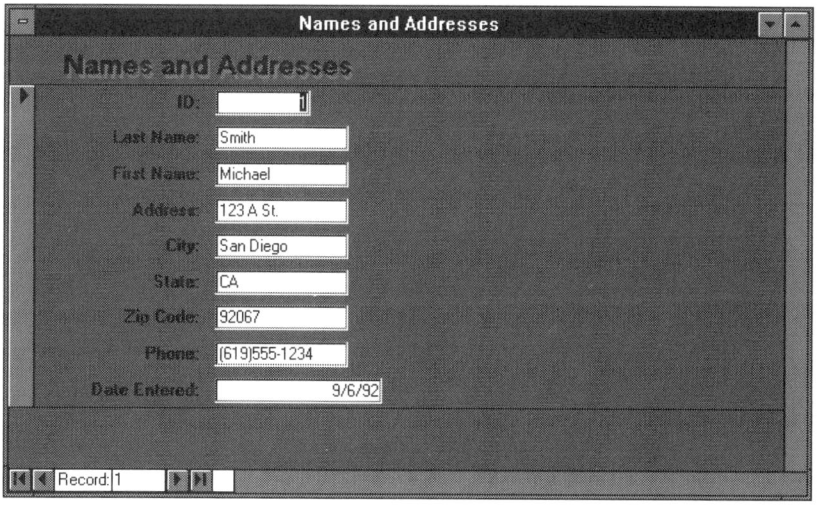

Printing the Current Form

If you want to print a copy of just the record that appears in form view at the moment:

1. Click the large Select Record button that runs the full height of the form window, to the left of the field names. Or, choose Edit ➤ Select Record.

2. Choose File ➤ Print from the menu bar.

3. In the **Print** dialog box that appears, choose Selection.

4. Choose OK.

TIP   If you skip Step 3 above, Access will print a form for each record in the table.

Saving the Form

To save the form you just created:

1. Choose File ➤ Close.

2. When asked about saving the changes you made to the form, choose Yes.

3. In the **Save As** dialog box that appears, type in a name for the form such as Add/Edit Names and Addresses, then choose OK.

The form is closed and its name appears in the database window (when the Form object button is selected.)

Opening a Saved Form

You can use the form to view, enter, or edit records in the table at any time. The form will always reflect the current data, so you need not recreate the form when you add, change, or delete table data. To open the form:

1. If it isn't already depressed, click the Form button in the database window for the Lessons database.

2. Click the Open button.

Whenever you're viewing data via a form, you can switch back and forth between datasheet view and form view using these buttons on the tool bar:

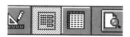

You can also use the standard Windows techniques to size and move either window. For instance, you can drag the lower right corner of either window down and to the right in order to enlarge the window. Sizing one of the windows automatically gives the other window the identical size.

When you've finished working with the table and form, you can close the table and save any changes from either the datasheet view or form view. Just choose File ➤ Close as usual, or double-click the Control-menu box in the view window.

You'll learn how to refine your form and how to create much fancier forms in Chapter 9. For now, let's turn our attention to yet another database object, the report.

Lesson 5: Creating a Report

Whereas a report is generally used for viewing and printing one record at a time, a report is generally used to print multiple records in whatever format you wish. As with forms, the easiest way to create a report format is with the report wizard ("ReportWizard").

You can also "attach" the report to the entire table or to a query. If you attach the report to the table, you can use the report to print all the fields and records in the table. If you attach the report to a query, you can use the report to print just the fields and records in the dynaset that's created by that query.

In this lesson we'll use the ReportWizard to create a report for printing a phone number list from the "All phone numbers" query you created back in Lesson 3. Here's how to get started:

1. In the database window for the Lessons database, first click the Report object button.

2. Click the New button.

3. In the **New Report** dialog box that appears, first click the drop-down list button that appears next to the empty text box.

4. Click on the *All Phone Numbers* query name.

5. Click the ReportWizards button.

6. From the first Wizard dialog box, choose *Single-column,* then click OK.

7. Click the >> button to move all the field names to the list box on the right.

8. Click the Next> button.

9. The next dialog box asks which fields you want to sort by. Click the > button twice to move the Last Name and First Name fields to the sort order list.

10. Choose the Next> button.

11. The next dialog box, shown in Figure 2.15, asks what kind of look you want to give to the report. Click any option for a sample of how the report will look.

12. For this example, choose *Executive,* then choose Next>.

13. From the next dialog box, click the Print Preview button to accept the suggested *All Phone Numbers* title and view a preview of how the report will look when printed.

FIGURE 2.15

This ReportWizard
screen lets you choose
a general appearance
for your report.

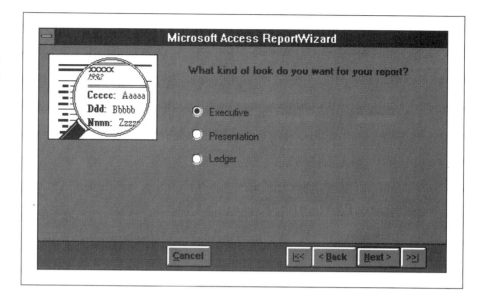

Saving the Report Format

To save the report format and return to the database window:

1. Choose File ➤ Close.

2. When asked about saving the report format, choose Yes.

3. Type a name such as Print a Phone List, and then choose OK.

As usual, the name you gave to the report appears in the database window.

Printing a Report

Keep in mind that when you create a report, all you are really creating is the *format* of the report. What this means is that, as with forms and queries, you can use that report format over and over again in the future, even after adding, changing, or deleting table data. Whenever you want to print a report:

1. Click the Report object button in the database window (if it isn't already selected).

2. Click the name of the report you want to print. (Your only choice right now is the *Print A Phone List* report you just created.)

3. Click the Preview button near the top of the database window.

4. Click the Print button in the tool bar.

5. Choose OK from the **Print** dialog box that appears.

6. To close the report preview window, choose File ➤ Close, or double-click the preview window's Control-menu box.

You'll learn how to create much fancier report formats in Chapter 12. For now, let's review some of the basic skills we've covered in these lessons.

Overview of Basic Procedures

This whirlwind tour of Access has been a sort of 90-10 deal—you've learned the 10 percent of Access's capabilities that you'll use 90 percent of the time. In particular, you should keep in mind the following points:

- A database is a collection of all the objects (tables, queries, forms, reports, and others still to be presented) that make up the entire collection of information you want to manage.

- When you first start Access, no database is open. You can choose File ➤ Open Database to open an existing database. A database window appears.

- To see what tables, forms, or other objects you've already created for the current database, first click the appropriate object button in the database window. Once selected, the button remains depressed, so a quick glance at the buttons will show you what type of object you're viewing at the moment.

- To use an existing object, click the name of the object, then choose Open (or, in the case of a report, click the Preview button).

- To change an object, click the name of the object you want to change, then click the Design button. (We'll talk about designing forms and reports in detail in Chapters 9 and 12).

- To create a new object, first make sure to click the appropriate object button, if it isn't already depressed, then click the New button.

- To close an object that's currently open on the screen, choose File ➤ Close, or double-click the object's Control-menu box.

Figure 2.16 recaps the uses of the various parts of the database window.

FIGURE 2.16

Basic steps for creating, opening, and changing database objects

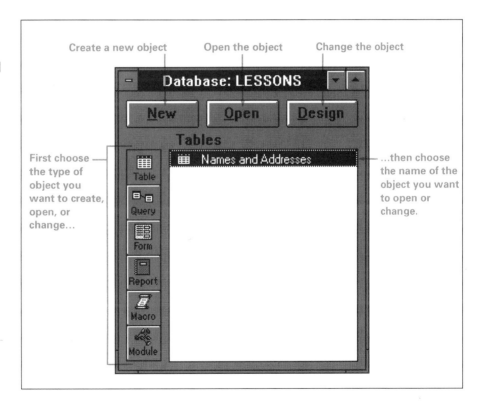

Moving On

Your Access program comes with a sample database designed around a hypothetical company named Northwind Traders. If you'd like to use the basic skills you've learned so far to explore that database, just choose File ➤ Open Database, then double-click the *nwind.mdb* file name.

In the chapters that follow, we'll get into all the topics we've covered here in much more depth, and create a sophisticated database similar to the Northwind Traders example. We'll start with the important topic of planning the entire database.

PART TWO

Managing Data

CHAPTERS

Designing a Database

f *ast* TRACK

A many-to-many relationship 69

describes a situation where many records in one table relate to many records in another table. In this case, a third table is used to define the relationships between the two tables.

A one-to-one relationship 71

refers to a situation where one record from one table refers to only one record in another table. Except in a few rare cases, the data from the two tables should probably be combined into one table.

AS MENTIONED in the lessons in Chapter 2, a simple application might require only a single table of information, such as a database for managing a list of names and addresses. There are many cases, however, in which a database might require several tables. For instance, a database for a retail business might include one table for storing customer information, another for inventory information, another for orders, and so forth.

The task of determining when and how to divide data into separate related tables is an important element of *database design*. Sometimes, it's obvious when data needs to be stored in separate tables. For instance, there's no reason why a retail business would want to try to store all its information about customers and inventory in a single table.

On the other hand, knowing exactly how to best divide up information into multiple tables can be tricky. In this chapter, we'll look at some basic design concepts, and examples of their use, to give you a foundation for designing your own databases.

Keep in mind that everything we'll be talking about here is a matter of *planning*—the kind of stuff you do with paper and pencil. After you've sketched out a database design on paper, you can go to your computer and start actually creating the tables, as we'll discuss in the next chapter.

The One-to-Many Relationship

The *one-to-many* relationship describes a database design where for every one item of data in one table, there may be many items of related information in another table. For instance, let's suppose you're a retail business, and you want to design a database to manage customers, orders, and inventory. The relationship between your customers and the orders they place is a classic example of a one-to-many relationship. After all, any *one* customer might place *many* orders over the course of time. Hence, you have a natural one-to-many situation.

Figure 3.1 shows how you could design two tables, named Customers and Orders, to divide information about customers and orders into two tables.

The Common, or Key, Field

The arrow connecting the Customers table and the Orders table indicates that Customer ID is the *common field,* or *key field,* that relates the two tables. The *1* in the figure indicates the table on the "one side," and the *M* indicates the table on the "many side." That is, for every one customer in the Customers table, there may be many orders in the Orders table.

Now there is one very important point to keep in mind about these two tables. Each customer must have a unique Customer ID. After all, if two customers in the Customers table have the ID 1002, how would we (or Access) know *which* customer 1002 placed a particular order in the Orders table?

FIGURE 3.1

Structures of the Customers and Orders tables, illustrating Customer ID as the common field that relates the two tables, with 1 indicating the table on the "one side," and M indicating the table on the "many side."

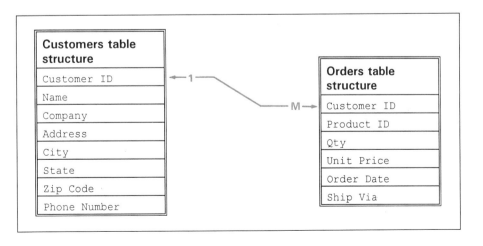

If each customer does have a unique ID, and we add some data to each table, we can easily tell which customer a particular order belongs to by looking at the customer ID in the Orders table, then locating that ID in the Customer table, as shown in Figure 3.2. (It's also easy to see in this figure how, for every one customer, there may be many orders.)

Another way to understand the importance of the key field is to imagine the two tables shown in Figure 3.2 after removing the key field, Customer ID, from one or both tables. If you were to do so, there would be no way to tell which record(s) in the Orders table goes with which record in the Customers table.

FIGURE 3.2

The sample Customers and Orders tables after adding some data to each one. The common field, Customer ID, which appears in both tables, tells us which customer placed each order.

Customers Table (one record per customer)

Customer ID	Name	Address	etc...
1001	Jane Doe	123 A St.	...
1002	Martha Miller	234 B St.	...
1003	Rocco Moe	11 Oak Ave.	...

Orders Table (one record per order)

Customer ID	Product ID	Qty	Unit Price	etc...
1001	MO-100	1	$18.00	...
1001	PA-100	1	$26.50	...
1001	SL-100	1	$25.00	...
1002	PA-100	1	$28.50	...
1002	PA-101	2	$15.00	...
1002	SL-101	1	$25.00	...
1003	PA-100	1	$18.00	...
1003	MO-101	1	$18.00	...
1003	SU-105	5	$17.50	...

N O T E

The *etc...* in Figure 3.2 simply refers to additional fields in the table structure that aren't shown in the figure.

The Relationship between Orders and Products

Another example of a one-to-many relationship can be found in the relationship between products and orders, as illustrated in Figure 3.3. In this example, the Products table stores information about products carried in inventory, with each record representing one product.

Notice that, once again, we're using the common field, Product ID in this example, to relate the two tables. Figure 3.4 shows how these two tables might appear after adding data to each one. Once again, it's easy to see exactly which product any given order is referring to simply by looking up the appropriate Product ID code in the Products table.

One of the advantages of using Access to manage these data is that you can use automatic updating to ensure that the Products table is always up to date. That is, Access can automatically subtract the quantities of items

FIGURE 3.3

Structures of the sample Products and Orders tables. Here, Product ID is the key field that relates the two tables.

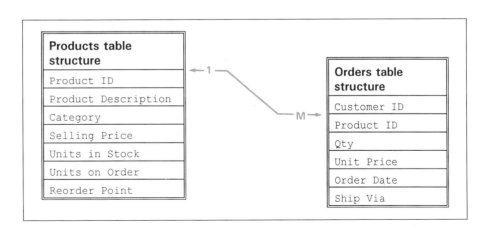

FIGURE 3.4

The Orders and
Products tables with
some sample data in
them. The Product ID
stored in each order
provides a link to
more information
about each product, in
the Products table.

Orders Table (one record per order)

Customer ID	Product ID	Qty	Unit Price	etc...
1001	MO-100	1	$18.00	...
1001	PA-100	1	$26.50	...
1001	SL-100	1	$25.00	...
1002	PA-100	1	$28.50	...
1002	PA-101	2	$15.00	...
1002	SL-101	1	$25.00	...
1003	PA-100	1	$18.00	...
1003	MO-101	1	$18.00	...
1003	SU-105	5	$17.50	...

M

Products Table (one record per product)

Product ID	Product Description	etc...
MO-100	Margo Moth Orchid	...
PA-100	Midnight Giant Orchid	...
SL-100	Callosum Orchid	...
etc...		

1

sold from the appropriate in-stock quantity in the Products table as orders
are filled. Thus, the Products table will always reflect the true quantity of
each item in stock.

N O T E

Chapter 16 talks about automatic updating in
detail.

In some cases, there might be a natural many-to-many relationship between tables, as we'll discuss next.

The Many-to-Many Relationship

The *many-to-many* relationship occurs in situations where records from one table might be refer to many records in another table, and vice-versa. A prime example is the relationship between customers and products. That is, *many* customers order *many* different products.

So how do we go about defining a many-to-many relationship between two tables? The only way to do so, actually, is by using a third table, and then setting up two one-to-many relationships between the third table and the first two tables. In this particular example, the Orders table *is* that third table, as shown in Figure 3.5.

Looking at some sample data in these tables (Figure 3.6) perhaps better illustrates the concept. That is, many customers order many products, and vice versa. The third table, Orders, provides the link between Customers and Products.

FIGURE 3.5

The one-to-many relationship between Customers and Orders and the one-to-many relationship between Products and Orders together define a many-to-many relationship between Customers and Products.

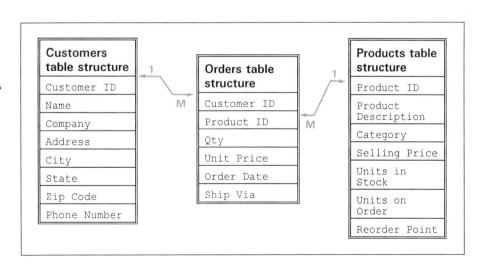

FIGURE 3.6

Sample data in the
Customers, Orders,
and Products tables.

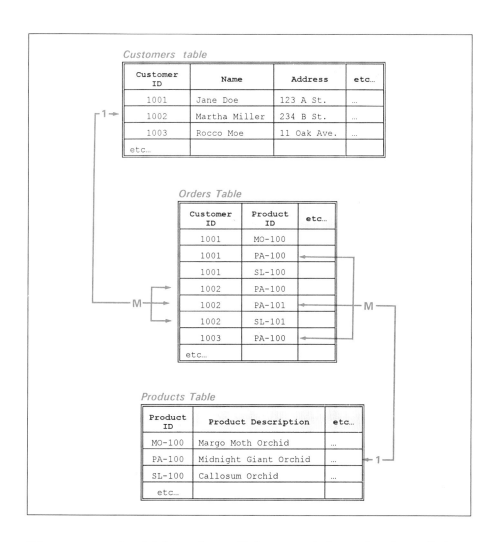

Now you may be thinking that splitting your information into all these
separate tables is going to be a problem in the long run. For instance, how
are you going to print and keep track of invoices, receipts, packing slips,
and so forth with the data all split up into three separate tables? Not to
worry! As you'll learn in upcoming chapters, Access will let you mix and
match the data from separate tables however you want. So you can view
and print the information from separate tables all at once, in whatever format you need.

The One-to-One Relationship

The one-to-one relationship means that for every one record in one table, there's exactly one record in some other table. For instance, in Figure 3.7, for every employee in the Employees table, there is exactly one record in the Employee Information table.

In many cases, this design is an indication that you could just put all the data into one table. However, in a few situations, this one-to-one

FIGURE 3.7

Here there is an exact one-to-one relationship between records in the Employees table and records in the Employee Information table.

Employees Table (one record per employee)

Employee ID	Name	Address	etc...
10001	Bill Adams	45 Willow St.	...
10002	Mandy Cohorts	P.O. Box 11	...
10003	Alec Fraser	714 Rainbow Dr.	...
10004	Tina Bulina	88 Arrow Hwy	...
10005	Frank Lee	9864 Temple St.	...

Employee Information Table (one record per employee)

Employee ID	Social Security Number	Salary	etc...
10001	323-45-6789	$25,500	...
10002	547-94-9504	$37,500	...
10003	504-60-4056	$45,500	...
10004	656-43-5049	$31,500	...
10005	652-45-3049	$61,600	...

design might make sense. For instance:

- If you need more than 255 fields (Access's limit) to define all the information for a single record, you can split the information into two tables. You still need to use a common field (like Employee ID in Figure 3.7) to link records from one table to the other table.

- If you need to limit access to some (but not all) of the information, the one-to-one design will do the trick. For instance, you could make the information in the Employees table accessible to everyone. Then you could password-protect the Employee Information table to limit access to the social security number, salary, and other data in that table.

Don't Use Multiple Tables to Categorize Data...

One thing you *don't* want to use multiple tables for is to categorize information. For instance, suppose you want to manage personnel information, and your company has several different departments.

Your first inclination might be to create one table, perhaps named Accounting, for people in the accounting department, then create a second table named Marketing for people in the marketing department, and so forth. This might be handy when you want to work with personnel data for people in a given department only. But it's going to be a pain when you need data for all employees, or employees from several departments.

You'd be much better off creating a single table, perhaps named Employee, that contains data for all the employees in the company. Include in that table a field, perhaps named Department, that describes which department the employee works in. Later, when you need to work with records for people in a single department, Access can easily isolate those records for you.

...Except in the Case Of

There are exceptions to every rule. For instance, you might want to create two tables with identical structures to store orders or other information. One table, perhaps named New Orders, would contain new, unfulfilled orders. A second table, perhaps named Old Orders, would contain fulfilled orders.

When an order is fulfilled, you could move its record from the New Orders table to the Old Orders table. Doing so would keep the size of the New Orders table down to small-and-speedy. Old Orders would act as a *history table*, to keep track of old, fulfilled orders. When you need to go back and check on a problem with some old order, you'll be able to find it in the Old Orders table. We'll look at examples of using history tables in Chapter 16.

Clues to Warn You When Multiple Tables Might Be Better

This background information about typical database designs should help you when you are sketching out your own database design. But even so, there are a few things you want to watch out for while designing your tables that will give you clues as to when you need multiple tables. We'll also point out some potential problems that come up if you *don't* use multiple tables.

Repeating Groups of Fields

When you finish planning all the fields for a single table, take a look at the fields in that table and look for any repetitive groups of fields. If you find any, you'll know right off the bat that you need to break that table into two or more tables. For instance, take a look at the table structure in Figure 3.8, which could be used to store information about orders, and notice the repetitive field groups.

What's wrong with this design? Well for one thing, since a table can contain a maximum of 255 fields, there is a limit to the number of products you can store for each customer. A second problem is that when you later

FIGURE 3.8

This table contains repetitive groups of fields for storing information about orders.

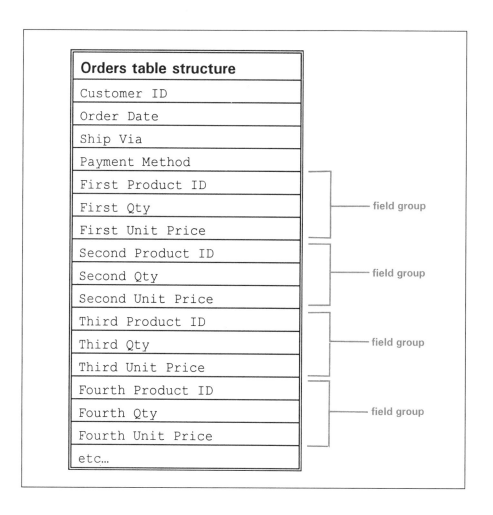

want to analyze, perform calculations on, print, or sort information about orders, you're sure to find it all very difficult with the orders spread across several fields in this manner.

Redundant Data

A second clue to look for in an existing table design is fields that repeatedly store the same information over and over again throughout multiple records. For instance, you might try to use the table structure shown in Figure 3.9 to store information about orders in a single table, where each record in the table represents a single "line item" on an order form.

Projecting into the future a bit, and imagining how this table will look when you start filling it with data later, may bring to light a potential problem. And that is, the information about the order as a whole—Date Ordered, Ship Via, and Payment method, is repeated throughout the first four records of the table, as shown in Figure 3.10.

Why is this a problem? For one thing, when entering orders, you're going to get tired of retyping the repetitive information with each line item in the order. If you need to change some piece of information about the order, such as the Ship Via method, you'd need to be very careful to make

FIGURE 3.9

Another attempt to store information about orders in a single table

Orders table structure
Customer ID
Order Date
Ship Via
Payment Method
Product ID
Qty
Unit Price

FIGURE 3.10

Storing information about Customers and Orders in the single table design shown in Figure 3.9 leads to repetitive information in multiple records.

Customer ID	Order Date	Ship Via	Payment Method	Product ID	Qty	Unit Price
1001	12/1/92	UPS	Check	MO-100	1	$18.00
1001	12/1/92	UPS	Check	PA-100	2	$26.50
1001	12/1/92	UPS	Check	SL-100	1	$25.00
1001	12/1/92	UPS	Check	SU-105	1	$17.50
1009	12/2/92	Mail	Invoice	MO-100	4	$18.00
1009	12/2/92	Mail	Invoice	MO-101	4	$25.50
1009	12/2/92	Mail	Invoice	MO-144	1	$49.95

These first four records represent a single order placed by Customer 1001. Data in the Order Date, Ship Via, and Payment Method fields is repeated throughout these four records.

sure you make that change in all the appropriate records (the first four records in Figure 3.10).

Solution to These Problems

The cure for both the repeating fields and redundant data is to use two tables to store information about orders. One table, perhaps named Orders, would contain information about the order as a whole. A second table, perhaps named Order Details, would contain one record for each line item on the order, as illustrated in Figure 3.11.

Information about the order as a whole placed on the "one" side of the relationship and information about order details placed on the "many" side of the relationship. We've created a new field, named Order ID, to link the information in the two tables. The standard one-to-many relationship ends up being the perfect solution to all the problems we encountered above.

FIGURE 3.11

Breaking information about orders into two separate tables eliminates repeating groups of fields and redundant data.

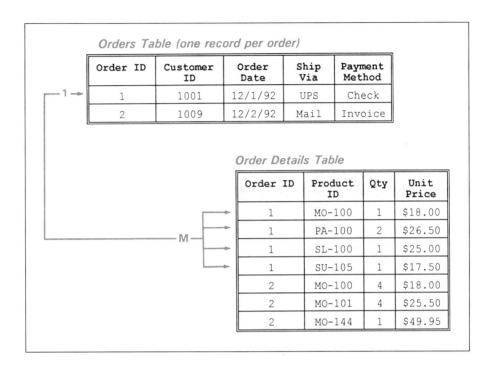

Orders Table (one record per order)

Order ID	Customer ID	Order Date	Ship Via	Payment Method
1	1001	12/1/92	UPS	Check
2	1009	12/2/92	Mail	Invoice

Order Details Table

Order ID	Product ID	Qty	Unit Price
1	MO-100	1	$18.00
1	PA-100	2	$26.50
1	SL-100	1	$25.00
1	SU-105	1	$17.50
2	MO-100	4	$18.00
2	MO-101	4	$25.50
2	MO-144	1	$49.95

The Bigger Picture

The bottom line in all of this is that you want to structure your tables so as to eliminate repeating groups of fields in a table and to minimize redundant data. To achieve this, your database design might end up with quite a few separate tables, with several one-to-many relationships between the tables.

Figure 3.12 shows an example, displaying the structures and relationships among the Customers, Products, Orders, and Order Details tables we've been describing in this chapter.

DESIGNING A DATABASE

FIGURE 3.12

The structures of, and relationships between, the Customers, Products, Orders, and Order Details tables

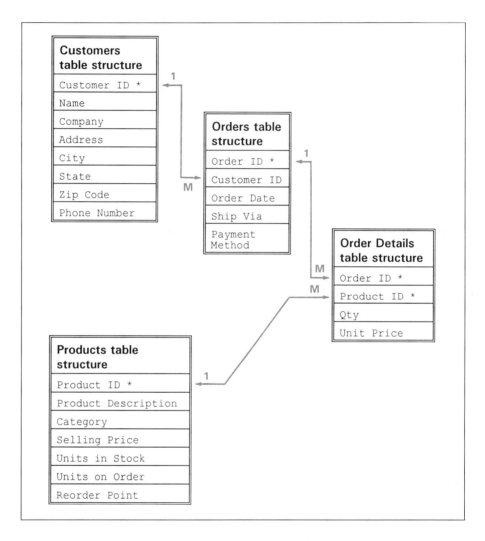

NOTE In Chapter 4 we'll build upon the design shown in Figure 3.12 in order to create a more powerful and realistic database for a retail business. In that chapter I'll also explain the meaning of the asterisks next to the field names.

The database design sketched out in Figure 3.12 has reached a kind of database design nirvana, because every field in every table describes information that's relevant only to its own subject. And there are no repetitive groups of fields or redundant data to struggle with down the road.

TIP In database terminology, the process of reaching this state of "database design nirvana" is often called *normalization.*

Keep in mind that this organization in no way limits how you can view or print the data. For example, Figure 3.13 shows a sample order-entry form built from these four tables of information. Even though the information on the form is organized into four different tables behind the scenes, the form looks very much like any standard printed order form.

What If I Get It Wrong?

Database design is always somewhat tricky, particularly for beginners, because your natural inclination will probably be to stick as much information as possible into a single table. But rest assured that your initial design is never cast in granite. Access is a very flexible tool, and you can change your database design at any time, add new tables, make refinements… whatever you need.

Sample order-entry form showing some data from the four separate Customers, Products, Orders, and Order Details tables.

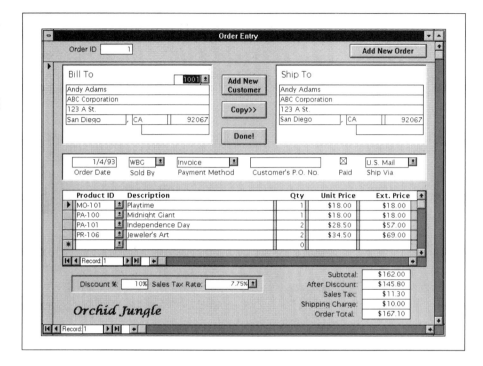

A pencil sketch of your initial design is probably sufficient for starters. Once you have a basic idea of what tables you need to create, and what fields you want to put into each table, you can further refine the contents of each table, then go to your computer and actually create the tables, as we'll discuss in the next chapter.

CHAPTER

4

Creating Access Tables

fast TRACK

To create the table   **99**

> be sure to open (or create) the database you want to put the
> table into. Then click on the Table object button and then
> the New button in the database window.

To define the primary key   **102**

> select the field(s) you want to use for the primary key, then
> click on the Primary Key button in the tool bar.

To save the table structure   **102**

> choose File ➤ Close, and provide a name (up to 64 characters,
> including blank spaces) when prompted.

To get online coaching while working with Access   **115**

> choose Help ➤ Cue Cards.

FIGURING out what tables you'll need, and roughly what fields will go into each table, is the first step of designing a database. The second step involves refining the structure of each table, and then starting up Access and actually creating the tables. These are the topics of this chapter.

Planning a Table

When you're concentrating on the design of individual tables, your best bet might be to stick with pencil and paper, so you can spend some time thinking, planning, and making adjustments.

Planning the Field Names

When deciding what fields to place in a table, keep in mind the following rules for defining field names:

- The maximum width of a field name is 64 characters, including blank spaces.
- Each field name must be unique. That is, no two fields within a table can have the same name.
- You can use letters, numbers, special characters, and blank spaces in a field name.
- You can can use punctuation characters *except* for periods (.), exclamation points (!), or square brackets [ ].

- A field name cannot contain leading spaces.

- If you wish, you can also write a lengthy description, which will later appear at the bottom of the screen, while defining each field name.

Let's suppose that you're designing a table, to be named Customers, that stores information about your customers. You might come up with the list of field names and descriptions shown in Figure 4.1.

Now you might be wondering why we would bother to split people's names into four fields: Honorific, Last Name, First Name, and MI (middle initial). Well, doing so will make it easier to manage the data later on. For example, storing each person's last name in a separate field makes it easier to later tell Access to "put the information into alphabetical order by last name" or to "find Smith."

Separating the fields also makes it easier to determine later exactly how to print them. For example, if you later want to print an alphabetical

FIGURE 4.1

The field names for a table of customer names, addresses, and other information, sketched out on a scratch pad

Field Name	Data Type	Description
Customer ID		Customer's unique ID (four digits)
Honorific		Mr., Mrs., Ms., Dr., etc.
First Name		Customer's first name
MI		Customer's middle initial
Last Name		Customer's surname
Department/Title		Customer's title or department
Company		Customer's company affiliation
Address		Customer's street address
City		Customer's city
State/Province		Customer's state or province
Zip/Postal Code		Customer's Zip or postal code
Phone		Customer's phone number
Fax		Customer's FAX number
Discount Rate		Customer's standard discount
Date Entered		Date this record entered

customer list, you could easily tell Access to list the last name followed by a comma, followed by the first name, like this:

Adams, Andy

Baker, Barbara

Carlson, Cara

It would be just as easy to tell Access to put the name in a different format—honorific followed by first name, middle initial, and then last name, like this:

Mr. Andy A. Adams

Ms. Barbara B. Baker

Mrs. Cara C. Carlson

Of course, if you think your particular needs might not require this flexibility in printing and sorting names, you could just store the entire name in a single field.

Planning the Data Types

Access stores different types of information in different formats. So when you are defining your table, you need to think about what type of information will be stored in each field. Your options are described below:

Text   Any combination of letters, numeric characters, spaces, and other characters. The length of a Text field can be anywhere from 1 to 255 characters. Examples of use: names, addresses, titles, product codes—basically, any short piece of text.

Memo   Same as text fields except that a memo field can contain up to 32,000 characters. Examples of use: résumés, job descriptions, product descriptions, journal abstracts—any text that requires more than 255 characters.

Number   Numbers that you may want to perform math on, such as totals, subtotals, averages, and so forth. They can accept only numeric characters (0–9), decimal points, commas, and negative signs (or hyphens). Alphabetic characters are not allowed in number fields. Examples of use: quantities, measurements, and so forth.

Currency   Numeric data representing dollar amounts. Currency data is like number data, except that all numbers are automatically rounded to two decimal places, and negative values are enclosed in parentheses. Examples of use: unit price, salary, hourly wage.

Counter   If you elect to use this data type, Access will automatically assign a unique number to each new record that you add to the table. The first record you add is numbered *1*, then next record is *2*, and so forth. Once assigned, the number in this field cannot be changed. Examples: order number, customer number; useful when you're not planning on using another numbering scheme.

Date/Time   Dates and times. Access automatically validates any entry, rejecting a date like 06/31/93 (June has only 30 days), and allows for date arithmetic, which means you can calculate the number of days between two dates, add or subtract days from a date, and so forth. Examples of use: date hired, billing date, due date.

Yes/No   This field accepts only two values: yes and no. Examples of use: Paid (yes or no), Active (yes or no), Posted (yes or no), Taxable (yes or no).

OLE Object   Objects that are placed in your table from other Windows applications that support OLE (Object Linking and Embedding). Use primarily for storing pictures and sound in a table. Examples of use: a picture or photo, clip art, a business chart, animation, a sound. You can also use this field to include less exotic objects such as a spreadsheet cell, an entire spreadsheet, or a word processing document.

You might jot down the data types as shown in Figure 4.2, which refer back to our Customers table.

Now you may be thinking "Wait a minute—you just said that the number data type is for numbers. Yet you just made Zip Code and Phone the

Field Name	Data Type	Description
Customer ID	Number	Customer's unique ID (four digits)
Honorific	Text	Mr., Mrs., Ms., Dr., etc.
First Name	Text	Customer's first name
MI	Text	Customer's middle initial
Last Name	Text	Customer's surname
Department/Title	Text	Customer's title or department
Company	Text	Customer's company affiliation
Address	Text	Customer's street address
City	Text	Customer's city
State/Province	Text	Customer's state or province
Zip/Postal Code	Text	Customer's Zip or postal code
Phone	Text	Customer's phone number
Fax	Text	Customer's FAX number
Discount Rate	Number	Customer's standard discount
Date Entered	Date/Time	Date this record entered

text data type." That's true, and the reason for doing so is that neither zip codes nor phone numbers are true numbers. Defining either of these as numbers would later prevent us from putting letters, leading zeros, and punctuation marks such as hyphens into the entries.

For example, if you defined Zip/Postal Code as a number field, you could not later store a hyphenated zip code like 92067-3384, or a foreign zip code like MJ3 OH4, or one with a leading zero like 01234 into that field. Similarly, if you'd made Phone a number field, you couldn't type in a simple phone number like (619)555-1212, because the field wouldn't accept the parentheses or the hyphen.

When to Use the OLE Object Data Type

If you're not already familiar with Object Linking and Embedding, you may be wondering just when you'd want to use the OLE Object data type.

The most common use of this data type is to store data that doesn't fit any of the other data types, namely pictures and sound. However, you can also use this data type to store text and numbers—with limitations.

To store lengthy pieces of text in an OLE Object field, you'll need to have a word processing or desktop publishing application that acts as an OLE server, such as Microsoft Word for Windows (Version 2.0). You can then use all the formatting features of your word processing software to create and edit the lengthy text stored in the OLE Object field. Doing so gives you much more formatting capability than a Memo field would.

The downside to using the OLE Object, rather than a Memo field, for storing lengthy text is that the text doesn't appear on your screen, nor can it be printed directly while you're using Access. Instead, the text document appears only as an icon.

By way of contrast, if you store a number from a spreadsheet in a table, you can view that number in Access when you use custom forms. However, you won't be able to perform any math with that number from within Access. So again, you'll only have limited access to numbers in a field if you use the OLE Object data type rather than the Number or Currency type to store those numbers.

Figure 4.3 shows a custom form illustrating the appearance of various types of fields in a sample table.

When to Use the Counter Data Type

The Counter data type automatically assigns a number to each new record that you enter into a table. Once assigned, that number never changes. Use this data type when you want to assign a unique value to every record in the table, and don't already have some numbering system in place to uniquely identify each record.

For instance, in a table that tracks orders, you might want to use a counter field to automatically assign an order number to each record. On the other

FIGURE 4.3

Examples of various data types on a custom form. OLE objects appear as icons only.

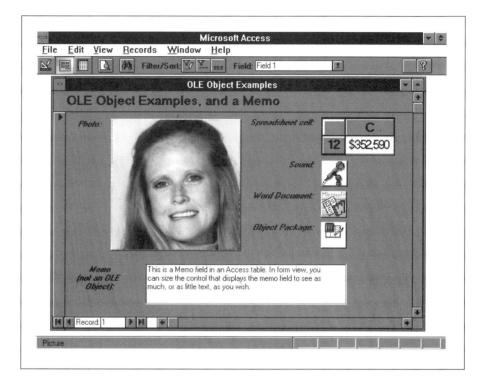

hand, in a table that stores information about products, you may want to use an existing part number or product code to uniquely identify each record. In that case, you wouldn't need to use a Counter field.

You may be thinking that I should have used the Counter data type for the Customer ID number in the Customers table, and let Access number the customers automatically as I enter them into the table. And you might indeed want to do that in your own Customers table. But for this particular example, I'd like to give each customer a four-digit ID code, starting at 1001. Since the Counter data type automatically assigns numbers starting at 1, that data type just isn't appropriate for the numbering scheme I want to use. So I decided to use the Number data type instead in this case.

TIP You can have your cake and eat it too by defining the Customer ID field as a Number field and adding at least one record with whatever starting number you want (e.g., 1001). Then, use techniques described under "Converting a Number Field to a Counter Field" in Chapter 18 to have future records automatically numbered in sequence.

What NOT to Put in Tables

While you're designing your tables, you want to try to avoid some of the common mistakes listed in the next three sections.

Don't Create a Field for a Calculated Item of Data

There's no need to create fields to store the results of a calculation. Instead, you need only define fields for the raw data, then let Access do all the calculations. For instance, when creating a table to track orders or sales, you'd want to include fields for the quantity and unit price. But you *wouldn't* want to include a field for the total price (or extended price), since Access can calculate that "on the fly"—by multiplying quantity and unit price whenever you print or view data.

Include Only Fields That Have a One-to-One Correspondence with Other Fields

As we discussed in Chapter 3, don't try to throw the whole kitchen sink into one table. Include only fields that are directly relevant to other fields in the table. For instance, in the Customers table, there's one address, city, state, zip code, and phone number for every name—a perfect one-to-one correspondence between fields. There's no need to put information about products or orders into the Customers table.

Never Include a Field That Will Contain the Same Information in Every Record

Suppose you're storing names and addresses for customers, and plan on printing form letters with your company's logo at the top of each letter. There's no need to include a field for storing a copy of your logo with each customer's name and address. As you'll see, you can just add your company logo to the top of the form letter design (once) when it comes time to print the letters.

Table Structure Limitations

Access provides a lot of leeway in designing tables, but there are a few limitations that you need to be aware of if you're planning on designing huge tables:

- A single record can contain a maximum of 255 fields.
- A single table can hold a maximum of 128MB of data.
- A single memo field can contain a maximum of 32,000 characters, or about 32 pages of double-spaced text.
- The maximum size of an OLE object stored in a field is 128MB.

As discussed later in this book, you can join up to 16 tables in a single query. So the real limitation of a database (i.e., all the tables combined) is about 16 times the limitation of a single table.

Planning a Primary Key

You can use what is called a *primary key* to help Access manage data more efficiently. By definition, a primary key is a field in the table that uniquely identifies each record in the table. But that primary key actually plays three roles in a table:

1. It prevents duplicate entries in the field(s) that make up the primary key.

2. It maintains a sort order of records based on the field(s) that make up the primary key.

3. It speeds up sorting and searching operations.

Of these three roles, the most important one to keep in mind is the first—the fact that no two records in the table can have the same data within primary key field(s). For instance, in our Customers table, you might think it a good idea to use the Last Name field as the primary key, so that Access keeps the records in the table alphabetized by people's last names. However, you'd create a bit of a problem for yourself if you did so: if you enter a record for John Smith, then later try to enter a record for Wanda Smith, Access will reject the second record, because there is already a Smith in the Last Name field of the table.

Finding the Right Primary Key

One way to identify the best primary key for a table is to first look at your overall database design, like the example presented back in Figure 3.12 of Chapter 3. Find the common field on the "one-side" of any one-to-many relationship between two tables, and you've found an ideal candidate for a primary key. After all, each record *must* contain a unique value in that field for the relationship to work, as we discussed back in Chapter 3.

If you refer back to Figure 3.12, you'll notice that I have already marked the ideal primary key fields with an asterisk (*). In almost every case, the primary key is the common field on the "one side" of a one-to-many relationship.

You'll also notice that I've marked two fields in the Orders table as a primary key. The next section explains why.

Multiple-Field Primary Keys

If there is no single field that uniquely identifies each record in the table, you may be able to use some combination of fields as the primary key. In that case, only records that have identical data in *all* the key fields are considered duplicates. For instance, suppose you make the Last Name, First Name, Middle Initial, Address, and Zip Code fields, combined, the primary key in the Customers table. In that case, you could enter two or more people with the name John Smith into the table, as long as they had different addresses and zip codes.

Looking back at our larger database design, we can certainly make the Order ID field in the Orders table a primary key, since we do want every order to have a unique identifying Order number. But we can't make the Order ID field a primary key in the Order Details table, since several records in that table might need the same Order ID number. (As you may recall, each record in the Orders table represents information about one order as a whole; such as who placed the order, the order date, and so forth. Each record in the Order Details table represents one product, quantity, and unit price line on the printed order form. If you need a reminder as to why we need to repeat the Order ID number in several records of the Order Details table, take a look at Figure 3.11 in Chapter 3.)

Thus, we have two choices for the Order Details table:

One would be to not define a primary key at all. But Access won't be able to process orders as quickly if we don't define a primary key.

The second choice would be to use the Order ID field in combination with one or more other fields as the primary key. For instance, in Figure 3.12 of the previous chapter we marked both the Order ID *and* Product ID fields as the primary key. There's really no reason for any two records on the Order Details table to have identical Order ID and Product ID values in these two fields.

Marking both the Order ID and the Product ID fields as the primary key in the Order Details table buys us a couple of advantages. For one, just the fact that we have defined a primary key for the table will speed up operations later. For another, this primary key will prevent us from accidentally entering the same record into the Order Details table twice, because it will reject the second, duplicate entry.

In your hand-written table plan, you might want to just indicate with an asterisk the field, or fields, that make up the primary key. In the Customers table we've been designing so far, we're going to be using the Customer ID field as the primary key, since we want to be sure that each customer has a unique identifying number.

At this point you've designed the Customers table sufficiently to go "online" and create it using Access. But before you do that, you need to either open the database that you want to put the table into or create a new database as described in the next sections.

Creating the Database

In Chapter 2 you created a small sample database named Lessons. But we're going to leave that database behind now and start building a larger, more complete database named Orchids. As you'll see, this database will be built around a hypothetical retail business named Orchid Jungle, which sells orchids.

Though this hypothetical business deals in orchids, its database design is generic enough to be adapted to just about any retail business that deals in customers, inventory, and orders. We'll look at the overall design of this larger database in just a few moments.

N O T E   I will be using the Orchids database as a continuing
example throughout the next few chapters. To help
you follow along, you might want to create this
database as it is presented, entering the information
as shown in the figures in the following sections.

Creating a Database

As you learned in the lessons in Chapter 2, you use File ➤ New Database,
in Access, to create a new database. Thus, to create the new Orchids
database, you would need to do the following:

1. If Access *isn't* currently running, start it now.

2. Choose File ➤ New Database.

3. Take a look at the current directory displayed under Directories in
    the **New Database** dialog box that appears. If you want to store
    your database on another directory, first double-click on the ap-
    propriate directory. (If the directory you want is a subdirectory
    and you don't see its name in the dialog box, double-click on the
    parent folder in the directory tree to expand the parent directory,
    then double-click on the name of the subdirectory you want to
    store the database on.)

4. In the File Name dialog box, double-click the suggested name
    (most likely *db1.mdb*) then type in your database name, **orchids**
    in our example.

5. Choose OK.

An empty database window for the new database appears.

N O T E   If you want several network users to share data, create a directory for the database on a network drive. See Chapter 20 for more information on networks.

Creating a Table

Before you create your table, make sure that the database that you want to put the table into is open (the name of the currently open database, if any, appears at the top of the database window). If you've been following along, the sample Orchids database should be open now. If the database you want isn't open, use File ➤ Open Database (in Access) to open it. Now you're ready to get started. To create a table:

1. Click the Table object button in the database window.

2. Click the New button in that window. You'll be taken to the table design window shown in Figure 4.4.

3. Type in a field name, then press Tab or click in the Data Type column.

4. In the Data Type column, click the drop-down list button or press Alt+↓ to view the list of data types (if the list isn't already open).

5. Choose the data type for the current field.

6. Press Tab or click in the Description column. You can type an optional description of the field you are defining here. For instance, if you are defining the Customer ID field, you could enter something like **Customer's unique ID (four digits)**. Later, when you actually start putting data into the table, this brief description will appear in the status bar to remind you of exactly what needs to be typed into this field.

7. Press Tab, or click in the Field Name column in the next row.

FIGURE 4.4

The table design
window

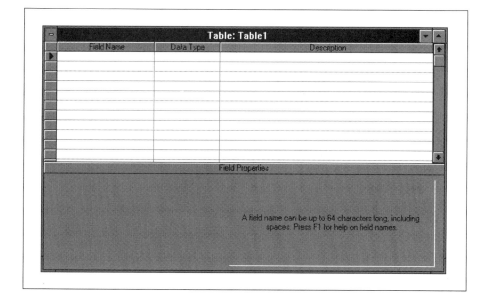

8. Repeat Steps 3 through 7 for each field in the table you're creating
at the moment.

Assuming you've planned your table on paper, defining it now on the
screen should simply be a matter of "filling in the blanks."

Making Changes and Corrections

To change existing text in a field, simply click wherever you need to make
a change and then type your change. (You can use the Backspace and
Delete keys to erase text.)

You can also use any of the techniques listed below to make changes and
corrections to rows, if need be, while designing your table:

* To select a row that you want to move or delete, first click the
field selector to the left of the field name. The entire row will be
selected (Figure 4.5).

FIGURE 4.5

Clicking the field selector to the left of a field name selects the entire row.

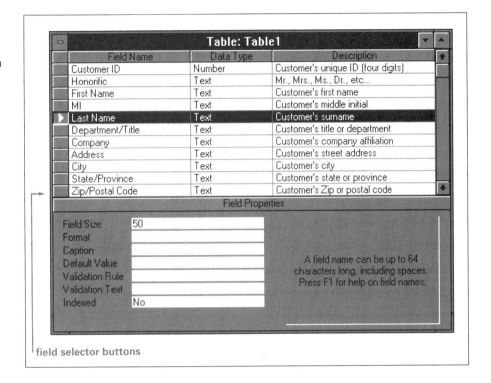

field selector buttons

- To delete a row that has been selected, press Delete or choose Edit ➤ Delete Row. (Choose Edit ➤ Undo Delete to restore a row if you delete it by accident.)

- To insert a new row at a selected row position, press Insert or choose Edit ➤ Insert Row.

- To move a selected row, click the field selector again, but this time hold down the mouse button. Drag the row to its new position, then release the mouse button.

TIP

Chapter 6 presents more information on changing and refining the structure of a table.

Choosing the Primary Key

To define the primary key for the current table:

1. Select the field that you want to define as the primary key, by clicking the *field selector button* to the left of the field name.

2. If you want to define multiple fields as the primary key, hold down the Ctrl key as you click the field selector of each additional field that you want to define as the primary key.

3. Click on the Primary Key button (shown at left) in the tool bar.

A key symbol appears in the field selector for the selected field(s), as shown in Figure 4.6. If you make a mistake, simply repeat the steps to redefine the key.

Saving the Table Structure

When you've finished defining your table, follow these steps to save it:

1. Choose File ➤ Close or double-click the Control-menu box in the upper left corner of the table design window. You'll see this dialog box:

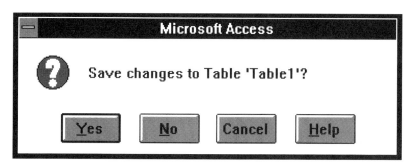

FIGURE 4.6

The Customer ID
field marked as the
primary key

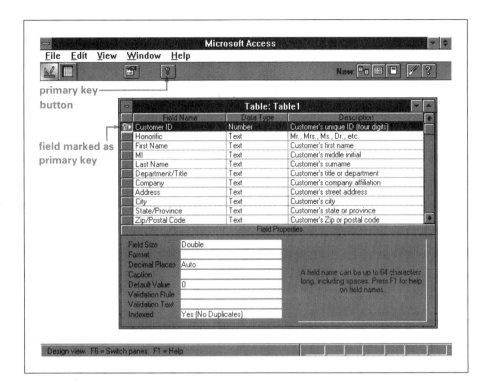

2. Choose Yes, and you'll be taken to the Save As dialog box.

3. Type the name of the table. The name you enter can be up to 64 characters in length, and may contain letters, numbers, and blank spaces. However, it *cannot* contain a period (.), exclamation point (!), brackets [ ], leading blanks, or ASCII control characters (ASCII values 0 through 32).

4. Choose OK.

5. If you *didn't* define a primary key for the current table, you'll see this dialog box:

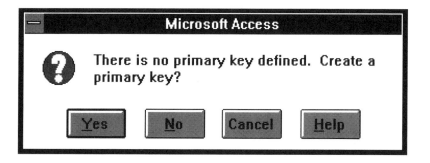

- If you simply forgot to define your own primary key, choose Cancel to return to the table structure and define your own primary key.

- If you choose Yes, Access will create a primary key for you, as described below.

- If you want to save the table structure without a primary key, choose No.

If you do choose Yes, Access will add a Counter field, named ID, to your table structure, and make it the primary key. However, if there's already a Counter field in the table, and you haven't defined some other field as the primary key, Access will just mark that Counter field as the primary key.

If you're in a quandary about whether or not to let Access create a primary key, just choose Yes to let Access do its thing. In the long run, your table operations will go more quickly and you'll have more flexibility in managing your data if the table has a primary key.

Once the table is saved, you can open it up and start adding data, as described in the next chapter. Optionally, if you want to create additional tables, you can start planning those tables now, and then create them, using the procedures we've just finished describing.

A More Complete Database Design: Designing Multiple Tables

The database design I presented back in Chapter 3 was a fairly simple one, only because I didn't want to further complicate the issue with too many tables and fields. That design illustrates the basics of one-to-many relationships. But in real life, you might want your database to contain quite a few more fields and tables.

The Orchids database we'll be using for examples from this point on will use a much more complete design, consisting of a few additional tables. Figure 4.7 illustrates the design.

Before we actually create all the tables in the Orchids database, we still need to think about data types and primary keys.

When your database contains multiple tables, you need to think especially hard about the data types of the common fields that relate the tables, as well as the primary key used within each table. Here are some important points to keep in mind, which we'll illustrate in a moment.

FIGURE 4.7

A more complete database design for a retail business. This is the design we'll be using for future examples throughout this book.

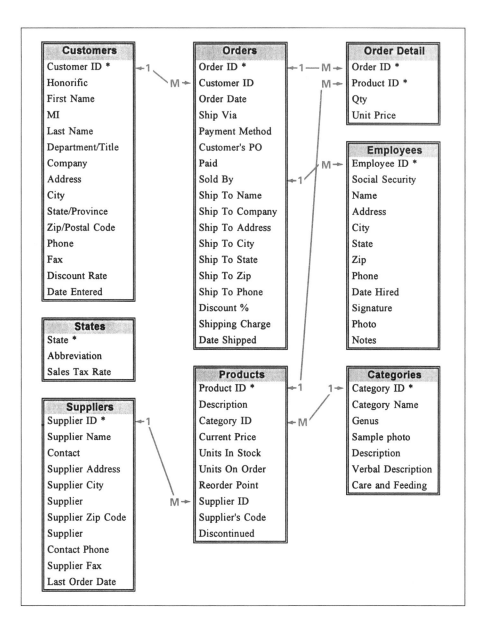

- When defining the data type for the key field (i.e., the common field—see Chapter 3) that links two tables, make sure that you give that field the same data type in both tables. *Exception:* If the key field on the "one side" of the relationship has the Counter data type, set the corresponding common field in the table on the "many side" to the Number data type, with the Long Integer property. We'll present an example and show you how to do this in a moment.

- You can mark the key field on the "one side" of the one-to-many relationship as the primary key for that table. In Figure 4.7, the primary key fields are marked with an asterisk (*).

- In the table on the "many side" of a one-to-many relationship, you *don't* want to mark the common field by itself as the primary key, as doing so would prevent you from entering many records with the same value into that field. Instead, try to mark the common field *plus* additional fields in that table as the primary key, so that you can enter multiple records with the same value in the common field. For instance, we marked both the Order ID and Product ID fields in the Order Details table as the primary key.

In the sections that follow I'll present the structure of each of the Orchids database tables to illustrate these important points. If you want to create these same tables, make sure you put them all into the Orchids database, or some other single database of your choosing.

NOTE

I've intentionally used a database design that's similar to the Northwind Traders example database (*nwind.mdb*) that came with your Access package. For one thing, it's a good general-purpose design. For another, if you want to try something out on your own without *creating* all the sample tables that follow and putting sample data into them, you should be able to experiment with just a little improvising here and there.

The Customers Table

We've already described the Customers table in depth. Figure 4.8 shows that table's structure in its entirety, on a high-resolution monitor so that you can see all the fields. Notice that Customer ID is the primary key, and that that field has the Number data type.

FIGURE 4.8

The full structure of the sample Customers table. Customer ID is the primary key, and its data type is Number.

Field Name	Data Type	Description
Customer ID	Number	Customer's unique ID (four digits)
Honorific	Text	Mr., Mrs., Ms., Dr., etc...
First Name	Text	Customer's first name
MI	Text	Customer's middle initial
Last Name	Text	Customer's last name
Department/Title	Text	Customer's title or department
Company	Text	Customer's company affiliation
Address	Text	Customer's street address
City	Text	Customer's city
State/Province	Text	Customers state or province
Zip/Postal Code	Text	Customer's zip or postal code
Phone	Text	Customer's phone number
Fax	Text	Customer's FAX number
Discount Rate	Number	Customer's standard discount
Date Entered	Date/Time	Date this record entered

Table: Customers

Field Properties

Field Size	Double
Format	
Decimal Places	Auto
Caption	
Default Value	0
Validation Rule	
Validation Text	
Indexed	Yes (No Duplicates)

The field description is optional. It helps you describe the field and is also displayed in the status bar when you select this field on a form. Press F1 for help on descriptions.

NOTE I'll use my high-resolution monitor only to display figures where standard VGA doesn't show enough information. Your screen won't show as much information at one time unless you also happen to be using a 1024×768 monitor.

The Products Table

The Products table stores information about products, with each record storing all the information about a single product. Its structure is shown in Figure 4.9. The primary key in this table is Product ID. That field is the Text data type because my sample product codes include letters, such as MO-100.

The Orders Table

The Orders table, shown in Figure 4.10, will contain one record for each order placed by a customer. Order ID is the primary key in this table, and

FIGURE 4.9

Structure of the Products table. Product ID is the primary key, and its data type is Text.

Field Name	Data Type	Description
Product ID	Text	Product identification number
Description	Text	Product name/description
Category ID	Text	Product category (link to Categories table)
Current Price	Currency	Current selling price
Units In Stock	Number	Quantity in stock
Units On Order	Number	Quantity on order
Reorder Point	Number	Reorder at what quantity?
Supplier ID	Text	Who supplies us? (link to Suppliers table)
Supplier's Code	Text	Supplier's product code, for reordering purposes
Discontinued	Yes/No	Yes if discontinued, No if actively selling

Table: Products

Field Properties

Field Size: 50
Format:
Caption:
Default Value:
Validation Rule:
Validation Text:
Indexed: Yes (No Duplicates)

The field description is optional. It helps you describe the field and is also displayed in the status bar when you select this field on a form. Press F1 for help on descriptions.

FIGURE 4.10

The Orders table for the Orchids database. Order ID is the primary key, and it has the Counter data type.

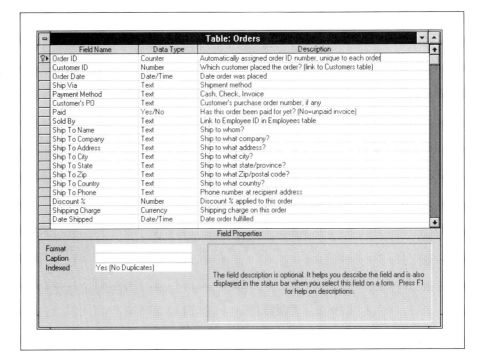

its data type is Counter. Access will automatically assign a unique order number to each order, starting at 1, with this data type.

The Order Details Table

The Order Details table, shown in Figure 4.11, will contain one record for each line item on an order form. Order ID is the field that links this table to the Orders table.

A couple of tricky things are needed in the Order Details table. For one thing, the Order ID field's data type must be Number, even though the Order ID field in the Orders table is Counter. The reason for this is that several records in this table are likely to have the same Order ID number; thus, we can't have Access automatically number the records.

Secondly, it's important that the Order ID field in both the Orders and Order Details tables have identical *properties*, (a topic we will discuss in more detail in Chapter 6). For now, you just need to be sure that when

FIGURE 4.11

The structure of the Order Details table. The Order ID and Product ID fields together make up the primary key for this table.

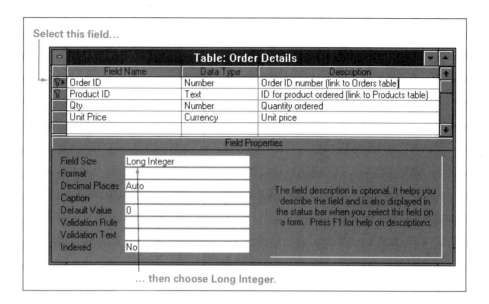

Select this field...

... then choose Long Integer.

you create the Order ID field in the Order Details table, you give it the Number data type. Then click the Field Size option down near the bottom of the window, and choose *Long Integer* from the menu that appears.

Double-check to make sure you did it right by verifying that the field selector is pointing to the Order ID number, and that *Long Integer* appears next to Field Size, as in Figure 4.11.

Finally, we can't use the Order ID field alone in this table as a primary key, because this table is on the "many" side of a relationship, which means that several records will need to have the same Order ID number. Therefore, and as discussed earlier, we've used Order ID and Product ID combined as the primary key.

The Employees Table

The Employees table, shown in Figure 4.12, stores information about employees. We'll use this table often to illustrate OLE objects and memo fields. The primary key in this table is Employee ID, and, since we'll be using the person's initials to uniquely identify each employee, its data type is text.

FIGURE 4.12

Structure of the Employees table, where Employee ID, a Text field, is identified as the primary key

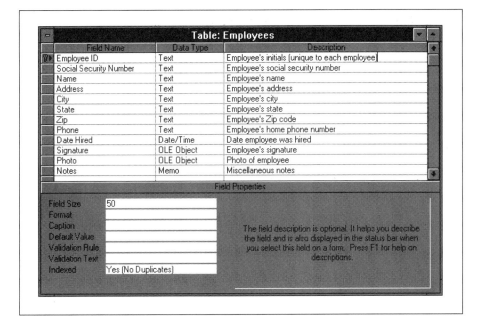

We'll also be storing the employee's initials in the Orders table, in a field named Sold By. We'll use this link later as a means of looking up an employee's initials while entering new orders.

The Categories Table

We'll use the Categories table to help us view products by category, and we'll also use it to demonstrate some fancy stuff with OLE fields. The structure of the Categories table is shown in Figure 4.13. Category ID is the primary key, and its data type is Text.

The States Table

The States table will provide a quick on-screen reference to two-letter state abbreviations and to sales tax rates in various states. The structure of the States table is shown in Figure 4.14, with the State field chosen as the primary key.

FIGURE 4.13

Structure of the
Categories table.
Category ID is the
primary key, and its
data type is Text.

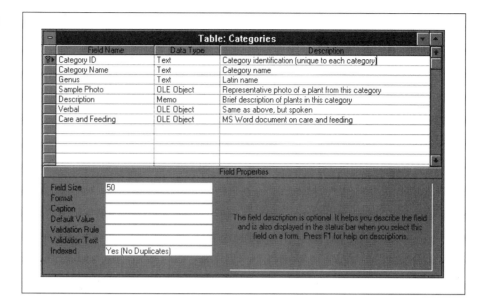

FIGURE 4.14

Structure of States
table, which will
come in handy as a
reference for looking
up two-letter state
abbreviations, and
sales tax rates in
various states

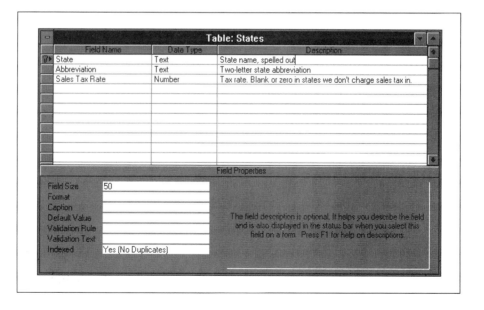

In my sketched-out database design I didn't include any "one-to-many" lines connecting the States table to any other tables, because the table can be used independently to look up information on an as-needed basis, as you'll see in Chapter 10.

The Suppliers Table

The Suppliers table stores information about companies that the Orchid Jungle purchases products from. The primary key here is the Supplier ID field, which is also used in the Products table to identify which supplier each product is ordered from. Figure 4.15 shows the structure of the Suppliers table.

FIGURE 4.15

Structure of the Suppliers table, which will contain one record for every company that the Orchid Jungle purchases supplies from

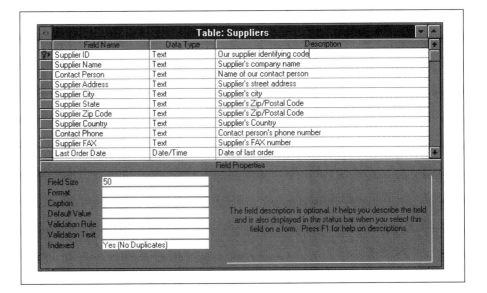

How the Database Window Will Look

After you create all of these tables, the database window will display all of their names, as shown below. Once again, all these tables will be stored within the single database file, which in this example we've named **orchids.db**.

Getting Help

 Like any Windows application, Access has a complete online help system. So, when working on your own, you can press F1, or choose Help ➤ Contents, or click the Help button (shown at left) on the tool bar, or the Help button in the current dialog box, if any, to get help.

N O T E Because all Windows applications use the standard Windows help system, there's really no need for us to describe it here. If you're new to Windows, see your Windows manual for more information on using Help.

Using "What Is...?"

 In addition to the standard help, Access offers "What is...?" help. To use this feature, just press Shift+F1. The mouse pointer will have a large question mark attached to it. Just click whatever button or object you have a question about to get help.

Using Cue Cards to Coach You

Access also includes a new level of help, called Cue Cards, that offer more of a step-by-step, question-and-answer kind of support. To call up the Cue Cards:

- Choose Help ➤ Cue Cards

The opening screen presents the simple question *What do you want to do?*, as shown in Figure 4.16. You answer by clicking the button next to whichever topic you want.

Once you pick a topic, you'll be given information, or perhaps additional topics to choose from. You can flip to the next cue card, when you're ready, simply by clicking the Next button at the bottom of the window.

Cue cards remain on the screen even if you click outside the cue card window. You can also move, size, or minimize the Cue Card window using the standard Windows techniques.

FIGURE 4.16

Cue cards provide coaching in a question-and-answer format.

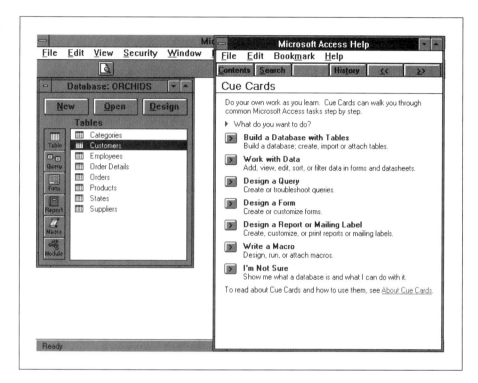

TIP

If you're using Windows 3.1, you can also keep the standard help screens in the forefront by choosing Help ➤ Always on Top from the Help window's menu bar.

When you want to close the Cue Cards, just double-click the Control-menu box in the upper left corner of the Cue Card window.

Summary

In this chapter we've covered in considerable depth all the details of creating tables. In the next chapter you'll learn how to open the tables and how to add, change, and delete data—in general, how to manage table data.

Entering, Editing, and Printing Data

fast TRACK

To change the contents of a field   **134**

> move the insertion point to the field, either by clicking on the field, or by pressing F2 if the field is selected. Then make your changes using standard Windows editing techniques.

To undo changes   **135**

> press Esc once to undo changes to the current field. Press Esc a second time to undo all changes to the record. Optionally, choose an Undo option from the Edit menu.

To delete a record   **136**

> click the record selector at the left edge of the record you want to delete, to select the entire record. Then press Delete or choose Edit ➤ Delete.

When entering data in a memo field   **151**

> press Ctrl+↵, rather than just ↵, when you need to end a short line, a paragraph, or insert a blank line.

To embed an object in an OLE field   **168**

> use the standard Windows cut-and-paste techniques to copy an object from an OLE server application into an OLE Object field in your table.

To link an object to an OLE field   **170**

> use the standard Windows cut-and-paste techniques to copy an object from an OLE server to the Clipboard, then use Edit ➤ Paste Link (rather than Edit ➤ Paste) to place the object in an OLE Object field in your table.

IN THIS chapter you'll learn how to open a table, add data to it, and make changes and corrections as needed. You'll also learn about cutting and pasting, linking and embedding, finding and replacing data, and other topics that go along with getting data into a table and maintaining it once it's there.

Opening a Table

The first step to entering or editing table data is, of course, to open the table:

NOTE   If the database the table is stored in isn't open yet, you need to use File ➤ Open Database to open the database first.

1. Click the Table object button in the database window.

2. Double-click the name of the table you want to open, or click the table name once than click the Open button.

The Datasheet View

The table opens in *Datasheet view,* where you can see multiple records (if there are any in the table), and as many fields as will fit across the screen. Figure 5.1 shows an example, where I've opened the Customers table described in the preceding chapter with some data already in it.

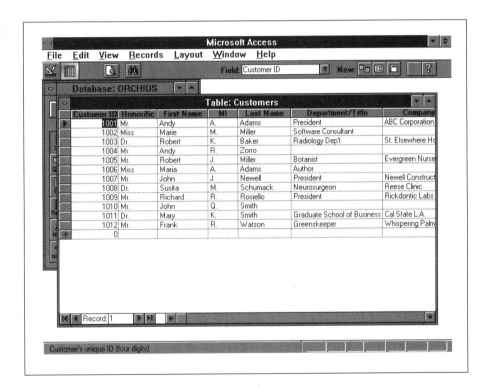

The menu bar and tool bar change to offer some new options. The roles of various buttons are shown below.

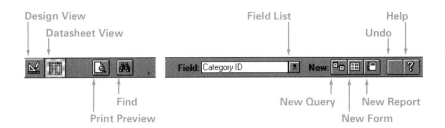

T I P

If you want to see the description of a tool bar button, move the mouse pointer to that button and hold down, *don't click,* the mouse button. As long as you keep the button pressed, a description appears in the status bar near the bottom of the screen. If you want to activate the button's feature, simply let go of the mouse button. If you *don't* want to activate the button's feature, move the mouse pointer off the button before releasing the mouse button. You can also press Shift+F1, then click on the tool bar button for which you want help.

Adding New Records to a Table

Generally, one of the first jobs in using a table is to put some data into it. Access always displays a blank record, with an asterisk indicator at the left, at the bottom of the datasheet. You can type a new record into that blank record at any time. To do so:

1. Move to the last (blank) record in the table, or choose Records ➤ Go To ➤ New, or press Ctrl++ (Ctrl with a plus sign.)

2. Type the contents of the current field. If your entry is wider than the column, text will scroll as you type.

3. Press Tab to move to the next field, or just click on the next field.

After typing in the last field for the record, you can press Tab once again to move to another blank record, and then enter another new record. As soon as you move the "focus"—the highlight—from the current record, that record is saved to disk.

NOTE If Access displays an error message and refuses to save your new record, see "Troubleshooting Data Entry and Editing Problems" near the end of this chapter.

Each field in a table will accept only values that make sense for that field's data type. Some guidelines to keep in mind:

- A Text field will accept any characters, including foreign language and other special characters (described below). By default, a Text field will accept a maximum of 50 characters, but you can increase that to up to 255 characters by changing the fields's *properties,* as discussed in Chapter 6.

- When typing an entry into a Number or Currency field, only valid numbers are acceptable. You cannot type letters or punctuation marks other than - (minus or hyphen), . (period), , (comma) and ( ) (parentheses used to identify a negative number) into these types of fields.

- The Yes/No field type will accept only the words *yes, true,* or *on* for Yes, and *no, false,* or *off* for No. This data type will also accept a number, converting 0 to No and any other number to Yes.

- A Date/Time field entry must conform to the date format specified in the International settings in the **Windows Control Panel**. In the United States, this is mm/dd/yy for dates (e.g., you can enter a value of 1/31/93), and hh:mm A/P for times (e.g., you can enter 12:30p or 12:30:00PM). You can press Ctrl+; (Ctrl-semicolon) to insert the current date, or Ctrl+: (Ctrl-colon) to insert the current time.

- A Counter field accepts no value, and cannot be changed.

- Pressing Ctrl+↵ inserts a carriage return. You can use this to end paragraphs and insert blank lines in Memo fields.

We'll discuss specific techniques for Memo and OLE Object fields a little later in this chapter.

Copying Data from the Previous Record

If you want the field that you're about to type data into to have the same value as the field immediately above, press Ctrl+' (Ctrl-apostrophe) or Ctrl+" (Ctrl-quotation mark).

Changing a Default Value

If the field you are about to type data into has a default value, you can just press Tab to accept that suggested value, or you can type in a new value. If you type in a new value, then decide to revert back to the suggested default value, press Ctrl+Alt+Spacebar.

Typing Special Characters

You can type foreign language and other special characters into any text or memo field. To use characters from the IBM Extended Character Set, follow these steps:

1. Position the insertion point where you want to type the special character.

2. Toggle the Num Lock key on if it is off.

3. Hold down the Alt key, and, while holding it down, type the character's three-digit number, as listed in Figure 5.2, *using the numeric keypad* (don't use the numbers at the top of the keyboard).

4. Release the Alt key.

Code	Text	Code	Text	Code	Text	Code	Text
128	Ç	140	î	152	ÿ	164	ñ
129	ü	141	ì	153	Ö	165	Ñ
130	é	142	Ä	154	Ü	166	ª
131	â	143	Å	155	¢	167	º
132	ä	144	É	156	£	168	¿
133	à	145	æ	157	¥	169	⌐
134	å	146	Æ	158	₧	170	¬
135	ç	147	ô	159	ƒ	171	½
136	ê	148	ö	160	á	172	¼
137	ë	149	ò	161	í	173	¡
138	è	150	û	162	ó	174	«
139	ï	151	ù	163	ú	175	»

TIP

If your printer supports multiple character sets, use the *PC-8* set to print characters shown in Figure 5.2. If you can't print or view those characters, try using the Character Map instead.

You can also cut-and-paste special characters from the **Windows 3.1 Character Map**. Here's how:

1. If Character Map is already open, you can just switch to it, and then skip the next step. Use Task List (Ctrl+Esc) or the Windows 3.1 "cool switch" (Alt+Tab) to get to Program Manager. (Alt+Tab works only in Windows 3.1, and only if the [windows] section of the win.ini file includes the command **CoolSwitch=1**.)

2. Open the Accessories group, and double-click the Character Map icon. The Character Map appears on the screen, as in Figure 5.3.

3. Open the Font drop-down list, and choose whatever font you're using to display text in the datasheet. (If you have never changed the font, this will most likely be *MS Sans Serif*.)

FIGURE 5.3

The Windows 3.1
Character Map

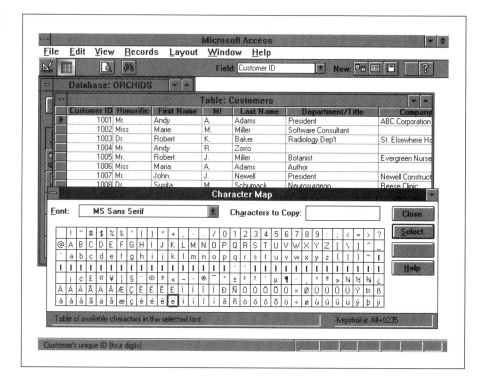

4. Click the character you want to copy, then choose Select. (You can repeat this step to select as many characters as you want.) The character(s) you select appear in the Characters to Copy: text box.

5. Choose Copy to copy the selected characters to the Clipboard.

6. Use Alt+Tab or the Task List (Ctrl+Esc) to switch back to Microsoft Access.

7. Choose Edit ➤ Paste, or press Ctrl+V to copy the character(s) into the field.

As an alternative, you can just use the Alt+*numeric keypad* method described above if you know the four-digit number for the character you want to insert from the Windows Character Map. (You use a three-digit number for ASCII extended characters, but a four-digit number for characters from the Windows Character Map.) For instance, typing Alt+0169 on the numeric keypad inserts a copyright symbol. For more information on using Character Map, refer to your Windows 3.1 documentation.

Hiding Existing Records While Adding New Ones

You can hide existing records entered in a previous session before entering new records. Doing so will help you to avoid inadvertently editing the existing records, and perhaps avoid any distractions that the old records might impose. To view only the new record you're entering into a table:

1. Choose Records ➤ Data Entry.

2. Type in as many new records as you wish.

3. To view all the records in the table again, choose View ➤ Show All Records.

Importing and Attaching Existing Data

If you already have data on your computer that you want to manage with Access, but that data is stored in some other format, chances are you can import it into Access, or attach it to an Access table, rather than retyping it in from scratch. See Chapter 19 for more information on these topics.

Navigating a Table

Once you've entered some data in a table, you can get around using your mouse and the various cursor positioning keys. Table 5.1 summarizes the navigation keys.

You can also use the menus and navigation buttons shown in Figure 5.4 to move through records and fields. (You'll see how to use the Record Selectors and Field Selectors a little later in the chapter.)

TABLE 5.1: Summary of keyboard techniques for navigating a table

KEY(S)	DESCRIPTION
↑, ↓	Moves to next/previous record (datasheet view) or next/previous field (form view)
Ctrl+↑, Ctrl+↓	Moves to top/bottom of column
←, →	Moves to next/previous character (insertion point) or next/previous field (selected data)
Ctrl+←, Ctrl+→	Moves one word left/right while insertion point is visible
Tab, Shift+Tab	Moves to next/previous field
↵	Moves to next field
Ctrl+↵	Ends short line or paragraph, or inserts a blank line, in memo or lengthy text field
PgUp, PgDn	Scrolls up/down one screen
Ctrl+PgUp, Ctrl+PgDn	Moves right/left on screen in datasheet view, to previous/next record in form view
Home, End	Moves to first/last field of record
Ctrl+Home, Ctrl+End	Moves to first/last field in table
F5	Selects record number box. Type in new number and press ↵ to go to that record position

Moving through Records

To move through records in a table:

• Choose Records ➤ Go To, then the record you want to go to: First, Last, Next, Previous, or New (for entering a new record).

• Or use the equivalent buttons near the lower left corner of the datasheet view window, as shown in Figure 5.4.

Tools for moving through and selecting records and fields in a table

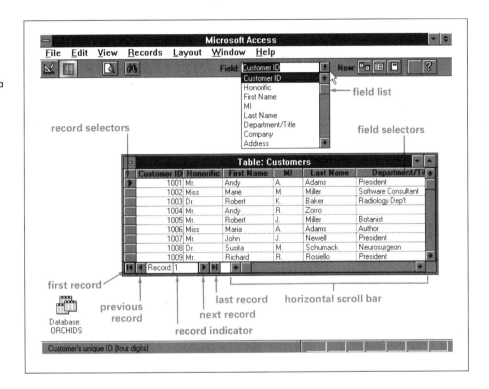

- You can specify a record by number by double-clicking the current record indicator or pressing F5, either of which allows you to type in a specific record number, then press ↵ to go to that record. For instance, if you enter **3** the focus will move to the third record in the table.

You can also use techniques described under "Finding the Data to Edit" later in this chapter to find a record that you want to view or edit.

Moving to a Field

If the table is wider than the window it's displayed in, you can use the horizontal scroll bar at the bottom of the datasheet window to scroll across fields. You can also click the drop-down list button next to the Field text box to view a list of fields in the table, as in Figure 5.4. After you open the list, just click the name of the field you want to move to.

Editing Records

Editing records is basically a matter of moving to the data you want to change and then typing your changes. Whenever you begin editing a record, the record indicator shows a pencil icon to indicate that the record is being edited.

Access follows the standard text-editing guidelines that all Windows applications share. But exactly how Access behaves while you're editing a record depends on whether you work with selected text or with the insertion point. Here are some specific guidelines:

- If you move to a field using the keyboard, the entire contents of the field are selected as soon as you get to the field.

- Similarly, if you click to the left of the first character in the field (when the mouse pointer has an arrow shape), the entire field is selected.

- When the field's entire contents are selected, anything you start typing immediately replaces the full contents of the field. Pressing Delete or Backspace erases the entire field's contents. Pressing ← or → moves to the next field.

- If you click *within* the field's contents, the field's contents are not selected; instead, the blinking insertion point appears at the character you clicked.

- When the insertion point appears, any new text you type is inserted at the insertion point, provided the Insert mode is active. If you're in Overwrite mode, new text replaces existing text on a character-by-character basis. Press the Insert key to toggle between modes. OVR appears in the status bar when you're in Overwrite mode.

- When the insertion point is visible, pressing Backspace erases the character to the left of the insertion point, and pressing Delete erases the character to the right of the insertion point. Pressing ← or → moves the insertion point within the field. (You can use Tab to jump from one field to the next, and Shift+Tab to jump to the preceding field.)

- Pressing F2 toggles between insertion-point (editing) mode and field-selection (navigation) mode.

- When the insertion point is visible, you can select part of a field to replace or delete using standard Windows techniques. For instance, you can press Shift+ an arrow key, or Shift+Home, or Shift+End to select part of the field. You can also drag the mouse pointer though the text you want to select, or double-click a word to select the entire word.

As with adding new records, any changes you make to the current record are saved when you move to another record.

Table 5.2 summarizes the editing keys and techniques.

Using Undo to Cancel a Change

Access keeps track of your recent changes to a field or record, and gives you ample opportunity to undo those changes. Options on the Edit menu let you choose how many changes to undo.

If you want to undo the changes that you just made to the current field, including restoring any text that you accidentally deleted, and you haven't moved out of that field, just choose Edit ➤ Undo Typing or click the Undo button in the tool bar.

If you've made several changes to the current field or record, but haven't yet moved to another record, you can choose Edit ➤ Undo Current Field to undo all the changes to the current field, or Edit ➤ Undo Current Record to undo all the changes to the current record.

You can also press Esc to undo the changes to the current field. Pressing Esc a second time will undo all the changes you made to the current record.

Once you move from the record you're editing to another record, the changes you made to that record are saved. But you can still undo the changes to the previous record by choosing Edit ➤ Undo Saved Record. However, this option is only available for a limited time. For instance, if you switch to another window, the option Undo Saved Record won't be available anymore.

TABLE 5.2: Summary of editing keys and techniques

KEY	DESCRIPTION
F2	Switches between insertion point and selection
Backspace	Deletes selection, or character to left of insertion point
Delete	Deletes selection, or character to right of insertion point
Insert	Toggles between insert and overwrite modes (insertion point)
Ctrl+' or Ctrl+"	Copies data from field above
Escape	Undoes changes to field (first press), then remaining changes to record (second press)
Ctrl++	Adds new record
Ctrl+-	Deletes current record
Ctrl+;	Inserts the current date
Ctrl+:	Inserts the current time
Shift+↵	Saves current record
Ctrl+Alt+Spacebar	Insert default value defined for the field (if any)

Deleting a Record

To delete entire records from a table:

1. Select the record you want to delete, using one of the following methods:

   • Click the record selector at the left of the record.
   • Or choose Edit ➤ Select Record.

- Or press Shift+Spacebar if there is already a field selected within the record you want to select. (If necessary, press F2 to select a field, then press Shift+Spacebar.)

You cannot undo entire record deletions, so use these techniques carefully!

The entire record will be selected, like the record for customer 1002 below:

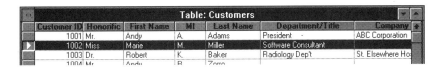

Customer ID	Honorific	First Name	MI	Last Name	Department/Title	Company
1001	Mr.	Andy	A.	Adams	President	ABC Corporation
1002	Miss	Marie	M.	Miller	Software Consultant	
1003	Dr.	Robert	K.	Baker	Radiology Dep't	St. Elsewhere Ho
1004	Mr.	Andy	B.	Zorro		

As an alternative to selecting the record(s) you want to delete, you can just press Ctrl+- (Ctrl-hyphen) to delete the current record (i.e., whatever record the focus is in at the moment.)

2. If you want to select multiple records to delete, press Shift+↑ or Shift+↓ to extend the selection. You can also drag the mouse pointer through several record indicators to select a group of adjacent records.

3. Press Delete or choose Edit ➤ Delete. You'll see this dialog box telling you how many records you've just tried to delete:

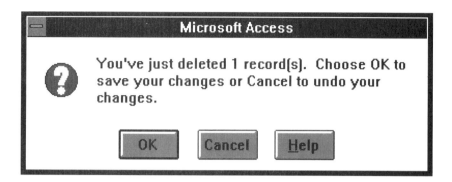

4. If you're sure you want to delete the record(s), choose OK. Otherwise, choose Cancel.

If your table contains a Counter field, you might be surprised to see that deleting records has no effect on the contents of a Counter field. That's because once entered, the contents of a Counter field never change. Access behaves this way to ensure integrity between multiple tables that use the Counter field as the common field between two or more tables.

How Do I Insert a Record between Records?

The answer to the question above is simple: you *don't*. This might seem odd, especially if you're a spreadsheet user. But there are two reasons why you don't need to insert records between existing records. For one, you can sort records into whatever order you wish at any time. For another, if the table has a primary key, records will be re-sorted by the primary key field every time you open the table. So if you insert a record into a specific position in the table, chances are it wouldn't be in that same position the next time you open the table anyway.

Therefore, there's really no reason to insert a record between existing records. Instead, just continue to add new records to the bottom of the table, and then sort the records however you wish later (Chapter 7).

Customizing the Datasheet View

You can change the width and order of columns in the datasheet, "freeze" columns, and do other tasks that might make entering and editing data a little easier.

Changing Column Widths

To widen or narrow a column:

1. Move the mouse pointer to the right side of the field selector at the top of the column you want to widen or narrow. The mouse pointer changes to a two-headed arrow with a bar down the middle, as illustrated below:

2. Hold down the mouse button and drag the column edge to the desired width. Then release the mouse button.

To size multiple columns all at the same time, you can use the following technique. Note that the columns must all be adjacent, and that they will all be changed equally.

1. Select the columns you want to resize. To do so, you can either drag the mouse pointer through the field selectors, or click the field selector of the first column, then Shift+Click the field selector of the last column you want to select.

2. Choose Layout ➤ Column Width. You'll see this dialog box:

3. Type the width you want (e.g., **20** to display 20 characters), or choose Standard Width to specify the default width. Then choose OK.

Moving Columns

As with resizing columns, you can move one or more columns at one time. To move columns:

1. First, select the column or columns you want to move:

   • If you want to move a single column, simply click its field selector. The entire column is selected, as in the example below:

   • If you want to move multiple (adjacent) columns, hold down the Shift key and click the field selector of the column you want to extend the selection to. Or you can just drag the mouse pointer through the field selectors to select multiple columns.

2. Click the field selector again, and drag the column(s) left or right. A solid bar indicates where the column(s) will appear (Figure 5.5).

3. Release the mouse button when the solid bar is at the position you want.

FIGURE 5.5

To move one or more columns, select the column(s) that you want to move, then drag the column(s) to a new position in the datasheet view.

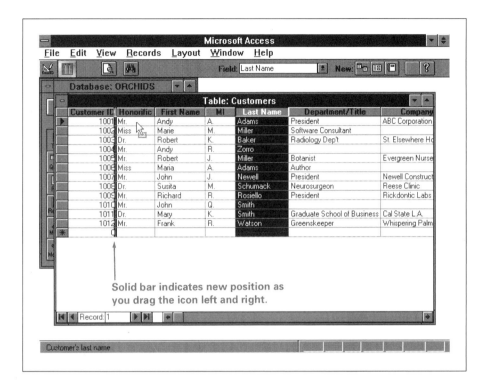

Solid bar indicates new position as you drag the icon left and right.

Hiding Columns

You can hide one or more columns to make it easier to focus on specific fields within the table.

1. Click the field selector for the column you want to hide, or, to choose multiple (adjacent) columns, Shift+Click on the columns you want or drag the mouse pointer through their field selectors.

2. Choose Layout ➤ Hide Columns.

Showing (Unhiding) Columns

To bring columns out of hiding:

1. Choose Layout ➤ Show Columns. You'll see this dialog box:

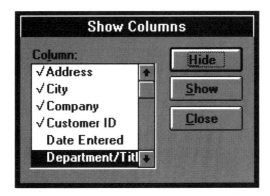

2. Click the name of the field you want to redisplay, then choose Show. Repeat this step for each column you want to display.

TIP   To redisplay all the columns, drag the mouse pointer through all the field names, or press Shift+Ctrl+End, then choose Show.

3. Choose Close to leave the dialog box.

"Freezing" Columns

When the table is wider than the screen, scrolling to the rightmost columns forces the leftmost columns off the edge of the window. This can make it difficult to know exactly what record you're editing, particularly if the information that best identifies the record is in the left columns.

You can *freeze* any columns so that those columns are always in view. For instance, when editing the Customers table, you might want to freeze the

Last Name and First Name columns so that the customer names are always visible. To freeze columns:

1. If necessary, move the fields that you want to keep in view to the leftmost column(s) of the datasheet view, using techniques described under "Moving Columns" earlier in this section.

2. Select the column you want to freeze by clicking the field selector at the top of the column. As usual you can select multiple columns using Shift+Click or by dragging the mouse pointer through the appropriate field selectors.

3. Choose Layout ➤ Freeze Columns.

Figure 5.6 shows an example where I dragged the Last Name and First Name fields to the leftmost column positions in the table. Then I froze those two columns. Even though the insertion point is now scrolled way

FIGURE 5.6

Moving the Last Name and First Name fields to the leftmost column positions, then freezing those columns, lets you scroll over to the columns near the right edge of the table and still see the customer's names.

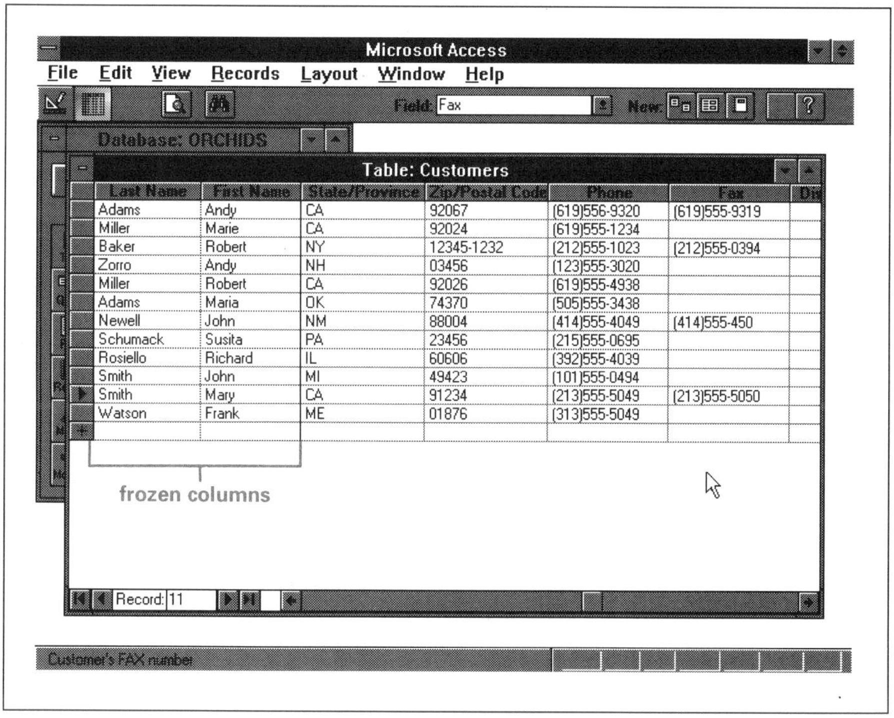

over to the Phone and Fax fields, you can still see the customers' names in the leftmost columns.

Unfreezing Columns

To unfreeze columns:

- Choose Layout ➤ Unfreeze All Columns.

Changing the Row Height

To change the row height in the datasheet view:

1. Move the mouse pointer to the line separating any two record selector buttons. The mouse pointer changes to a vertical two-headed arrow split by a horizontal bar, as illustrated below:

	Customer ID	Honorific	First Name
▶	1001	Mr.	Andy
	1002	Miss	Marie
	1003	Dr.	Rubert
	1004	Mr	Andy

2. Hold down the mouse button, drag the icon up or down, then release the mouse button.

As an alternative to dragging, you can:

1. Choose Layout ➤ Row Height to view this dialog box:

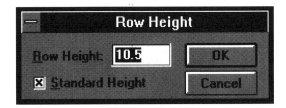

2. Type in the new row height, or choose Standard Height to reestablish the default height, then choose OK.

Changing the Font in a Datasheet

To change the font in a datasheet:

1. Choose Layout ➤ Font.

2. From the Font dialog box choose a font, Font Style, Size, and any effects you want.

3. Choose OK.

Figure 5.7 shows an example where I chose the TrueType Lucida Handwriting font, at 12 points. I also removed the grid lines, as discussed in a moment, in that example.

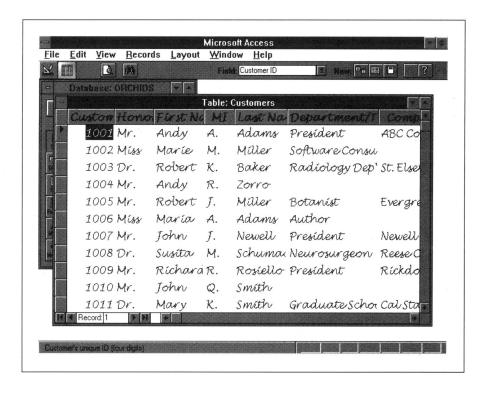

If you want to return to the standard font, repeat the steps and choose *MS Sans Serif* as the font (or a similar font if this is not listed for your setup), *Regular* as the Style, *8* as the size, and no effects.

Hiding or Showing the Gridlines

To hide or show the grid lines in the datasheet view:

1. Choose Layout ➤ Gridlines.

This option acts as a toggle, so you can choose it first to hide, then to display, the grid lines.

Saving or Canceling Your Datasheet Settings

If you customize the datasheet view, you'll see this dialog box when you close the table:

NOTE Though this looks like the standard Windows dialog box for saving changes to data, it's not. Remember, Access saves any changes you make to your data on a record-by-record basis. This dialog box is actually asking if you want to save the customization changes you made to the datasheet *view*.

If you want to keep the customization settings for future sessions, choose Yes. Otherwise choose No.

You can also save the changes to the table view at any time by choosing File ➤ Save Layout.

Printing the Table

In Chapter 12 you'll learn techniques for printing your data in a wide variety of formats. But if you just want to print a quick copy of the data in your table:

1. Choose File ➤ Print to get to the **Print** dialog box.

2. If your printer can print in landscape mode (sideways), and your table is wide, you can switch to landscape mode by choosing Setup, then Landscape (under Orientation), and then OK.

3. Choose OK to start printing.

The Form View

The datasheet view is just one way to view, enter, and edit records. You can also use *form view*, which generally shows only one record at a time. We'll discuss forms in depth in Chapter 9, but here we can introduce them, show you how to create a simple form, and how to enter and edit data with a form.

Creating a Quick Form

You can use the FormWizard to create a quick form on the fly:

1. Starting at the datasheet view for the table you want to create a form for, click the New Form button (shown at left) in the tool bar. Or, choose File ➤ New ➤ Form.

2. If the name of the table that you want to create a form for doesn't already appear in the Select A Table/Query text box, use the drop-down list to choose the appropriate table name.

3. Click the FormWizards button.

4. Choose *Single-column*, then choose OK.

5. To place all the fields on the form, click the >> button in the next dialog box. Or choose specific fields to include by clicking the field name, then clicking the > button.

6. Choose the Next button.

7. Choose any one of the available "looks" from the next dialog box, then choose Next again.

8. In the next box, you can enter a name for the form, or just accept the suggested name.

9. Click the Open button.

Access creates and opens a simple form for the table. Figure 5.8 shows an example of a quick form with the Shadowed look, created for the Products table.

FIGURE 5.8

A sample form
created for the
Products table

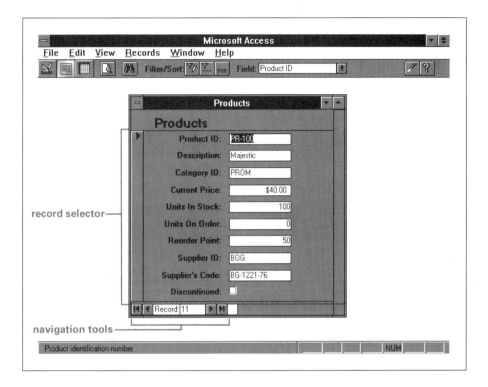

Navigating and Editing with a Form

For the most part, in form view you use the same techniques described
so far for entering data in datasheet view. A few exceptions are listed
below:

- The ↑ and ↓ keys scroll through fields in the form, rather than
  through records in the table. You can press Ctrl+PgUp and
  Ctrl+PgDn to scroll from record to record. You can also use the
  various buttons near the lower left corner of the form window,
  and options on the Record ➤ Go To menu, to move through
  records, or to add a New Record.

- You can click in any field to move the insertion point to it, or click
  on the field name next to the field's contents to select the field's
  contents.

- The Yes/No data type appears as a check box in form view, as below. Clicking that check box inserts an X (which means Yes) or clears the check box (which means No).

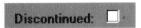

NOTE   A form can also have control buttons, list boxes, and combo boxes. For more information on these options, see Chapter 10.

- To delete the record that's currently displayed in the form, click on the Record Selector button along the left edge of the form window (see Figure 5.8), or choose Edit ➤ Select Record. Then press Delete or choose Edit ➤ Delete.

Switching between Form and Datasheet Views

When you're in form view, you can switch to datasheet view by clicking the Datasheet View button in the tool bar or by choosing View ➤ Datasheet. To switch back to form view, choose View ➤ Form, or click the Form View button.

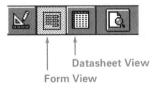

Datasheet View

Form View

Closing a Form View

To remove the form from the screen, simply close it by choosing File ➤ Close, or by choosing Close from the form window's Control-menu box, or by pressing Ctrl+F4. If you've just created the form, you'll see this dialog box:

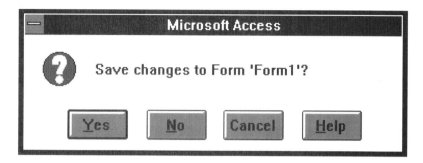

Unless you've spent some time customizing the form, as discussed in Chapter 9, you can just choose No to abandon the form. Later, you can recreate the form as needed using the FormWizard described earlier.

If you do want to save the form, however, choose Yes and enter a name up to 64 characters, including spaces.

Entering and Editing Memo Field Text

If you want to type a lengthy passage of text into a memo field, your best bet might be to first create a custom form (Chapter 9) that displays several lines of text in the memo field. Or you might want to increase the row height in datasheet view. Either way, you'll be able to see much more text as you're typing and editing.

When typing the text, use the general techniques you use in all Windows applications and word processors. For instance, when typing a paragraph, don't press ↵ to end each line. Instead, just let Access word-wrap each line for you.

NOTE When you do get to the end of a paragraph, or want to end a short line, or insert a blank line, press Ctrl+⏎, rather than just ⏎. Pressing ⏎ will finish the entry and move you to the next field.

Finding the Data to Edit

As your table grows, just finding the data you want to view or edit can be a job in itself. The next sections describe a couple of techniques that you can use to find, and optionally replace, data without scrolling around for it.

Finding a Record

To find a record based on the contents of a field:

1. If you want to search a particular field, such as Last Name, move to that field.

2. Click the Find button (shown at left), or choose Edit ➤ Find.

3. Type whatever it is you want to search for (e.g., **smith** if you're looking for that name.)

4. Choose Find First.

Access will find the first record in the table (if any) that matches your request. If the dialog box is covering the data that Access has found, just move the dialog box out of the way by dragging its title bar to a new location on the screen. For instance, in Figure 5.9 I've used the **Find in Field:** dialog box to locate the first Smith in the Customers table, then dragged the dialog box down a bit so I could see the data behind it.

If the record that Access finds isn't the one you want, choose Find Next to find the next record that matches your request. You can keep doing so until Access reports that it has reached the end of the dynaset. At that point, you can either choose Yes to restart the search from the top of the

FIGURE 5.9

A search for smith has located the first Smith in the Customers table.

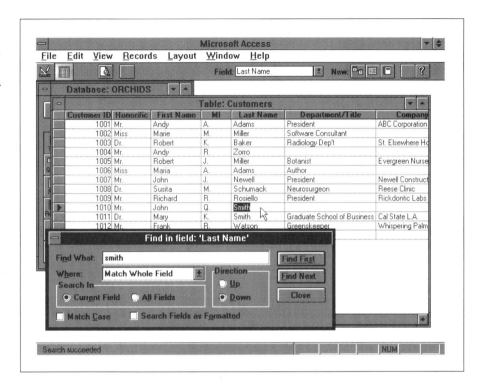

table, or choose No to end the search. When you're done, you can click the Close button in the Find in Field: dialog box to close it.

There are several options in the Find in Field: dialog box that you can use to broaden or narrow the search to your liking, as discussed next.

Matching All or Part of the Field

The drop-down list next to the Where option in the Find in Field: dialog box lets you determine what portion of the field you want to search:

- **Any Part of Field**: The text you type need only exist somewhere within the field. For instance, a search for **smith** will match *Smith* and *Smithsonian*, as well as *Blacksmith*.

- **Match Whole Field**: Only exact matches are found. For example, a search for **smith** will find only *smith* (and *Smith*, if you haven't checked the Match Case check box at the bottom of the dialog box), but not *Blacksmith*.

- **Start of Field**: Only first letters need to match. For example, a search for **smith** will find *Smith* as well as *Smithsonian*, but not *Blacksmith*.

TIP If looking for a particular street in an Address field, such as ocean view, be sure to choose *Any Part of Field* since the street name will likely be embedded within the address (e.g., *1234 Ocean View Lane*).

Searching One or All Fields

The Search In options let you decide how much of each record you want to search:

Current Field: Searches only the field that the focus is on at the moment. (The name of that field appears in the title bar of the Find in Field: dialog box.)

All Fields: Searches all the fields in the table.

Enabling or Disabling Case Sensitivity

If you want the search to be case-sensitive, choose the Match Case option. Otherwise, leave this option cleared.

As an example, if you *don't* choose Match Case, a search for **smith** would find *smith*, *Smith*, *SMITH*, and any other combination of upper and lowercase letters that spell *smith*. If you *do* choose Match Case, a search for **smith** would find only *smith*, not Smith or SMITH, and not any other combination of upper/lowercase letters that spell *smith*.

Searching Fields as Formatted

As you'll learn in the next chapter, you can change the format of a field without changing its underlying data. For instance, you can format a

Date/Time field to display dates in the long, *Saturday, January 16, 1993*, format rather than the short, *1/16/93*, format.

You can also search a field for either its underlying data or its formatted data. For instance, you could search for the date **1/16/93** regardless of whether the dates are displayed in the short or long format.

NOTE If you choose the All Fields option, Access automatically searches the fields as formatted.

If you specifically want to search the data in the format currently shown, you need to choose the Search Fields as Formatted option. For instance, after choosing that option you could enter **Saturday** as the value to search for, and then choose *Start of Field* as the Where option. Access would then locate records that start with the word Saturday.

Choosing a Direction

The Direction options in the Find in Field: dialog box let you perform the search either from the current record toward the top of the table (Up) or from the current record toward the end of the table (Down).

Using Wildcards

You can also broaden the search by using the wildcard characters shown in Table 5.3. (As you'll see in Chapter 7, you can also use these wildcard characters in queries.)

Finding and Replacing Data

You can globally change the data in several records by using the Find and Replace options. One very important point to keep in mind for these options is that once you make a global change to a table, there's no way to undo that change. Therefore, you'd be very wise to make a backup copy of the table before you even begin the Find and Replace procedure. See Chapter 18 for information on making backup copies of tables.

TABLE 5.3: Wildcard characters you can use in the Find What portion of a Find or Replace dialog box

WILDCARD	STANDS FOR	EXAMPLE
?	Any single character	**Sm?th** will match *Smith, Smyth, Smath,* and so forth.
*	Any characters	**Sm★** will match *Smith, Smithereens, Sm'ores.*
#	Any numeric digit	**9## Oak St.** will match any address in the range of 900 Oak St. to 999 Oak St.
[]	Any characters in the brackets	**Sm[iy]th** will find *Smith* or *Smyth,* but not *Smath.*
–	Any characters within the range (must be within brackets)	**[N-Z]** will match any text beginning with the letters N through Z, provided that the Start Of Field option is also selected.
!	Any character except (must be used in brackets)	**[!N-Z]** will match any text that doesn't start with the letters N through Z, provided that the *Start Of Field* option is also selected.

Once you've made your backup, you can open the original copy of the table and follow these steps to perform the Find and Replace operation:

1. Move to the field that you want to find and replace data in, starting at the first record in the table, or whatever record marks the place where you want to start replacing data.

2. Choose Edit ➤ Replace. You'll see the **Replace in Field:** dialog box:

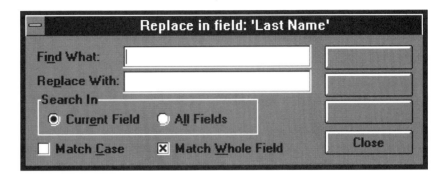

3. Type the value you want to search for, then press Tab or click on the Replace With text box.

4. Type the new replacement value.

5. If you're sure you want to make the change to all the records, choose Replace All and skip to Step 7.

6. If you want to verify the change in each record, choose Find Next. If necessary, you can drag the dialog box out of the way so that you can see the data that Access is about to change. Then ...

   • If you *do* want to change the current record, choose Replace.
   • If you *don't* want to change the current record, choose Find Next.

7. When Access gets to the end of the table you'll see the message indicating this. You can choose No if you're done.

8. If you chose Replace All in Step 5, you'll be given one last chance to undo the changes. Remember, if you choose OK here, the only way to undo the changes will be to replace the current copy of the table with the backup copy you made before performing the find and replace operation.

9. To close the Replace in Field: dialog box, just click its Close button.

As an example of using Find and Replace, suppose two different people in the company enter customer names and addresses. One person spells out the city name *Los Angeles*, and another uses the abbreviation *L.A.*. For consistency, you decide that you'd prefer to use Los Angeles throughout the table.

In that case, you'd move the insertion point into the City field of the Customers table, then choose Edit ➤ Replace. Then you'd fill in the Replace in Field: dialog box as below before choosing the Replace All or Find Next option to proceed with the operation.

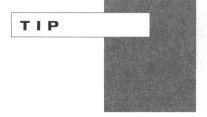

TIP

Action queries (Chapter 8) provide much more flexibility for changing data throughout a table. For instance, with a query you could increase or decrease the current price of all products within a given category by 10 percent.

Like the Find in Field: dialog box, the Replace in Field: dialog box provides options that let you search just the current field or all fields, match upper/lower case exactly, and match either the whole field or just part of the field. You can also use the wildcard characters described earlier (Table 5.3) in the Find What text box to broaden the search.

Cutting and Pasting Data

You can use all the standard Windows cut-and-paste techniques to move and copy data in tables, as well as to move and copy data to and from Access and other applications.

NOTE   See your Windows documentation for information on cutting and pasting to and from non-Windows applications.

Selecting Access Data to Cut and Paste

Before you can move or copy data, you need to select the data using any of the techniques listed in Table 5.4. However, if you specifically want to move or copy data from a table, you need to select a single field, part of a field, or an entire record. If you select a column or several columns, the Cut and Copy options on the Edit menu will be dimmed and unavailable.

TABLE 5.4: Techniques for selecting data

TO SELECT...	DO THIS...
Part of field contents	Drag mouse pointer through a portion of the field, or use Shift+→, Shift+←, Shift+Home, or Shift+End.
Word to left or right	Press Shift+Ctrl+→, or Shift+Ctrl+←

T A B L E 5.4: Techniques for selecting data (continued)

TO SELECT...	DO THIS...
Full field contents	Move to the field with an arrow key, or press F2 to switch from insertion-point mode to selection mode, or click the field name in form view.
Entire record	Click the record indicator at the far left edge of the record, or choose Edit ➤ Select Record, or press Shift+Spacebar when a field is selected.
Multiple records	Drag the mouse pointer through appropriate record selectors, or extend the selection by Shift+clicking the record to extend the selection to, or hold down the Shift key while clicking adjacent record selectors, or extend the selection using Shift+↓ or Shift+↑.
Entire Column	Click field selector at top of column, or press Ctrl+Spacebar once text is selected (press F2 first, if necessary).
Multiple columns	Drag mouse pointer through field selectors, or Shift+click multiple field selectors, or press Ctrl+Spacebar to select column, then Shift+→ or Shift+← to extend selection.
Entire table (in datasheet view)	Choose Edit ➤ Select All Records.
Using function key	Press F8 to extend selection (EXT appears in status bar). Selects word, field, record, entire table with each successive press.
To cancel selection	F2 or Esc.

Moving or Copying from Field to Field

To move or copy data from one field to another:

1. Select a portion of the field, or the full field contents.

2. To *move* the selected data, choose Edit ➤ Cut or press Ctrl+X. To *copy* the selected data, choose Edit ➤ Copy or press Ctrl+C.

3. Move to the destination field and choose Edit ➤ Paste or press Ctrl+V.

To Move or Copy Data to Another Application

If you want to move or copy data to another Windows application, select the data you want to move or copy. The selected data can be part of a field, an entire field, an entire record, or several records. Then choose Edit ➤ Copy to copy, or Edit ➤ Cut to move.

Load the other Windows application, position the insertion pointer to wherever you want to place the data from the table. Then choose Edit ➤ Paste.

Figure 5.10 shows an example, where I selected customers 1003 through 1008 in the Customers table in Microsoft Access. After choosing Edit ➤ Copy, I then ran Microsoft Excel, opened a blank spreadsheet, and used Edit ➤ Paste to paste the data into the spreadsheet. (Notice that Access automatically copies the field names from the table to the Clipboard when you choose Edit ➤ Copy or Edit ➤ Cut.)

TIP

If you paste data into a Word for Windows document, you can then select the pasted data within the document, then click the Table button to put the data in a Word table.

FIGURE 5.10

Data copied from an Access table into an Excel spreadsheet

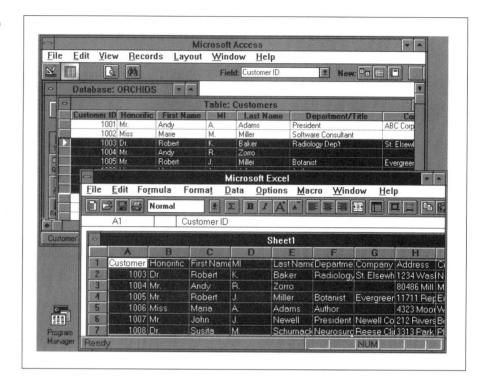

Pasting Data into an Access Table

You can copy or cut data from any Windows application, and paste that data into a field in your Access table. The exact method you use depends on if you want to paste in the contents of a single field or the contents of several fields and records.

Pasting Data into a Field

Pasting data into a single field is quite easy. You start the application that you want to paste data from, and open the appropriate document file. For instance, you can open a word processing document or a spreadsheet that contains the data you want to copy. Then, within that application:

1. Select the data you want to paste using whatever techniques are appropriate for that application. For instance, in a word processing document, you can drag the mouse pointer through the text you want to select. In a spreadsheet, you can click the single cell that you want to copy.

2. Choose Edit ➤ Copy from that application's menu bar to copy the selection to the Windows Clipboard.

3. Switch to Access using Alt+Tab or the Task List (Ctrl+Esc), and move to the field within the Access table that you want to paste data into.

4. Choose Edit ➤ Paste or press Ctrl+V.

If you paste data from a word processing document into a Memo field or Text field in Access, you'll lose fonts, some special characters, and other features that Memo fields do not support.

T I P   If you don't want to lose all the formatting features, you can store the document in an Access OLE Object field rather than a Memo field.

Pasting In Records

The basic procedure for pasting multiple fields and records into a table is similar to that for pasting in a field. The basic steps are:

1. In the application you're copying *from,* select the data that you want to paste into the Access table, using techniques appropriate to the application. You can choose multiple cells in a spreadsheet, multiple rows and columns in a word processing document or table within a document, or multiple records from another Access table.

2. If you want to *add* the selected data to your Access table, choose Edit ➤ Paste Append. If you want to *replace* data in the Access table with the incoming data, select the records you want to replace. Then choose Edit ➤ Paste or press Ctrl+V.

CAUTION

If you choose Edit ➤ Paste without first selecting the records that you want to replace, Access will attempt to put all the fields and records into a single field in the table!

Though the basic procedure is fairly simple, pasting a record or multiple records into an Access table can be tricky because the order of fields in the incoming data is important.

If you paste data into a datasheet view, the pasted data is entered in column-by-column order. This is true even if you're pasting from another Access table into the current table. If the order of fields in the current datasheet view doesn't match the order of fields in the data you're about to paste in, you need to rearrange the fields in the datasheet first. That is, make sure the left-to-right order of fields in the datasheet matches the left-to-right order of fields in the data you're about to paste in.

TIP

You may find it easiest to *import* or *attach* records to an Access table, as opposed to using cut-and-paste. See Chapter 19 for more information.

On the other hand, if you paste data into a form, *and* you're pasting from some other Access table, Access will match field names in the form to the field names in the incoming data. Thus, the order of fields doesn't matter when you're pasting into a form.

Except for one big difference, the same basic principles work when you're pasting rows and columns from a spreadsheet or word processor into a table. The difference is this: spreadsheets and word processors don't use field names, per se. However, you can treat any *column headings* that you've typed into the document as though they're field names by including those column headings in the selection that you copy to the Clipboard. Whether or not you can (or want to) do that depends on three things:

- If the column headings at the top of the document (Note that I'm using the term "document" here to refer to the spreadsheet or to the word processing document you want to copy data from) exactly match field names in the Access table, and you *can* include them in the selection, do so before copying to the Clipboard. Then make a mental note that the Clipboard contains field names.

- If you *can't* include column headings in the selection (because you're not selecting data near the top of the document), just select the data you want to copy to Access and ignore the column headings. Make a mental note that the Clipboard does not contain field names.

- If the column headings in the document don't exactly match field names in the Access table, and you don't want to change the existing column headings, exclude those column headings from the selection before copying to the Clipboard. Then make a mental note that the Clipboard does not contain field names.

TIP You can view use the Clipboard Viewer in the Main group of the Windows Program Manager to view the contents of the Clipboard at any time.

At this point, you've copied data to the Clipboard and are ready to Paste Append it into your Access table. Your best choices now are as follows:

- If the Clipboard includes field names, go to the form view then choose Edit ➤ Paste Append.

- If the Clipboard does not include field names, go to datasheet view and arrange columns so that their left-to-right order matches the left-to-right order of the incoming data. Then choose Edit ➤ Paste Append.

Let's take a look at an example of the last option, where the incoming data does not include field names.Figure 5.11 shows a small sample table in a Word for Windows document. Each row has a unique customer ID associated with it. (I added that column so that I wouldn't later run into any problems with duplicate or blank values in the Customer ID field later, which is a primary key in my Access table.) I've already selected the rows and column I want to copy to my Access table, as you can see in the figure.

After selecting the text to copy, I'd choose Edit ➤ Copy from the Word for Windows menu bar to copy that text to the Windows Clipboard. Then, I need to get to Access and open the table that I want to paste the data into, Customers in this example.

Because the columns in the Word for Windows table are in ID, First Name, Last Name, and Phone number order, I first need to rearrange columns in the Access table. There's no need to change the underlying structure of the table. Just drag columns around so that the first four

FIGURE 5.11

A small table in Word for Windows, with customer ID numbers, names, and phone numbers

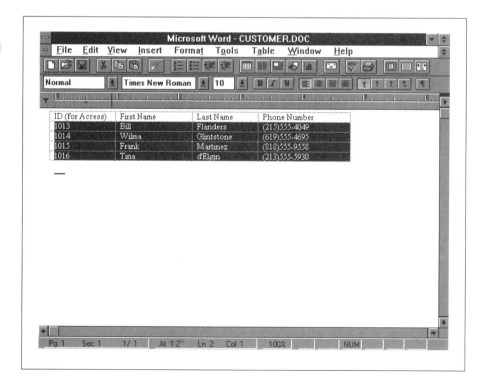

columns in the datasheet view match the order in the Word for Windows table.

Once the columns are in order, I first click on any field just to make sure no data is selected in the Access table, then choose Edit ➤ Paste Append from Access's menu bar. Access pastes in the available data, as shown in Figure 5.12. Additional columns to the right of the pasted-in data are still empty because there is no data to paste into them in this example.

FIGURE 5.12

After ensuring that Customer ID, First Name, Last Name, and Phone (in that order) are the first four columns in the datasheet view, I can Paste Append the records from the Word for Windows table into my Access table.

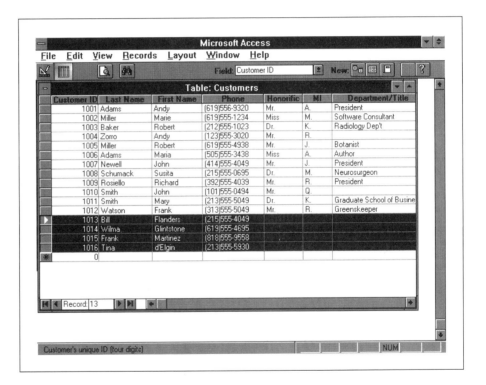

Potential Problems with Cut-and-Paste

The rules that apply for entering data from the keyboard also apply when you're cutting-and-pasting into a table. For instance, you can't put null values or duplicate values in a primary key field, you can't put text into a numeric field, and so forth.

If any record that you're paste-appending into the table breaks these rules, Access will display a messages indicating the problems. Records that could not be appended will be stored in a separate table named **Paste Errors**.

If that situation arises, you can refer to the section "Troubleshooting Data Entry and Editing Problems" later in this chapter for some guidelines on what is, and what isn't, acceptable data for a table. Then you can perhaps modify the data in the Paste Errors table so that it meets all the requirements, then paste-append the data from the Paste Errors table into your table.

Storing Data in OLE Object Fields

Object Linking and Embedding (OLE), a feature born with Windows 3.1, allows multiple applications to share data in the form of *objects*. An object can be an entire document file, such as a picture, sound, spreadsheet, or word processing document, or just a portion thereof. Object Linking and Object Embedding differ in these respects:

- When you *embed* an object in an Access table, Windows maintains a connection between the embedded object in the Access table and the source application that was used to create that object. However, the copy of the object that is in your Access table is totally separate from the original object, so changing the original object has no effect on the copy that's in your Access table.

- When you *link* an object into an Access table, Windows maintains a link to both the original source object *and* the application that was used to create it. Therefore, any changes you make to the original object, whether from Access or the original application used to create it, will be reflected in your Access table.

Remember that you can cut-and-paste data into any field in an Access table. But you can only link or embed to an OLE Object data-type field. Also, you can only link and embed objects from applications that support

OLE as a server. If you're not sure whether or not a particular application supports OLE as a server, check that application's documentation.

TIP

The Windows 3.1 Paintbrush and Sound Recorder applications, and the Microsoft Graph application that comes with Access, support OLE as a server.

Finally, you also need to be aware that the embedded (or linked) object will look different in datasheet and form view. In datasheet view, a brief description of the type of object appears in the field. In form view, you'll see the actual object if it's a picture, graph, or spreadsheet cell; you'll see an icon if the object is a sound or word processing document.

Figure 5.13 shows an example comparing the datasheet and form views of OLE Objects using the same table. In the upper window, the record containing information about the PROM category of orchids is selected. The OLE fields Sample Photo, Verbal, and Care and Feeding contain only descriptions of the fields contents. (I customized the sample form shown in Figure 5.13 to better display the sample data. You'll learn how to do that in Chapter 9.)

The lower window shows the same record in form view. The embedded PaintBrush picture is fully visible, the embedded Word document and sound appear as icons.

NOTE

The Description field in Figure 5.13 is the Memo data type. You can see much more of that field in form view than you can in datasheet view.

FIGURE 5.13

Only descriptions of objects appear in datasheet view (top of screen). Form view (bottom of screen) shows the entire object, or an icon representing the object.

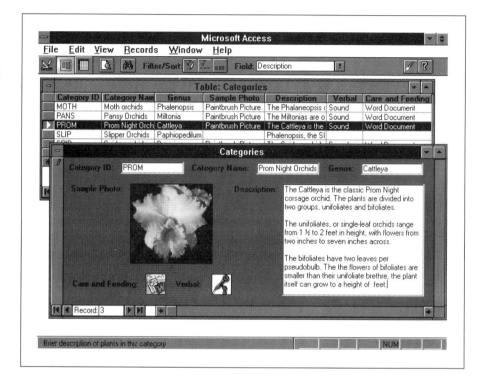

Using Cut-and-Paste to Link and Embed

If you want to link or embed an object into a field, you can follow the procedure described here. This technique will also let you link or embed a portion of a larger document into your Access table.

Assuming you're starting from Access, with the insertion point in the OLE Object field that you want to put an object into, follow these steps:

1. Start, or switch to, the *source application*, i.e. the one you used to create the object that you want to link or embed.

2. Use the File ➤ Open (or equivalent) commands in the source application to open the object that you want to link or embed. For instance, you might open a spreadsheet, word processing document, picture (in PaintBrush), or sound (in Sound Recorder).

- If the object doesn't exist yet, you must create it *and* save it to give it a file name.

3. If appropriate in the current application, select whatever it is you want to link or embed using whatever selection method is appropriate for the application you're using. For instance, in Figure 5.14 I've loaded a scanned photograph named *slipper.bmp* into PaintBrush, and selected most of the photo using the Pick (scissors and square) tool. (The dotted outline bordering the frame defines the cutout.)

- You wouldn't select anything if the object is a sound in the Sound Recorder application.

4. Choose Edit ➤ Copy from the source application's menu bar. This will copy the object (or selected portion) to the Windows Clipboard.

FIGURE 5.14

A scanned photo loaded into PaintBrush and selected using the Pick (scissors and square) tool

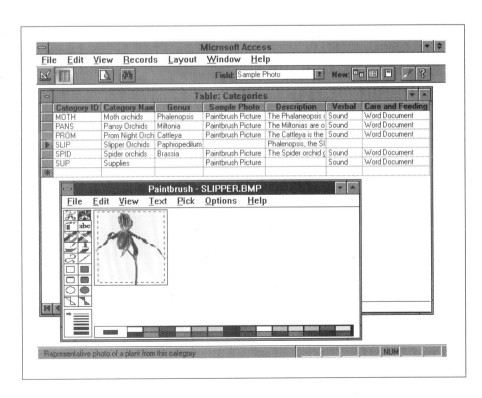

5. Don't close the current application. Instead, switch back to Access using Task List (Ctrl+Esc) or Alt+Tab.

NOTE   It doesn't matter which view you use to paste data into the table. If you paste pictures and sound into a table in datasheet view, you'll always be able to see the pictures and icons when you switch to form view.

6. Move the insertion point to the OLE Object field that you want to put the object into. Then:

   • If you want to *embed* the object, choose Edit ➤ Paste.
   • If you want to *link* the object, choose Edit ➤ Paste Link.

If you chose Edit ➤ Paste in the steps above, you're done. If you chose Paste Link, you'll see the dialog box below. Just choose OK to proceed. A copy of the object is placed in the field, appearing as just a description if you happen to be in datasheet view, or as a picture or icon if you happen to be in form view.

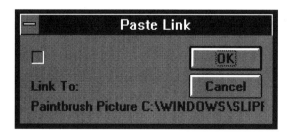

Summary of Steps

Let's take a moment to review the basic steps now, and clarify the distinctions between cut-and-paste and OLE:

1. You can use cut-and-paste to copy data from any application into any field in an Access table. That is, the field you're pasting into can be any data type.

2. If the field you're pasting into happens to be an OLE Object field, then the object is *embedded* in the field, and Access maintains a connection to the original source application.

3. If the field you're pasting to happens to be an OLE Object field *and* you chose Paste Link rather than Paste as the last step, then the object is *linked* to the Access table, and Access maintains a link to both the source application and the original source object.

You'll see how these different techniques affect your later editing of the object in a moment.

Embedding an Entire Object into a Field

If you're sure you want to embed, rather than link, an object into an OLE Object field, *and* you want to embed the entire object into the field, you can use this shortcut procedure to embed the object without leaving Access:

1. In Access, move to the OLE Object field in the table that you want to embed the object into. (You can be in either datasheet view or form view.)

2. Choose Edit ➤ Insert Object. You'll see the **Insert Object** dialog box as below. (The Object Types listed in this box will differ depending on the applications installed on your system.)

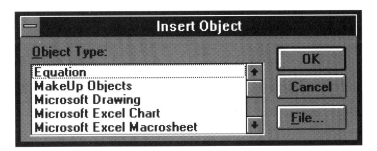

3. In the Object Type list, choose the type of object you want to embed.

TIP If you don't see the exact application you want, you can pick one that supports the type of object you're embedding. For instance, if you've scanned a photo and saved it as a bitmap (.bmp) file, you can choose Paintbrush Picture as the Object Type.

4. Click the File button.

5. In the **Insert Object from File:** dialog box that appears, choose the drive and directory location of the object you want to embed.

6. Choose the file name of the object you want to embed from the list under File Name.

7. Choose OK.

That's all there is to it. As usual, you'll only see a description of the object when you're in datasheet view. But you'll see the object, or its icon, whenever you're in form view.

Editing an OLE Object

If you want to view, change, or print an OLE object that's in your table:

1. Double-click the OLE Object field. If the object is a sound or animation, Access will play it. Otherwise you'll be taken to the source application for that object. Then:

   • If you embedded the object in the field, the title bar of the source application indicates that you are editing "*(object type)* in Microsoft Access." Any changes you make will affect only the copy of the object that's in your Access table.

   • If you linked the object, the title bar of the source application will show the name of the original file (e.g., *slipper.bmp*), indicating that you are about to edit the copy in your Access table *and* the original source object.

2. When you've finished changing the object, you can choose File ➤ Exit from the source application's menu bar to return to Access.

We'll talk in more detail about OLE, and techniques specific to spread-sheets, word processing documents, pictures, sounds, and graphs in Chapter 19. For now, the basic steps described so far should allow you to store pictures, sounds, and other objects in any OLE Object field in your Access table.

Troubleshooting Data Entry and Editing Problems

For the remainder of this chapter we'll look at some common problems that you might encounter when entering and editing data, and how you can rectify those problems.

Duplicate Key Message

If the record you just entered into the table duplicates the contents of the primary key field in some other record, you'll see this message when you try to move to another record:

NOTE This message also appears if the contents of a field duplicate an entry in an indexed field that doesn't allow duplicates, as described in Chapter 6.

Your only recourse is to choose OK to return to the table. Then you need to either edit the record so that it no longer duplicates the other record, or delete the new record using Edit ➤ Undo Current Record.

If the root of the problem lies in the way you defined the primary key or indexes, you can change the structure of the table to redefine the key (this will be discussed in Chapter 6).

Can't Have Null Value in Index

If you see the message "Can't have Null value in index" when you attempt to leave a record, that means you've left the primary key field in the current record empty. You'll need to choose OK to return to the table. Then, fill in the primary key field (or indexed field) that requires a value, or, if you just want to delete the entire new record, choose Edit ➤ Undo Current Record.

Value Isn't Appropriate for This Field Type

If you see a message indicating that the value you entered isn't appropriate for the field type, you need to choose OK and then enter appropriate data. See the section "Adding New Records in Datasheet View" earlier in this chapter for a reminder about what's appropriate to the various data types.

New Records Seem to Disappear

Keep in mind that if the table has a primary key, Access maintains an ongoing sort order based on the field(s) that define the primary key. But it doesn't re-sort the table until after you close it.

So even though new records will always be at the bottom of the table when you're first entering them, they'll be in their proper sort-order position the next time you open the table. You can scroll around to find those records to verify that they're in the table.

Data Fails Validation Rule

If you've defined a validation rule for a field (Chapter 6), and the new data in the field fails the validation rule, you'll see the message below, or whatever custom message you defined for the field:

You'll need to modify the field value so that it passes the validity check, or delete the entire record, before you can move onto another field.

If the data is indeed valid, and it's your validity check that's at fault, you'll need to change the field's validity check properties, as discussed in the next chapter.

Indicator Shows a "No" Symbol

 If you share data with other users on a network, and another user has locked a record that you want to edit, that record's indicator will look like the international No symbol, shown at left. You'll need to wait for that other user to unlock the record before you can change it.

TIP See Chapter 20 for more information on using Access on a network.

Access Won't Let You Add or Change Any Data

If you can't change any data in the table, the most likely cause is that the Allow Editing option is deselected. Choose Records from the menu bar, and take a look at the Editing Allowed options. If that option *isn't* checked, select it. Then try editing the table again.

If you're using a form, it may be that field properties on the form are intentionally set to prevent editing. See Chapter 10 for more information on forms and field properties.

If the entire database has the read-only attribute, you cannot change any data in any tables. You use the File ➤ Properties commands in the Windows File Manager, or the DOS ATTRIB command to change the Read/Write status of a database.

Summary

In this chapter you've learned a lot about adding data to a table, editing and deleting data, and getting around in a table. We've also discussed ways of customizing the datasheet view, and introduced you to forms, another way of viewing and editing data.

Finally, you've also learned how to use the standard Windows cut-and-paste and Object Linking and Embedding (OLE) techniques within Access to help with editing and data entry.

In the next chapter, we'll look at some techniques for changing and refining the overall design of the table.

Refining Your Table Structure

○ **To minimize data entry and editing errors in a field**   203

change the field's *Validation Rule* property. You can also create "Validate Text" to appear on the screen when an entry breaks a validation rule.

○ **To speed up processing down the road**   208

create an index, using the *Indexed* property, for any fields that you'll be using often to search or sort the data in the table.

○ **To create multi-field indexes**   211

choose View ➤ Table Properties, or click the Properties button in the tool bar. List the names of the fields, separated by semi-colons, next to one of the available index options.

○ **To set up the relationships between tables**   217

get to the database window, then choose Edit ➤ Relationships. Choose the table on the "one side" of a one-to-many relation-ship as the Primary Table (you must already have defined the primary key for this table). Then choose the table on the "many side" of the relationship as the Related Table. Then choose the common field under Select Matching Fields. You can also check the Enforce Referential Integrity option if you want to activate that now.

AS YOU add and edit data in your table, you may find that there are certain changes and refinements you can make to the underlying design of the table. For instance, you might need to add some fields to a table, or delete some fields that you're not really using. Or, you may find that you need more than 50 characters in a text field. Or, if you find you're entering the same data into a field in most records, such as the current date, you might want to make the current date a default value so you don't have to type it in over and over again. In this chapter we'll look at various ways to refine the design of your tables, including defining field properties.

Changing the Design of an Existing Table

Changing the design of a table is simply a matter of returning to the design view of your table. You can do so in either of two ways:

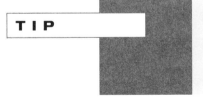

TIP

If the table you're about to change contains a significant amount of data, you'd do well to make a backup copy of the table, as discussed in Chapter 18, before changing the table's design.

- If the table is currently open, just click the design view button in the tool bar, as shown below:

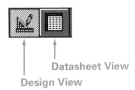

Datasheet View

Design View

- If the table isn't open, click the Table button in the database window. Click the name of the table you want to change, and then click the Design button.

You'll see the underlying design of the table, as in the example shown in Figure 6.1 where the Products table's design is shown.

NOTE   The terms "table design" and "table structure" mean the same thing: the fields and properties that define the table, as opposed to the data stored within the table.

Inserting, Deleting, and Moving Fields

You can move, insert, and delete fields using the same techniques you used when first defining the table design. However, if the table already contains data, keep in mind that *deleting* a field from the table design will delete all the data that you've put into that field. Access will present a message warning you of this, and you can just choose Cancel at that time if you change your mind and decide not to delete the field.

FIGURE 6.1

Design view for the sample Products table

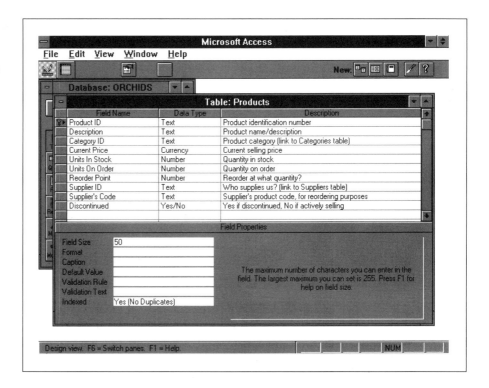

TIP

See "Making Changes and Corrections" in Chapter 4 if you need a reminder on how to insert, move, and delete fields in the table design window.

Switching between Datasheet and Design Views

You can easily switch back and forth between datasheet and design views by clicking the Datasheet View and Design View buttons on the tool bar. If you make any changes to the table design, you'll be asked if you want to save those changes before being taken to the design view. As usual, you can choose Yes to save your changes, or Cancel to stay in the design view.

Closing the design view window will also save any changes you make to the table's design. As usual, you'll be given an opportunity to save, or cancel your changes.

Changing Field Properties

Adding, changing, and rearranging fields is just one way to refine your table design. You can also make more subtle refinements to individual fields by changing *field properties*. You can use the method summarized in Figure 6.2 and described below to change a field's properties:

1. Click the name of the field you want to change the properties for. (Make sure you do this first, or you might assign the properties to the wrong field!)

FIGURE 6.2

To change a field's properties, *first* click the field that you want to change, then choose whatever field property you want to change.

First click the field for which you want to change the properties...

Table: Products		
Field Name	Data Type	Description
Product ID	Text	Product identification number
Description	Text	Product name/description
Category ID	Text	Product category (link to Categories table)
Current Price	Currency	Current selling price
Units In Stock	Number	Quantity in stock
Units On Order	Number	Quantity on order
Reorder Point	Number	Reorder at what quantity?
Supplier ID	Text	Who supplies us? (link to Suppliers table)
Supplier's Code	Text	Supplier's product code, for reordering purpo
Discontinued	Yes/No	Yes if discontinued, No if actively selling

Field Properties

Field Size	6
Format	
Caption	
Default Value	
Validation Rule	
Validation Text	
Indexed	Yes (No Duplicates)

A field name can be up to 64 characters long, including spaces. Press F1 for help on field names.

...then choose the property you want to change

2. Choose the property you want to change, from the options near the lower left corner of the screen, either by clicking the property name or the text box to the right of the property name.

- In some cases a drop-down list button will appear to the right of the text box, as below. Click this button, then choose the property you want.

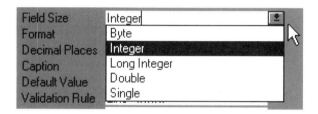

- If a drop-down list button does not appear (as in the case of assigning a default value, or a validation rule or text), you need to type in an entry following the guidelines we'll present in later sections.

Table 6.1 summarizes the kinds of properties you can assign to a field, and the data types that each property is applicable to. We'll talk about each of the properties in detail in the sections that follow.

TABLE 6.1: Summary of properties that you can assign to fields

PROPERTY	USED TO...	DATA TYPES
Field Size	Limit the length of a text entry, or size of a number	Text, Number
Format	Determine the appearance of the field	All except OLE Object
Decimal Places	Specify how many decimal places to show	Number, Currency, Counter
Caption	(Optional field title used in forms and reports)	All

TABLE 6.1: Summary of properties that you can assign to fields (continued)

PROPERTY	USED TO...	DATA TYPES
Default Value	(A suggested value that's placed in the field automatically, but can be changed)	All except Counter and OLE Object
Validation Rule	Restrict data that can be entered into a field, and ward off errors	All except Counter
Validation Text	(Message displayed when an entry fails the validation rule)	All except Counter
Indexed	Speed up sorting and querying operations	All except Yes/No and OLE Object

Assigning a Size to a Field

You can assign a maximum field size to text and number fields to limit the size of the entry and to determine how much disk space the field will use.

Sizing Text Fields

The field size for a Text field limits the number of characters you can type into the field. By default, Access allows you to type a maximum of 50 characters into a text field. But you can change that value to any length between 1 and 255. So if you know for sure that a particular text field might require more than 50 characters, you'll certainly want to change the field's *Field Size* property.

TIP

Memo fields, like text fields, can contain text. But the maximum length is 32,000, rather than 255 characters.

If you know for a fact that a particular text field will never be more than a certain number of characters in length, you may want to reduce the size of the field accordingly to help reduce data entry errors. For instance, if your table includes a Product ID field of the Text data type, and all your product codes are six characters in length, you could limit the size of that field to six characters. Doing so would help prevent someone from entering a longer (and, therefore, incorrect) entry into that field, because, as soon as you (or whoever) starts typing beyond the sixth character, Access will start beeping.

CAUTION

If your table already contains data, and you reduce the size of a text field, any existing data that is longer than that size will be truncated (cut off) to fit within the new field size. See "Cautions on Changing the Table Design" later in this chapter for more information.

For the benefit of those readers who have experience with other database management systems, I should point out that Access stores *only* the characters you type into a text field in the table. For instance, even if you leave the size of the State/Province field set at 50, then later type the state abbreviation CA into that field, that field will consume two bytes, not 50 bytes. Thus, there's no penalty for making the size of a text field larger than it needs to be. (For the truly hard-core database folks, suffice it to say that Access uses the Indexed Sequential Access Method (ISAM), rather than the fixed-length or random-access method of storing data.)

Sizing Number Fields

You can also use the *Field Size* property to determine the range of acceptable entries in a Number field, and how much disk space the field will consume. Table 6.2 lists your options.

TABLE 6.2: Field Size settings for Number fields

FIELD SIZE	RANGE	DECIMAL PLACES	STORAGE SIZE
Byte	0 to 255	None	1 byte
Integer	−32,768 to 32,767	None	2 bytes
Long Integer	−2,147,483,648 to 2,147,483,647	None	4 bytes
Single	-3.4×10^{38} to 3.4×10^{38}	7	4 bytes
Double	-1.797×10^{308} to 1.797×10^{308}	15	8 bytes

To conserve disk space, you'll want to use the smallest size that can accommodate the numbers you'll be storing in the field. For example, you can assign the *Byte*, *Integer*, or *Long Integer* property to any whole-number "quantity" fields in a table that don't require a decimal point.

On the other hand, if any of the numbers stored in the field require decimal places, you'll need to use the *Single* or *Double* property, as these are the only two that support decimals. For dollar amounts, however, you can use the Currency, rather than Number, field type.

Be Careful to Size Common Fields Equally

If you change the field size property of a field that acts as the common field in a relationship between two tables, you should make certain that you assign the same size to the common field in *both* tables. For instance, in our example of setting the field size of the Product ID field in the Products table to a length of 6, you'd also want to set the size of the Product ID field in the Order Details to a length of 6, as in Figure 6.3.

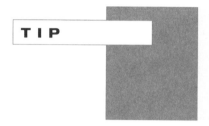

T I P

Refer to Figure 4.7 in Chapter 4 if you need a reminder on how we've defined the relationships between the various tables in our sample database design. In fact, you might want to flag or photocopy that page for easy future reference.

Likewise, if you were to change the properties of the Customer ID field in the Customers table to *Integer*, you'd want to be sure to change the properties of the Customer ID field in the Orders table to *Integer* as well.

FIGURE 6.3

The design of both the Products and Order Details table. The common field that links the two tables, Product ID, is the Text data type, with a length of 6 in both tables.

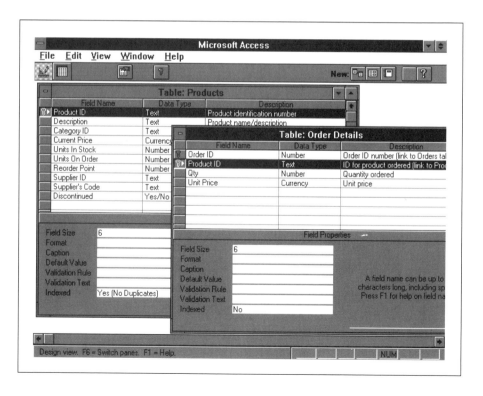

The one exception, which we've mentioned before, concerns the use of the Counter data type. If the common field on the "one side" of the one-to-many relationship is the Counter data type, the equivalent field on the "many side" of the relationship should be the Number data type, with the *Long Integer* field property assigned to it, as in Figure 6.4. That way, both tables will store a four-byte number in the common field.

FIGURE 6.4

When the common field on the "one side" of a one-to-many relationship is a Counter field, the equivalent field on the "many" side should be the Number data type, with the Long Integer field size, as in the Orders and Order Detail tables shown here.

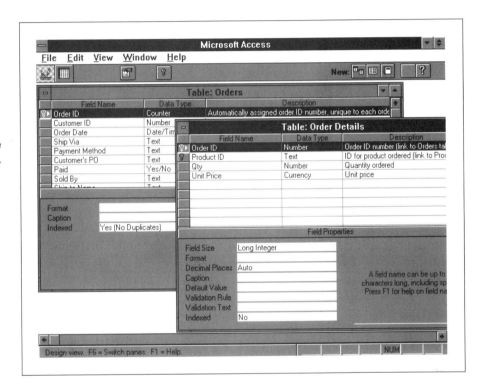

Assigning Format Properties to Control Appearance

You can also assign formatting properties to control the appearance of data in the field. The formatting options available to you depend on the data type of the field.

Formatting Number, Currency, and Counter Fields

Table 6.3 lists formatting properties that you can assign to Number and Currency fields. The second column shows a sample number that might be typed into the field, and the third column shows how that field would appear on the screen. Keep in mind, however, that the *Decimal Places* property, described later, will also affect the appearance of a number.

N O T E   Whereas the *Field Size* property determines how large and how small a number you can put in a field, the *Format* property simply determines how that number will look on the screen and when printed.

If you don't explicitly assign a format to the field, Access uses the General format.

TABLE 6.3: Format properties that you can assign to Number, Currency, and Counter fields

FORMAT	FIELD'S CONTENTS	WILL APPEAR AS...
General	1234.56	1234.56
	-1234.56	-1234.56
Currency	1234.56	$1,234.56
	-1234.56	($1,234.56)
Fixed	1234.56	1235
Standard	1234.56	1,234.56
Percent	0.075	7.50%
	5	500.00%
Scientific	1234.56	1.2E+03

CAUTION

If the table already contains data in a numeric field, and you assign a format with a smaller range of values to that field, you might lose some data in the table. See "Cautions on Changing the Table Design" later in this chapter.

Custom Numeric Formats

You can also define your own custom numeric format. When planning this format, you can use any of the symbols listed in Table 6.4 to define parts of the number.

TABLE 6.4: Symbols used to define a custom format for Number, Currency, and Counter fields

SYMBOL	DESCRIPTION
. (period)	Decimal place
, (comma)	Thousands separator
0	Digit placeholder (displays 0 if no digit)
#	Digit placeholder (displays nothing if no digit)
$	Displays a dollar sign
%	Multiplies value by 100 and appends percent sign to end of number
E- or e-	Scientific notation with a minus sign next to negative numbers
E+ or e+	Scientific notation with a plus sign next to positive numbers
;	Separates positive, negative, zero, and null formats
"	Literal text displayed with number

You can actually define up to four formats, each separated by a semicolon, for a single number or currency field. The first format is used if the number is positive, the second format is used if the number is negative, the third format if the number is zero, and the fourth if the number is null (i.e., the field is empty), as illustrated in the example below:

Field Size	Single
Format	#,###.0;[#,###.0];0.0;"N/A"
Decimal Places	2

If we set the *Decimal Places* property (described in the following section) to **2,** here's how various numbers would be displayed using the custom format shown:

IF FIELD CONTAINS	IT WILL APPEAR AS
1234.5	1,234.50
-1234.5	1,234.50)
0	0.00
(nothing)	N/A

If you want to use the general format for any one of the options, include the semicolon anyway. Also, if you want to use a foreign currency, you can type that symbol into the format using the Alt+*numeric keypad* method or the **Windows 3.1 Character Map** as discussed in Chapter 5.

For example, the following format displays the number with a leading Yen sign if the number is positive, with a leading Yen sign and enclosed in quotation marks if the number is negative, and in general format if the number is zero or blank. (The Yen sign is character 0165 in the MS Sans Serif font.)

    ¥#,###.00;(¥#,###.00);;

To enter a custom format for a numeric field, click the Format Property text box, and type in the custom format. (That is, you can ignore the drop-down list.)

You can also include literal text in the format, by enclosing that text in quotation marks. For example, this format contains the literal text *Cust ID* and a blank space:

"Cust ID "####

When displaying a record that contains the number *1234* this format would display the field's contents as

Cust ID 1234

Deciding How Many Decimal Places to Display

When you're formatting a numeric, currency, or counter field, *and* you've defined the Format property for the field as something other than *General Number*, you can also determine how many decimal places of accuracy you want to show. For instance, you could choose *Standard* as the Format and *2* as the *Decimal Places* property to display all numbers with two decimals of accuracy (e.g., 1,234.56).

The default option, *Auto*, determines the number of decimal places automatically, based on the data type and the Format property you've assigned to the field.

Formatting Date/Time Fields

By default, data you enter into a date/time field is displayed in General Date format, which matches the short format that's currently defined in the International settings of the **Windows Control Panel**. Optionally, you can choose to display a date/time field in any of the formats shown in Table 6.5.

Custom Date/Time Formats

You can also create a custom format for formatting a date/time field using the symbols listed in Table 6.6.

TABLE 6.5: Format properties for display data in a date/time field

FORMAT	EXAMPLE
General Date	3/31/93
Long Date	Wednesday, March 31, 1993
Medium Date	31-Mar-93
Short Date	3/31/93
Long Time	2:00:00 PM
Medium Time	02:00 PM
Short Time	14:00

TABLE 6.6: Symbols for defining a custom date/time format

SYMBOL	DISPLAYS	SYMBOL	DISPLAYS
:	Time separator	q	Quarter, as a number (1-4)
/	Date separator	y	Day number in year (1-366)
c	Same as standard General Date format	yy	Last two digits of year (01-99)
d	Day of month as a number (1-31)	yyyy	Full year (0100-9999)
dd	Day of month as two-digit number (01-31)	h	Hour (0-23)
ddd	First three letters of weekday (Sun-Sat)	hh	Two-digit hour (00-23)
dddd	Full name of weekday (Sunday-Saturday)	n	Minute (0-59)

TABLE 6.6: Symbols for defining a custom date/time format (continued)

SYMBOL	DISPLAYS	SYMBOL	DISPLAYS
ddddd	Same as standard Short Date format	nn	Two-digit minute (00-59)
dddddd	Same as standard Long Date format	s	Second (0-59)
w	Day of week as a number (1-7)	ss	Two-digit second (00-59)
ww	Week of the year (1-53)	tttt	Standard Long format
m	Month as number (1-12)	AM/PM	AM or PM (uppercase)
mm	Month as two-digit number (01-12)	am/pm	am or pm (lowercase)
mmm	Month abbreviation (Jan-Dec)	a/p	a or p (for am/pm)
mmmm	Full month name (January-February)	AMPM	AM/PM designator defined in Control Panel International settings

As with numbers, you can include literal text in the format by enclosing that text in quotation marks. Here are some examples of custom date formats, and how they would display the entry *1/15/93 12:00:00 PM*:

FORMAT	EXAMPLE
ddd, mmm d, yyyy	Fri, Jan 15, 1993
dddd, hh:mm AM/PM	Friday, 12:00 PM

FORMAT	EXAMPLE
"Quarter " q, yyyy	Quarter 1, 1993
hh:mm:ss	12:00:00

Defining a Format for Yes/No Fields

If you're assigning the format property to a field with the Yes/No data type, your options are True/False, Yes/No, and On/Off. If you don't use any of those formats, the field displays 0 for No, or -1 for Yes.

Defining a Format for Text and Memo Fields

You can define a two-part custom format for text and memo fields. The first part of the format defines how the field's contents appear when the field contains text. The optional second part defines how the field appears when the field is empty. Use a semicolon (;) to separate the two parts.

You can use any of the symbols listed in Table 6.7, as well as literals that you want to embed in the entered text.

As an example, you could define the format of a Phone Number field as

(@@@)@@@-@@@@

TABLE 6.7: Symbols used for defining the format of a Text or Memo field

SYMBOL	MEANING
@	A character or a space is required
&	No character required (can be left blank)
<	Converts all characters to lowercase
>	Converts all characters to uppercase

When entering a phone number into this field you wouldn't need to type in the parentheses or hyphen. For instance, if you type **6195551234** Access would instantly convert your entry to **(619)555-1234**.

Suppose you want to always display product codes, such as MO-100, with uppercase letters. Assigning the **>** format property to that field would ensure that every entry is displayed in uppercase letters.

If you want a blank field to show a message indicating that the field has been left blank, use a two-part format. For instance, this format displays whatever entry you type into the field normally. But if you leave the field blank, the message **N/A** (for Not Available) appears in that field instead.

> @ ;"N/A"

Assigning a Descriptive Caption

The caption property defines an alternative field name for the field. For instance, if you have a field named Paid, you could assign the caption **Paid Yet? (Yes or No)** to that field. Later, when viewing the table in datasheet view, this caption would appear at the top of the column where the shorter field name, Paid, would normally appear.

Similarly, any new forms that you create for the table after changing the caption will display the caption, rather than the field name, next to the field. (Any forms that you've already created and saved are unaffected.)

Assigning Default Values to Speed Data Entry

A default value is a "suggested" entry that appears automatically while you're entering data into a new record. You can either accept this suggested value (by moving on the next field) or change it (by typing in a new value). This can be a great time-saver if you find yourself entering the same data into a field often.

For example, suppose that you do most of your business in Los Angeles. So, when entering customer information you find yourself entering *Los Angeles, CA* over and over again.

You could define **Los Angeles** as the default value for the City field, as in Figure 6.5. And then go on to assign **CA** as the default value for the State field.

Access uses zero as the default value for any number fields. So when you're entering records, a zero appears in any number field that you leave blank. You can remove the zero from the field's *Default Value* property if you prefer to have Access display nothing when you leave the number field blank.

You can also use an *expression* that starts with an equals sign (=) to define a default value for a field. Table 6.8 shows some examples of default values, both with and without expressions.

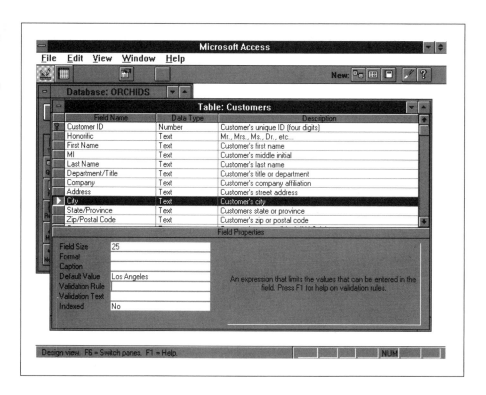

TABLE 6.8: Examples of default values

DEFAULT VALUE	DATA TYPE	SUGGESTED VALUE IN FIELD
CA	Text	CA
1	Number	1
=Date( )	Date/Time	Current date
=Now( )	Date/Time	Current date and time
=Time( )	Date/Time	Current time
=Null( )	Date/Time	Null value (empty)
=-1	Yes/No	Yes

Keep in mind that changing the default expression for a field has no effect on any records that you've already entered into the table. Instead, the default will appear only in new records you add in the future. Or, if you select a text field that already has some value, and press Ctrl+Alt+Spacebar, Access will replace the current value in that field with the default value.

N O T E   Expressions are covered in more detail in Chapter 17.

Assigning Validation Rules to Minimize Errors

The *Validation Rule* property lets you define a range of acceptable values for a field. This can help minimize the likelihood of errors and faulty data being entered into your tables during data entry and editing. You can also use validation rules to disallow the entry of certain types of values into a field. For instance, you could prevent "back-dating" of entries in a date/time field, or limit the dollar amount entry in a currency field to some maximum value.

The *Validation Text* property lets you assign a custom message that will appear on the screen should a field's entry fail the validation rule. If you leave the *Validation Text* property empty, Access displays a generic error message when an entry fails the validation rule.

T I P When entering or viewing a lengthy expression in a properties text box, you can press Zoom (Shift+F2) to work in a larger window. Choose OK from the Zoom box to return to normal view.

For example, suppose you assign the validation rule **>=Date( )** (greater than or equal to today's date) to a date/time field, and also assign the *Validation Text* property **Sorry, no backdating allowed here!** to that same field. If you later try to enter a date that's earlier than the current date into that field, Access will display the message shown in Figure 6.6. The 6/15/92 date in the newly added record at the bottom of the table is the faulty date in this example.

The person entering the data would then choose OK, and would have to re-enter a valid date before Access would let them move on to another field.

The validation rule that you define is an expression. Chapter 17 discusses expressions in depth, but here are some guidelines that are specific to entering validation expressions:

* The expression can use any of the standard comparison operators such as **=** (equals), **>** (greater than), **<** (less than), **<>** (not equal to), **And**, **Or**, **Like**, and so forth.

* Any date within the expression must be surrounded by # signs (e.g., **>=#1/1/93#**).

* Text within an expression should be enclosed in double quotation marks (**"**).

FIGURE 6.6

The validation text
appears in a message
box when the entry in
a field fails a
validation rule.

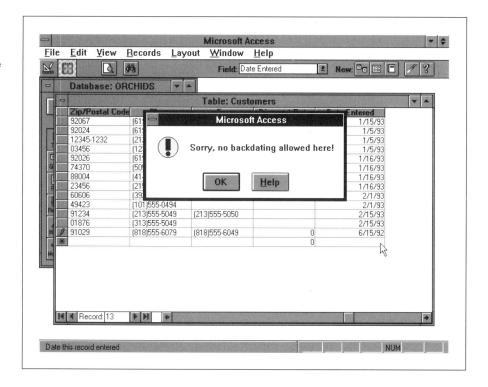

- The expression can use a *function* such as **Date( )**.

- You can use the **Like** function to limit the entry to certain
  characters, where **?** accepts any single character, ***** accepts
  any characters, and **#** accepts numeric digits only.

- You can refer to another field in the same table by enclosing the
  field name in square brackets **[ ]**.

Table 6.9 shows some examples of validation expressions.

Figure 6.7 shows an example where I've used the validation rule **Like**
"####" in the Customer ID field of both the Customers and Orders
table, to ensure that the field always contains a four-digit number. I've
also entered appropriate Validation Text in each table. Of course, if you're

TABLE 6.9: Examples of validation expressions

VALIDATION RULE	ENTRY MUST BE...
>=Date( )	Greater (later) than or equal to today's date
<>0	Some value other than zero
>0	A positive number greater than zero
>="A" And <"N"	Text starting with the letters A through M
"U.S." Or "Canada"	Either U.S. or Canada
Between 0 and 10000	Between 0 and 10,000
Between #1/1/93# And #12/31/93#	A date in 1993
In ("Check", "Cash", "Invoice")	The word *Check*, *Cash*, or *Invoice*.
Like "####"	A four-digit number
Like "(###)###-####"	In U.S. phone number format, such as (510)555-3232
Like "??-###"	Two characters, followed by a hyphen, followed be a three-digit number (e.g., SU-100)
<=[Order Date]+30	A date that is no more than 30 days past the date stored in a the field named Order Date

expecting to have more than 9,000 customers in your Customers table, you'd want to allow more characters in the field. For instance, **Like "#####"** would allow a Customer ID number as high as 99,999. You'd also want to assign the *Long Integer* field size property to the field, so you're not limited to a maximum value of 32,767.

FIGURE 6.7

The validation expression *Like "####"* assigned to the Customer ID field of the Customers and Orders tables, to require that each entry be a four-digit number.

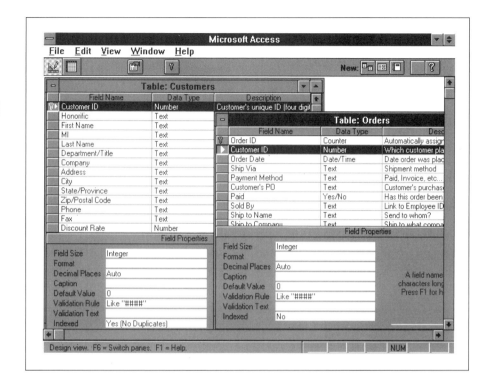

Note that validation rules aren't case-sensitive. For example, the validation rule **"U.S." Or "Canada"** will accept *U.S.*, *u.s.*, *CANADA*, *Canada*, or any other combination of upper and lowercase letters.

TIP

You can use macros in forms (Chapter 15) to impose more stringent validation rules, and to prevent a field from being left empty.

Be aware that Access doesn't validate fields that you intentionally leave empty. Also, Access does not validate entries that you've already put into the table. And perhaps most importantly, know that Access validates a field *before* any Format property that you assigned to that field is executed. Therefore, you cannot use the Format property to automatically insert characters that the validation rule requires.

Creating Indexes for Faster Performance

Though indexes are entirely optional, they can be great time-savers when you start working with large amounts of data, because they greatly speed sorting and searching for data. But to appreciate how Access uses an index, you first need to understand how it does things *without* the aid of an index.

Usually, when Access needs to find a bit of information in a table, it laboriously reads through each record of the table on disk, until it happens to find the record you're looking for. For instance, if you ask Access to find the record for John Smith, and John Smith is the 495th record in the table, Access must read through the first 494 records from disk before it finds John Smith. This is akin to trying to find information about a topic in a book by flipping through all the pages until you stumble upon the topic you're looking for.

On the other hand, if you create an index for the field, Access stores a copy of the index (or as much as it can fit) in memory (RAM). That index is organized much like the index at the back of a book—sorted into alphabetical (or some other) order. The position of each record in the table is also included in the index, in much the same way the index at the back of a book includes page numbers describing where topics are located.

NOTE   Unlike most spreadsheet programs, which tend to store all the data you're working with in memory (RAM), databases always work on data that's still stored on the disk. That why databases let you manage so much more data than spreadsheets do.

So let's say you define an index that's based on the Last Name and First Name fields in the Customers table. When you open the table and ask to find the record for John Smith, Access need only look up the name John

Smith in the index in memory. This takes only a fraction of a second, because Access need not use the disk drive at all to read through the index.

When Access finds John Smith in the index, it will know John Smith is in the 495th record. It can then skip over the first 494 records when it accesses the disk, thereby saving the considerable amount of time that would have otherwise have been required to read through all those records.

So you see, Access uses the index in memory in much the same way that you'd use the index at the back of a book: to find out where some information is and then to skip straight to the appropriate page (i.e., record).

Unlike the index at the back of a book, which you personally use to look up information, you never actually see the contents of an Access index. Instead, Access uses the index behind the scenes, when appropriate, to speed things along on its own.

You can create as many indexes for a table as you wish. However, creating too many indexes can actually slow things down, because Access needs to put a little time into maintaining each index. Therefore, you'll get maximum performance out of Access if you pick your indexed fields wisely.

So Which Fields Do I Index?

When deciding which fields are the best candidates for an index, you need to ask yourself two questions:

- Will I use this field often to look up information in the table?
- Will I use this field often to sort (alphabetize) records in the table?

If you can answer yes to either or both of these questions, then the field is a good candidate for an index. But before you make a final decision, you need to ask yourself one more question:

- Is the field already defined as the primary key?

If the answer to *that* question is Yes, then you don't want to create an index for that field, because Access has already done so.

Creating a Single-Field Index

To create an index for a single field in a table, click the field name, then click the *Indexed* property and open the drop-down list. You'll see the options shown at the bottom of Figure 6.8 and described below.

Yes (Duplicates OK)   Creates an index that *doesn't* require that each record have a unique value in the field (the most likely choice).

Yes (No Duplicates)   Creates an index that, like a primary key, does not allow multiple records to have the same value in the field.

No   The field won't be indexed (removes a previously defined index).

FIGURE 6.8

Options for creating an index for a single field

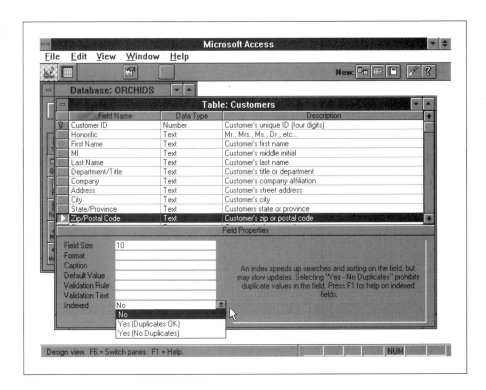

NOTE The index for the primary key field is automatically *Yes (No Duplicates)*. You cannot change that without losing the primary key.

A good candidate for a single-field index in the Customers table might be the Zip/Postal Code field, particularly if you need to pre-sort data into zip code order for bulk mailing. Or, if your company does telemarketing, you might want to occasionally sort records into phone number order, so that records are grouped by area code. In that case, the Phone field would be a good candidate for a single-field index.

TIP You cannot create an index for Yes/No, Memo, or OLE Object fields.

Keep in mind that just *defining* an index doesn't re-sort the records in the table. Instead, Access will *use* the index to speed the sorting of the table when you request to do so later. You'll learn how to sort in the next chapter.

Creating a Multiple-Field Index

You can also create an index that's based on multiple fields. Why would you want to do this? Well let's say that you plan to print customer lists or a directory with names alphabetized by Last Name, First Name, and Middle Initial, like the phone book.

Creating separate indexes for these three fields wouldn't help much when it comes time to sort your records into alphabetical order. But creating a single index based on all three of those fields would speed up the sort significantly.

To create an index based on multiple fields:

1. Click the Properties button (shown at left) in the tool bar, or choose View ➤ Table Properties. You'll see the **Table Properties** dialog box.

2. Click the first available Index slot (e.g., *Index1* if you haven't created any multi-field indexes).

3. Type the names of fields that you want to include in the index, separated by semicolons, and in "most important" to "least important" order.

N O T E   Remember, you cannot include Memo, Yes/No, or OLE Object fields in an index.

4. When you're done, press Alt+F4 or double-click the Control-menu box in the Table Properties dialog box to close its window.

N O T E   Multiple-field indexes never disallow duplicate entries. Also, you can create a maximum of five multiple-field indexes for a table.

Figure 6.9 shows an example where I've created an index for the Customers table based on the Last Name, First Name, and MI (middle initial) fields. (I zoomed in on the expression by pressing Shift+F2.)

The order of the field names is important, and, as mentioned above, should be listed in "most important" to "least important" order. For instance in Figure 6.9 I specified the field names as

Last Name; First Name; MI

FIGURE 6.9

A multiple-field index
based on the fields
Last Name, First
Name, and MI
(middle initial)

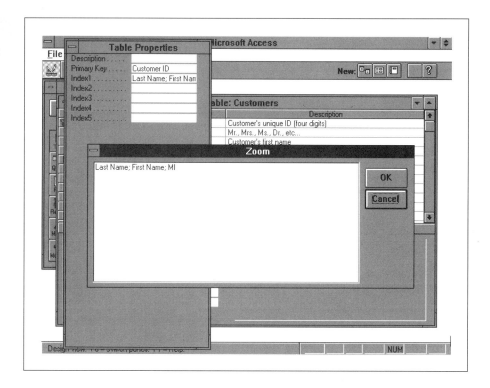

This tells Access that I'm going to want to list records in alphabetical order by last name. Within identical last names, I want records listed alphabetically by first name, and finally by middle initial. In other words, I want them alphabetized like this:

Adams, Andy A.

Adams, Andy B.

Adams, Carla V.

Baker, Richard

Baker, Zeke

Carlson, Charles B.

Carlson, Charles R.

Carlson, Michelle P.

etc...

Again, just defining the index won't change the order of records in the table. But later sorts based on the indexed fields will be faster.

Saving the Modified Table Design

Once you've changed the design of the table, you can save the new design by switching to Design View or closing the design window, and choosing Yes when prompted to save your changes.

Cautions on Changing the Table Design

If your table already contains a significant amount of data when you decide to change its design, there are a few things to keep in mind so that you don't inadvertently lose any data you've already stored. We'll look at some potentially troublesome changes in the sections that follow.

Changing a Field's Data Type

If you change the data type of a field in such a way that the fields cannot accept as much data, you're likely to lose some data in that field. In particular:

- If you change a data type from Text to some other data type, you'll lose any characters or data that aren't appropriate for the new data type. For instance, if you change from Text to Number, you'll lose any nonnumeric characters that have already been stored in the field.

- If you change a field from Memo to Text, you'll lose any text that doesn't fit into the smaller Text field. For instance, if you keep the field size at 50 in the Text field, you'll lose any text beyond the 50th character in the Memo field.

Changing a Field's Field Size Property

Changing the *Field Size* property of a field that already contains data can also lead to data loss. For instance, if you originally allowed a field size of 50 in a Text field, then reduce the size to 10, any text beyond the 10th character will be lost when you save the new table design.

Similarly, if you change the field size of a Number field to a smaller size, you may lose data in that field. For instance, if you change the field size from *Double* to *Integer*, you'll lose the decimal value in each field, and any values greater than 32,767, the largest value an Integer field can store.

Adding a Primary Key or Index

If you decide to change an existing field to a primary key after you've already added data to the table, or if you base a "No Duplicates" index on an existing field in a table, Access will delete any records that duplicate existing values in the field. If you're not careful, you could lose a significant amount of data this way.

So before you use an existing field as a primary key or indexed field, take a look at the existing data in the field and see if there are already any duplicate entries.

TIP

The easiest way to see if a field already contains duplicate entries is to first sort the table on that field, using a query (Chapter 7). That way, any duplicates will be grouped together in the resulting dynaset.

If the duplicate entries are mistakes, change them so that they're no longer duplicate entries before you change the table's design. If the field *needs* to have duplicate entries, don't use that field as the primary key or as the field for a "No Duplicates" index.

Last Chance to Avoid Data Loss

If the changes you make to the table design are likely to lead to data loss, Access will provide a warning, as in the example below, before it saves the new table design:

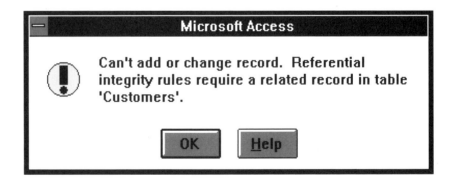

Read carefully whatever message appears in the message box before you opt to proceed. If you have any doubts, choose Cancel to return to the table design window without saving your changes. Again, your safest bet when changing the design of a table that already contains a significant amount of data might be to first make a backup copy of all the data in the table.

Assigning Relationships among Tables

When you later start creating queries, forms, and reports to mix and match data from multiple tables, you'll find that you need to tell Access what relationships exist between the tables as you go along. As an alternative to doing this over and over again in the future, you can just tell Access what relationships exist up front. Though entirely optional, this is the easiest way to do things, particularly if you have your sketched-out database design, like our Figure 4.7 back in Chapter 4, handy.

Also, you need to complete a couple of jobs before you start on this endeavor:

- The common field on the "one side" of a one-to-many relationship must already be defined as the primary key for that table.

- The data types and properties of the common field should be the same in both tables (except in the case of the Counter to Long Integer Number relationship that we've discussed before.)

You might also want to think about whether or not you want Access to enforce *referential integrity* between the related tables, as discussed next.

Enforcing Referential Integrity

Referential integrity is a way of ensuring that data in two related tables is valid. More specifically, it means that the table on the "many side" of a one-to-many relationship cannot contain data that does not relate to data in the table on the "one side" of the relationship. Here are some examples:

- If you enforce referential integrity between Customers and Orders, you can only enter orders for customers who already exist in the Customers table. (This helps prevent you from entering invalid customer ID numbers in the Orders table.)

- If you enforce referential integrity between Products and Order Details, you can only enter order detail records for Product ID codes that exist in the Products table. (This prevents you from entering invalid Product ID codes in the Order Details table.)

- If the Orders table contains one or more records for a given customer, you cannot delete that customer from the Customers table. (Thus, any outstanding orders will always refer to an existing customer.)

- If the Order Details table contains one or more records for a given product, you cannot delete that product from the Products table. (Thus, any outstanding orders will always refer to existing products.)

In other words, referential integrity is yet another means of minimizing the likelihood of problems, errors, and faulty data creeping into your database.

Defining the Relationships

When you are ready to define the relationships, and optionally the referential integrity, between two tables, follow these steps:

1. Close any open design view or datasheet view windows, so that you're starting from the database window.

2. If necessary, click the Table button in the database window to view a list of table names. Then click the name of the table that's on the "one side" of the relationship that you want to define.

3. Choose Edit ➤ Relationships. You'll see the Relationships dialog box, with the table you selected in the previous step chosen as the *Primary table,* and its primary key listed under *Primary Key Fields:,* as in the example shown in Figure 6.10.

FIGURE 6.10

The Relationships dialog box lets you define the relationship between the primary key of the table on the "one side" of a one-to-many (or one-to-one) relationship and the equivalent field in another table.

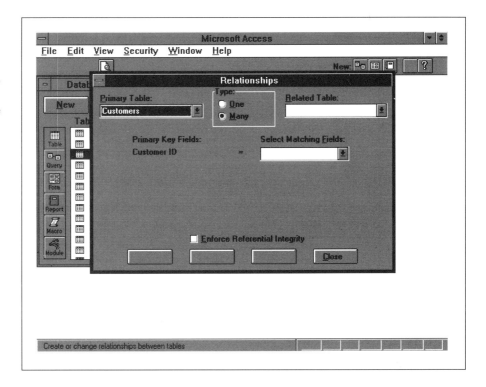

CAUTION

You cannot select a table that does not have a primary key as the Primary Table in a relationship. If you want to define a one-to-one relationship between two tables, both tables must have a primary key.

4. Choose the type of relationship between this table and the other table from the option button under *Type:*. That is, if there's a one-to-many relationship between this table and the other, choose Many. If there's a one-to-one relationship, choose One.

5. Click the drop-down list button under *Related Table*, and choose the table on the "many side" of the relationship.

6. Choose the table that you want to relate the primary table to (most likely, the table on the "many side" of the one-to-many relationship). Optionally, you can click the Suggest button to let Access suggest a matching field. (If the suggestion is correct, skip the next step.)

7. Click the drop-down list button under *Select Matching Fields,* then choose the name of the field in the Related Table that matches the primary key field in the primary table.

CAUTION

If you cannot find a matching field, the most likely problem is that the data type and/or field size of the common field is not the same in both tables. You'll need to close the Relationships dialog box and change the design of one or both tables so that the two fields match before you can define a relationship between the tables, as we discussed earlier under "Be Careful to Size Common Fields Equally."

8. If you want to enforce referential integrity between these two tables, choose the Enforce Referential Integrity check box. (You won't be able to do this if existing data in the table already violate the relationship.)

9. Choose the Add button to finish the job.

10. You can click the Close button now to close the dialog box if you wish. Optionally, you can define additional relationships without first returning to the database window by choosing another table under Primary Table, and then repeating steps 4 through 8.

Figure 6.11 shows the relationship between our sample Customers and Orders tables defined in the Relationships dialog box. In that example, Customers is on the "one side" and Orders is on the "many side" of a one-to-many relationship. In this example we've defined Customer ID as the matching field, and opted to enforce referential integrity.

FIGURE 6.11

The one-to-many relationship between Customers and Orders, based on the common Customer ID field, defined in the Relationships dialog box. I've also opted to enforce referential integrity in this example.

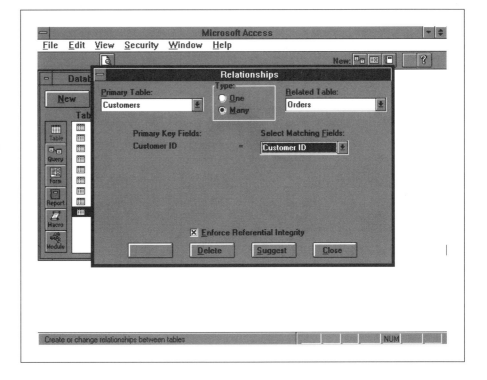

As another example, Figure 6.12 shows the relationship between our sample Products and Order Details tables, which is based on the Product ID field, defined in the Relationships dialog box.

And as a third example, Figure 6.13 shows the relationship between the Orders and Order Details tables, based on the Order ID field, defined in that dialog box.

You won't see any immediate results when you define the relationships between tables in this manner. However, you'll see why they're useful in the next chapter.

There are obviously more relationships between the tables in the database design I concocted in Chapter 4 (Figure 4.7) than are shown here. If you're following along and creating all the same tables that I'm creating, you can either define the relationships between those tables now, or just skip it for now. Remember, defining the relationships between tables at

FIGURE 6.12

The one-to-many relationship between Products and Order Details, based on the common Product ID field, defined in the Relationships dialog box

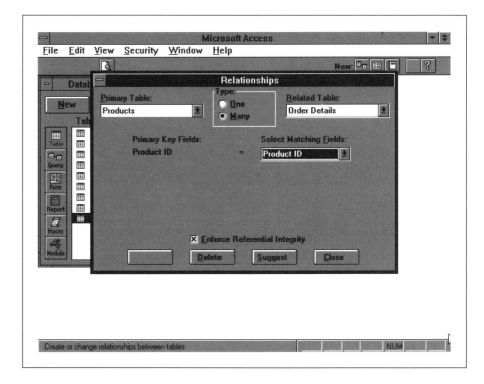

this point is entirely optional. You can define relationships on-the-fly as needed later if you wish.

NOTE

Actually, the Relationships dialog box is the only way to enforce referential integrity between tables. So perhaps I should say that defining relationships between tables is optional only if you don't want to enforce referential integrity.

FIGURE 6.13

The one-to-many relationship between Order and Order Details, based on the common Order ID field, defined in the Relationships dialog box

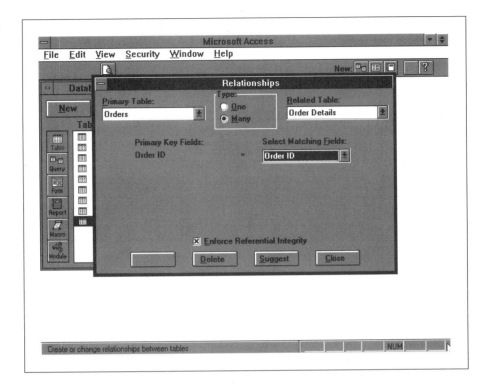

Additional Restrictions on Related Tables

Defining a relationship between two tables imposes a few additional limitations on those tables. But again these limitations exist solely to prevent you from making mistakes:

- You cannot delete the table that you've defined as the primary table in a relationship.

- You cannot delete the common field from either table once you've defined the relationship.

- You cannot change the data type of the common field in either table once you've successfully defined a relationship.

If you do need to do any of the above, you'll first need to delete the relationship, as described in a moment.

Changing or Deleting a Relationship

If you need to delete the relationship between a pair of tables, go through the same steps you went through when first defining the relationship. That is, choose the primary table, related table, and matching field that describe the relationship you want to change or delete.

If you simply want to change the referential integrity status of the relationship, click that option. If you want to delete the relationship, choose the Delete button.

What Happens If I Break Referential Integrity?

Remember that once you've defined a referential integrity relationship between two tables, you're limited to entering only data that meets the integrity requirements. If you break a referential integrity rule while entering or editing data, you'll see a message indicating the problem, as in the example below:

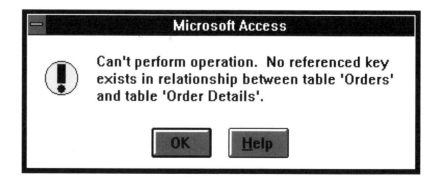

You'll need to choose OK, then change the data in the common field so that it matches a value in the other table. Or, delete the current record, then add the appropriate record to the other table.

For instance, if you enter an order for a non-existent customer into the Orders table, you'll either need to correct the Customer ID number in the Orders table so that it reflects an existing customer, or go add that customer number to the Customers table.

Admittedly, this can get to be confusing when you're only viewing one table at a time. But it gets to be easier, and makes much more sense, when you start designing forms that can really take advantage of referential integrity.

A Note on Foreign Keys

The designers of Access have tried to keep database terminology to a minimum in dialog boxes and menu commands. But there is one term that you might come across in a help screen or Cue Card that bears defining—and that's the term *foreign key*.

As you know, whenever there is a one-to-many relationship between two tables, there needs to be a common field that relates the records in one table to appropriate records in the other table. On the "one-side" of the relationship, that common field is called the *primary key,* or sometimes just the *key field,* or even just the *key*. The equivalent field on the "many side" of the relationship is called the *foreign key*.

For instance, in our Customers table, the Customer ID field plays the role of the primary key, uniquely identifying each customer in the table. In the Orders table, the Customer ID field acts as the foreign key that describes exactly which customer each order belongs to.

Summary

By this time you're probably beginning to think "Wow, here I am at the end of Chapter 6, and I'm *still* defining my database." That's true, but that's just the nature of the beast. In fact, there are entire books dedicated solely to database design that hardly bother to talk about how you go about *managing* the data at all.

We're not going to follow suit on that. We're finished with designing databases and tables. From here on out we're going to be talking about all the objects that you can create to *manage* your database, starting with queries in the next chapter.

Sorting and Querying Your Data

fast TRACK

N THIS chapter you'll learn many techniques for *querying,* or asking questions about, data in your tables. Access offers a graphical *query by example* (*QBE*) tool that you can use to view selected fields and records in a table, sort records into whatever order you want, and also to perform calculations. You can also use a query to join data from multiple tables into a single dynaset.

Creating a Query

The first step to creating a query, also called a "select query" (so named because it lets you select the fields and records that you want to view), is to get to the **Select Query:** window.

There are several ways to get to this window, and you should certainly feel free to use whatever method seems most convenient at the moment:

- If the table that you want to query is already open, just click the New Query button (shown at left) in the tool bar, or choose File ➤ New ➤ Query. Then skip to "The Select Query: Window" discussion below.

- *Or* click the name of the table you want to query in the database window, then click the New Query button or choose File ➤ New ➤ Query. Then skip to "The Select Query: Window" discussion below.

- Or, follow these steps:

    1. Click the Query object button in the database design window.
    2. Click the New Query button.
    3. The **Add Table** dialog box shown below appears, listing the names of all the tables, and any previously saved queries, in the current database.

TIP   As we'll discuss later, you can base any new query on the dynaset from any previously saved query.

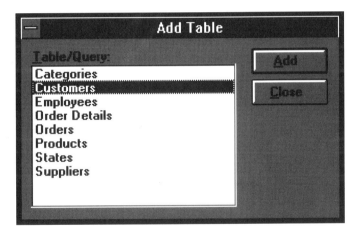

    4. Choose the name of the table (or dynaset) you want to query, then click the Add button (or just double-click the table name). You can repeat this step to query multiple related tables, as we'll discuss a little later in the chapter.
    5. Choose Close from the Add Table dialog box.

Regardless of which method you use to start the query, you'll be taken to the Select Query: window.

The Select Query: Window

N O T E Although the title of this query window shows the title "Select Query:", the window is known by the more generic name "the query window" in the Access manuals and the help files. For the sake of consistency, we'll use the more generic term hereafter.

Like most Access windows, the query window offers its own tool bar, menu bar, and other options. The names of buttons used in working with the query are shown below. The various parts of the query window itself are identified in Figure 7.1.

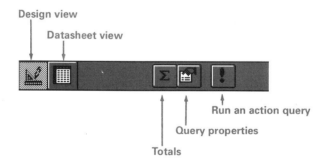

Design view
Datasheet view
Totals
Query properties
Run an action query

The field list that appears in the upper left corner of the query window includes the names of all the fields in the table you chose to query (the Customers table from Chapter 4 in this example).

FIGURE 7.1

The Select Query:
window (also referred
to simply as "the
query window") with
a field list for the
Customers table open
in the upper portion of
the window

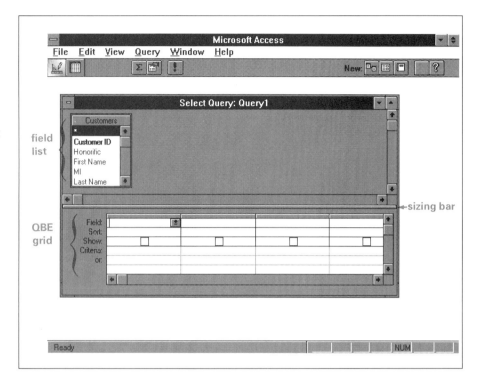

TIP   You can widen the field list window just as you
would any other window, by dragging its right
border toward the right.

Choosing Which Fields You Want to View

Once you're in the query window, your first step will be to decide which
fields you want to view in the results of the query. In some situations, you
might want to view all the fields in the table. In other situations, you might

want to view only certain fields. For instance, you might want to view only the names and phone numbers to generate a phone list.

Selecting Individual Fields to View

To choose specific fields to view:

- Drag a file name from the field list to any column in the QBE grid.
- *Or* click any field name slot, then click the drop-down list button that appears, and choose a field name from the list.
- *Or* type a field name into any field name slot.

Figure 7.2 illustrates the first two methods.

FIGURE 7.2

You can choose a field to view by dragging its name from the field list, or by clicking a field name cell and choosing a field name from the drop-down list.

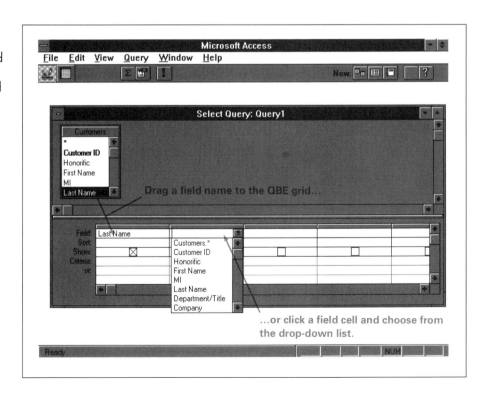

If you prefer, you can choose several field names from the field list by holding down the Ctrl key as you click field names. Or, you can click one field name, then hold down the Shift key and click another field name to extend the selection through several field names. Then just drag any one of the selected field names to a field name cell.

Selecting All the Fields

You can also copy all the field names from the field list to the QBE grid in one fell swoop. And yes, you guessed it, there are a few different ways to do it:

1. Double-click the title bar at the top of the field list to select all of its field names:

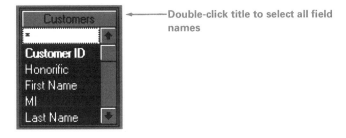
Double-click title to select all field names

   Or drag the mouse pointer through all of the field names,
   Or click the first field name and press Ctrl+Shift+End to select all the field names.

2. Then drag any selected field name to a field name cell in the QBE grid.

TIP

The asterisk (*) at the top of the field list plays a special role that we'll talk about in Chapter 8.

Inserting, Deleting, and Moving QBE Columns

Here are a few basic techniques you can use to rearrange the QBE grid in case you change your mind after you've gotten started:

1. To move or delete a field, first click the field selector just above the field name in the QBE grid, as shown below:

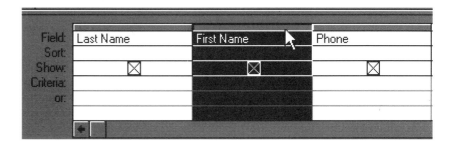

TIP

You can select multiple columns by dragging the mouse pointer through several field selectors, or by holding down the Shift key while clicking the field selector of the column you want to extend the selection to.

2. To move the selected column, click the field selector a second time, then drag the column left or right to its new position. To delete the selected column(s), press Delete or choose Edit ➤ Delete. (Optionally, choose Edit ➤ Delete All to remove all the field names from the QBE grid.).

If you want to insert one of the field names from the field list between two columns in the QBE grid, just drag the field name from the field list into whatever column position you want the field to be in. Additional columns will shift to the right to make room for the new field.

Running the Query

Once you've chosen one or more field names to view, you can run the query to see the results. For example, in the QBE grid below, I've opted to display just the fields named Last Name, First Name, Phone, and Fax from the Customers table:

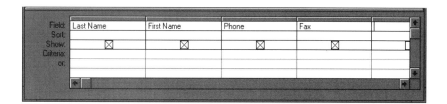

To run the query you can do any of the following:

- Click the Datasheet view button (shown at left—the second button from the left in the tool bar).

- *Or* choose View ➤ Datasheet.

A *dynaset* appears, displaying only the selected fields from the table. For example, Figure 7.3 shows the dynaset resulting from the query shown just above.

What *Is* a Dynaset?

The dynaset that results from a query looks very much like the datasheet view of the table, except that it contains only the fields you've requested to see. The reason it's called a dynaset is because it contains a *dyna*mic sub*set* of the all the records in the table.

It's a subset because it doesn't necessarily contain *all* the fields and records from the table, just the particular fields and records you're interested in viewing at the moment. It's dynamic because it contains "live data"—that is, unlike some database management systems, which display a *copy* of the data in the table, a dynaset displays a subset of the actual table.

FIGURE 7.3

The results of a query are displayed in a *dynaset*.

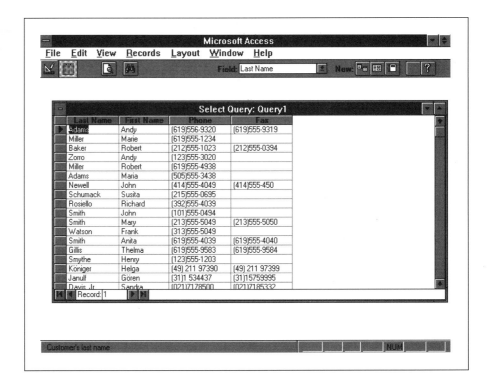

NOTE

We'll talk about how you can use a query to view specific records, as well as specific fields, just a little later in this chapter.

This is a terrific convenience, because it means that if you happen to notice a typo or other item of data that needs to be changed, you can change it right here, on the spot. (In other database management systems, changing data on the spot here in the query results would be a waste of time, because you'd only be making the change in this separate copy of the data rather than in the original table where the change is actually needed.)

But this is just the tip of the proverbial iceberg. As you'll see in upcoming chapters, the fact that a dynaset contains live data has far-reaching and powerful beneficial effects on the designing of forms and reports.

Printing the Dynaset

You can "quick print" the dynaset on your screen as you would any other table. That is, choose File ➤ Print to get to the **Print** dialog box. If necessary you can use the Setup button to change the selected printer, margins, paper orientation, and so forth. When you're ready to begin printing, choose the OK button from the Print dialog box.

Returning to the Query Window

When you're done viewing the results of the query, you can return to the query window, if you so desire, to change or refine the query. To do so:

- Click the Design button (shown at left—the first button in the tool bar).
- *Or* choose View ➤ Query Design.

Closing and Saving a Query Window

When you've finished with your query, just close either the query window or the dynaset window with the usual techniques, such as choosing File ➤ Close, or by double-clicking the appropriate window's Control-menu box, or by pressing Ctrl+F4.

You'll be asked if you want to save the current query. If you think you might use the query again in the future, you can choose Yes, then provide a standard Access name (up to 64 characters, including blank spaces). For instance, you could name the sample query I just showed you something like **Customer phone numbers**.

When you save a query, Access saves *only* the query design, not the resulting datasheet. That way, when you re-use the query in the future, it operates on whatever data happens to be in your table at that time. Thus, if you've added, changed, or deleted records since the last time you used the query, the results of the query will display up-to-date information.

Reusing a Saved Query

If you did save the query, you can reopen it by following these steps:

1. Click the Query object button in the database window (Figure 7.4). A list of all the saved queries in the database appears.

2. If you want to view the query's current dynaset, double-click the name of the query you want to open, or click its name and choose Open. If you want to view or change the query's design, click the Design button.

Regardless of which of the last two options you use to open the query, you can switch back and forth between the query design and the resulting dynaset using the Design View and Datasheet View buttons in the tool bar. You can also change the query design, using the same general techniques you used to create it.

FIGURE 7.4

As with any database object, you can click the Query object button to view all saved queries. Then click Open to see the selected query's dynaset, or Design to see the query's design, or New to create a new query.

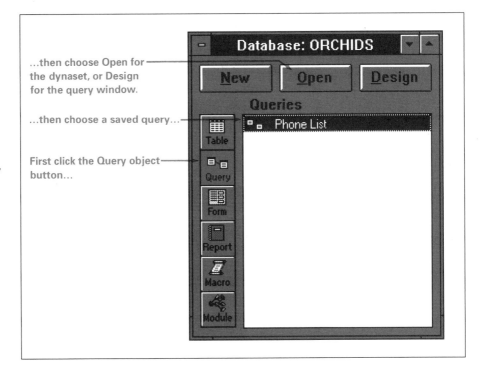

Customizing the Dynaset

While you're viewing the dynaset that results from a query, you can customize its appearance using the same techniques you'd use to customize a datasheet. For instance, you can move and change the width of columns, use options on the Layout menu to change the font and gridlines, and so forth.

However, any changes you make to the dynaset will be used in the current session only, and won't be saved when you save the query. Therefore, you don't want to spend too much time perfecting the appearance of a dynaset.

To make permanent changes to the appearance of a dynaset, you need to design a form that's based on the query. We'll talk about how you do that in Chapter 11.

Sorting Records

Choosing particular fields that you want to view is just one capability of queries. You can also use a query to *sort* records in a table. Sorting, in database terminology, means the same thing it does in everyday language. For instance, you can sort the records in your table into alphabetical order by people's names. Or you can sort the records into chronological date order, or some other numerical order. For example, you could sort the Products table from smallest (cheapest) to largest (most expensive) Unit Price order. To sort records:

1. Open (or create) a query design window, and select the fields you want to view.

2. Click the Sort cell under the name of the field that you want to sort the records by, then click the drop-down list button that

appears. You'll see the options shown and summarized below:

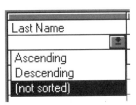

Ascending Sort records in smallest to largest order (e.g., smallest number to largest number, A to Z for text, or earliest to latest date).

Descending Sort records in largest to smallest order (e.g., largest to smallest number, Z to A for text, or latest to earliest date).

(not sorted) Don't sort on this field.

The QBE grid below shows an example where I've opted to sort records into ascending order by the Last Name field. Figure 7.5 shows the resulting dynaset after running the query. As you can see, the records are indeed in alphabetical order by last name.

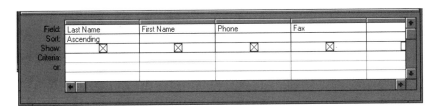

Using a Sort to Organize Data into Groups

Sorting the records in a table naturally groups records with identical values together. For instance, in the dynaset shown in Figure 7.5, all the Smiths naturally fall together because the names are alphabetized.

Now let's say that you are going to start a telemarketing project, and want to start calling people within certain area codes. How could you group records together by area codes? Just get to the query window, set the Last

FIGURE 7.5

Dynaset resulting from
a query that sorts
records into ascending
order by last name

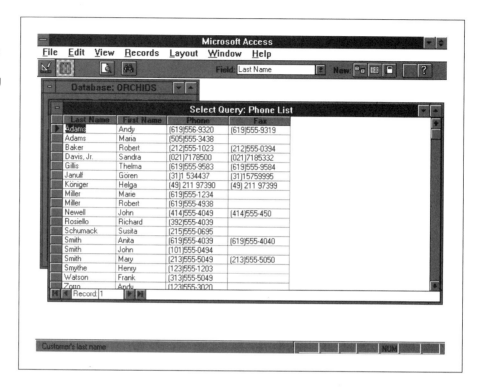

Name field to *not sorted*, then sort the Phone field into ascending or descending order, as in the QBE grid below. Then run the query.

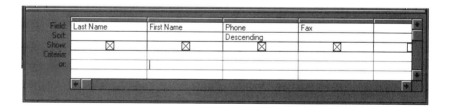

Sorts-within-Sorts

You can sort on multiple fields in a query to achieve a sort within a sort. The most common example of this type of sort order is the telephone directory, where entries are alphabetized by last names, then by first name within identical last names, and by middle initial within identical first and last names.

To sort on multiple fields in a query, select either an ascending or descending sort order for every field you want to sort on. For instance, to sort customer names and addresses into Last Name, First Name, and MI fields, you'd arrange the QBE grid like this:

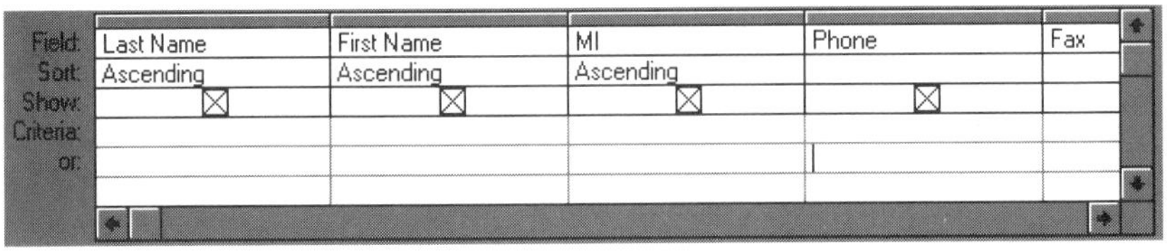

When you run the query, the records will be sorted by all three fields. For instance, as you can see in Figure 7.6, Smith, John Q. comes before Smith, John Z. And of course, all the other records are in alphabetical order as well.

FIGURE 7.6

Records in the Customers table sorted by Last Name, First Name, and Middle Initial

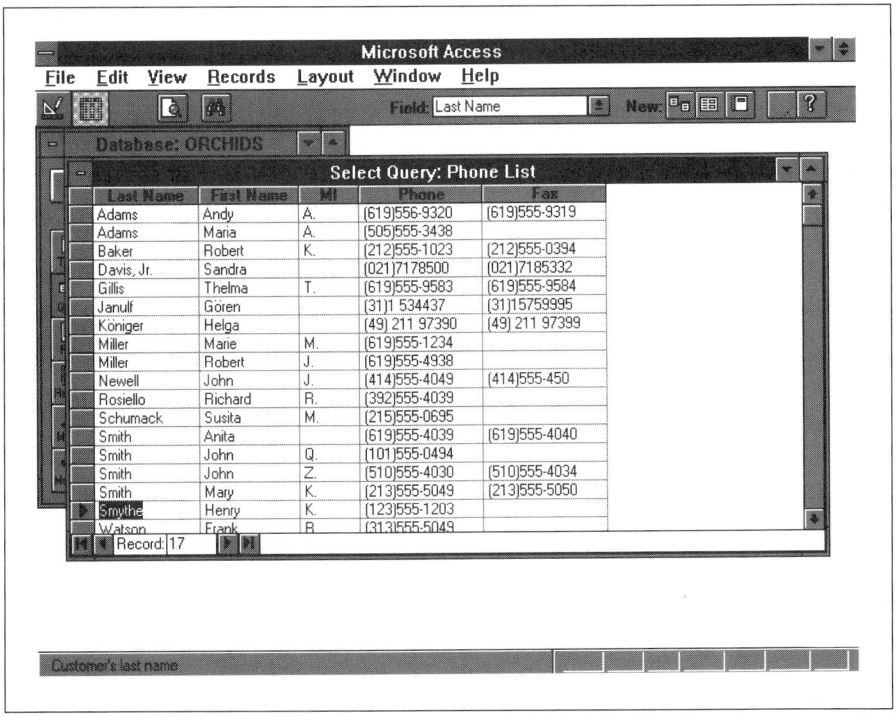

Be aware that the order of *columns* in the QBE grid affects the final sort order of the records. Access uses the leftmost sorted column for the "main" sort order, the first column to the right of that as the second sort order, and so forth.

For instance, in the QBE grid below, First Name is in the leftmost column, MI is the second column, and Last Name is the third column. All three fields are marked for sorting into ascending order.

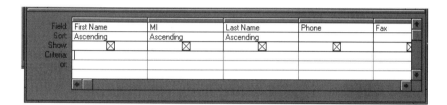

When you run the query, records in the dynaset will be alphabetized by people's *first names*, then by middle initial, then by last name, as in Figure 7.7.

Using a Query to Search for Records

You can use a query to search for, and isolate, particular records in a table. For instance,

* In the Customers table, you might want to view all customers in a certain city, state, or zip code range, or customers who haven't placed any orders in the last six months.

* In the Orders table, you might want to view all unpaid orders that are more than 30 days past due, or recent orders for a certain product, or orders placed by a certain customer.

FIGURE 7.7

Records in this dynaset are sorted by First Name, rather than Last Name, because First Name is in the first column.

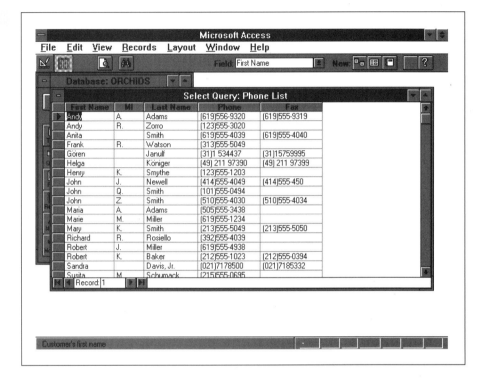

* In the Products table, you might want to look through products within a given category only, or products within a certain price range, or products that need to be reordered.

To search for or isolate records:

1. In the QBE grid, click the Criteria cell in the field you want to search.

2. Type in the *criterion expression* that exemplifies the information you're looking for, keeping in mind the following:

   * If you are searching a number, currency, or counter field, do not include a currency sign or thousands separator. For instance, to search for a value of $10,000, you would type **10000**.

- When searching a date/time field, you can be flexible about the format of the date, but the left-to-right order of the month, date, and year should match that defined in the International settings of the Windows **Control Panel**. For instance, in the United States, you could enter **3/31/93** or **3 March 1993** or **3-Mar-93** or **Mar 3 93**. Access will place # signs around whatever date you enter when you move to another cell or run the query.

- When searching a text field, you can (usually) just type the text you're looking for. Access will place double-quotation marks around the text when you run the query. In some cases, however, you'll want to put in the quotation marks yourself, as discussed later under "Searching for Operators and the Words And and Or."

- To search a Yes/No field, you can enter **-1**, **Yes**, **True**, or **On** to search for Yes, or **0**, **No**, **False**, or **Off** to search for No.

- You can use any combination of operators, wildcard characters, and other options (described in the following section) in the criterion expression.

3. When you've finished entering search criteria, run the query in the usual manner.

Using Operators to Search for Records

You can use a wide variety of *operators* and *wildcards* to help you find exactly the information you need in a query. For future reference, they're all listed in Table 7.1 with brief examples.

You can also use the mathematical operators listed in Table 7.2 to help you find exactly the records you're looking for and to perform calculations. The **&** operator works with text, as you'll see a little later in the chapter.

TABLE 7.1: Operators and wildcard characters you can use in queries

OPERATOR	MEANING	EXAMPLE	INTERPRETATION
COMPARISON OPERATORS			
=	Equals	=smith	Equals smith
>	Greater than	>5000	Greater than 5,000
<	Less than	<1/1/93	Less (earlier) than January 1, 1993
>=	Greater than or equal to	>=M	Greater than or equal to the letter *M*
<=	Less than or equal to	<=12/31/92	Less than or equal to December 31, 1992
<>	Not equal to	<>CA	Does not equal CA
Between	Between two values (inclusive)	Between 15 and 25	A number from 15 to 25
In	Within a set of values	In (NY PA NJ)	New York, Pennsylvania, or New Jersey
Is Null	Field is empty	Is Null	Records that have no value in this field
Is Not Null	Field is not empty	Is Not Null	Records that *do* have a value in this field
Like	Matches a pattern	Like MO-*	Records that start with *MO-* followed by any other characters

TABLE 7.1: Operators and wildcard characters you can use in queries (continued)

OPERATOR	MEANING	EXAMPLE	INTERPRETATION
LOGICAL OPERATORS			
And	Both are true	>=1 And <=10	Between 1 and 10
Or	One or the other is true	CA or NE	Either California or Nevada
Not	Not true	Not Like MO-???	Records that don't start with *MO-*
WILDCARD CHARACTERS			
?	Any single character	P?-100	Values that start with *P*, followed by any single character, followed by *-100*
★	Any characters	(619)*	Any text that starts with *(619)*, e.g., Phone or FAX numbers
REFERENCE TO ANOTHER FIELD			
[*field name*]	Some other field in the QBE grid	<[Units In Stock]	Records where this field's value is less than the value in the Units In Stock field

TABLE 7.2: Mathematical operators

OPERATOR	MEANING
+	Addition
-	Subtraction
*	Multiplication
/	Division
\	Integer division
^	Exponent
Mod	Remainder of division (modulo)
&	Join two strings (text)

Searching for a Specific Value

If you want to search for a specific item of information, you simply need to type whatever you want Access to find into the Criteria cell of the appropriate field, and then run the query. For instance, suppose that you want to isolate records for California residents in the Customer table. You'd first need to drag the State/Province field (and any other fields you want to view) to the QBE grid. Then enter **CA** or **"CA"** or **="CA"** into the Criteria cell for that field, as below.

Field:	Last Name	First Name	MI		State/Province	City	
Sort:	Ascending	Ascending	Ascending				
Show:	☒	☒	☒		☒		
Criteria:					CA		
or:							

NOTE If you don't put quotation marks around text, Access will put them in for you as soon as you leave the cell or run the query. Similarly, if you don't put an equals sign (=) in front of a search criterion, Access just assumes you *meant* equals.

When you run the query, only records that have (exactly) CA in the State/Province field will appear in the dynaset, as in the example below:

Last Name	First Name	MI	State/Province	City	Phone	Fax
Adams	Andy	A.	CA	San Diego	(619)556-9320	(619)555-9319
Gillis	Thelma	T.	CA	Rancho Santa Fe	(619)555-9583	(619)555-9584
Miller	Marie	M.	CA	Encinitas	(619)555-1234	
Miller	Robert	J.	CA	Encinitas	(619)555-4938	
Smith	Anita		CA	Encinitas	(619)555-4039	(619)555-4040
Smith	Mary	K.	CA	Los Angeles	(213)555-5049	(213)555-5050
*						

Be aware that this kind of search will only find values that are the same length and that have the same spelling as the criterion (though upper/lowercase doesn't matter). For instance, searching for **Ocean** in the Address field won't find *Ocean Vista Way* or *123 Ocean Lane,* because neither of those addresses is the same length as just the word Ocean. (Rather, each only *contains* the word Ocean.) You can use wildcard characters to extend the search to words that don't exactly match the length of the criterion.

CAUTION When you switch from a dynaset back to the QBE grid, be sure to erase any existing criteria that you don't want to use in the next search before entering the new search criteria. Just drag the mouse pointer through the old criterion and press Delete.

Searching for Partial Text

When querying a field, you can use the **?** wildcard character to match any single character, and **★** to match any group of characters. For instance, to search for product codes starting with the letters PO in the Products table, you would set up a query window for that table as below:

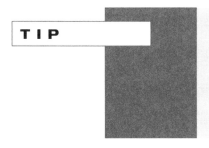

Field:	Product ID	Description	Current Price	Category ID	
Sort:					
Show:	☒	☒	☒	☒	
Criteria:	PO*				
or:					

Whenever you use wildcard characters, Access will automatically add the **Like** operator to the front of the query criterion, and enclose the criterion in quotation marks (in a text field), or # symbols (in a date/time field.) For instance, Access will convert the criterion **PO★** to

    Like 'PO*'

You can always use the ★ operator to broaden a search that failed to find data on the first try. For example, suppose a search for **Davis** in the Last Name field of a table doesn't yield any results. Yet you're pretty sure there's a Davis in the table somewhere. Changing the criterion to **Davis★** or **"Davis★"** might find a *Davis, Jr.* or *Davis III* in the table.

T I P

If you originally entered your phone numbers with the area code in parentheses, as in the Customers table, you could search for all the phone numbers within a certain area code, such as 619, with the criterion (619)* or Like "(619)*" in the Phone field of the QBE grid.

You can use the ★ character to stand for any portion of a date as well. For instance, the criterion:

    1/*/93

in a date/time field would isolate records with dates in January of 1993.

Searching for Embedded Text

If the text you want to search for is embedded within the field, use a ✶ character both in front of and after the criterion. For example, suppose you want to locate records for all customers on Moonglow St. (or Moonglow Rd. or whatever) in the Address field of the Customers table. Since the word moonglow is undoubtedly embedded within the addresses (for example, *123 Moonglow St.*), you could use either **✶moonglow✶** or **"✶moonglow✶"** as the search criterion, like this:

Field:	Department/Title	Company	Address	City	State/F
Sort:					
Show:	☒	☒	☒	☒	
Criteria:			"moonglow"		
or:					

Searching Memo and OLE Fields

The ✶ character is also useful for finding text in memo fields. For instance, a search for **✶spanish✶** would find the word *spanish* embedded in a lengthy memo field.

Although there's no official documentation on it, I've also found that this kind of search will work in an OLE Object field, provided that the OLE Object contains text, such as a Word document, and that the object has been embedded in, rather than linked to, the field. Which all makes sense, because Access will store a copy of the entire document in the OLE Object field if it's embedded in the field.

Searching for Empty or Non-Empty Fields

To search for records that have no value in a field, you can use the **Is Null** criterion. For example, if you leave the Country field in the Customers table empty for addresses within the United States, running a query with **Is Null** in the Country field, as below, will isolate records within the United States. Running a query with **Is Not Null** in that field would isolate addresses outside the United States.

Field:	State/Province	Zip/Postal Code	Country	Phone	Fax
Sort:					
Show:	☒	☒	☒	☒	
Criteria:			Is Null		
or:					

TIP

You can use Is Null in an OLE Object field to locate records with no object in that field, and Is Not Null to isolate records that do have some object in that field.

Hiding a Field from a Dynaset

If you want to include a field in the QBE grid so that you can put a criterion in it, but not display the contents of that field in the dynaset, just deselect the Show check box beneath the field name. For example, the criterion below requests that only records with blank Country fields be displayed in the dynaset, but the Country field itself won't be included in that dynaset.

Field:	State/Province	Zip/Postal Code	Country	Phone
Sort:				
Show:	☒	☒	☐	☒
Criteria:			Is Null	

Searching for Ranges of Values

The comparison operators you saw in Table 7.1 let you extend a search to include a range of values. For example, suppose you want to isolate customers in a particular county, such as San Diego, and you know that zip codes in that county range from 92003 to 92086. To isolate records in that zip code range, you would enter the search criterion **Between 92003 And 92086-9999** into the Criteria cell of the Zip/Postal code field, as shown below.

Field:	State/Province	Zip/Postal Code	Country	Phone
Sort:				
Show:	☒	☒	☒	☒
Criteria:		Between 92003 And 92086-9999		
or:				

T I P

I didn't use the Zip+four code (the Post Office's extended zip code system) at the low end of the scale, because 92003 is the smallest zip code at that end of the scale. I did use Zip+four at the high end, because 92086-9999 is actually the highest possible Zip code at that end of the scale.

The **Between** operator works with a date/time field as well. For instance, the criterion **Between (1/1/92 And 3/31/93)** in a date/time field would isolate records that have dates in the first quarter of 1993.

Suppose you want to help a customer find a gift for under $25.00. You could create a query for the Products table to isolate records with appropriate values in the Unit Price field, like this:

Field:	Description	Category ID	Current Price	Units In Stock	Units O
Sort:					
Show:	☒	☒	☒	☒	
Criteria:			<25		
or:					

Of course, you could be a little more selective in your search by changing your **<25** to **Between 15 And 25.**

Searching Based on a Calculation

You can use the mathematical operators to base a search on the results of a calculation. In many cases, you'll probably want to use the contents of some other field or fields in the table in your calculation.

For instance, to see only products that need to be reordered in the Products table, you'd want to find records that have a Reorder Point value that's greater than the sum of the values in the Units In Stock and the Units On Order fields. Here's how you could set up such a QBE screen, using our sample Products table.

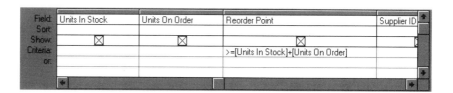

Field:	Units In Stock	Units On Order	Reorder Point	Supplier ID
Sort:				
Show:	☒	☒	☒	
Criteria:			>=[Units In Stock]+[Units On Order]	
or:				

Let's take a closer look. First of all, I widened the Reorder Point column in the QBE grid so that you could see the entire criterion. Then I entered this expression:

    >=[Units In Stock]+[Units On Order]

TIP

To widen or narrow a QBE column, drag the vertical bar to the right of the field name, as with a datasheet. You can also zoom in on a criterion by pressing Shift+F2.

In English, the criterion means that I want to see records where the value in this field, Reorder Point, is greater than or equal to the sum of the Units In Stock and Units On Order fields. Notice that I've enclosed the names of those fields in square brackets, as required. The results of the query are shown in Figure 7.8.

Searching for Ranges of Dates

You've already seen how you can use wildcards and operators to search for dates. For instance, the search criterion ***/*/93** would find all records with 1993 dates. The expression **Between 1/1/93 And 3/31/93** would find all records with dates in the first quarter of 1993. The criterion **<=12/31/92** would find dates on, or before, December 31, 1992.

You can also search for records with dates that are relative to today's date using the **Date( )** function. Using **Date( )** alone as the criterion in a date/time field would find records that contain exactly today's date. You can specify dates a certain number of days from now by adding a plus sign (+) and the number of days, or adding a minus sign (-) and subtracting the number of days from **Date( )**. For instance **Date( )+30** results in a

FIGURE 7.8

Only products that need to be reordered appear in this dynaset of the Products table.

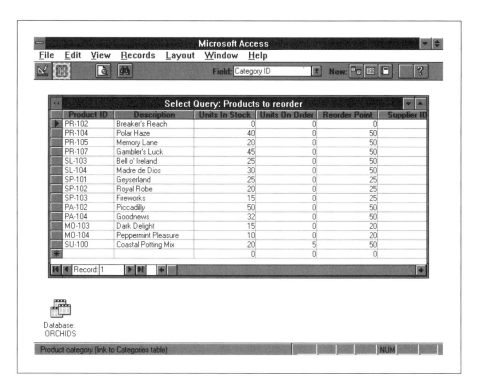

date that's 30 days in the future. The expression **Date( )-60** results in the date 60 days ago. Table 7.3 shows examples of how you could use this date arithmetic to find records that fall within a range of dates relative to today's date.

TABLE 7.3: Examples of expressions using Date( )

CRITERION	DATES INCLUDED IN DYNASET
Date( )	Exactly today's date
<=Date( )	Today, and all dates before
>=Date( )	Today, and all dates after
Between Date( ) And Date( )-30	Dates within the last 30 days
Between Date( ) And Date( )+30	Dates within the next 30 days
Between Date( )-60 And Date( )-30	Dates between 30 and 60 days ago
Between Date( )+60 And Date( )+30	Dates between 30 and 60 days from today
<Date( )-90	Dates that are more than 90 days earlier than today

You can also use the **DateAdd( )** function to specify a range of dates based on some interval other than days. For example, the expression:

    Between DateAdd("m"-2,Date( )) And Date( )

would find records with dates from the last two months. So if the current month is March, this expression would find records with dates ranging from January 1 to the current date. for more information on DateAdd( ) and other functions, see Chapter 7.

Performing "And/Or" Searches

In some situations, you want your queries to produce only records that meet *all* the query criteria. For instance, when you are specifically trying to locate information about Andy Adams in San Diego, you would want to structure your query so that it searches only for records that contain Adams in the Last Name field *and* Andy in the First Name field *and* San Diego in the City field.

In other situations, you might want to find records that match *any* of the search criteria. For instance, you want to locate customers who purchased either a MOTH *or* a SLIPPER orchid (or both).

The basic techniques you use in the query window to specify "And" and "Or" relationships among query criteria are summarized below:

- To specify an "And" relationship among multiple fields, place the query criteria in the same row of the QBE grid.

- To specify an "Or" relationship among multiple fields, place the query criteria in separate rows of the QBE grid.

- To specify an "And" relationship in a single field, use the **And** operator.

- To specify an "Or" relationship in a single field, use the **Or** operator, or use the **In** operator, or *stack* the criteria in the QBE grid.

Defining "And" Relationships across Several Fields

When you want to isolate records that match several search criteria in different fields, place those search criteria in the same row. For example, the query shown in Figure 7.9 asks for records that have Adams in the Last name field *and* Andy in the First Name field *and* San Diego in the City

FIGURE 7.9

An "And" search to
find records for Andy
Adams in the city of
San Diego. There is
an "and" relationship
between the query
criteria, because all
the criteria are on
the same row of the
QBE grid.

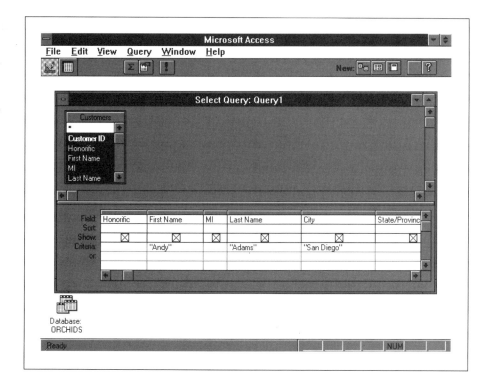

field. The resulting dynaset would display records for any Andy Adams living in San Diego.

Looking at another example, suppose you want to isolate unpaid orders that are between 30 and 60 days past due in the Orders table. You'd need to use the criterion **Between Date( )-30 And Date( )-60** in the Order date field, and **No** in the Paid field, both on the same row in the QBE grid for the Orders table, as below:

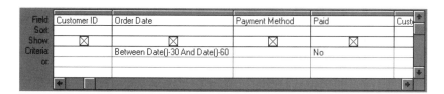

Defining an "And" Relationship in a Single Field

If you want to specify an "And" relationship among search criteria in a single field, separate the query criteria with a comma. In most cases, using multiple search criteria only makes sense when searching for ranges using comparison operators, or for small pieces of text within a larger text or memo field.

For instance, the query criterion **>=4/1/93 And <=6/30/93** in a date/time field would find records with dates in the second quarter of 1993. You may find it more intuitive to use the more English-like expression **Between 4/1/93 And 6/30/93**, which means exactly the same thing.

If you wanted to search the Notes field of the Employees for people who speak *both* French and Spanish, you could use the query criterion ***Spanish* And *French***. Access would add the **Like** operators, as below. When you run the query the resulting dynaset will include records that have both the word *Spanish* and the word *French* in the Notes field. Records that contain only *French*, or only *Spanish*, or neither, would be excluded from the dynaset.

Field:	Signature	Photo	Notes	
Sort:				
Show:	☒	☒	☒	☐
Criteria:			Like '"*spanish*"' And Like '"*french*"'	
or:				

Defining "Or" Relationships across Several Fields

If you want to search for records that contain certain values *or* other values, place the query criteria on separate rows of the QBE grid. For example, to find customers that have either San Diego in the City field *or*

714 as the area code in their phone numbers, you would put the two query criteria on separate rows of the QBE grid, as below:

Field:	Address	City	State/Province	Zip/Postal Code	Country	Phone
Sort:						
Show:	☒	☒	☒	☒	☒	☒
Criteria:		"San Diego"				
or:						Like "(714)*"

You might think of each row in the QBE grid as a separate question that the query asks of the table. For instance, when running the query shown above, Access will first ask "Does this record have San Diego in its City field?" Then it will ask "Does this record's Phone field start with (714)?" If it can answer Yes to either or both questions, it includes the record in the dynaset. If it cannot answer yes to either question, that record is excluded from the dynaset.

When setting up this type of query, you need to think carefully about exactly what the question in each row of the QBE grid is going to ask. For example, suppose you want to look at all the Smiths in the states of New York and New Jersey. Your first thought might be to set up the QBE grid as below.

Field:	Last Name	Department/Title	Company	State/Province	Address
Sort:					
Show:	☒	☒	☒	☒	☐
Criteria:	"Smith"			"NY"	
or:				"NJ"	

However, the results of this query would actually display all the Smiths in New York, and every customer in New Jersey, regardless of last name. Why? because the first question asks "Does this record have Smith in the Last Name field, and NY in the State field?" But the second question only asks "Does this record have NJ in the State field?"

The correct way to locate all the Smiths in New York and New Jersey is below. In that version both "questions" ask if the Last Name field contains Smith before checking on the contents of the State field.

Field:	Last Name	Department/Title	Company	State/Province	Address
Sort:					
Show:	☒	☒	☒	☒	☐
Criteria:	"Smith"			"NY"	
or:	"Smith"			"NJ"	

Defining an "Or" Relationship in a Single Field

If you want to search for any one of several given values in a field, you can either stack the values in separate rows or use the **Or** operator or the **In** operator. For instance, the QBE grid below would find records that have *NY* or *NJ* or *PA* in the State/Province field:

Field:	Last Name	Department/Title	Company	State/Province	Address
Sort:					
Show:	☒	☒	☒	☒	☐
Criteria:				"NY"	
or:				"NJ"	
				"PA"	

As an alternative to stacking the criteria, you could use the single criterion:

    NY Or NJ Or PA

or the criterion:

    In ("NY", "NJ", "PA")

Going back to our earlier Employee table example, if you wanted to locate records that have either *Spanish* or *French* in the Notes field, you would either stack the query conditions, or separate them with the **Or** operator, like this:

Field:	Date Hired	Signature	Photo	Notes	
Sort:					
Show:	☒	☒	☒	☒	
Criteria:				Like "*spanish*"	
or:				Like "*french*"	

Troubleshooting "And/Or" Queries

When building criteria that use "And" and "Or" logic, remember that the way you might think about the query in plain English may *not* be the way to express it in a query. For example you might think to yourself, "I want to view California and Washington residents." Then you define the query criterion as:

CA And WA

When you run the query, however, the dynaset will be empty, regardless of how many CA and WA residents are actually in the table. Why? Because it is impossible for the State field in any single record in the table to contain both CA *and* WA. Therefore, Access can never answer Yes when it asks "Does this record have CA in the State field, *and* WA in the State field?"

To isolate records for California and Washington residents, you need to structure the query so that it looks for records that have either CA *or* WA in the State field, like this:

CA Or WA

or by using the **In** operator, like this:

In (CA, WA)

Searching for Operators and the Words And and Or

If the text you're looking for is the same as an operator listed in Table 7.1, Access will naturally interpret it as an operator rather than text. For instance, let's suppose you want to search for the company name *Bash and Loam*. When you run the query or move to another field in the query grid, Access will convert that criterion to:

"Bash" And "Loam"

because it thinks that the word "And" in this phrase is an operator. To prevent (or fix) this, enclose the entire criterion in quotation marks, like this:

"Bash and Loam"

Creating Calculated Fields

If you want a query to perform a calculation for you, and display the results of that calculation in the dynaset, create a *calculated field* in the QBE grid. That is, move to an empty field cell, and type in an expression that will do the calculation you want into the Field cell (not the Criteria cell) of that column. When referring to other fields in the QBE grid, be sure to enclose their names in square brackets [ ]. For instance, the expression for multiplying the quantity times the unit price would be **[Qty]*[Unit Price]**.

You can also give the calculated column its own heading in the dynaset, and use that heading as a field name in still other calculations. Just precede the calculation with the heading you want to use, followed by a colon, like this:

Extended Price:[Qty]*[Unit Price]

You could then use Extended Price as a field name in another calculated field. For instance, to add 7.75% sales tax to the extended price in the next column over, and display that result, you could enter this formula:

With Tax:[Extended Price]*1.0775

You can use the **CCur** function to format the result as a currency field if you wish. For instance, to display the results of the Extended Price calculation in currency format you would enter the expression as:

Extended Price: CCur([Qty]*[Unit Price])

N O T E   CCur( ) and similar functions are covered in more depth in Chapter 17.

A sample QBE grid, based on the Order Details table created in Chapter 4, using two calculated fields named Extended Price and With Tax, is shown below:

Field:	Qty	Unit Price	Extended Price: CCur([Qty]*[Unit Price])	With Tax: CCur([Extended price]*1.0775)
Sort:				
Show:	☒	☒	☒	☒
Criteria:				
or:				

Figure 7.10 shows the results of running this query. Extended Price and With Tax look like any other fields in the dynaset, but are actually just the results of calculations based on the Qty and Unit Price fields to the left.

N O T E   You cannot change the contents of a calculated field in a dynaset. But you can change any other fields, including, in this example, Qty and Unit Price. The calculated field will be recalculated automatically.

FIGURE 7.10

A dynaset based on
a query of the Order
Details table, where
Extended Price and
With Tax are
calculated fields

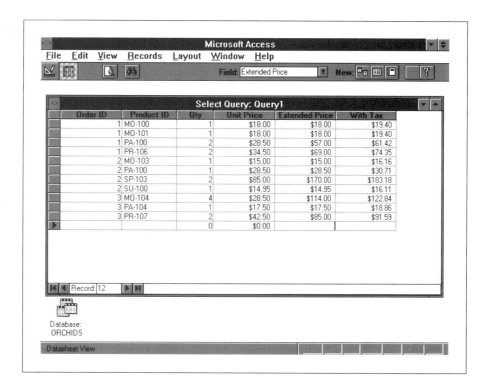

For information on computing totals, subtotals, averages, and similar calculations, see "Totals, Averages, and Other Summary Calculations" in Chapter 8.

Calculations with Text Fields

You can use the **&** operator to join text and fields into a single calculated field. Any field names in the QBE grid must be enclosed in square brackets, as usual. Any text, including any blank spaces you want to add, must be enclosed in quotation marks.

In most cases, you'll probably want to use text expressions in reports, such as when printing form letters, envelopes, and mailing labels. But as food for thought, and for future reference, Table 7.4 shows some examples of text expressions using field names from the sample Customers table, some literal text (e.g., **"Dear   "**), and the **&** operator.

TABLE 7.4: Examples of expressions using field names from the Customers table and the & operator to join text

EXPRESSION	DISPLAY EXAMPLE
[First Name]&" "&[Last Name]	Andy Adams
[Last Name]&", "&[First Name]	Adams, Andy
"Dear "&[First Name]&":"	Dear Andy:
[Honorific]&" "&[First Name]&" "&[MI]&" "&[Last Name]	Mr. Andy A. Adams

Here's an example using the Customers table, where the first column in the QBE grid contain the expression

    [Last Name]&",   "&[First Name]

I've opted to sort this field in ascending order. I've also included the Company Phone fields in the QBE grid.

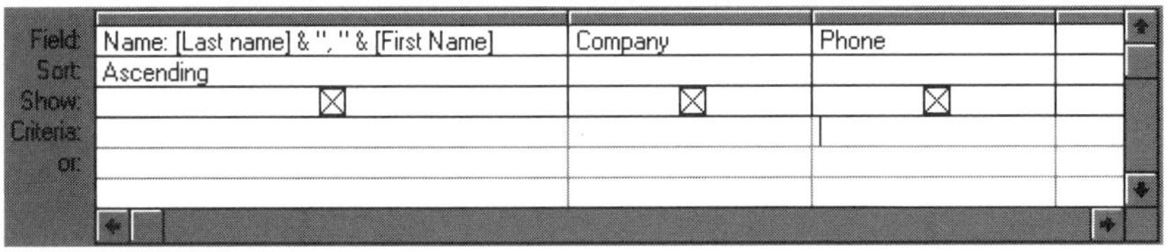

The first few records from the resulting dynaset are shown below:

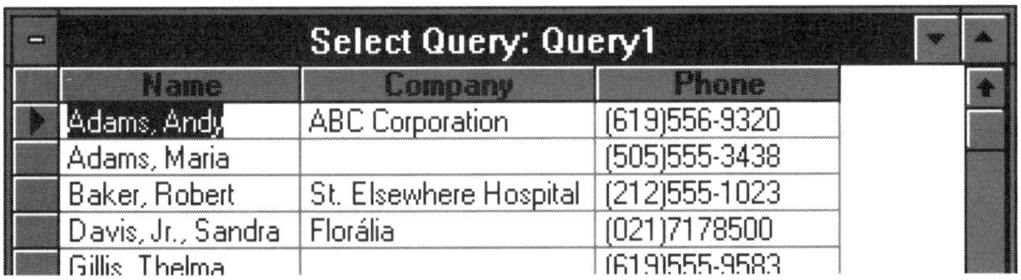

Viewing Only Unique Values

Normally, when you query a table, Access shows you all the records that match what you're looking for (or every record in the table if you don't enter search criteria). For instance, a query of just the State/Province field would list the contents of that field for every record in the table, as in the left-hand side of Figure 7.11.

In some situations, however, you might prefer to eliminate duplicate views of the same data in the dynaset so you can see just the unique values in the field. That is, you might be more interested in knowing just what states are represented in the table, and not as interested in which state each and every record contains, as in the right-hand example of Figure 7.11.

FIGURE 7.11

A "regular" query shows all records, including duplicates. A Unique Values query eliminates duplicates, giving you an overview of what values are represented in the table.

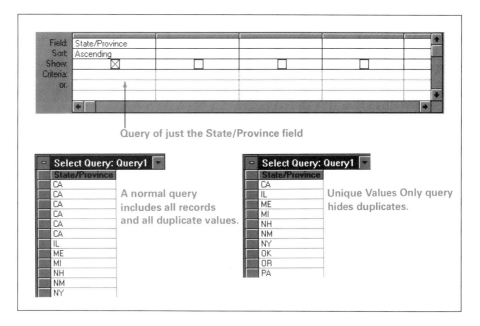

To isolate unique values in a query:

1. Choose View ➤ Query Properties or click the Query Properties button (shown at left). You'll see this dialog box:

2. Choose the Unique Values Only option, then choose OK.

Before you run the query, be sure that the QBE grid includes only the field you want to view unique values in. For instance, if you want to see all the unique states, you would make the State/Province field in Customers the only field in the QBE grid.

TIP

In the next chapter you'll learn how to construct a query that answers the question "How many customers are there in each state?"

Optionally, if you want to know what unique combinations of values exist, choose all the fields that define the combination of fields. For instance, if you include both City and State/Province fields in the QBE grid, and turn on Unique Values Only, only unique combinations of those fields will appear. That is, Portland, Maine would not be considered the same as Portland, Oregon, but each would appear only once in the dynaset.

Don't Forget to Deactivate Unique Values!

The Unique Values Only property is "sticky"—once you select it, it stays turned on in the current query window. This can be confusing if you later use the same query window to perform some other query. To prevent confusion, be sure to turn Unique Values Only back off when you've finished with it.

Querying Multiple Tables

In all the chapters up to this point I've been promising that even though you might store your data in separate related tables, you can still "mix and match" that data however you want later. In this section, you'll start learning how to do that with queries.

The procedure to create a query for multiple tables is virtually identical to that for querying a single table. That is, if you start from the database window and go through the **Add Table** dialog box, you can just choose each table that you want to query from that dialog box before closing it.

If you are already at the query window, and want to add a table, you can choose Query ➤ Add Table to return to the Add Table dialog box, and choose more tables. An even simpler method is to:

1. Click any visible portion of the database window.
2. Click the Table object button in the database window to view the names of tables in this database.
3. Drag the name of whatever table you want to add from the database window to the upper portion of the query window.
4. When you're done adding tables, click any visible portion of the query window to bring it back to the foreground.

After you've dragged tables into the query window, you can drag them into whatever positions are most convenient for you.

Joining the Tables

Before you can actually run a query with multiple tables, you need to tell Access how the tables are related. There are two ways to do this:

- If you've already set up the relationship between two tables, as discussed under "Defining the Relationships" near the end of Chapter 6, Access *joins* the tables automatically, and you'll see the *join lines*. You don't need to do anything else.

- If you haven't already set up the relationship between the two tables, you need to click the name of the common field in one of the tables, then drag the icon to the name of the equivalent field in the other table. Access draws the join line when you release the mouse button (see below).

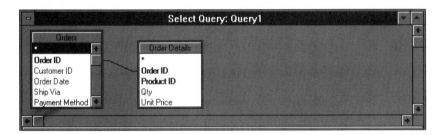

The one disadvantage of using the latter approach to join tables "on the fly" is that Access can't really check to see if the join you've defined makes any sense. That is, it will accept just about any join, and even run the query for you. But the resulting dynaset will be empty or inaccurate if the join you've defined doesn't make any sense. So if you can define the relationships between tables "up front," you can ward off potentially confusing results.

Deleting a Join

If you need to delete a join between two tables, first click the join line you want to delete. The line darkens when you do this. Then press the Del key.

Choosing Fields to Display or Search

Once you've joined several tables in a query, you can choose the fields you want to display, choose fields to sort on, and enter criteria in the QBE grid just as though you were querying only a single table. Access handles all the jobs of "pulling together" the data from the tables automatically behind the scenes. By default, Access performs an *equi-join* where only records that have matching values in the tables are pulled together. The examples that follow will help to illustrate this.

First, let's suppose that the Orders table and the Order Details table (two separate tables) each contain the data shown in Figure 7.12. (Some of the fields in the Orders table are scrolled out of the window.) There is a one-to-many relationship between these two tables, with Order ID being the field that links the two tables. There are currently three outstanding orders in the Orders table. In Order Details, there are four line items for Order #1, four line items for Order #2, and three line items for Order #3.

FIGURE 7.12

Current contents of the Orders and Order Details tables

Table: Orders

Order ID	Customer ID	Order Date	Ship Via	Payment Method	Customer's PO	Paid
1	1001	1/4/93	UPS	Cash		Yes
2	1007	1/4/93	Fed Ex	Invoice		No
3	1013	1/4/93	UPS	Purchase Order	11-332-22	No
(Counter)	0					

Record: 4

Table: Order Details

Order ID	Product ID	Qty	Unit Price
1	MO-100	1	$18.00
1	MO-101	1	$18.00
1	PA-100	2	$28.50
1	PR-106	2	$34.50
2	MO-103	1	$15.00
2	PA-100	1	$28.50
2	SP-103	2	$85.00
2	SU-100	1	$14.95
3	MO-104	4	$28.50
3	PA-104	1	$17.50
3	PR-107	2	$42.50
*		0	$0.00

Record: 1

Now suppose I set up a query as shown in Figure 7.13. Notice that the join line connects the common Order ID field of the two tables. I've dragged the Order ID, Customer ID, and Order Date fields from the Orders field list, and the Product ID, Qty, and Unit Price fields from the Orders table field list into the QBE grid.

When I run the query, I get data from both tables in the resulting dynaset (Figure 7.14). For instance, I can see the Customer ID and Order Date for every record in the Order Details table, even though that information is actually stored in the separate Orders table.

Now, suppose you would like to see the product description, as well as the Product ID, in this dynaset. Well, the product description is stored in the Products table, so you need to add another table to the query. You would click the design button to return to the query design, then add the Products table to the query, either by dragging its name from the database window, or by choosing Query ➤ Add Table and choosing *Products* as the table to add.

FIGURE 7.13

Query of both the Orders and Order Details tables.

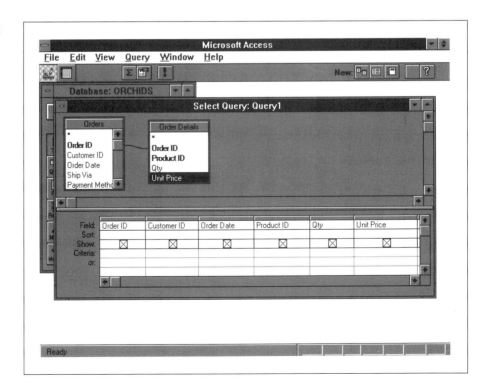

FIGURE 7.14

Results of the query
shown in Figure 7.13,
showing all Order
Details, with Order
Date and Customer ID
from the Orders table

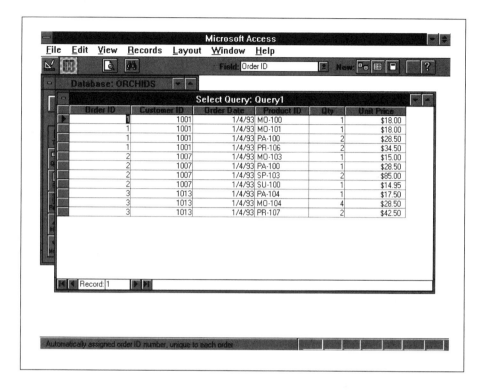

If you hadn't already predefined the relationship between Order Details
and Products, you would need to draw a join line to connect the Product
ID fields from these two tables, as in Figure 7.15. If you had already
defined that relationship, the join line would appear automatically.

In Figure 7.15, I've also dragged the Description field from the Products
table field list to the Qty column of the QBE grid, so *that* field is now inserted between Product ID and Qty in the grid.

Now when I run the query, I get the same results as before, but this time
I can see the description of each product in each order, as shown in Figure 7.16.

Now, perhaps you're thinking that if you can display the product description from the Products table, couldn't you also display the customer's
name and address, rather than just the Customer ID field? Absolutely! As
before, you need to return to the query design window, and add the Customers table to the query. It doesn't really matter where you place any of

FIGURE 7.15

The Products table added to the query, and the Description field from that table's field list added to the QBE grid

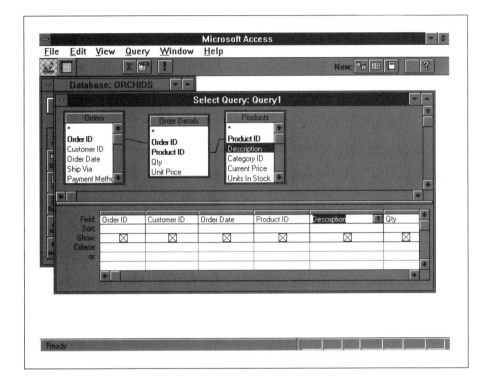

the tables in the query, but in Figure 7.17 I dragged the Orders, Order Details, and Products field lists to the right, and dragged in the Customers table to the left of those, only so you could better see the join lines connecting the Customer ID fields in the Customers and Orders table. As usual, if you hadn't already defined this relationship, you'd need to draw that join line yourself.

I also dragged the First Name and Last Name fields from the Customers table field list into the grid, so I could see them in the resulting dynaset. (The Description, Qty, and Unit Price columns are now scrolled out of view, but are still in the QBE grid.)

FIGURE 7.16

Results of the Query shown in Figure 7.15. I've changed column widths slightly so you could see all the fields in this dynaset.

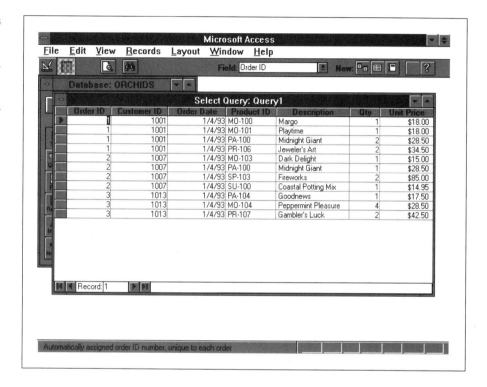

Running this query presents the same results as the previous query, but now I can see customers' names in the resulting dynaset, as shown in Figure 7.18 (where I've changed some column widths so you could see the entire dynaset.)

TIP

As you'll see in Chapter 12, joining the Customers, Products, Orders, and Order Details tables is the first step to printing packing slips, invoices, receipts, and other reports that require data from all four tables.

FIGURE 7.17

Customers table added to the sample query, with a join line connecting the Customer ID fields in Customers and Orders. I also dragged the Last Name and First Name fields from the Customers table into the QBE grid.

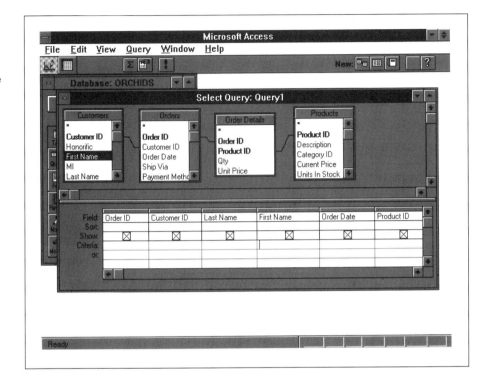

Using the QBE Grid with a Multi-Table Query

Adding multiple tables to a query does not in any way limit what you can do down in the QBE grid. You can still drag whatever fields you wish from any field list into the grid. And you can use all the sort options, the Show box, search criteria, and calculated fields described earlier in this chapter.

Viewing Table Names in the QBE Grid

When querying multiple tables, some fields appear in more than one table. For instance, the Customer ID field appears in both the Customers and Orders tables. You might find it handy to include table names, as well as field names in the QBE grid for such a query, so that you know which table each field is coming from.

FIGURE 7.18

Results of the query shown in Figure 7.17, where Customer Last Name and First Name fields are included in the dynaset

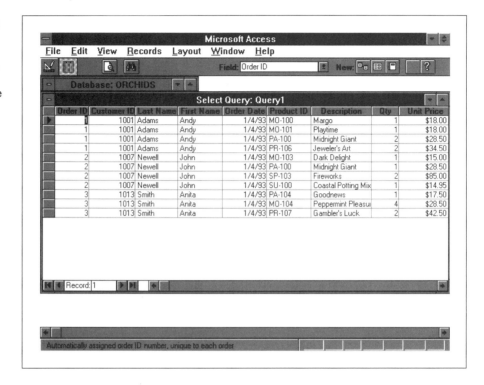

To turn on table names, just choose View ➤ Table Names. A new row, titled *Table*, appears below the Field row. As you add new fields to the QBE grid, the name of the table that the field came from appears below each field name, as below:

Field:	Order ID	Customer ID	Last Name	First Name	Order Date	Product ID
Table:	Orders	Orders	Customers	Customers	Orders	Order Details
Sort:						
Show:	☒	☒	☒	☒	☒	☒
Criteria:						
or:						

TIP   You can change the entry in the Table cell by clicking and then choosing a new table name from the drop-down list.

Another Multi-Table Join Example

Figure 7.19 shows a sample query, based on four tables, that uses calculated fields, an ascending sort, and a search criterion as described below:

* The first column contains the expression (only partially visible):

  Name:[Last Name]&",   "&[First Name]

  and I've opted to sort records by this field into ascending order.

FIGURE 7.19

Query of four tables that includes calculated fields, an ascending sort order, and a search criterion

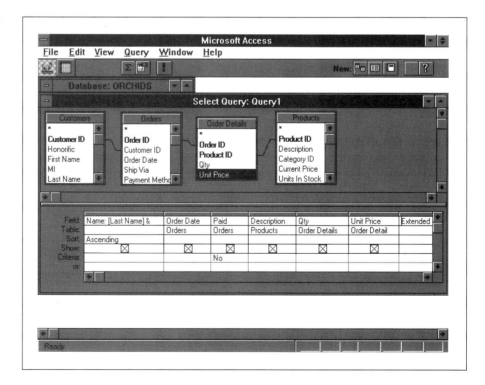

- The Paid field, from the Orders table, contains the search criterion **No**, to limit records to unpaid orders.

- The last column (also only partially visible) contains the expression:

  Extended Price:CCur([Qty]*[Unit Price])

- Table names appear under field names in the QBE grid, because I chose *V*iew ➤ Table *N*ames to activate that feature.

Figure 7.20 shows the results of the query. Only records that have *No* in the Paid field are displayed; the records are sorted by name; and the calculated Name and Extended Price fields show their calculated values.

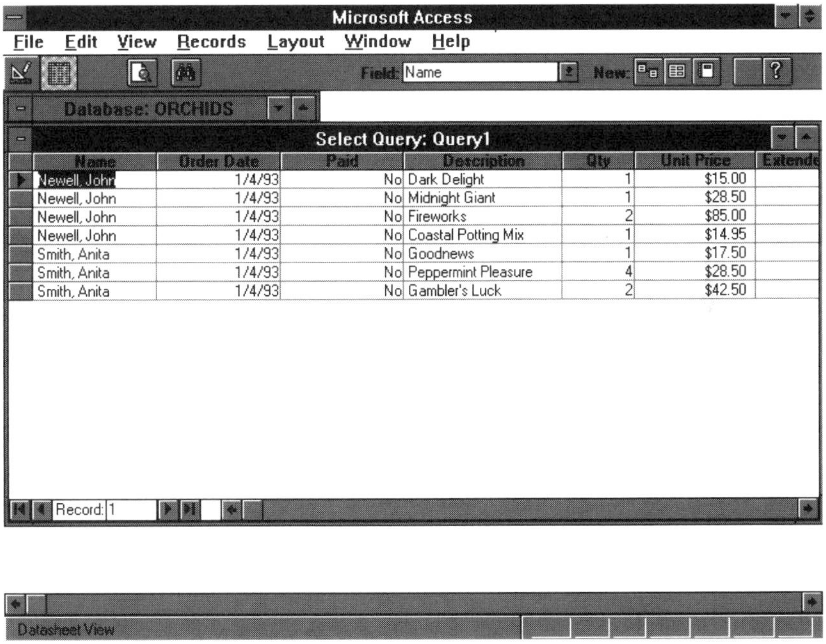

FIGURE 7.20

Results of the query shown in Figure 7.19 above

Making the Join in a Many-to-Many Relationship

As we mentioned back in Chapter 3, a many-to-many relationship between two tables is really composed of two one-to-many relationships between two (or more) tables. If you want to join two tables that have a many-to-many relationship, you must include the table (or tables) that "bridge the gap" between the tables, even if you don't care to see data in those in-between tables.

For example, there is a many-to-many relationship between customers and products, since many products are ordered by many customers, and vice versa. If you want to ask the question, "Which customers have purchased which products?", your first inclination might be to start a query with just the Customers table and the Products table, as below:

But there is no common field that links the Customers table to the Products table, so there is no way to make a sensible join line between these two tables.

To see who has purchased what, you need to use *orders* to bridge the gap between customers and products. In this particular database design, orders are divided into two separate tables, Orders and Order Details. So you actually need to use both those tables to bridge the gap.

Of course, you don't need to *view* data from the Orders and Order Details tables if you don't want to. For instance, in the QBE grid in Figure 7.21,

FIGURE 7.21

To answer the question "Who has ordered what?", you need to "bridge the gap" between the Customers and Products tables using the Orders and Order Details tables. Then, as usual, you can just choose whichever fields you want to display.

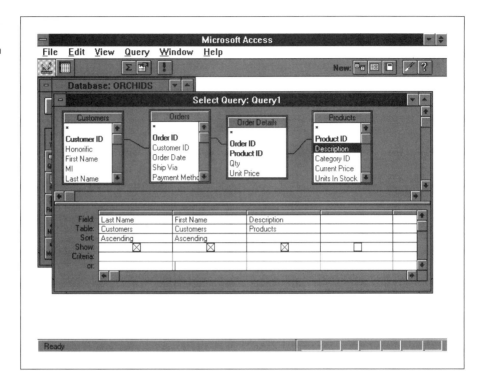

I've dragged only the Customer ID, Last Name, and First Name fields from the Customers table, and the Product ID and Description fields from the Products table into the QBE grid. The resulting dynaset, Figure 7.22, answers the question "Who has ordered what?"

What Is an Equi-Join?

As I mentioned earlier, when you perform a query Access does an *equi-join*. This means that only records that have *equi*valent values in the common fields of related tables will appear in the resulting dynaset.

FIGURE 7.22

Dynaset resulting
from the query shown
in Figure 7.21,
answering the
question "Who has
ordered what?"

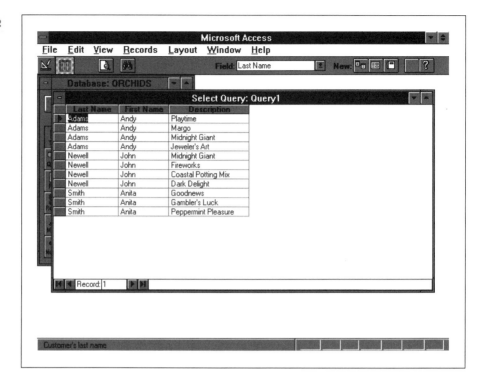

For instance, suppose you want to view brief information about customers, and about the orders they've placed. You could query just the Customers and Orders tables, as in Figure 7.23.

When you run this query, you get the results shown below. Only three customers appear, because currently these are the only customers who have outstanding orders. If you prefer to view *all* the customers, whether they have outstanding orders or not, you would have to use an *outer join*, rather than an equi-join, as described in the next section.

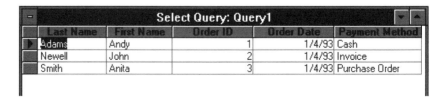

FIGURE 7.23

A query of Customers and Orders, using an equi-join

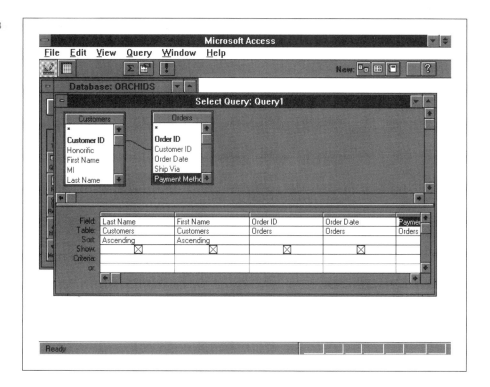

Creating an Outer Join

An *outer join* is one that shows all the records in a table, even if there are no equivalent records in a related table. To set up an outer join:

1. If the tables in the query window aren't connected by a join line yet, create a join line (as described in the section "Joining the Tables" earlier in this chapter) between the common fields that link the two tables.

2. Double-click the join line that you want to change. You'll see a dialog box like the one below, but with table names reflecting the tables currently in your query window:

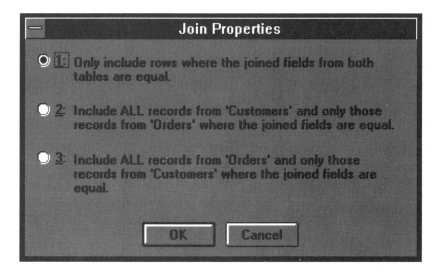

3. Your options are explained within the dialog box, and are summarized below:

- **1:** Performs the standard "equi-join" (the default choice).
- **2:** Performs an outer join where all records from the table on the left will be included in the dynaset whether or not there are matching fields in the table on the right (this is called a *left outer join*).
- **3:** Performs an outer join where all records from the table on the right will be included in the dynaset whether or not there are matching fields in the table on the left (this is called a *right outer join*).

4. Click whichever option you want, then choose OK.

The join line changes to an arrow, pointing *from* the table that will be displaying *all* of its records, *to* the other table. For instance, if you changed the join line from our previous query to a left outer join, the join line would appear as below:

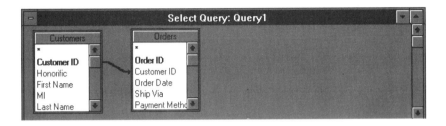

Running the query displays the dynaset shown in Figure 7.24. This time, every customer is listed. The Order ID, Order Date, and Payment Method fields are simply left empty for customers who have no outstanding orders.

FIGURE 7.24

The results of a left outer join between Customers and Orders. The Order ID and Order Date fields for customers who have no outstanding orders are empty.

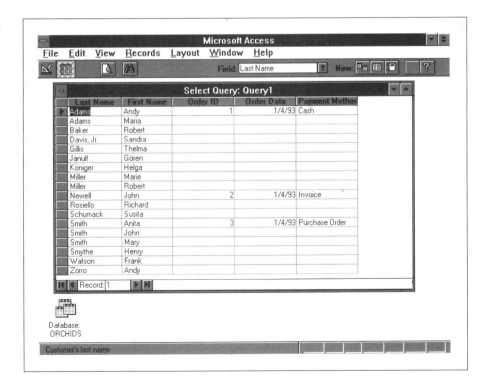

Keep in mind that the direction of the arrow is important. For instance, if I were to return to the query design, double-click the join line, and choose option 3, the arrow would point *from* Orders, *to* Customers (an outer right join), as below:

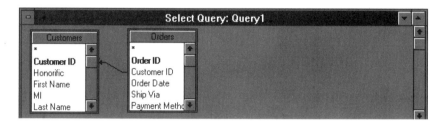

The results of this query are a horse of a different color, as shown below. But the results are good because they mean that, for every Customer ID in the Orders table, there is a matching Customer ID in the Customers table.

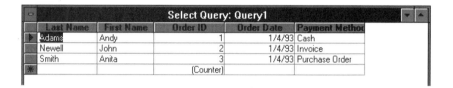

Had the resulting query come up with empty Customer ID, Last Name, and First Name fields, that would be an indication that there are outstanding orders for customers who do not even exist in the Customers table.

NOTE

The blank record marked with a * at the bottom of every dynaset is just the extra record that's made available for adding new data. It's not an indication of a non-matching record in an outer join.

Creating a Self-Join

You can also join a table *to itself* in a query. This is a something of a mind-boggling technique that really only makes sense in those rare situations where a field within the table refers to some other field within the same table. But just so you know it's possible, I show you an example of how to do it.

To create a self-join, drag two (or more) copies of the table into the query window. Access will automatically add a number to each duplicated table's name to distinguish among the tables. Add a join line between the field that contains the reference to whichever field in the other field list contains matching values. Then run the query as usual.

To present an example, we'll stray from the business side of our hypothetical Orchid Jungle company for a moment, and take a look at what the folks in the nursery might be doing. Suppose the technicians create a table like the one shown in Figure 7.25 to keep track of individual plants in their breeding program. Each plant has a Plant ID number. Some plants are hybrids (a cross between two other plants), and they use the Plant ID number to identify the parents of those hybrid plants. For instance, the parents of plant MO-100 are plants MO-001 and MO-002.

In this example, the contents of the Parent 1 and Parent 2 fields refer to the Plant ID field, which is in this same table. Using a self-join, you could create a dynaset that links the contents of the Parent 1 and Parent 2 fields to other copies of the Plants table, just as though the Plant ID field were in a separate table. First, you'd create a query for the Plants table, then drag (or add) two more copies of that table to the QBE grid. These second copies would automatically be renamed to Plants_1 and Plants_2.

Then you'd connect the Parent 1 field to the Plant ID field of one of those tables, and the Parent 2 field to the Plant ID field of the second table. Next you would convert both lines to right outer join lines. Drag to the

FIGURE 7.25

Table to keep track of plants and their parents. The identification number in the Parent 1 and Parent 2 fields refers to the Plant ID field in this same table.

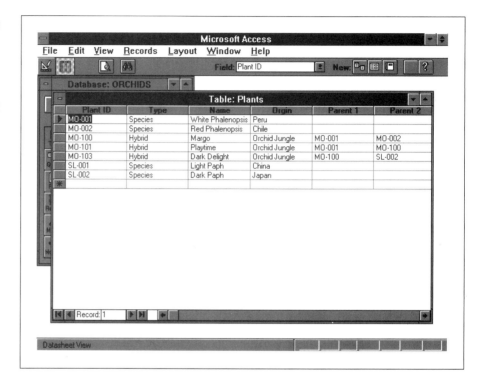

QBE grid the names of fields you're interested in viewing, as in Figure 7.26. In this example I've included the Plant ID, Type, and Name fields from the Plants table, and the Name and Origin fields from the Plants_1, and Plants_2 tables in the grid. I've also limited the display to records that have Hybrid in the Type field.

The results of the query are shown in Figure 7.27. Each record in the dynaset shows the Product ID, Type, and name of a hybrid plant. Each record also displays the name and origin of that plant's parents.

FIGURE 7.26

A self-join between the Plants table and two additional copies of that table, linking Parent names to Plant ID codes as right outer joins

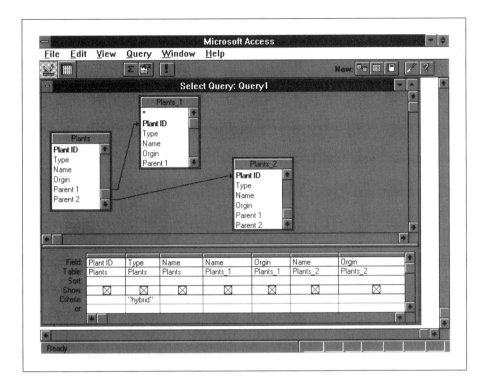

Using the Query Window to Print a Database Diagram

As sort of an added bonus, you can use the query window to create a handy summary of your database design, like the example shown in Figure 7.28. Here's how you could create the same:

• Drag all the tables that you want to include in the design to the query window.

FIGURE 7.27

Results of the self-join shown in Figure 7.26, where the names of parents, rather than their product ID codes, are displayed in the dynaset

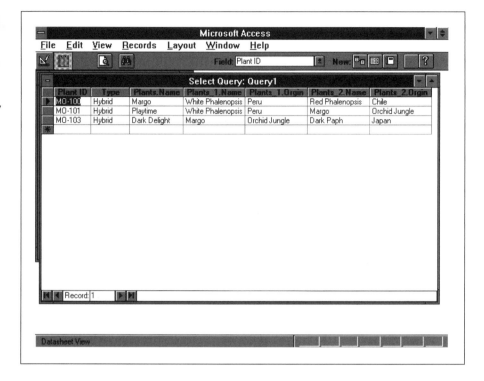

- Maximize or enlarge the window as much as necessary, then drag down the split bar that separates the upper and lower halves of the window, to give yourself maximum room to work in.

- You can move and size each field list window using standard techniques.

- If you haven't already defined the relationship between a pair of tables, you can draw join lines now by dragging, as described earlier.

- When you are happy with your screen, save the query by choosing File ➤ Close, and entering a name such as **Database Design Overview**.

FIGURE 7.28

A summary database design created and displayed via a query window

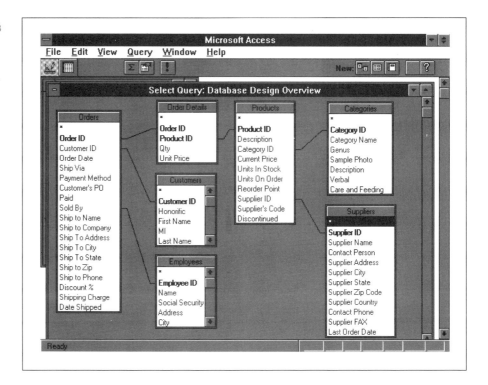

Whenever you want to view this screen in the future, click on the Query object button in the database window, then click on *Database Design Overview,* and click the Design button. Size and position the window to your liking. If you want to print the display, you'll need to use the "Screen Capture-to-PaintBrush" method described in Chapter 18.

NOTE

If you don't drag any fields into the QBE grid, you'll only be able to open the query in design view. Attempting to run the query would display the message "Query must have at least one output field."

Summary

In this chapter we've covered all the basics of "select queries," so named because they let you select the fields and records that you want to view. As you've seen, you can also use queries to determine a sort order for records in the table.

You've also learned how to join multiple tables in the query window, so that you can treat the data in separate tables as though it were in a single table. In the next chapter we'll look at more advanced querying techniques.

CHAPTER

8

Working with Sets
of Data

*f*ast
TRACK

MOST of the time, you'll want to use queries to do the very things you learned to do in the previous chapter—choose fields and records to view, sort records, join data from separate tables into a single dynaset, and so forth.

But as you'll learn in this chapter, a query can do much, much more. For instance, you can use a query to total and subtotal records in a table, and to cross-tabulate data. You can design *action queries* to automatically change, copy, and delete multiple records in one fell swoop. And you can design *parameter queries* that ask what you're looking for when you run them.

Totals, Averages, and Other Summary Calculations

In the previous chapter we talked about calculated fields, which let you create a new field that contains a calculation based on the contents of another field. A *summary calculation* is different in that it computes some value, such as a sum or average, on multiple records within a table. The basic procedure for performing summary calculations is as follows:

1. Starting at the query window, drag any fields that you want to group by, or perform calculations on, to the QBE grid.

2. Click the Totals button in the tool bar. A new row titled Total: appears in the QBE Grid with *Group By* in each column of this row, as shown below.

3. If you want to use a field for grouping (or categorizing, or subtotaling) data, leave that field's Total cell set to *Group By*.

4. If you want to perform a summary calculation in a field, click that field's Total cell and choose one of the summary options listed in Table 8.1.

TABLE 8.1: Summary operators used in queries

SUMMARY OPERATOR	COMPUTES	WORKS WITH DATA TYPES
Avg	Average	Number, Currency, Counter, Date/Time, Yes/No
Count	Number of non-blank values	All
First	Value in first record	All
Last	Value in last record	All
Max	Highest value	Number, Currency, Counter, Date/Time, Yes/No, Text
Min	Smallest value	Number, Currency, Counter, Date/Time, Yes/No, Text
StDev	Standard deviation	Number, Currency, Counter, Date/Time, Yes/No
Var	Variance	Number, Currency, Counter, Date/Time, Yes/No
Sum	Total	Number, Currency, Counter, Date/Time, Yes/No

TIP

If you don't want to use a particular field for grouping or calculating, you should exclude that field from the QBE grid.

5. Run the query in the usual manner (click the Datasheet button.)

Some examples of summary calculations are presented in the sections that follow.

Basing a Calculation on All the Records in the Table

If you want to perform a calculation on all the records in a table, you first need to make sure that none of the columns in the QBE grid contains *Group By*.

For instance, suppose you just want to count how many customers are in the Customers table. To do that, you'd need to create a query for the Customers table, drag a field to the QBE grid, and set its Total: cell to *Count*, as in Figure 8.1.

Running this query produces the dynaset shown below, which tells you that there are 18 records in the Customers table.

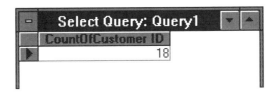

A query to count how many records are in the Customers table. Because there are no Group By cells, the calculation will be based on all the records in the table.

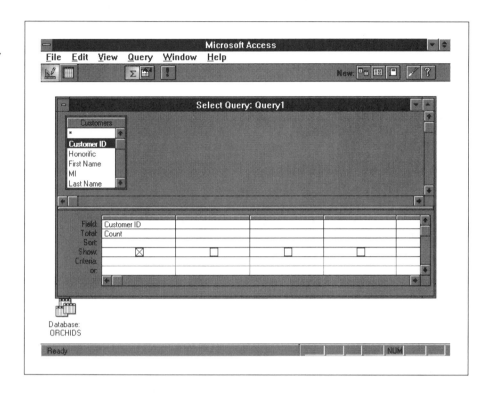

NOTE

More specifically, the dynaset shows you how many non-blank Customer ID's there are in the Customers table, since summary calculations exclude blank records. We'll discuss the effects of blank fields on summary calculations in more detail under "Effects of Zeros and Blanks on Summary Calculations" later in this chapter.

You can perform calculations on as many fields as you wish, and include multiple copies of the same field in the QBE grid. For instance, the query shown in Figure 8.2, which is based on the Products table, will calculate the total number of products listed in the Products table (*Count*), the lowest-priced product (*Min*), the highest-price product (*Max*), and the Average price (*Avg*).

FIGURE 8.2

This query, based on the Products table, counts how many records are in the Products table, and calculates the lowest, highest, and average Current Price.

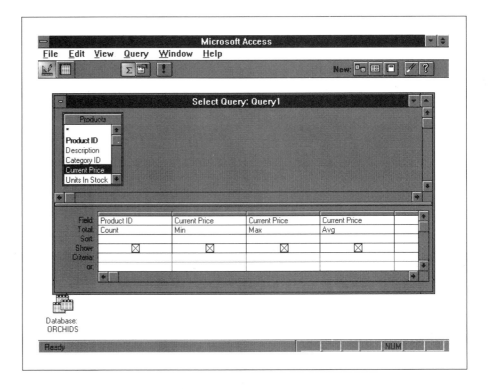

The results of this query are shown below. I've widened the columns a bit in that example so you can see the full column headings that Access uses in the dynaset to indicate the type of calculation in each column (e.g., CountOfProduct ID, MinOfCurrent Price, and so forth.)

Basing the Calculations on Groups

You can also perform summary calculations on groups of records, rather than all the records in the table. To do this, you need to drag the field that you want to base the grouping on into the QBE grid, and choose *Group By* in that field's Total cell.

For instance, going back to the Customers table, you might want to ask "How many of my customers live in each state?" In that case you'd need to add the State/Province field to the QBE grid, and use that column as the Group By field, as below:

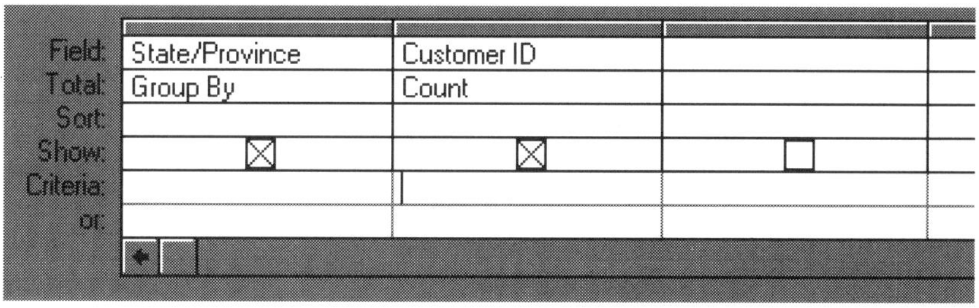

Field:	State/Province	Customer ID	
Total:	Group By	Count	
Sort:			
Show:	☒	☒	☐
Criteria:			
or:			

The resulting dynaset would show how many records there are within each state/province. In the example shown below, two records have no entry in the State/Province field (probably because they're non-U.S. entries), six records have CA in the State field, and so forth. (Because our sample table is small, there are relatively few states represented.)

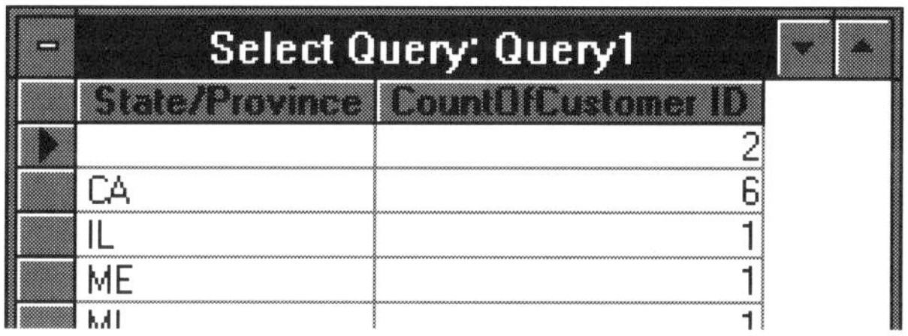

Select Query: Query1

State/Province	CountOfCustomer ID
	2
CA	6
IL	1
ME	1
MI	1

If you include several Group By fields, those fields combined define a group. For example, if your Customers table is quite large, and you want to count how many customers are in each city, you could group by the City and State fields, as below:

Field:	City	State/Province	Customer ID
Total:	Group By	Group By	Count
Sort:			
Show:	☒	☒	☒
Criteria:			
or:			

TIP Another way to think of the Group By field is as the field used for subtotaling.

The resulting count would be based on each city and state combination.

TIP If you based the grouping on City alone, Portland would be defined as a single group. But if you use City and State combined, Portland Oregon and Portland Maine would be defined as two separate groups.

Looking at our earlier Products table example, you might want to know the count, lowest-priced, highest-priced, and average of current price of products within each product category. In that case, just group the records by the Category ID field, as below:

Field:	Category ID	Product ID	Current Price	Current Price	Current Price	
Total:	Group By	Count	Min	Max	Avg	
Sort:						
Show:	☒	☒	☒	☒	☒	
Criteria:						
or:						

The results of this query are shown below. The first record tells us that there are five products within the MOTH category. The least expensive one is $16.00, the most expensive is $49.50, and the average price in that category is $24.30. The records that follow provide the same information for other product categories.

Category ID	CountOfProduct ID	MinOfCurrent Price	MaxOfCurrent Price	AvgOfCurrent Price
MOTH	5	$16.00	$49.50	$24.30
PANSY	5	$15.00	$28.50	$20.90
PROM	8	$25.00	$42.50	$35.25
SLIPPER	5	$20.00	$67.50	$36.50
SPIDER	4	$20.00	$85.00	$57.38
SUPP	1	$14.95	$14.95	$14.95

Specifying Search Criteria in Group By Fields

You can specify search criteria in the Group By field of a summary query just as you would any other query. For instance, if you want to display price statistics but are only interested in the PROM and SLIPPER categories of orchids, just place the appropriate search criterion in the Group By field, as in the example below:

Field:	Category ID	Product ID	Current Price	Current Price	Current Price	
Total:	Group By	Count	Min	Max	Avg	
Sort:						
Show:	☒	☒	☒	☒	☒	
Criteria:	"Prom" Or "Slipper"					
or:						

Access would do the grouping and calculations, but only display the PROM and SLIPPER groups.

Specifying Search Criteria in Summary Fields

When specifying search criteria in a field that contains a summary calculation operator, you have your choice as to when the criterion is applied: either before or after the calculation.

Selecting Records Based on the Calculation

In some situations, you'll want the query to perform a calculation first, and then select records based on the results of the calculations. For instance, you might want to display categories of products with an average price that's greater than $20.00. For that kind of a query, just enter the search criterion in the Criteria cell of the field that you're doing the calculation in.

The query below tells Access to "Calculate the average price of products in each category, then show me only those categories that have an average price that's greater than $25.00".

Field:	Category ID	Current Price	
Total:	Group By	Avg	
Sort:			
Show:	☒	☒	
Criteria:		>25	
or:			

Selecting Records Before the Calculation Takes Place

In some other situations, you may want to limit the records that are included in the calculation. That is, you want Access to "weed out" certain records first, then perform the calculation based on those records that haven't been weeded out. For this kind of query, you use the **Where** operator, which acts as sort of the "pre-filter" for the rest of the query.

For instance, if you wanted to weed out discontinued products (i.e., records that have the word *Yes* in the Discontinued field), you would first drag the Discontinued field into the QBE grid. Then change its Group By operator to **Where**, and specify **No** as the criterion for this field, like this:

Field:	Category ID	Current Price	Discontinued	
Total:	Group By	Avg	Where	
Sort:				
Show:	☒	☒		☐
Criteria:			No	
or:				

NOTE The Show box in the Where column needs to be deselected.

When you run the query, all calculations in the dynaset will be based on only those records that have the word *No* in the Discontinued field. Records that have the word *Yes* in that field would have been weeded out before any calculations took place.

Effects of Zeros and Blanks on Summary Calculations

As a general rule of thumb, Access does not include blank values in a summary calculation. It does, however, include any zero values in a numeric field in a calculation. This fact can have a substantial effect on the outcome of some calculations.

If I can stray from our Orchid business example for a moment here, perhaps a statistical example would help to best illustrate this. Suppose you have a table of test scores (or some other statistical data) as below:

Table: Test Scores	
Name	**Score**
Wanda Wilcox	100
Brian Jones	90
Wilma Divin	75
Ted McGoo	80
Fred Flipper	0
Fanny May	0
Ozzie Osgood	0
Ted Mostable	0
	0

Then you set up a query to do some statistical measures on these scores. Here the QBE grid below will count how many records are in the table, and calculate the average, lowest, and highest score:

Field:	Score	Score	Score	Score
Total:	Count	Avg	Min	Max
Sort:				
Show:	☒	☒	☒	☒
Criteria:				
or:				

When you run this query, you get these results:

Select Query: Query1			
CountOfScore	**AvgOfScore**	**MinOfScore**	**MaxOfScore**
8	43.125	0	100

The zero scores are heavily influencing the calculation results in this dynaset. In particular, the average score is low because all the zeros are included in the calculation. Though the calculation is correct, it may not be the information you're looking for, particularly if the zero scores are based on absenteeism.

On the other hand, let's suppose that you leave the Score field empty for any absentee test takers, like this:

Table: Test Scores	
Name	**Score**
Wanda Wilcox	100
Brian Jones	90
Wilma Divin	75
Ted McGoo	80
Fred Flipper	
Fanny May	
Ozzie Osgood	
Ted Mostable	

Running the same query on this collection of data produces a much different result, as shown below, because the blank fields are excluded from the calculation:

Select Query: Query1			
CountOfScore	**AvgOfScore**	**MinOfScore**	**MaxOfScore**
4	86.25	75	100

Record: 1

Including Blank Values in a Count

When you use Count to count how many records there are in a table, remember that any empty fields will be excluded. For instance, getting back to our Customers table, suppose you use this query to count how many records there are in the Customers table:

Field:	Country		
Total:	Count		
Sort:			
Show:	☒	☐	☐
Criteria:			
or:			

When you run the query, the results would actually tell you how many records there are in Customers that *don't* have a blank value in the Country field. And that, indeed, might be useful information.

However, when it's important that the query count exactly how many records are in the table, including any blanks, you can use **Count(★)** in the Field cell of the column. As with any calculated field, you can give this expression a name, such as **Total Records**. Then change the Total cell to **Expression**, like this:

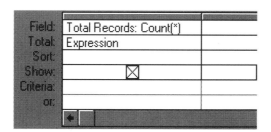

Field:	Total Records: Count(*)	
Total:	Expression	
Sort:		
Show:	☒	
Criteria:		
or:		

When you run the query you'll know for certain that the resulting dynaset shows you exactly how many records there are in the table.

Summarizing a Calculated Field

You can include calculated fields in a summary calculation. However, if you want to use several calculated fields, the expression in each calculated field should refer only to other "real" fields being used in the tables, not to names assigned to other calculated fields.

This isn't too terribly inconvenient, however, since you can just substitute the calculation for the expression name. For instance, in earlier queries I used this expression to calculate extended price:

        Extended Price:CCur([Qty]*[Unit Price])

Then I used:

        With Tax:CCur([Extended Price]*1.0775)

to calculate sales tax. To avoid using the expression name *Extended Price* in the second expression, simply replace that name with the actual calculation, like this:

        With Tax:CCur([Qty]*[Unit Price]*1.0775)

NOTE   If you misspell a field name within the square brackets, or refer to a field that's not in one of the tables included in the query window, Access will treat that field as a *parameter* and prompt you for its value when you run the query. You can choose Cancel to ignore that request, then correct the faulty field name.

Sales tax, of course, is a rather nebulous thing in most states, and in fact you might not even want to bother with it when summarizing order information. On the other hand, perhaps you *do* want to take into consideration discount and shipping charge when calculating order totals. We'll take a look at some advanced queries that include that information next.

Creating Your Own Calculation Expressions

As you gain experience with expressions and Access *functions,* you may want to design your own summary expressions for analyzing data. There are dozens of functions you can use. Chapter 17 discusses expressions and functions in general. But here we'll present some examples as food for thought in creating your own advanced summary queries.

To create a custom summary expression:

1. Make sure you've activated totaling by clicking the Totals button in the tool bar.

2. Move to a blank column in the QBE grid, and choose *Expression* in the Total cell of that column.

3. Enter an expression into the Field cell of this column. (You can use Zoom, Shift+F2, as usual if you plan on entering a lengthy expression.)

4. Run the query in the usual manner after entering the expression.

Now let's take a look at some examples.

Calculating Order Totals with Discount and Shipping

When creating your own custom summary expressions, you can use *aggregate functions,* such as **Sum( )** and **Avg( )**, to have part of an expression be based on several records, while another part of the expression is based on some constant value.

Figure 8.3 shows an example dynaset that's based on a query that uses custom summary expressions. The information presented in the dynaset tells us some very specific information about current orders in the Orders and Order Details tables. For instance, the first record shows us the subtotal (or detail total), $162.00, for order #1. The discount rate on that

FIGURE 8.3

A dynaset that calculates and shows order totals with Discount and Shipping Charge

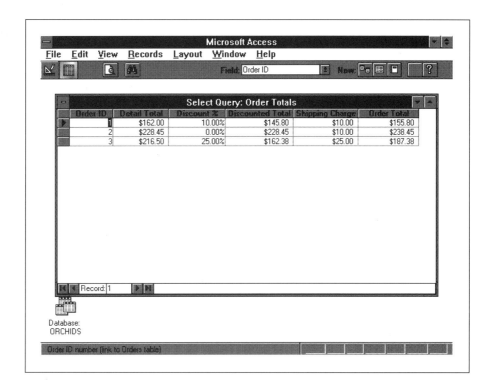

order is 10%, so the discounted total is $145.80. The Shipping charge on that order is $10.00, so the final order total is $155.80. The records that follow show the same information for other orders.

Figure 8.4 shows the query that generated this dynaset. The actual expressions I used in the Field cells of the QBE grid in Figure 8.4 are too wide to fit entirely within the query window, so I'll explain how each column was calculated below.

The first column contains only the field name *Order Detail,* and this is used as the Group By field to group order details by order number.

The second column shows the *Detail Total,* and its Field cell contains the expression:

    Detail Total: CCur(Sum([Qty]*[Unit Price]))

FIGURE 8.4

The query used to create the dynaset shown in Figure 8.3. The expressions used in Field cells are too wide to display in the QBE grid, but each is explained in text.

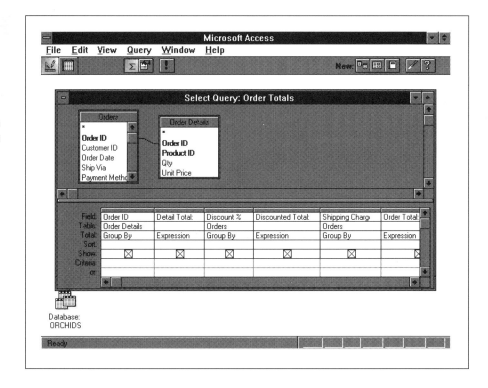

This expression calculates and displays the sum of the extended price (Qty times Unit Price), and displays that result in currency format, using the **CCur** function.

The Field cell in the third column is simply the *Discount %* field name from the Orders table, dragged down from the Orders table in the usual manner.

The fourth column, *Discounted Total,* contains the expression:

Discounted Total: CCur(Sum([Qty]*[Unit Price])*(1-[Discount %]))

Looking at this expression one piece at a time, the first part,

Sum([Qty]*[Unit Price])

calculates the total extended price, using the same expression that the Detail Total column used. The next part of the expression,

*(1-[Discount %])

subtracts the Discount percent from 1 (e.g., if the Discount percent is 10%, the result here is 90%). Multiplying the subtotal by that 90% gives you the discounted total. The whole expression is inside a **CCur** function, to format the result as in currency format.

The fifth column contains only the field name *Shipping Charge,* dragged down from the Orders table in the usual manner.

The last column contains the rather hefty expression:

> Order Total: CCur(Sum([Qty]*[Unit Price])*(1-[Discount %])+[Shipping Charge])

This is the same expression used to calculate the discounted total, with **+[Shipping Charge]** tacked on to the end to add the shipping cost.

Calculating Percentage of the Whole

You can use custom expressions to perform percentage-of-the-whole queries. For instance, the dynaset below shows information about current orders broken down into product categories. The *Orders in Category* column shown how many products within the category were ordered, and the *Percent of Whole* column shows each category's contribution to all orders expressed as a percent. The *Total Orders* column is the same in each row because that column shows the total number of outstanding orders (i.e., 4 + 3 + 2 + 1 + 1 equals 11). So the first record in the dynaset tells us that there were 4 orders for products in the MOTH category, which accounts for 36% of total orders (4/11 expressed as a percent.)

Category ID	Orders In Category	Total Orders	Percent Of Whole
MOTH	4	11	36%
PANSY	3	11	27%
PROM	2	11	18%
SPIDER	1	11	9%
SUPP	1	11	9%

Select Query: Orders by Category [%]

Record: 1

Figure 8.5 shows the query I used to display that dynaset. The expressions used in the Field cells are too large to show in the figure, so I'll explain each one below.

FIGURE 8.5

Query used to calculate each product category's contribution to all orders as a percent. Expressions in the Field cells are cut off, but are explained in text.

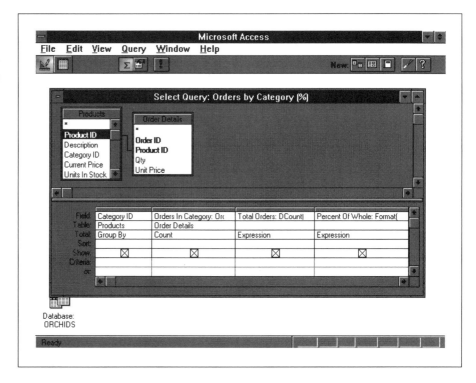

To create the first column in the QBE grid, I just dragged the *Category ID* field name from the Products table field list to the QBE grid in the usual manner. Then I chose it as the Group By field.

To create the second column, I dragged the *Order ID* field from the Order Details table into the Field cell. Then I changed that field name from Order ID to *Orders In Category* by entering the expression below:

    Orders In Category: Order ID

The text in front of the colon, **Orders in Category**, is the name that will appear in the dynaset. Order ID is the actual field that will be used in the query. Notice that the Total cell in this column contains *Count,* to count how many orders are in each product category.

The third column is the trickiest one. To create that column I chose *Expression* from the Total cell, then entered this expression into the Field cell:

    Total Orders: DCount("*","Order Details")

Total Orders, to the left of the colon, is just the name I've given to the expression. **DCount( )** is one of Access's *domain aggregate* functions. Like Count, it counts how many. **DCount ("*","Order Details")** tells Access to count all the records in the Order Details table. But given that **DCount** is a domain aggregate function, it will override a Group By expression. Therefore, every row in the resulting dynaset will display the total count of records in the Order ID field (11 in this example).

Other domain aggregate functions are discussed in Chapter 17.

The Field cell in the last column contains the expression:

Percent of Whole: Format([Orders In Category]/[Total Orders], "0%")

When typing an expression into a Field cell, don't split the expression into two or more lines. Some expressions shown here are broken into two lines simply because they're too wide for the margins of this book.

Looking at this expression from the inside out:

[Orders In Category]/[Total Orders]

performs the basic math needed to calculate the percentage by dividing the contents of the Orders In Category column by the larger value in the Total Orders column.

That calculation is contained within a **Format( )** function, which lets you determine the format of a number. In this example, I've specified **0%** as the format, so numbers would be presented as percentages. The **Percent of Whole:** that precedes the expression is just the name I gave to the column.

You might also be interested in a breakdown by dollar amount rather than just the number of orders in each category, like this:

Category ID	Category Sales	Total Sales	Percent
MOTH	$165.00	$606.95	27.19%
PANSY	$103.00	$606.95	16.97%
PROM	$154.00	$606.95	25.37%
SPIDER	$170.00	$606.95	28.01%
SUPP	$14.95	$606.95	2.46%

Select Query: Orders by Category [Dollar %]

Here the Total Sales column displays the total dollar sales of all the orders, and the Percent column indicates each category's dollar percentage contribution to all orders.

The query used to create that dynaset is similar to the previous example, with the Products and Orders table joined at the top of the query window. But the QBE grid looks like this:

Field:	Category ID	Category Sales: CCur(Sum(	Total Sales: CCur(DSum(	Percent: Format([Categi
Table:	Products			
Total:	Group By	Expression	Expression	Expression
Sort:				
Show:	☒	☒	☒	☒
Criteria:				
or:				

Again, the expressions in each Field cell are too wide to display, so here's what they are:

- The first column contains the Category ID field dragged down from the Products table.

- The second column contains the expression:

  Category Sales: CCur(Sum([Qty]*[Unit Price]))

  to sum the quantity times the unit price and display the result in currency format.

- The third column contains the expression:

  Total Sales: CCur(DSum("[Qty]*[Unit Price]","Order Details")) which uses the domain aggregate function **DSum( )** to calculate the grand total of quantity times unit price in the Order Details table.

- The fourth column contains the expression:

Percent: Format([Category Sales]/[Total Sales],"0/00%")

which displays the percent.

Grouping by Month, Quarter, or Some Other Time Interval

You can also use expressions and functions in the Group By column of a query. For instance, you can group on any part of a date/time field, which means that you can group and total information by month, quarter, year—whatever. Table 8.2 lists some examples, where *field* refers to the name of the date/time field you want to group on.

Figure 8.6 shows an example that would group orders by month (though the query won't do you much good until you have several month's worth of data to work with!).

TABLE 8.2: Examples of using the Format function to define time intervals for grouping

EXPRESSION IN FIELD CELL OF GROUP BY COLUMN	GROUPS BY
Format ([*field*],"ww")	Week of year (1-53)
Format ([*field*],"mmm")	Month
Format ([*field*],"q")	Quarter
Format ([*field*],"yyyy")	Year
Format ([*field*],"hh")	Hour

FIGURE 8.6

A query to group orders by month, and display the total sales (quantity times unit price) per month

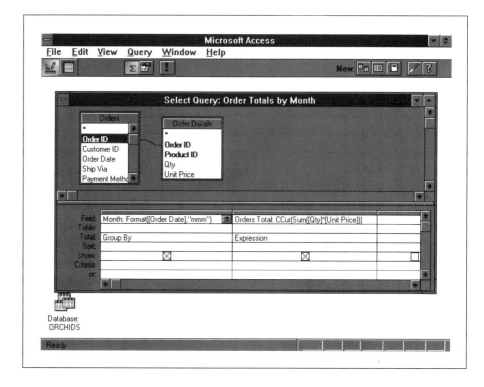

Grouping on Part of a Text Field

You can use the **Left( )** function to group by the first few characters of a text field, rather than the entire text field. For instance, in the QBE grid below, the grouping would be based on the first two characters in the Product ID field.

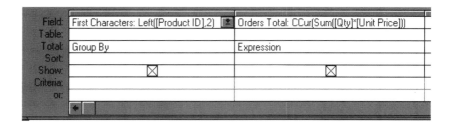

In that example the Field cell contains the expression:

First Characters:Left([Product ID],2)

where **First Characters** is simply the name I've given to the expression. The actual expression,

Left([Product ID],2)

isolates the first two characters in the Product ID field. The resulting dynaset would group records by the first two characters of the Product ID field. For instance, product ID's starting with the letters *MO* would be in one group, product ID's starting with the letters *SL* would be in another group, and so forth.

A Quick Peek at Available Functions

The point of all these heady arithmetic and grouping examples is this: There is much more to queries than first meets the eye! Access offers dozens of functions, and enormous flexibility in creating expressions, that can help you to categorize and calculate data in any way imaginable. You can get a quick overview of the available functions by opening Help (F1), choosing Search, and looking up *Functions: Reference*.

When creating your own expressions, it's important to follow all the rules of proper syntax. If you don't already have experience with creating expressions in a spreadsheet or some other kind of application, be sure to read up on expressions in Chapter 17 before venturing forth and creating your own calculation expressions.

Creating Crosstab Queries

A *crosstab query* lets you cross-tabulate data in a row-by-column fashion. For instance, Figure 8.7 shows the dynaset from a query that asks the question "Who has ordered how many of what?" One version shows the results of a regular select query, where both customer names and product names

FIGURE 8.7

Comparison of a regular query and a crosstab query. In the crosstab query, customer names are listed across the top of the dynaset, rather than down the rows.

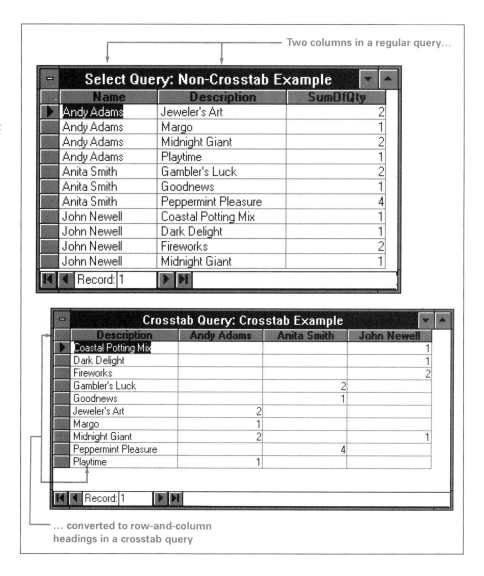

Two columns in a regular query...

Select Query: Non-Crosstab Example

Name	Description	SumOfQty
Andy Adams	Jeweler's Art	2
Andy Adams	Margo	1
Andy Adams	Midnight Giant	2
Andy Adams	Playtime	1
Anita Smith	Gambler's Luck	2
Anita Smith	Goodnews	1
Anita Smith	Peppermint Pleasure	4
John Newell	Coastal Potting Mix	1
John Newell	Dark Delight	1
John Newell	Fireworks	2
John Newell	Midnight Giant	1

Record: 1

Crosstab Query: Crosstab Example

Description	Andy Adams	Anita Smith	John Newell
Coastal Potting Mix			1
Dark Delight			1
Fireworks			2
Gambler's Luck		2	
Goodnews		1	
Jeweler's Art	2		
Margo	1		
Midnight Giant	2		1
Peppermint Pleasure		4	
Playtime	1		

Record: 1

... converted to row-and-column headings in a crosstab query

are listed down the first two columns. The second version shows the crosstab version of this same query, where customer names are listed across the top, and product names are listed in rows. To create a crosstab query:

1. Create a query, choose tables for the query, and drag the names of any fields you want to use in the query to the QBE grid, in the

usual manner. You can also specify any search criteria you need in the QBE grid.

2. Choose Query ➤ Crosstab. Access adds to rows to the QBE grid: one named Total, the other named Crosstab.

3. Click the Crosstab cell in the column that you want to use as row headings, and choose *Row Heading* from the drop-down list. You can use several fields as row headings, but at least one of those rows must have *Group By* in its Total cell.

4. Click the Crosstab cell in the column you want to use as Column Headings, and choose *Column Heading* from the drop-down list. (You can only use one field as the column heading.)

5. The Total cell above the Column Heading cell must contain *Group By*. If it doesn't, click that Total cell and choose *Group By* from the drop-down list.

6. Click the Crosstab cell in the column you want to use for summary values (e.g., Total or Average), and choose *Value* from the drop-down list.

7. Click the Total cell above the Value cell, and choose the type of summary calculation you want, such as *Sum*. Don't choose *Group By* for this field.

8. If you want to use additional fields for grouping, but don't want those fields to appear in the resulting dynaset, change the Crosstab cell for those fields to **Not Shown**.

9. Run the query.

Figure 8.8 shows the query used to create the crosstab example back in Figure 8.7. The Field cell in the first column contains the expression

    Name:[First Name]&" "&[Last Name]

and is earmarked as the Column Heading cell to display customer names across the top of the resulting dynaset. The second column uses the Description field from the Products table as row headings. The third column sums the Qty field in the Order Details table, to calculate how many of each product the customer has ordered.

FIGURE 8.8

Crosstab query
window used to create
the crosstab example
shown back in
Figure 8.7

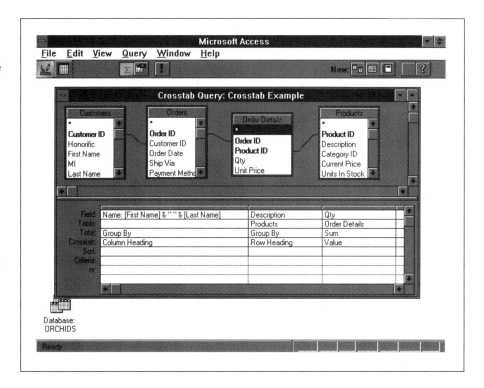

NOTE

The Orders and Order Details tables are included in
the query shown in Figure 8.8 to make the join
between Customers and Products, as discussed in
Chapter 7.

Using Fixed Column Headings
in Crosstabs

Normally, Access will automatically determine crosstab column headings
from whatever data is available in the table, and then sort (alphabetize)
those headings in left-to-right order across the columns. If you prefer, you
can predefine exactly what column headings you want, and the order

you want them in. Doing so not only gives more control over the appearance of the resulting dynaset, but can also make large crosstab queries run faster. To create your own column headings:

1. Create, and run, the crosstab query. You may want to print a copy of the resulting dynaset (File ➤ Print ➤ OK) so you have a hardcopy of valid column names (which you may need later).

2. Return to the crosstab query's design window and click the Query Properties button, or choose View ➤ Query Properties.

3. Choose Fixed Column Headings from the **Query Properties** dialog box that appears.

4. Click the text box or press Tab, and type in column headings in the order you want them to be displayed in the dynaset. Separate each heading with a semicolon (;) or new line (press Ctrl+↵ after typing each heading). The spelling of the column headings you enter must *exactly* match that of the actual headings (which should be on the hardcopy of the dynasheet you just printed out).

N O T E   In other words, you can change the left-to-right *order* of column names using fixed headings, but you cannot change the spelling of those column names.

5. Choose OK.

Now you can run the query to view the results with the fixed column headings.

A perfect example of when you'd want to use fixed column headings is when you group data by month or day of the week, and want the month or day names listed in chronological order, as below:

Product	Jan	Feb	Mar	Apr	May	Jun	Jul	Aug
Coastal Potting Mix	$1,400.95	$3,434.00	$1,323.00	$989.00	$454.00	$656.00	$545.00	
Dark Delight	$1,500.00	$121.00	$767.00	$767.00	$656.00	$454.00	$767.00	
Fireworks	$680.00	$545.00	$1,232.00	$454.00	$767.00	$878.00	$1,786.00	
Gambler's Luck	$970.00	$543.00	$654.00	$1,287.00	$543.00	$656.00	$654.00	
Goodnews	$275.00	$2,056.00	$877.00	$1,645.00	$1,767.00	$1,978.00	$654.00	

Figure 8.9 shows the query window used to create that crosstab.

NOTE

The sample dynaset assumes that order data has been collected through the month of July—well beyond the tiny Orders and Order Details tables we've been using up to this point. August and the months beyond are still empty.

The expressions used in the QBE grid are:

- **Column Heading:** The Field cell for the column heading contains

  Month: Format([Order Date], "mmm")

FIGURE 8.9

Crosstab query to calculate order totals by product and month.

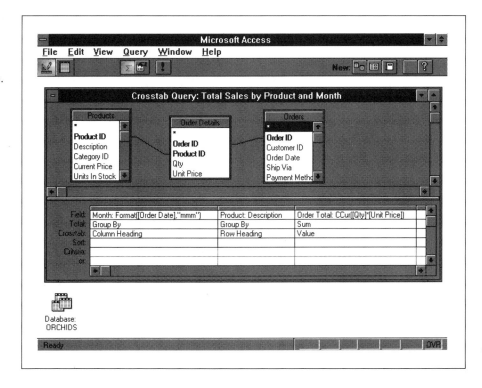

which displays the contents of this date/time field in the format *Jan, Feb, Mar,* and so on. Since this is also the Group By expression, calculations will be based on each month's data.

- **Row Heading:** The Field cell for the Row Heading is *Product: Description.* This tells Access to use the contents of the Description cell for this column, but to give the column the heading *Product* (which just looks a little better in the resulting dynaset).

- **Value:** The Field cell for the Value column contains the expression

Order Total: CCur([Qty]*[Unit Price])

to calculate the extended price and display it in currency format. The Total cell in this column contains *Sum,* to total those extended prices.

Since month names are to be used as column headings in this example, and we don't really want them alphabetized across the top of the dynaset (e.g., *Apr, Aug, Dec, Feb,* and so on). So to put those month names in chronological order (e.g., *Jan, Feb, Mar,* and so on), you'd want to change this query's properties and enter the month names in the order you want them displayed, as below:

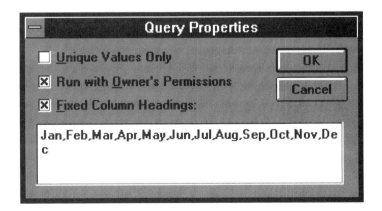

Using the Asterisk in a QBE Grid

Any time you're viewing a query window, the first item in a field list will be an asterisk, which stands for "all fields." As an alternative to dragging all the field names from the top part of the query window into the QBE grid, you can just drag the asterisk.

The Field cell in the column will then contain the table name followed by a period and the asterisk, as shown in Figure 8.10. When you run the query, the resulting dynaset will contain all the fields in the table.

One advantage of using the asterisk as opposed to specific field names is that the resulting dynaset will *always* contain all the fields in the table. So

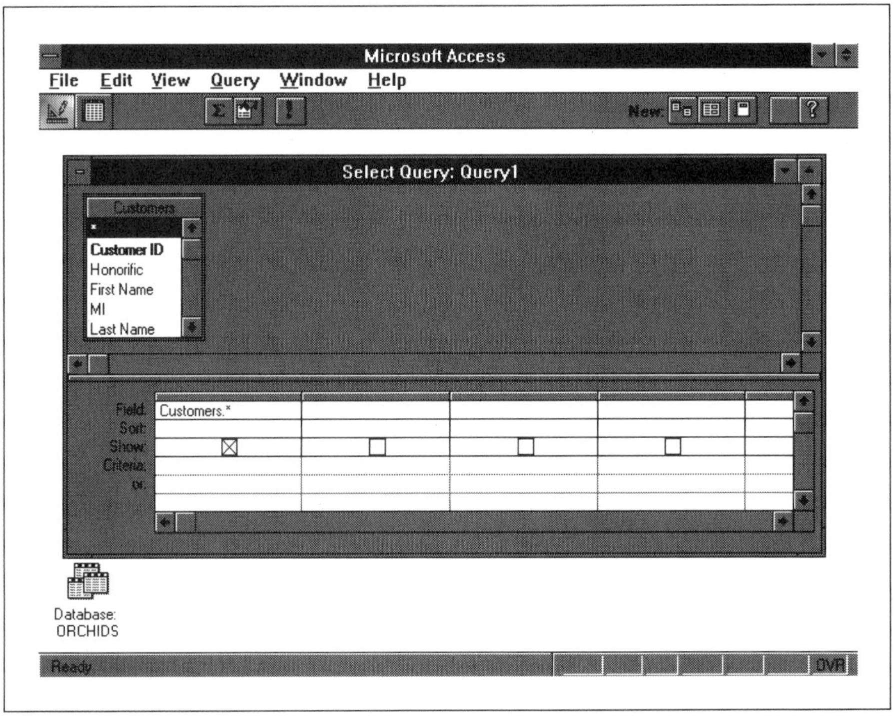

FIGURE 8.10

You can drag the asterisk from the field list to the QBE grid as an alternative to dragging all the field names.

let's say you save the query, and then at some future time you alter the structure of the table that the query is based on—perhaps you add or delete some fields. When you run that saved query in the future, the query will use whatever fields are now in that table's structure.

You can still sort and search on fields when you use the asterisk. However, you must drag the fields that you want to use for sorting into the QBE grid. Furthermore, to prevent the field from appearing twice in the dynaset, you should deselect the Show check box for these fields.

N O T E   The field would appear twice in the dynaset because the asterisk will automatically display every field in the table, then the selected Show option would display the field again.

For instance, if you want to display all the fields from the Customers table, and want to sort records by Zip Code, and limit the display to records entered on or after 2/1/93, you could set up the QBE grid as below:

Field:	Customers.*	Zip/Postal Code	Date Entered	
Sort:		Ascending		
Show:	☒	☐	☐	
Criteria:			>=#2/1/93#	
or:				

In all our sample queries up to this point, we've been very selective about what fields we want to see in the resulting dynaset. So there was no reason to use the asterisk to display every field in a dynaset.

When you start designing more advanced queries, and particularly when you start designing action queries (described next), you might want to use the asterisk to ensure that the query always operates on the current structure of the underlying table, and that all the fields are included in the query operation.

Creating Action Queries

The select queries and crosstab queries that you've seen up to this point all have one thing in common: none of them changes the underlying data in the table in any way. They each *show* the data in some unique way, but none of them alters or deletes any of that underlying data.

By comparison, an *action query* does change or delete data in a table. In Access, there are four different types of action queries:

- *Update queries* change the data in a group of records.
- *Delete queries* delete records from a table.
- *Append queries* copy a group of records from one table to another.
- *Make-table queries* create a new table from a group of records in another table.

Warning: Action Queries Are Fast!

The most important thing to keep in mind about action queries is that, not only do they make many changes to the data in your tables, they also do it very quickly. If you run an action query and suddenly realize you've just made a drastic mistake, you're out of luck. Chances are, the action query will be done making its changes before you even finish saying "whoops."

There are two things to keep in mind that will help you to avoid (or at least recover from) mistakes you might make with action queries:

- Always design and run the query as a select query first, so you can see what data will be changed (or deleted) when you run the query. Don't convert the select query to an action query until the dynaset displays only the records you want to delete or change.
- Always keep a backup copy of your database handy. You can also make a quick backup copy of just the table you're going to change. Both techniques are covered in Chapter 18.

TIP

If you just want to make a quick backup copy of a table, click the Table button in the database window, then click the name of the table you want to copy. Choose Edit ➤ Copy, then choose Edit ➤ Paste. Type a name for the copy of the table, then choose OK.

Using an Update Query to Change Multiple Records

Update queries let you change data in all the records, or just selected records in a table. This is generally much faster than changing one record at a time. For example, you could create an update query to increase the unit price of all products in a table, or just the products in a given category, by 10 percent. Or, you could create an update query to change the Date Shipped field to a specific date after all the orders have been fulfilled.

Creating a Select Query to Preview an Update Query

As with any action query, your best bet is to start out by creating a select query that you can use to preview which records will be changed. To do so:

1. Create a regular select query for the table you want to update.

2. Drag the field(s) you want to update, as well as any fields you'll need to use to specify search criteria.

3. Specify the search criteria (unless you want to change all the records in the table).

4. Run the query.

Looking at an example, let's say you want to increase the current price of all products in the SLIPPER category of our Products table by 15 percent. First, you'd set up the query as in Figure 8.11. Notice that I've dragged the Category ID field, which I need to specify search criteria, the Description field (just so I can see the names of all the products I'm going to change the price of), and the Current Price field (the one I'm going to change later) in the QBE grid.

When I run this query, I can take a look at the dynaset, which would look something like the one below, to verify that these are indeed the records I want to change.

Select Query: Query1		
Category ID	**Description**	**Current Price**
SLIPPER	Callosum	$25.00
SLIPPER	Constellation	$25.00
SLIPPER	Yerba Buena	$20.00
SLIPPER	Bell o' Ireland	$45.00
SLIPPER	Madre de Dios	$67.50
		$0.00

If the records that appear in the dynaset are *not* the records you want to change, you'll need to go back to the query design, and change or define the appropriate selection criteria until you get it right. Make sure you don't proceed with the update query until the dynaset shows only the records you want to change.

Changing the Select Query to an Update Query

When you're satisfied that the records in the dynaset are the exact records you want to change, you can change the select query to an action query:

1. From the dynaset, click the Design View button to return to the query's design window.

FIGURE 8.11

A select query for the
Products table that
isolates records in the
SLIPPER category

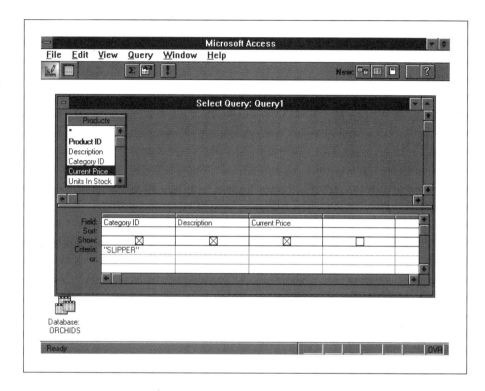

2. Choose Query ➤ Update. The QBE grid now contains a row
   named *Update To:*, and the title bar of the query window changes
   from *Select Query* to *Update Query.*

3. Click the Update To cell under the name of the field that you want
   to change, and enter a new value for the field, or an expression
   that will calculate the change you want to make.

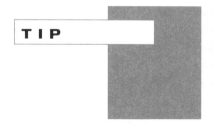

TIP

If you're nervous about getting the expression
right, you might want to try running the entire
update procedure on a backup copy of the table
first, so you don't do the wrong calculation on
important data.

4. Click the Run button in the tool bar, or choose Query ➤ Run.

5. A dialog box appears telling you how many records will be updated.

6. Choose OK if you're ready to proceed with the query.

When you choose OK, Access will either complete the query or, if it encounters problems, will display an "Errors were encountered…" message, described under "Troubleshooting Action Queries" later in this chapter.

Getting back to our example of increasing the Current Price by 15 percent, you'd need to put the expression:

[Current Price]*1.15

into the Update To cell of the Current Price column, as below.

Field:	Category ID	Description	Current Price
Update To:			[Current Price]*1.15
Criteria:	"SLIPPER"		
or:			

When you click the Run button, Access would inform you that it plans to update five rows in the table (i.e., the five records in the SLIPPER category of products). Choosing OK runs the query and performs the update.

T I P

If you plan on using this same update query again in the future, use File ➤ Save to save it now, before changing back to a select query.

To check the results of the update:

1. Change the update query back to a select query by choosing Query ➤ Select.

2. Run the select query with the usual Datasheet button (or View ➤ Datasheet) to view records that have changed.

In this example, changing the update query back to a select query, and running that query displays the dynasheet shown below. The Current Price in each record has indeed been increased by 15 percent.

Select Query: Query1		
Category ID	**Description**	**Current Price**
SLIPPER	Callosum	$28.75
SLIPPER	Constellation	$28.75
SLIPPER	Yerba Buena	$23.00
SLIPPER	Bell o' Ireland	$51.75
SLIPPER	Madre de Dios	$77.63
		$0.00

We'll take a look at additional examples of update queries in Chapter 16. For now, let's take a look at another type of action query.

Using a Query to Append Data to Another Table

An *append query* copies all or some records from one table to the bottom of another table, as illustrated in Figure 8.12. This capability is handy when you use separate tables with similar structures to manage data. For instance, you might have a Customers table of all your active customers. As new customers come in and apply for credit, you might store their data in a separate table, perhaps named Applicants, so you can work with their records independently. When convenient, you can append records for approved customers to the larger Customers table without retyping their data.

Append queries are also useful for storing data in *history tables*. For instance, you could store all your active, unfulfilled orders in one set of tables. When a group of orders is fulfilled and all the processing is done,

FIGURE 8.12

An append query copies records from one table to the bottom of some other, existing table.

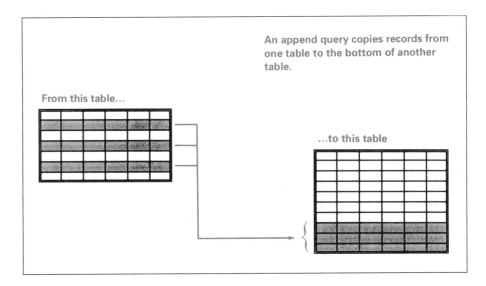

An append query copies records from one table to the bottom of another table.

From this table...

...to this table

you could move those records to the history tables. This prevents your active orders table from growing excessively large, while keeping a backup of old, fulfilled orders for future reference as needed.

NOTE   In Chapter 16 we'll look at ways of automating the task of moving old orders into history tables.

An append query only makes sense if the two tables involved have similar structures and field names. But they need not have identical structures. In general:

- If the table you're copying from has more fields that the one you're appending to, excess fields are ignored and are not appended.

- If the table you're copying from has fewer fields than the one you're appending to, fields with matching names are updated and any additional fields are left blank.

When designing an append query, you work directly with the table that you'll be appending records *from,* so that you can choose exactly which fields and records you want to append to the other table. As usual, your best bet is to start out by designing a select query that defines the records you want to append, and then change that to an action query that does the actual appending.

Designing a Select Query to Preview an Append Query

Your first step to designing an Append query will be to design a select query, and then test it, to verify that only the records you want to append to another table will be selected. The general steps are:

1. Create a query for the table that you want to move or copy records *from*.

2. Drag all the fields that you want to copy to the other table into the QBE grid.

3. If the table you are appending to has a primary key, be sure to drag the equivalent field in the current table to the QBE grid. (The one exception would be if the primary key in the table you'll be appending records to is the Counter data type, as discussed under "Appending Records with a Counter Field" later in this section.)

N O T E

If the two tables involved in an append query have identical structures, you can use the asterisk instead of field names in QBE grids. Use the * in both the Field cell and the Append To cell. If the QBE grid also includes criteria for selecting records, the Append To cell for those criteria should be left blank, because the * will already be appending to all the fields in the table.

4. Specify search criteria that describe the records you want to append. If you don't specify criteria, all the records from the current table will be appended to the other table.

5. Run the query with the usual Datasheet button to preview the fields and records that will be appended.

Now you need to inspect the dynaset to ensure that all the fields that you want to append, and only the appropriate records, are included. If the dynaset does not show the records you want to append, you'll need to change the query and try again.

Changing the Select Query to the Append Query

When you're sure only the records you want to append are included in the select query's dynaset, you can convert the select query to an append query:

1. If you are still in the dynaset, click the Design View button to return to the query design.

2. Choose Query ➤ Append. You'll see this dialog box:

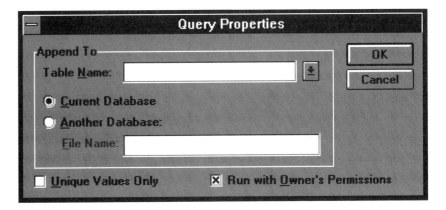

3. If the table you're appending data to is in the current database, accept the default Current database and skip to Step 3 now. If the table you want to append records to is in a different database, choose Another Database and then type the location and name of the database you want to send data to (for instance, you might want to send it to **c:\access\mydata.mdb**).

TIP For information on exporting records to non-Access databases, see Chapter 19.

4. Choose the name of the table you want to append records to from the drop-down list.

5. If you've set up a secure system on a network, you can choose *Run With Owner's Permission* to prevent users with restricted rights from running the query.

6. If you want to copy unique values only, choose that option. The uniqueness will be determined by the entire combination of fields in the QBE grid. (See "Viewing Only Unique Values" in Chapter 7 for a discussion of uniqueness in this context.)

7. Choose OK. The QBE grid now contains an *Append To:* row and the title bar of the query window now displays *Append Query.*

8. Access suggests fields in the table to append the current fields to based on identical field names. If you want to change a suggested field name, click its Append To cell, then choose an alternative field from the drop-down list.

NOTE If you're appending records to a non-Access database, you'll need to type in field names. See Chapter 19.

9. To perform the append, click the Run button or choose Query ➤ Run.

If Access doesn't encounter any problems with the query, you'll see a message indicating how many records will be appended to the other table. To proceed with the append, choose OK. Otherwise, choose Cancel. If you see an error message instead, indicating a problem, see "Troubleshooting Action Queries" below for help.

You can save an append query as you would any other. When you want to append new records that match the query's search criteria in the future, just run the query again.

To verify that the records were appended, just open the table that you appended the records to and look for the new records.

NOTE   Remember that if the table you appended to has a primary key, the records will appear in sorted order when viewing the table's contents. So even though the records have been appended to the bottom of the table, they will appear in their proper sort-order position when you're viewing that table's dynasheet.

An Append Query Example

Let's suppose that you use the Customers table that we've described before to store information about active customers. You also create a table, perhaps named Applicants, to store information about new customers who have applied for credit. This Applicants table has the same basic structure as the Customers table, but includes one extra Yes/No field named Approved.

As new customers come in, you add their records to the Applications table, rather than directly to the Customers table. When a given applicant's credit rating is approved, you change the contents of the Approved field from No to Yes. For instance, of the four customers in the Applicants table shown below, two have been approved:

Approved	Customer ID	Honorific	First Name	MI	Last Name	Department/Title	
No	1019	Dr.	Wilson	J.	Jones	Department of Biology	E
Yes	1020	Miss	Ellen		Parker		E
No	1021	Ms.	Anne	T.	Funicello		
Yes	1022	Mr.	Sari	U.	Fell	Owner	E
	0						

When it comes time to append these records to the Customers table, you first want to design a select query that isolates records with Yes in the Approved field, as in Figure 8.13.

N O T E   Access will copy *only* those fields that are included in the QBE grid to the other table. So be sure that *you* include all the appropriate fields in your QBE grid.

When you run this query, the resulting dynaset will indeed display only records with Yes in the Approved field.

FIGURE 8.13

A select query, based on the Applicants table, that will isolate records that have Yes in the Approved field.

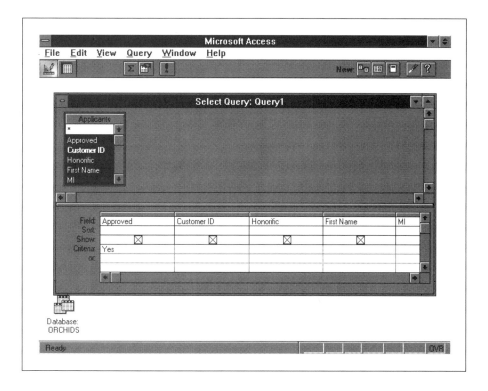

TIP

For occasional copying or moving records from one table to another, you can use the Paste Append technique described back in Chapter 5.

Next you would return to the query design window, and choose Query ➤ Append to convert the select query to an append query, and specify *Customers* as the table to append records to. Access adds an *Append To:* row. Each cell in this row will contain the name of the field in the Customers table that matches the equivalent field in the Applicants table. The Append To: cell for the Approved field will be blank, however, because (in this example) the Customers table doesn't have an equivalent field (see below).

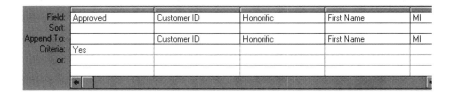

Field:	Approved	Customer ID	Honorific	First Name	MI
Sort:					
Append To:		Customer ID	Honorific	First Name	MI
Criteria:	Yes				
or:					

To run the query, you would now click the Run button (!). Access would display the message "2 row(s) will be appended." When you choose OK, Access executes the query.

To verify the append, open the Customers table and look for the records of the customers you added. Here you can see that approved customers 1020 and 1022 have indeed been appended to the Customers table.

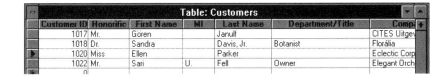

Table: Customers						
Customer ID	Honorific	First Name	MI	Last Name	Department/Title	Comp:
1017	Mr.	Gören		Janulf		CITES Uitgev
1018	Dr.	Sandra		Davis, Jr.	Botanist	Florália
1020	Miss	Ellen		Parker		Eclectic Corp
1022	Mr.	Sari	U.	Fell	Owner	Elegant Orch
0						

Keep in mind that the two records from the Applicants table have been *copied*, not *moved*, to the Customers table. Since those customers are no longer applicants, you could now delete them from the Applicants table, using a delete query (described momentarily) if you wish.

Appending Records with a Counter Field

As you may recall, if a table contains a Counter field, Access automatically assigns a counter value to each new record that you type into the table. For instance, the first record you type in is numbered 1, the next record is 2, and so forth.

When you're appending records to a table that contains a Counter field, you can let Access either assign counter values in this same manner or you can copy append records with their existing counter values.

If you want Access to assign Counter values to the records as they come into the table, exclude the Counter field (if any) from the QBE grid when designing the append query. When you run the query, Access will automatically fill in the Counter field of each new record as it is appended to the table.

If you want to retain the counter values from the current table in the new table, include the counter field in the QBE grid when you're designing the append query. When you run the append query, the records in the table you appended to will have the same Counter values that they did in the original table.

Keep in mind, however, that if the Counter field is a primary key in the table you're appending to, each incoming record will need to contain some value that doesn't generate a key violation, as described under "Troubleshooting Action Queries" later in this chapter.

Using a Query to Delete Records

As you know, you can delete individual records from a table's datasheet by selecting records and pressing the Delete key. But if you want to delete all the records that meet some search criterion, you might find it easier to use a delete query.

Designing a Select Query to Preview Records to Delete

As with other action queries, you'll want to start off by designing a select query that isolates the records you want to delete:

1. Create a query for the table that you want to delete records from.

2. Drag the asterisk (*) from the field list into the QBE grid.

3. Also, drag any fields for which you need to specify criteria from the field list into the QBE grid.

CAUTION

A delete query always deletes entire records, it doesn't just delete the contents of specific fields. The fields in the QBE grid are used only for defining search criteria.

4. Enter the criteria that define the records you want to delete.

5. Use the Datasheet View button to preview the records.

Any records that appear in the dynaset at this point will be deleted when you run your delete query. If the dynaset isn't showing just the records you want to delete, be sure to adjust the query until only the records you plan to delete appear in the dynaset.

Changing the Select Query to a Delete Query

To change the select query to a delete query:

1. If you're still viewing the dynasheet, switch back to the query design window.

2. Choose Query ➤ Delete. A *Delete* row appears in the QBE grid and the title bar of the query window shows *Delete Query*.

3. The word *From* appears beneath the name of the table that you'll be deleting records from. Check this carefully to make sure the records will be deleted from the table you intend.

4. The word *Where* appears in all criteria columns. Don't change that.

5. To delete the records, click the Run button or choose Query ➤ Run.

You'll see a message indicating the number of records that will be deleted. If you're ready to proceed, choose OK to delete the records. Otherwise, choose Cancel if you want to return to the QBE grid without deleting any records.

CAUTION You can't "undo" a delete query, so think before you click!

A Delete Query Example

Referring back to the example of the Applicants and Customers tables, let's suppose that after appending the selected records to the Customers table, you want to delete them from the Applicants table.

First you'd need to create the select query for the Applicants table, drag the asterisk to the QBE grid, and also drag the Approved field to the QBE grid, since you need that field to define the criterion. Enter **Yes** in the Criteria cell of the Approved column to isolate records that have that value in that field, as below:

Field:	Applicants.*	Approved		
Sort:				
Show:	☒	☐	☐	☐
Criteria:		Yes		
or:				

You can run this select query with the Datasheet button, as usual, to make sure you'll be deleting the correct records. Then return to the query window and choose Query ➤ Delete to create the Delete query. The word *From* appears beneath *Applicants.** to indicate that you'll be deleting records from the Applicants table. The word *Where* appears in the Criteria column of the Approved field, as below:

Field:	Applicants.*	Approved		
Delete:	From	Where		
Criteria:		Yes		
or:				

When you run the query (using the Run button or Query ➤ Run), the records will be deleted from the table. You can then save this query if you think you'll want to re-use it in the future.

When you reopen the Applicants table in the future, the records that contained *Yes* in the Approved field will be gone. The customers still pending approval, however, will still be in that table, as below.

Table: Applicants

Approved	Customer ID	Honorific	First Name	MI	Last Name	Department/Title	
No	1019	Dr.	Wilson	J.	Jones	Department of Biology	E
No	1021	Ms.	Anne	T.	Funicello		
	0						

The Beauty of Append and Delete Queries

This business of creating an append query to copy records to a table, then creating a delete query to delete those same records from the original table, might seem like a pretty elaborate technique to follow just to move some records from one table to another. After all, you could use Edit ➤ Cut and Edit ➤ Paste Append (Chapter 5) on the spur of the moment to do the same job.

But here's the beauty of the thing. Suppose you save both the append query and the delete query that we created in the above two examples. Furthermore, let's say you need to move applicants from the Applicants table to the Customers table quite often.

You could create a macro (Chapter 16) that runs the append query, then runs the delete query. From that point on, you could move all the approved customers—whether it be just a few or several hundred, from the Applicants table to the Customers table with just a few button clicks!

Creating a New Table from a Query

A make-table query creates an entirely new table from the results of a query. You might find this kind of action query helpful when you need to work with a copy of a dynaset, table, or crosstab containing data that was "frozen" at a specific date or time, such as the close of business at the end of the month or quarter.

You can then print reports and graphs based on this frozen copy of the data at your leisure, without being concerned about new data coming into the table and changing totals, averages, or any other calculations.

You can also use a make-table query to create an editable copy of the dynaset that results from a summary, crosstab, or unique values query.

A make-table query is also handy for exporting data to non-relational applications. For instance, you can create a query that combines data from several separate tables, then copy the resulting dynaset to a new table. You could then export that combined data to a spreadsheet or other application that doesn't allow you to combine data from multiple related tables.

The procedure for creating a make-table query is virtually identical to that for an append query. The results are different, of course, because whereas an append query copies records from the dynaset to some other existing table, a make-table query creates an altogether new table from the data in a dynaset. To create a make-table query:

1. First, create a select query that contains the fields you want to copy to the new table, and also specify any criteria that select records you want to copy—or no criteria, if you just want to copy all the records. (See "Copying a Crosstab to a Query" below for additional information on using a crosstab in a make-table query.)

2. Run the select query with the usual Datasheet button to verify that the dynaset contains the records you want to copy to a new table. If necessary, adjust the query until the dynaset display exactly the information you want to copy to another table.

3. To convert the select query to a make-table query, return to the query design window and choose Query ➤ Make Table. You'll see this dialog box:

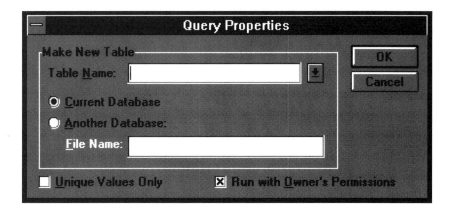

4. If you want to create an Access table in the current database, accept the default Current Database and skip to Step 5 now. If you want to store the new table in another database, choose Another Database, and enter the location and name of the other database (e.g., **c:\access\mydata.mdb**) in the File Name text box.

TIP For information on exporting records to non-Access databases, see Chapter 19.

5. Enter a name for the new table you want to create in the Table Name text box. Or, if you want to replace some existing table with the data you're about to copy, choose the name of the table you want to overwrite.

6. If you've set up a secure system on a network, you can choose *Run With Owner's Permission* to prevent users with restricted rights from running the query.

7. If you want to copy unique values only, choose that option. The uniqueness will be determined by the entire combination of fields in the QBE grid. (See "Viewing Only Unique Values" in Chapter 7 for a discussion of uniqueness in this context.)

8. Choose OK. The title bar of the QBE grid now shows *Make Table Query* rather than *Select Query.*

9. Click the Run button, or choose Query ➤ Run to run the query.

If you chose the name of an existing table in Step 5 above, Access will ask for permission before deleting the current copy of that table. Choose Yes if you're sure you're willing to replace that table. Access will then display a message indicating how many records will be placed in the new table. Choose OK to proceed.

To verify that the query worked, open the table that you specified in Step 5 above. It should contain an exact copy of the dynaset you saw when running the original select query.

Creating a Table from a Crosstab

If you want to copy the results of a crosstab query to a new table, you need to first save and name the crosstab query, then base the make-table query on the crosstab query. For instance, suppose you created the crosstab shown back in Figure 8.9, and then saved that query with a name such as **Order Totals by Month**.

To copy the crosstab's dynaset to a table, you first need to click the Query button in the database window to view a list of all the saved queries. Then click on the name you gave the crosstab query, then click the New Query button (or choose File ➤ New ➤ Query).

The query window displays column names from the crosstab in the field list. Drag the asterisk (or all the field names) to the QBE grid, as in Figure 8.14.

FIGURE 8.14

Query window based
on a previously saved
query named Order
Totals by Month

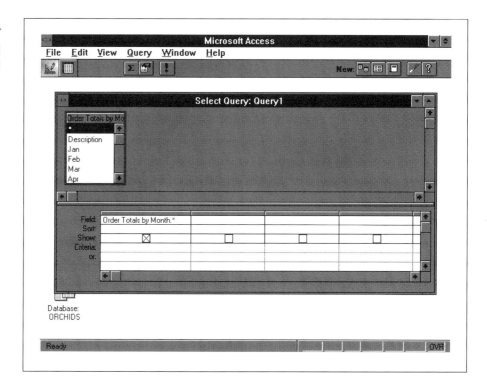

Choose Query ➤ Make Table, and enter a name for the new table. (It must
be different from the name of the query. For instance, you might enter
Orders Totals By Month On 3/31/93, substituting the current date in
your table name. Choose OK.

Click the Run (!) button. To verify that the query worked, return to the
database window and click the Table object button. Then double-click on
the name you gave the new table to open the table.

NOTE

Because the copy of the data you're viewing at this
point is in a table rather than a dynaset, clicking the
design button will take you to the table design
window, rather than the query design window.

Running a Saved Action Query

When you save an action query, its name is listed in the database window with other queries (that is, when the Query object button is selected). However, action queries have an exclamation point next to their icons, as shown below:

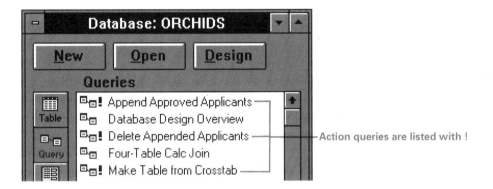

To run an action query from the database window, you can either double-click its name in the query window, or highlight its name and choose Open.

Access will display a message indicating how many records will be changed or deleted by the query, or, in some cases, will display a general message indicating that the query will change data. You can choose OK to proceed with the action, or Cancel to cancel the query.

If Access has any problems completing the query, you'll see an error message to that effect, as described in the next section.

If you want to view or change the action query's design, click its name in the database window, then click the Design button. Remember that once you're in the query window, you use the Run button (!), not the Datasheet button, to run an action query.

Troubleshooting Action Queries

The same rules that apply when you're entering or editing data from the keyboard apply to action queries. If you run an action query that breaks any of those rules, Access will inform you that errors were encountered, and tell you how many fields were deleted, how many records were lost (not updated or appended), and how many records couldn't be changed because they were locked, as in the example below:

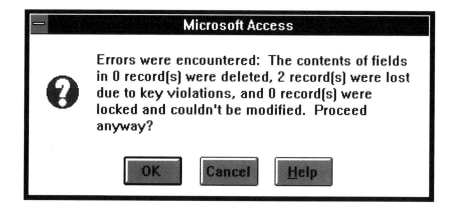

This message is actually somewhat misleading because it implies that the query has already been executed and the errors have already occurred. Luckily, however, the errors really only occurred during a sort of "dry run" of the action query. The message should actually say *will be* where it says *were*, because if you choose Cancel, the query won't be executed, and none of the listed errors will occur.

So your best bet, at this point, would be to cancel the query, then go back the query, or the original data, and try to fix any potential problems before running the query. Here are the most common causes of errors, and their solutions.

The Contents of Fields Were Deleted

If the message indicates that the contents of any fields were deleted, the most likely cause is that an update or append query is trying to enter data that isn't appropriate for the data type of the field. For instance, if you're trying to append text data into a number field, Access will delete the contents of any records that contain data that cannot be interpreted as a number.

If you're running an append query, check to see that the data types in the table you're appending to match the data types of the table you're appending from. Or, if you're running an update query, make sure that the update value is the correct data type for the field. Then try the query again.

Records Lost Due to Key Violations

Remember that if the table you are updating or appending to contains a primary key, two rules always apply to that table:

1. Each record must have a unique value in the field or fields that define the primary key.

2. The primary key cannot contain null values.

If you design an append query or update query that breaks either of those rules, the offending records will be reported as "lost." In an append query, this simply means that the records weren't appended to the table that you're copying records *to*, but those records still exist in the table you're appending *from*—so the term "lost" isn't quite as harsh as it sounds!

The best solution would be to cancel the query, and go back to the table you're appending records from. Change the data in that table so that it doesn't violate either of the rules concerning primary keys, then rerun the query.

If you've predefined the relationship between two tables, and have enforced referential integrity, the action query must also adhere to those rules. For instance, a delete query cannot delete records from the "one side" of a one-to-many relationship if there are any records on the "many" side of the relationship that are related to that record.

Records That Were Locked

If you're using Access on a network, and another user has locked records that your action query is attempting to modify, Access will report how many records are locked and couldn't be updated. Your best bet at that point, as usual, would be to cancel the query. Otherwise, it will be hard to tell which records have, and which records haven't, been updated by the query. Then you can run the update query later when nobody else on the network is using the table(s) involved in the action query.

Creating Parameter Queries

You can build some added flexibility into your queries by using *parameters* in place of specific criteria. A parameter acts as a sort of placeholder that you can fill in with specific information when you run the query. Rather than changing the query each time you want to look up some specific information, you can just run the query as-is, and then fill in the value you want to search for.

To define a parameter:

1. Create a query and drag field names that you want to view, sort, or search on to the QBE grid as usual.

2. Click the Criteria cell of the field you want to search, and enter a parameter rather than a specific value. The parameter must be enclosed in square brackets, must not be the name of an existing field, and is best worded as a question.

N O T E   If you don't spell the parameter query in the list exactly as you spelled it in the QBE grid, Access will prompt you for both spellings, as though they were two entirely separate parameters.

3. Choose Query ➤ Parameters. You'll see the **Query Parameters** dialog box. Here's an example of one, already filled in to show some examples of parameters and data types:

4. In the Parameter column, type the parameter *exactly* as you typed it into the Criteria cell, but without the square brackets.

5. Choose a data type for the parameter from the Data Type column. (The data type you choose should match the data type of the field that the parameter is in.)

6. Choose OK.

The query in Figure 8.15, based on the Customers table, presents an example. The parameter *[What last name?]* appears in the Criteria cell for

FIGURE 8.15

The parameter
[What last name?]
will appear in the
message box when
you run this query, so
that you can decide
on-the-fly what you
want to search for
whenever you run
the query.

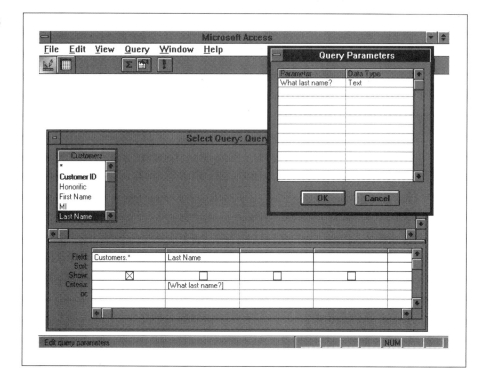

the Last Name column. You can also see that same parameter defined
in the Query Parameters dialog box.

Now let's suppose that you save this query. Any time you run it in the future, with the usual Datasheet button or by double-clicking its name in
the database window, Access will first display this message:

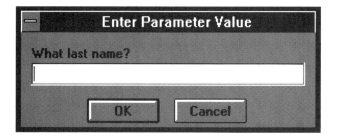

You could type in any name of your choosing, such as **Smith**, then choose OK. The resulting dynaset will display only records that contain the last name Smith.

You can use the parameter as part of a search criterion as well. For instance, you could replace the criterion shown in Figure 8.15 with:

    Like [Search for what last name?]&"*"

When you run the query, Access would show the same message. But your entry will be substituted into the larger **Like** expression. So if you entered **Smith**, Access would convert that to

    Like Smith*

before running the query, and display records that begin with the letters *smith*. Similarly, changing that expression to

    Like "*"&[Search for what last name?]&"*"

would extend the search to include records with *smith* embedded anywhere in the Last Name field (i.e., **Like *smith***).

The same basic idea works with other data types as well. For instance, you could use this criterion in a numeric field to prompt for some number, then have the query display only data that's greater than or equal to that number:

    >=[Lowest value?]

You could enter this parameter into a date/time field to ask for a range of dates, and then display records within that range:

    Between [Starting Date?] And [Ending Date?]

Just remember that, in addition to defining the parameter in the Criteria cell of the QBE grid, you need to define the data type of the parameter in the Query Parameters list. Also, notice that our last example contains two separate parameters, *[Starting Date?]* and *[Ending Date?]*. In the Query Parameters list, you'd need to define each of these on a separate row, and assign the date/time data to each one.

Using Parameter Queries for What-If? Scenarios

You can also include a parameter in a calculation expression, by enclosing the parameter in square brackets just as you would a field name. This is very handy for trying out "what-if" scenarios.

For example, Figure 8.16 shows a query that is based on the Products table and that uses two parameter queries. The first parameter appears in the Field cell of the last column, though isn't fully visible. The complete expression in that cell is:

> After Increase: CCur([Current Price]*(1*[Increase current price by what percent?]/100))

(typed in as one long line.) The figure also shows the Query Parameters box for the query. (Once again, the *Increase by what percent?* parameter is truncated in the figure.)

FIGURE 8.16

Query with two parameters: one in the last column of the QBE grid (partially obscured), and another in the Criteria cell of the Category ID column

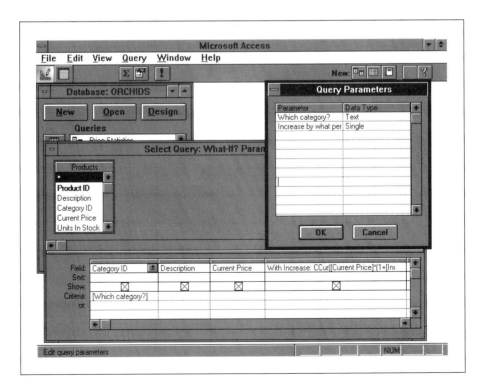

TIP

Access always prompts for parameters in the order that you list them in the Query Properties box.

When you run this query, Access will ask for which category you want to view, and then an increase amount. (You'd omit the % sign when entering the increase amount.)

The resulting dynaset would display the current price of each product in that category, as well as what the price will be if you increase it by 10 percent.

Viewing a Query's SQL Statement

SQL (pronounced *sequel*) stands for *Structured Query Language*, and is a widely used standard for querying databases across many platforms, from microcomputers to mainframes. Whenever you create a query, Access creates an equivalent SQL statement for the query.

You can view that SQL statement by choosing View ➤ SQL whenever you're at a query window. For instance, the last query shown above would display this SQL statement:

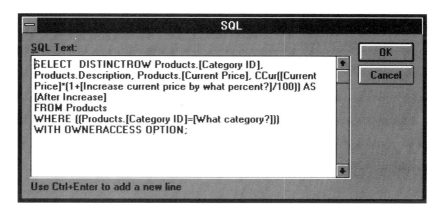

```
SQL Text:
SELECT  DISTINCTROW Products.[Category ID],
Products.Description, Products.[Current Price], CCur([Current
Price]*(1+[Increase current price by what percent?]/100)) AS
[After Increase]
FROM Products
WHERE ((Products.[Category ID]=[What category?]))
WITH OWNERACCESS OPTION;
```

Use Ctrl+Enter to add a new line

That statement might not mean much to you if, like most Access users, you're not familiar with SQL. In fact, you don't *need* to know anything about SQL.

Nonetheless, the SQL statement can come in handy later when you're designing forms, reports, and macros. You can copy the SQL statement to one of those other objects by following these steps:

1. Select the entire SQL statement either by dragging the mouse through it, or by pressing Ctrl+Home, then Shift+Ctrl+End.

2. Press Ctrl+Ins (or Ctrl+C in Windows 3.1). The statement is copied to the Clipboard.

3. Choose Cancel in the SQL box to close that dialog box

4. Go to wherever you want to place a copy of the SQL statement and press Ctrl+V to paste the copy.

We'll look at some examples in upcoming chapters.

When a Query Gets Too Complicated, Consider Using Two

Remember that it's never necessary to create one grand, complicated query to get the results you're looking for. When your query starts getting too complicated, consider using two. For instance, suppose you create a query that joins data from the Customers, Products, Orders, and Order Details tables, and calculates the extended price of each order total. You save this query with the name **Four-Table Calc Join**.

When you want to ask questions about the data in that query's dynaset, it's not necessary to change that query at all. Instead, just create a new query based on that query. That is,

1. Go to the database design window.

2. Click the Query object button to display the names of all your saved queries.

3. Click the name of the query you want to base a new query on (*Four-Table Calc Join* in this example).

4. Click the New Query button or choose File ➤ New ➤ Query.

The field list for the new query contains the names of all the fields in the query's dynaset. Now you can drag field names and define sort orders and criteria, as you would in any other query. For instance, in Figure 8.17 I added the criterion **>100** to the Criteria cell in the Extended Price column to have this query limit the dynaset to order details over $100.00.

FIGURE 8.17

This select query is based on another saved query, named "Four-table calc join," that calculates order totals from four tables.

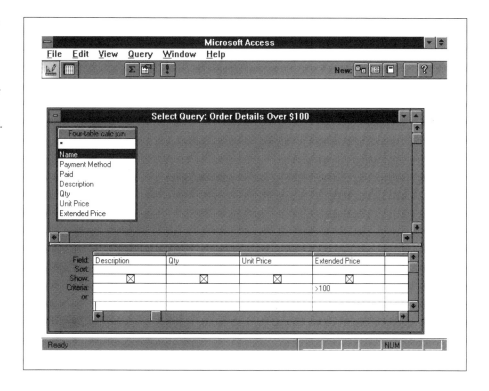

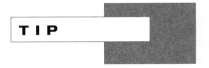

TIP   You could also use a parameter in this second query, to make it even more flexible.

Next you could save *this* query with another name, such as **Orders over $100** (don't include a period in the name). Now you could run this query at any time with the usual techniques. Access will "know" that this query needs data from the first query, and will automatically run that first query behind the scenes so that the results in the second query are accurate and up to date.

Summary

There's really no limit to the ways in which you can use a query to combine, view, calculate, and change data in your tables. In many ways, the query is the main tool you'll use to manage the data in a database. As you'll see, you can use queries to help you design fancy forms and beautifully formatted reports that display the information you want to see, in whatever format you want to see it.

PART THREE

Personalizing Forms and Reports

CHAPTERS

CHAPTER

9

Creating Custom Forms

fast TRACK

IN **EARLIER** chapters we covered some basic techniques for creating forms with FormWizards, and using those forms to manage data. In this chapter we'll look more deeply into forms, focusing on techniques that you can use to tailor forms to your particular work needs and personal taste.

What Is a Form?

A form offers an alternative way of viewing and working with data in your table. Unlike the datasheet view, which always displays data in rows and columns, a form can display data in just about any format. Perhaps the most common use of a form is to create a "fill-in-the-blanks" view of your data that resembles a paper form that your company already uses.

Figure 9.1 shows an example, displaying data from the Customers table in the datasheet view and in form view. In the datasheet view, you can see as many records and fields as will fit into the window. In the form view, you can focus on one record at a time, and generally see all the fields for that one record.

In addition to letting you view one record at a time, forms also offer advantages over the datasheet view. For instance, with a form you can:

- Display graphical data such as photos, charts, and icons.

- Use combo boxes, option buttons, and other Windows "graphical controls" to simplify data entry and editing.

FIGURE 9.1

Datasheet view displays your data in a tabular format. Form view generally shows just the data for a single record in a "fill-in-the-blanks" format, like a paper form.

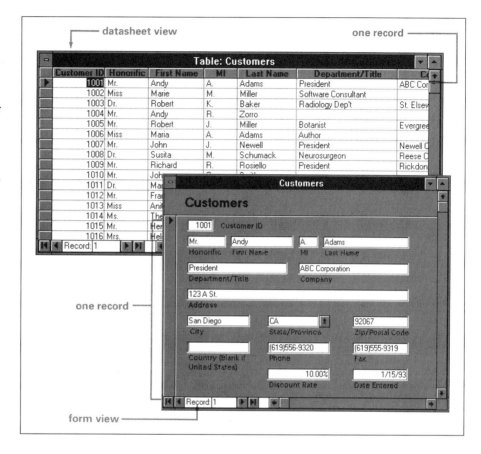

* Automatically compute and display totals and other types of calculations.

* Display data from multiple related tables in a format that's easy to understand.

Creating a Form

There are two ways to create a form: You can create it from scratch or you can use a FormWizard. As you learned in Lesson 4 of Chapter 2, and as elaborated in Chapter 5, the FormWizards provide a quick and easy way to create a form. You can use the form that the Wizard creates "as-is," or tailor that resulting form to your liking.

To create a form (either with or without a Wizard), follow these steps:

1. Choose File ➤ New ➤ Form, or go to the database window and click the Form button, then click the New button in the database window. You'll see the **New Form** dialog box.

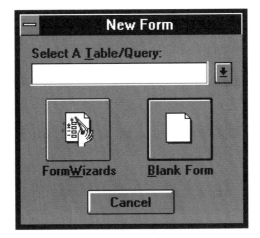

2. Click the drop-down list button, then click the name of the table or query you want to base the form on, following these guidelines:

   • If you want to create a form to view, edit, or graph data from a single table, choose a table name.

   • If the data you want to view or edit with the form is in several different tables, choose the name of a query that joins those tables (see Chapter 11 for more information).

TIP

If the table or dynaset that you want to base the form on is already open, you can just click the New Form button in the tool bar to start creating a form.

3. If you want to create the form from scratch, choose the Blank Form button, then skip the remaining steps.

4. If you want to use a Wizard, click the FormWizards button, and then choose the type of form you want to create, as summarized below:

> **Single-Column Forms** This Wizard helps you create a single-column form that displays all the fields from one record in a table in vertical format. This is the Wizard you'll use for creating a standard "fill in the blanks" form for view and editing data one record at a time.

> **Tabular** This Wizard helps you design a form that's organized into row-and-column format, like a datasheet. You can use this wizard to create a custom datasheet view for a table or dynaset that's independent of the default datasheet view. This type of form is discussed in Chapter 11.

> **Graph** The Graph Wizard takes you through the steps required for viewing data in a bar graph, pie chart, or other type of graph. See Chapter 13 for information on using this Wizard.

> **Main/Subform** This Wizard helps you to design a form that displays data from multiple tables in a format that's easy to understand as discussed in Chapter 11.

5. Choose OK after choosing a Wizard.

6. In the next dialog box, choose any or all of the available fields to include on your form, then choose Next.

7. In the next dialog box, choose any one of the available "looks", then choose Next.

8. If you want to change the title that will appear at the top of the form, type in a new title.

9. To view the finished form, click the Open button. To go to the design view, where you can start changing the appearance of the form immediately, choose Design.

If you used a Wizard, the form appears on the screen after a brief delay, either in form view or design view, depending on which option you chose in Step 9 above.

If you opted to start with a blank form, you'll be taken directly to an empty form design window. In that case, you'll need to add *controls* to the form before you can actually start using the form, as described under "Adding Bound Controls to Display Data from the Table" later in this chapter.

Three Ways to View a Form

Whenever you're using a form, the tool bar offers these three buttons for choosing how to view the form:

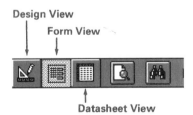

To switch to another view, just click the appropriate button:

Form View   The mode used for viewing, entering, changing, printing, and deleting data in the underlying table, using the basic navigation and editing techniques described under "Navigating and Editing with a Form" in Chapter 5.

Design View   Acts as an "artist's palette" for personalizing the form to your liking, as discussed in this chapter.

Datasheet View　Displays the underlying table or dynaset in the familiar row-and-column format you've seen in preceding chapters.

An Overview of the Form Design View Window

As mentioned, the design view is like your artist's palette, where you can create, change, and design the form to your liking. The design view offers several tools to help you be creative. Figure 9.2 points out some of these tools. (Don't worry if your screen doesn't look exactly like the figure.) As

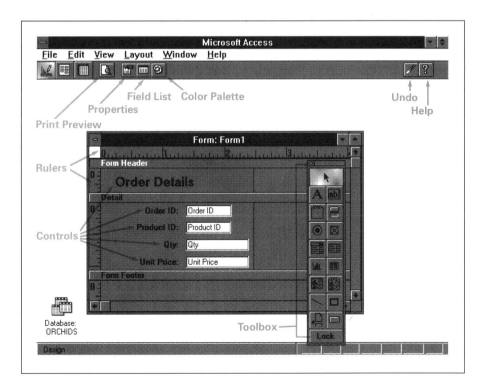

you'll see, you can hide and display tools at will so they're out of your way when you don't need them.

As with any window, you can move and size the form design view window using standard Windows techniques. You can also use the vertical and horizontal scroll bars at the edge of the window to scroll to any parts of the form that aren't currently visible.

The Rulers

The horizontal and vertical rulers, which appear only in design view, help you to keep track of the size of the form and the positions of the various controls on the screen. You can turn the rulers on and off by choosing View ➤ Ruler.

The Tool Bar

In addition to the Design, Form, and Datasheet buttons described earlier, the design view window's tool bar includes buttons for displaying and hiding other tools: The Properties sheet, the Field List, and the Color palette. There are also the standard Undo and Help buttons.

The Toolbox

The toolbox offers tools for creating new controls, and is available when you're designing reports as well as forms. So we'll talk about the Toolbox in depth in Chapter 10, but here are some basic techniques you can use to view, hide, or move the toolbox as necessary.

- To hide the toolbox, or bring it out of hiding, choose View ➤ Toolbox.

- To move the toolbox out of the way, drag its title bar (just above the pointer tool) to a new location.

The Form Header, Footer, and Detail Bands

Any single-column form that you create with a Wizard will automatically be divided into three sections:

- **Header band**: Any text or controls within the Header band appear once at the top of the form within the window and once at the top of each printed form. Wizard puts the form title (*Customers* in Figure 9.1) in a Header band.

- **Detail band**: Appears once for each record in the table, both on the screen and on printed copies of the form. Data from the table appears in the Detail band when you use a Wizard to create the form.

- **Footer band:** Text and controls within the Footer band appear once at the bottom of the form window (if space within the window permits), and appear only once when printing, beneath the last printed form. This band is empty when you first create a form with a Wizard.

The Header and Footer bands are optional, and pertain to both forms and reports. So we'll discuss the role of the bands, and techniques for managing them, in more detail in Chapters 10 and 12. For now, it's sufficient to know that:

- Wizards always place the form title (the title *Customers* in Figure 9.1) in the form Header band, and leaves the form Footer band empty.

- You can increase or decrease the size of the form Header or Footer band by dragging the *bottom* edge of the band up or down. For example, to increase or decrease the height of the form Header band, move the pointer to just above the Detail band's bar, until the two-headed arrow appears, then drag up or down.

- You can add or remove the form Header and form Footer bands, as a whole, by choosing Layout ➤ Form Hdr/Ftr.

About Controls

The *controls* in design view show you where various objects in the form appear. There are three fundamental types of controls:

- **Bound controls**: Controls that display data that's stored in the underlying table are called *bound controls,* because they're "bound" to the table. As you move from record to record in form view, the contents of the bound controls changes to reflect the data in the current record. The form in Figure 9.2 shows bound controls for the fields Order ID, Product ID, Qty, and Unit Price in the Order Details table.

- **Unbound controls**: Controls that are not in any way tied to the underlying table are call *unbound controls.* For instance, Order Details in the form Header band in Figure 9.2 is an unbound control that shows the form title, as opposed to data within the table.

- **Calculated Controls**: A calculated control computes a new value based on data in the table, and displays the results of that calculation on the form. For instance, you might add a calculated control to the form shown in Figure 9.2 to calculate and display the following extended price:

([Qty]*[Unit Price].)

Basic Skills for Using the Form Design View

If you used a Wizard to create a form, chances are you'll probably want to learn to move, size, and color controls to reassign the form to your liking. Before you can do any of that, you need to know how to *select* the control(s) you want to work with.

N O T E   If you started with a blank form, rather than a form created by a Wizard, your first job will be to add some controls to the blank form. See "Adding Bound Controls to Display Data from a Table" later in this chapter.

Selecting a Single Control

To select a single control, just click it. Most controls consist of two parts: a *label*, which is typically the field name or caption from the table, and a *text box*, where the data from the underlying table appears in the form. You can select either the label or the text box. Both will then have *move handles*, but the selected one will have *size handles*, as below.

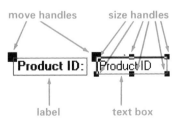

Selecting Several Adjacent Controls

If you want to select a group of adjacent controls, position the pointer just outside the top or bottom control that you want to select. Then hold down the mouse button and drag the pointer through, or around, the controls that you want to select. A frame appears as you drag the mouse pointer. When you release the mouse button, objects within that frame will be selected, and the frame will disappear.

Only items that are within the frame will be selected, and they will have sizing handles. For instance, if you drag the mouse through just the text boxes, only the text boxes will have sizing handles. The corresponding labels, however, will have move handles. (See Figure 9.3 for examples.)

Selecting Non-Adjacent and Overlapping Controls

To select several non-adjacent or overlapping controls, hold down the Shift key and click each control you want to select (see Figure 9.3).

Selecting All the Controls

If you want to select all the controls and labels on the form, choose Edit ➤ Select All.

Deselecting Controls

To deselect all the currently selected controls, click any neutral area on the form (i.e., where there is no control or label). To deselect *some* of the currently selected controls, Shift+Click each control that you want to deselect.

FIGURE 9.3

To select several adjacent controls, drag the pointer around or through them. To select non-adjacent controls, Shift+click each control.

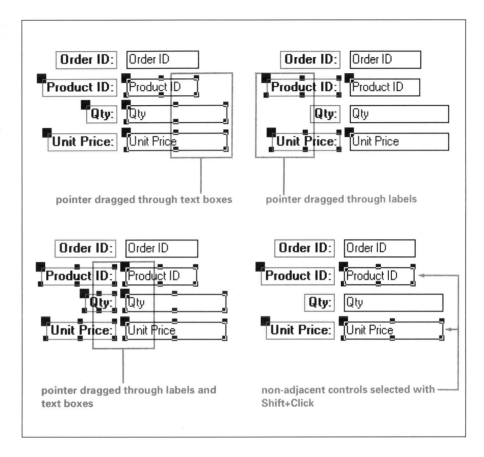

pointer dragged through text boxes   pointer dragged through labels

pointer dragged through labels and text boxes   non-adjacent controls selected with Shift+Click

Moving Controls

You can move a control anywhere within the form window. If you want to keep the control's text box and its label together while moving:

1. If you used a Wizard to create the initial form with the Chiseled, Shadowed, or Boxed look, the chiseled lines, shadows, and boxes are separate unbound controls. You'll want to include those controls in the selection before moving the control.

2. Select the control(s) that you want to move.

3. Move the pointer to a control's border, so that the "full-hand" icon appears.

4. Hold down the mouse button, drag the frame that appears to the new location for the control(s), then release the mouse button.

If your form has a colored background, you can still drag controls outside of that colored area. Access will automatically resize the colored background area after you complete the move.

If you want to move a single control, you can select and move in one step. Position the pointer to the control's border, hold down the mouse button (the "full hand" pointer should appear), and just start dragging.

Moving Just the Text Box or Label

If you want to move just the text box(es), or just the labels(s):

1. Select the text box(es) or label(s) you want to move.

2. Move the pointer to the move handle of whichever item you want to move. The pointer changes to a hand with just the index finger touching the move box.

3. Drag the item into position, and release the mouse button.

This technique is particularly handy for moving a label to a different position in relation to its text box. For instance, you might want to put a label beneath its text box, as below:

Canceling a Move

If you're not too thrilled with the results of a moved control, just choose Edit ➤ Undo Move or press Ctrl+Z to cancel the move. Optionally, you can press Esc to cancel a move that's in progress.

Moving Controls between Bands

You can move an entire control into, and out of, footer and header bands. But if you want to move just the label or just the text box to another band, you'll need to use cut-and-paste. The easiest way to do this is to select the control(s) you want to move and choose Edit ➤ Copy. Then click within the band you want to move the control to and choose Edit ➤ Paste. The control appears near the upper left corner of the band, but you can drag it into whatever position you want within the band. You can then delete just the label, or just the text box.

Maintaining Alignment As You Move

To move a control without affecting its alignment in relation to other controls, hold down the Shift key before, and during, the move. For instance, if you want to move a control up or down without changing its horizontal alignment, hold down the Shift key, then start moving the control up or down. As long as you keep the Shift key depressed, you'll only be able to move in whatever direction you started moving.

Checking Your Progress

As you're working with the form's design, you might want to check to see how things will look on the finished form. To do so, just click the Form View button or choose View ➤ Form. To return to the form design, click the Design button or choose View ➤ Form Design.

Saving Your Work As You Go

Whenever you've achieved some result in your form design that's worth keeping (or just before you try something you're nervous about), you can do a quick save of your form by choosing File ➤ Save. If you've never saved the form, you'll be prompted for a name. Fill in a valid Access name (up to 64 characters, with spaces), and choose OK. If you've already named the form, choosing File ➤ Save saves the form as it appears right now, without prompting for another name.

Changing a Label

If you want to change the text of a label, first select the label (so it has size handles.) Then click the label again. The pointer changes to an I-beam. You can then delete text with the usual Backspace and Delete keys, and type in any new text. When you're done, click anywhere outside the label.

Sizing Controls

You can size a control in much the same way that you size a window—by dragging its corner or border:

1. Select the control you want to resize.
2. Move the pointer to any size handle on the control.
3. Drag the sizing handle until the control is the size you want, then release the mouse button.

Deleting Controls

To delete a control and its label:

1. Select the control(s) you want to delete.
2. Press Delete or choose Edit ➤ Delete.

To delete just the label(s):

1. Select the label(s) only (so that only the label has sizing handles).
2. Press Delete or choose Edit ➤ Delete.

To undo the most recent deletion, choose Edit ➤ Undo Delete.

Aligning Controls

There are two ways to keep controls aligned neatly on the form: you can align the controls to the grid, and you can align the controls to each other.

Viewing the Grid

The grid acts much like graph paper, giving you checkpoints for aligning the various controls on your form. You can turn the grid on and off using the View ➤ Grid options on the menu.

N O T E   If you used a Wizard to create the form, you'll need to change the grid's "fineness" (its spacing) before you can actually view the grid.

Changing the Grid Spacing

You can control how finely or coarsely you want the grid to align controls by changing the form's grid properties. However, you'll only be able to *see* the grid if you use set the fineness to 16 dots or fewer per inch.

N O T E   I'll talk about properties, and the Properties sheet, in more detail in the next chapter.

The Wizards usually set the grid to about 64 dots per inch, which is great for aligning things closely on the form. But you can't see the grid when it's set that fine. To change the grid's fineness:

1. Click the Properties button (shown at left) in the tool bar, or choose View ➤ Properties to bring up the *Properties sheet.*

2. Choose Edit ➤ Select Form (or click the gray area outside the form background) to set properties for the entire form.

3. Locate the *Grid X* option and change it to 16 or some smaller value.

4. Locate the *Grid Y* option and set it to 16 or some smaller number.

5. Close the properties sheet by double-clicking its Control-menu box or by choosing View ➤ Properties again.

Now you can use View ➤ Grid normally to hide and display the grid, even if you used a Wizard to create the form.

Snapping Existing Controls to the Grid

To align controls that are already on the form to the grid:

1. Select the control(s) that you want to align to the grid.
2. Choose Layout ➤ Align ➤ To Grid.

Sizing Controls to the Grid

You can also size existing controls to the grid, to fix minor discrepancies in the sizes of controls:

1. Select the control(s) that you want to size to the grid.
2. Choose Layout ➤ Size To Grid.

Snapping to the Grid While Sizing and Moving

You can use Snap To Grid to keep controls aligned to the grid as you are sizing and moving them. Normally, Snap To Grid is turned on as soon as you enter the form design window, so any controls you move or size will snap to the grid (even if the grid isn't visible at the moment). That is, controls will jump from grid point to grid point as you move and size them by dragging.

To activate or deactivate Snap To Grid, choose Layout ➤ Snap To Grid. The Snap To Grid option is a toggle, meaning it's either on (checked) or off (unchecked).

When Snap To Grid is active, you can temporarily override it by holding down the Ctrl key as you move or size a control.

Aligning Controls to Each Other Horizontally

You can also align controls to each other. To align controls horizontally:

1. Select the controls that you want to align horizontally, preferably by dragging the pointer around them, so that all labels and text boxes are selected, as in the example below:

2. Choose Layout ➤ Align.

3. To align along the bottom of the lowest control, choose Bottom. Otherwise, to align along the top edge of the highest control, choose Top.

Below, I aligned to Bottom, so the bottom of the Discount Rate control is aligned to the bottom of the Date Entered control:

Aligning Controls to Each Other Vertically

You can also align controls, or just labels, or just text boxes vertically by selecting the objects you want to align and choosing either Left or Right from the Layout ➤ Align menu. This is particularly handy for correcting minor vertical misalignments.

Here's an example. The label and text box in the Order ID control below are nicely aligned and spaced apart, but the labels and controls beneath Order ID are not aligned equally. To align the controls below Order ID vertically with the Order ID control, you would first drag the pointer through the labels to select just the labels, as below:

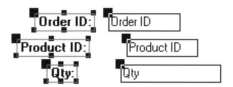

Choosing Layout ➤ Align ➤ Right aligns the right edge of each label to the right edge of Order ID label, as below:

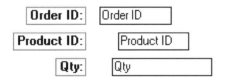

Selecting just the text boxes next, and choosing Layout ➤ Align ➤ Left, would align the left edges of all the text boxes to the left edge of the leftmost text box, the Order ID text box in this example. Thus, the text boxes would now be neatly aligned next to the labels, as below:

As with moving, sizing, and deleting, you can choose Edit ➤ Undo Align to undo an unsatisfactory alignment change. If labels and text boxes tend to overlap when you use the Layout ➤ Align options, first try getting the text boxes and controls into approximate alignment by individually dragging their move handles. Then try using Layout ➤ Align to refine that alignment.

Changing the Font and Justification

You can change the font and justification of text in controls by using tools that appear on the tool bar after you select one or more controls:

1. Select whichever control(s) you want to change. As usual, you can choose just the labels, just the text boxes, or both.

NOTE The buttons for selecting fonts and text justification appear on the tool bar only when you have selected one or more controls on the form.

2. To change the font, use the tool bar options shown below to choose a typeface and/or size, and to select any combination of boldface, italics, and underline:

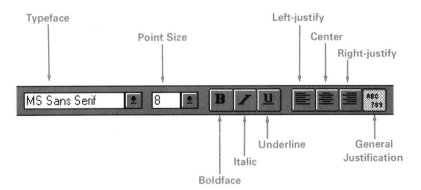

CREATING CUSTOM FORMS

3. To change the justification, choose one of the alignment options in the toolbar: Left, Right, Centered, or General. (General alignment aligns text to the left, and numbers to the right within their boxes.)

Sizing the Control to the Font

If you increase or decrease the size of the font significantly, you can quickly resize the surrounding box to better fit the new font:

1. If the controls are still selected, skip this step. Otherwise, select the control(s) that you want to resize.

2. Choose Layout ➤ Size to Fit.

As an example of changing fonts, I first selected just the labels shown below (not the text boxes) by dragging the pointer through them. Then I chose *Lucida Calligraphy, 8 points* as the font, with no boldface, italic, or underlines. I then chose Layout ➤ Size to Fit to ensure that each label's box was sized to fit the text within it:

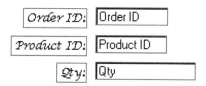

NOTE

Only fonts that you purchased and installed on your system for use in Windows will be available in the list of fonts. Lucida Calligraphy is one of the fonts from Microsoft's TrueType Font Pack.

Changing Colors and Special Effects

To change the colors and special effects of controls:

1. Select whatever controls you want to change colors in. As usual, you can select just the labels, just the text boxes, or both.

2. Click the Color Palette button (shown at left) or choose View ➤ Palette to view the palette. (If necessary, you can drag the palette by its title bar so it doesn't cover the control you're changing.)

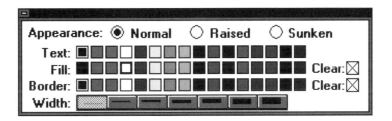

3. Choose appearances and colors as follows:

    Appearance Choose *Normal*, *Raised*, or *Sunken*, as below:

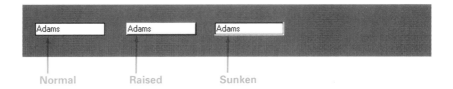

    Text Choose a color for the text (the actual letters).

    Fill If you want the background color of the control to match the color of the form, choose the *Clear* option. Otherwise, deselect the Clear option and choose a color from the Fill row.

    Border If you want to hide the control's borders (in form view) choose the *Clear* option. If you want to be able to see the borders, choose a color from the Border row.

Width: Choose a width for the border. (The border will only be visible if its color isn't set to *Clear*.)

Changing the Form's Background Color

You can also use the palette to change the color of the form background:

1. If the color palette isn't already visible, choose View ➤ Palette or click the color palette button in the tool bar.

2. Click the form background color within the section you want to re-color, i.e., within the form Header or Detail band. Make sure no controls are selected.

3. Choose a color from the Fill row in the Color Palette.

You can leave the color palette on the screen and choose other controls to color, if you like. Or, if you want to remove the palette, choose View ➤ Palette again, or double-click its Control-menu box.

Adding Bound Controls to Display Data from the Table

When you create a form with a Wizard, the Wizard automatically places bound controls for fields from the underlying table onto the form. But there are several situations where you might need to add a bound control to the form to display some field from the underlying table.

For instance, if you initially decided to exclude a field while going through the Wizard, you might change your mind and want to add it later. Or you might delete a control, then later decide you were better off leaving it in.

Then again, if you create the form from scratch, without the aid of a Wizard, the form won't have any controls on it initially. You'll need to add controls yourself.

To add a control to display data from the underlying table:

1. Make sure you're in the form design window.

2. Choose View ➤ Field List or click the Field List button (shown at left) in the toolbar. A field list for the underlying table opens up, as in Figure 9.4.

3. Select the field(s) you want to add to the list:

   • Click a single field name.,

   • *Or* Ctrl+click multiple field names.

   • *Or* Shift+click a range of field names.

   • *Or* double-click the field list's title bar to select all the field names.

FIGURE 9.4

To add bound controls for displaying data from the table to a form, first open the field list. Then drag the field named from the list onto the form.

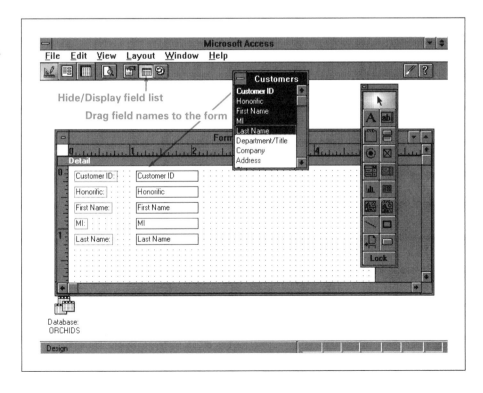

4. Drag the field name(s) from the list into the form, positioning the pointer to where you want the left edge of the text boxes (not the labels) to be. For example, to align the field near the left edge of the form, move the pointer about one inch from the left edge of the form before you release the mouse button. That will leave an inch for the label to the left of the text box.

Access adds the control(s) to the form. You can size, move, delete, align, and change the controls once they're on the form using any of the methods described earlier.

Closing and Saving a Form

When you're done working with a form for the time being, you can close and save it as you would any other object:

1. Choose File ➤ Close while viewing the form, or double-click the form window's Control-menu box.

2. If you've changed the design of the form, Access will ask if you want to save those design changes. Choose Yes if you want to save the current form design.

3. If you've never given the form a name, type a descriptive name, up to 64 characters (with spaces), then choose OK.

Opening a Saved Form

Once you've closed and saved a form, you can open it as you would any other object.

TIP

Opening a form automatically opens its underlying table. You need not open the table first.

1. Choose the Form button in the database window. A list of all saved forms appears.

2. Double-click the name of the form you want to open. Or, click the name of the form, then click Design if you want to open the form to make changes.

3. You can move and size the form's window, if necessary, using standard Windows techniques.

Practice Makes Perfect

Knowing *how to* arrange, size, and align controls, and how to change fonts, colors, and other properties, is one thing. But to get the hang of it you really need to practice. A good way to get that practice is to use the FormWizard to create a single-column form, with the Standard or Embossed look, and use that as your starting point.

You can do wonders with just the techniques we've discussed so far. For instance, Figure 9.5 shows a sample form (in form view, not design view) based on the Customers table that I initially created using the single-column FormWizard and an embossed look. In design view, I used techniques described earlier in this chapter to move, position, size, and change controls to my liking.

Figure 9.6 shows another example, where I created a form for the Categories table, again using the single-column FormWizard as a starting point. Once again, I used the basic techniques described earlier in this chapter to move, size, and position controls on the form.

FIGURE 9.5

A sample form based on the Customers table, initially created with a single-column FormWizard, and redesigned using basic techniques described earlier in this chapter.

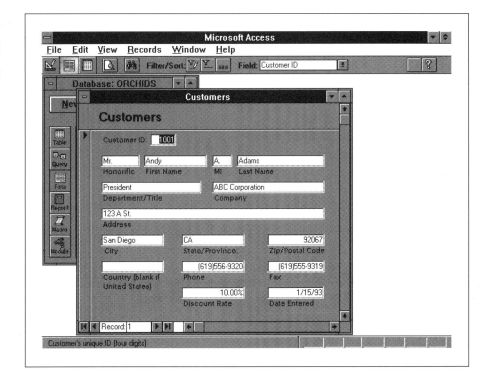

The sample form in Figure 9.6 looks quite a bit fancier than the one in Figure 9.5, but that's only because the underlying table structure contains OLE Object and Memo data type fields. Specifically,

- The flower picture and the icons at the bottom of the form are OLE Objects that are stored in the underlying table (Categories), using OLE techniques described in Chapter 5.

- The Description field is a memo field.

FIGURE 9.6

A sample form based on the Categories table, initially created using a single-column FormWizard, and redesigned using the basic techniques described earlier in this chapter.

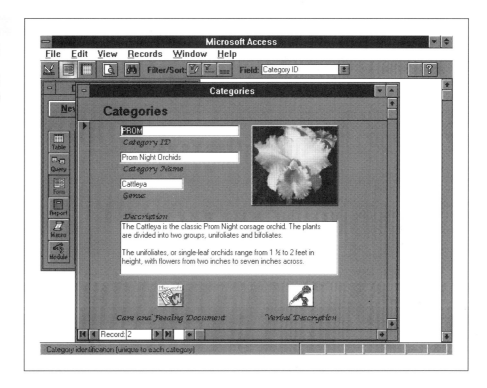

Even though the *table* in Figure 9.6 contains this fancier data, the techniques I used to design the *form* are the same techniques I've already described in this chapter.

Special Techniques for Form View

There are a couple of special techniques that you can use in form view while you're managing data with your completed form.

Using Filter/Sort to Select and Sort Records

Whenever you're viewing or editing data in form view, (and even if you switch to datasheet view while a form is open), the Filter/Sort options will be available in the tool bar. These let you perform a temporary, instant query of the table data.

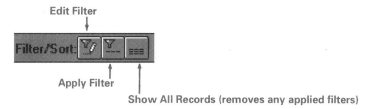

Edit Filter

Apply Filter

Show All Records (removes any applied filters)

To use the Filter/Sort buttons:

1. Click the Edit Filter button, or choose Records ➤ Edit Filter/Sort to view the *filter window.*

2. As in a regular query, drag the names of any fields that you want to use for sorting or selection criteria to the grid.

3. Choose sort orders and enter selection criteria as you would in a normal query. For instance, Figure 9.7 shows a QBE grid designed to limit records to those with dates in February of 1993, and to sort records into ascending alphabetical order by name.

4. Click the Apply Filter button or choose Records ➤ Apply Filter/Sort.

As you scroll through records, only records that meet the criterion will appear, and they'll be presented in the sort order you specified.

Removing a Filter

When you want to see all the records in the table again, just click the Show All Records button, or choose Records ➤ Show All Records.

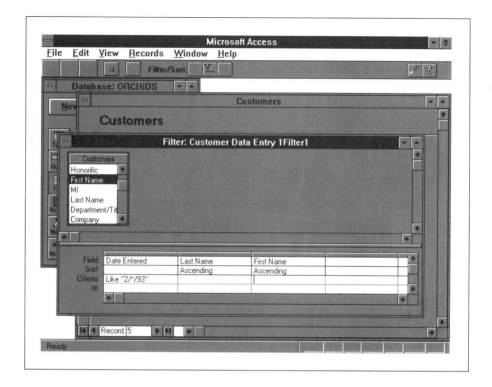

Saving a Filter as a Query

Access assumes that you used Filter/Sort to create a temporary query on the fly, so it doesn't save the filter when you close the form. But if you think you might want to use the filter again in the future, you can save it as a query:

1. With the form still open, get back to the filter window by clicking the Edit Filter button or choosing Records ➤ Edit Filter/Sort.

2. Choose Files ➤ Save As Query.

3. Enter an Access name and choose OK.

The filter is saved in a query, and will be available in the list of other saved queries when you choose the Query button in the database window. You can then reload that query into the form's filter window, as needed, or use it as a regular stand-alone query, as though you originally created it in the standard query window.

Using a Saved Query as a Filter

You can load a query into the filter window of the current form, regardless of whether you originally created that query from a filter or from the standard query window. However, the query that you load into a filter window must meet certain requirements:

- It must be based on the same table as the form, and may not contain any additional tables.
- It cannot contain totals, and it must be a select query—not an action query or crosstab.

To load the query into the filter window of a form:

1. Open the form in form view, and get to its filter window.
2. Choose File ➤ Load From Query.
3. Choose the name of the query you want to copy, then choose OK.
4. Choose the Apply Filter button, or Records ➤ Apply Filter/Sort.

Quick-Printing a Form

In Chapter 12 we'll get into all the details of printing and using print preview to display the information you want from your *tables*. For now, however, you can learn the basics of "quick-printing" data from a *form*.

1. Open the form in form view.

2. If you want to print just a single record, scroll to that record, then click the large Record Select button at the left edge of the form window, or choose Edit ➤ Select Record.

3. Choose File ➤ Print. Now you can do any of the following:

   - If you want to print just the currently selected record, choose Selection, then choose OK.

   - If you want to print all the records, or all the records that pass the criteria you've applied in a filter, choose *All*, then choose OK.

Because the form is graphical, it may take a while for the printer to get going.

Changing the Tab Order of Fields on a Form

When you use a form in form view, you can press Tab and Shift+Tab to move from field to field. If you've rearranged the fields on the form in design view, the focus might move through fields in a somewhat haphazard order. To correct that, or to define your own custom tab order:

1. Open the form (if it isn't already open) and switch to design view.

2. Choose Edit ➤ Tab Order to get to the **Tab Order** dialog box.

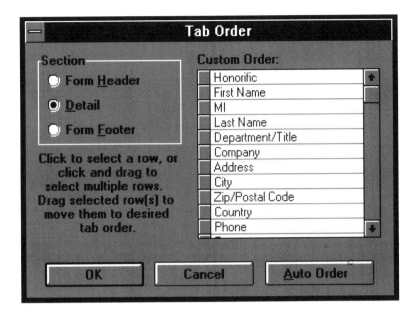

3. If you simply want Access to correct the current tab order so tht the focus moves through fields in the normal left-to-right, top-to-bottom order, choose Auto Order, then choose OK, then skip the remaining steps.

4. If you want to define your own order, rearrange the order of field names accordingly by clicking and dragging, as instructed on the form.

5. Choose OK.

As usual, you can test the new tab order by switching to form view and trying it out.

Tips for Managing Forms

For the remainder of this chapter, we'll look at some general tips and techniques for managing your forms.

Copying a Form to Another Table or Database

If you have two tables with similar structures, and want to copy a form that you created for the one table to the other table:

1. If the form you want to copy is currently open, close and save it.

2. Go to the database window and click the Form button to view the list of form names.

3. Click the name of the form you want to copy, then choose Edit ➤ Copy.

TIP

If you want to copy the form to a table in another database, choose File ➤ Open Database to open that other database now, and click the Form button in that database's window.

4. Choose Edit ➤ Paste, type in a name for the new form, and choose OK.

5. Now click the name of the form you just created, then click the Design button to view that form in design view.

6. Choose Edit ➤ Select Form.

7. Choose View ➤ Properties or click the Properties button.

8. Change the first option in the properties sheet, *Record Source,* to the name of the table you want to base this copy of the form on.

9. Make the same change to the *Caption* option.

T I P You can double-click the entry in Record Source, press Ctrl+C to copy it to the Clipboard, then double-click the current Caption entry, and press Ctrl+V to paste in the replacement.

10. You might also want to change the text in the form header band using the standard techniques to change a label (double-click the label and make your changes).

11. Choose File ➤ Close and choose Yes to save your changes.

Deleting or Renaming a Form

You can delete or rename a form as you would any other object:

1. Click the Form window in the database window to view form names.

2. Click the name of the form you want to rename or delete.

   - To rename the form, choose File ➤ Rename and enter the new name for the form.
   - To delete the form, press the Delete key.

Copying or Converting a Form to a Report

If you want to convert a form to a report, or use a form as the starting point for designing a report with a similar structure:

1. Open the form you want to copy in design view.

2. Choose File ➤ Save As Report, enter a name for the report, and choose OK.

3. Close the form and return to the database window.

When you click the Report button in the database window, the form will be listed as a report, and you can treat that copy of the report as you would any other report.

Summary

The techniques you've learned in this chapter will put you well on your way to designing forms that are perfectly tailored to your own needs and tastes. In the next chapter we'll look at more advanced techniques for designing and personalizing forms.

10

Creating Visually Exciting Forms

fast TRACK

To add a regular bound control to a form   **432**

drag the field's name from the field list onto the form. For other types of controls, use tools in the toolbox.

To create a calculated control   **434**

choose the Text Box tool from the toolbox, then choose wherever you want to place the control on the form. Then enter an expression, starting with an equal sign (=), into the Control Source property of the properties sheet.

To create bound graphical controls   **439**

such as combo boxes, option buttons, and check boxes, choose the appropriate tool from the toolbox. Then click and drag the appropriate field name from the field list onto the form.

IN THIS chapter I'll look at more techniques for designing and personalizing forms. As you'll see, you can use a wide variety of controls and properties to make your forms visually exciting and easy to use.

In a nutshell, controls and properties are what it's all about. You design a form by creating controls and assigning properties to those controls. It's really quite simple once you get the hang of it. But it certainly helps to have an understanding of what those buzzwords, *controls* and *properties,* are really all about. Let's start with properties.

Working with Form Properties

Every object on the form design screen, including labels, text boxes, and the form itself, has certain *properties,* or characteristics, assigned to it. For instance, the font and colors are properties that you can assign to a control.

You can view all the properties for a given object whenever the form is open in design view, by following either of these steps:

- Double-click the text box, label, or report section that you want to view the properties of.

- Select a single label, text box, or other object, then click the Properties button (shown at left), or choose View ➤ Properties.

The properties sheet appears, showing all the properties for the current control or section, as in the example shown in Figure 10.1.

FIGURE 10.1

A sample properties sheet, showing properties assigned to a text box on the form

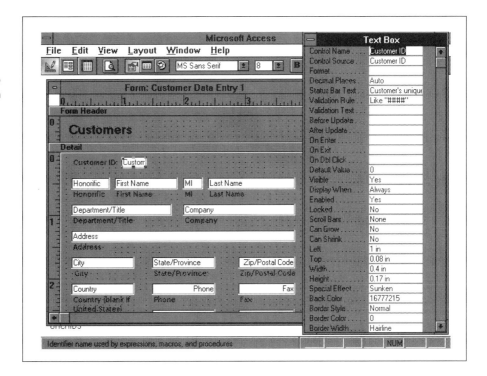

As you create more sophisticated forms, you'll surely be visiting the properties sheet more frequently. Here are some general points to keep in mind about this sheet:

- You can move and size the properties sheet using the standard Windows techniques.

- The properties-sheet title bar always shows what type of item you're assigning properties to, such as Text Box, Label, Form, or Section.

- If you select multiple controls, the properties sheet will be empty, because each control has its own unique properties, and the sheet can only show the properties of one control at a time.

- To change a property, click the appropriate option within the properties sheet. Type in a new value or choose an option from the drop-down list (if a drop-down button appears).

TIP Once you've chosen an item in the properties sheet, the status bar presents a brief description of what that property controls. Pressing Help (F1) takes you to the Help screen for that specific property.

* Any property that you change within the properties sheet takes effect as soon as you leave the option by pressing Tab or clicking some other part of the screen.

* You can change colors, fonts, size, and other properties using techniques described in the preceding chapter, even while the properties sheet is open. Both the form itself and the properties sheet, will reflect those changes.

* You can use the Zoom key (Shift+F2) to zoom in on any properties that might contain lengthy text, such as the Status Bar Description property.

* The properties sheet is always on top of the form design window. To close the properties sheet to get it out of the way, click the Properties button in the tool bar again, or choose View ➤ Properties again.

With these basics in mind, let's take a look at some properties you can use in a form.

Format, Validation, and Default Values in Forms

If you click the text box for a bound control on your form, and view its properties sheet (as I did back in Figure 10.1), you'll notice that the sheet offers several properties that you may have already assigned to fields in the underlying table, including

* Format
* Decimal Places
* Status Bar Text (same as the Description column in the table design)

- Validation Rule
- Validation Text
- Default Value

N O T E   If you need a reminder on the roles played by any of these properties, refer to "Changing Field Properties" in Chapter 6.

When you first create a form, the controls within the form inherit these properties from the underlying table design. But you can change any of the properties for a field, within the form design, using the same basic techniques and types of expressions you used in the table design.

The *difference* between assigning those properties here in the form and assigning them in the table design is that the properties you assign within the form come into play *only* when you're using the form. That is, the properties that you assign within the form override the properties you assigned in the table design, but only while you're using the form in form view.

Thus, when you go back to your original table design, or work with the table in datasheet view without the form being opened, the properties you assigned in the table design come back into play.

Changing Properties for the Entire Form

The properties sheet shown back in Figure 10.1 shows the properties for a single text box on the form. But you can also assign properties to the form as a whole. To get to the Form properties sheet:

1. In design view, choose Edit ➤ Select Form, or double-click the gray area outside the form's background (but within the design window).

2. Open the properties sheet (if it isn't already open).

NOTE

Remember, the properties sheet, palette, and field list are all *toggles* that you can open (display) or hide (close) at any time in design view, using buttons on the tool bar or options on the View menu.

The title bar of the properties sheet will display the title Form and present a whole new set of properties, as shown in Figure 10.2. Let's take a look at how you can use some of those properties to change the appearance of your form.

FIGURE 10.2

The Form properties sheet, made available by selecting Edit ➤ Select Form, displays properties assigned to the form as a whole.

Changing the Default View

The Default View property for the form lets you choose any one of three default views, which will come into play when you switch to form view:

Single Form   Only one record at a time appears within the form in form view, regardless of the size of the form's window.

Continuous Form   As many records as will fit within the form window are visible.

Datasheet   Fields from the form are shown in datasheet view when you first open the form. But the form's properties are still in effect, and you can click the Form View or Design button to switch instantly to the form or design view.

Figure 10.3 shows a small sample form, named Employee Rolodex, in the three different views. In particular, notice how the continuous form setting displays two records within the form window. The Single Form setting displays only one record, even though there's enough room for another record within the form window.

Changing the Default Editing Status

While changing the properties of the form as a whole, you can also choose one of the following default editing modes. The editing mode will be in effect as soon as you open the form in form view.

Allow Edits   The Editing Allowed option on the Records menu is selected as soon as you open the form, so data can be added, changed, and deleted at will.

Read Only   The Editing Allowed option on the Records menu is deselected when you first open the form, so no editing is permitted. Choosing Records ➤ Editing Allowed, however, instantly changes the form back to full editing status.

FIGURE 10.3

Examples of
continuous form,
single form, and
datasheet views of a
sample form named
Employee Rolodex

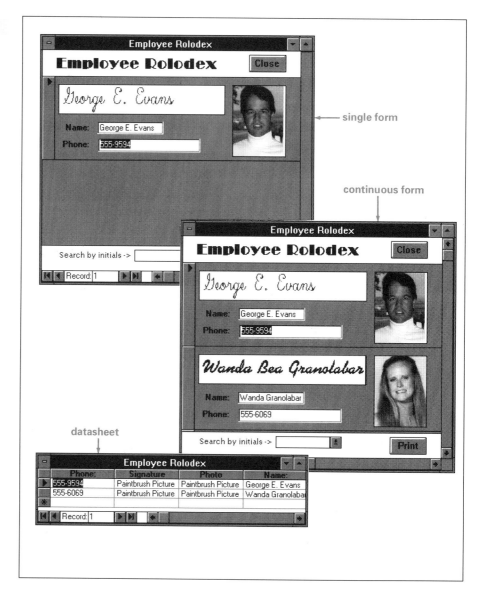

Data Entry   Selects Records ➤ Data Entry as soon as you open the form, so that existing records are hidden, and only new records can be added and edited. Choosing Records ➤ Show All Records at that point reverts to normal editing.

Making a True Read-Only Form

Suppose you want to create a form that *never* allows the person who is using the form to edit data in the table. In that case, you need to get to the Form properties sheet, and set the Default Editing property to Read Only and the Allow Editing property to Unavailable, like this:

| Default Editing . . . | Read Only |
| Allow Editing . . . . | Unavailable |

When using the form in form view, the Editing Allowed option on the Records menu will be deselected, and also dimmed and unavailable for selection.

Changing the Form Window's Title Bar

To change the title that appears in the title bar of the form's window, in form view, delete the current entry next to Caption in the Form properties sheet. Then type in whatever new title you want to give to the window.

Changing the Form's Underlying Table or Query

You can use the Record Source property on the Form properties sheet to choose a different underlying table or query for the form. For an example of where this property comes in handy, see "Copying a Form to Another Table or Database" in Chapter 9.

Form Header and Footer Sections

As mentioned in the previous chapter, a form that you create with a Wizard always has a form header and footer. The header contains the form title that you define while using the Wizard. The form footer is always empty.

Regardless of whether you use a Wizard to create the form or not, you can actually divide your form into as many as five separate sections:

Form header   Use the form header to display information that appears once at the top of all the forms. You might use this header for a form title, your company name and address, or even buttons and other controls (described later in this chapter) to make the form easier to use. The form header normally appears once at the top of the form window, and also once atop any records that you print with the form.

Page header   A page header never appears on the screen, but appears once at the top of each printed page when you use the form to print records. Use this section to create a page heading of column titles, page number, or any other information that you want to appear at the top of the page.

Detail section   The detail section displays the data from the table, both on the screen and in the printed report.

Page footer   The page footer never appears on the screen, but does appear at the bottom of each printed page. Like the page header, you can use this section to print page numbers, the current date and time, and any other information you want to print at the bottom of each page (using calculated controls with the =Page, =Date() , and =Now() functions).

Form footer   The form footer appears at the bottom of the design window (if space permits), and also once, after the last record, when you print the form. Like the form header, you can use this section to add titles, buttons, and other unbound controls.

Adding and Deleting Sections

A form always has a detail section, but the header and footer sections are optional. To insert and delete headers and footers:

1. In the form design view, choose Layout from the menu bar.

The Page Hdr/Ftr and Form Hdr/Ftr options will be checked if those sections are already in the form or unchecked if those sections are not in the form.

2. To insert or delete a pair of sections, click the appropriate option. To leave the setting as is, click outside the menu.

CAUTION   You can't "undo" deleted sections!

If you delete a pair of sections, Access will first present a warning indicating that deleting the sections will also delete the controls within them. If you want to delete those controls, choose OK. If you change your mind, choose Cancel.

Sizing Sections

To change the height of a section:

1. Move the mouse pointer to the *bottom* of the section you want to resize, until the pointer becomes a two-headed arrow. For

instance, to resize the form header, put the two-headed arrow at the bottom of that section, like this:

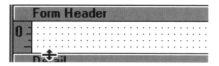

2. Drag the icon up or down until the section is the size you want, then release the mouse button.

Coloring a Section

To color a section within the form:

1. Click the bar at the top of the section that you want to color, or click any empty area within the section.

2. Open the color palette by choosing View ➤ Palette or by clicking the Color palette button on the tool bar.

3. Choose a color from the Fill row.

Filling Sections

For the most part, you always want to put bound controls, which represent data that comes directly from the table, into the detail section of the form. But you can add unbound controls, such as labels, calculated controls, and pictures, to the headers and footers using tools in the toolbox, described a little later in this chapter. For example, Figure 10.4 shows a sample form, in design view, with all five sections filled in.

When you switch to form view, the form header and footer will be visible, but the page header and footer will not be visible, as in Figure 10.5.

A report design with the form header/ footer and page header/footer sections filled in.

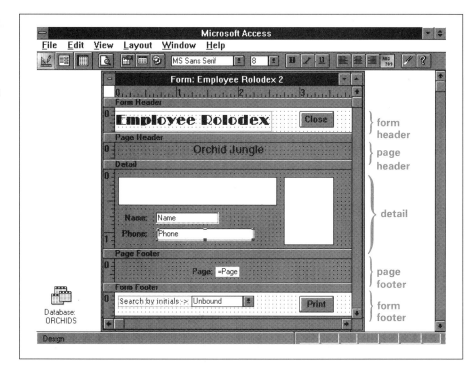

There are two ways to view a page header and form footer in a form, either by actually printing the form or by switching to Print Preview. To use Print Preview, choose File ➤ Print Preview, or just click the Print Preview button (the magnifying glass over a page). Once in Print Preview, you can do any of the following:

- Move the mouse pointer, which looks like a magnifying glass in Print Preview, to any area of the page that you want to zoom in on, and then click the mouse button.

- Use the Zoom button to switch between full-page and close-up views.

- Use the Setup button to choose a printer, orientation, and so forth.

- Use the Print button to print the forms.

- Click the Cancel button to leave Print Preview and return to your previous view of the form.

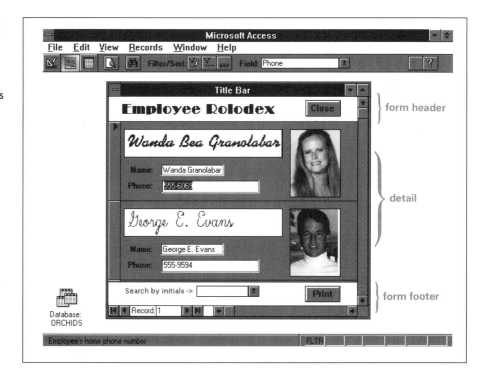

Figure 10.6 shows the sample form in full-page Print Preview. Though the page is tiny, it does give you a good idea of where the various header and footer sections will appear. You can zoom in, as necessary, on any section that you want to inspect more closely.

Changing Section Properties

You can set various properties for sections within the form by following these steps:

1. Double-click the bar at the top of the section, or double-click within the section (but not on a control within that section).

2. The properties sheet's title bar shows Section when you're assigning properties to the section as a whole.

FIGURE 10.6

Print Preview gives you a bird's-eye view of where various sections of the form will appear when you print the form.

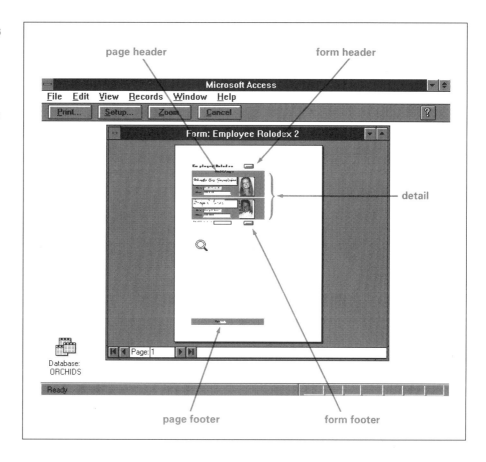

As usual, the meaning of each option in the properties sheet is displayed in the status bar when you choose that option. You can press Help (F1) to get more in-depth help with the property.

Hiding the Form Header and Footer Bands

The Display When property, which is available when you're changing the properties of the form header or form footer section, lets you decide when these sections are displayed. For instance, if your form header and footer contain buttons or other controls that aren't really useful on a printed form, you can hide those sections when printing. Just choose the Display When property in the properties sheet, and choose Screen Only from the list that appears. Repeat the same procedure for the form footer band.

Using the Toolbox to Create Controls

Whereas the properties sheet lets you change characteristics of items that are already on your form, the toolbox plays a much different role. It lets you *create* new controls for the form.

These tools lets you add bound, unbound, and calculated controls to a form. As mentioned in the previous chapter, you can choose View ➤ Toolbox to turn the toolbox on and off, and you can move it around by dragging its title bar.

Also, as mentioned in the previous chapter, you can create a "regular" bound control for a field simply by dragging the name of the field from the field list onto the form. The Toolbox lets you create other kinds of controls, which you can use to enhance the appearance and usability of your form. Here's a summary of what's available in the toolbox:

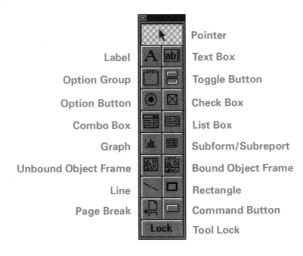

Pointer   Deselects a previously selected tool to get you back to the normal mouse pointer. You use the pointer to work with controls that are already on the form. All the other tools let you create new controls.

Label   Use this tool to add descriptive, unbound text to a form.

Text Box   Use this tool to add a calculated control, or a bound control for displaying data from the table.

Option Group   Use this tool to add a group of mutually exclusive options consisting of option buttons, check boxes, or toggle buttons.

Toggle Button   Use this tool to create a toggle button.

Option Button   Use this tool to create an option button.

Check Box   Use this tool to create a check box.

Combo Box   Use this tool to create a text box with a drop-down list.

List Box   Use this tool to create a list box.

Graph   Use this tool to add a graph to the form (see Chapter 13).

Subform/Subreport   Use this tool to create a subform or subreport (see Chapter 11).

Unbound Object Frame   Use this tool to put an independent picture on the form.

Bound Object Frame   Use this tool to display pictures and icons stored in the table.

Line   Use this tool to draw lines.

Rectangle   Use this tool to draw rectangles.

Page Break   Use this tool to create a page break on the form.

Command Button   Use this tool to create your own command buttons.

Tool Lock   Use this tool to keep the current tool selected until you select some other tool.

CREATING VISUALLY EXCITING FORMS

Figure 10.7 shows a sample form (in form view) with just a few of the types of controls that you can create with the toolbox added to it.

Before you start using the toolbox, here are some things you might want to know to make your work a little easier, as described next.

Setting Default Properties for Tools

When you use the toolbox to add controls to a form, Access will automatically assign certain default properties to each control you create. If you already know what properties you're going to want these new controls to

FIGURE 10.7

A sample form with labels, a calculated control, a combo box (open), and command buttons—just a few of the controls you can add to a form with tools from the toolbox

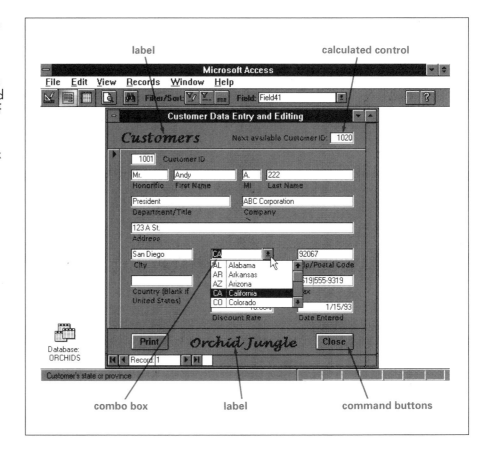

have, you can preassign the defaults before you create the controls. That way, if you add several similar controls to the form, they'll all have the same properties right off the bat.

To change the default properties for a control:

1. Make sure the toolbox is visible.

2. Open the properties sheet if it isn't visible (click the Properties button or choose View ➤ Properties).

3. Click whatever button in the toolbox you want to apply new properties to. The properties sheet heading and options change in accordance with the currently selected tool. Now you can do any of the following:

   • If the tool has color characteristics, open the color palette and choose default colors, borders, and special effects.

   • If the tool has font characteristics, choose font, style, and justification options from the tool bar.

   • Change any other properties by selecting options directly from the properties sheet.

You can then close the properties sheet, if you need to get it out of the way. Any new controls that you create with that tool in this form will now have the default characteristics that you assigned to the tool.

Copying an Existing Control's Properties to the Defaults

Another way to change the default properties for a tool is to copy the properties you've assigned to an existing control on the form into the default properties sheet for that tool. For instance, suppose you create an unbound label, then give it a certain color and font. You could copy that label's properties to the default values for the Label tool so that any additional labels you create have the same properties.

To copy a control's properties to the defaults:

1. Select the control that already has the properties that you want to use as the default.

2. Choose Layout ➤ Change Default.

Remember, only new controls that you create, of the same type, will have the new default properties.

Applying Default Properties to Existing Controls

If you change the default properties for a tool *after* you've already created some controls with that tool, and you want to go back and assign those properties to the controls you've already created, follow these steps:

1. Select the controls that you want to apply the new defaults to.

2. Choose Layout ➤ Apply Default.

How Tool Defaults Are Saved

When you change the defaults of a tool, those new defaults are saved as part of the current form. So even if you close and reopen the form, any new controls that you create will have the new default properties.

However, the default properties apply only to the current form. Other forms will continue to have whatever default properties you assigned in those forms.

Duplicating Controls

In some situations, you might want to create several tools of the same type. For instance, you might want to put several check boxes or option buttons on the form.

One way to do that would be to select the tool you want, then click the Tool Lock button. Then you can create multiple controls of the same type simply by clicking where you want each control to be. To unlock the tool, click Tool Lock again, then click the Pointer or some other tool.

You can also follow these steps to copy any control that you've already placed on the form:

1. Click the control that you want to copy.

2. Choose Edit ➤ Duplicate.

3. Drag the copied control to wherever you want it on the form.

How to Use the Tools

Regardless of which tool you want to use, the basic procedure you'll follow goes like this:

1. If you plan to replace a control that's already on the form with the new control, you might first want to delete that control to make room for the new one.

2. Click the tool that represents the type of control you want to create (e.g., Label, Text Box, Option Group). The pointer changes to an icon to represent the type of control you're creating, with a + sign. What you do next depends on whether or not you want to bind the control that you are creating to a field in the underlying table.

N O T E   Remember, a *bound control* is one that displays data from a field in the underlying table. An *unbound control* is on the form, but is independent of data in the underlying table.

- If you want to create a bound control, first open the field list (if it isn't already open), then click and drag the name of the field that you want to bind the control to onto the form. Place the icon where you want the upper-left corner of the control (not the attached label) to appear.

- If you want to create an unbound control, move the pointer directly into the form so that the + sign is where you want the upper-left corner of the control (not the attached label) to be. Then drag a box that approximates the size you want the control to be, or just click to create a default-size control.

Once the control is on the form, you can use any of the standard techniques to move and resize it, or change its color, font, or any other properties.

Adding Your Own Text to a Form

You can add your own text, such as a description, instructions, your own company name, whatever, to a form using the Label tool. The label is unbound and *static,* meaning that it doesn't change as you scroll through records in the table.

Labels that you create with the Label tool are also freestanding, which means that they are not connected to a control on the form. Thus, you can size and move the label in the form design independently of any other controls or text boxes.

NOTE   The titles *Customers* and *Orchid Jungle* in Figure 10.7 are examples of unbound labels.

To create a label:

1. Click the Label tool (shown at left) in the toolbox. The pointer changes to an A with a + sign.

2. Position the + sign where you want the upper-left corner of the label to appear.

- To create a label that's automatically sized to the text you want to type, just click the mouse button and then start typing.
- Or, to presize the box, drag the mouse pointer until the label is whatever size you want, then release the mouse button, and type your text.

If you want to type several lines of text into the label box, press Ctrl+↵ (rather than just ↵) to end the current line or to insert a blank line. If you presized the control, text will wrap within the box, and the box will grow in height, rather than in width, as you type new text.

You can then move or size the control, and change its font, color, or properties, using the standard techniques. To change the text within the control, select the control, then click where you want to make changes and make your changes. You can choose Layout ➤ Size to Fit to adjust the size of the control to the new text.

Attaching a Label to a Control

If you delete the label from a bound control, then change your mind and want to reattach a label, you can do so with the Label tool:

1. Click the Label tool, then click anywhere on the form and type whatever text you want into the label box.
2. Press ↵ to select the label.
3. Choose Edit ➤ Cut from the menu.
4. Select the text box (or other control) that you want to attach the label to.
5. Choose Edit ➤ Paste.

The label will now be attached to the text box. Thus, when you select the control in design view, both the label and the text box will be selected, so you can move them about the form in unison.

Adding a Calculated Control

A calculated control contains an expression and displays the results of that expression in form view. As in queries, the expression can contain field names (enclosed in square brackets), arithmetic operators, functions, and constants (such as 0.015 for 15%). You can also use the ampersand (&) to combine text in an expression (e.g., [First Name]&" "&[Last Name]).

N O T E   Expressions in general are discussed in Chapter 17.

Keep in mind that, when you're in form view, the calculated control displays the results of a calculation, but you cannot change the contents of that field on the form. Therefore, you wouldn't want to use an expression like [First Name]&" "&[Last Name] to display names on the form if you want to edit names when you're using the form to enter and edit data later.

To create a calculated control:

1. Click the Text Box tool (shown at left) in the toolbox.

2. Move the pointer into the form, then do either of the following:

   - To create a default-size control and label, click wherever you want the upper-left corner of the text box to be (leaving about an inch of blank space to the left for the label).

   - Move the pointer to where you want the upper-left corner of the text box to be (leaving about an inch of empty space to the left for the label), then drag the mouse until the box is the size you want.

3. Click inside the text box to get to the blinking insertion point.

4. Type in a valid expression, starting with an = sign.

5. To change the contents of the neighboring label, click the label to select it. Then click inside the label and add and delete text. (If you don't want the label, press Delete after you select the label.)

Examples of Calculated Controls

The sample form back in Figure 10.7 contains a calculated control in the form header. The expression in the text box is

=DMax([Customer ID],"Customers")+1

Here I used the DMax domain aggregate function to calculate the largest Customer ID number in the Customer ID field of the Customers table. The +1 at the end of the expression simply adds that number. The information is useful because, when adding a new customer to the table with the form, you can glance up at this field to see what the next available (unused) Customer ID number is.

NOTE   If you changed the Customer ID field from the Number data type to the Counter data type, the next available customer ID number wouldn't be particularly useful, because new customers would be assigned Customer ID numbers automatically! See "Converting a Number Field to a Counter Field" in Chapter 18 for more information.

Figure 10.8 shows a more complex form, named Order Summary, that displays information about a single order. This form is based on a query that combines information from the Orders, Customers, and Order

FIGURE 10.8

The Order Summary form displays summary information about an order.

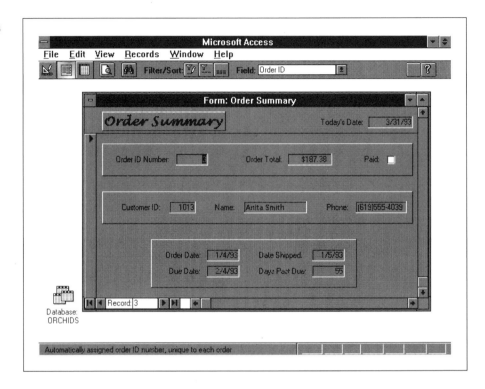

Details table. I'll discuss techniques for basing forms on multiple queries in the next chapter. But here, I'll focus on the calculated controls used in the form, as described below:

Today's Date   Contains the expression

=Date()

Name   Contains the expression

[First Name]&" "&[Last Name]

Due Date   Contains the expression

=[Date Shipped]+30

which calculates and displays the date 30 days past the shipped date.

Days Past Due: Contains the expression

=IIF(Not [Paid] And (Date()>[Date Shipped]+30),Date()-([Date Shipped]+30),0)

The IIF (immediate "if") function that this expression uses follows the general syntax IIF (*this is true, then do this, otherwise do this*), where commas separate the three main parts within the parentheses. In English, this expression says, "If the order is not paid yet, and today's date is more than 30 days past the ship date, then show the number of days that have transpired between today and the due date. Otherwise, just show zero."

The Order Total is calculated within the underlying query in a calculated field named Order Total. The field on the Order Summary form that displays the Order Total simply displays the contents of that field, and hence need not have its own calculation expression.

TIP I added the raised boxes around Order Summary and the various parts of the form using the Rectangle tool.

Zooming In on Complex Expressions

When you're entering a lengthy expression into a calculated control, you can get to the zoom box by going through the properties sheet.

1. Select the calculated control. If you've already started typing the expression, press ⏎. Otherwise, just click the control as usual. (If the expression is incomplete, you'll need to complete it, or delete it, before you can select the control.)

2. Click the Properties button or choose View ➤ Properties.

3. Click the Control Source option.

4. Press Zoom (Shift+F2). You'll be in the zoom box.

5. When you've finished editing the expression, choose OK to close the zoom box (or Cancel to abandon your changes).

6. Close the properties sheet (double-click its Control-menu box or press Alt+F4).

Check Boxes, Option Buttons, and Toggle Buttons

If your table contains a Yes/No field, you can use a check box, option button, or toggle button to insert a Yes or No into the field in the underlying table. Examples are shown below:

Data within the underlying Yes/No field is set as follows:

- If the check box is checked, the field contains Yes. If the check box is cleared (has no X), the field contains No.
- If the option button is selected (contains a dot), the field contains Yes. If the option is cleared, the field contains No.
- If the toggle button is depressed, the field contains Yes. If the toggle button isn't depressed, the field contains No.

If you use the check box, option button, or toggle button for a data type other than Yes/No, Access stores 0 in the field for a "No" value and -1 for a "Yes" value.

To add one of these controls to the form, click the appropriate tool for the type of control you want to create, as shown below:

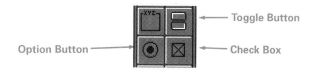

* If you want to bind the control to a field in the underlying table, click the name of the field that you want to bind the control to, and drag that field name onto the form.

* If you want to create an unbound control, just click the form where you want to place the control.

As usual, you can then change the label, and move the control using the standard techniques.

Special Techniques for Command Buttons

If you've created a command button, and just clicked for a default-size button, the button will initially be quite large. However, it will be selected and have sizing handles, so you can just resize it on the spot.

To put a label on the button, or change any text you've already put into the button:

1. Select the button, then click inside the button and type the button's label.

2. Press ↵ after typing to select the button.

3. Optionally, you can choose font options from the tool bar, or a text color from the palette.

4. To resize the button to fit the label, choose Layout ➤ Size to Fit.

You can also change the text on a button by going to its properties sheet and changing the Caption property. Optionally, you can add a picture to the button using the Picture property. See "Displaying a Picture on a Button" later in this chapter.

Converting an Unbound Control to a Bound Control

If you create an unbound option button, check box, or toggle button, then later decide to bind it to a field in the underlying table, select that control and get to its properties sheet. Choose the Control Source property, and choose the name of the field that you want to attach the control to from the drop-down list.

Adding Option Groups to a Form

An option group displays several mutually exclusive option buttons, toggle buttons, or check boxes. This is a handy way to present data when only a few options are available. But if the option group is bound to a field, the underlying field in the table should be the Number data type, because the option buttons will store a numeric value in the field: 1 for the first option button, 2 for the second option button, and so forth.

For instance, you could change the Payment Method field of the Orders table to the Number data type in the table design. Then you could store the value 1 for Check, 2 for Cash, or 3 for Invoice in that field. Then you could create an object group consisting of option buttons on a form for entering a payment method into that field, as below:

N O T E   If the Orders table already contains data with text entries, such as Check, Cash, Invoice, you would first want to convert those entries to numbers (1, 2, or 3) in datasheet view. *Then* go to the table design and change that field's data type to Number on the table design screen. As an alternative, you can leave the Payment Method field as the Text data type, then use a list box or combo box to display options.

The group can contain toggle buttons, rather than option buttons, as below:

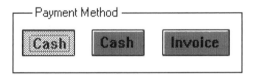

The group can contain check boxes, rather than option buttons, as below. However, it's not standard Windows practice to use check boxes for mutually exclusive options, so you might want to stick with option or toggle buttons to be Windows CUA (Common User Access) compatible.

To create an option group:

1. If you plan to bind the option group to a field that's already represented by a control on the form, first delete that control.

2. Click the option group button in the toolbox.

3. If you want the option group to be bound to a field, click the name of that field in the field list, then drag that field name into the form. If you want the group to be unbound, just click

wherever you want the option group to appear in the form, without going through the field list.

Access displays an empty option group box on the form, with the name of the bound field (if any) as the label, as below, or a generic label if you didn't bind the group to a field. You can change the size and shape of the box now, if you wish, using the Size handles. For instance, I gave the empty option group box below a rectangular shape by dragging its Size handles.

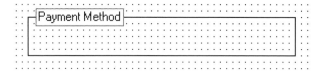

Next, you need to fill the option group with buttons or check boxes:

1. Click the Toggle Button, Option Button, or Check Box tool in the toolbox.

2. Click the Tool Lock tool at the bottom of the toolbox.

3. Move the pointer into the option group box. The box changes color, indicating that the control you're about to place will be within the object group.

4. Place each button or check box in the box by positioning the pointer within the box and clicking the mouse button.

5. To unlock the tool, click the Tool Lock tool after placing all the buttons or check boxes, then click the Pointer tool at the top of the check box.

In the example below, I placed three option buttons in the option group:

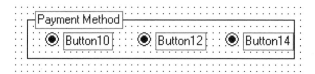

Next, you need to change each option's label to whatever you want the button or check box to represent on the form. Open the properties sheet, then click the label that you want to change (or in the case of a toggle button, just click the button). Then change the Caption property to the appropriate label. For instance, I changed the labels attached to each option below by clicking each label and changing its Caption property (you needn't change the Control Name property). After changing each label, you can use Layout ➤ Size to Fit to fit the surrounding box to the label.

To see what value each option in the group represents, click the button or check box (not the attached label), and take a look at the Option Value property. By default, the first option has an option value of 1, the second has an option value of 2, and so forth. In the example below, you can see that the third option button (selected) will have an option value of 3. That is, when I select that option in form view, Access will store the number 3 in the underlying Payment Method field of the table.

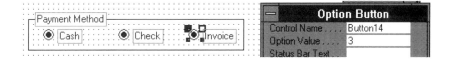

T I P If you want the option group to have a default value, select the option group by clicking its frame. Then set the Default Value property to one of the acceptable values, such as 1.

Finally, you can move, size, and align the options within the group, and the group box itself, so everything fits nicely. You can also use the color palette to color the group and give its border a special effect, perhaps

Raised. Here's the completed option group, in form view, after a little tidying up and coloring:

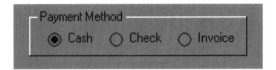

Adding a List Box or Combo Box to a Form

As you may already know from your day-to-day use of Windows, a list box presents a list of possible entries in a field. The list is always open and presents the only acceptable entries for the attached text box (if any). For example, the list under the Payment Method field below offers three possible options for that field: Cash, Check, or Invoice.

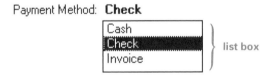

A combo box is a text box that has an optional drop-down list button attached to it. When using a combo box, you can either type an entry into the text box or click the drop-down list button and select an entry from the list that appears. The State/Province field shown below uses a combo box. In the example on the left, the list is closed. On the right, the list is open.

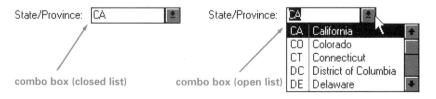

One advantage of a combo box is that it takes up less room on the form, because the attached drop-down list can be opened and closed at will. Another advantage of a combo box is that you have your choice of either limiting the entry in the attached text box to an item that matches something in the list or allowing the text box to contain anything. For instance, in the combo box that has states and their abbreviations, the drop-down list provides a quick reference to looking up the two-letter abbreviation for a state or territory within the United States. However, the State/Province field can actually contain anything, including a province or territory outside the United States.

Where Does the List Come From?

The items that appear in the list can come from any of the following:

Records from table or dynaset   The list can display selected fields and records from another table or dynaset. This type of list is generally preferred when the list is lengthy, or when you want the person using the form to be able to look up information that changes. For instance, if the list were designed to help the person using the form to look up a product ID number, you'd want to base the list on the Products table so that the drop-down list always shows current product information.

Fixed values   A set of values defined within the form's properties. You'll most likely use this type of list when there are very few items to display in the list, and the contents of the list never change.

Field names   A drop-down list can also display the field names from a table. This type of list, however, makes sense only when used in conjunction with macros.

Creating a Query to Use as a List

If you want the list to display records from a table, a good starting point is to design a query that displays fields and records as you want them to appear in the drop-down list. When designing this query, you want to

• Make sure that the field that contains the data that you want to appear in the text box is in the first (leftmost) column of the QBE grid.

- Include any other fields that you want to display in the drop-down list in the QBE grid as well.

- Define the sort order of rows in the drop-down list, by defining a sort order for records in the QBE grid.

After defining the query, you'll want to run it to make sure it displays the data you want the drop-down list to display. Then close and save the query so that you can attach the list or combo box to it later when working on your form. We'll take a look at an example in a moment.

Creating the List Box or Combo Box

Before you create a list box or combo box, be aware that when you create a bound combo box, you're also creating a label and text box for the field. Therefore, if there is already a control on the form for the field you intend to bind the combo box to, you should delete that control first.

With a list box, you have the choice of whether or not you want to include an associated text box. Most Windows dialog boxes do have a text box associated with a list box. So if you plan to bind the list box to a field in the table, and there is already a control for that field on the form, you need not delete that control.

T I P

When positioning a list or combo box on the form, leave about an inch of empty space to the left for the attached label.

So now, to actually create the list box or combo box, you want to start out with the form in design view and then follow these steps:

1. Click the Combo Box tool or List Box tool in the toolbox, depending on which type of control you want to create.

combo box ⟶   ⟵ list box

2. If you want to bind the list box or combo box to a field in the underlying table, click that field's name in the field list, then drag that field name onto the form. If you want to create an unbound list or combo box, just click wherever you want to place the control without going through the field list.

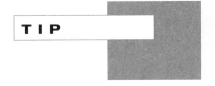

T I P

You only need to create an unbound combo or list box if you are going to attach a macro to its After Update property.

The control appears on the form. But before you can switch to form view and use the list or combo box, you need to assign its properties, as discussed in the upcoming sections.

Choosing the Row Source Type

Use the Row Source Type property to define where the rows in the list will be coming from:

Table/Query   The rows in the drop-down list come from records in a table or query. If you choose this option, the Row Source property must be set to the name of a table or query.

Value List   The rows in the drop-down list come from the properties sheet. If you choose this option, the Row Source property must contain the values to display in the list.

Field List   Each row in the drop-down list displays the name of a field in a table or dynaset. If you choose this option, the Row Source property must be set to the name of a table or query.

Defining the Row Source

The row source defines the actual source of the rows displayed in the drop-down list. If you chose Table/Query or Field List as the Row Source Type, choose the name of the query (or table) that contains the records that you want to display in the list.

If you chose Value List as the Row Source Type, type the values that you want to appear in the list, separating each item with a semicolon. For instance, if you want the drop-down list to display the three items Check, Cash, Invoice, you would type those options as shown next to Row Source below:

Defining the Column Count

Use the Column Count property to define how many columns you want to appear in the drop-down list. If the row source is a table or query, the Column Count property defines how many columns from the table or dynaset, from left to right, will appear in the list.

If the row source is a value list, the Column Count property will stagger items in the list across columns. For instance, if the Row Source Type is Value List, the row source is arranged in the order

First;Second;Third;Fourth;Fifth;Sixth

the Column Count is 2, and the column widths are each 0.5 inches, the list will look like this:

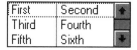

Choosing Whether or Not to Display Column Heads

If you set the Column Heads property to Yes, the list will have headings that describe what's in each column. If you set this option to No, the list won't have column headings. The headings themselves come from the row source:

• If the Row Source is a table or query, field names from the underlying table are used as column headings.

- If the Row Source is a value list, the first entry or entries in the list become the column heads (and cannot be selected from the list).

In the example below, I activated column heads to show the field names, Abbreviation and State, from the underlying query in the drop-down list. I also widened the first column to 0.75 inches and widened the list to 2 inches, to better display the column heads.

Defining Column Widths

Use the Column Width property to define the width (in inches) of each column in the list. Separate each measurement with a semicolon. For instance, in the Column Widths option below, I typed 0.75;1 for the column widths. Upon leaving that option, Access changes my entry to 0.75 in; 1 in, as shown:

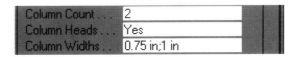

N O T E   If you prefer to work in centimeters, follow each entry with cm, e.g., 1cm;3cm.

If you want to hide a column from the table or query, set its width to zero (0). Even though the column won't appear in the list, you can still make it the Bound To column to copy its value from the list into the field.

Choosing the Bound Column

The Bound Column property defines which column in the list contains the data that will actually be copied into the text box that the list is attached to. Keep in mind that the text box always *displays* data from the first column in the drop-down list. But if you set the Bound Column property to some value other than 1, the field will actually *contain* the data from the specified column.

For instance, suppose you were to go back to the query for displaying state names and abbreviations, and reverse the columns so that the *first* column displays the state name, spelled out, and the second column displays the abbreviation. After you save that query and return to the form (and change the measurements on the combo box to widen the first column and narrow the second), the combo box looks like the one below:

Even if you set the Bound Column entry to 2 for this combo box, the text box will continue to *show* the spelled-out state name—California in the example above—because the spelled-out state name is in the first column of the list. Changing the Bound Column entry to 2 has no effect on the fact that the combo box always displays data from the first column in the list.

However, when you choose an item from the list, Access will actually *store* the data from the second column, the state abbreviation in this case, in the field. You'd see that the field actually contains the abbreviation, rather than the full name, *only* when viewing or printing data without this particular form.

This can make for a rather confusing situation, since the field seems to contain one thing when you're using the form, yet something else when you're not using the form. But this capability is not without merit. The beauty of it is that while using the form, you can see the "spelled-out" information, but the underlying table need only store the more compact abbreviation, which saves disk space.

Perhaps a more realistic example would be a field that uses some coding method, such as 1 for Cash, 2 for Check, and 3 for Invoice, to prevent you from having to spell out those words throughout the table. If you create a list or combo box that lets the person using the form choose one of those options, you can have the best of both worlds. That is, the underlying table will store the brief code 1, 2, or 3. But the person using the form would see the spelled-out equivalent Cash, Check, or Invoice, which is more meaningful.

Defining the Number of Rows to Display

By default, a list will display up to a maximum of eight rows, and a scroll bar appears if there are more than eight items in the list. You can use the Number Of Rows property to increase or decrease the maximum number of rows that the list displays.

Defining the List Width

This property defines the width of the list (not the attached text box). If you've defined the width of each column in the list, using the Column Widths property, the ideal List Width would be the sum of those column widths, plus about an extra 0.25 inches for the scroll bar that appears in the list.

TIP　　The scroll bar appears only when the list contains more rows than can fit in the box.

Limiting the Entry to a List Item

The Limit To List property, which is available only for a combo box, lets you decide whether or not the attached text box can contain only values from the list, or any value. The default setting is No, which allows the text box to contain any text. If you want the text box to contain only values that are included in the list, change this property to Yes.

For instance, I left the Limit To List property for the State/Province combo box set to No, because the person using the form might need to enter some province or territory name that's not in the list. The purpose of that combo box is simply to help the person using the form look up a state abbreviation as needed—not to limit what he or she can type into the field.

A Sample List Box

Earlier I showed how you could use an option group to display the options Cash, Check, Invoice for the Payment Method field. But, as explained, doing so requires changing the Payment Method field's data type to Number in the underlying table. If you don't want to store the numeric abbreviations in the field, you can leave the field as the Text data type and use a list box (or combo box) to present the three options.

Visually, the best way to do this on the form is to use the same method that most Windows dialog boxes use, where both the list and the selected item from the list appear on the form. For instance, in the example below I show the name of the field, Payment Method, the current entry in the field, Invoice, in bold, and the list box of options just below that field. I didn't frame Invoice in bold, however, because I want it to be apparent to the person using the form that the option is to be selected from the list box, not typed onto the form.

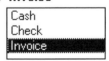

In this example, I'm using two controls for the Payment Method field: the standard text-box control to display what's in the field and a list box to allow the user to select an entry for the field.

At the form design screen, I started out by dragging just the Payment Method field from the field list onto the form, to create the standard text box. I made this a "read-only field" so that the person using the form wouldn't think they need to type an entry into the field, and to prevent the field from even being selectable by setting its Enabled Property to No, its Locked property to Yes, its borders clear, and the contents of the text box Bold (see "Creating a Read-Only Field" later in this chapter).

Then I clicked the List Box tool, dragged the Payment Method field from the field list onto the form, to just below the text box control for the Payment Method field, like this:

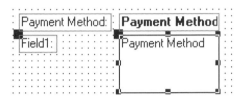

With the list box selected, I changed the first few properties as shown below:

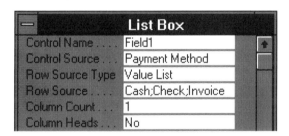

Then I deleted the attached Field1 label by selecting just the label and pressing Delete. Then I sized and moved the box, switching back and forth between design view and form view from time to time to check my progress, until I got just the look I wanted.

NOTE

If you create a list box for a field that doesn't already have a text box control, you can just drag that field name from the field list to the form to create the text box control for that field.

A Sample Combo Box: Looking Up State Abbreviations

The combo box for displaying two-letter state abbreviations is based on the States table (whose structure was shown in Chapter 6). As mentioned, this handy combo box lets you look up a two-letter state abbreviation while entering a United States address in the State/Province field.

To create this combo box, I first created the States table, and added a record for each state and territory within the United States. Then I created the query shown in Figure 10.9 for the States table.

- Abbreviation is the leftmost column in the QBE grid, because this is the field that contains the text that I want to actually copy into the form.

- The Sort By field in the Abbreviation field is set to Ascending so that the list will be alphabetized by that field for easy lookup.

FIGURE 10.9

A query, based on the States table, that defines the fields used in a combo box that I'll be adding to a form

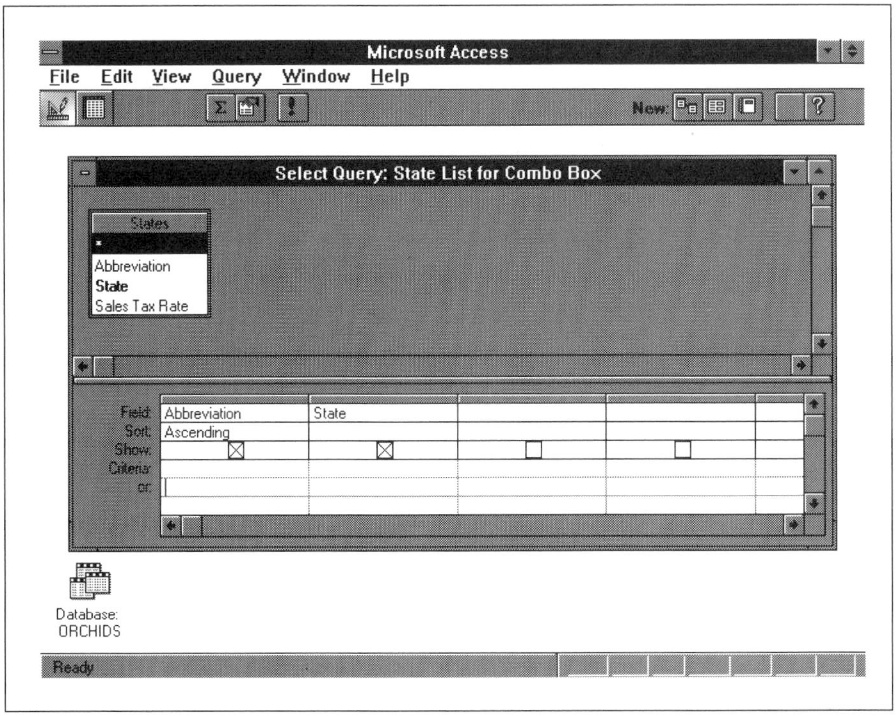

TIP

Access has a tendency to shift columns used for sorting over to the left of the QBE grid. To prevent this column arrangement from carrying over to a list box or combo box, arrange columns to your liking. Then copy the query's SQL statement to the list box's or combo box's Row Source property, as described in a moment.

Running this query shows that the selected fields and records are in the order that I want them to appear in the combo box, as Figure 10.10 shows. (Only the first 17 records fit in the window, but the dynaset contains records for all the states and territories.)

I then closed and saved that query with the name *State List for Combo Box*.

FIGURE 10.10

Results of the query shown in Figure 10.9

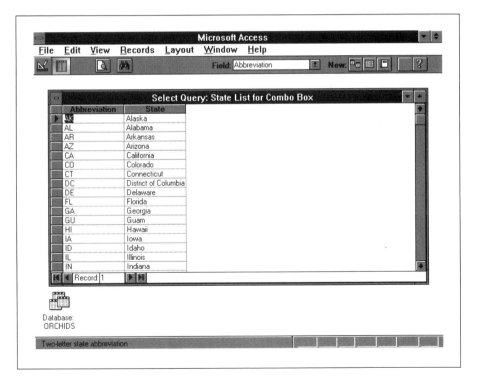

Then, I opened the form for entering customer data, in design view, and deleted the current control for displaying the State/Province field, because the Combo Box tool will create its own text box for that field. Then I clicked the Combo Box tool in the tool bar, clicked the State/Province field in the field list, and dragged that field name onto the form, as in Figure 10.11 (the combo box is next to the control for the City field). I also set the properties for that combo box as shown in the figure.

Remember, the combo list doesn't do anything in design view. To test it out, you need to switch to form view first.

FIGURE 10.11

Combo box for the State/Province field selected on the form, with its properties defined

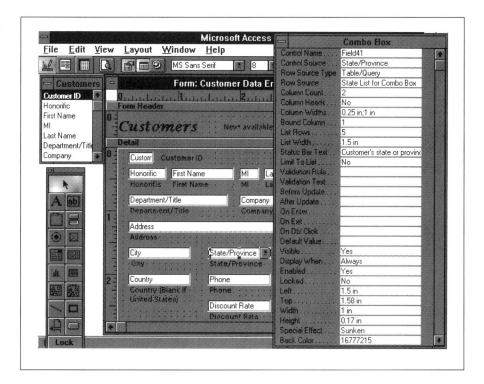

Using a SQL Statement to Display a Combo Box

You can use an SQL statement, rather than the name of a query, as the row source for a list box or combo box. Doing so will make the list or combo box independent of the original query, which offers two advantages:

- You can delete the query after you've created the list box or combo box, so you needn't build up a long list of queries just to support the lists.

- You need not worry that some other user is going to change the query that the list is based on, and therefore you can rest assured that the list will always look the same.

To use a query's SQL statement, rather than the query itself, for a list box or combo box:

1. First open the query in design view, and choose View ➤ SQL.

2. Select the entire SQL statement either by dragging the mouse pointer or by pressing Shift+Ctrl+End. Make sure the entire statement is selected, as in the example shown in Figure 10.12.

FIGURE 10.12

A SQL statement selected, and ready to copy to the Clipboard

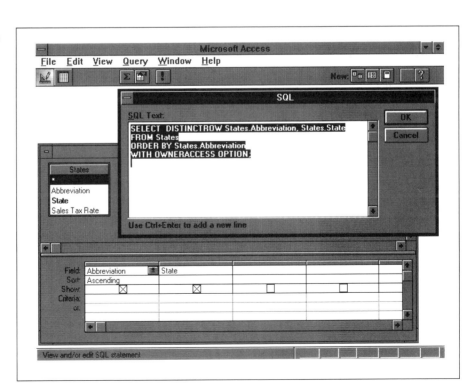

3. Press Ctrl+C to copy the SQL statement to the Windows Clipboard.

4. Choose OK to close the SQL dialog box, then close the query.

5. Open the form, in design view, and select (click on) the control for the list box or combo box that you want to copy the SQL statement to.

6. Open the properties sheet for the list or combo box.

7. Select the Row Source property (*not* the Row Source Type property), and zoom in on it (press Shift+F2).

8. Press Delete to delete the query name (make sure you delete the entire name).

9. Press Ctrl+V to paste the SQL statement into the Row Source property.

10. Choose OK to return to the properties sheet.

When you close the form, be sure to choose Yes when asked about saving changes. You can then delete the original query, if you wish. The form's list box or combo box will use the embedded SQL statement to query the underlying table. If you don't delete the original query, do keep in mind that *changing* that query will have no effect on the list box or combo box in the form, as that list is now independent of the original query.

Drawing Lines and Rectangles

You can use lines and rectangles to further refine the appearance of your form and to separate information into easily recognizable groups. For instance, I used some raised rectangles in the Order Summary form in Figure 10.8 to separate some information into groups. The form in Figure 10.13 shows some more uses of lines and rectangles, and a drop-shadow look as well.

FIGURE 10.13

A form with an unbound OLE object (the flower logo), a drop shadow on the company name, a line, and a couple of rectangles

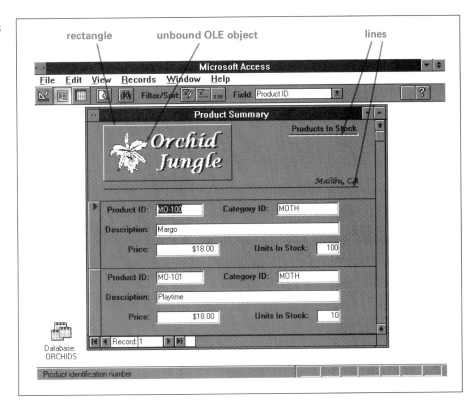

Drawing a Line

To draw a line in your form, make sure you're in design view, then follow these steps:

1. If you want to draw a straight vertical or horizontal line, hold down the Shift key. (If you plan to angle the line, don't hold down the Shift key.)

2. Click the Line tool.

3. Move the pointer to where you want to start the line, then drag a line in whatever direction you want to draw.

4. Release the mouse button when the line is drawn, then release the Shift key (if you started holding it down in step 1).

The line will be drawn (and selected) as soon as you release the mouse button. If you want to change the color or thickness of the line, use the color palette.

Drawing a Rectangle

To draw a rectangle on the form, in design view:

1. Click the Rectangle tool.

2. Move the + pointer to where you want the upper-left corner of the rectangle to be, then drag the pointer until the rectangle is the size you want, and release the mouse button. Optionally, you can just click to draw a default-size rectangle.

Initially, the rectangle will be opaque and cover anything behind it. To change the rectangle, be sure to select it (so it has sizing handles), then do any of the following:

- From the color palette, choose a border thickness, border color, and fill color. If you want the rectangle to be transparent, so you can see any controls behind it, set its Fill color to Clear.

- To give the rectangle a raised or sunken look, choose the appropriate appearance from the color palette.

- If you want to fill the rectangle with a color but put objects behind the rectangle on top of the rectangle, choose Layout ➤ Send To Back.

If the rectangle surrounds other controls, and you want to move the rectangle and all the controls within it as a group, you first need to select the rectangle and the items within it as adjacent controls. To select all the controls, either drag the mouse around the entire rectangle or use Shift+click. Then you can drag all the selected controls with the full-hand icon.

If you want to use the Rectangle tool to create a deep line (as under Products In Stock in Figure 10.13), you may need to turn off Snap To Grid, or hold down the Ctrl key as you drag the rectangle, so you can get the small height. Then choose Sunken from the Appearance options of the color palette.

Creating the Shadowed Look

To create a drop-shadow look, create the object and then make a duplicate of it using Edit ➤ Duplicate. Color the duplicate using the color palette, then drag it into position in relation to the first copy of the object. If Snap To Grid is on, you may need to hold down the Ctrl key while you drag to get the close alignment that you'll need.

For instance, to create the Orchid Jungle title, I first colored the section background gray by selecting the section and choosing the gray Fill color from the color palette. Then I created an unbound label containing the word Orchid, using the Label tool. I set the font to Lucida Calligraphy 20pt, set its Fill color to the same color as the background, and then chose Layout ➤ Size to Fit.

Then I chose Edit ➤ Duplicate to make an exact copy of that label. Then I chose white as the Text color in the color palette, and clear as the Fill color, which ends up looking like this:

Then I held down the Ctrl key to override Snap To Grid and dragged the white word Orchid until it partially overlapped the black one until I got just the look I wanted.

You can use a similar method to create a drop shadow behind a text box or other control. However, you first need to create a rectangle, using the Rectangle tool, that's the same size as the control. Give that rectangle whatever Fill color you want from the color palette. You might also want to set its Border color to clear in the color palette. In the example below, I created a gray rectangle that's the same size as the text box for the Product ID text box:

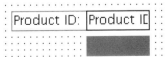

Drag the rectangle so that it's partially covering, though slightly offset, from the text box. You'll need to use a very fine grid, or use the Ctrl key to override snap-to-grid as you drag the rectangle to get it aligned as closely as you want.

Then choose Layout ➤ Send To Back to put the rectangle behind the text box. Switch to form view, and voila!, you have your drop shadow:

TIP The shadowed look in the FormWizards will automatically create the rectangular drop shadows behind all the text boxes on the form.

Adding a Picture to a Form

To add an unbound picture to a form, such as the logo at the top of Figure 10.13, you first need to create the picture either by scanning it to a bitmap file or by drawing it in an application that lets you create a bitmap, such as Paintbrush. While scanning or drawing the picture, try to size it as closely to whatever size you want to use in the form. Be sure to save the completed picture with the .bmp (bitmap) extension before adding it to your form.

Once you've created and stored the picture, there are many ways that you can link it to or embed it in a form (or in a report). I'll go into all the possibilities in Chapter 19, but here's the quick-and-dirty method for getting the job done:

1. Choose the Unbound Object Frame tool (shown at left).

2. Move the pointer into the form, and drag a box that's whatever size you want the picture in the form to be. When you release the mouse button, you'll see the **Insert Object** dialog box, as below

(though object types in the list will depend on what OLE applications are available on your system):

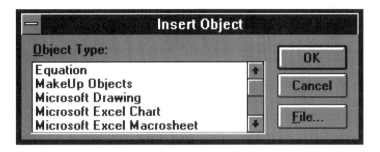

3. Choose the type of object you want to embed (e.g., Paintbrush Picture for a bitmap), then click the File button.

4. Go to the drive and directory where the picture is stored, then double-click its name in the File Name list.

CAUTION

The Paintbrush application in Windows 3.0 doesn't support OLE. OLE is only available in Windows 3.1 and subsequent releases.

If the picture doesn't fit the frame well, try setting the frame's Scaling property, in the properties sheet, to Zoom or Scale, and then resize the box to best fit the picture. I'll discuss the Clip, Zoom, and Scale properties in detail in Chapter 19.

If you want the background color of the picture to match the background color of the form, you need to recolor the original picture. Changing its Fill color in Access won't do the job. To change the object's background color, double-click the object on your form (in design view) to return to the source application. Then use *that* application to fill in or change the background color. Then choose File ➤ Exit and return to Microsoft Access from the source application's menu bar, and choose Yes to return to Access.

If you need more information, be sure to read up on Object Linking and Embedding in Chapter 19.

Displaying the Contents of an OLE Field

 When you drag the name of an OLE object field from the field list onto the form, Access automatically creates a Bound Object Frame control for displaying the contents of that OLE Object field in your table. You really don't need to use the Bound OLE Object Frame tool (shown at left) in the toolbox to create this type of control.

However, you might plan on adding controls for several OLE Object fields to the form and want them all to have the same properties. In that case, you can change the default properties for the Bound Object Frame tool in the toolbox, using techniques described in "Setting Default Properties for Tools" earlier in this chapter. For instance, you might change the default Special Effect property for Bound Object Frames to Raised, to give the controls a raised appearance. Then, any new Bound Object Frame controls that you add to the form will have that property. Or, you can use Layout ➤ Apply Default to copy the new defaults to any bound object frames that you've already added to the form.

Keep in mind that, unlike unbound object frames, you don't fill a bound object frame while you're in design view. Instead, just leave that frame empty. When you switch to form view, the control will display any pictures or icons that you've stored in the underlying OLE Object field of the table.

Adding Command Buttons to a Form

You can add a command button to a form, and then later attach a macro that performs some action when you click the button. For instance, you can create buttons to print the form, close the form, filter records, whatever. The button won't *do* anything until you create a macro and attach it to the button. But you can place the button on your form, just to get it sized and positioned, before you create the macro:

1. With the form open and in design view, click the Command Button tool (shown at left).

2. Move the pointer into the form, and either click for a default-size button or drag to draw a button sized to your liking. Initially, the button face will have a generic name, as below:

3. To change the text on the button, you can either click the button again and change the default name or change the Caption property in the properties sheet for the button.

If you want to resize the button to better fit the text you put on its face, you can select the button and choose Layout ➤ Size to Fit.

Displaying a Picture on a Button

If you want the button face to show a picture rather than text, you first need to create that picture, at whatever size you want it to be on the button. Then, in design view on your form, follow these steps:

1. Select the button that you want to put the picture on.

2. Open the properties sheet.

3. Select the Picture property, and enter the full path and file name of the picture that you want to put on the button.

4. Optionally, you can choose Layout ➤ Size to Fit to resize the button to fit the picture.

If you use Paintbrush to create (or edit) the picture that you want to put on the button, be sure to size the picture's drawing area to whatever size you want the button to be on the picture. Also, keep in mind that the picture's background will show up on the button, so you may want to color the background of the picture accordingly. For example, in Figure 10.14, I sized the drawing area to a small picture and colored in the background with the gray color.

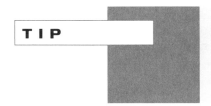

TIP

In Paintbrush, you use the Paint Roller tool to color the background. To reduce the size of the drawing area, define a small cutout around the picture, and use Edit ➤ Copy To to copy just the cutout to a file.

When you've finished creating the picture, you can exit Paintbrush and save the picture. Then go back to your form in Access, and follow the

FIGURE 10.14

A picture in Paintbrush to be used on a button face. The drawing area around the picture is just slightly larger than the picture, and its background is the color of the button.

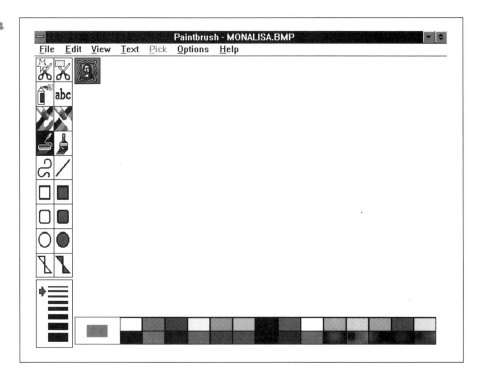

procedure described earlier to put the picture on the button. Here's an example where I put the picture shown in Figure 10.14 on a button and used Layout ➤ Size to Fit to resize the button to the picture:

Attaching a Macro to a Button

Remember, the button won't do anything until you assign a macro to it and only when you're in form view. I'll discuss how to create a macro in Chapter 14. But in case you've already been there and created a macro, all you need to do now to attach the macro to the button is to select the button. Then open its properties sheet, choose the On Push property, and select the appropriate macro name from the drop-down list.

Adding a Page Break to a Form

If a form is just too large to display on the screen, you can insert a page break into the form to break it into two or more screens. When using the form in form view, you can press PgDn to scroll down to the next page and PgUp to scroll up to the previous page. You can still scroll through the form with the scroll bars as well. The page break just gives you the option of flipping from page to page in the form with the PgUp and PgDn keys.

To add a page break to a form:

1. In design view, select the Page Break tool from the toolbox.

2. Click the place where you want to insert the page break.

Access inserts a page-break symbol in the form, as shown below, into the form design. You can select, move, and delete the symbol as necessary, as you would any other control.

The page-break symbol doesn't appear at all in form view. However, you can use the PgUp and PgDn keys to scroll quickly from one page of the form to the next in form view. Also, you can continue to use Ctrl+PgDn and Ctrl+PgUp to scroll through records, without changing pages on the form, while in form view.

Creating Read-Only Fields

When you're designing more advanced forms, you might want to make one or more fields on the form read-only, where the form displays some value from the underlying table, but the person using the form cannot change that value. For instance, when displaying a form that includes product information, you might want the user to be able to view, but not change, the Product ID number.

There are two field properties that you can use to make a field read-only:

Locked   If Yes, the field cannot be changed. If No, the field can be changed.

Enabled   If Yes, the field can have the focus. If No, the field is dimmed and unavailable on the form, and cannot have the focus.

There are four possible combinations of these properties, as summarized in Table 10.1.

TABLE 10.1: Combinations of the enabled and locked properties, and how they affect a field on the form

ENABLED	LOCKED	APPEARANCE	EFFECT IN FORM VIEW
Yes	No	Normal	The normal setting, where the field can have the focus and be edited.
Yes	Yes	Normal	The field can have the focus, but its contents cannot be changed. (The contents can be copied to the Clipboard.)
No	Yes	Normal	The field cannot have the focus, so there is no way to change or copy its contents.
No	No	Dimmed	Same as above, but the field is dimmed.

To assign any combination of properties to controls on your form, follow the standard techniques for changing properties:

1. In design view, select whatever controls you want to change.

2. Open the properties sheet.

3. Choose whatever combination of Enabled and Locked properties best defines how you want to treat the field.

Fields That Are Always Read-Only

Keep in mind that certain fields on the form are *always* read-only and cannot be changed. This includes

• A calculated field from the underlying query

• Any field that's the result of a summary (total), crosstab, or Unique Values Only in the underlying query

- Certain fields on queries that are based on multiple tables, as described in the next chapter

- Any field displayed by a calculated control in the form

By default, read-only fields look like all the other fields on the form. You may want to change that appearance, as described next.

Design Considerations for Read-Only Fields

A form might have any combination of editable fields and read-only fields. As a consideration to the person using the form, you might want to change the appearance of read-only fields so that they don't look exactly like the other editable fields on the form.

For instance, the Next Available Customer ID field at the top of the Customers form shown in Figure 10.7 (and below) is a calculated field. That field is for information purposes only and therefore need not (and cannot) be changed by the person using the form. However, the field looks just like all the editable fields in the main section of the form.

To prevent confusion, you could change the appearance of the field in design view. For instance, you might want to select the control for that field in design view, then change its border color to clear, its Fill color to the same color as the form background, its appearance to Normal, and its font to Bold. Doing so will make it more obvious to the person who is using the form that the field is for information only.

Whether or not you want to prevent the focus from even getting into the calculated field depends on whether or not you want the person who is using the form to be able to copy data from that field.

Creating a Form Template

When you start a form from scratch, without the aid of a Wizard, Access uses certain default settings that are defined in a template, named *Normal,* to define certain properties for the form. For instance, the new blank form will have a white background, no headers or footers, a grid fineness of 10×12, and so forth.

You can create your own template for new, blank forms. This is handy when you plan on creating several similar forms from scratch, because you won't have to redefine the same settings in each new form you create.

You can either use an existing form as the template for future forms or create a form from scratch with the characteristics you want future forms to inherit. Characteristics that you can pass on to the template include

- Form and page headers and footers (whether they're on or off)
- The height of each section in the form
- Colors for each section of the form
- Default properties for tools in the toolbox, as described earlier in "Setting Default Properties for Tools."
- Properties assigned to the form as a whole using the Edit ➤ Select Form properties sheet

Once you've defined the characteristics that you want to pass on to the template, you need to close and save the form. Then, to use those characteristics as the template for future blank forms:

1. From the database window, choose View ➤ Options.

2. Choose Form & Report Design to get to the options shown below:

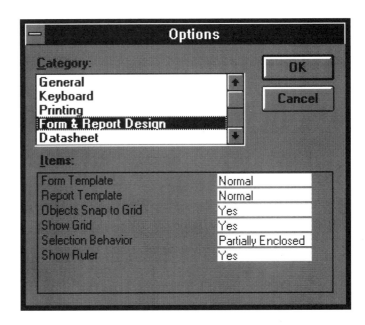

3. Choose the Form Template option, delete the Normal entry, and enter the name of the form that you want to use as the template.

4. Choose OK.

Note that the template will only be used in forms that you create in the current database. If you want to use the same template in another database, you need to copy the form that defines the template to that other database. See Chapter 18 for information on copying objects between databases.

To revert to the previous template, repeat the steps and set the Form Template option back to *Normal*.

Summary

As you can see, Access forms are extraordinarily flexible. There are countless ways to combine controls and properties to get exactly the look and behavior you want in a form. And as I said at the beginning of this chapter, the whole process can be summed up as simply this: You design a form by creating controls and assigning properties to those controls.

Once you get the hang of it, you can throw some real muscle into the works by basing your forms on queries and combining data from multiple tables. Doing *that,* as you may have guessed, is the subject of the next chapter!

Designing Multitable Forms

f a s t TRACK

N THIS chapter we'll be looking at ways of combining data from multiple related tables onto forms. As you'll see, this is where you can reorganize into more familiar formats all that data that's been split into multiple tables on the screen.

Here we'll be pulling together many techniques described in previous chapters. In fact, if you've skipped much material up to this point, you may find quite a few of the concepts and techniques described here to be well over your head! That's the way it is in database management—you have to learn certain basic skills before you can move on to more advanced skills. If you've got your queries and forms down pat, though, you should be able to move right along through this chapter.

Creating Main/Subform Forms

One way to display data from multiple tables in a form is by using Access's *Main/Subform* feature. You can create such a form with or without the aid of FormWizards. To illustrate Main/Subform, let's take a look at how you'd use a Wizard to create one first.

Creating a Main/Subform with a FormWizard

You can use the Main/SubFormWizard to create a multitable form between any two tables or queries that have a one-to-many relationship. You'll want base the main form on the table that's on the "one side" of the relationship and base the subform on the table that's on the "many side" of the relationship, as you answer the questions posed by the Wizard. Here are the steps to follow:

1. Starting from the database window, click the New Form button or choose File ➤ New ➤ Form.

2. In the **New Form** dialog box that appears, choose the table or query that's on the "one side" of the one-to-many relationship under Select A Table/Query, then click the FormWizards button.

3. Choose *Main/Subform* when prompted for an Access Wizard, then choose OK.

4. The next dialog box asks "Which table or query contains the data for the subform?" Choose the table or query that's on the "many side" of the one-to-many relationship. Then choose the Next button.

5. Choose the fields that you want to display on the main form with the >, >>, <, and << buttons, then click the Next button.

6. Choose the fields that you want to display in the subform, and then click the Next> button.

7. Choose a "look" for the form, then choose Next.

8. Optionally, enter a new form title in the Form Title text box.

9. Click either the Open button to go straight to form view, or the Design button to go straight to design view.

10. Before Access displays the form, you'll see this dialog box:

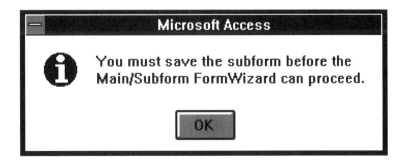

11. Choose OK, enter a name for the subform, then choose OK.

12. If Access cannot establish a link between the two tables, you'll see a message indicating so. Choose OK, then see "Defining the Link between the Main Form and Subform" for information on establishing the link between the two tables.

Figure 11.1 shows an example where I based the main form on the Suppliers table, and based the subform on the Products table.

Be aware that if the main form displays many fields, the subform may be scrolled out of view. You can use the vertical scroll bar on the form window to scroll down to the subform in that case. General techniques for a

FIGURE 11.1

A form created with the aid of the Main/SubFormWizard, using selected fields from the Suppliers table on the main form and selected fields from the Products table on the subform

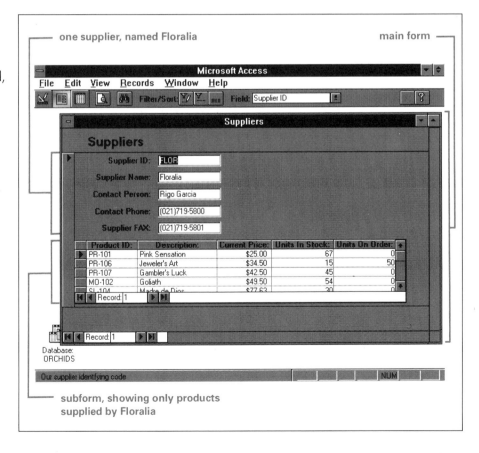

multitable form are discussed under "Using the Multitable Form" a little later in this chapter.

You can also use, in design view, the standard techniques for rearranging controls on a form in design view, as described under "Changing the Main Form and Subform" later in this chapter.

Creating a Main/Subform without a Wizard

You can also create a multitable form without the aid of the Main/Subform Wizard. To do so, you need to

- Create the main form, based on a table or query, using standard techniques for creating any form. Leave room for the subform, then close and save the main form.
- Create the subform alone using standard techniques. Close and save the subform.
- Reopen the main form in design view, and drag the name of the subform from the database window onto the form.
- If necessary, define the links between the main form and subform.
- Save the completed form.

We'll take a look at each of these steps in more detail in the sections that follow.

Creating the Main Form

You can create the main form for a multitable form by either using the Single-Column Wizard or starting from a blank form. Just make sure to leave enough room on the form for the subform that you'll be adding later.

Figure 11.2 shows a sample main form, in form view, based on the Categories table. As you can see, I've left enough room at the bottom of the form to add a subform.

After creating the main form, just close and save it normally.

FIGURE 11.2

A sample form, based on the Categories table, to be used as the main form in a multitable form

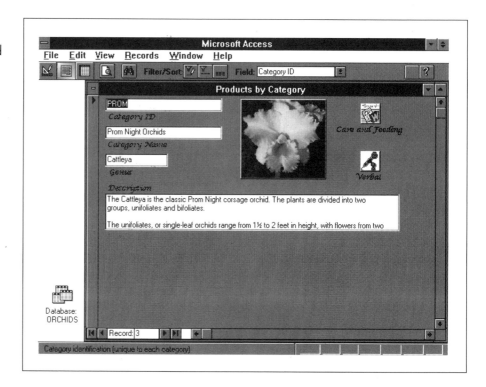

Creating the Subform

The subform in multitable form is a separate form that you create and save independently of the main form. The subform can be a datasheet view of the underlying table, or a more polished form with graphical controls, a header and footer, and so forth. The choice is yours. After all, it's your form!

Using a Datasheet as a Subform

If you want to use only a datasheet view of a table as a subform, you still need to create a form. However, it doesn't matter how you arrange controls in the form's design screen. All that matters is that the Detail section of the form design contain controls for all the fields that you want the subform to display.

For instance, Figure 11.3 shows a subform that I created by starting with a blank form, and dragging field names to the detail section of the form.

FIGURE 11.3

Controls for a subform
dragged to a blank
form, in design view

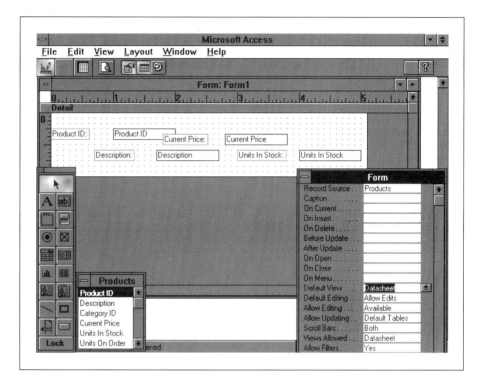

The controls are in no particular order, and don't have any special properties assigned to them, because I plan on using only the datasheet view in the subform.

Switching the datasheet view (not form view) using the Datasheet button, or by choosing View ➤ Datasheet, displays the fields that I've dragged onto the form in datasheet view, as in Figure 11.4.

If you don't bother to design the subform neatly, you may want to ensure that the person using the form sees only the datasheet view of the form. To do that, you need to:

1. Get back to design view and choose Edit ➤ Select Form.

2. Open the Properties sheet for the subform (using the Properties button or View ➤ Properties.)

FIGURE 11.4

Datasheet view of the
form in Figure 11.3
above

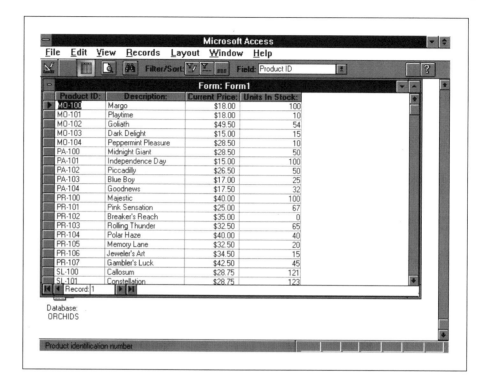

Database:
ORCHIDS

3. Change the Default View property for the form to *Datasheet.*

4. Change the Views Allowed property to *Datasheet.*

Once you've completed those steps, the Form View button on the tool bar
will be unavailable, and you'll be able to switch only between design view
and datasheet. Later down the road, the only view available to the person
using the form will be datasheet view.

NOTE   See "Switching Views in the Subform" later in this
chapter for more information on view switching in a
subform.

Remember to close and save the form after setting the properties, so that
you can use it as a subform later.

Using the Tabular FormWizard to Create a Subform

As an alternative to using just the datasheet view of a table as the subform, you can create a more polished subform with controls arranged to your liking. If you want the subform to display multiple records from the table on the "many side" of a one-to-many relationship, you can use the Tabular FormWizard to create the initial form.

The step-by-step procedure for using the Tabular Wizard is virtually identical to that for using the Single-Column Wizard. That is, you start from the database window, choose File ➤ New ➤ Form, select the table or query that you want to base the subform on, and then choose *Tabular* when asked which Wizard you want. From there, you can select field names and a look for the form as you would normally. The end result is different, however, because:

- The Tabular Wizard arranges controls horizontally across, rather than vertically down, the Detail section.
- Field labels (captions) are listed across the form Header section, rather than next to each field, and the labels don't have a colon (:).
- The Tabular Wizard sets the Default View property for the form to *Continuous Form,* rather than *Single Form,* so that the form displays multiple records.

After the Wizard has finished creating the form, you can make whatever changes you wish in design view to personalize the form. For instance, Figure 11.5 shows an example of a form based on the Products table, in form view. I used the Tabular Wizard with the Standard look to create the initial form. Then, in design view, I rearranged controls and resized the form Header and Detail sections to achieve the look shown in the figure.

Keep in mind that it's not *necessary* to use the Tabular Wizard to design the subform—you can design the subform however you wish. But if you want subform to display multiple records, be sure to choose Edit ➤ Select Form, and change the Default View property to *Continuous Form.*

On the other hand, if you want the subform to display only one record at a time, set its default view to *Single Form.* Later, you can switch between datasheet and form view in the subform to view all the records, or just one record in the subform.

FIGURE 11.5

A sample form, in form view, based on the Products table. I initially created this form with the Tabular FormWizard, with the Standard look, then made slight modifications in design view to achieve this look.

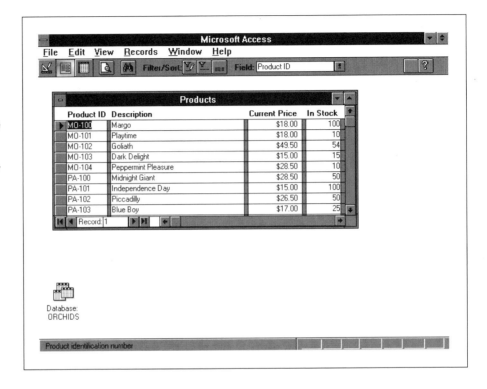

After creating the subform, be sure to close and save it, so you can add it to the main form later.

Adding the Subform to the Main Form

After you've created, closed, and saved both the main form and the subform, you can follow these steps to join them together into a single form:

1. Open the main form in design view.

2. Switch back to the database window, and click the Form object button to view your list of form names.

3. Drag the name of the subform from the database window onto the main form, with the pointer positioned at approximately where you want the upper left corner of the subform to appear.

4. The subform is just like any other control on the form (see Figure 11.6). You can select it, move, and size it as you would any other control. You can also delete its attached label, if you wish.

5. Open the **Subform/Subreport Properties** sheet, either by selecting the subform's control and clicking the Properties button, or by double-clicking on or near the edge of the subform's control.

6. Take a look at the *Link Child Fields* and *Link Master Fields* properties. In some cases, these will already be set to the fields that link the main form to the subform, in which case you can leave the settings as they are. If either or both of those properties are empty, change the properties as described in the next section.

Another way to add a subform to a main form, without going through the database window, is to open the main form in design view, and click the Subform/Subreport button (shown at left) in the toolbox. Then click within the main form at whatever position you want the upper left

FIGURE 11.6

A subform control on a main form. You can use the standard techniques to select, size, and move the subform's control.

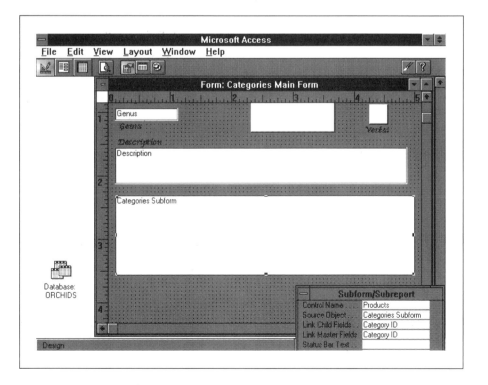

corner of the subform to appear. A control for the subform appears. You'll need to change the control's Source Object property, on the Properties sheet, to the name of the subform.

Defining the Link between the Main Form and Subform

When you add a subform to a main form, Access will automatically link the forms, provided the following conditions have been met:

- Both the main form and subform are based on tables, rather than queries, and you've predefined the relationship between the tables (as discussed in Chapter 6).

- The table on the "one side" has a primary key, and the table on the "many side" contains a field with the same name and data type as that primary key.

If you're not certain as to whether or not Access has automatically defined the link, you should check the subform's Properties sheet and, if necessary, define the linking fields yourself. Here's how:

1. Open the main form in design view. (I'll be assuming here that you've already added the control for the subform to the main form.)

2. Select the control for the subform (so it has sizing handles).

3. Open the Properties sheet using the Properties button or View ➤ Properties.

4. In the Link Child Fields property, type the name of the field that links records in the table on the "many side" of the relationship to records in the table on the "one side."

5. In the Link Master Fields property, type the name of the field in the form that links records in the table on the "many side" of the relationship to records in the table on the "one side" of the relationship.

The *Control Name* for the subform should be the name of the table or query that the subform is based on; the *Source Object* is the name of the subform itself. For instance, in the properties below, the subform is based on the Products table, and the Source Object is the form named *Categories subform*. Category ID is the field that links these two tables.

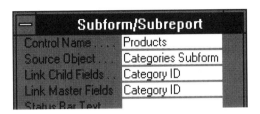

After you've defined the linking fields, Access will use those fields to limit records displayed in the subform to those that match the value currently displayed in the main form.

NOTE   In the main/subform relationship between Supplier and Products, discussed in the FormWizard example at the beginning of this chapter, the Control Name would be *Products*, the Source Object would be whatever name you assigned to the subform while using the Wizard, and the Child and Master linking fields would both be *Supplier ID*.

For instance, when the main form is showing the record for the PROM category, the subform will display only those records that also have the word *PROM* in the Category ID field. When you scroll to another record in the main form, such as the SLIPPER category, the subform will display only those products that have the word *SLIPPER* in the category ID field.

Using a Main/Subform

After you've added the subform to the main form and defined the linking fields, you can switch to form view to view the finished form. For instance, Figure 11.7 shows how the form shown back in Figure 11.6 looks in form view. You can close and save the finished form using the standard File ➤ Close commands.

FIGURE 11.7

The form shown
in Figure 11.6, in
form view

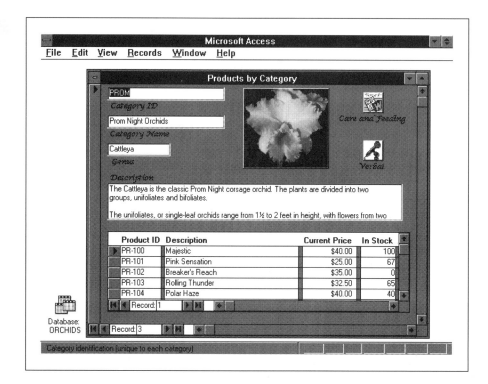

To use the multitable form, first open it just as you would any other form. The main form and subform each has its own separate navigation tools and record indicator in the lower left corner. As you scroll through records on the main form, the subform will show only records that have identical values in the field that links the two forms. For instance, if you were to scroll from the PROM category to the SLIPPER category, only the records for products in the SLIPPER category would appear in the subform.

Switching between the Main Form and Subform

To move the focus into any field on the main form, or subform, just click whichever field you want to edit (not the empty space between fields.) Optionally, you can open the Field drop-down list in the tool bar and choose the name of the subform, or *(Parent)* if you're in the subform, to move the focus into either form.

Switching Views in the Subform

If you have not set properties in the subform to prevent view switching, you can follow these steps to switch views within the subform:

1. In form view, move the focus into any field in the subform.

2. Choose View ➤ Subform Datasheet.

You can change the subform's properties to enable or disable the *Subform Datasheet* command on the View menu, to allow or disallow view switching in the subform. See "Controlling View Switching in the Subform" later in this chapter.

Changing the Main Form and Subform

To change the main form's design, or reposition or resize the subform, open the main form in design view. You can then use standard techniques to change any control on the main form, including the control that displays the subform.

Changing the Subform

To change the subform, you can either open the subform by itself in design view, make your changes, and then save the subform. Optionally, you can open the combined Main/Subform in design view, and follow these steps:

1. Click anywhere on the main form, away from the subform control, to make sure that the subform isn't selected.

2. Double-click inside the subform's control. The design view of the subform opens, as in the example shown in Figure 11.8.

   • To change the form view of the subform, make whatever changes you wish to the subform, using standard design techniques.

FIGURE 11.8

Double-clicking the subform's control in design view opens the subform itself in design view.

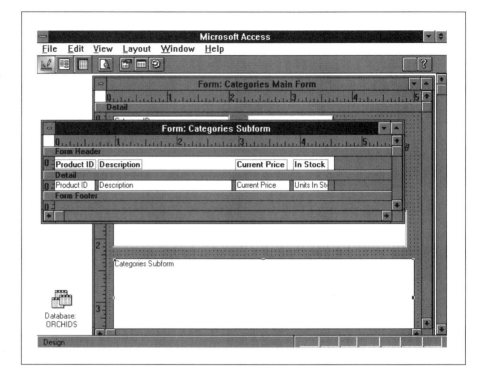

- To change the datasheet view of the subform, click on the Datasheet View button in the tool bar. Then you can arrange columns, change their widths, and use other standard techniques described under "Customizing the Datasheet View" in Chapter 5.

3. When you've finished making changes, choose File ➤ Close to close the subform and save your changes.

4. On the main form, click the edge of the subform's control to select it, then click inside the subform's control.

5. Press ↵ to load the latest version of the subform into the main form.

6. Switch to form view to verify your changes.

Controlling View-Switching in the Subform

You can change the properties of the subform to control switching between form view and datasheet view in the subform. To do so, bring the subform into design view, as described in the first two steps of the preceding section. Then open that form's Properties sheet and choose Select ➤ Form. Change the Default View and Views Allowed properties as below:

- To allow datasheet view only (no form view), set the Default View and Views Allowed properties both to *Datasheet*.

- To allow only form view (no datasheet view), set the Default View property to *Continuous Form* for multiple records or to *Single Form* for one record at a time. Then set the Views Allowed property to *Form*.

- To allow switching between form view and datasheet view, set the Default View property to whichever view you want to appear when the form is first open; either *Continuous Form* or *Single Form* for form view, or *Datasheet View*. Then set the Views Allowed property to *Both*.

Be sure to complete Steps 3 through 6 from the preceding section to save your changes and update the subform control.

Basing Forms on Queries

The Main/Subform approach to designing multitable forms is very much geared toward displaying a single record from the table on the "one side" of a relationship, and multiple related records from the table on the "many side." But that's not the only way to display data from multiple tables on a form. You can also create a query that displays data from multiple tables, and base the form on that query:

1. Starting from the datasheet window, choose File ➤ New ➤ Query or click on the New Query button to create a query.

2. Add all the tables that contain fields that you want to include on the form, and link the tables with join lines.

3. In the query window, drag to the QBE grid any field names that you want to include on the form.

4. Optionally, you can use any of the standard techniques to define a sort order, criteria, calculated fields, and totals in the current query window.

5. You might want to run the query to ensure that the dynaset includes all the fields and records that you want to include on the form. This is important because the form you'll be designing will be based on this dynaset. (In fact, the form will be just another way of viewing the data in this dynaset, just as a form that's based on a regular table is just another way of viewing the data in that table!)

6. When you're satisfied with the query, close and save it.

7. Use the New Form button, or choose File ➤ New ➤ Form to create a new form.

8. When prompted for the Table/Query name, choose the name of the query you saved in Step 6 above. You can then start with a blank form, or use a Wizard to create the form.

When you get to the form design screen, you can use any of the techniques described in the previous chapters to design the form to your liking.

The Order Summary Form: Linking Data from Three Tables

Figure 11.9 shows a sample Order Summary form that displays data from three different tables—Orders, Order Details, and Customers—on a single form.

To create the form in Figure 11.9, I first created the query shown in Figure 11.10, which joins the Order Details, Orders, and Customers tables. There are more fields in the QBE grid than I can show in the figure. The grid actually contains the following fields: Order ID, Customer ID, Order Date, Date Shipped, Paid, Discount %, Shipping Charge, First Name,

FIGURE 11.9

FIGURE 11.9

The Order Summary form displays information about individual orders, using data from the Customers, Orders, and Order Details tables.

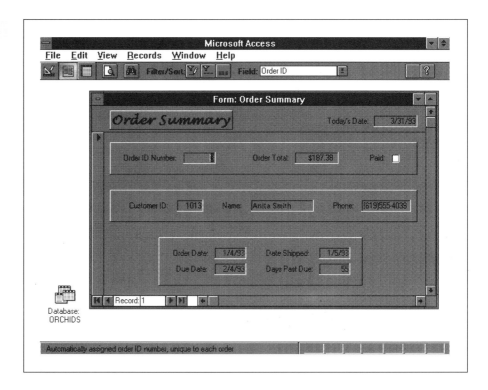

Last Name, and Phone, all of which contain **Group By** in the Total cell. The last column in the QBE grid (visible in the figure), contains the expression necessary to calculate the order total.

If you want to use the Order Summary form to view only unpaid, overdue orders, you could enter appropriate criteria into the QBE grid. For instance, below I put the criterion **No** in the Paid column and the criterion **<=Date( )-30** in the Shipping Date column to isolate orders that are unpaid and were shipped 30 or more days ago.

Last Name	Order Date	Paid	Date Shipped	Discount %	Shipping Charge
Customers	Orders	Orders	Orders	Orders	Orders
Group By	Group By	Group By	Group By	Group By	Group By
☒	☒	☒	☒	☒	☒
		No	<=Date()-30		

FIGURE 11.10

The query used to join tables to create the Order Summary form shown in Figure 11.9. (Some fields in the QBE grid are scrolled off the screen.)

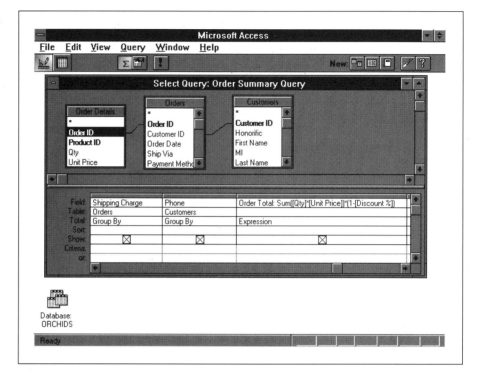

To create the form, I first saved and closed the query. Then I based the form on that query, and used the standard techniques to design the form. I used some calculated controls within the form to display the current date, customer's name, due date, and days past due, as explained under "Examples of Calculated Controls" in Chapter 10.

Which Fields Can Be Edited?

When you base a form on a query, it's important to remember that the same rules that apply to what can and what can't be edited in the resulting dynaset apply to the form. After all, the form *is* just another way of viewing the data in the dynaset. For future reference, Table 11.1 summarizes what fields, in general, can and cannot be edited in the resulting dynaset or form.

The additional restrictions listed in Table 11.2 apply if the query contains multiple tables.

To summarize the information presented in Tables 11.1 and 11.2, suffice it to say that you *can* edit any non-calculated field on the "many side" of a one-to-many relationship in the dynaset or form that's based on the query.

Referring back to my Order Summary form, the entire form is read-only, mainly because of the "Group By" totals in the underlying query. So while the form is useful for viewing order summary information, you can't use it to change order information.

You *could* create a similar form that does allow editing. However, you would need to create a query that *doesn't* include the Order Details table,

TABLE 11.1: Fields that can and fields that can't be edited in a dynaset or form

TYPE OF QUERY	WHICH FIELDS CAN BE EDITED?	COMMENTS
select query based on one table	all	Except as noted below
calculated field	non-calculated fields	Calculated fields can't be edited, but non-calculated fields can still be edited.
query with summary calculations, crosstab, or unique values	none	No fields can be edited, because the dynaset is showing results of calculations or analyses, not raw data.

TABLE 11.2: Fields that can and fields that can't be edited in multitable queries. (Restrictions from Table 11.1 also apply here.)

TYPE OF QUERY	WHICH FIELDS CAN BE EDITED?
query based on two tables with a one-to-one relationship	all
queries based on two tables with a one-to-many or many-to-one relationship	fields in the table on the "many" side of the relationship only
queries based on two tables with a one-to-many relationship, but no fields from the table on the "many" side are included in the dynaset	all
query based on a self-join	none
multitable queries with no primary key or unique index on the "one" side of a one-to-many relationship	none

doesn't include a column for calculating the order total, and doesn't include any Group By calculations. Then you could base the form on that query and design it like the one I've shown, but without the Order Total calculation.

N O T E

Another way to show the order total in the Order Summary form would be to store the order total in the Orders table. But to ensure that the order total is always correct, you'd need to devise some macros (Chapter 16) that recalculate that total whenever data in the table changes.

Pulling It All Together: An Order Entry Form

At the outset of this chapter we developed a couple of Main/Subform examples where both forms were based on tables. But the fact is, you can base the main form or the subform, or both, on queries rather than on tables. This simple fact gives you an extraordinary flexibility in designing multitable forms.

For instance, the fancy order form shown in Figure 11.11 is a Main/Subform, where both forms are based on queries. That form includes several features described in the previous chapters, including combo boxes, calculated controls, and command buttons (which I'll talk about more in Chapter 15). For the moment, however, we'll just focus on the underlying queries.

FIGURE 11.11

An order entry form where both the main form and the subform are based on queries

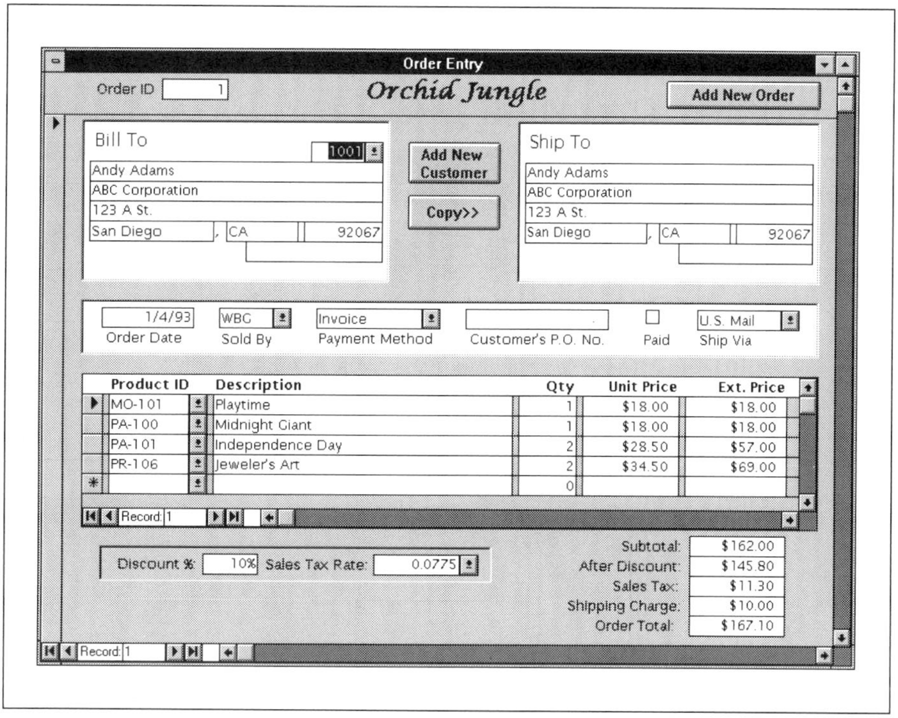

N O T E

I'm using my higher resolution monitor to display the Order Entry form in this section. On a standard VGA monitor, you'd need to do some scrolling to view the entire form, unless you use very small fonts while designing the form.

The Order Entry Main Form

Figure 11.12 shows the query that the main form for the Order Entry form is based on. The QBE grid contains quite a few fields: Order ID, Customer ID (from the Orders table), Company, Address, City, State/Province, Zip/Postal Code, Country, Phone, Fax, Discount Rate, Order Date, Sold By, Ship Via, Payment Method, Customer's PO, Paid, Ship To Name, Ship To Company, Ship To Address, Ship To City, Ship To State, Ship To Zip, Ship To Country, Discount %, Shipping Charge, and

FIGURE 11.12

The Order Entry Main Form Query, which combines data from the Orders and Customers table

Date Shipped. There's also a calculated field in the query to combine the Last Name and First Name fields, as you can see in the figure.

NOTE

As discussed later in this chapter, if you need to charge different sales tax rates on different orders, you might want to add a field named Sales Tax Rate to the Orders table. Then, include that field in the QBE grid. When creating the main form later, you can then add a Sales Tax Rate control to the form, like the one shown in Figure 11.11.

I saved this query with the name **Order Entry Main Form Query**. Then I designed the main form based on that query, as shown in Figure 11.13

FIGURE 11.13

The Order Entry main form, in design view

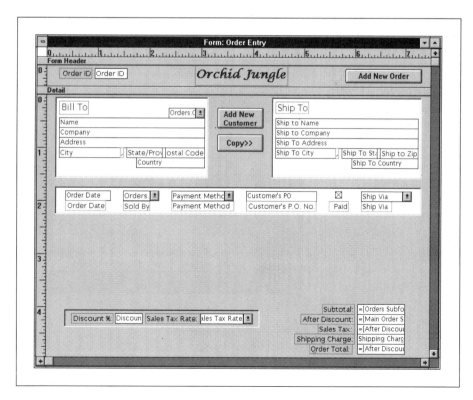

(where you can see the form in design view). The calculated controls at the bottom of the form are discussed under "Using Expressions in Forms" later in this chapter.

I saved and closed the form with the name Order Entry.

The Order Entry Subform

The subform in the order entry form is based on the query shown in Figure 11.14. This form combines data from the Order Details and Products table, and the QBE grid contains the fields Order ID, Product ID (from the Order Details table), Description, Qty, Current Price, Unit Price, and the expression

Extended Price: [Qty]*[Unit Price]

in the Field cell of the last column of the QBE grid.

FIGURE 11.14

The Orders Subform Query combines data from the Order Details and Products tables, and is used as the basis for the subform on the Order Entry form.

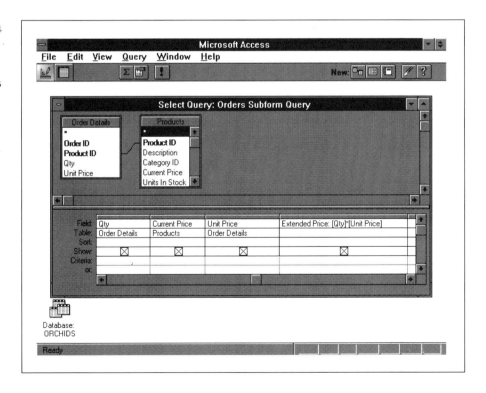

After creating the query, I closed it and gave it the name **Orders Subform Query**.

In Chapter 15, I'll show you how to create a macro that automatically copies the contents of the Current Price field of the Orders table into the Unit Price field of the Order Details table.

Then I used the Tabular FormWizard to create a form, based on the Orders Subform Query, that includes the fields Product ID, Description, Qty, Unit Price, and Extended Price. I sized and arranged the controls as shown in Figure 11.15. I also set the properties of the controls for the Unit

FIGURE 11.15

The Orders Subform in design view, initially created with the Tabular FormWizard, then rearranged and customized to get the look I wanted

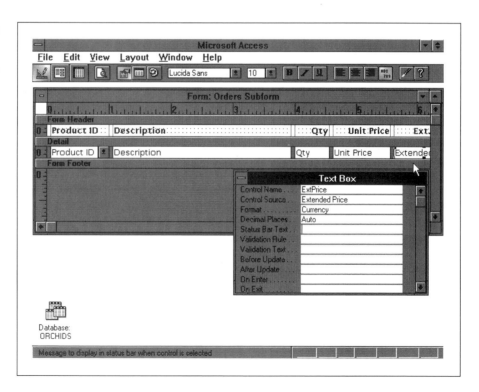

Price and Extended Price fields to Currency format, Auto decimals, as you can see in the Properties sheet for the Extended Price field's control.

When I was happy with the appearance of the subform, I closed it and saved it with the name **Orders Subform**.

Next it was time to add the Orders Subform to the Order Entry form. I reopened the Order Entry form in design view, and dragged the Orders Subform form onto that main form, then moved and sized it into position, as described earlier in this chapter. Also, I set the relationship between the main and subform to the Order ID field, as you can see in Figure 11.16.

Next it was time to focus on creating the calculated controls to do the necessary arithmetic.

FIGURE 11.16

The control for the Orders Subform added to the Order Entry form, and the Order ID field defined as the linking field in the subform's property sheet

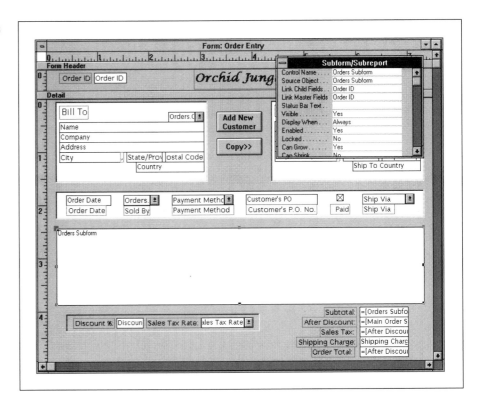

Using Expressions in Multitable Forms

In Chapter 10, under "Adding a Calculated Control" I showed how you can add a calculated control to a form using the text box tool that contains an expression starting with the equals sign (=). A calculated control on a form can contain just about any expression to perform some calculation on data in the underlying table or query.

In a Main/Subform situation, you may want the main form to display the results of a calculation that's based on the subform. For instance, in my order entry form, the order subtotal, which appears on the main form, is actually the total extended price of records displayed in the subform.

There are two ways you could go about displaying that order subtotal on the main form:

- Use a **DSum( )** function with a criterion to calculate the order subtotal directly on the main form.

- Or, calculate the order subtotal using a **Sum( )** function in the subform. Then hide that calculation in the subform, and display a copy of that calculation on the main form.

Of the two options, the one using **Sum( )** in the subform is faster (and easier), because the records that you need to base the calculation on are already isolated in the subform. So we'll focus on that method here.

Totaling Values in a Subform

To perform a calculation in a subform, you need to add the appropriate calculated control to that subform. Here's how you'd do that using my order entry subform example:

1. Open the Orders subform in design view.

2. Increase the height of the form footer section so you can put a control into that section.

3. Use the Text Box tool on the tool bar to create a control in the form footer section.

4. Open the Properties sheet for the new text box.

5. Set the Control Name property to a name that will be easy to remember in the future. (You'll need to refer to this control by that name later if you want to display its contents on the main form.) In Figure 11.17, I named this control **Order Subtotal**.

6. In the Control Source property, enter the calculation expression. For example, in Figure 11.17 I put the expression

=Sum([Extended Price])

into the Control Source option, to have the control calculate the sum of the extended price.

7. Optionally, set the format and number of decimal places for the control. (I used Currency, Auto decimal places in this example.)

FIGURE 11.17

The Order Subtotal calculated control added to the Orders Subform's form footer band

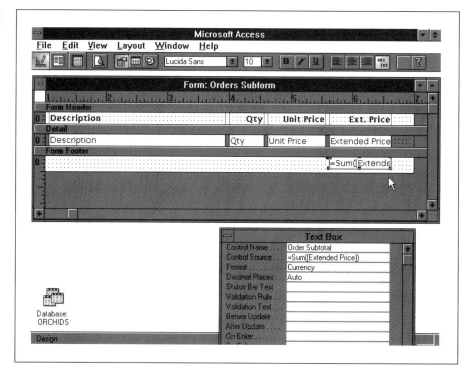

8. To check the results of the calculation, you can switch to form view and scroll down to the form footer.

9. Switch back to design view.

Now, if you want to display the results of that calculation on the *main* form rather than on the *sub*form, you need it to make its results "invisible" on the subform. To do that in this example:

1. Click on any empty area in the form footer, or on the bar at the top of the form footer.

2. Open the Properties sheet for the form footer section, and change the Visible property to *No*, as below:

Now if you switch to form view, you won't *see* the form footer, and hence you won't see the order subtotal. But rest assured, it's there; you can now close and save the subform.

Displaying a Subform's Control on the Main Form

To display the contents of a control from the subform on the main form, you need to add a calculated control (using the Text Box tool) to the main form. The expression you use in the calculated control needs to use an *identifier* to refer to data that's in the subform, following the basic syntax:

=[*subform name*].Form![*control name*]

- *subform name* is the name of the subform (as defined in its Control Name property)

- The period is an operator that identifies the name that follows as an Access object or property (as opposed to a user-defined name)

- Form is the Access object type (a form in this example)

- The exclamation point (!) indicates that what follows is a user-defined name (i.e., one that you created)

- *control name* is the name of the control on the subform, as defined in that control's Control Name property

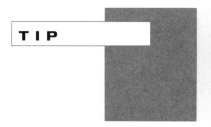

T I P

Amazingly, you can use the exclamation point and the period to refer to virtually *any* object in your Access database—not just calculated controls in subforms. See "Identifiers" in Chapter 17 for a more general discussion of this topic.

For example, you could create a calculated control on the Order Entry main form that contains the expression

=[Orders Subform].Form![Order Subtotal]

to display the contents of the Order Subtotal control that you placed on the subform earlier. Thus, that calculated control on the main form would display the order subtotal that you previously made "invisible" in the subform. As usual, you'd use the Text Box tool from the toolbox to put that calculated control onto the main form. Here are the exact steps:

1. Open the main form (*Order Entry* in this example) in design view.

2. In the toolbox, choose the Text Box tool.

3. Click wherever you want to position the calculated control on the main form. An empty text box control appears.

4. Open the Properties sheet, and change the Control Name property to whatever name you want to give this control. In this example, you could name the control **Main Order Subtotal** to avoid confusion with the control named **Order Subtotal** on the subform.

5. In the Control Source property, enter the expression:

=[Orders Subform].Form![Order Subtotal]

6. Optionally, change the Format and Decimal Places properties to whatever appearance you want, as in Figure 11.18.

FIGURE 11.18

A calculated control named Main Order Subtotal, added to the main form to display the contents of the Order Subtotal control from the subform

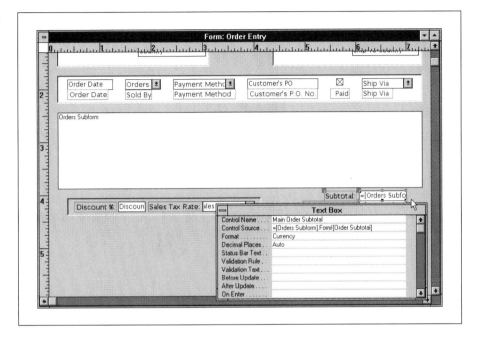

7. You can also size and move the control, and change its appearance properties, using the standard techniques.

Figure 11.18 shows how the main form looks in design view at this point, with the new calculated control selected, and its Properties sheet open.

At this point you can switch to form view to see the results.

Calculated Controls on the Order Entry Form

Once you've added the Main Order Subtotal control to the main form, you can create other calculated controls to calculate the rest of the information that's needed on the form. When creating those calculated controls, you can refer to the contents of the Order Main Subtotal control by its name, just as you can refer to a field in the underlying table or query by its name. For instance, the expression

=[Main Order Subtotal]*0.0775

in a calculated control would multiply the order subtotal by 7.75 percent, to calculate sales tax.

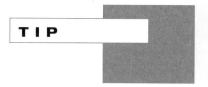

TIP

Remember that you might also want to set the Enabled Property to *No*, and Locked Property to *Yes*, in the calculated controls.

Table 11.3 lists the other calculated controls used on my order-entry form example, including the label, Control Name, and Control Source expression used in each one. There, I've assumed that all orders are charged 7.75 percent sales tax. However, we'll look at other ways of dealing with sales tax in a moment.

TABLE 11.3:   Calculated controls on my sample Order Entry form, each created with the Text Box tool in the toolbox

LABEL ON THE FORM	CONTROL NAME	CONTROL SOURCE EXPRESSION
Subtotal	Main Order Subtotal	=[Orders Subform].Form![Order Subtotal]
After Discount	After Discount	=[Main Order Subtotal]*(1-[Discount %])
Sales Tax	Sales Tax	=[After Discount]*0.0775
Order Total	Order Total	=[After Discount]+[Sales Tax]+[Shipping Charge]

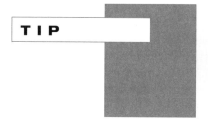

TIP

Note that [Discount %] and [Shipping Charge] in Table 11.3 are names of fields in the underlying query. [Main Order Subtotal], [After Discount], [Sales Tax], and [Order Total] are names of controls on the form.

Caution: Nulls Propagate

One thing you need to be aware of is that a *zero* and a *null* (blank field) are not the same. If any part of an arithmetic expression is a null, the results of the entire expression will be null. Furthermore, any other calculated controls that refer to that null value will also end up being blank. This is called *null propagation* because if the first calculation in a series is null, that null value carries over to all subsequent expressions.

By default, Access sets the default values for numeric fields to zero, so that if you leave the field blank, it still ends up containing a zero. In complex expressions, you can use the **IIF( )** function with the **Is Null** operator to test for a null value and replace it with a zero.

TIP

The example Northwind Traders database included with Access includes an Access Basic function, named NullToZero, that you can copy to your own database to convert nulls to zeros.

Handling the Sales Tax Problem

Sales tax is always something of a stickler in an application that deals with sales or orders, because sales tax rules vary from state to state, and they change with time. While I can't tell you exactly how to handle sales tax in your particular state, I can give you some food for thought that might help you figure out ways of dealing with sales tax in general.

On the one hand, if all of your orders are local, and are subject to the same sales tax rate, you can use the technique I used above to add a constant sales tax, such as 7.75 percent, to each order right on the form, like this:

    =[Main Order Subtotal]*0.0775

On the other hand, if you need to charge different sales tax rates on different orders, this constant 0.0775 won't do you much good. You'll need to replace that with an expression that calculates the correct sales tax for your particular state.

For instance, let's suppose that your particular state requires that you charge 7.75% on orders shipped within the state and no sales tax on orders shipped outside the state. In that case, you can use the IIf() (immediate if) function to calculate sales tax based on the contents of the Ship To State field. As an example, if you only need to charge sales tax in the state of Ohio, the calculated control for determining sales tax on the order entry form would contain the expression

=IIf([Ship To State]="OH",[After Discount]*0.0775,0)

which translates to "If the ship to state is "OH" (Ohio), then calculate sales tax as the [After Discount] value times 7.75%. Otherwise, calculate sales tax as zero."

Now, if you need to charge different sales tax rates in different states, it gets to be a bit trickier. For starters, you'd want to add a field, perhaps named Sales Tax Rate, to the Orders table, as a Number field with the Percent format property.

N O T E Refer to Chapter 6 if you need a reminder on how to change the structure of a table and how to set the Format property of a field.

You would also need to include that Sales Tax Rate field in the QBE grid of the Order Entry Main Form Query. And you'd need to add a bound control to the Order Entry form that lets you enter the appropriate tax rate to the Sales Tax Rate field of the Orders table. Finally, you would change the calculated control that determines the sales tax amount on the Order Entry form to

[After Discount]*[Sales Tax Rate]

which calculates sales tax, in dollars, based on the contents of the After Discount control on the form, and the contents of the Sales Tax Rate field in the current record of the Orders table.

Now, the one drawback here is that you, or whoever is entering order information, needs to know the appropriate sales tax rate to charge in each state. Or, as an alternative to memorizing sales tax rates, you could store that information in the States table (which I originally structured in Chapter 4), and add a record for each state in United States to that table.

If you don't charge tax in a particular state, leave its Sales Tax Rate field set at zero. If you do charge sales tax in a particular state, enter the appropriate rate into the table. For example, here are the first few records of the States table, where I've listed 5.5% as the sales tax rate for Arizona, and 7.75% for California. Other states have zero sales tax rates because I don't charge sales tax in those states.

Abbreviation	State	Sales Tax Rate
AL	Alabama	0.00%
AK	Alaska	0.00%
AZ	Arizona	5.50%
AR	Arkansas	0.00%
CA	California	7.75%
CO	Colorado	0.00%

Table: States

After making the appropriate changes to the States table, you can use it as the list in a combo box in the Sales Tax Rate control on your order entry main form to help you find sales tax rates. When defining the query for this combo box, use the criterion **>0** in the Sales Tax Rate column so that only those records show up in the combo box, as in this example:

Sales Tax Rate:	0		Afte
	0.055	Arizona	
	0.0775	California	

N O T E

When using the form and combo box later, you need to enter a zero into the combo box if no tax is to be applied. A null in that field or control would propagate to the order total.

When adding the combo box to your Order Entry form, be sure to bind it to the Sales Tax Rate field in the underlying Orders table. That way, whatever sales tax rate you choose from the combo box will be stored in the Orders table. This is important, because any reports or calculations that you create later will need to have the correct tax rate stored in the Sales Tax Rate field of the Orders table.

Now, I hate to confuse an already complicated issue, but I should point out that there is yet another way to handle the problem of charging different sales tax rates in different states. And that is, rather than enter the sales tax rate yourself, you could just have the calculated control look up the sales tax rate in the States table. You wouldn't need a combo box, or a Sales Tax Rate field in the Orders table at all. Instead, you would just replace the Sales Tax expression shown back in Table 11.3 with the expression below, which looks up the sales tax rate based on the contents of the Ship To State field:

```
=[After Discount]*DLookUp("[Sales Tax Rate]","States",
"[Abbreviation]=[Ship To State]")
```

(Remember that this should all be entered on one line.) If you need to base the calculation on the "bill to" state, rather than the "ship to" state, you'd use this expression instead:

```
=[After Discount]*DLookUp("[Sales Tax Rate]'","States",
"[Abbreviation]=[State/Province]")
```

The only potential problem would be if the order is being shipped out of the country: when this is the case, there wouldn't be a matching state in the States table. In that case, the **DLookup** function would result in a null, which in turn would nullify the Sales Tax calculation and the Order Total calculation.

If you copied the **NullToZero( )** function from the Northwind database into your own database, you could solve that problem by enclosing the entire expression in the NullToZero function, like this:

```
=NullToZero([After Discount]*DLookUp("[Sales Tax
Rate]","States",'"[Abbreviation]=[State/Province]"))
```

See the section on *domain aggregate functions* in Chapter 17 for more information. In particular, it's important to note that current changes to a record do not force a recalculation of the function or its criterion. So you may need to "requery" the form, by pressing Shift+F9, to update any domain aggregate functions on the form. Optionally, you can attach a *Recalc* macro to the After Update property of any controls on the form that alter fields referenced by the domain aggregate function's criterion expression.

Finally, there's that *other* tricky sales tax problem where some products are taxable while others are not. The solution to that problem is to add a Yes/No field, perhaps named Taxable, to the Products table design. Then, for each record in the Products table, set that field to *Yes* for taxable items and *No* for nontaxable items.

Next you would need to use two calculated controls in the Orders Subform footer: The Order Subtotal described earlier, plus a calculated control, perhaps named Taxable Subtotal, that contains an expression like this:

    =DSum("[Extended Price]","Orders Subform Query","[Taxable]")

This expression tells Access to total the Extended Price field in the underlying query, but include only records that have *Yes* in the Products field.

Then, in the main form, you could create calculated controls that base the sales tax calculation on just the Taxable Subtotal field in the Orders Subtotal subform, perhaps like this (for 7.75 percent tax rate):

    =[Orders Subform].Form![Taxable Subtotal]*0.0775

or like this, if your table includes a Sales Tax Rate field or control:

    =[Orders Subform].Form![Taxable Subtotal]*[Sales Tax Rate]

Again, all I can give you here are some ideas for working out solutions of your own. The main trick is learning what's available in expressions, and learning how to construct expressions that calculate the results you need.

N O T E   Chapter 17 discusses expressions in general.

Combo Boxes on the Order Entry Form

In addition to the Sales Tax Rate combo box, I've added a few other combo boxes to the Order Entry form, using the techniques described in Chapter 10. Here's a quick overview of some of those combo boxes, as suggestions for creating your own order entry forms.

The Customer ID combo box helps you to look up a Customer ID number by name while entering an order. This combo box is bound to the Customer ID field of the underlying query. When opened, it displays customer ID, names, and addresses with the names alphabetized for easy lookup, as below:

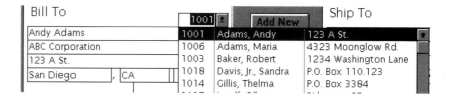

N O T E   You can't type a customer name and address directly into the Order Entry form, because the Customer data is on the "one side" of a one-to-many relationship. Chapter 15 describes how to create a macro and attach it to the Add New Customer button, to allow entry of new customers on-the-fly.

The combo box for the Sold By control is bound to the Sold By field, and displays data from the Employees table, as below:

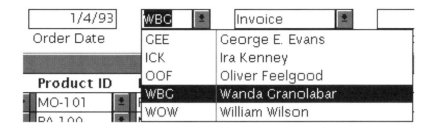

The Payment Method and Ship Via combo boxes are both simple Value List combo boxes that display only a small set of alternative choices, as below. Each combo box is bound to the field by the same name in the underlying query.

The Product Id combo box is defined in the Orders Subform subform, and is bound to the Product ID field of the underlying query. When opened, it displays product ID's and descriptions, with products listed in alphabetical order as shown below:

Product ID	Description
MO-101	Playtime
MO-104	Peppermint Pleasure
PA-102	Piccadilly
PR-101	Pink Sensation
MO-101	Playtime
PR-104	Polar Haze
PR-103	Rolling Thunder
SP-102	Royal Robe
SL-102	Yerba Buena

You'll see this Order Entry form again, in Chapter 15, where we'll add some macros to make it even more useful and pleasant to use.

Summary

If you're thinking that there's virtually no limit to the ways in which you can combine Access queries, forms, and expressions to get exactly what you want, I'd say your thinking is right on the mark. The trick to total mastery lies in learning to use those design screens fluently, and becoming familiar with Access expressions and functions. The first takes practice—the second takes study.

If you're an experienced DOS database management guru, and you're thinking that all of this is *nothing* like what you've experienced in the past, I'd say "Welcome to the world of object-oriented database management!" It gets even better.

Printing Custom Reports

fast TRACK

To preview a report   **533**

click the Print Preview button in the tool bar. Within print preview, you can zoom in and out by clicking anywhere on the report, or by clicking on the Zoom button. To leave print preview, choose Cancel.

To add or delete page or report headers and footers   **535**

in design view, choose File ➤ Page Hdr/Ftr or File ➤ Report Hdr/Ftr.

To sort and group data in a report   **542**

open the report in design view, and choose View ➤ Sorting And Grouping, or click the Sorting and Grouping button on the tool bar. Choose fields for sorting and grouping, and Ascending or Descending sort order. To use a field for grouping, change its Group Header and/or Group Footer property to Yes.

To calculate subtotals and totals in a report   **556**

use the Group/Total ReportWizard to create the report. Or add your own group footer sections to the report design. Then use the Text Box tool to add calculated controls containing **=Sum**(*field name*) expressions to the group or report footer sections.

To display only subtotals and totals   **560**

without the detail records, set the detail section's Visible property to No.

SO FAR, you've learned about three of the main objects you can create in your Access databases—*tables*, *queries*, and *forms*. In this chapter, we're going to be looking at yet another object, the *report*.

As you'll see, creating a report is much like creating a form. In fact, the basic skills you learned for creating forms will carry over quite nicely to creating reports.

What Is a Report?

In a nutshell, a report is a formatted, printed presentation of data from a table (or tables). Like a form, a report can be based on a table or on a query. For instance, if you want to display data from multiple tables in a report, you can join the tables in a query, then base the report on the query.

Unlike forms, reports are geared toward printing, and not for entering and entering data. When you create a report, you're deciding how you want the data to look on the printed page. As you might expect, Access offers total flexibility in designing reports to your liking.

Like a form, a report always displays current, up-to-date data. That is, you design and save the *format* of a report. Once you've done that, you can use the report repeatedly in the future to print current data in the table(s).

Creating a Report

As with forms, you can create reports with or without the aid of a Report-Wizard. There are three ReportWizards that you can use:

- **Single-Column** Lists fields from the underlying query vertically down the page, like a single-column form.

- **Groups/Totals** Lists fields horizontally across the page. Optionally, you can define fields to group records together (e.g., group products by product category, or group orders by month). Access automatically adds controls to calculate totals and subtotals of numeric and currency fields to the report.

- **Mailing Labels** Lets you arrange fields, and add punctuation, to define the appearance of data on each label. Also lets you choose from among several commonly used label formats.

You can also design a report completely from scratch, without the aid of a Wizard. To create a report:

1. Choose File ➤ New ➤ Report, or click on the name of the table or query that you want to base the report on, then click on the New Report button in the tool bar. The **New Report** dialog box appears.

2. Select the name of the table or query that you want to base the report on (if you used the New Report button, the table or query name will already be selected).

3. Choose ReportWizards to use a Wizard. Or, to start from scratch, choose *Blank Report* and skip the remaining steps.

4. Choose the type of report you want to create—*Single-Column*, *Groups/Totals*, or *Mailing Label*—then choose OK.

5. Read and follow the instructions in each page of the Wizard screens, and look to the example at the left side of the window for examples. Choose Next after choosing options from each screen.

6. When you get to the last Wizard screen, choose *Print Preview* to view the report in print preview mode, or choose *Design* to go straight to the reports design screen.

7. If you want to print the report, choose File ➤ Print, then choose OK.

8. If you want to save the finished report, choose File ➤ Close, then choose Yes. Enter an Access name, up to 64 characters, for the report.

If you use a Wizard, remember that once you leave the last Wizard screen, you can't back up and make changes with the Wizard. If you want to make any changes to the report format, you'll either have to do so in the report design window or close the report without saving it, and then try again, using the Wizard.

If you don't use a Wizard, you'll need to add controls yourself, using the same basic techniques you use in forms. For instance, to add a bound control from the underlying table or query, drag a field name from the field list. To create other types of controls, you can use tools from the toolbox. You can save and close the report at any time with the usual File ➤ Close commands from the menu.

Using and Changing a Saved Report

After you've created, saved, and closed a report, you can re-open and re-use it as you would any other object in the database:

1. Click on the Report button in the database window.

2. Click on the name of the report you want to open.

   • To preview the report on the screen, choose the Preview button.

- The print the report, choose File ➤ Print, then OK.
- To change or view the report's design, click on the Design button.

Designing Reports

You create, change, or design a report in the report design screen. The design view for a report looks much like the design view for a form. Text and data that appear on the printed report are represented by controls in design view. For instance, if you use the Single-Column Wizard to create a report for printing data from the Customers table, the report design will contain controls for printing the form title, current date, lines, and fields from the underlying table.

In the example shown in Figure 12.1, the control for displaying data from the Honorific field from the underlying table is selected. The Properties sheet and toolbox are also displayed on the screen.

The tool bar contains the buttons shown below. When you select a control, the tool bar will also show the usual tools and buttons for setting the font, weight (*Bold, Italic, Underline*), and alignment of the text of data within the control.

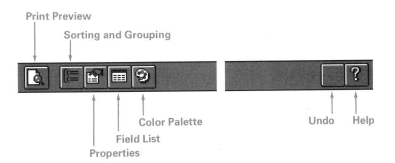

FIGURE 12.1

A sample report in
design view

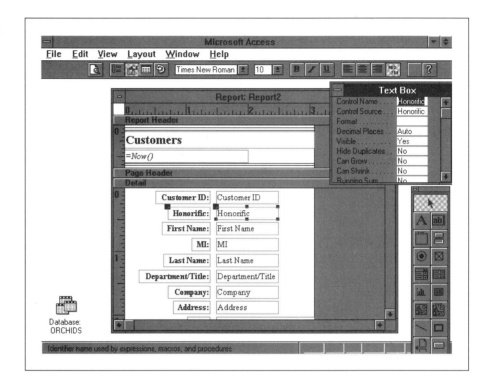

Basic Skills for Designing Reports

The skills and concepts you learned back in Chapters 9 and 10 for designing forms also apply to designing reports. Here's a quick summary of basic techniques for managing objects on the reports design screen:

- You can create, select, move, size, align, and format controls on a report using the same techniques you use when designing forms.

- Like a form, a report can contain bound controls that show data from the underlying table or query, unbound controls to show freestanding labels and pictures, and calculated controls that show the results of calculations.

- Add bound controls by dragging field names from the field list. Use the toolbox to add unbound controls, or to bind graphical controls such as check boxes and option buttons to fields. Create calculated controls using the Text Box tool in the toolbox, and an expression starting with an equals sign (=).

- Draw lines and rectangles using the Line and Rectangle tools in the toolbox.

- Hide or display the toolbox by choosing View ➤ Toolbox.

- Hide or display the Properties sheet by choosing View ➤ Properties, or by clicking the Properties button.

- To change the properties of a control, select the control before or after opening the Properties sheet.

- To change the properties of the report, select Edit ➤ Select Report, then open the Properties sheet (if it isn't already open). Or double-click on the gray background within the report area.

Setting Up the Printer for a Report

Because reports are geared toward printing, you also need to think about the printed page layout—margins, page size, and so forth. To change or define the page layout:

1. Starting from the report design, choose File ➤ Print Setup. Or, in print preview, click on the Setup button.

2. Choose options from the **Print Setup** dialog box, as discussed below, and/or click on the More button to change column layouts (Figure 12.2).

FIGURE 12.2

The Print Setup dialog
box with the More>>
options displayed

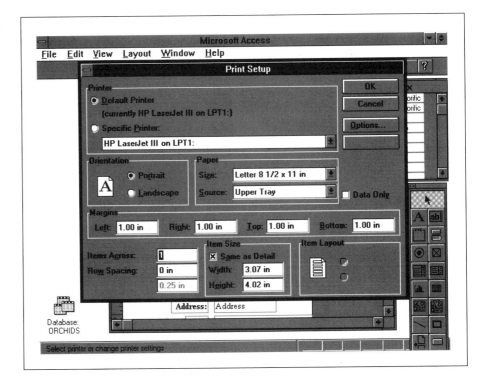

3. You can also choose the Options button to change settings that are specific to your particular printer.

4. Choose OK when you're done.

The options in the Print Setup dialog box are summarized below:

- **Printer**   Choose Default to have the report printed on the default printer (as defined in the Windows Control Panel), or select Specific Printer, then choose the printer you want to use to print the report. (The available printers are those that you've installed via Windows.)

- **Orientation**   Choose Portrait for "normal" (vertical) printing, or Landscape to print sideways on the page.

- **Paper**   Choose an available paper size and source, as relevant to your particular printer, from the options listed.

- **Data Only**   Choose this option to print data only, without grid-lines, borders, or graphics.

- **Margins**   Specify Left, Right, Top, and Bottom settings, as measured from the edge of the page.

TIP   The Mailing Label ReportWizard will set the options in the More dialog box for you.

The options in the **More** dialog box are:

- **Items Across**   Specify the number of columns to print across the page.

- **Row Spacing**   Specify the distance between items on the page, such as the empty space between mailing labels.

- **Column Spacing**   Specify the distance between columns (if Items Across is greater than one), such as the empty space between mailing labels.

- **Item Size**   Choose *Same As Detail* to print all of the report (or form). Or, if you're printing labels, clear the Same As Detail check box, and enter the Width and Height measurement of one label.

- **Item Layout**   If you've specified more than one column, choose *Horizontal* to arrange columns horizontally. Choose *Vertical* to print "snaking columns."

When you close the report format, any changes you made are saved with the report.

Preventing Blank Pages

Once you've determined the left and right margins for the report, and the page width, you need to keep in mind that anything beyond the right margin will print on a spillover page. Any "blank" report area beyond the right margin will also print on spillover pages, causing your report to be printed with a blank page between each page.

To prevent spillover pages, keep the report size within the margins. For instance, if you're printing on 8.5×11-inch paper (in portrait), and you've set 1-inch left and right margins, that leaves you a page width of 6.5 inches. If you size the report area to 6.5 inches, as in Figure 12.3, you won't have any spillover pages.

Be aware that, if any existing lines or other controls extend past the page width, you'll need to resize, move, or delete them before you can narrow the report to the page width you want.

FIGURE 12.3

Sizing the report to the page prevents spillover pages (including blank ones).

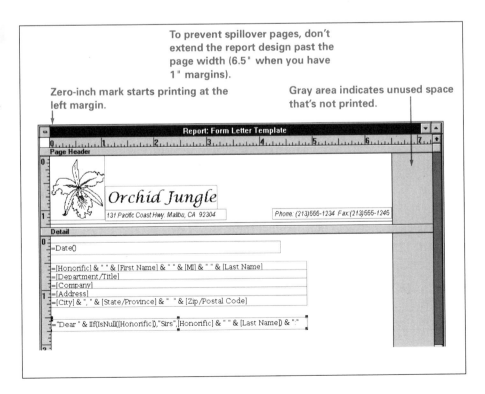

Checking Your Progress with Print Preview

When you're in the report design window, you can check to see how the report is shaping up from time to time by switching to Print Preview. Click on the Print Preview button, or choose File ➤ Sample Preview for a close-up preview, or File ➤ Print Preview for a preview of the entire page. You'll be taken to the Print Preview window (Figure 12.4). There you can:

* Click on the Print button to get to the **Print** dialog box and start printing.

* Click on the Setup button to get to the **Print Setup** dialog box and change page layout options.

FIGURE 12.4

You can check your progress as you design a report by switching to the Print Preview window.

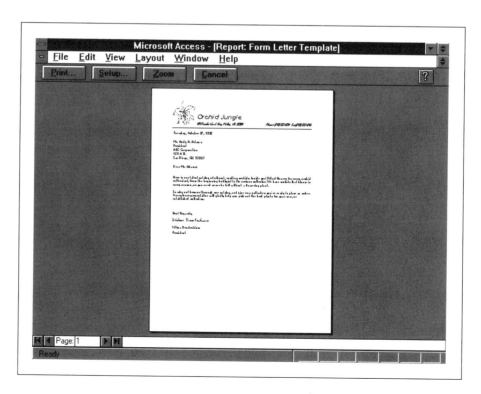

- Click on the Zoom button, or click anywhere on the report, to switch between full-page view and sample preview.
- Scroll through pages, or go to a specific page using the scroll buttons and page-number box in the lower left corner of the Print Preview window.
- Click on the Cancel button to return to the report design.

TIP   You can check for spillover pages before printing by scrolling through pages in Print Preview.

Report Sections

Like a form, a printed report is divided into sections. Each section plays a specific role in the report, as summarized below:

- **Report Header**   Printed once, at the beginning of the report.
- **Page Header**   Printed at the top of each page.
- **Group Header**   Printed at the top of a group of related records. Typically used to identify the group.
- **Detail**   Printed once for every record in the underlying table or query. This is where you usually place bound controls to display data from the underlying table or query.
- **Group Footer**   Printed at the end of a group. Typically used to display subtotals.
- **Page Footer**   Printed at the bottom of each page. (Useful for displaying page numbers.)
- **Report Footer**   Printed once at the end of the report. In reports with totals and subtotals, you can use this section to display grand totals.

Adding and Deleting Report and Page Sections

As with forms, you can choose Layout ➤ Page Hdr/Ftr, and Layout ➤ Report Hdr/Ftr to insert or remove the page header and footer or the report header and footer. (We'll talk about adding group headers and footers in a moment.)

Moving and Copying Controls between Sections

As in forms, you can move controls and their labels between sections by selecting the control and dragging. However, if a control has an attached label, and you want to move just the control, or just the label, you need to use cut-and-paste.

Sizing Sections

As with forms, you size sections by dragging the *bottom* of the section up or down. Remember, any blank space you leave in a section appears as blank space on the printed report as well!

Formatting Pages with Sections

You can change properties of sections within the report's design to control the vertical layout of each printed page. To change a section's properties:

- If the Properties sheet is already open, just double-click on the section, or on the bar across the top of the section.
- If the Properties sheet isn't already open, double-click on the report section or on the bar across the top of the section.

The Properties sheet is titled **Section** when you're changing the properties of the a section (Figure 12.5). Different sections offer different properties, but here's a brief description of what the main properties are:

- **Force New Page** You can force Access to start printing a new page before, after, or both before and after printing the section. The default is *None*—i.e., Access doesn't force a new page.

- **New Row or Col** In a multicolumn report, determines when Access switches to a new row (in a horizontal layout) or column (in a vertical "snaking" layout). Can be used with group headers and footers to start each group in a new row or column. Your options are *Before Section*, *After Section*, and *Before & After*. The default is *None*, where Access breaks to a new row or column only when the current row or column is completely filled.

FIGURE 12.5

Double-clicking on a section, or on the bar at the top of a section, displays the section's Properties sheet.

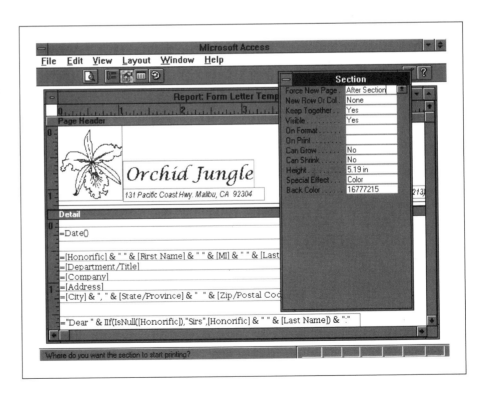

- **Keep Together** If set to *No* (the default), Access will split the contents of the section across two pages if there isn't room on the current page to print the entire section. If set to *Yes*, and there isn't enough room to print the entire section on the current page, Access moves to the next page before printing the section.

T I P Changing the detail section's Keep Together property to *No* eliminates any empty space that appears at the bottom of each printed page.

- **Visible** The default is *Yes*, where the section is always visible. You can change this to *No* to make the section invisible. (Useful when you want to hide a detail section and display only subtotals and totals.)

- **On Format** Lets you specify a macro or Access Basic module to run *before* the section is formatted for printing.

- **On Print** Lets you specify a macro or Access Basic module to run *after* the section is formatted, but before it's printed.

- **Can Grow** Determines whether the section can grow to accommodate all the data in the section (*Yes*), or if the section maintains a consistent size (*No*). When printing labels, this should always be set to *No* to ensure that each label is printed at the same height.

- **Can Shrink** Determines whether the section will shrink to best fit the data printed within (*Yes*), or will always be printed at a consistent size (*No*). When printing labels, this too should be set to *No* to ensure that each label is printed at the same size.

- **Height** You can set the height of the section by dragging the bottom of the section, or by placing an exact measurement in this property.

• **Special Effect** and **Back Color**   Change these properties with the Appearance and Fill options in the color palette.

Controlling Page Breaks

You can force Access to skip to a new page anywhere in report design. For instance, if you want to use the report header as a separate cover page, you can end that report section with a page break. If you want each record in the report to be printed on a separate page, you can end the detail section with a page break. You can use the Force New Page property described above to control page breaks.

Optionally, if you want to break to a new page within a section, use the Page Break tool in the tool bar to insert a page-break control wherever you want the new page to begin.

Omitting the Page Header and Footer from Certain Pages

In some cases, you might not want to print page headers and footers on the report header or footer. A perfect example of this is in the Catalog report that's in the sample Northwind database (*nwind.mdb*) that came with your Access package. That report uses a two-page report header to display a cover sheet and introductory page at the beginning of the report, and uses the report footer to print an order form. Within the body of the report (but not on the cover sheets or order form), a page footer is used to print page numbers and a logo at the bottom of each page.

To choose whether or not you want the page header and/or footer to print in the report header and/or footer:

1. In report design, choose Edit ➤ Select Report, then open the Properties sheet. Or, just double-click on the gray area in the form's background.

2. Choose the Page Header option, or Page Footer option, and choose whichever option describes where you want to print page headers and footers. Your options are shown below.

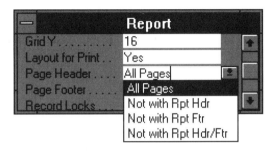

Formatting the Appearance of Fields

To change a field's font, alignment, color, or special effect, select the field (or fields) in design view, and use the font tools, alignment buttons, and/or color palette to make your changes (just as you'd do in a form).

You can also control the size of printed fields, as discussed in the next two sections.

Squeezing Out Blank Lines and Spaces

Empty fields in a table will often print as blank lines in your report. For instance, if you create a mailing label format without the aid of a Wizard, you might find that a record with blank Department/Title and Company fields prints like this:

Mr. John Q. Smith
(blank)
(blank)
65 Overton Hwy
Holland, MI 49423

To squeeze out the blank lines, go to the report's design view, and select the control that displays the field. Then open the Properties sheet and change the control's Can Shrink property to *Yes*. This tells Access to "print nothing" (not even a blank line) if the underlying field is empty.

To ensure that no blanks are *ever* printed, change the Can Shrink property for *all* the controls in the report to *Yes*.

When printing labels, you always want each label to be printed at the same size. Therefore, you should change the Can Shrink properties of the *controls* to *Yes*, to squeeze out the blanks, but leave the Can Shrink property of the *section* to *No*, so that each label is printed at the same size.

Printing Lengthy Memo Text

If your report includes a memo field, and you want to ensure that the entire field's contents are printed, set the Can Grow property for the control that displays the memo to *Yes*.

When you set the Can Grow property for a control to Yes, Access also sets the Can Grow property for the report section to Yes, so that both the control and the section can expand to accommodate the data.

Formatting Numbers and Dates

To change the format or numbers and dates, change the Format property of the control that displays the number or date. That is, in design view, select the control that contains the number or date that you want to format. Then open the Properties sheet and choose an option from the Format property, as below:

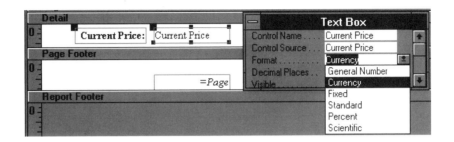

TIP   You can also design your own custom formats, as discussed under "Assigning Format Properties to Control Appearance" in Chapter 6.

Sorting and Grouping Data

As we discussed back in Chapter 7, sorting records in a table is a natural way to group like information together. For instance, if you sort records in the Products table by Category ID, all the records in each category will naturally be grouped together.

One of the more powerful features of reports is that you can add group headers and group footers, to appear at the top and bottom of each group. For instance, rather than printing the category name repeatedly in the left column of the report, you could place the category name in a group header, above the records. You can also use a group footer to display information at the end of the group. This is particularly handy for displaying subtotals and totals, as in Figure 12.6.

FIGURE 12.6

You can include group headers and footers in a report, to appear at the top and bottom of each printed group.

Current Inventory ◄——— report header

27-Oct-92

Category ID: MOTH ◄——————— group header (at top of each group)

Product ID	Description	Current Price	In Stock	On Order	Value
MO-100	Margo	$18.00	100	0	$1,800.00
MO-101	Playtime	$18.00	10	15	$450.00
MO-102	Goliath	$49.50	54	0	$2,673.00
MO-103	Dark Delight	$20.00	15	0	$300.00
MO-104	Peppermint Pleasure	$16.00	10	0	$160.00

group footer (at bottom of each group) ——► **189   15 $5,383.00**

Category ID: PANSY

Product ID	Description	Current Price	In Stock	On Order	Value
PA-100	Midnight Giant	$28.50	50	0	$1,425.00
PA-101	Independence Day	$15.00	100	0	$1,500.00
PA-102	Piccadilly	$26.50	50	0	$1,325.00
PA-103	Blue Boy	$17.00	25	50	$1,275.00
PA-104	Goodnews	$17.50	32	0	$560.00
			257	**50**	**$6,085.00**

Category ID: PROM

Product ID	Description	Current Price	In Stock	On Order	Value
PR-100	Majestic	$40.00	100	0	$4,000.00
PR-101	Pink Sensation	$25.00	67	0	$1,675.00
PR-102	Breaker's Reach	$35.00	0	0	$0.00
PR-103	Rolling Thunder	$32.50	65	0	$2,112.50
PR-104	Polar Haze	$40.00	40	0	$1,600.00
PR-105	Memory Lane	$32.50	20	0	$650.00
PR-106	Jeweler's Art	$34.50	15	50	$2,242.50
PR-107	Gambler's Luck	$42.50	45	0	$1,912.50
			352	**50**	**$14,192.50**

Category ID: SLIPPER

Product ID	Description	Current Price	In Stock	On Order	Value
SL-100	Callosum	$28.75	121	0	$3,478.75
SL-101	Constellation	$28.75	123	0	$3,536.25
SL-102	Yerba Buena	$23.00	55	0	$1,265.00
SL-103	Bell o' Ireland	$51.75	25	0	$1,293.75
SL-104	Madre de Dios	$77.63	30	0	$2,328.75
			354	**0**	**$11,902.50**

Category ID: SPIDER

Product ID	Description	Current Price	In Stock	On Order	Value
SP-100	Featherhill	$20.00	50	0	$1,000.00
SP-101	Geyserland	$49.50	25	0	$1,237.50
SP-102	Royal Robe	$75.00	20	0	$1,500.00
SP-103	Fireworks	$85.00	15	0	$1,275.00
			110	**0**	**$5,012.50**

Grand Total :   report footer ——► **1262   115 $42,575.50**

Page 1

You can group on up to 10 fields, or expressions, to print groups within groups. You can also include fields to sort on, without group headers and footers, to sort within the group. For instance, the products within each category in Figure 12.6 are sorted (alphabetized) by Product ID.

A quick way to get the hang of grouping and sorting is by using the Group/Totals Wizard to create some reports that use grouping. For instance, you might try basing a Group/Totals field on the Products table, using the Category ID as the field to group on, "Normal" when asked how to group, and Product ID as the field to sort on. When you get to the last Wizard screen, open the report in design view. Then switch back and forth between print preview and design view to see how the Wizard designed the report, and how it would look when printed.

As an alternative to using a Wizard, you can define sorting and grouping fields in the report design yourself. Here's how:

1. In the report design view, click on the Sorting and Grouping button in the tool bar, or choose View ➤ Sorting and Grouping to get to the **Sorting and Grouping** dialog box.

2. Click in the Field/Expression column, then use the drop-down list to choose a field to sort or group on.

3. If you want to sort in descending, rather than ascending, order click on the Sort Order column, and choose *Descending*.

4. If you want to use the field for grouping, and want a group header, change the Group Header property at the bottom of the dialog box to *Yes*.

5. If you want a group footer, change the Group Footer property at the bottom of the dialog box to Yes.

6. Optionally, change the Group On and Group Interval properties to define the size of the group, as discussed under "Setting Group Ranges and Intervals" later in this chapter.

7. You can repeat Steps 2 through 5 to define up to ten levels of grouping and sorting.

Initially, Access leaves the group header and/or footer section empty. So in print preview, you just see empty space between the groups. You can add controls to the sections to display whatever information you want in the section. For instance, Figure 12.7 shows the design of the report shown back in Figure 12.6, with groups defined and with the header and footer sections filled in.

The group header section for the category ID field contains the expression:

="Category ID: " & [Category ID]

which displays the text *Category ID:* followed by a blank space and the contents of the Category ID field in the underlying table.

The detail section contains controls from the underlying table, Products in this example. There's also one calculated control, created with the Text Box tool from the toolbox, that contains the expression:

=[Current Price]*([Units In Stock]+[Units On Order])

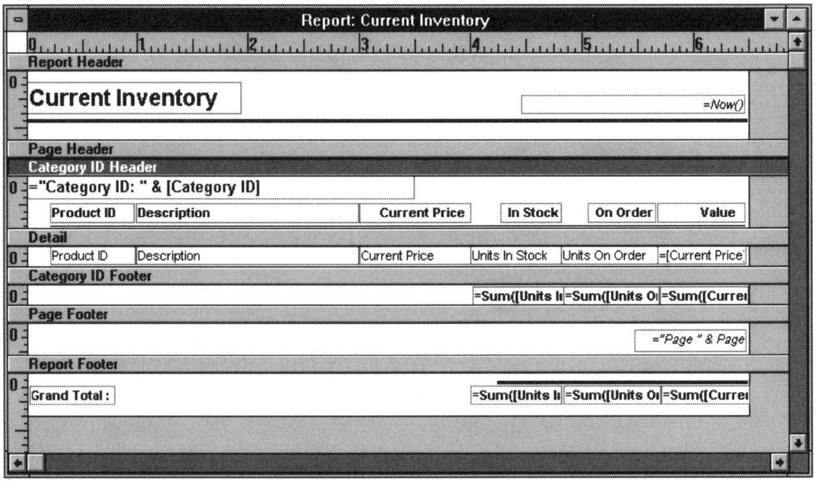

FIGURE 12.7

The report design for the Current Inventory report shown in Figure 12.6

The group footer section for the Category ID field contains the calculated controls (also created with the Text Box tool in the toolbox) that contains the expressions:

```
=Sum([Units In Stock])
=Sum([Units On Order])
=Sum([Current Price]*([Units In Stock]+[Units On Order]))
```

Because these expressions are in the Category ID footer section, they calculate the sums for each group, and display the results of the calculations at the bottom of each group.

The report footer section also contains calculated controls, with identical **=Sum( )** expressions. However, since those expressions are in the report footer section, they base their calculations on all the records in the report, and appear only once at the end of the report.

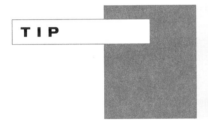

TIP   If you use the Group/Totals Wizard to create a report, Access automatically creates group headers and footers for each field that you group on, and automatically adds controls for totaling all the numeric and currency fields in the report.

Arranging Fields in the Sorting and Grouping Box

Keep in mind that when you want to group and sort on multiple fields, you want to list fields in the Sorting and Grouping dialog box in most-important to least-important order. For example, if you were basing the report on the Customers table, and want to sort records by people's last names, and by first name and middle initial within identical last names (like the phone book), you'd list the field names like this:

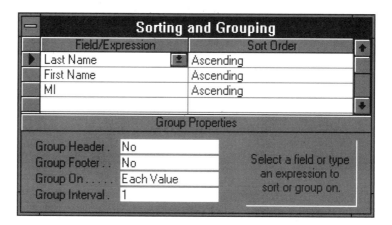

If you need to rearrange rows in the Sorting and Grouping dialog box, click on the row selector at the left of the row you want to move. Then click a second time, and drag the row to its new position. You can also press Delete to delete the selected row, or press Insert to insert a new row at the selected row's position.

You can add or delete a group header or footer for any field by changing its properties at the bottom of the dialog box. Fields that have group headers and/or footers are indicated with the grouping icon in the row selector, as shown below:

Grouping icon ———→

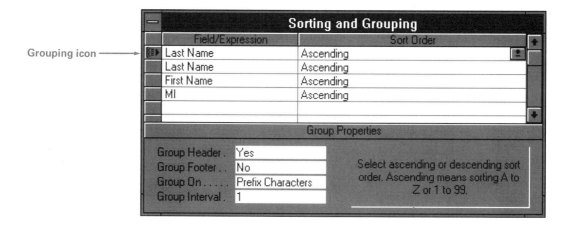

Defining Group Ranges and Intervals

Normally, a group will be based on the full contents of the field, or expression, in the underlying table or query. For instance, in our sample report shown back in Figure 12.6, each category name defines a single group.

You can also group on ranges and intervals. If the group is based on a text field, you can group on just the first letter, or first few letters. If the group is based on a date/time field, you can group records by week, month, quarter, or some other unit of time.

You change the group range and interval by changing the Group On and Group Interval properties at the bottom of the Sorting and Grouping dialog box. Or, if you use the Group/Total ReportWizard to create the report, the Wizard will prompt you for grouping ranges and intervals.

Grouping On Part of a Text Field

If your group is based on a text field or expression, you can group on the first character, or first several characters. In the example shown in Figure 12.8, records are grouped by the first character.

In the report's design, shown in Figure 12.9, the Last Name field is used for grouping. The Group On property is set to *Prefix Characters*, and the Group Interval is set to *1*, to base the grouping on the first character of each last name. The last name, first name, and middle initials are also included, but only for sorting. Table 12.1 summarizes the settings for all the group fields in the report.

In case you're wondering why the Last Name field is listed twice, keep in mind that the group field is only looking at the first character in each last name. Using the Last Name field for sorting ensures that records within each group will be alphabetized by the complete last name (as well the first name and middle initial, in this example).

The single letter printed at the top of each group is printed by a calculated control in the group header. The expression for that control is:

    =Left([Last Name],1)

FIGURE 12.8

A customer phone list, with records grouped by the first letter of the person's last name

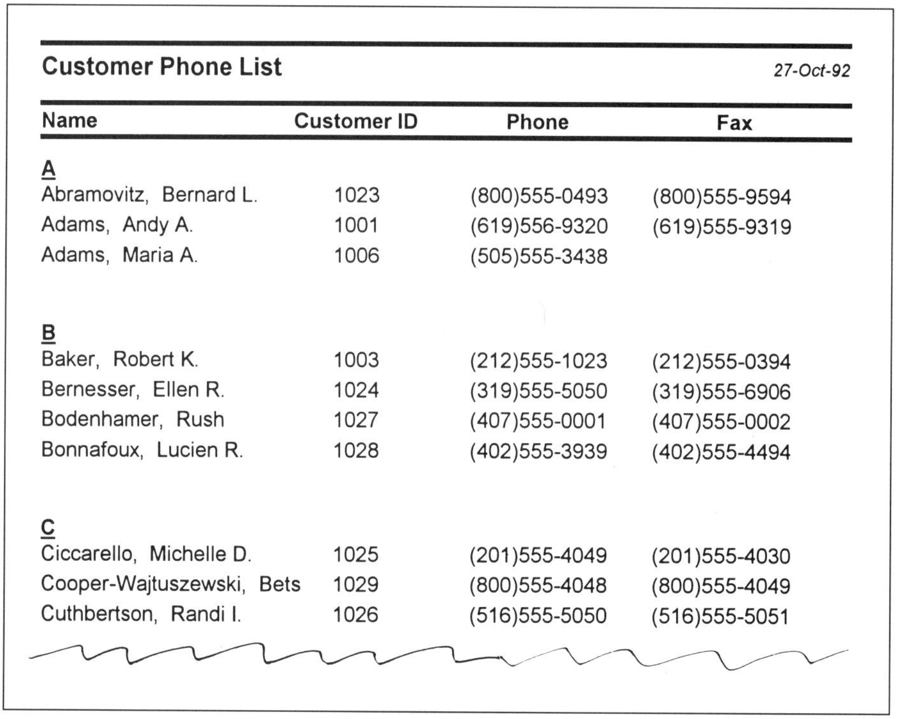

Customer Phone List			27-Oct-92
Name	**Customer ID**	**Phone**	**Fax**
A			
Abramovitz, Bernard L.	1023	(800)555-0493	(800)555-9594
Adams, Andy A.	1001	(619)556-9320	(619)555-9319
Adams, Maria A.	1006	(505)555-3438	
B			
Baker, Robert K.	1003	(212)555-1023	(212)555-0394
Bernesser, Ellen R.	1024	(319)555-5050	(319)555-6906
Bodenhamer, Rush	1027	(407)555-0001	(407)555-0002
Bonnafoux, Lucien R.	1028	(402)555-3939	(402)555-4494
C			
Ciccarello, Michelle D.	1025	(201)555-4049	(201)555-4030
Cooper-Wajtuszewski, Bets	1029	(800)555-4048	(800)555-4049
Cuthbertson, Randi I.	1026	(516)555-5050	(516)555-5051

TABLE 12.1: Sorting and Grouping fields for the Customer Phone List report

FIELD/ EXPRESSION	SORT ORDER	GROUP HEADER	GROUP FOOTER	GROUP ON	GROUP INTERVAL
Last Name	Ascending	Yes	No	prefix characters	1
Last Name	Ascending	No	No	each value	1
First Name	Ascending	No	No	each value	1
MI	Ascending	No	No	each value	1

FIGURE 12.9

The design of the customer phone list report shown in Figure 12.8, with the Sorting and Grouping dialog box open

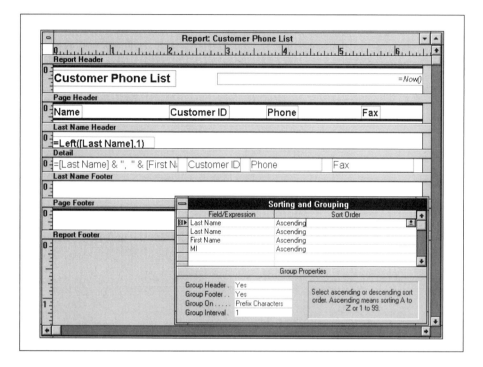

bolded and underlined. (The **Left( )** function displays the leftmost character(s) of a string.) The names themselves are printed by a calculated control in the detail section. The expression in that control is:

    =[Last Name]&", "&[First Name]&"   "&[MI]

Grouping on a Numeric Field

If the group is based on a number, currency, or counter field, you can group by ranges of numbers. For example, the sample Gift Ideas report shown in Figure 12.10 is grouped on the Current Price field, with the Group On interval set to *10*.

Table 12.2 summarizes the Sorting and Grouping fields used in the Gift Ideas report design. The Current Price field is listed twice: first to define the group interval of 10, and a second time to sort records by the full contents of the field within each group. The Description field sorts records by product name (the Description field) within identical prices.

FIGURE 12.10

A sample report with
records grouped on
Current Price, with the
Group On property
set to Interval, and the
Group Interval set to 10

Gift Ideas

Price	Description	Product ID	Genus	In Stock
$10 to $19				
$16.00	Peppermint Pleasure	MO-104	*Phalaenopsis*	10
$18.00	Margo	MO-100	*Phalaenopsis*	100
$18.00	Playtime	MO-101	*Phalaenopsis*	10
$20 to $29				
$20.00	Dark Delight	MO-103	*Phalaenopsis*	15
$23.00	Yerba Buena	SL-102	*Paphiopedilum*	55
$25.00	Pink Sensation	PR-101	*Cattleya*	67
$28.75	Callosum	SL-100	*Paphiopedilum*	121
$28.75	Constellation	SL-101	*Paphiopedilum*	123
$30 to $39				
$32.50	Memory Lane	PR-105	*Cattleya*	20
$32.50	Rolling Thunder	PR-103	*Cattleya*	65
$34.50	Jeweler's Art	PR-106	*Cattleya*	15
$35.00	Breaker's Reach	PR-102	*Cattleya*	0
$40 to $49				
$40.00	Majestic	PR-100	*Cattleya*	100
$40.00	Polar Haze	PR-104	*Cattleya*	40
$42.50	Gambler's Luck	PR-107	*Cattleya*	45
$49.50	Goliath	MO-102	*Phalaenopsis*	54
$50 to $59				
$51.75	Bell o' Ireland	SL-103	*Paphiopedilum*	25
$70 to $79				
$77.63	Madre de Dios	SL-104	*Paphiopedilum*	30

1

TABLE 12.2: Sorting and Grouping fields used in the Gift Ideas report shown in Figure 12.10

FIELD/ EXPRESSION	SORT ORDER	GROUP HEADER	GROUP FOOTER	GROUP ON	GROUP INTERVAL
Current Price	Ascending	Yes	No	interval	10
Current Price	Ascending	No	No	each value	1
Description	Ascending	No	No	each value	1

The expression used in the group header of this report's design is:

="$"&([Current Price]\10)*10 & " to $"&((([Current Price]*10)\10)*10-1

If you use the Group/Totals Report Wizard to create a report like this, the Wizard will create a similar expression automatically. (In this example, I just added the dollar signs to the expression that the Wizard created.)

Grouping by Date and Time

If you group on a date/time field, you can organize the groups by any time interval ranging from a minute to a year. For instance, Figure 12.11 shows data about orders, organized into months (January, February, and March) and broken down by salesperson within each month.

The report in this figure is unique in a couple of ways. For one thing, it's based on a query that joins the Employees, Orders, and Order Details tables. It also "hides the details," showing just the totals and subtotals. We'll discuss both those topics in a moment. For now, let's just take a look at the grouping fields, summarized in Table 12.3.

TABLE 12.3: Sorting and Grouping fields used in the Monthly Sales report shown in Figure 12.11

FIELD/ EXPRESSION	SORT ORDER	GROUP HEADER	GROUP FOOTER	GROUP ON	GROUP INTERVAL
Order Date	Ascending	Yes	Yes	month	1
Name	Ascending	No	Yes	each value	1

FIGURE 12.11

Sales grouped by
month and salesperson

Monthly Sales

January of 1993

George E. Evans :	$7,373.75
Oliver Feelgood :	$3,734.45
Wanda Granolabar :	$5,982.10
Subtotal for January :	$17,090.30

February of 1993

George E. Evans :	$11,075.00
Oliver Feelgood :	$2,903.02
Wanda Granolabar :	$9,691.20
Subtotal for February :	$23,669.22

March of 1993

George E. Evans :	$4,825.45
Oliver Feelgood :	$4,776.70
Wanda Granolabar :	$5,532.70
Subtotal for March :	$15,134.85

Grand Total :	$55,894.37

The first field, Order Date, defines the grouping by month, where Group On is set to *Month* and Group Interval is set to *1*. The second group is based on the Name field in the Employees table, to sort records by employee name within each month.

Calculations in Reports

A report, like a form, can contain calculated controls. The expression within the calculated control can be any valid Access expression, and you can include any of the many functions that Access offers, including **Sum ( )**, **Avg( )** (average), **Count( )**, and so forth.

To add a calculated control to the report design:

1. If the toolbox isn't already visible in design view, (choose View ➤ Toolbox to display it.

2. Click on the Text Box tool (shown at left) in the toolbox.

3. Move the pointer into the report design, within whatever section you want to place the calculated control, and with the **+** sign wherever you want to put the calculated control.

4. Click to create a default-size text box, or drag a rectangle to indicate the size you want the text box to be.

An unbound text box appears. It might also have an attached label, depending on the defaults for the report you're designing. If need be, you can delete the label by selecting just the label and pressing Delete.

You can enter an expression into the text box in either of two ways:

- Select the text box, and then click again to move the insertion into the text box. Type the expression, starting with an equals sign (=) into the box.

- *Or*, select the text box, and then open the Properties sheet. Type the expression—starting with an equals sign (=)—into the Control Source property. You can also give a more meaningful name to the control, such as Monthly Subtotal rather than Field24, by changing the Control Name property at the top of the Properties sheet.

TIP

When you use the Control Source property in the Properties sheet to enter or change an expression, you can also use the Zoom feature (Shift+F2).

The calculation can be virtually any Access expression. As usual, you can refer to fields in the underlying table or query, or to names of controls on the report, by enclosing their names in square brackets.

Adding Page Numbers and Dates

If you want the calculated control to display the current date, use the expression **=Date( )**, or **=Now( )** in that control. You can then choose the Format property for that control to determine how you want the date to look.

If you want the calculated control to display the current page number, place the expression **=Page** in the calculated control. You'll probably want to place this control in the page header or page footer section, so that it's printed at the top or bottom of each page.

Resetting the Page Number

You can do a little basic math with =Page to reset the page number if necessary. For instance, suppose your report has two cover pages, like the Catalog example in the Northwind database. You want to print page numbers in page footers *after* these cover pages, with the first page being page 1.

First, you'd need to use Edit ➤ Select Report and open the Properties sheet to set the Page Footer properties to *Not With Rpt Hdr*, so the page numbers don't appear until after the cover sheets are printed. Then, in the page footer, create a calculated control like this:

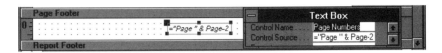

The first two pages will print without page numbers, then the third page will print page numbers, but starting at 1, rather than 3.

Manipulating Text and Dates

Calculated controls can contain expressions that join and manipulate text. For instance, the expression below:

[Honorific]&" "&[First Name]&" "&[MI]&" "&[Last Name]

displays data from the Honorific, First Name, MI, and Last Name fields in this format:

Mr. Andy A. Adams

N O T E   To insert freestanding text that's *not* based on a calculation or a field, use the Label tool, rather than the Text Box tool, as discussed in "Adding Your Own Text to a Form" in Chapter 10.

You can use the many Access *string functions*, such as **Left( )**, **Right( )**, and **Mid( )** to print a portion of text. (Chapter 17 serves as a reference to Access functions and expressions.) You saw an example earlier in this chapter where we used the **Left( )** function to display the first letter of a person's last name in the group header.

You can also use **IIf( )** to make a decision about what to print, based on the contents of a field. For instance, you could use this expression in the salutation of a form letter:

```
="Dear  " & IIf(IsNull([Honorific]),"Sirs",[Honorific] &  "  " & [Last Name]) & ":"
```

In English this says:

> *"Print the word **Dear** followed by a blank space. Then, if the Honorific field is empty, print the word **Sirs;** otherwise, print the Honorific and the Last Name. Then print a colon at the end."*

Thus, if the Honorific field in the current record is empty, the salutation comes out looking like this:

Dear Sirs:

If the Honorific field isn't empty, the salutation is printed in this format:

Dear Mr. Adams:

You can also perform date arithmetic, and use the many date functions to isolate a part of a date, in a calculated control's expression. For instance, to print just the month name from the Order Date field, you'd use the expression:

```
Format([Order Date],"mmmm")
```

For examples of expressions that perform date arithmetic, see "Examples of Calculated Controls" in Chapter 10. For more information on expressions and functions in general, refer to Chapter 17.

Calculating Totals and Subtotals

To calculate totals and subtotals in reports, you add calculated controls to the appropriate sections of the report's design. You can use the **Sum( )** function for a total or subtotal. You can also use other aggregate functions, such as **Avg( )**, **Count( )**, and so forth, to calculate averages, counts, and other statistical measurements.

It's important that you place the calculated control in the section that you want to base the calculation on. Keep in mind that:

- If the calculated control is in the header or footer section of a group, the calculation is based on the records in that group only (i.e., it is a subtotal).

- If the calculated control is in the report footer section, the calculation is based on all the records, in all the groups (i.e., it is a grand total).

- If the calculated control is in the detail section, the calculation is based on the current record only (hence it shouldn't use a **Sum( )** or other aggregate operator).

As an example, the detail section in the sample report design below contains the expression:

=[Qty]*[Unit Price]

which is the familiar expression for calculating the extended price of a single record in the Order Details table.

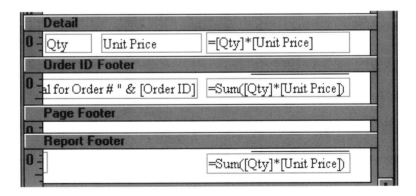

Both the Order ID footer, and the Report Footer include calculated controls that contain the expression:

=Sum([Qty]*[Unit Price])

Though the expressions are identical, the one in the Order ID footer section sums and displays the total of extended price for the current group only. The same calculated control, in the report footer, calculates the sum of the extended price for all the records in the report.

Performing the Calculation in a Query

If you're basing the report on a query, you might want to consider using calculated fields in the query design to do whatever calculations you need. That way, any expressions that you use in the report design need only refer to the name of the calculated field in the underlying query. Thus, you won't need to use complicated expressions in your report design. And, you can take advantage of totaling and crosstab capabilities of queries.

For instance, take a look at the query shown in Figure 12.12. Notice that I've included a calculated field named Total Sale in the QBE grid, which

FIGURE 12.12

Total Sale is a calculated field in the query.

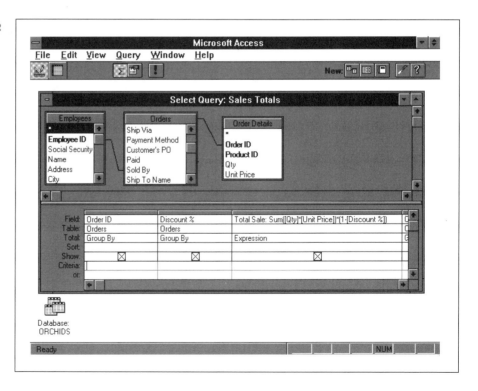

calculates the total sale based on the sum of the extended price and the discount applied to the order.

NOTE The QBE grid shown in Figure 12.12 also includes the Name field from the Orders table, and the Order Date field from the Orders table, for inclusion on the Monthly Sales report.

If you base a report on this query, the report can refer directly to the Total Sale field in any expressions you use in the form, as in Figure 12.13.

FIGURE 12.13

The design of the Monthly Sales report, based on the query shown in Figure 12.12

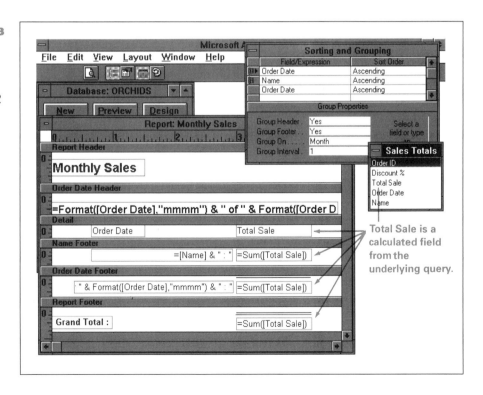

Naming and Formatting Calculated Controls

Remember that after you create a calculated control with the Text Box tool, you can give that control a name, and set its Format property to control its appearance. For instance, in the example below I've named the calculated control Sales Rep Total, and have given it the Currency format.

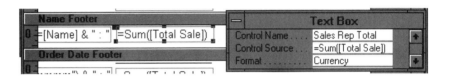

In general, you can refer to the control name in another expression, as we'll discuss under "Calculating Percentages" later in this chapter. (Keep in mind, though, that a **Sum( )** or other aggregate function can't refer to a control name—those can only refer to field names in the underlying table or query, or expressions based on those underlying field names.)

Hiding the Details

When you want to create a summary report that shows only the totals and subtotals, like our sample Monthly Sales report, you can just hide the detail section. But it's a good idea to print a copy *with* the detail section included first, so you can check your math and make sure you've done all the calculations in the report and/or underlying query first. (After all, like any program, Access just does whatever calculations you tell it to—it's up to *you* to make sure it does the correct calculations for the task at hand!)

When you are ready to hide the detail section, just double-click on the detail section's title bar in the report design. Then set its Visible property to *No*, as below. The section will still appear in the report design, but will be invisible in the printed copy.

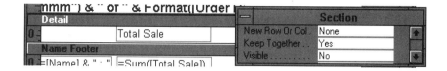

Fixing Rounding Errors

Be aware that even though the Currency format *displays* data with two decimal places of accuracy, it bases its calculations on four places of accuracy. This can occasionally cause totals to be off by a penny. You can use the **CLng( )** data type conversion function (Chapter 17) to minimize rounding errors.

Calculating Percentages in Reports

When Access prints a report, it actually makes two passes through the report. On the first pass, it calculates all the subtotals and totals. On the second pass, it can perform calculations based on those totals and subtotals. This means that, as in a spreadsheet, you can include calculated controls that refer to other calculated controls that appear "later" in the report. For instance, you can create calculated controls that refer to the grand total at the bottom of the report, even though those grand totals don't actually *appear* until the end of the report. This is perfect for calculating percentages.

To calculate percentages, you first need to assign a control name (using the Control Name property in the Properties sheet) to any controls that you want to refer to in other calculations. For instance, Figure 12.14 shows Control Names assigned to various calculated controls in the Monthly Sales report.

Once you've assigned names to those controls, you can refer to them in calculated controls as you would refer to a field name—by enclosing the

FIGURE 12.14

Control Names,
assigned via the
Properties sheet, to
various controls in our
sample Monthly Sales
report

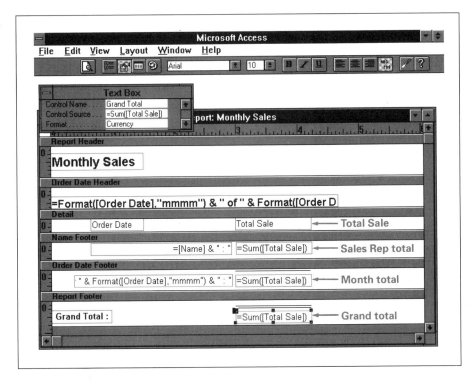

control's name in square brackets in an expression. For instance, the expression below:

=[Monthly Total]/[Grand Total]

determines the monthly total as a percent of the grand total.

CAUTION

Keep in mind that you *cannot* refer to control names
in aggregate and domain aggregate functions.
Thus, an expression like *=Sum([Monthly Total]/
[Grand Total])* is not allowed, because Monthly Total
and Grand Total are names of controls on the
report, not names of fields in the table.

Figure 12.15 shows a modified version of the Monthly Sales report, which includes a column indicating what percent of the monthly total each sales rep contributed. It also includes the total percent that each month contributes to the grand total.

Figure 12.16 shows the design of that report.

Here's a summary of changes made to the original version of the report (after assigning control names as described earlier):

- In the Order Date header section, added the column titles *Sales Rep*, *Total Sales*, and *% of this Month*, using the Label tool in the toolbox. Also added an underline using the Line tool in the toolbox.

- In the Name footer section, added the calculated control at the far right using the Text Box tool, containing the expression:

  =[Sales Rep Total]/[Month Total]

  Also set its Format property to *Percent*, and Decimal Places to zero.

- In the Order Date footer section, used the Text Box tool to add a calculated control that contains the expression:

  =Format([Order Date], " mmmm ")&'s percent of Grand Total

  to display the text next to the percentage calculation.

- Also in the Order Date footer section, used the Text Box tool to create a calculated control containing the expression:

  =[Monthly Total]/[Grand Total]

  Also set its Format property to *Percent* and Decimal Places to zero. Then used the color palette to change its border from clear to black.

Running Sums in Reports

You can convert any number or currency field in your report to a running sum, to calculate totals on a record-by-record basis. To do so:

1. Select the field you want to convert to a running sum.

Monthly Sales

January of 1993

Sales Rep	Total Sales	% of this Month
George E. Evans :	$7,373.75	43%
Oliver Feelgood :	$3,734.45	22%
Wanda Granolabar :	$5,982.10	35%
Subtotal for January :	$17,090.30	
January's percent of Grand Total:	31%	

February of 1993

Sales Rep	Total Sales	% of this Month
George E. Evans :	$11,075.00	47%
Oliver Feelgood :	$2,903.02	12%
Wanda Granolabar :	$9,691.20	41%
Subtotal for February :	$23,669.22	
February's percent of Grand Total:	42%	

March of 1993

Sales Rep	Total Sales	% of this Month
George E. Evans :	$4,825.45	32%
Oliver Feelgood :	$4,776.70	32%
Wanda Granolabar :	$5,532.70	37%
Subtotal for March :	$15,134.85	
March's percent of Grand Total:	27%	
Grand Total :	$55,894.37	

FIGURE 12.16

The design of the
report shown in
Figure 12.15, which
includes percentage
calculations

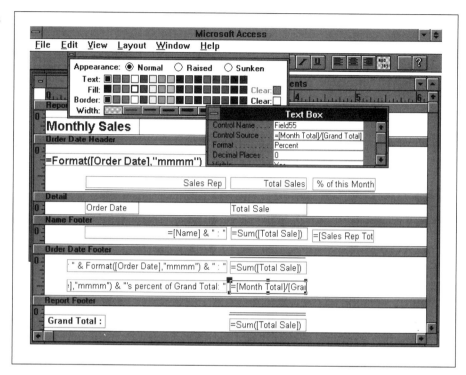

2. Open the Properties sheet, and change the Running Sum property
as below:

- If you want the running sum to continue through all records
displayed in the report, choose *Over All*.

- If your report contains group headers and footers, and you
want the running sum to be reset to zero at the top of each
group, choose *Over Group*.

The rightmost column in the report shown in Figure 12.17 uses the Running Sum property to calculate a running total of sales in the rightmost
column.

FIGURE 12.17

Portion of a sample
report (in print
preview) that uses a
running sum to keep
a running total of
sales by date.

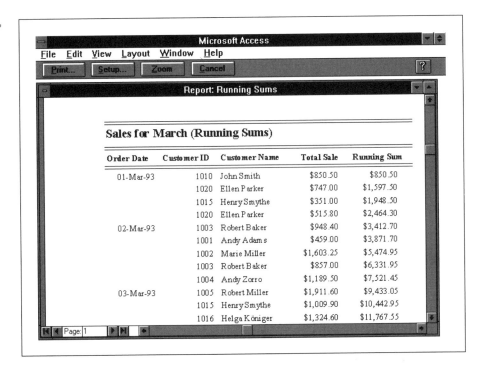

TIP

Search Access's help system for *RunningSum*
(one word) to find some other examples of using
the Running Sum property.

Hiding Duplicate Values

If you sort by a field in your report design, and don't use a group header
and/or footer to introduce or end the group, your report will normally list
duplicate values in the field. If you simply want to hide the duplicate
values, without creating a group header or footer:

1. In the report design, select the field that you want to hide dupli-
    cates in.

2. Open the Properties sheet, and change the Hide Duplicates property to *Yes*.

Doing that tells Access to hide the contents of the field if those contents are identical to the record above. For example, I used Hide Duplicates in the Order Date field of the report shown in Figure 12.17 to prevent duplicate dates from appearing in the Order Date column. The detail section for that report is shown below, in design view:

Hide Duplicates property set to Yes   Running Sum property set to Over All

General Techniques for Printing

As with any object, you use File ➤ Print to print a report:

1. If the report *isn't* open in Print Preview or design view, just click on the Report object button in the database window, then click on the name of the report that you want to print.

2. Choose File ➤ Print to get to the **Print** dialog box (shown below). Then choose from among any of the options offered, as described below.

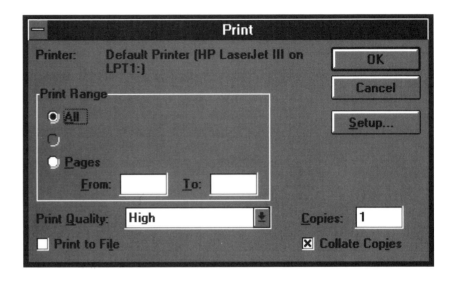

* To print the entire report, choose All under Print Range. Otherwise, choose Pages and indicate the range of pages that you want to print in the From and To text boxes.

* Optionally, choose a Print Quality. A low print quality is usually fastest, but doesn't print graphics. A higher quality is slower, but prints text and graphics at the sharpest quality.

* To print to a file rather than to the printer, choose the Print To File check box. You'll be prompted for a file name after you choose OK.

* To print multiple copies, indicate the number of copies that you want to print in the Copies text box.

* If you opt to print more than one copy, you can also select or deselect the Collate Copies check box. (You can press F1 for help if you're not familiar with this option.)

3. Choose OK when you're ready to start printing.

After a brief delay, Access will begin printing the report.

Printing to a File

If you choose the Print To File check box in the Print dialog box, Access will prompt you for a file name after you choose OK to start printing. If you want to store the file in your Access database, provide an Access name (up to 64 characters). If you want to print to a regular file on the disk, provide a complete path and file name (e.g., **a:\myreport.txt**).

The file you print will be formatted for the currently selected printer. Thus, you can print the report later, directly from DOS, to the appropriate printer port using the DOS copy command—for instance:

copy a:\myreport.txt >prn

If you want to print a report to an ASCII text file, first install the *Generic/Text Only* printer driver (or a similar driver) via the Printers option in the **Windows Control Panel**. Then, in Access, select that printer driver, using the Setup button in the Print dialog box, before you print the report to the file.

Examples of Access Reports

If you've been reading along from the start of this chapter, you're probably thinking "Whew! That's a lot of stuff to think about. *How* do I apply all that stuff to get the report format I want?"

For starters, your best bet is to practice creating some reports with the Wizards. The Wizards are fast and relatively easy. So even if your report doesn't come out quite as expected, you can always just close it, without saving it, then start over. Or, if you get the report in the general ballpark of what you want, you can then just modify the format that the Wizard created and refine the report's design to your liking.

It also helps to look at examples of other reports. For the remainder of this chapter, I'll present some general examples, and describe the most significant features of each one. Remember, you can also explore the sample reports in the Northwind and other sample databases that came with your Access package for additional insights.

Printing Mailing Labels

You can create a report to print mailing labels using the Mailing Label ReportWizard. The Wizard will prompt you for fields to include on the label, and allow you to insert spaces and punctuation as necessary. You'll also be able to choose from a variety of label sizes.

The Wizard takes care of placing the controls on the report design, and also sets up the margins, Items Across, and other necessary settings in the Print Setup dialog box for the report.

Printing Envelopes

If your printer has the capability, you can print data directly on envelopes.

- In the Print Setup dialog box, under the Paper options, choose an *Envelope* paper size, and the Source for the envelopes.

- If you need to include a return address on each envelope, set the Left and Top margins to some small size, such as .25 inches.

- In the report design window, eliminate the report header and footer, and page header and footer sections, using the appropriate commands on the Layout menu. The report need only have a detail section.

- Set the detail section's Force New Page property to *After Section* (or put a page break at the bottom of the detail section).

- In the report design window, place the return address text in Label controls. Optionally, you can include a picture in an unbound OLE Object frame, as in the example shown in Figure 12.18.

FIGURE 12.18

A sample report
design for printing on
envelopes

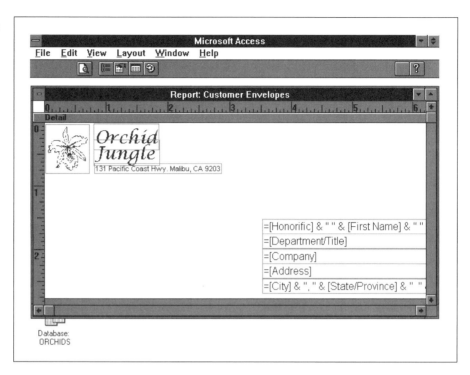

TIP You can cut and paste controls for displaying names
and addresses from a mailing label report into the
report for printing envelopes.

- Place the controls for displaying each customer's name and
  address about $1\frac{1}{2}$ to 2 inches from the top of the envelope,
  and about $3\frac{1}{2}$ inches from the left edge of the envelope, as in
  Figure 12.18.

- Set the Can Shrink property for each control in the detail section
  to *Yes* to prevent blank lines and spaces.

Creating Form Letters

Form letters, like the example shown in Figure 12.19, are also fairly easy to create in Access. Some basic tips:

- You won't need a report header or footer section, so you can delete these from the report design if you wish.

- If you want Access to print the letterhead, design a place for the letterhead in the page header section. (If you're printing on letterhead stock, leave enough empty space in the page header so that text in the detail section starts printing past the preprinted letterhead.)

- Place the date, or a text box containing the expression **=Date( )** at the top of the detail section, followed by controls for displaying the recipient's name and address (and the salutation) near the top of the detail section.

- Use the Label tool in the tool box to create a control for the body of the letter. You can put a maximum of 2,048 characters in the label. So, if necessary, you can use a separate label for each paragraph in the letter.

- You can also use Label controls to print the letter closing, and optionally use an unbound OLE Object frame to paste in a digitized copy of your signature.

- Put a Page Break at the bottom of the detail section, or change the detail section's Force New Page property to *After*, so that each letter is printed on a separate page.

- Be sure to set the width of the report to whatever width your margin settings provide. For instance, if you set the left and right margins to 1 inch in Print Setup, the maximum width of your letter will be 6.5 inches, as in the Figure 12.19.

FIGURE 12.19

A sample form letter,
in design view

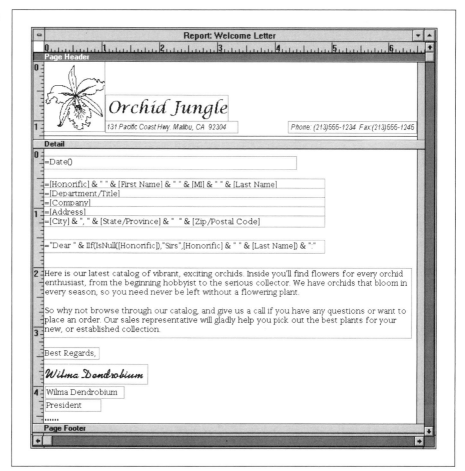

Using Your Word Processor to Create a Letter

You can use your word processor to create the body of the letter, check its spelling, and so forth. It would be a good idea to define the font in your word processor to match whatever font you plan to use in the form letter.

You can then cut and paste text from the word processing document into the Access letter. Remember, however, that an Access label can contain a maximum of 2,048 characters, so you might need to cut and paste one paragraph at a time.

To cut and paste, select a paragraph in your word processor, then press Ctrl+C or choose Edit ➤ Copy in your word processor. Switch to Access, and use the Label tool to create a control that's as wide as your report. Choose Edit ➤ Paste or press Ctrl+V to paste in the text from the Clipboard. If necessary, press ↵ to select the control, then choose a font from the tool bar. If the lines don't wrap properly within the Label control, just move the insertion point to the end of each line, and press Delete or Backspace to delete the (invisible) newline character at the end of each line.

Using Your Word Processor to Print Form Letters

Copying text *from* your word processor into Access for printing form letters has one disadvantage: you can't change the font or appearance of text *within* the label control that displays that text.

As an alternative to using Access to print the form letters, you can export data from the Access table to a file that your word processor can use as a "mail merge" or "secondary merge" file. Then use your word processor to create and print the form letter.

First, check your word processor's documentation to see what type of data formats you can use for merging. (Most support ASCII, or DOS delimited-text formats.) Then see Chapter 19 in this book for information on exporting data from your Access tables.

Invoices, Receipts, and Packing Slips

Designing reports for invoices, receipts, and packing slips is largely a matter of creating a query that includes data from the necessary tables, and then basing the report on that query. Figure 12.20 shows a sample printed invoice from the Orchids database.

Figure 12.21 shows the query that the invoice report is based on. The QBE grid contains all the fields necessary to print the invoice (though most are scrolled out of view). I included some calculated fields in the

FIGURE 12.20

A sample invoice, printed from the Orchids database

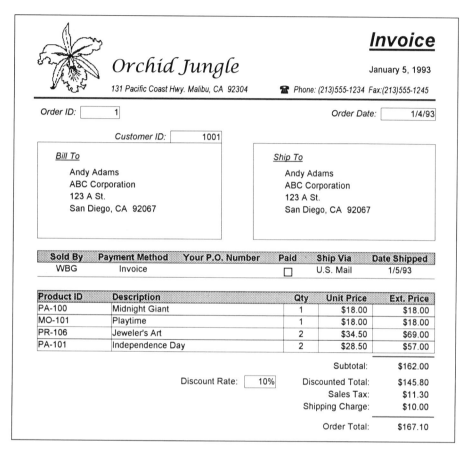

query, just to avoid having to do the calculations in the report design. So, in addition to "regular" fields from the field lists, the QBE grid in this example also contains the calculated fields shown below:

* Customer Name: [First Name] & " " & [Last Name]

* Customer CSZ: [City] & ", " & [State/Province] & " " & [Zip/Postal Code]

* Ship To CSZ: [Ship To City] & ", " & [Ship To State] & " " & [Ship To Zip]

* Extended Price: [Qty]*[Unit Price]

The report design for printing invoices is shown in Figure 12.22.

FIGURE 12.21

Query used to print invoices. (Most of the fields in the QBE grid are scrolled out of view.)

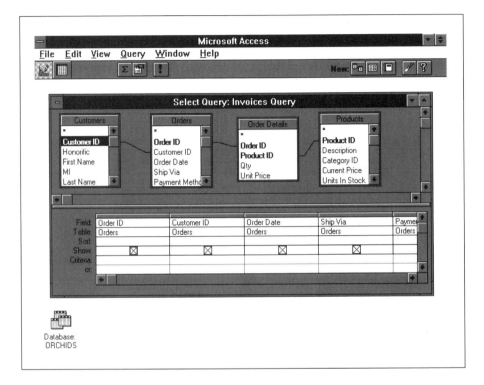

Here's a summary of the basic organization of the report:

- The page header section includes the information to be printed at the top of each invoice. The text box containing the **IIf** function prints the word *Receipt* at the top of the report if the Paid field contains *Yes*. Otherwise, that text box prints the word *Invoice*.

- In the **Sorting and Grouping** dialog box, I created a group based on the Order ID field, and have included both a group header (Order ID Header) and group footer (Order ID Footer) in the report design.

- The Order ID header prints information that's relevant to the order as a whole: the Order ID, Order Date, Bill To, Ship To, Sold By, Payment Method, Customer's PO, Paid, Ship Via, and Date Shipped fields from the underlying query. This section also contains labels that act as column headings for order details.

FIGURE 12.22

Report design, based on the Invoices query shown in Figure 12.21, used to print the sample invoice.

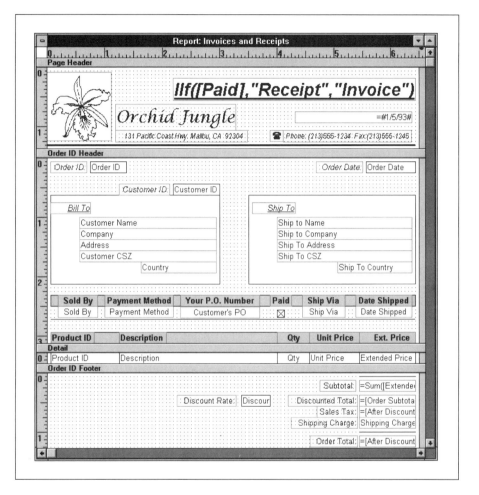

- The detail section displays the Product ID, Description, Qty, Unit Price, and Extended Price fields from the underlying query.

- The Order ID footer section displays calculations required at the bottom of the invoice. Table 12.4 lists the control names and expressions used in those text boxes. Each of those controls is formatted as currency in its Properties sheet.

- The Force New Page property for the Order ID footer section is set to *After*, to ensure that each invoice is printed on a separate page.

N O T E

If you included a Sales Tax Rate field in your Orders table, you'd want to include that field in the QBE Grid for the underlying query. Then use the expression =[After Discount]*[Sales Tax Rate] in the Sales Tax calculated control in the Order ID footer section of the report.

TABLE 12.4: Calculated controls in the Order ID footer section of the Invoices and Receipts report

LABEL	CONTROL NAME	CONTROL SOURCE
Subtotal	Order Subtotal	=Sum([Extended Price])
Discounted Total	After Discount	=[Order Subtotal]*(1-[Discount %])
Sales Tax	Sales Tax	=[After Discount]*0.0775
Shipping Charge	Shipping Charge	Shipping Charge
Order Total	Order Total	=[After Discount]+[Sales Tax]+[Shipping Charge]

To explore a similar invoice and query, open the Northwind database that came with your Access package, and take a look at the Invoices query and the Invoice report.

Printing in Columns

If you want to print in columns, you might find it easiest to use the Mailing Labels Wizard to design the report, since it takes care of all the Print Setup options required to print in columns.

When the Wizard is done, you can add report and page footers and/or groups as necessary to design the report to your liking. Figure 12.23 shows an example where I've included a page header and footer, and also a group header based on the first letter of each person's last name.

If you want to eliminate blank space caused by blank fields, set the detail section's Can Shrink property to *Yes*, and also set the Can Shrink property for each control within the detail section.

FIGURE 12.23

The report design for the columnar Customer Directory report shown in Figure 12.24

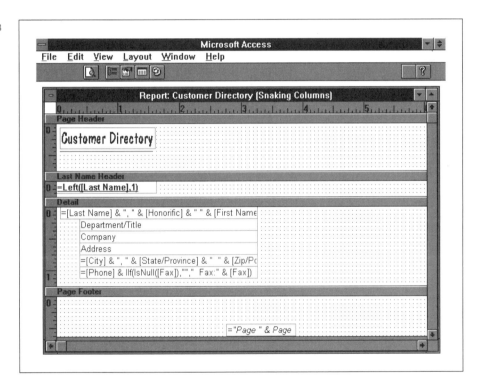

Snaking Columns

When you use the Wizard to create a columnar report, it alphabetizes (or sorts) horizontally, across columns, based on whatever fields you chose to sort on. If you prefer snaking columns, where records are alphabetized vertically down columns, as in Figure 12.24, open the report in design

FIGURE 12.24

A two-column customer directory with snaking columns. The names are alphabetized vertically down each column, rather than horizontally across columns.

Customer Directory

A

Abramovitz, Mr. Bernard L.
   4567 Cochituate Road
   Framingham, MA 01701
   (800)555-0493 Fax:(800)555-9594

Adams, Mr. Andy A.
   President
   ABC Corporation
   123 A St.
   San Diego, CA 92067
   (619)556-9320 Fax:(619)555-9319

Adams, Miss Maria A.
   Author
   4323 Moonglow Rd.
   Wyandotte, OK 74370
   (505)555-3438

B

Baker, Dr. Robert K.
   Radiology Dep't
   St. Elsewhere Hospital
   1234 Washington Lane
   New York, NY 12345-1232
   (212)555-1023 Fax:(212)555-0394

Bernesser, Miss Ellen R.
   Accounts Payable
   Flowers-R-Us
   1121 Parsons Dr.
   Hiawatha, IO 52233
   (319)555-5050 Fax:(319)555-6906

Bonnafoux, Mr. Lucien R.
   5078 S. 105th St., Suite 200
   Omaha, NE 68173-2234
   (402)555-3939 Fax:(402)555-4494

C

Ciccarello, Ms. Michelle D.
   1131 Maywood Ave
   Maywood, NJ 07607
   (201)555-4049 Fax:(201)555-4030

Cooper-Wajtuszewski, Miss Betsy K.
   Director
   Center for Womens Rights
   P.O. Box 8818
   Buffalo, NY 14226-8818
   (800)555-4048 Fax:(800)555-4049

Cuthbertson, Mrs. Randi I.
   Fashion Consultant
   Cuthbertson Designs
   P.O. Box 7701
   Manhasset, NY 11030-0393
   (516)555-5050 Fax:(516)555-5051

D

Davis, Jr., Dr. Sandra
   Botanist
   Florália
   P.O. Box 110.123
   Niterói, Rio de Janeiro 24.001
   (021)7178500 Fax:(021)7185332

---

view. Choose File ➤ Print Setup and go to the More>> options. Then choose Vertical under the Item Layout options.

Summary

Reports, like forms, are a means of presenting data in your tables and queries in an organized, meaningful manner. The main difference between forms and reports is that forms are used mainly for presenting information on the screen, while reports are used for printing.

Yet a third way to present data from your tables and queries is through graphs, the topic of our next chapter.

CHAPTER

13

Graphing Your Data

*f*ast TRACK

A linked embedded graph   **594**

is one that's linked to the table or query that underlies the form or report, and changes from record to record.

To change the colors, appearance, position, or other properties of a graph   **603**

change its control using standard techniques in design view.

To resize or customize an existing graph   **604**

double-click the graph in design view. This starts Microsoft Chart, which lets you change the graph's colors, axes, legend, size, graph type, and so on. When you're finished, choose File ➤ Exit And Return To Microsoft Access, then choose Yes.

If you don't want a graph to show current data   **610**

but prefer that it show data from some specific point in time, convert the graph's frame to a picture at that point.

To graph data from other applications   **610**

select the Unbound Object tool from the toolbox, then click and drag to define the size of the graph. Select *Microsoft Graph* from the next dialog box, then choose OK to start Microsoft Graph.

BUSINESS graphs, such as pie charts and bar charts, display data in a compact, visual format that's easy to understand. Graphs can also uncover important trends and relationships that might otherwise be hidden in large amounts of data.

To graph your Access data, you use Microsoft **Graph**, a separate application that comes with Access (as well as with several other Microsoft products). Though separate, Microsoft Graph is actually an *embedded* application, meaning that you can use it only from within some other application, such as Access or Excel. Microsoft Graph actually creates the graph as an OLE object, which you can then embed and display in an Access form or report.

In this chapter we'll look at the various ways in which you can create and embed graphs in forms and reports, and how you actually go about creating a graph. We'll start with the most important first step of deciding *what* you want to graph.

Choosing the Data You Want to Graph

Creating graphs is simple, *if* you go about it in an organized manner. The first step is to decide *which* data in your table you want to base the graph on. If all the fields that you want to base the graph on are in a single table, you can just base the graph on that table.

However, it's quite likely that the specific fields that you want to base the graph on will be in separate tables. In that case, you'll need to create a query to join the tables, then base the graph on that query.

NOTE Throughout this chapter I'll assume that you already know how to create and save queries, topics that are covered in depth Chapters 7 and 8.

Be sure to join all the tables you'll need to gain access to the fields you want to graph. Then drag fields that will be used in the graph into the QBE grid. Be sure to include the following fields:

- At least one field for categorizing the data. For instance, if you're graphing sales by product category, include the Category ID field. If you're graphing salesperson performance, put Employee ID or Sold By in the QBE grid.

- A field for a second category if you want two horizontal axes in the graph. For instance, if you want to view sales by product category *and* by month, you'd include a date/time field, such as Order Date, in the QBE grid.

- The field, or calculated field, that you want to total or average in the graph. This should be a numeric or currency value that Access can total or average and also plot on the graph. Put this into the third column.

If you wish, you can add additional numeric or calculated fields beyond the third column, and include those in the graph. Figure 13.1 shows an example where I've joined several tables from the Orchids database in a query (note the join lines). Here, I've included only two fields in the QBE grid:

- **Category ID**   I want to graph total orders by product category, so I've made this the first column in the QBE grid.

- **Extended Price**   The second column contains an expression named Extended Price, which is for the numeric values that will actually be summed and graphed.

You could create any two-dimensional business graph using just these two columns in the QBE grid. For example, Figure 13.2 shows a pie chart that's based on the query shown in Figure 13.1, where each slice of the pie shows total sales of each product category.

FIGURE 13.1

The QBE grid in this query includes just two fields, Category ID and Extended Price (a calculated field).

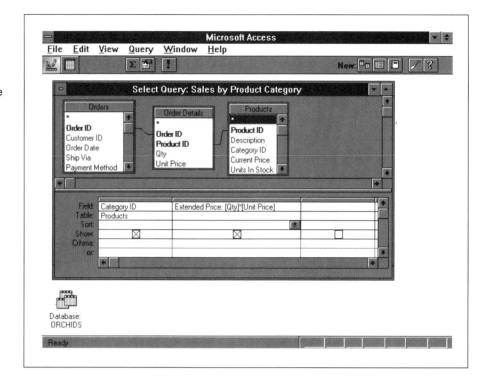

Now suppose you want to graph total sales by employee (the Sold By field in the Orders table). Furthermore, you want to break sales down by month. In that case, you'd need to include three columns in the QBE grid: Sold By, Order Date, and Extended Price, as in Figure 13.3. (The Products table isn't required in this query, because all the fields we need are in the Orders and Order Details table.)

Now your graph would have two horizontal axes, one for dates and one for employees, as in the example shown in Figure 13.4.

Notice that in both of the examples above, I'm graphing just the extended price ([Qty]*[Unit Price]). If you want to include discounts, shipping charges, and/or sales tax in the graph, you need to create the appropriate expressions and totaling queries. The section titled "Calculating Order Totals with Discount and Shipping" in Chapter 8 presents an example of a query that calculates an entire order total.

FIGURE 13.2

A pie chart based on the query shown in Figure 13.1. Each slice of the pie represents the total sales in one product category.

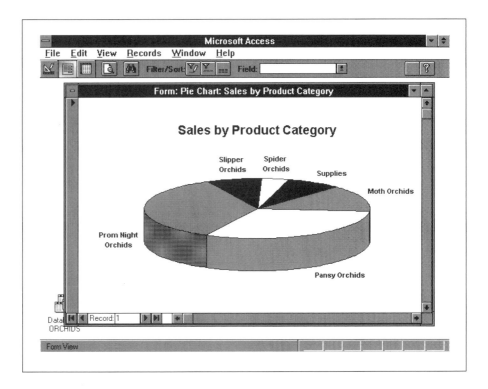

You can base the graph on a crosstab or totals query.

Optionally, you can use techniques described in Chapter 16 to store the order total with each record in the Orders table, then base the graph on that Order Total field.

Saving the Query

When you've finished creating the query, you should close and save it. Keep in mind that when you save a query, you save only its design. So, as the data changes in the table in the future, any graphs that you have based

FIGURE 13.3

The QBE grid contains the columns for the Sold By, Order Date, and Extended Price fields.

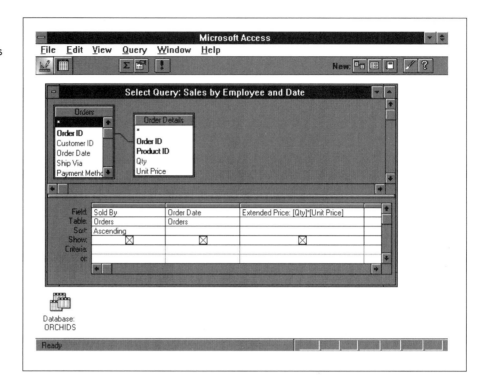

on that query will also change, to display current, up-to-date data in the table. This, of course, is a great feature because it means that you need not re-create the graph in the future when you want to take a look at current trends in your data. Instead, just open the form that the graph is in!

TIP

If you *don't* want the graph to change over time, but prefer that it display data at a particular point in time, you can separate it from its underlying table or query, as described under "Changing the Graph to a Picture" later in this chapter.

FIGURE 13.4

A graph based on the query shown in Figure 13.3. This graph has an axis for the Order Date field, and another axis for the salesperson's initials.

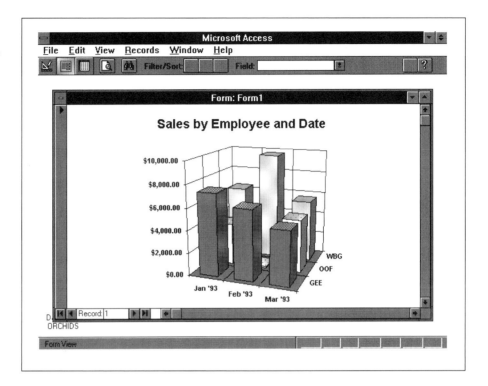

Freestanding and Embedded Graphs

Once you've decided which fields you want to include on the graph, and have created and saved the appropriate query, you need to decide *how* you want to display the graph. There are two main types of graphs you can create:

- A *freestanding graph* fills a form window, and is not used as part of a larger report or form (like Figures 13.2 and 13.4 above).

- An *embedded graph* is part of a larger report or form (see Figure 13.6 later in this chapter).

We'll look at the freestanding graph type first, since it's the easiest to create. Later we'll build upon those skills to show you how to create a graph that's embedded in a form or report.

Creating a Freestanding Graph

To create a freestanding graph, you can start right from the database window and use the GraphWizard. Assuming you've already created and saved the query that you want to base the graph on, you would:

1. Click on the New Form button on the tool bar, or choose File ➤ New ➤ Form.

2. From the drop-down list, select the table or query that you want to base the form on.

3. Click on the FormWizards button.

4. Select the Graph Wizard, then choose OK.

5. Choose the type of graph you want to create by clicking on the sample graph of your choosing (Figure 13.5).

6. Under Totals in the same dialog box, choose the type of calculation you want the graph to be based on—either *Sum* or *Average*. Then click on Next>.

7. You'll be prompted for fields to include in the graph. Choose fields in the usual manner. If you're basing the graph on a query that already contains all the fields you need in the graph, you can just click on **>>** to include all the query's fields on the graph.

8. What happens next depends on the type of graph you're creating, and whether or not you've included a date/time field in the graph. Follow the instructions on each Wizard screen:

   • If prompted, specify which field(s) you want to use as labels across the X axis, then choose Next>.

FIGURE 13.5

The first screen from the GraphWizard displays sample graphs to choose from.

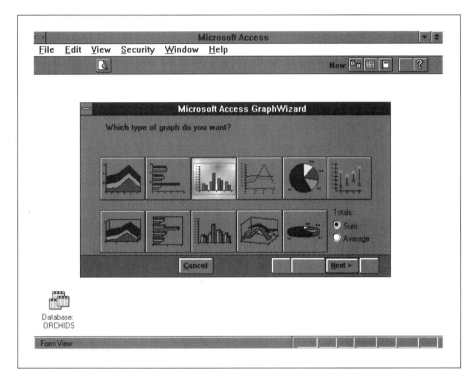

- If prompted, specify whether categories should appear along the category axis and/or in the legend, then click Next>.
- If prompted, specify how you want to group the dates (by quarter, month, week, day, hour, minute, etc.). You can also limit the graph to a range of dates by choosing *Use Data Between* and then specifying a range of dates to include. (Optionally, just choose *Use All Data* to include all records in the graph.

9. Choose Next>, then type a title, up to 50 characters in length, for the graph. Then choose the Open button to see the finished graph in form view, or the Design button to change the design of your graph.

Be aware that you cannot return to the GraphWizard after completing Step 9 above. If you're not happy with the graph, simply close the form without saving it. Then begin again, either by changing and re-saving the query, if necessary, or by running the GraphWizard based on the same query.

Using the Freestanding Graph

Remember that any freestanding graph you create is actually displayed in a form. So when the graph is open, you can switch back and forth between form view and design view with the usual buttons or option on the View menu. When you're in form view, you can print the graph with the usual File ➤ Print commands. (I'll talk about ways of customizing the graph in design view later in the chapter.) You can close and save the graph with the usual File ➤ Close commands. To reopen the graph in the future, first click the Form button in the database window, then double-click the name of the form. The graph will show current data in the table (unless you convert it to a picture, as described under "Changing the Graph to a Picture" later in this chapter).

Embedding a Graph in a Report or Form

An embedded graph is one that is included in a report or a larger form. To create such a graph, you start from the form or report design window, rather than from the database window. Also, you start out with the Graph tool in the design window, rather than the database window.

When creating an embedded graph, you have another two choices about how to display the graph:

* You can embed an *unlinked graph*, which doesn't change from record to record.

* You can embed a *linked* graph, which does change from record to record.

You use a unlinked embedded graph when you want to display multiple copies of the same graph. For instance, Figure 13.6 shows a couple of

FIGURE 13.6

An unlinked, embedded graph is the same in each record, or in each printed report. Here the graph displays sales for every salesperson in the first quarter of 1993.

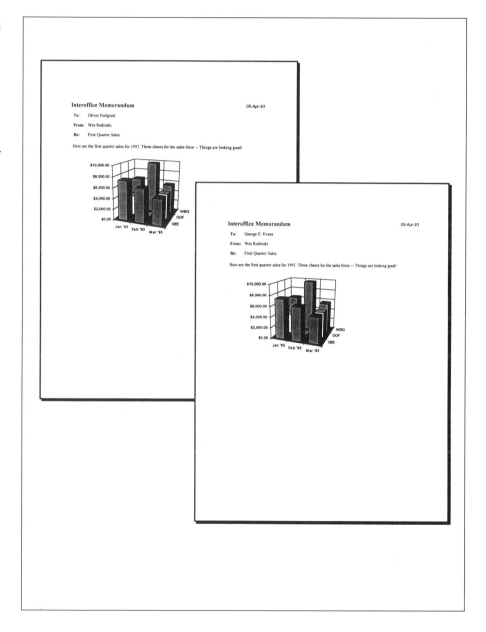

memos, each addressed to a different employee. Each memo displays a copy of the same graph.

You use a linked graph when you want to create a graph that changes from record to record as you scroll through records. For instance, by linking the same graph shown in Figure 13.6 above to a form that shows data from the Employees table, you can display data for just the employee whose data you're viewing at the moment, as in Figure 13.7.

When you scroll to another record, the same graph shows the sales performance of *that* employee only, as in Figure 13.8.

Notice that when the graph *isn't* linked, it displays the graph with two horizontal axes: one for the date, and one for the employee initials. When the graph *is* linked, only the date axis appears, because the graph is displaying data for only one employee.

FIGURE 13.7

A graph that's linked to the Employee ID field of the Employees table shows the sales for one employee at a time, Wanda Granolabar (WBG) in this example.

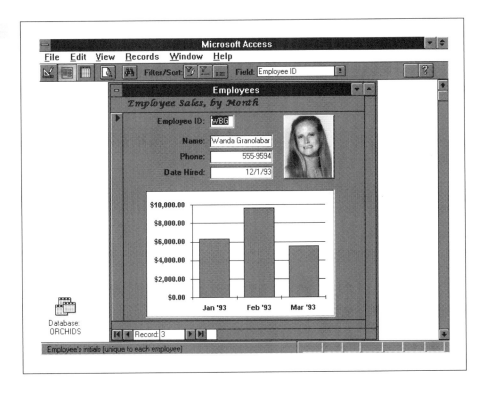

FIGURE 13.8

Scrolling to another record shows the same graph, but only for employee George Evans (GEE) in this example.

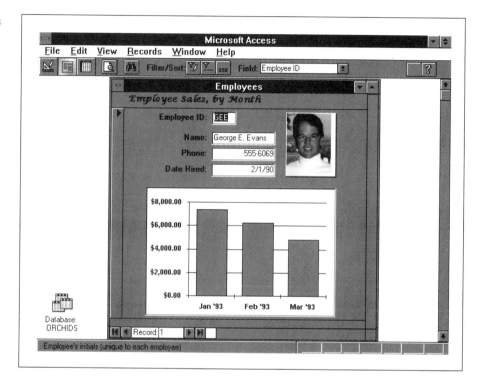

Here's the basic procedure for creating either a linked or unlinked embedded graph:

1. Create the report or form that you'll be placing the graph in. Be sure to leave enough room for the graph.

2. If you need to base the graph itself on a query, create a query for the graph.

3. In design view, reopen the report or form that you want to embed the graph in, and use the Graph tool in the toolbox to create and embed the graph.

We'll look at each step a little more closely in the next three sections.

Step 1: Create the Report or Form

You can use the standard techniques to create the form or report that will contain the graph, based on whatever table (or query) you wish. Just be sure to leave enough room for the graph that you'll be embedding later.

For instance, Figure 13.9 shows a form, in form view, that I created based on the Employees table (not a query). It includes the Employee ID, Name, Phone, Date Hired, and Photo fields from the table. I've left some empty space at the bottom of the form.

When you've finished designing the initial form or report, you can close and save it to get it out of the way, for the time being, if convenient.

FIGURE 13.9

Sample form based on the Employees table, in form view. I've left some empty space for the graph I'll be embedding later.

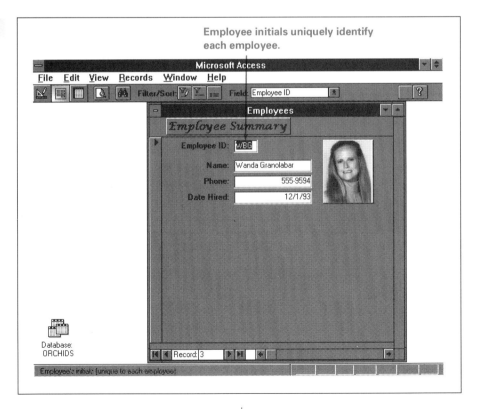

Step 2: Create the Query for the Embedded Graph

The basic technique for creating a query for an embedded graph is the same as described earlier under "Creating a Query to Base the Graph On." However, if you want the graph to change on a record-by-record basis, you must include the field that links the graph to the report or form, as this is the field that will tell the graph *which* data to display. For instance, when creating a graph of total sales to embed on the form shown back in Figure 13.9, you need to include the field that links the data from that query to the Employees table. In this example, the Sold By field in the Orders table contains the employee initials that identify which employee took each order. Therefore, the query that you want to base the graph on must include that field, as in the example shown in Figure 13.10.

FIGURE 13.10

When creating a linked graph that changes on a record-by-record basis, you need to include the field that links the graph to the report or form.

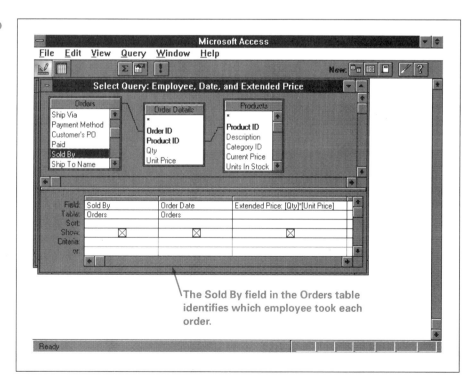

The Sold By field in the Orders table identifies which employee took each order.

If you don't want the graph to change on a record-by-record basis, you need not be concerned about providing a linking field. But you still need to create a query for the graph if the graph is based on fields that come from more than one table.

Once you've created the query for the graph, you can close and save it.

Step 3: Embed the Graph

Now that you have a report or form to put the graph in, and a query to base the graph on, you can create the graph and embed it into the report or form. When embedding a graph in a form or report, you always use the Graph tool, in design view, to get started. Here are the exact steps:

1. In design view, open the form or report that you want to embed the graph into, and display the toolbox. (Choose View ➤ Toolbox if the toolbox is hidden.)

2. Select the Graph tool (shown at left) from the toolbox.

3. On the form or report design, click where you want the upper-left corner of the graph to appear, or drag to define the size of the graph. The **Microsoft Access** GraphWizard screen will appear.

4. In the text box near the top of the Wizard screen, choose the query that you created earlier to base the graph on (or a table, if you're not basing the graph on a query.)

N O T E   When you're creating an embedded graph, notice that the first dialog box in the GraphWizard includes a text box for selecting the table or query that you want to base the graph on.

5. On the same screen, choose the type of graph that you want, and also choose either *Sum* or *Average*. Then click on the Next> button.

6. Choose the fields that you want to include on the graph. (Again, if you've already done this in the underlying query, just click **>>** to select all the fields.)

7. Click on the Next> button.

8. As previously described, if you included a date/time field in the graph, you can opt to display dates along the category axis or in the legend, then click Next>. You can choose how to group the data (i.e., by month, week, year, and so forth), from the next dialog box. You can also choose a range of dates to include. Then choose the Next> button.

9. Next you'll see the dialog box below. Choose Yes only if you want to create a graph that changes from record to record. Choose No if you want the graph to look the same on each copy of the printed report or form. (If you chose No, skip to Step 13.)

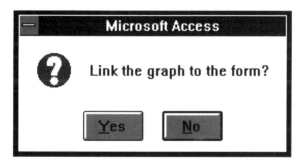

10. In the next dialog box, click the name of the field in the form that links the form to the graph.

11. Under Graph Fields, click the name of the corresponding field from the graph, then click the <=> button. The selected fields will

appear under Link(s), as in the example below where I've linked the form to the graph via the Employee ID and Sold By fields:

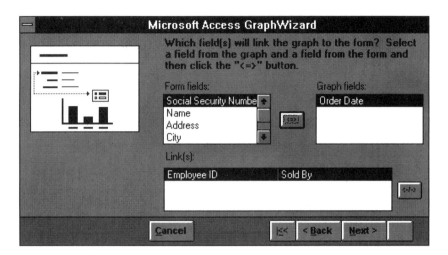

12. Click on the Next> button.

13. Optionally, enter a title to appear at the top of the graph, then click on the Design button.

NOTE Both the Employee ID field in the Employees table and the Sold By field in the Orders table are the text data type with a Size of 3 characters. Even though the fields have different names, they can be used as the common field to link orders to employees, based on employee initials.

A embedded object frame for displaying the graph appears on the form or report. You can size and move that frame as necessary using the standard techniques. To view the finished result, switch to form view (if you're working with a form) or print preview (if you're working with a report).

Fixing the Linking Fields

If you chose to link the graph to the form or report, and Access displays a message indicating a problem with the Link Child Fields and Link Master Fields properties, here's how to fix that problem:

1. If the error dialog box is on the screen, choose OK to close it.

2. Switch to design view, and select the control that displays the graph (click it once, so it has sizing handles.)

3. Open the Properties sheet if it isn't already opened (View ➤ Properties).

4. Change Link Child Fields to the field(s) in the graph that link the graph to the form or report.

5. Change Link Master Fields to the field(s) in the graph that link the graph to the form or report.

Figure 13.11 shows an example where I've set the properties for my sample form to Sold By and Employee ID, the fields that link orders to customers.

Once you've finished all of the above, you can switch between print preview, form view (if you're using a form), and design view. Use File ➤ Print to print, and other standard techniques to open and close the form or report as usual. In design view, you can change the properties of the graph's frame (control), or actually customize the graph, as discussed next.

Customizing a Graph

Chances are, your graph won't look exactly the way you want it to the moment you finish creating it. But you can customize the graph by changing its properties in design view, or by going into Microsoft Graph and making more refined changes to the graph, as described in the next two sections.

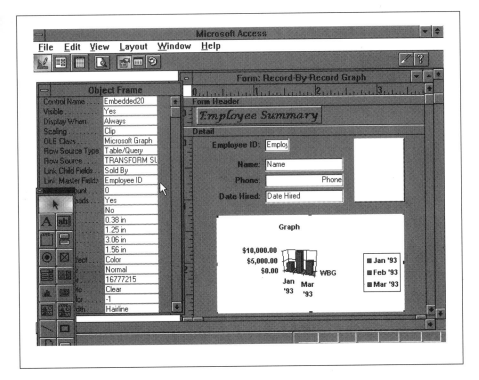

Changing the Graph's Size, Position, and Properties

You can make some changes to the size and appearance of the graph right in the report design or form design screen. Just open the form or report that the graph is in, in design view, then click on the graph or its frame. Once the frame is selected, you can:

- Change its fill color, border color, and general appearance using the standard options on the color palette.

- Move and size the frame using the standard techniques for moving and sizing controls. (However, to change the actual size of the graph, use Microsoft Graph, as described in the next section.)

- Change other properties of the frame by opening the Properties sheet, using the Properties button or View ➤ Properties.

When working directly with the Properties sheet, always set the Scaling property to *Clip* for graphs, as this provides the fastest display. You can change the size of the graph in Microsoft Graph, then use Layout ➤ Size To Fit to fit the frame to the resized graph.

TIP

If you create a freestanding graph and then decide to add more fields to its form later, you can change the graph's Record Source property to the name of the table or query that you based the graph on. Then you can use the field list in the form design view to add new controls to the form.

Using Microsoft Graph to Customize the Graph

To makes changes directly to the chart, you use Microsoft Graph. To get started:

1. In design view, open the form or report that the graph is displayed in.

2. Double-click the graph.

You'll be taken to Microsoft Graph, as shown in the example in Figure 13.12.

Microsoft Graph has its own menu bar and help system. Its desktop contains two windows; a desktop window and a chart window. To customize the chart, first make sure the chart window is in front (click on it if necessary). You can then choose options from the menu bar or double-click areas of the chart to tailor those areas. For example, double-clicking a data series on a bar graph opens the **Area Patterns** dialog box shown in Figure 13.13. From here you can change the patterns and colors of the selected series of data.

FIGURE 13.12

Double-clicking a graph in design view takes you to Microsoft Graph, where you can customize the graph.

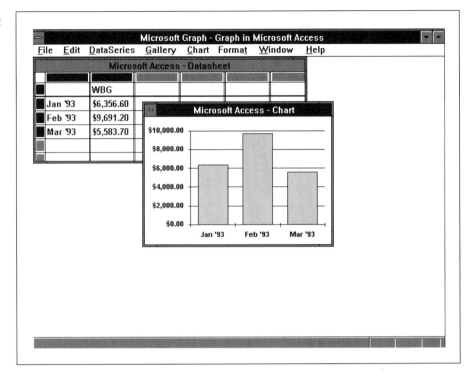

NOTE   A data series is a group of related data points in a row or column. In graphs, a data series appears as a set of bars, columns, lines, or other markers (depending on the graph type). Graphs can have one or more data series.

Here are some tips for customizing the graph:

- To change the size of the graph, resize the chart window to whatever size you want the graph to be, by dragging that window's borders. (Choose Window ➤ 100% View to make sure you're sizing the chart at the correct magnification.)

FIGURE 13.13

The Area Patterns
dialog box appears
when you double-click
on a data series.

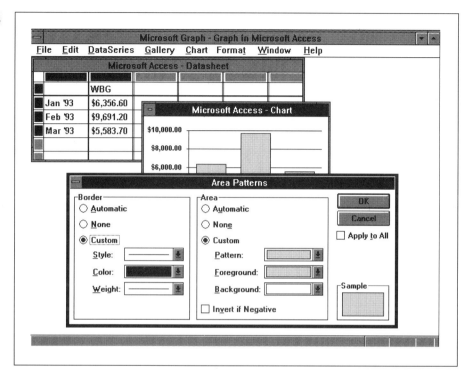

- To change the graph type, select an appropriate option from the Gallery menu. For greater control over the graph type, choose Format ➤ Chart.

- To switch the horizontal axes, choose DataSeries ➤ Series In Rows or DataSeries ➤ Series In Columns.

- To change the color of a data series, double-click the data series you want to change.

- To delete the legend, click on the legend and then press Delete (or choose Chart ➤ Delete Legend). To restore the legend, choose Chart ➤ Add Legend.

- To customize the location of the legend, choose Format ➤ Legend, then choose a location from the **Legend** dialog box.

- To customize an axis, double-click on the axis. You'll see the **Axis Patterns** dialog box shown in Figure 13.14. You can then change the font (click on the Font button), text orientation (click on the Text button), and scaling (click on the Scale button) for the selected axis.

    - If the tick labels are too crowded on the Y- axis, double-click on the axis to get to the Axis Patterns dialog box. Then click on the Scale button, then increase the Major Unit for scaling. For instance, if you double that number, only half as many tick marks will be listed down the Y axis.

    - To improve a crowded X axis, you can double-click the axis, then choose the Text button and select a vertical text orientation.

FIGURE 13.14

The Axis Patterns dialog box allows you to change the appearance of the axis and tick labels.

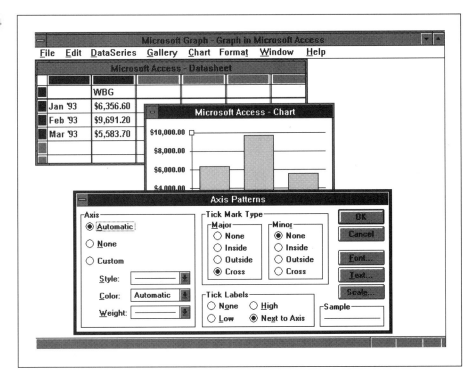

When you're finished making changes, choose File ➤ Exit And Return To Microsoft Access, then answer Yes when asked if you want to update the graph in Microsoft Access. Remember that if you changed the size of the graph, you can choose Layout ➤ Size To Fit when you get back to the axis if you want to resize the frame to better fit the new graph size.

For more information on using Microsoft Graph, please refer to the *Microsoft Graph User's Guide* that came with your Access program.

Changing the Graph Title

The graph title is the one item on the graph that tends to be a bit "sticky." Even if you change or delete that title in Microsoft Graph, it has a tendency to show up again when you switch to form view.

To change the graph title, or to get rid of it once and for all, you can change the graph's SQL statement. To do so, open, in design view, the form or report that displays the graph. Then click the graph's control, and open the properties sheet. Click the Row Source property, then press Zoom (Shift+F2) to view the entire entry. You'll see a SQL statement that starts out something like this:

SELECT DISTINCTROW [*fieldname*] AS [*graphname*], FROM...

where *graphname* is the title that appears at the top of the graph. You can change the graph title by changing the *graphname* within the brackets. For example:

SELECT DISTINCTROW [*fieldname*] AS [My Graph], FROM...

changes the graph title to **My Graph**. To delete the graph title, you can change *fieldname* to the word **Null**, and delete the AS [*graphname*] portion of the SQL statement, like this:

SELECT DISTINCTROW Null, FROM...

Changes you make to the SQL statement won't take effect until you switch to form view. If you find you've done more harm than good, close the form without saving your changes to retain the original SQL statement.

Changing the Graph to a Picture

Normally, your graph will always display current, up-to-date information from the underlying table. If you prefer to fix or freeze the data for the graph display, you can convert it to a picture:

1. Open the form or report that displays the graph.

2. Switch to design view, then click on the graph to select it.

3. Choose Edit ➤ Microsoft Graph Object ➤ Change To Picture.

CAUTION

Once you change the graph to a picture, there's no way to undo that change. Use this technique with care!

Graphing Data from Other Applications

So far, we've focused on graphs that display data from tables and queries. However, your reports and forms can also graph data from other applications.

Embedding Graphs from Other Applications

You can follow these steps to create a graph that uses data from another source, such as Microsoft Excel, Lotus 1-2-3, or data you've typed directly into the datasheet window.

1. Open your form or report in design view.
2. Choose the Unbound Object frame tool (shown at left).
3. On the form or report design, click where you want the upper left corner of the graph to appear, or click and drag to define the size of the graph. The **Insert Object** dialog box appears, listing all the OLE applications on your computer.

N O T E   Chapter 19 explains object linking and embedding (OLE) in more detail.

4. Select *Microsoft Graph* from the dialog box, then click OK.

Microsoft Graph opens with some sample data displayed in the datasheet window. You can simply change the existing data as needed, then click on the chart window to see the results.

If you prefer to clear out the existing data and type in or import data from another application, first clear all the existing data. To do so, choose Edit ➤ Select All, choose Edit ➤ Delete Row/Col, click OK, then click in the cell where you want to begin importing or typing data.

- To enter data into a cell, select the cell you want to edit by clicking it or using Tab and the arrow keys to reach the desired cell, then begin typing. Anything you type replaces the existing contents of the cell.

- To import a text or spreadsheet file, choose File ➤ Import Data, then choose the file you want to import.

- To import data from a Microsoft Excel chart, choose File ➤ Open Microsoft Excel Chart, choose OK when asked if you want to overwrite existing data and chart specifications, then choose the file you want to import.

NOTE Text files have *.csv* or *.txt* extensions; spreadsheet files have *.wks*, *.wk1*, *.wr1*, *.xls*, or *.slk* extensions; Microsoft Excel charts have *.xlc* extensions.

After importing or typing in your data, you can click on the chart window to view and customize your graph as desired. When you're finished, choose File ➤ Exit And Return To Microsoft Access, then answer Yes when asked if you want to update the graph in Microsoft Access. The graph will appear in your Access form or report. If necessary, resize it in the design window, or return to Microsoft Chart and resize the chart window.

Linking Graphs Developed in Other Applications

Graphs developed in other applications that support OLE can also be linked to unbound object frames in forms and reports, and to OLE Object fields in tables. Please see Chapter 19 for more information on using OLE to link and embed objects.

Summary

The main trick to graphing your Access data is deciding exactly *which* data you want to graph. Once you've done that, the GraphWizard will lead you through the steps necessary to describe *how* you want that data to be graphed. Graphs can be displayed alone in a form, or embedded into a report or form. To embed a graph, you start from the report or form design screen, and use the Graph tool in the toolbox to create, and embed, the graph.

Once created, graphs are easy to change. Just double-click the graph in design view to start Microsoft Graph. Then tailor the graph's colors, titles, axes, legends, graph type, dimensions, and other features as needed. When you're finished, choose File ➤ Exit And Return To Microsoft Access, then Yes.

In the last five chapters we've been describing various ways of viewing and calculating data in forms, reports, and graphs. Starting with the next chapter, we're going to look at ways to automate various Access tasks with the aid of *macros*.

PART FOUR

Using Macros to Simplify Your Work

Creating and Using Macros

fast TRACK

MACROS can play many roles in automating and simplifying the use of tables, queries, forms, and reports in a database. You can automate virtually any task with a macro, and reduce it to a simple mouse click.

For example, suppose you find yourself going through the same rigmarole every day to print invoices and update your product inventory. As an alternative to going through that rigmarole, you could create a macro that performs the necessary steps for you. Then, all you need to do is run that macro with a couple of mouse clicks to get the job done.

In this chapter, we'll cover all the basic skills, options, and concepts involved in creating and using macros. Then we'll look at specific examples in the next two chapters and in Chapter 21.

What Is a Macro?

A macro is a single action, or collection of several actions, stored as a database object. You *create* a macro by going to the macro window and defining a list of actions for the macro to carry out. When you *run* the macro, Access "plays" all the actions in that macro.

If you're accustomed to using macros in other applications, such as word processors, be aware that Access macros are not of the "record some action then play it back" variety. Also, in Access, there are two basic ways to run a macro: either directly from the database window or by using some *event*, such as the click of a button or a change of data in a form, to trigger the macro into action (Figure 14.1).

FIGURE 14.1

You can run Access macros directly from the database window, or from controls and command buttons on a form.

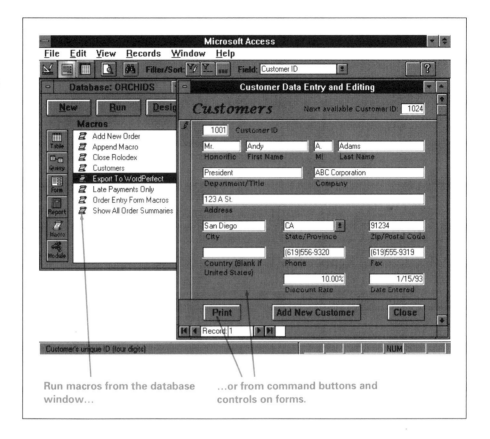

Run macros from the database window...   ...or from command buttons and controls on forms.

Handy Uses of Macros

You can use macros for a wide variety of tasks, including the following:

- Simplifying lookups and queries: You can create macros that help the person using a form or report find the information they need without going through a query.

- Coordinating forms and reports: With macros, you can synchronize forms and reports to make them work together, and to copy data from one to the other.

• Verifying data entry: Macros can check the contents of an entry in a form for verification, and provide more flexibility and power than the Validation Rule property you assign in table design or form design. A macro can also change the entry for consistency, for example, converting lowercase letters in a postal code to uppercase letters.

• Automating data transfer: If you regularly import or export Access data, you can create a macro to do the job with just a click of a button.

• Automating updating tasks: You can create macros to automate a series of action queries, and to automate those tasks that require copying, moving, and updating multiple records in tables.

• Building custom applications: You can simplify the overall use of your database by creating forms with command buttons and custom menus that trigger macros to perform common tasks. Doing so makes it easier for people with minimal computer skills to manage data in your database.

Creating a Macro

The first steps to creating a new macro are virtually identical to the steps for creating any other database object:

1. Starting in the database window, click the Macro object button.

2. Click the New button in the database window.

TIP You can also choose File ➤ New ➤ Macro from the menu bar to create a new macro.

You'll be taken to the macro window, which I'll discuss next.

The Macro Window and Tool Bar

First let's look at the tools for creating macros: the macro window and tool bar, shown in Figure 14.2. The title bar of the macro window shows Macro:, followed by the name of the macro you're designing (which is just Macro1 when you're creating your first macro).

The Action column is where you list actions that you want the macro to perform. There are two ways to specify actions, as I'll describe in a moment.

FIGURE 14.2

The macro window, where you create and edit your macros

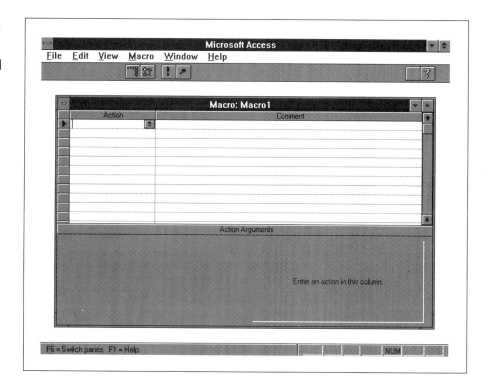

TIP

You can widen or narrow the Action column, as necessary, by dragging the line that separates the Action heading from the Comment heading to the left or right.

The second column, Comment, is where you store a plain-English description of what each action does. Though entirely optional, the Comment column is useful for keeping notes to yourself, or for anyone else who might later view or change the macro, about the purpose of each action within the macro.

The lower portion of the macro window, though initially empty, is where you specify *action arguments*, which describe which object the action should operate on and other information that is pertinent to the action. I'll discuss the arguments area in more detail a little later.

The tool bar for the macro window includes the buttons shown below. I'll describe the role of each button as I go along in this chapter.

Creating Macro Actions

An *action* is some task that the macro performs, such as opening a table or sounding a beep. There are two ways to assign actions to a macro: either by dragging the name of an object from the database window to the appropriate cell in the Action column or by clicking a cell in the Action column and choosing an action from the drop-down list.

Using Drag-and-Drop to Create an Action

If you want the macro to perform an action that opens a table, form, query, or other database object:

1. Size and position the macro window so that you can see both the database window and the Action column of the macro window on the screen.

2. In the database window, click the object button for the type of object you want the action to open.

3. Drag the name of the object that you want the macro to open from the database window to a cell in the Action column of the macro window.

When you use this technique, Access adds the appropriate action to the Action column and also fills in the Action arguments for that action. You can type in your own, plain-English description in the Comment column. For instance, in Figure 14.3 I dragged the report name Customer Mailing Labels from the database window to the first row in the Action column. Then I typed the description shown in the Comment cell.

N O T E   If you drag a table, query, form, or report name to the Action cell, Access will *open* that object when you later run the macro. If you drag the name of another macro to the Action cell, Access will *run* that macro when you later run the macro you're developing at the moment. (In other words, a macro can run another macro.)

FIGURE 14.3

I dragged the object name Customer Mailing Labels from the database window to the first cell in the Action column of the macro window, and I typed in the optional comment.

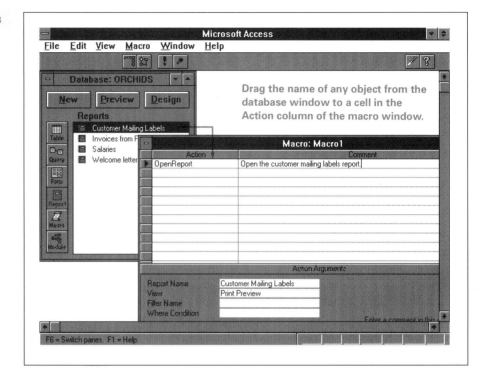

Adding an Action Using the Drop-Down List

The drag-and-drop method is useful only for creating a macro action that opens an object. To create other types of macro actions:

1. Click the cell in the Action column where you want to place a new action.

2. Click the drop-down list button that appears, and choose the action you want (see Figure 14.4).

3. If the action you chose requires arguments, you'll need to fill in the arguments as described in the next section, "Assigning Arguments to an Action."

4. Optionally, fill in the comment next to the action to describe what role the action plays.

FIGURE 14.4

You can also create, or change, a macro action by clicking the Action cell and choosing an action from the drop-down list.

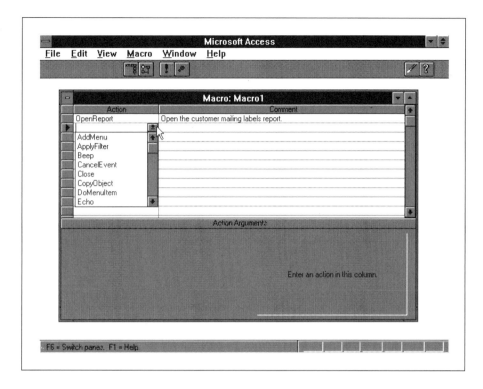

Assigning Arguments to an Action

Some actions require additional information to work correctly. For instance, an action such as OpenReport needs to know (at least) *which* report to open and *how* to display the report (i.e., in Print Preview, design view, or straight to the printer). To change an argument for an action:

1. Make sure that the row indicator is on the action that you want to assign or change the action for.

2. Click the argument you want to change.

T I P   You can also press the F6 key to switch between the upper and lower panes of the macro window.

3. If the argument offers a drop-down button, you can click that button, then choose an argument from the list. If the argument doesn't offer a drop-down button, you need to type the argument yourself.

You can also change certain arguments by dragging names from the database window. For instance, if the argument is asking for the name of an object (e.g., Table Name, Report Name, Form Name), you can click the appropriate object button in the database window, then drag an object name from the database window to the argument. This drag-and-drop method is, however, entirely optional, since the drop-down list for the argument will provide the names of all the appropriate objects in the current database.

Getting Help with Macro Actions and Arguments

The basic skills of knowing *how* to create actions and set their arguments is one thing. But choosing the *correct* action and arguments requires that you know what's available. By far, the easiest way to learn about actions and arguments is simply to use the online help for further information, as necessary. Here are some tips:

- The hint box in the lower-right corner of the macro window always provides a brief description of the action or argument that the insertion point is in.

- For more extensive help with an action or argument, move the insertion point either to the action or the argument you want help with, then press Help (F1).

The Help screen displays the name of the current action (e.g., Open-Report Action in Figure 14.5) and a description of each action argument.

FIGURE 14.5

For help with a macro action and its arguments, click the action or any argument, then press F1 for help.

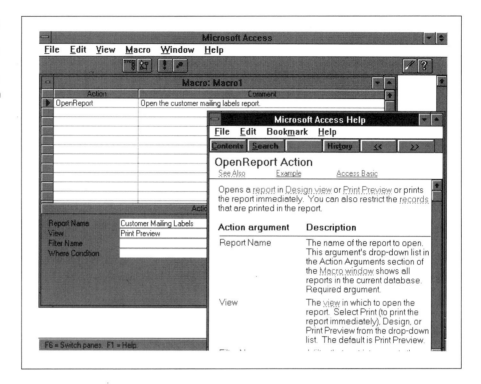

TIP

Remember that in Windows 3.1 you can choose Help ➤ Always on Top to prevent other windows from hiding the Help screen.

The sample macros I present in the next two chapters will also help you to learn more about the various macro actions and their arguments.

Changing, Rearranging, and Deleting Actions

It's important to keep in mind that Access always executes macro commands in the order that you place them in the macro. That is, it executes the first (topmost) action first, then the next action down, and so forth, until it has executed all the actions within the macro. If necessary, you can move, delete, and insert rows in your macro by following these steps:

1. Select a row by clicking its row selector (the gray box to the left of the Action column, as shown below):

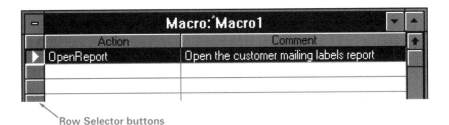

Row Selector buttons

Or, select several rows by dragging the pointer through several row selectors.

2. Then do any of the following:

- To delete the selected row(s), press Delete or choose Edit ➤ Delete.
- To insert a new row, press the Insert key or choose Edit ➤ Insert Row.
- To move the row(s), click the row selector again, hold down the mouse button, and drag the row(s) to the new position.
- To copy the selected row(s), choose Edit ➤ Copy, select the row position for the copied row, then choose Edit ➤ Paste.
- To undo any of the changes above, click the Undo button or choose Edit ➤ Undo.

Closing and Saving the Macro

Once you've finished creating a macro, you can close and save it as you would any other object:

1. Choose File ➤ Close, or double-click the macro window's Control-menu box.

2. If you haven't previously saved the macro, you'll be prompted for a name. Enter an Access name, up to 64 characters including spaces, and choose OK.

The macro is added to the list of macro names in the database window.

Running a Macro

To have the macro actually perform the actions that you've assigned to it, you *run* (or *execute*) the macro. There are many ways to run macros, and as you'll see in upcoming chapters, the correct way to run a macro really depends on what the macro is designed to do. But, if your macro is designed to be run from the database window, there are several ways you can run it.

Running a Macro from the Database Window

To run a macro, starting at the database window:

1. Click the Macro object button in the database window.
2. Double-click the name of the macro you want to run, or select the name of the macro you want to run, then choose the Run button.

Running a Macro from the Menus

If the database window is covered or minimized at the moment, you can run a macro by going through the menus:

1. Choose File ➤ Run Macro.
2. Open the drop-down list next to the Macro Name text box, and choose the name of the macro you want to run.
3. Choose OK.

Running a Macro from the Macro Window

If you're currently creating or editing a macro in the macro window, and want to give it a quick test run:

1. Click the Run button (shown at left) in the macro window's tool bar.

2. If you have never saved the macro or have changed it since it was last saved, you'll need to save the macro before Access will run it. Just choose Yes to proceed.

Umpteen Other Ways to Run a Macro

You can also assign macros to certain events, so that the macro is executed as soon as the event occurs. For instance, you can attach a macro to a custom command button on a form, so that the macro is executed as soon as the person using the form clicks that button. Or you can assign a macro to the Before Update, After Update, On Enter, On Exit, or On Dbl Click property of a control on a form, so that the macro is executed in response to specific activity on the form. We'll look at ways in which you can assign macros to events in the next two chapters.

Changing a Saved Macro

You can edit an existing macro at any time in much the same way you edit any other database object:

1. In the database window, click the Macro object button.

2. Click the name of the macro you want to change.

3. Choose the Design button.

The macro reappears in the macro window, and you can add, change, delete, move, or copy rows using the techniques described earlier in this chapter.

Performing an Action If...

In some situations, you might want your macro to perform an action only under certain conditions. For instance, suppose you want to create a macro that checks the contents of the Zip/Postal Code field on a form as soon as the person who is using the form moves the insertion point from that field. *If* (and only if), the Zip/Postal code is empty (null), you want the macro to display a warning message. If that field is not empty, you want the macro to do nothing (or something else).

To add conditions to a macro, you first need to get to the macro window for whatever macro you want to assign the conditions to, as discussed in "Changing a Saved Macro" earlier. Then, follow these steps:

1. If you haven't already done so, open the Conditions column by choosing View ➤ Conditions or by clicking the Conditions button (shown at left) on the tool bar.

2. In the Conditions column, just to the left of the command that you want to make conditional, enter a *condition expression* that determines when the action will be executed.

3. If you want other actions below the current action to be dependent on the same condition, type an ellipsis (three periods) in the Conditions cell next to each of those actions.

As an example, take a look at the macro actions below. The first three actions—MsgBox and the two GoToControl actions—will be executed *only* when the condition proves true. In this example, those actions will be executed only if the Zip/Postal Code field is empty when the macro is executed. The SetValue action is always executed, because it is not dependent on the condition.

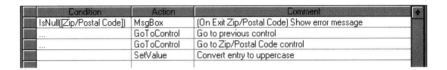

Condition	Action	Comment
IsNull([Zip/Postal Code])	MsgBox	(On Exit Zip/Postal Code) Show error message
...	GoToControl	Go to previous control
...	GoToControl	Go to Zip/Postal Code control
	SetValue	Convert entry to uppercase

Once you add conditions to a macro, the Conditions column remains open, even when you close and reopen the macro. You can hide the Conditions column using the Conditions button or View ➤ Conditions. But the conditions will still be effective when you run the macro and will again be visible when you reopen the column.

Creating Macro Groups

As mentioned, you can attach macros to controls and command buttons on forms. For instance, the form shown in Figure 14.1 contains three buttons. And you might want to add some other macros to that form, such as a macro to prevent the Zip/Postal Code field from being left empty.

Given that a single form might have many macros associated with it, and a given database might contain many forms, you can see how your collection of macros could grow to be quite large.

To avoid having a huge list of macro names appear in the database window, you can group all the macros that naturally belong together under one macro name. For instance, you might want to group all the macros that go with the Customers Data Entry form under a single macro name, such as *Customers*.

To group a set of macros under a single name:

1. Create a new macro or open an existing macro to get to the macro window.

2. Click the Macro Names button (shown at left) in the tool bar, or choose View ➤ Macro Names. A new column, titled Macro Name, appears in the window.

3. Type a name next to the first action for each macro in the group. If the macro contains several actions, leave the Macro Name cell empty beneath the macro name.

Figure 14.6 shows an example, where the macro name in the title bar is Customers. But that name really identifies the group of macros listed in the Macro Name column: Print, Add New Customer, Close, and No Blank Zip.

Running a Macro That's in a Group

If a macro object actually contains several named macros, you need to refer to a specific macro by its group name and specific name, separated

FIGURE 14.6

Four macros, named Print, Add New Customer, Close, and No Blank Zip, grouped together under the macro named Customers

Macro Name	Condition	Action	Comment
Print		DoMenuItem	(Print button) Select the current record
		Print	Print the current record
Add New Customer		GoToRecord	(Add New Customer button) Go to new, last rec
		SetValue	Copy Next Available ID to Customer ID
		GoToControl	Go to the Honorific control
Close		Close	(Close button) Close the form
No Blank Zip	IsNull([Zip/Postal C	MsgBox	(On Exit Zip/Postal Code) Show error message
	...	GoToControl	Go to previous control
	...	GoToControl	Go to Zip/Postal Code control
		SetValue	Convert entry to uppercase

Action Arguments

Object Type   Form
Object Name   Customer Data Entry

Enter a comment in this column.

F6 = Switch panes. F1 = Help.

by a period. For instance, when attaching the Close macro to the command button on the Customers Data Entry form, you'd refer to the macro as

Customers.Close

If you try to run a macro group using the Run button in the macro window tool bar or database window, Access will run only the first macro in the group. It's best to attach all the macros in the group to their respective buttons and controls on a form (or report), and then test and run the macros from that form (or report).

NOTE If you leave the first action in the macro window empty, Access won't run any of the macros in the group when you use the Run button.

Attaching Macros to Forms and Reports

Once you've created a macro, you can attach it to forms and reports. We'll look at examples in the next chapter, but for now, here are the basic steps to follow:

1. If you're in the macro window, choose File ➤ Save to save your current changes. (You can close the macro window as well—it doesn't need to be open for you to be able to attach its macros to a form or report.)

2. Open, in design view, the report or form that you want to attach the macro to.

   - If you want the macro to respond to a *form event,* select the entire form (Edit ➤ Select Form).

- If you want the macro to respond to an event in a particular control or command button on the form, select that control or command button (click it once).
- If you want the macro to respond to the opening or closing of a report, choose Edit ➤ Select Report.
- If you want the macro to respond to events in a report section, select the report section by clicking within the section or the bar at the top of the section.

3. Open the properties sheet if it isn't already open (click the Properties button or choose View ➤ Properties).

4. Select the appropriate On... property, such as On Push for a command button or On Exit for a control (as discussed in the next chapter).

5. Click the drop-down list button that appears, then select the name of the macro, or the name of the macro group that contains the macro, that you want to assign to the event.

6. If you chose the name of a macro group in the preceding step, add a period and the name of the specific macro that you want to assign to the event.

For instance, suppose you want the Close command button in the Customers Data Entry form to run a macro named Close in the macro group named Customers. In that case, you'd choose Customers as the macro name in Step 5, then add .*Close* to that name, as in the example shown in Figure 14.7.

To run the macro after assigning it to an event:

1. Switch to form view (or report view).

2. Make the event occur.

For instance, if you assigned the macro to the On Push property of a command button, click that button.

FIGURE 14.7

The macro named Close in the group named Customers assigned to the On Push property of a command button on the form

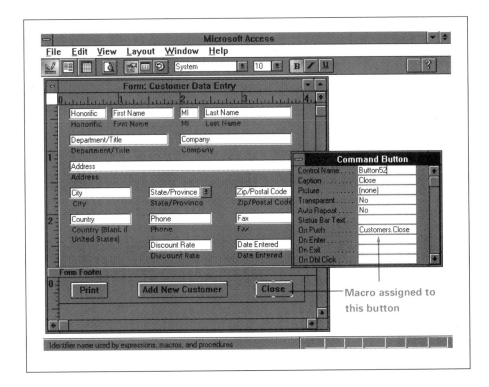

Macro assigned to this button

Again, we'll look at many examples, and describe the various events that you can assign macros to, in more detail in the next chapter. For now, it's sufficient to have a general idea of how you go about attaching macros to events on forms and reports, and how to run those macros.

Referring to Forms and Report Controls in Macro Expressions

As you'll see in upcoming chapters, a macro can refer to controls on forms and reports. For instance, the arguments for the SetValue action below refer to two controls on a form, named Customer ID and Next Available.

Specifically, this action, when executed, will copy the contents of the control named Next Available on the current form to the control named Customer ID on this same form.

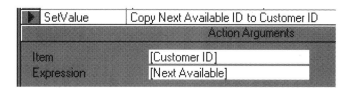

NOTE

You can find out the name of a control (or change it) by opening the form or report in design view. Select the control, and open its properties sheet. The Control Name is the first property in the properties sheet.

Referring to a control simply by enclosing its name in square brackets works *only* when you want the expression to refer to controls on the form or report that you've run the macro from.

In some cases, you might want to refer to controls that *aren't* in the form or report that you ran the macro from. For instance, you might want to run the macro from the database window, have it actually open the form or report, and *then* manipulate controls within that form or report. Or you might want a macro that's run from a particular form or report to refer to controls in some *other* form or report.

In either case, you need to refer to the control by its object type, name, and control name, using the identifier expression ! and the general syntax

    Forms![*formname*]![*control name*]

for a control on a form, or

    Reports![*reportname*]![*control name*]

for reports.

Three points to keep in mind:

* The *formname* or *reportname* that the expression refers to must be open when the macro is running (you can have the macro open the form or report with an OpenForm or OpenReport action).

* The *controlname* that expression refers to is the name assigned to the control as its Control Name property in the form's or report's design.

* The square brackets are only required if the *formname, reportname,* or *controlname* contains spaces. But it's a good idea to always use the square brackets as a matter of habit, so you won't forget them when you do need them!

As an example, if you wanted to refer to the control named Next Available on the Customers Data Entry form from within a macro that *wasn't* run from that form, you'd need to refer to that control as

Forms![Customers Data Entry]![Next Available]

You can use this identifying scheme in any macro expression, whether it be as an action argument or as a condition in the Conditions column of the macro window. You'll see some examples in upcoming chapters.

Responding to Problems in Macros

It's pretty unlikely that every macro you write will run perfectly right off the bat. Most of the time, creating a successful macro is a matter of running, testing, and debugging the macro until it works.

The very first thing you want to do, to avoid confusion and misleading errors, is to make sure that you always run the macro within the context it's intended for. For instance, if you assign a macro to a command button on a form, the only way to test and run the macro correctly is to open that form, in form view, and click the command button. That way, you'll know right off the bat that any errors in the macro *aren't* caused by running it in the wrong context.

When an error does occur in a macro, you'll see an error message and/or the Action Failed dialog box. For instance, here's a sample error message indicating that the macro currently running attempted to use a control that doesn't exist (the control name *Honorific* is misspelled in this example, which is the cause of the error):

Look to this error message for clues to help you diagnose the problem, then click the OK button. Most likely, Access will then display the Action Failed dialog box, as in the example below:

Here you can see a more specific description of exactly where the macro failed—the macro name (*Customers.Add New Customer* in this example), the Action that Failed (*GoToControl*), and the Arguments you've assigned to that control (*Honorfic*, misspelled in this example).

Your only option, in this case, is to choose the Halt button to leave the Action Failed dialog box. Then reopen the macro, and make whatever changes are necessary to fix the error.

Debugging Macros

Some problems in macros are easier to diagnose and fix than others. If the problem within a macro isn't readily apparent when the error occurs, you can single-step through the macro to watch every action it takes, one step at a time. That way, you can trace all the actions in the macro as they occur, and you will have a better feel for all the actions that preceded the error when the error occurs.

To single-step through a macro:

1. Open the macro window for the macro you want to test and debug.

2. Click the Single Step button (shown at left) on the tool bar, or choose Macro ➤ Single Step.

3. Run the macro, but be sure to do so within its appropriate context. For instance, if the macro is attached to a command button on a form, open that form in form view, and click the command button that the macro is assigned to.

The Macro Single Step dialog box appears, as in the example below:

Macro Single Step	
Macro Name: Customers.No Blank Zip	Step
Action Name: MsgBox	Halt
	Continue
Arguments: Can't leave Zip/Postal Code field empty, Yes, Warning!, Whoops!	

TIP You can also turn on single stepping by pressing Ctrl+Break while the macro is running.

The dialog box shows you the name of the macro that you're running and the action and its arguments *before* it actually executes the action. You have three options at this point:

- Step: Run the action that's shown in the dialog box. If that action *doesn't* cause an error, the next action in the macro appears in the Macro Single Step dialog box. If that action *does* cause an error, an error message appears and you're taken to the Action Failed dialog box.

- Halt: Stops running the macro before executing the current action, and closes the Macro Single Step dialog box (this is the only available option when you get to the Action Failed dialog box).

- Continue: Turns off single-stepping and runs the rest of the macro normally.

In general, you'll want to take a close look at every action before you choose the Step button, so you get a clear idea of every action that the macro is taking. When you run the action that is causing the problem, the error will still occur, and the Macro Single Step dialog box will change to the Action Failed dialog box. But, at this point, you should have a better idea of all the actions that led to the error, which in turn should help you to diagnose and solve the problem.

Don't forget that, if the macro contains conditions, those conditions will be in effect even while you're single-stepping through the macro. Even though the Macro Single Step dialog box *shows* those actions, it won't actually *execute* them if the condition proves false.

For instance, suppose you assign the condition IsNull([Zip/Postal Code]) to certain actions in a macro, then you single-step through the macro with data in the Zip/Postal Code field, so that IsNull([Zip/Postal Code]) proves to be false. The Macro Single Step dialog box will still show the actions that you've assigned that condition to, but it won't run those actions when you click the Step button. Therefore, if you specifically want to test the conditional actions in a macro, make sure the condition that the actions are dependent on proves true when you run the macro.

Summary

Learning the nuts and bolts of how to create, run, and debug macros is a good way to get your feet wet. In the next two chapters, we'll look at some specific macro techniques and examples, to help you create some useful macros for your own databases.

Using Macros with Forms and Reports

fast TRACK

ONE HANDY use of macros is to customize and automate your forms and reports. That is, you can develop small macros that automate certain tasks. Then, you can attach those macros to certain *events* that occur while you're using the form or printing the report. When the event occurs, the macro is triggered (run) as soon as the event occurs.

In this chapter we'll look at the various events that you can assign macros to. Then we'll look at some examples of macros and the events that they're attached to, to give you some food for thought in creating your own macros.

Using Macros with Forms

When you're using a form, in form view, Access recognizes certain actions that you take as *events.* You can assign a macro to an event so that when the event occurs, the macro is triggered into action.

For example, if you create a command button on a form, you can attach a macro to the On Push property of that button. In form view, clicking that command button instantly runs the macro.

NOTE   You can also attach Access Basic functions to events on forms and reports. Use = followed by a user-defined function name and parentheses, e.g., =MyFunction( ).

Responding to Form Events

You can attach macros to events that occur on a record-by-record basis in the form, or to the form as a whole. To do so:

1. Open the form in design view.

2. Double-click the gray form background, or choose Edit ➤ Select Form and open the properties sheet (if it isn't already open).

3. Make sure you're viewing the properties sheet for the form as a whole (the title of the sheet is Form, as in Figure 15.1).

4. Click on an event option, as summarized in Table 15.1.

5. Use the drop-down list to choose the macro that you want to assign to that event.

FIGURE 15.1

To assign macros to events on the form as a whole, or to events that occur on a record-by-record basis, use the Form properties sheet.

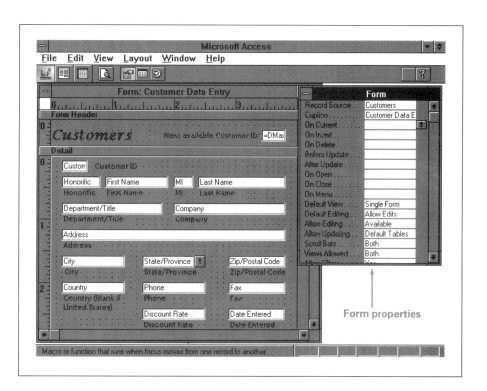

TABLE 15.1: Form and record events that can trigger macros

EVENT	FORM PROPERTY	WHEN EVENT OCCURS
Opening the form in form view	On Open	When the form is first opened, but before it displays any data. *Example:* You want to display a message about the form before the form appears on the screen.
Moving the focus to a different record	On Current	Before the focus moves into a new record to make it the current record. *Example:* You want the focus to appear in a particular field of the upcoming record.
Inserting a new record	On Insert	When you start entering data in a new record. *Example:* You want to fill in certain fields of the new record automatically.
Deleting a record	On Delete	After you choose to delete a record, but before the record is deleted. *Example:* You want to display a custom message for confirming a deletion.
Changing a record, but before changes are saved	Before Update	When you move the focus out of a record that you've just changed, but before the changes are saved to disk. *Example:* You want to verify changes to the record before saving those changes.
Changing a record after changes are saved	After Update	When you move the focus out of a record that's been changed, and those changes have been saved to disk. *Example:* You want to change data in some other form based on changes to the current form.
Closing the form	On Close	When the form is closed, but before it disappears from the screen. *Example:* You want to display some other form or report before, or after, the current form is closed.

Responding to Events in Individual Controls

You can also attach macros to individual controls on the form. For instance, you can have the macro be triggered as soon as the focus enters or leaves a particular field in the table, or when the *user* (i.e., the person using the form) clicks a command button that you've added to the form. To assign a macro to an individual control:

1. Open the form in design view.

2. Select the control (not the label) that you want to assign the macro to.

3. Choose View ➤ Properties or click the Properties button to open the properties sheet (Figure 15.2).

4. Choose the event you want to assign the macro to (Table 15.2).

5. Open the drop-down list, and choose the macro that you want to assign to the selected control.

Control properties

Selected control

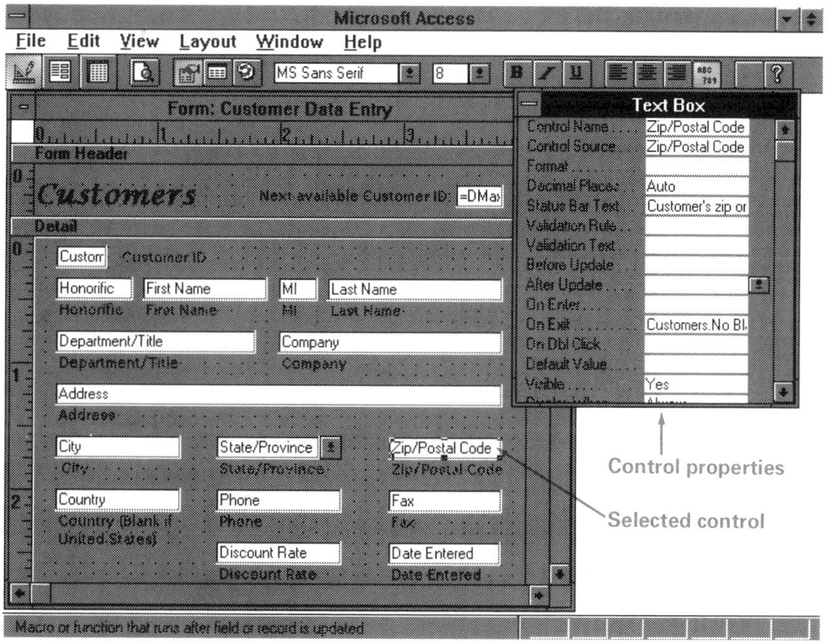

TABLE 15.2: Form control events that can trigger a macro

EVENT	CONTROL PROPERTY	WHEN EVENT OCCURS
Moving the focus to a control on the form	On Enter	When you try to move to a control, but before the control gets the focus. *Example:* You want to display a message or enter a value into a field before the insertion point goes into the field.
Pressing a command button on the form	On Push	When you click the command button. *Example:* To close the form as soon as the button is pushed.
Changing data in a control, without saving the change	Before Update	When you change data in a control, then leave the control, but before that change is saved to disk. *Example:* You want to verify the change before it's saved.
Changing, and saving, data in a control	After Update	After you change the contents of a control and Access has saved those changes. *Example:* You want to recalculate other controls on the form after saving data in the current field.
Double-clicking a control	On Dbl Click	When you double-click the control. *Example:* You want to display custom pop-up instructions about what goes in the field.
Leaving a control	On Exit	When you leave a control, but before the focus moves to the next field. *Example:* You want the focus to always go to a specific field after leaving the current field.

Macros Used with the Customer Data Entry Form

A good way to get a feel for how to design macros is to look at some examples. Figure 15.3 shows a sample Customer Data Entry form with

FIGURE 15.3

A sample form, based
on the Customers
table, that includes
some buttons and uses
macros

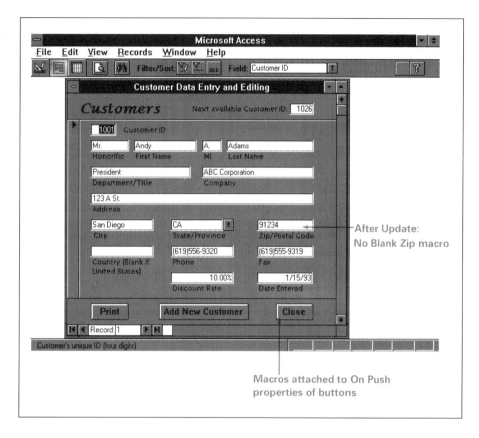

some custom buttons attached. I've also attached a macro to the Zip/Postal control in the form; I will talk about this macro in this chapter.

The form itself is based on the Customers table shown in Chapter 4. I added the custom buttons in form view, as discussed in Chapter 10.

I stored the macros for this form in a macro group named Customers, shown in Figure 15.4. Remember that, when viewing the macro window, you can only see the action arguments for the currently selected macro action. But I'll describe the action arguments assigned to each action as we look at the various macros in more detail in the sections that follow.

FIGURE 15.4

A group of macros, named Customers, attached to buttons and the Zip/Postal Code control on the Customer Data Entry form

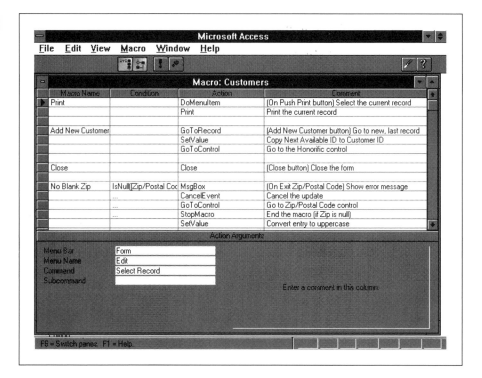

Using DoMenuItem to Choose Menu Commands

When creating a macro, you can use the DoMenuItem action to have the macro choose commands from whatever menus are available while the macro is running. To make sure you know exactly what menus and commands will be available when the macro is running, you need to get to that situation and take a look at the menus yourself. For instance, if the macro will be used in form view, you should open the form in form view and take a look at what's available in the menus there.

Then, when you return to the macro window, choose DoMenuItem as the macro action. Then:

- In the Menu Bar action argument, choose whichever menu bar will be available when the macro is executed (e.g., Form if the macro will be executed in form view).

- In the Menu Name action argument, choose which menu you want the macro to make a selection from (i.e., the name that appears in the menu bar, such as File or Edit).

- In the Command action argument, choose the specific command that you want the macro to perform.

- If the command you specified above leads to another menu, choose the Subcommand action argument and the command that you want the macro to perform.

Macro to Print the Current Form

The Print button on the Customer Data Entry form prints the current form when clicked. To do this, the macro chooses Edit ➤ Select Record from the menu bar and then prints the current selection.

The macro named Print in the Customers group does the job. The actions, and action arguments assigned to each action in that macro, are summarized in Table 15.3.

TABLE 15.3: Actions and action arguments in the Print macro

ACTION	ACTION ARGUMENT	SET TO
DOMENUITEM	Menu Bar	Form
	Menu Name	Edit
	Command	Select Record
PRINT	Print Range	Selection
	Print Quality	High
	Copies	1
	Collate Copies	Yes

NOTE In macro listings like Table 15.3, I've omitted action arguments that you'd leave empty in the macro window.

After creating and saving the Print macro, you need to open the Customer Data Entry form in design view. Then, select the Print button on the form, open the properties sheet, and specify Customers. Print as the On Push property of that button, as below:

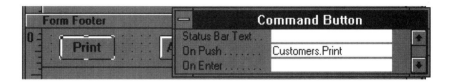

Remember, pressing the command button will trigger the macro *only* when you're in form view (not design view).

Using SetValue to Change Data and Properties

A macro can store data in a control on a form. For example, you might want the macro to copy data from one field to another, or from a control on the form to a field in the underlying table or query.

You use the SetValue action in a macro to change either the value or property of a control on the form. SetValue has two action arguments:

Item Defines the control, field, or property whose value you want to set (this can be any control *other than* a calculated control). If you want to change a property, include the control name in square brackets followed by a period and the property name, e.g., [Red Flag].Visible.

Expression Defines the value that you want to set in the control. If you're changing a property, the value must be a valid entry for that control, e.g., Yes or No for the Visible property.

Macro to Add a New Customer

You can use the GoToControl, GoToPage, and GoToRecord macro actions to move the focus to a particular control, record, or page in a form. For instance, the Add New Customer button in the Customer Data Entry form makes it easy to add a new customer to the Customers table. When the user clicks that button, a macro moves the focus to a new blank record, then copies the next available customer ID number to the Customer ID field. The user can then simply type in the new customer information.

In that form, the control that displays the next available customer ID number uses the **DMax( )** function to determine the next available number, as described in Chapter 10. Be sure to give that control a name, such as Next Available, in the Control Name property of the properties sheet.

NOTE   If you use a Counter rather than Number field to store the Customer ID, Access will automatically number customers for you. The SetValue action in Table 15.4 is then unnecessary. In fact, it generates a "Can't Set Value" error message, because you can't change the contents of a Counter field.

The macro that's attached to the Add New Customer button on the Customer Data Entry form is named Add New Customer and contains the actions and arguments shown in Table 15.4.

The GoToRecord action, with the New argument, moves the focus to a new, blank record. The SetValue action copies the contents of the Next Available control to the Customer ID field. The GoToControl action moves the focus to the Honorific field.

After creating the macro, you would attach it to the On Push property of the Add New Customer button, with the fully named Customers.Add New Customer, in the Customer Data Entry form.

TABLE 15.4: Actions and action arguments in the macro attached to the Add New Customers button on the Customer Data Entry form (Figure 15.3)

ACTION	ACTION ARGUMENT	EXPRESSION
GOTORECORD	Record	New
SETVALUE	Item	[Customer ID]
	Expression	[Next Available]
GOTOCONTROL	Control Name	Honorific

Macro to Close the Form

The action for the Close macro in the Customers group uses the action Close, with the Object Type argument set to Form, and the Object Name argument set to Customer Data Entry. To put this macro into action, attach the macro named Customers.Close to the On Push property of the Close button on the Customer Data Entry form.

Requiring an Entry in a Field

If you want to ensure that a particular control on a form is never left blank, you can attach a macro to the On Exit event of that field's control. Include a condition in the macro that displays a message box (using the MsgBox action), informing the user that the field cannot be left blank. Then have the macro put the focus back into the field.

Macro to Require a Zip/Postal Code Entry

The No Blank Zip macro in the Customers macro group prevents the Zip/Postal Code field in the Customers table from being left blank. The conditions, actions and action arguments used in the No Blank Zip macro are summarized in Table 15.5.

TABLE 15.5: Conditions, actions, and action arguments in a macro attached to the After Update property of the Zip/Postal Code field in the Customer Data Entry form

CONDITION	ACTION	ACTION ARGUMENT	SET TO
ISNULL([ZIP/ POSTAL CODE])	MsgBox	Message	Can't leave Zip/Postal Code field empty
		Beep	Yes
		Type	Warning!
		Title	Whoops!
...	CancelEvent		
...	GoToControl	Control Name	Zip/Postal Code
...	StopMacro		
	SetValue	Item	[Zip/Postal Code]
		Expression	UCase([Zip/Postal Code])

In this macro, the condition IsNull([Zip/Postal Code]) checks to see if the field is empty (null). If so, the macro displays the message box shown below, using the MsgBox action:

NOTE   You can also use Is Null (two words) *after* a control name to test for a null value. For example, [Zip/Postal Code] Is Null means the same thing as IsNull([Zip/Postal Code]).

The CancelEvent action prevents the update from occurring. That is, the event that triggered the macro, Update, is canceled, so the blank contents of the field are not accepted. The GoToControl action then puts the insertion point back into the State/Province control, and the macro stops (StopMacro).

As an added little bonus, the last action in the macro, SetValue, is executed only when the Zip/Postal code *isn't* left blank (its Condition column doesn't contain an ellipsis). This action converts the entry to uppercase, using the **Access UCase( )** function. So a valid entry like *m3h 2hj* is automatically converted to *M3H 2HJ.*

Using a Macro to Hide or Display Data

One of the more interesting things you can do with a macro is to change the Visible, Locked, and Enabled properties of a control on a form, based on some condition. As mentioned earlier, you can use SetValue to change the properties.

Hiding or Displaying a Red Flag

The ability to hide or display a control is particularly handy for calling attention to records that meet certain criteria. For instance, the Order Summary form in Figure 15.5 shows a red flag *only* for payments that are past

FIGURE 15.5

The red flag appears when the current order is past due. Otherwise, the flag is invisible.

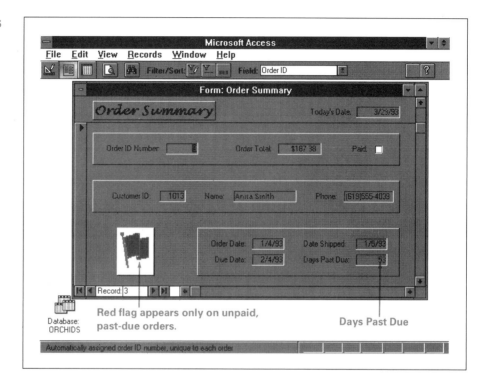

Red flag appears only on unpaid, past-due orders.

Days Past Due

due, calling attention to those orders. The red flag is invisible on orders that are paid up or not past due.

The macro to hide or display the red flag, which we'll name Red Flag Macro in this example, is shown below:

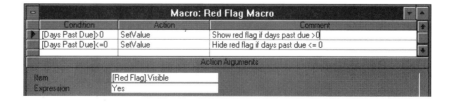

Notice that this macro contains two condition statements: one that's true when Days Past Due is greater than zero; the other that's true when Days Past Due is less than or equal to zero. The conditions, actions, and action arguments for this macro are listed in Table 15.6.

To put the macro into action, I opened the Order Summary form (originally presented in Chapter 10) in design view. I then used the Unbound Object Frame tool to add a control to the form to display the little red flag (which I happened to have in my clip-art collection). I opened the properties sheet and set the Control Name for that control to Red Flag.

Then, I selected the control that displays the number of days past due and assigned the control name Days Past Due to that control (in the Control Name property of the properties sheet). Lastly, I selected the form (Layout ➤ Select Form) and assigned the macro name Red Flag Macro to the On Current property of the form, as in Figure 15.6. This ensures that the macro to hide or display the red flag is executed each time the person using the form moves from one record to the next.

TABLE 15.6: Conditions, actions, and action arguments for the Red Flag macro

CONDITION	ACTION	ACTION ARGUMENT	SET TO
[DAYS PAST DUE]>0	SetValue	Item	[Red Flag].Visible
		Expression	Yes
[DAYS PAST DUE]<=0	SetValue	Item	[Red Flag].Visible
		Expression	No

FIGURE 15.6

The Order Summary form in design view after adding the Unbound Object Frame control to display the red flag and setting the form's On Current property to the Red Flag Macro name

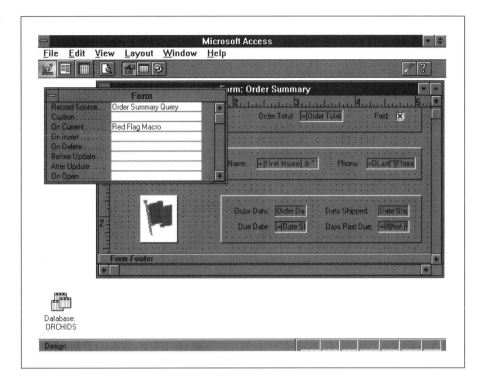

Macros Used with the Order Entry Form

The Order Entry form, originally presented in Chapter 11 and shown in Figure 15.7, uses a number of macros to simplify data entry.

FIGURE 15.7

The Order Entry form uses several buttons and macros to simplify data entry and editing.

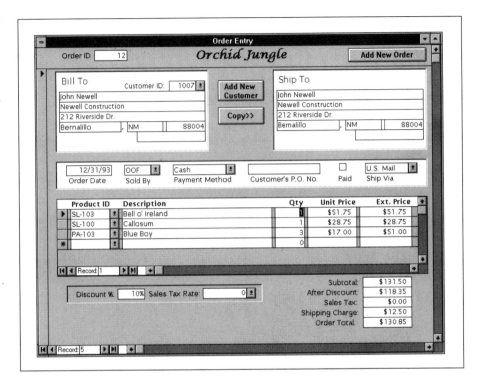

NOTE

I've patterned my Order Entry form and macros after the Orders form and Orders macro group in the Northwind database that comes with the Access package. So if you'd like to explore a "live" example of a similar form, open the Orders form in the Northwind database.

I stored all the macros for the Order Entry form in a macro group named Orders. Figure 15.8 shows the first four macros in that macro group. We'll look at those macros in the sections that follow.

FIGURE 15.8

Four of the macros
in the Orders macro
group, used with
controls in the Orders
and Orders Subform
forms

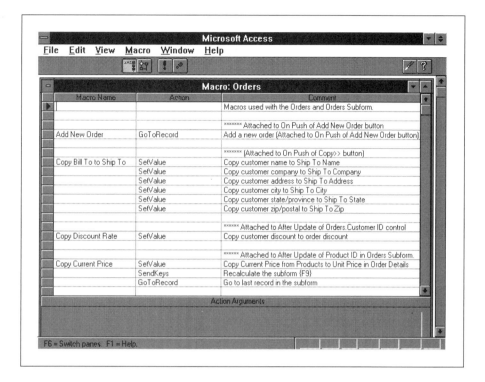

The Add New Order Button

The Add New Order button in the Orders macro simply moves to a new record in the underlying query, so the user can enter a new order. The macro is named Add New Order in the Orders macro group and contains the action and arguments shown in Table 15.7.

TABLE 15.7:   The action and action arguments used in the Add New Orders macro of the Orders macro group

ACTION	ACTION ARGUMENT	SET TO
GOTORECORD	Object Type	Form
	Object Name	Order Entry
	Record	New

After creating the macro, you'd attach it to the On Push property of the Add New Orders command button on the Order Entry form, with the full name Orders.Add New Order.

Macro Assigned to the Copy>> Button

A click on the Copy>> button of the Order Entry form copies data from the Bill To portion of the order form to the Ship To portion. The macro that does the job is named *Copy Bill To to Ship To*. Its actions and arguments are summarized in Table 15.8.

This macro uses a series of SetValue actions to copy data from the Name, Company, Address, City, State/Province, and Zip/Postal Code fields to equivalent "Ship To" fields in the underlying query. (In this example, the underlying query is named Order Entry Main Form Query, as discussed in Chapter 11.)

TABLE 15.8: Actions and action arguments in the Copy Bill To to Ship To macros in the Orders macro group

ACTION	ACTION ARGUMENT	SET TO
SETVALUE	Item	[Ship To Name]
	Expression	[Name]
SETVALUE	Item	[Ship To Company]
	Expression	[Company]
SETVALUE	Item	[Ship To Address]
	Expression	[Address]
SETVALUE	Item	[Ship To City]
	Expression	[City]
SETVALUE	Item	[Ship To State]
	Expression	[State/Province]
SETVALUE	Item	[Ship To Zip]
	Expression	[Zip/Postal Code]

The macro is attached to the On Push property of the Copy>> button in the form, with the full name *Orders.Copy Bill To to Ship To.*

Copying the Discount Rate

Another handy macro on the Order Entry form copies the customer's standard discount rate (stored in the Discount Rate field of the underlying query) to the Discount % field of the order (the Discount % field in this same query). The macro, named Copy Discount Rate, uses a single SetValue action to do this:

```
SetValue
        Item:       [Discount %]
        Expression:    [Discount Rate]
```

NOTE   The QBE grid in the underlying query must contain both fields. In this example, the QBE grid in the underlying Order Entry Main Form Query must include both the Discount % field from the Orders table and the Discount Rate field from the Customers table.

The macro is assigned to the After Update property of the Customer ID field, so the discount rate is updated right after the user chooses a customer ID number to identify whom the order is billed to.

Note that if two fields in the underlying query have the same name, you need to specify which table the field is based on. For instance, suppose we had assigned the field name Discount % to the discount rate field in both the Customers and Orders tables. In that case, the SetValue action above would need to be defined like this in the macro:

```
SetValue
        Item:       [Orders.Discount %]
        Expression:    [Customers.Discount %]
```

Determining the Unit Price

On the Order Entry form, the Unit Price of any given product is quite likely to be the same as the Current Price that's stored in the Products table. Thus, it would be very convenient to have the order form automatically look up the current price of a product in the Products table, and then set the value of the Unit Price control to that value.

There is one slight problem in doing this, however. Since the Products table is not included in the query that underlies the Order Entry subform (where the Unit Price control is placed), to do the job, the macro would need to open the Products table independently of the underlying query and look up the Current Price there.

When you need to look up information in a table that's not currently open, you use the **DLookup( )** domain aggregate function. Thus, to have the macro automatically look up that current price and copy that value to the unit price, the Copy Current Price macro uses SetValue with the Item and Expression action arguments shown in Table 15.9.

After creating the macro, you'd open the Order Entry subform in design view and assign the macro to the On Update property of the Product ID control in the Orders Subform. (I'll talk about the roles played by the SendKeys and GoToRecord options later in this chapter, under the general topic of using macros to recalculate a form.)

TABLE 15.9: Actions and action arguments used to look up the current price of a product in the Products table and copy that value to the Unit Price control on the Order Entry Subform

ACTION	ACTION ARGUMENT	SET TO
SETVALUE	Item	[Unit Price]
	Expression	DLookup("[Current Price]","Products","[Product ID]=Form.[Product ID]")
SENDKEYS	Keystrokes	{F9}
	Wait	Yes
GOTORECORD	Record	Last

More Order Entry Form Macros

Figure 15.9 shows some more handy macros used with the Order Entry form and its subform. These macros are also in the Orders macro group (I've just scrolled down to those macros in the figure).

FIGURE 15.9

Additional macros
in the Orders macro
group, used with
the Orders form and
Orders Subform form

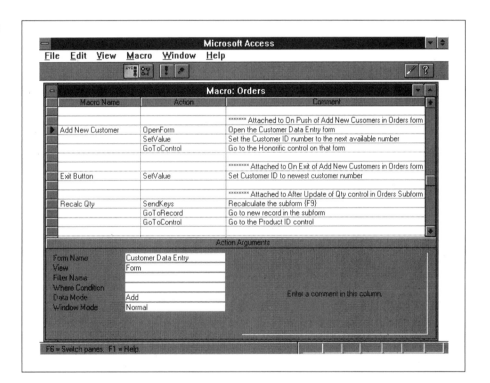

Opening Another Form

In some situations, you might want to make it easy for the person using a particular form to pop over to some other form, either to look up information or to make an entry.

For example, suppose the person using the Order Entry form needs to enter an order. But the customer for that order is new, and their name and address isn't in the Customers table yet. Clicking the Add New Customer button on the Order Entry form (Figure 15.7) takes the user directly to the Customer Data Entry form, where he or she can enter the new customer. Upon closing that form, the user is returned to the Order Entry form, where they can then complete the rest of the order.

N O T E   The Bill To information in the Order Form comes from the Customers table, via the underlying query. Selecting a Customer ID from the drop-down list on the form displays all the information for that customer in the Bill To section.

The actions and action arguments for the Add New Customer button are listed in Table 15.10. That macro is attached to the On Push property of the Add New Customer button in the Orders form (*not* the button in the Customer Data Entry form).

Let's take a look at each of these actions. The OpenForm action opens the Customer Data Entry form, in the Add data mode to add new records. SetValue sets the Customer ID number for the record to the next available Customer ID number. This action assumes that the next available ID

TABLE 15.10:   Actions used in the macro to add a new customer to the Customers table before entering a new order for that customer

ACTION	ACTION ARGUMENT	SET TO
OPENFORM	Form Name	Customer Data Entry
	View	Form
	Data Mode	Add
	Window Mode	Normal
SETVALUE	Item	Forms![Customer Data Entry].[Customer ID]
	Expression	Forms![Customer Data Entry].[Next Available]
GOTOCONTROL	Control Name	Honorific

number is displayed in a control named Next Available on the form (and is also necessary only if Customer ID *isn't* a Counter field). GoToControl moves the focus to the Honorific control, where the user can start typing in the new customer information.

The Exit Button Macro

The Exit Button macro in the Orders macro group fills in the Bill To information on the form with data for the new customer. That macro is attached to the On Exit property of the Add New Customers button on the Orders form (*not* the Add New Customer button on the Customer Data Entry form).

All this macro needs to do to fill in the Bill To section of the order form is to position the record pointer to the largest customer ID number in the underlying query (assuming that customer ID numbers are assigned sequentially). The action and its arguments in the Exit Button macro are listed in Table 15.11.

TABLE 15.11: The action and its action arguments used in the Exit Button macro

ACTION	ACTION ARGUMENT	EXPRESSION
SETVALUE	Item	[Orders.Customer ID]
	Expression	DMax("[Customer ID]","Customers")

Recalculating with Macros

When your form is based on a query and contains one or more calculated controls, you may find that the calculations aren't updated immediately when you change data. You can recalculate a form at any time by pressing Requery (Shift+F9). Or, if you're in a subform, you can press F9 to recalculate just the subform.

If you're using a macro, you can use the SendKeys action to press these (and any other keystrokes) for you. You may find, however, that when the macro finishes recalculating a subform, it sends the insertion point up to the first record in the subform. I'm not sure if this is a bug or a feature, but it can be an annoyance.

One way around this minor annoyance is to use a GoToRecord action to send the insertion point back to a specific record after the recalculation takes place. For example, the Copy Current Price macro (Table 15.9 above) ends with these two actions:

```
SendKeys
    Keystrokes:    {F9}
    Wait:          Yes
GoToRecord
    Record:        Last
```

The SendKeys action presses the F9 key to recalculate the subform after the first action in the macro copies the Current Price from the Products table to the Unit Price control of the subform. It also sends the focus back up to the first record of the subform.

To counteract that, the GoToRecord action puts the insertion point back down into the last record of the subform, where the last change was most likely made. Setting the Wait argument to Yes in the SendKeys action ensures that the focus is moved *after* the recalculation takes place.

Recalculating Orders After Changing the Quantity Sold

The Recalc Qty macro in the Orders macro group is attached to the After Update property of the Qty control in the Orders Subform. That macro contains the actions and arguments listed in Table 15.12.

This macro recalculates the subform after the quantity changes. Then it moves the insertion point to the Product ID control in the next blank record, so the user is ready to type in the next line item on the order.

TABLE 15.12: Actions and action arguments used in the Recalc Qty macro, attached to the After Update property of the Qty control in the Orders Subform

ACTION	ACTION ARGUMENT	SET TO
SENDKEYS	Keystrokes	{F9}
	Wait	Yes
GOTORECORD	Record	New
GOTOCONTROL	Control Name	Product ID

Other Ways to Recalculate

There are numerous other ways to recalculate forms and subforms and to control the position of the insertion point. If you get the urge to explore, you might want to take a look at the Orders forms in the Northwind database (*nwind.mdb*) and Order Entry database (*ordentry.mdb*), which come with your Access package.

Recalculating Domain Aggregate Expressions

If a control on your form uses a domain aggregate function, you might also want to recalculate that control with a macro. For instance, suppose that rather than using a Sales Tax Rate field in the Orders table to store the sales tax rate, you use a calculated control, named Sales Tax Rate, on the Order Entry form to look up the sales tax rate from the States table. The expression to look up the sales tax rate might look something like this (as discussed in Chapter 11):

```
=DLookUp("[Sales Tax Rate]","States","[Abbreviation]=
[Ship To State]")
```

Because the expression uses a domain aggregate function, it won't be updated automatically when the contents of the Ship To State control changes. To fix the problem, create a macro that recalculates just the control that contains the **DLookup** function. For instance, if the expression is stored in a calculated control named Sales Tax Rate, the macro would contain the following action:

```
Requery
    Item: [Sales Tax Rate]
```

Attach the macro to the After Update property of the Ship To State control, to ensure that the Sales Tax Rate control is updated whenever you change the Ship To State.

NOTE Search for *requery* in Access's help for more information on using the Requery action in a macro.

Using Macros with Reports

You can attach macros to events that occur when opening, closing, and printing reports, using the same basic techniques you use in forms. Open the report in design view, choose Edit ➤ Select Report, and then open the properties sheet. Table 15.13 summarizes the report events that you can attach macros to.

You can also attach macros to individual sections within the report, by selecting the section and opening its properties sheet in design view. Table 15.14 summarizes the "section events" that you can attach macros to.

Showing the Due Date on Invoices Only

As an example of formatting a report section, suppose you want to show the due date at the bottom of printed invoices. For emphasis, you want to

TABLE 15.13: Report events that can trigger a macro

EVENT	REPORT PROPERTY	WHEN EVENT OCCURS
Opening the report	On Open	When the report is first opened, but before it starts printing. *Example:* To have the macro ask for specific records to print before printing begins.
Closing a report	On Close	When the report finishes printing, or the Print Preview window is closed. *Example:* To have a macro flag printed invoices so they're not printed again in the future.

TABLE 15.14: Events that occur as a report section is being formatted or printed, which you can use to trigger a macro

EVENT	SECTION PROPERTY	WHEN EVENT OCCURS
Laying out a section, before printing	On Format	As Access is laying out the report section. *Example:* To hide, display, or change the properties of a control in the section before printing it.
Printing a section	On Close	After Access has laid out the report section, but just before printing the section. Only sections that are actually printed trigger the event. *Example:* To flag only those records that have actually been printed in a report.

show the border around the message. Your remittance policy is that all payments are due 30 days after the date that the invoice is printed.

If the order is paid (i.e., the Paid field in the Orders table contains Yes), you should hide the message and the surrounding border.

NOTE

If you don't care about hiding and displaying the border surrounding the message, you could just add a test box to the Invoices and Receipts report that contains the expression =IIf(Paid,"Thank You","Please remit payment by " &Date( )+30). You wouldn't need a macro to hide or display the control in this case.

Your first step would be to create a macro that contains two conditions, one to test for paid orders and another to test for unpaid orders. The macro, which I've named Remittance Macro in this example, is shown below.

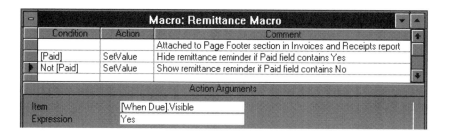

The conditions, actions, and arguments in the Remittance macro are listed in Table 15.15.

TABLE 15.15: Conditions, actions, and action arguments used in the Remittance macro

CONDITION	ACTION	ACTION ARGUMENT	SET TO
[PAID]	SetValue	Item	[When Due].Visible
		Expression	No
NOT [PAID]	SetValue	Item	[When Due].Visible
		Expression	Yes

Then, in the Order ID footer of the Invoices and Receipts report, you'd add a calculated control (using the Text Box tool in the report's design) that contains the appropriate expression, such as = *"Please remit payment by "&Date( )+30*. Then you'd select the control, open the properties sheet, and enter **When Due** as the Control Name.

Finally, to attach the macro to the report section, you'd select the Order ID footer section, by double-clicking the bar at the top of the Order ID section. Then, you'd set the On Format property for that section to Remittance Macro. When you printed or previewed the report, the remittance message would appear only on unpaid orders.

Summary

In this chapter we've looked at some examples of using macros with forms to simplify data entry and editing for the person using the form. We've also looked at a macro that's attached to a report section. You'll see some more examples of using macros with reports in upcoming chapters.

You can find many more examples of using macros with forms and reports, and for importing and exporting data, in the appropriate sections of the *Microsoft Access User's Guide,* which comes with your Access package.

For now, I'd like to turn your attention to another topic that concerns macros. It *isn't* discussed in your Access documentation but certainly is well worth knowing about: automatic updating.

Automatic Updating with Macros

fast _TRACK_

To keep a database running at top speed   **696**

store only new data in the tables used for the bulk of data entry and editing. Move older data to *history tables*.

To move data into history tables   **697**

create Append and Delete queries to copy records to the history table, and then delete those records from the original table. You can create a macro to run the queries to simplify the job, and ensure that the queries are run in the proper sequence.

Storing calculated totals in a table   **702**

can simplify the job of creating queries based on those totals. You can automate the task of keeping calculated totals up to date using queries and macros.

To hide action query warning messages   **707**

when running the query from a macro, precede the OpenQuery action in the macro with a SetWarnings action, set to No.

AUTOMATIC updating is a means of making your database work harder and more intelligently. It's not really a built-in feature of Access, but rather a means of using queries, macros, and other objects together to simplify and automate common tasks.

In this chapter, we'll look at some examples of automatic updating to streamline common tasks in the Orchids database. These examples should give you some good ideas for developing your own automatic updating schemes.

Sending Letters to New Customers Only

It's often convenient to have Access recognize the difference between new and old data. For instance, let's suppose you store all your customer data in one table, named Customers. Every once in a while, you want to print Welcome letters and labels just for the new customers. Sounds simple, right?

The question is, how do you discriminate between old and new customers? Or, more specifically, how do you discriminate between customers whom you have already sent Welcome letters to and those you haven't?

One way to do this is to store new customers in one table and "old customers" in another table. But this causes some problems because now you've got customer data in two separate places.

Another solution is to keep track of the last time you printed Welcome letters. Then, create and use parameter queries to ask for records with certain dates, and print letters only for those records. But this approach leaves *you* with the responsibility of keeping track of which customers have, and have not, received Welcome letters.

A third solution is to add a field, perhaps named Welcomed, to the structure of the Customers table, with a Default Value of No, as in Figure 16.1.

N O T E   See Chapter 6 if you need a reminder on how to change the structure of an existing table.

FIGURE 16.1

A field named Welcomed, with the Yes/No data type, added to the structure of the Customers table

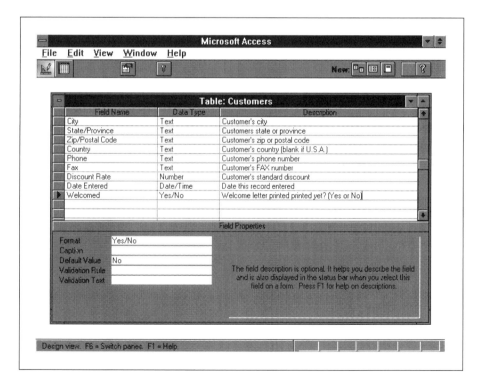

As you add new records to the Customers table, leave the contents of the Welcomed field set to No. Then you can create a macro that does three things:

- Prints Welcome letters only for records that have No in the Welcomed field
- Prints labels (or envelopes) for these same customers
- Changes each No to Yes in the Welcomed field, to indicate that the Welcome letter has been printed

So now the whole job of keeping track of which customers have already received Welcome letters is completely automatic. That is, each time you run the macro, Access prints letters only for customers who haven't received the letters yet. Access also *flags* (identifies) those customers as having been sent the letters.

N O T E   The field that identifies which records have and have not been through an automatic updating procedure is often called a *flag*.

Creating the Letters and Labels

Of course, you need to create the form letter and mailing label or envelope format for the report you want to print. In this example, we'll assume that the report for printing the Welcome letters is named Welcome Letter, and that the report for printing mailing labels is named Customer Mailing Labels.

Chapter 12 presents examples of reports for printing form letters, mailing labels, and envelopes from the Customers table.

Creating a Macro to Flag Welcomed Customers

After Access has printed Welcome letters and labels for new customers, we want it to automatically change the Welcomed status of those customers from No to Yes. Figure 16.2 shows the update query that would do the job. In this example, I've named that query Flag Welcomed Customers. After creating the query, you can just close and save it (there's no need to run it from the database window; we'll create a macro to run that query automatically).

FIGURE 16.2

An update query, named Flag Welcomed Customers, to change the contents of the Welcomed field in the Customers table to Yes

	Microsoft Access
File Edit View Query Window Help	

Update Query: Flag Welcomed Customers

Customers
*
Customer ID
Honorific
First Name
MI
Last Name

Field:	Welcomed			
Table:	Customers			
Update To:	Yes			
Criteria:				
or:				

Database: ORCHIDS

Ready

In the query window, you choose Query ➤ Update
to change a select query to an update query, as
discussed in Chapter 8.

Pulling It All Together with a Macro

Finally, you can create a macro to automate the entire job of printing Welcome letters and labels, and flagging customers for whom letters have been printed. The one shown in Figure 16.3, which I've named Print Welcome Letters and Labels, will do the job. As usual, you can only see the action arguments for one action in macro window.

FIGURE 16.3

The Print Welcome Letters and Labels macro. Action arguments for this macro are listed in Table 16.1.

```
┌─────────────────────────────────────────────────────────────────────┐
│  ─                        Microsoft Access                       ▾ ▴  │
│  File   Edit   View   Macro   Window   Help                           │
│  ┌──────────────────────────────────────────────────────────────┐    │
│                                                             ?         │
│  ┌─  Macro: Print Welcome Letters and Labels               ▾ ▴  │     │
│  │        Action              Comment                            │     │
│  │                    Print Welcome letters for new customers only (Welcomed = No) │
│  │  MsgBox            Tell user to load paper for printing letters. │  │
│  │  OpenReport        Print the Welcome letter, for records that have No in the Welcomed field. │
│  │  MsgBox            Tell user to load mailing labels.          │     │
│  │  OpenReport        Print the labels for records that have No in the Welcomed field. │
│  │▶ OpenQuery         Run the Flag Welcomed Customers query to change No to Yes in the Welcomed field. │
│  │                                                               │     │
│  │                     Action Arguments                          │     │
│  │  Query Name     Flag Welcomed Customers                       │     │
│  │  View           Datasheet                                     │     │
│  │  Data Mode      Edit                                          │     │
│  │                              Enter a comment in this column.  │     │
│  └──────────────────────────────────────────────────────────────┘     │
│  F6 = Switch panes.  F1 = Help.                                        │
└─────────────────────────────────────────────────────────────────────┘
```

Table 16.1 lists the action arguments assigned to each action in the macro. (Note, however, that there are two OpenReport and two MsgBox actions in the macro. The order of actions listed in the table matches the order of those actions in the macro.)

TABLE 16.1: Actions and action arguments in the Print Welcome Letters and Labels macro

ACTION	ACTION ARGUMENT	EXPRESSION
MSGBOX	Message	Load paper for printing letters, then choose OK.
	Beep	Yes
	Type	Information
OPENREPORT	Report Name	Welcome Letter
	View	Print
	Where Condition	[Welcomed]=No
MSGBOX	Message	After all the letters are printed, load the mailing labels in the printer, then choose OK.
	Beep	Yes
	Type	Information
OPENREPORT	Report Name	Customer Mailing Labels
	View	Print
	Where Condition	[Welcomed]=No
OPENQUERY	Query Name	Flag Welcomed Customers
	View	Datasheet
	Data Mode	Edit

Testing the Macro

To test the macro, you need first need to open the Customers table, and make sure that at least one record in the table has No in the Welcomed field (since the macro prints only those records). Then, run the macro. The first MsgBox action displays the message shown below:

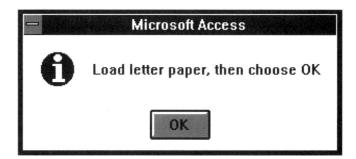

When the paper is loaded, choose OK. At that point, the OpenReport action in the macro is executed. That action opens the Welcome Letters report and starts printing. However, the Where condition in the action argument limits the printing to new customers—those with No in the Welcomed field.

After all the letters are sent to the Windows Print Manager, the second MsgBox action in the macro is executed and displays this message:

Chances are, the printer will still be printing letters, so you'll want to wait until all the letters are printed. Then, load the mailing labels (or envelopes) into the printer, and click the OK button. At that point, the second OpenReport action in the macro is executed, which prints the Customer Mailing Labels report for the same set of customers.

Finally, the OpenQuery action is executed in the macro, which runs the Flag Welcomed Customers macro. You'll see the first standard message that appears whenever you run an update query, as below:

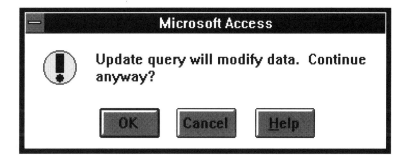

T I P

You can use the SetWarnings action in a macro to hide the standard messages that action queries display, as discussed a little later in this chapter.

Choose OK, and you'll see the second message, indicating how many records will be updated. Again, you can choose OK to proceed, letting the update query do its job. When the macro is done, you'll be returned to the database window.

At that point all your letters and labels will be printed. If you open the Customers table and scroll through records, the Welcomed field in every record will contain Yes.

Subtracting Units Sold from Units In Stock

Another very handy automatic updating technique involves keeping track of Units In Stock in the Products table automatically. For instance, you might want to have Access subtract the quantity of units shipped with each order (the Qty field in the Order Details table) from the Units In Stock quantities in the Products table.

This procedure is often called *posting* the orders. The one thing you want to be sure to do when creating a posting scheme is to make sure that no orders are posted more than once. You can do that by adding a Yes/No field, perhaps named Posted, to the structure of the Order Details table, as in Figure 16.4.

FIGURE 16.4

A Yes/No field, named Posted, added to the structure of the Order Details table

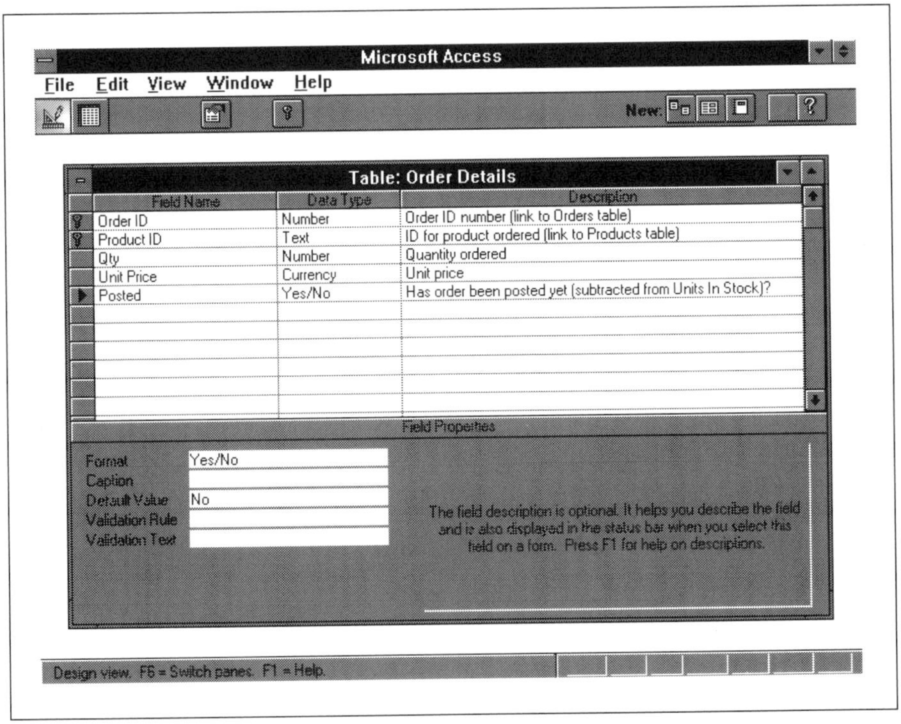

Now your posting scheme needs to do two things:

* Subtract the quantity of a product shipped from the Units In Stock field in the Products table, for unposted orders only.

* Change the Posted field from No to Yes to indicate that the record has been posted.

For instance, Figure 16.5 shows some sample data in the Products and Order Detail tables *before* posting orders. Notice that there are currently 100 units of product MO-100 in stock and 50 of product PA-100 in stock. The Order Details table indicates that 5 of product MO-100 and 10 of product PA-100 have been ordered. Notice, too, that the Posted field in each Order Detail record contains No.

FIGURE 16.5

Products and Order Details tables before posting orders. The Posted field in each record of the Order Details table contains No, to indicate that those orders haven't been posted yet.

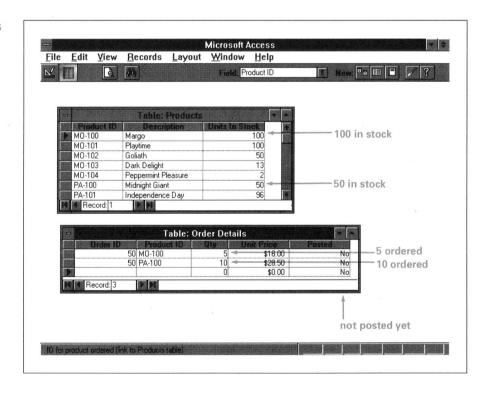

Figure 16.6 shows both tables *after* posting orders. Now the Products table shows that there are 95 of product MO-100 in stock, because 5 have been sold, and 40 of product PA-100 in stock, because 10 have been sold. The Posted field in both Order Details records has also been changed to Yes, to indicate that the quantity of each of those records has been subtracted from the In Stock quantity in the Products table.

FIGURE 16.6

After posting orders, the In Stock quantities of products MO-100 and PA-100 have been reduced to reflect order quantities. Records in Order Details are flagged as Yes, to indicate that those orders have been posted.

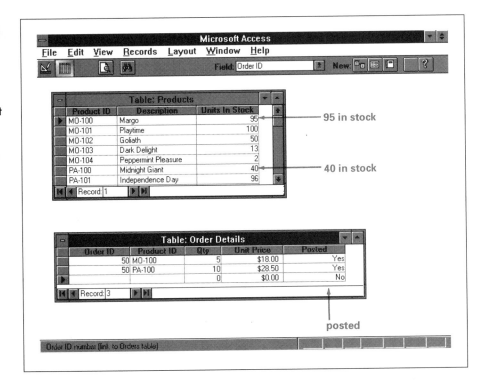

The Posting Query

Next, you need to create a query to subtract quantities sold from units in stock, and flag the appropriate records in Order Details to indicate that they've been posted. Figure 16.7 shows just the query to do the job, which I've named Subtract Order Qty From Units In Stock in this example.

FIGURE 16.7

The Subtract Units Sold From Units In Stock query subtracts the quantity sold (Qty) in the Order Details table from the Units In Stock in the Products table.

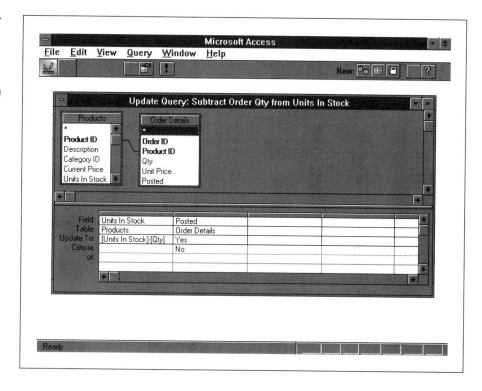

Notice that this is an update query (not a select query). Perhaps it seems too simple to do the job, but it works because of the following:

* The Products and Order Details tables are joined by their common field, Product ID.

* The Criteria cell in the Posted field limits records to those that have No in the Posted field. Access imposes the criterion before it does the updating.

* The Update To cell in the QBE grid updates the Units In Stock field to its current value, minus the contents of the Qty field.

* The Update To cell in the Posted field changes the contents of the Posted field from No to Yes.

NOTE If you need reminders on how to create and run action queries like the ones presented in this chapter, refer to Chapter 8.

When creating queries like the example shown in Figure 16.7, you need to make sure to run and test them quite carefully. You might want to experiment with a small amount of sample data in a separate database until you get the query just right. When you're sure the query does the job you need it to do, you can copy it into your real database.

Using History Tables to Speed Data Entry

If you store all your orders in the Orders and Order Details tables throughout the year, those tables are likely to become quite large as the months roll by. As the tables grow larger, processing takes longer.

To keep your database running at top speed, you can use *history tables* to store orders that have been fulfilled (and posted). That is, you can continue to store new, outstanding orders in your Orders and Order Details tables. But then at some point, perhaps right after printing invoices and receipts, you can move all those records to the history tables.

Creating the History Tables

Creating the history tables for fulfilled orders and order details is a simple matter of copy-and-paste. Starting at the database window, follow these steps:

1. Click the Table Object button in the database window.

2. Click on the Orders table, and choose Edit ➤ Copy.

3. Choose Edit ➤ Paste.

4. Enter a name for your history table, such as Order History.

5. Choose Structure Only from the Paste options, then choose OK.

6. Click on the Order Details table name.

7. Choose Edit ➤ Copy, then Edit ➤ Paste.

8. Enter a name for the history table, such as Detail History.

9. Again, choose Structure Only from the Paste options, then choose OK.

Using Append and Delete Queries to Copy Posted Records

Moving records from one table to another is actually a two-step process. First you *append* records from one table to the other, using an append query. Then you delete those records from the original table, using a delete query.

If you're using automatic updating to subtract quantities sold from units in stock, you'll want to build some extra safety into these queries to ensure that only posted orders are moved into the history tables. In this example, you'd want to use criteria that isolate records that have Yes in the posted field, so that unposted records are not moved into the history tables.

Figure 16.8 shows the append query for appending records from the Order Details table to the Detail History table. While creating this query, you'd specify Order History as the table to append records to (after choosing Query ➤ Append), as shown in the figure. Notice the use of the Criteria cell in the Posted field in the QBE grid, to ensure that only posted records are appended to the history table.

To append records from the Orders table to the Order History table, you can use a similar append query, as in Figure 16.9. Notice that you need to include the Order Details table in the query so that you can use the Posted field as a criterion in the query.

FIGURE 16.8

The query to append
records from the
Order Details table to
the Detail History table

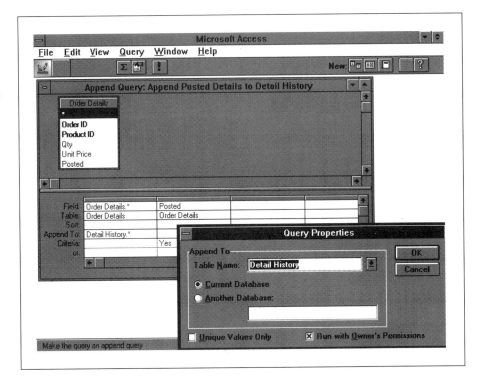

After the Append queries have done their jobs, you can use Delete queries
to delete appended records from the Orders and Order Details tables. The
delete query for deleting orders is shown below:

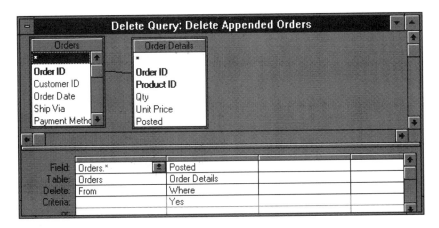

FIGURE 16.9

The query to append
records from the
Orders table to
the Orders History
table.

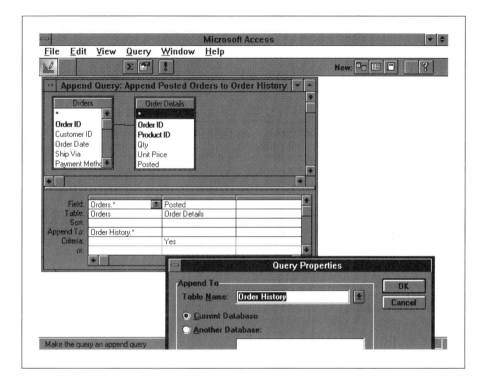

You need the Posted field from the Order Details table to isolate records
to delete in the Orders table, so make sure you delete records from the Orders table *before* you delete records from the Order Details table. Also,
remember that if you've defined referential integrity between two tables,
you cannot delete records from the table on the "one side" if there are corresponding records on the "many side." You can remove referential integrity restrictions by choosing Edit ➤ Relationships from the database
window (see Chapter 6).

Next, you need to create the delete query for deleting posted records from the Order Details table, as below:

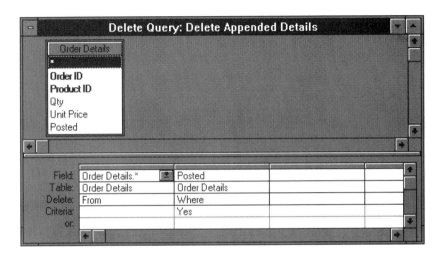

Creating a Posting Macro

After you have created all the queries for subtracting order quantities from in stock quantities and have moved posted records, you'll almost certainly want to create a macro to run them all. Doing so not only reduces the whole procedure to a single action but also ensures that the queries will always be run in the proper sequence.

Figure 16.10 shows a macro, named Post And Move Orders, that will do the job. Table 16.2 shows the action arguments used in each line of the macro. (The order of actions in the table matches the order of actions in the macro.)

FIGURE 16.10

The Post And Move
Orders macro runs the
action queries for
posting orders and
moving them to
history tables.

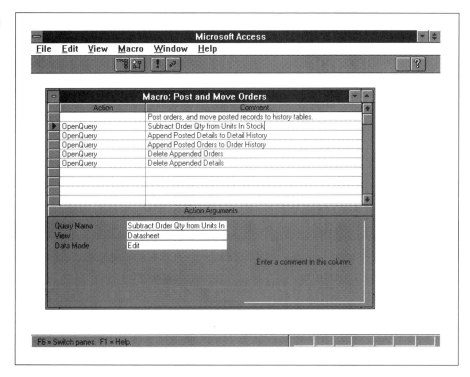

TABLE 16.2: Actions, action arguments, and expressions in the Post Orders
macro (in the same order as shown in Figure 16.10)

ACTION	ACTION ARGUMENT	EXPRESSION
OPENQUERY	Query Name	Subtract Order Qty From Units In Stock
	View	Datasheet
	Expression	Edit
OPENQUERY	Query Name	Append Posted Details To Detail History
	View	Datasheet
	Expression	Edit

TABLE 16.2: Actions, action arguments, and expressions in the Post Orders macro (in the same order as shown in Figure 16.10) (continued)

ACTION	ACTION ARGUMENT	EXPRESSION
OPENQUERY	Query Name	Append Posted Orders To Order History
	View	Datasheet
	Expression	Edit
OPENQUERY	Query Name	Delete Appended Orders
	View	Datasheet
	Expression	Edit
OPENQUERY	Query Name	Delete Appended Details
	View	Datasheet
	Expression	Edit

Storing Calculated Totals in the Order History Tables

In Chapter 4, I recommended against storing the results of calculations in tables. I did so because you can use queries, forms, and reports to perform current, up-to-date calculations on "raw data."

The disadvantage of storing only raw data in the table is that anybody who uses the database needs to enter complex expressions in queries to analyze sales and order totals. For example, suppose a sales manager wants to do a quick query and graph based on total sales, or order totals. If only the raw data is stored in the table, that sales manager will need to know how to create sophisticated query expressions to calculate the needed totals.

You, as the local database management guru, can make life easier for the sales manager and other personnel by storing precalculated sales and order totals in the table. Other personnel can then use those precalculated totals in their queries, without entering the expressions required to calculate those totals.

There is one risk involved in storing the results of a calculation in the table: The results of the calculations are not updated automatically when the changes are made to the data in datasheet view. Here are some measures you can take to minimize the risks:

* Store the results of calculations only in the Order History table, where data is less likely to change.

* Devise a security scheme that grants permission to *change* the Order History tables to yourself and others who understand that the calculated fields are not updated automatically. Allow other users to *read* and analyze the history tables without making changes to them.

* Create forms for the Order History table that update the calculated fields on a record-by-record basis. For instance, you can attach a SetValue macro to the OnCurrent property of a form to update the underlying fields as changes are made. (But remember that changes made in datasheet view won't update those fields.)

* Create a macro that updates all the calculated totals in the table. That way, you'll know all the totals are correct and up to date as soon as the macro finishes its job.

Regardless of which measures you take to keep the calculated totals up to date, you'll almost certainly want to create the macro to quickly calculate all the totals. In this example, you'd first want to change the structure of the Order History table to include the new fields. For example, in Figure 16.11 I've added two new Currency fields named Total Sale and Order Total to the Order History table.

FIGURE 16.11

Two Currency fields, named Total Sale and Order Total, added to the structure of the Order History table

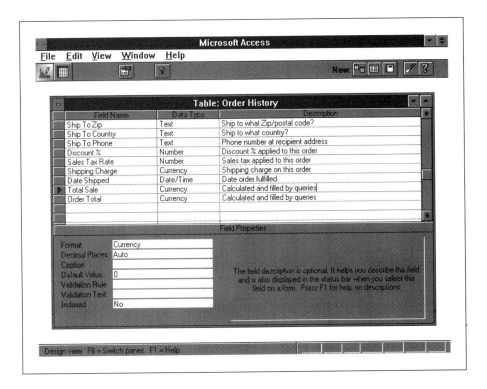

Creating the Query to Calculate Totals

Your next step would be to create a make-table query that calculates the total sale and order total. Join the Order History and Detail History tables at the top of the query, as in Figure 16.12. Include the necessary fields and calculations in the QBE grid, as listed in the example shown in Table 16.3.

FIGURE 16.12

The query to join the Order History and Detail History tables and calculate totals

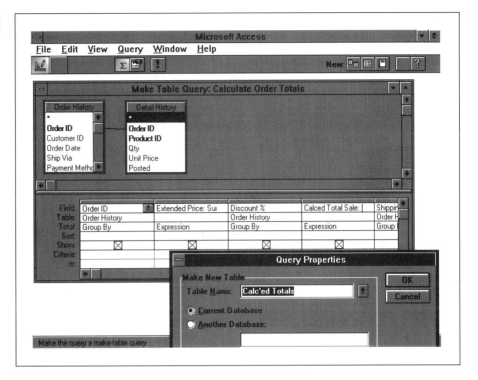

TABLE 16.3: Fields and calculated fields in the QBE grid shown in Figure 16.12. Omit the last three fields if you don't have a Sales Tax Rate field or want to exclude sales tax from order totals.

TABLE	TOTAL	FIELD
Order History	Group By	Order ID
	Expression	Extended Price: Sum([Qty]*[Unit Price])
Order History	Group By	Discount %
	Expression	Calced Total Sale: [Extended Price]*(1-[Discount %])
Order History	Group By	Shipping Charge
	Expression	Calced Order Total:[Calced Total Sale]+[Shipping Charge]
Order History	Group By	Sales Tax Rate
	Expression	Sales Tax: [Sales Tax Rate]*[Calced Total Sale]
	Expression	Order Total With Tax: [Calced Order Total]+[Sales Tax]

NOTE

In Table 16.3, I'm assuming that Sales Tax Rate is a field in the Order History table that contains the sales tax rate, as a percentage, for each order. If you haven't created a Sales Tax Rate field, or you don't want to include sales tax in the calculated order totals, omit the last three fields from the QBE grid.

Convert the select query to a make-table query, specifying the name of some table that will store the results of the calculation. In Figure 16.12, I've named that table Calc'ed Totals.

Copying Calculated Totals into Order History

The next step would be to create a query that updates the Total Sale and Order Total fields in the Order History table with values from the Calc'ed Totals table. This would be an update query, as in the example shown in Figure 16.13.

If you included sales tax in your make-table query, and you wanted to include sales tax in the Order History table's Order Total field as well, you would update that field from the Order Total With Tax field, as below:

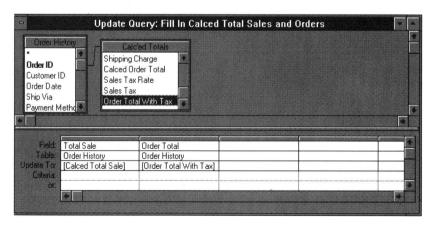

FIGURE 16.13

An update query to update the Total Sale and Order Total fields in Order History from the Calc'ed Totals table

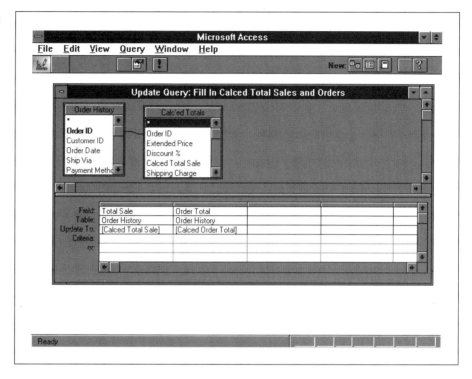

Keep in mind that you need to run the make-table query first, then the update query. As in the previous updating examples, you can create a macro to run both queries. You might also consider adding the necessary actions to the end of the Post And Move Orders macro, described above, so that the totals are filled in right after you post and move orders to the history tables.

Hiding Action Query Warnings

When a macro opens an action query, you'll see the usual warnings about records being changed or updated before the action query is executed.

You can hide all those warnings using the SetWarning action in the macro, so that the macro just runs the queries without prompting for permission. You might also want to add an Hourglass action to the macro. That action will change the mouse pointer to the Hourglass "Wait" icon, so that whoever runs the macro will know to wait until the macro is done before he or she tries to use the mouse again.

Figure 16.14 shows a modified version of the post-and-move orders query described earlier that includes the SetWarning and Hourglass actions. I've also added OpenQuery actions to the macro to do the job of storing precalculated totals in the Order History table.

The two actions in the modified macro are the following:

```
Hourglass
      Hourglass On:   Yes
SetWarnings
      Warnings On:   No
```

FIGURE 16.14

A modified version of the post-and-move-orders query that hides action query prompts and warnings, and also runs the queries for storing precalculated totals in the Order History table.

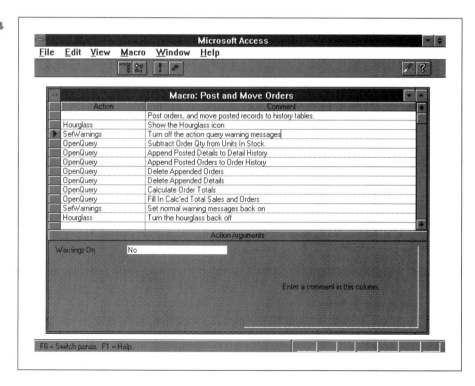

The new OpenQuery actions, near the bottom of the macro, are the following:

```
OpenQuery
     Query Name:   Calculate Order Totals
     View:   Datasheet
     Data Mode:   Edit
OpenQuery
     Query Name:   Fill in Calced Total Sales and Orders
     View:   Datasheet
     Data Mode:   Edit
```

The last two actions in the macro are the following:

```
Hourglass
     Hourglass On:   No
SetWarnings
     Warnings On:   Yes
```

These turn off the hourglass and set the warning messages back to their normal status of Yes.

Summary

In this chapter we've looked at examples of combining Update queries and macros to automate and streamline some common tasks in the Orchids database. When we start looking at techniques for building applications (Chapter 21), you'll see how to simplify these tasks even more, by reducing them to a simple mouse click on a button.

PART FIVE

Special Topics

CHAPTERS

17

Reference to Access Expressions

fast TRACK

Use the ! identifier operator to precede   724

the name of something you created, such as the name of a form or a control. For example, Forms![MyForm]![Date Entered] refers to a control named Date Entered on a form named MyForm.

Use the . (dot) operator to precede   724

the name of an Access object or property. For example, Forms![MyForm]![Date Entered].Visible refers to the Visible property of a control named Date Entered on a form named MyForm.

To see a list of Access functions, and examples of their use   727

search help for *functions: reference*.

To perform calculations on all the records in the currently open table or query   729

use the aggregate functions **Sum**, **Avg**, **Count**, and so forth.

To perform calculations based on all or some of the records in an unopened table or query   730

Use domain aggregate functions such as **DSum**, **DAvg**, **DLookup**, and so forth.

EXPRESSIONS play many roles in Access, and are used in virtually every type of database object. For instance, you use expressions to define validation rules and default values in the table design window. In queries, you can use expressions to define calculated fields and criteria. In the form and report design windows, you use expressions to define the contents of calculated controls that you create with the Text Box tool.

What Is an Expression?

An expression is a calculation that results in a single value. For instance, the expression

    [Qty]*[Unit Price]

multiplies the contents of two fields, named Qty and Unit Price, and results in a single value: the product of that multiplication.

An expression can contain any combination of Access operators, object names (identifiers), literal values, and constants. For example, the expression below contains a function, a couple of object names, two operators, and a literal value:

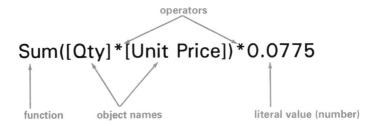

operators

Sum([Qty]*[Unit Price])*0.0775

function   object names   literal value (number)

Help with Expressions

In some situations, such as when you're creating a calculated control in a form or report, you need to precede the expression with an equals sign (=). In other situations, such as when you're entering an expression in the Criteria cell of a query, you don't need the leading equals sign.

 If in doubt about how to construct an expression in a particular situation, just press F1, or click the Help button (shown at left) in the tool bar, for more information and examples.

Once you're in the help system, you can also choose the Search button to look up information about specific parts of an expression. For instance, you can search help for specific *operators* or *functions*. I'll point out more specific words you can search for in the sections that follow.

Object Names

The *object name* portion of an expression can refer to any of the following:

* The name of a field in the underlying table or query
* The name of a control on a form or report
* A table or query name

If the name contains a blank space, you must surround that name with square brackets. For instance, in the expression below, [Date Entered] is the name of a field in the underlying table:

    [Date Entered]>=#1/1/93#

If the name does not contain a blank space, you can omit the square brackets. However, it's a good idea to get into the habit of using square brackets at all times, so that you don't forget them when you do need them.

When entering an expression in the Criteria cell of a query, the object name is assumed to be the field name defined at the top of the column. For instance, the expression

>=#1/1/93#

in the Date Entered column of a query's QBE grid assumes that you want to search for dates in the Date Entered field of the table. There is no need to include the field name [Date Entered] in the expression.

In some situations, you need to use the *identifier* operators ! and . (dot) to more accurately describe an object. (See "Identifiers" later in this chapter.)

Literal Values and Constants

A *literal value* in an expression is a specific item of data. In some situations, such as when you're entering an expression into the Criteria cell of a query, Access will automatically add *delimiters* (punctuation symbols) around literal values. In other situations, such as when you're defining a validation rule, you need to add the delimiters yourself. The punctuation marks you use for delimiters are described in the following sections.

Numbers

When specifying a specific *number*, type the number into the expression without any surrounding punctuation. For instance, in the expression below, Qty is a field name, >= is the operator, and the number 100 is a literal value:

[Qty]>=100

Notice that the number is not enclosed in quotation marks.

Text

When entering literal *text* into an expression, enclose the text in double quotation marks. (In many cases, Access will automatically add the quotation marks if you leave them out.) For instance, in the expression below:

[Last Name]="Jones"

the name Jones is a literal value.

N O T E

See "Aggregate Functions" later in this chapter for information on entering literal text into the criteria portion of an aggregate function.

Dates and Times

Dates and *times* are surrounded by the **#** symbol in an expression. If you leave them out, Access will usually insert them for you. Here's an expression that specifies dates between February 1 and February 15, 1993:

Between #2/1/93# And #2/15/93#

Constants

A *constant* is like a literal value, but one that Access has defined. There are five constants in Access: **Null**, **Yes**, **No**, **True**, and **False**. Don't use quotation marks or other delimiters around constants. For instance, in the Criteria cell of a query, the expression

Is Null

isolates records with empty (null) data in the field. The expression

Is Not Null

isolates records that do not have empty data in the field. The expression

Yes

in the Criteria cell of a Yes/No field in the QBE grid isolates records that have **Yes** (or **True**, or **-1**) in that field.

When using constants in settings *other than* the Criteria cell of a query, include the name of the field you want to search. For instance, the expression

> [Country] Is Null

isolates records that have blank values in the Country field. The expression

> [Country] Is Not Null

isolates records with non-empty values in the Country field.

If the field referred to in the expression is the Yes/No data type, it's not necessary to use the **Yes** and **No** constants. For instance, the expression

> [Posted]

means the same as [Posted] = Yes or Posted = True. The expression

> Not [Posted]

is equivalent to [Posted] = No or Posted = False.

Operators

The *operators* in an expression describe what type of action the expression should perform, or how the expression should compare two values. You can search the help system for the term *operators* for quick assistance in finding information on an operator. Tables 7.1 and 7.2 in Chapter 7 also provide examples of operators.

Arithmetic and Text Operators

The *arithmetic* (mathematical) operators perform mathematical calculations on numbers. For example, the following expression multiplies the contents of a field named Sales Tax Rate by a field or control named Order Subtotal:

[Sales Tax Rate]*[Order Subtotal]

A special version of the arithmetic addition operator is used to join strings of *text*. This is the **&** operator, known as the *concatenation* operator. For instance, you could use the following expression to display the salutation in a letter:

"Dear "&[First Name]&":"

where [First Name] is the name of a field in the underlying table or query.

The arithmetic operators are summarized below:

OPERATOR	PURPOSE
^	Raise one number to the power of another
*	Multiply two numbers
/	Divide two numbers
\	Divide numbers, return integer portion of result
+	Add two numbers
- (hyphen)	Subtract two numbers, or negate a number
Mod	Divide two numbers and return the remainder
&	Concatenate (join) two strings (text values)

Comparison Operators

The *comparison* operators compare values. For example, the expression

>=#/1/1/93#

—used in the Criteria cell of the QBE grid in a query—isolates records that have dates that are greater (later) than or equal to January 1, 1993.

The comparison operators are summarized below:

OPERATOR	MEANING
<	Less than
<=	Less than or equal to
>	Greater than
>=	Greater than or equal to
=	Equal
<>	Not equal

Miscellaneous Operators

Access categorizes the operators summarized below under the heading of "Miscellaneous Operators":

OPERATOR	MEANING
Between…And	Value falls within a range (inclusive)
In	Value is included within a set of values
Like	Text matches a pattern (used with wildcard characters ? and *)
Is	Comparison is true (e.g., Is Null)
Is Not	Comparison is not true (e.g., Is Not Null)
!	Precedes a user-defined object name in an identifier (see "Identifiers" later in this chapter.)
.	Precedes the Access name for an object or property (see "Identifiers" later in this chapter.)

Logical Operators

The *logical* operators combine comparison expressions to create a single, multiple-criterion comparison. These operators are most often used in the Conditions column of a macro, in the *criteria* portion of a domain aggregate function, or in a query's Criteria cells. The logical operators are summarized below:

OPERATOR	MEANING
And	Both comparisons are true.
Or	One comparison or the other is true.
Xor	One comparison or the other is true, but not both. (This is known as "Exclusive Or.")
Not	The comparison is not true.
Eqv	Bitwise comparison of two numeric expressions. ("Equivalence"—used only in Access Basic)
Imp	Bitwise comparison of two numeric expressions. ("Implication"—used only in Access Basic.)

Identifiers

You can use identifiers in expressions to refer to control names, field names, and properties on forms and reports. The simplest identifier is an object name, the name of a field in the underlying table or query, or control on the current form or report. For instance, the following identifier refers to a field or control named Customer ID:

[Customer ID]

The identifier operators allow you to identify objects more precisely. You need to use identifier operators:

- To resolve ambiguous field references
- To refer to a control on a subform from a main form
- In the Condition column of a macro, to refer to a control on a form or report other than the one the macro was started from
- In the expression of a macro **SetValue** or **FindRecord**, to refer to a control on a report or form other than the one that the macro was started from

An identifier expression can consist of the following components:

- The type of object you're referring to: **Forms**, **Reports**, or **Screen**.
- The name of the object you're referring to, enclosed in square brackets.
- The **!** operator, to indicate that what follows is the name of something that you've created, such as a form, report, control, or field.
- The **.**(dot) operator, to indicate that what follows is an Access property (e.g., .Visible refers to the Visible property of a control).

The object type portion of an identifier can refer to any of the following:

- **Forms** Followed by **!** and the name of a form that is currently open.
- **Reports** Followed by **!** and the name of a report that is currently open.
- **Screen** Followed by **.** (dot) and either **ActiveForm** or **Active-Report** to refer to a property on whatever form or report is in the active window on the screen. (Search Help for Screen Object for more information.)

N O T E   You can identify a broader range of objects, including dynasets and methods, using the . (dot) identifier in Access Basic.

When creating an identifier in an expression, start with the most general object, and work toward the more specific. For instance, the identifier

Forms![Order Summary]![Due Date]

identifies the control named Due Date on an open form named Order Summary. The expression

Forms![Order Summary]![Due Date].Visible

refers to the Visible property of the Due Date control on the form named Order Summary.

Resolving Ambiguous Field References

You can use identifier operators to resolve *ambiguous field reference* errors in an expression. For instance, suppose two tables named Products and Order Details are joined in a query, and both those tables include a field named Unit Price. The expression

Extended Price:[Quantity]*[Unit Price]

causes the message "Ambiguous field reference," because Access isn't sure *which* Unit Price field the expression is referring to.

To fix the problem, return to the expression and precede the field name with a table name and identifier operator. If the table name contains a blank space, enclose it in square brackets. For instance, the corrected expression

Extended Price:[Quantity]*[Order Details]![Unit Price]

specifically refers to the Unit Price field from the Order Details table, and thus resolves the ambiguity. You could also use [Order Details].[Unit Price] in this example, because the square brackets around the name Unit Price tell Access that Unit Price is a field name rather than a property.

Identifying Subform Controls

You can use an identifier to refer to a control on a subform when you're entering a calculated control for the main form. Use the Text Box tool on the main form to create the control, and enter an expression using the following general syntax:

[*subform name*].Form![*subform control name*]

For instance, the expression

[Orders Subform].Form![Order Subtotal]

refers to a control named Order Subtotal on a subform named Orders Subform.

Identifying Objects in Macro Expressions

When you launch a macro from a command button or event on a form or report, Access assumes that any object names used in expressions within that macro are referring to controls and fields on the form from which the macro was launched. To refer to controls on other forms or reports, you must use identifiers in the macro conditions and expressions.

For instance, suppose you launch a macro from a form named Order Entry Subform. That macro, in turn, opens a form named Products. To refer to a control on the Products form, you must use an identifier. For instance, the macro condition expression below refers to the Unit Price control on the Order Entry form, and the Current Price control on the Products form (both forms must be open when the condition is evaluated):

[Unit Price]=Forms![Products]![Current Price]

Access Functions

A *function*, in Access, performs some calculation on data, and returns the result of that calculation. There are well over 100 functions available in Access.

Help with Functions

In this section, we'll cover some of the more commonly used functions. However, for a more complete list, search the help system for *functions: reference*. For information on the syntax of a function, and examples of its use, search the help system for the specific function name.

Financial Functions

Common financial functions are summarized below:

CALCULATION	FUNCTION NAME
depreciation	DDB, SLN, SYD
future/present value	FV, PV, NPV
internal rate of return	IRR, MIRR
loan payment	IPmt, NPer, Pmt, PPmt, Rate

Math Functions

Access provides many of the mathematical and trigonometric functions offered in spreadsheets. Search the help system for *math functions* for more information.

Date/Time Functions

The most commonly used date functions are summarized below. Search help for more information on a particular function.

CALCULATION	FUNCTION NAME
current date	Date
current date and time	Now
date/time format	Format, Format$
number of days between dates	DateDiff
time interval (day, week, year, etc.)	DatePart
serial date	DateSerial

String Functions

Functions that perform their calculation on text (*strings*) are summarized below. You can search the help system for the function name for more information.

CALCULATION	FUNCTION NAME
embedded characters	Mid
ending characters	Right
leading characters	Left
length	Len
lowercase conversion	LCase
null	IsNull
trim ending blanks	Trim
trim leading blanks	LTrim
uppercase conversion	UCase

Logical Functions

Two *logical* functions, **IIF** and **Choose**, allow an expression to make a decision. The **Choose** function selects a value from a list based on the contents of its first argument. For instance, suppose your table contains a field named Payment Method containing a number, and each number represents a particular type of payment: 1 for Cash, 2 for Check, 3 for Invoice. The following expression in the Criteria cell of a query would display the appropriate word, rather than the number, in the resulting dynaset:

    Choose([Payment Method],"Cash","Check","Invoice")

The **IIF** function performs a test, then returns either the first argument, if the test proves true, or the second, if the test proves false. The syntax of IIF is as follows:

IIF(*this is true,return this,otherwise return this*)

For example, the expression below tests to see if the State/Province field is empty. If that field is empty, the expression returns a blank space. If the field is not empty, the expression returns a comma and a blank space:

    IIF ([State/Province] Is Null," ",", ")

Aggregate Functions

The *aggregate* functions (also called *summary functions* and *SQL aggregate functions*) perform statistical calculations on data in a table or query.

CALCULATION	FUNCTION
average	Avg
count (how many)	Count
first/last record in table or dynaset	First, Last
highest/lowest value	Min, Max
standard deviation	StDev, StDevP

CALCULATION	FUNCTION
sum (total)	Sum
variance	Var, VarP

It's important to keep in mind that aggregate functions can only operate on fields in the underlying table or query. You cannot refer to the name of a control on a form or report in an aggregate function. For more information and examples, search the help system for *SQL: aggregate functions*, or the name of the specific function you need help with.

Domain Aggregate Functions

The *domain aggregate* functions are similar to the aggregate functions. However, a domain aggregate function can base its calculation on any table in the current database—including an unopened table. You can include all the records, or a range of records, in the calculation. To base the calculations on all the records in a table, use the syntax:

> *dfunction("expression","domain")*

To base the calculation on specific records in the table, use the syntax:

> *dfunction("expression","domain","criteria")*

The descriptors used in the syntax forms above are described below:

* *dfunction* is the name of the domain aggregate function.

* *expression* is the name of the field that you want to base the calculation on, or an expression that refers to field names.

* *domain* is the name of the table or query that contains the records that you want to base the calculation on. The domain can also be expressed as a SQL statement.

* *criteria* (optional) is the expression that defines the records to include in the domain.

Note that the double quotation marks surrounding each argument in the function are part of the syntax. For instance, note the use of double quotation marks in the expression below:

> DLookup("[Tax Rate]","States","[Abbreviation]=[State]")

If you want to use a literal text value in the criteria portion of a domain aggregate function, enclose that text in single quotation marks. For instance, the expression below looks up CA in the Abbreviation field of a table named States, and returns the value stored in the Tax Rate field of the table:

DLookup("[Tax Rate]","States","[Abbreviation]='CA'")

TIP   Another way to interpret the expression above— i.e., in English—would be "Look up the Tax Rate in a table named States, where the Abbreviation field in that table contains CA."

The domain aggregate functions are summarized below. For information on a particular function, search the help system for the function name.

CALCULATION	FUNCTION
average	DAvg
count (how many)	DCount
first/last	DFirst, DLast
largest/smallest value	DMin, DMax
look up (find)	DLookup
sum (total)	DSum
standard deviation	DStDev, DStDevP
variance	DVar, DVarP

Data Type Conversion Functions

The *data type conversion* functions, summarized below, convert that data type of a value to some other data type.

CONVERT TO	FUNCTION
currency	CCur
double precision number	CDbl
integer	CInt
long integer number	CLng
single precision number	CSng
string (text)	CStr
variant (Access Basic only)	CVar

Fixing Rounding Errors

Access stores currency values to four decimal places of accuracy (even though it only displays two decimal places of accuracy). This can lead to results that appear to be off by a penny or so, due to rounding errors. For instance, suppose you use the expressions below to calculate the extended price and subtotal in an order form or report:

Extended Price: =[Qty]*[Unit Price]

Subtotal: =Sum([Qty]*[Unit Price])

Later, when using the form or report, you might notice that some calculations are off by a penny. To fix the rounding error, you could change the expressions to:

Extended
Price: =CLng([Qty]*[Unit Price]*100)/100

Subtotal: =Sum(CLng([Qty]*[Unit Price]*100)/100)

The sample **Invoices** report in the Northwind database uses similar expressions to calculate extended price and order subtotal, with discounts.

Summary

This chapter has presented an overview of Access operators, identifiers, functions, and other components that make up an expression. Perhaps the most important point to keep in mind in regard to these components is that any time you need to enter an expression, you can press F1 (Help) for relevant help. You can also use the Search feature within the help system to search for information about, and examples of, specific operators and functions.

Managing Your Access Environment

fast TRACK

To back up a database   **738**

close the database, and use your backup software or the Windows File Manager to copy the database *.mdb* file to the backup hardware of your choosing.

To compact a database   **739**

and reclaim space left behind by deleted records and objects, first close the database. Choose File ➤ Compact Database, choose the name of the database you want to compact, then enter a valid DOS file name for the compacted copy of the database.

To encrypt a database   **740**

so that it can only be opened and viewed in Access, first close the database. Then choose File ➤ Encrypt/Decrypt Database. Choose the name of the database you want to encrypt or decrypt, then enter a valid DOS file name for the encrypted or decrypted copy.

To restore a corrupted database   **741**

close any open databases, then choose File ➤ Repair database. Select the name of the database you want to repair, and choose OK. When the repair work is done, you should be able to open the database with the usual File ➤ Open Database commands.

To copy an object within the current database   **742**

choose the object that you want to copy, then choose Edit ➤ Copy. Then choose Edit ➤ Paste, and enter a name for the new copy of the object.

N THIS chapter we'll look at general-purpose tools and techniques for managing Access databases and objects. We'll also look at techniques for changing Access defaults, and getting around some of the printing limitations that you may have noticed on the design screens!

Backing Up a Database

Perhaps it goes without saying that making backups of your database is important. After all, if you only keep one copy of your database around, and some problem with the disk makes the file unreadable, you're going to lose all the work you've put into the database. This would be particularly disastrous with an Access database, since *every* object you create within a database is stored in *one* large database file!

Exactly where you back up a database to, and how often you do it, is up to you. If the database is small enough, you can back it up to a floppy. Or, you can use a file compression program to create a compressed copy of the database, and back that up to a floppy. For larger databases, you'll need to back up to a tape drive or perhaps a hard drive with removable disks.

You may also want to keep a second backup copy of the database on your local hard disk. That way, if you make a change to the original copy of the database that somehow corrupts that original copy, you can quickly copy the local backup to the original file name, without bothering with external drives or tape devices.

Backing up a database is basically a matter of copying the entire database, which has the *.mdb* extension, to the backup device:

1. Close the database by choosing File ➤ Close Database.

2. If other users on the network share data in the database, make sure all other users also close the database, so there are no open copies on the system.

3. Switch to whatever program you use to make backups, be it the Windows File Manager, a tape drive system, or a DOS program.

4. Copy the *.mdb* file to the backup destination of your choosing, then switch to a DOS session.

If you've set up a security system in Access, you should also back up the *system.mda* file on your Access directory. This file contains important password and account information that Access needs to open the database.

Compacting a Database

As you delete records, macros, tables and the like from your database, the space these objects formerly took up tends to stay in the database. To reclaim this wasted space, you can *compact* the database.

During the compaction, Access will need as much available disk space as the database itself requires. You can check the size of the database, and the available disk space, with the Windows File Manager. When you're ready to compact the database:

1. If the database you want to compact is open, choose File ➤ Close Database to close it. (Any users on the network should also close the database.)

2. Choose File ➤ Compact Database.

3. Choose the drive, directory, and name of the database that you want to compact, then choose OK.

4. Type in a name for the compacted version of the database, then choose OK.

You can use the original database name in Step 4 above to compact the original copy of the database.

Encrypting a Database

Encrypting a database is a means of ensuring that the database can only be opened and viewed in Access. Though this doesn't prevent another Access user from tampering with the database, it does prevent an unauthorized user from viewing or tampering with the database using another application or utility program.

For instance, if you plan to transmit a copy of a database to another user, or store a copy off-site, you might want to encrypt the database to prevent prying eyes from viewing the database contents with a simple Edit program.

While you *can* open an encrypted database without decrypting it first, the database will be slower in its encrypted state. Therefore, if you receive a copy of an encrypted database from another Access user, you might want to decrypt it before you start using it.

To encrypt or decrypt a database:

1. If the database you want to encrypt or decrypt is currently open, choose File ➤ Close Database. If you're using Access in a multi-user environment, all the other users must also close the database.

2. Choose File ➤ Encrypt/Decrypt Database.

3. Choose the name of the database you want to encrypt or decrypt, then choose OK.

4. Type a valid DOS file name for the encrypted (or decrypted) copy of the database. You can omit the *.mdb* extension. Also, you can use the original database name if you want to encrypt that copy of the database.

5. Choose OK.

Access automatically determines whether or not the database is already encrypted. If the database isn't encrypted, Access encrypts it. If the database is already encrypted, Access decrypts it.

Restoring a Damaged Database

As with any application, you should always exit Access before turning off your computer, to make sure that all your database objects are saved to disk. If a power outage or some other mishap occurs that corrupts the open database, you may have trouble opening the database next time you start Access. You can repair the corrupted database by following these steps:

1. Close any open databases using File ➤ Close Database.

2. Choose File ➤ Repair Database.

3. Choose the drive, directory, and name of the database you want to repair, then choose OK.

Once the repair is done, you should be able to open the database with the usual File ➤ Open Database commands.

Copying Objects within a Database

You can also copy objects within a database. This is very handy for making a quick backup copy of a table, report, form, or other object that you're about to change, just in case your changes do more harm than good.

Copying an object within a database is a simple matter of cut and paste:

1. In the database window, click on the object button for the type of object you want to copy (e.g., Table, Query, Form, etc.)

2. Click on the name of the object you want to copy, then choose Edit ➤ Copy.

3. Choose Edit ➤ Paste.

4. Enter a name for the backup copy, then choose OK.

Deleting and Renaming Objects

To delete or rename an object in a database, click on (in the database window) the name of the object you want to delete or rename. Then...

- To rename the object, choose File ➤ Rename, type in the new name, then choose OK.

- To delete the object, press Delete or choose Edit ➤ Delete. Then choose OK when asked for verification.

To undo a deletion or a rename, click on the Undo button in the tool bar, or choose Edit ➤ Undo.

N O T E　To delete or rename an entire database, use the Windows File Manager or DOS commands to delete or copy the database's *.mdb* file.

Copying Objects from Database to Database

You can use the same technique as above to copy objects from database to database. That is, follow Steps 1 and 2 above, then use File ➤ Open Database to open the database that you want to copy the object to. Then follow Steps 3 and 4.

As an alternative to switching back and forth between databases, you can *export* an object from the current database to an unopened Access database. See "Exporting an Access Object to Another Access Database" in Chapter 19.

Copying Objects to Another Computer

In some cases, you might want to copy an object to an Access database that's on another computer, and the only way to do so is via floppy disks. For instance, let's say you have two copies of the same database, one at home and one at the office. You design a report or form at home, and then want to copy *just* that form or report to the office copy of the Access database.

To do so, you can use File ➤ New Database to create a "holding database" perhaps named **Transfer** on the floppy disk (e.g., *a:\transfer.mdb*). Then you can copy and paste, or export, objects from the Access database on your hard disk to that database on the floppy.

Then later, you can import, or cut and paste, objects from the *a:\transfer.mdb* database to the database on the hard disk at your office.

Converting a Number Field to a Counter Field

As discussed back in Chapter 4, the counter data type automatically numbers new records that you add to a table, starting with 1. This is a great convenience, except if you want to use a four- or five-digit number to identify each record in a table. In that case, you'd want to start numbering records at 1000 or 1001, or 10000 or 10001.

To do this, you need to first create the table with a number field to store that number. Then open that table, and add at least one record to it, with whatever starting number you want. For instance, in the example below, I originally created the Customers table with the Customer ID field as the number data type. Then I added the first record where, as you can see, I assigned the number 1001 to the first customer.

Table: Customers					
Customer ID	Honorific	First Name	MI	Last Name	Department/Title
1001	Mr.	Andy	A.	Adams	President
0					

Once you've added that first record to the table, you can convert the data type of the numeric type. But you can't do that simply by going back to the table design screen. Instead, you need to make a copy of the table's structure, change the data type in the empty copy of the table, and then copy the records from the original table to the new table structure. Here are the exact steps:

1. Close the table, using File ➤ Close, after entering at least one record with the starting number that you want to use.

2. In the database window, choose the name of the table you just closed, then choose Edit ➤ Copy.

3. Choose Edit ➤ Paste.

4. Choose Structure Only, then enter a name for the copy of the table (such as **Customers with Counter** in this example), and choose OK.

5. Click on the name of the copy you just made (*Customers with Counter* in this example), then click on the Design button.

6. Change the data type of the number field to **Counter**.

7. Choose File ➤ Close, then Yes, to close this copy of the table.

8. Click on the name of the original table (*Customers* in this example), and choose Edit ➤ Copy.

9. Choose Edit ➤ Paste.

10. Choose Append Data To Existing Table.

11. In the Table Name text box, type the name of the table that has the counter data type (**Customers with Counter** in this example.)

12. Choose OK.

Now you can open the copied table (*Customers with Counter* in this example) to verify that it contains the records that you copied from the original table. Then you can delete the original copy of the table (*Customers* in this example), and use File ➤ Rename to rename the new copy of the table to the original table name.

Personalizing Access

You can personalize your Access work environment by changing certain defaults in Access. All of the defaults are set in the **Options** dialog box. So to get started, you want to:

1. Start at the database window, and choose View ➤ Options. You'll see the Options dialog box as shown in Figure 18.1.

FIGURE 18.1

Choosing View ➤ Options takes you to the Options dialog box, where you can change numerous default settings in Access.

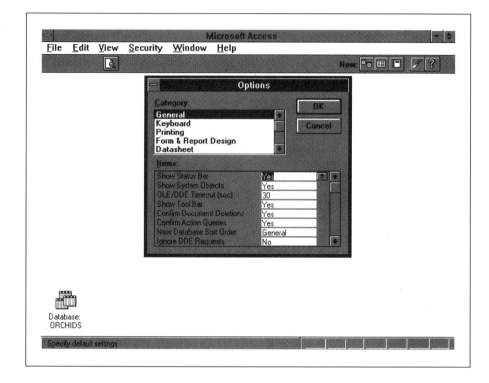

2. Choose a category, then change an option, as described in the sections that follow.

Changing the General Desktop Options

The General category in the Options dialog box offers options for changing basic desktop features and behaviors. The options are summarized below:

- **Show Status Bar**   Choose *Yes* to display the status bar, *No* to hide it.

- **Show System Objects**   Choose *Yes* to display, or *No* to hide, the names of system objects that Access uses internally. When displayed, the names of these objects appear along with other table names in the database window. The names of the system objects all start with the letters *MSys*.

- **OLE/DDE Timeout (sec)**   Possible settings range from 0 to 300 seconds. In the event of either an OLE or DDE communication failure, Access will reattempt the operation after the specified number of seconds elapse.

- **Show Tool Bar**   Set to *Yes* to display or *No* to hide the tool bar.

- **Confirm Document Deletions**   Set to *Yes* to have Access prompt for permission before deleting an object.

- **Confirm Action Queries**   Yes/No control to determine whether or not Access displays the warning box before executing an action query.

- **New Database Sort Order**   Sets the alphabetic sorting of new databases to *General* (for English), or *Traditional Spanish*, *Dutch*, or *Nordic* languages. To change the sort method for an existing database, make the change here, then compact the existing database.

- **Ignore DDE Requests**   Yes/No control to tell Access to ignore or respond to DDE requests from other applications that support Dynamic Data Exchange.

- **Default Find/Replace Behavior**   Controls the default mode of operation when you use the Edit ➤ Find or Edit ➤ Replace command. A *Fast Search* only looks in the current field and matches the entire field, while a *General Search* looks in all the fields and can match any part of a field.

- **Default Database Directory**   Determines which directory Access stores, and searches, for databases. The default is the dot (period) which stands for the current directory.

- **Confirm Record Changes**   Yes/No control to determine whether or not Access prompts for permission when you delete or paste records.

Changing the Keyboard Behavior

You can change the behavior of certain keys on the keyboard to make Access behave more like other databases you might already be familiar with.

NOTE Because Access follows the Windows Common User Interface (CUA) standards for keyboard behavior, you may be better off learning the default keyboard, rather than trying to make Access behave like a DOS application.

- **Arrow Key Behavior**   Determines whether pressing ← and → moves to the next field or to the next character within the field.

- **Move After Enter**   Determines whether pressing ↵ moves to the next field or to the next record, or has no effect.

- **Cursor Stops at First/Last Field**   Determines whether or not pressing ← or → when the insertion point is in the first or last field of a row moves to the next or previous record (*No*), or keeps the insertion point in the current field (*Yes*).

- **Key Assignment Macro**   Determines the name of the auto-executed key-assignment macro that Access looks for when you first open a database. The default is *AutoKeys*.

Changing Printer Default Margins

The Printing defaults let you assign default margin settings for new reports and forms. The settings don't affect existing forms and reports. The measurement can be expressed in inches (in), centimeters (cm), or *twips*, which is $\frac{1}{1440}$ of an inch.

Changing Form and Report Design Defaults

The Form & Report Design category lets you change the defaults used in the form and report design screens. Your options are:

- **Form Template**   The default is *Normal*, an internal, general-purpose template. You can create your own form template, as discussed in Chapter 10.

- **Report Template**   As with forms, you can define your own report template, and assign its name here.

- **Objects Snap To Grid**   Determines whether or not the Snap To Grid option on the Layout menu in the form and report design screens is initially turned on (*Yes*) or off (*No*).

- **Show Grid**   Determines if the Grid option on the View menu is initially turned on (*Yes*) or off (*No*) in report and form design screens.

TIP   As discussed in "Viewing the Grid" in Chapter 9, the grid is visible only when it's set to 16 or fewer dots to the inch, and the View ➤ Grid command is turned on.

- **Selection Behavior**   Choosing *Partially Enclosed* tells Access to select any control that you drag the pointer through in the design screen. Choosing *Fully Enclosed* tells Access to select only controls that are completely contained within the frame you draw while dragging the pointer.

- **Show Ruler**   Determines whether or not the Ruler is turned on when you first enter the form or report design screen. (Regardless of the default setting, View ➤ Ruler within the design screen will still turn the Ruler on or off.)

Changing Datasheet View Defaults

The Datasheet options let you change the default appearance of the datasheet view when you first open a table.

- **Default Gridlines Behavior**   Determines whether or not gridlines appear in the datasheet view.

- **Default Column Width**   The default width of each column in the datasheet view, ranging anywhere from 0 to 22 inches.

- **Default Font Options**   The default *Font Name*, *Size*, *Weight*, *Italic*, and *Underline* options let you choose the default font used in datasheet view.

Changing Query, Macro, and Module Defaults

The three options in the Query Design category are summarized below:

- **Restrict Available Fields**   Determines whether a field list in a new query that's based on another query displays only fields from the underlying query's QBE grid (*Yes*), or displays all the fields from that query's underlying table (*No*). Can also be set using View ➤ Query Properties in the query design screen, if the current query is based on another query.

- **Run With Owner's Permission(s)**   Determines whether or not the Run With Owner's Permission property is set to *Yes* or *No* by default in new queries. In a secured database, setting this option to *Yes* restricts viewing of underlying tables, and running of action queries, to users who have been granted permission. You can choose View ➤ Query Properties to change this default setting within any given query's design window.

- **Show Table Names**   Determines whether or not the View ➤ Tables Names option is initially on (*Yes*) or off (*No*) when you first enter the query window.

Macro Design Defaults

The Macro category determines a couple of default settings for the macro window:

- **Show Macro Names Column**   Determines whether or not View ➤ Macro Names is turned on (*Yes*) or off (*No*) when you first enter a new macro window.

- **Show Conditions Column**   Determines whether or not View ➤ Conditions is turned on (*Yes*) or off (*No*) when you first enter a new macro window.

Module Design Options

The Module Design options determine the default characteristics of the module design window, used for creating Access Basic procedures and functions:

- **Syntax Checking**   When set to *Yes*, the syntax of each line you enter in the Module window is checked at the time that you enter it. If *No*, syntax is checked only when you execute the module.

- **Tab Stop Width**   Specifies the width of a tab in spaces (from 1 to 30) used in the Module window.

Changing Multi-User Defaults

The Multi-User category of options, used only in a network environment, are described in Chapter 20.

Changing Screen Colors

Like most Windows applications, Access inherits its general desktop color scheme from the **Windows Control Panel**. To choose a new color scheme, switch to the Windows Program Manager and open the Main group. Then open the Control Panel, open the Color applet, and choose your color scheme there.

Printing Design Screens

When you're viewing a table structure or other design screen, the File ➤ Print options generally are not available. There are two ways to get around this. One is to copy the screen to the Clipboard, then use **Paintbrush** or some other application to print that screen. The other method is to use the **Database Analyzer** that came with Access. Each technique is described below.

Screen Capture to Clipboard

To do a "screen dump" of the current design screen to the printer:

1. Arrange the design screen to see whatever information you want to print, then press PrintScreen on your keyboard (or Shift+Print-Screen on some keyboards). A copy of the screen is sent to the Windows Clipboard.

2. If you want to use Paintbrush to print the screen, switch to the Windows Program Manager, open the Accessories group, and run PaintBrush.

3. Maximize PaintBrush to full-screen size.

4. Choose Options ➤ Image Attributes, then click on the Default button. Also, choose either *Black and White* or *Colors*, then choose OK.

5. Choose File ➤ New, then choose View ➤ Zoom Out.

6. Choose Edit ➤ Paste, then click on any tool in the toolbox at the left side of the screen.

7. Choose View ➤ Zoom In, then choose File ➤ Print, and then choose OK.

If you have any problems, or need more information, see your Windows documentation for more information on using the PaintBrush application.

Using the Database Analyzer

Database Analyzer is an extra tool that comes with Access. Although it is copied to your hard disk when you perform a normal installation, it isn't readily available in Access, possibly because it's a fairly advanced tool that's geared toward more sophisticated database users. But if you're comfortable with editing *.ini* files, you can set up and use the database analyzer quite easily.

Installing the Database Analyzer

To install the database analyzer:

1. Exit Access and get to the **Windows Program Manager**.
2. Use **Windows Notepad** to edit the *msaccess.ini* file that's stored on your Windows directory.
3. Locate the *[Libraries]* group, and place the following command beneath the [Libraries] heading:

   analyzer.mda=
4. Exit Notepad and save the modified *msaccess.ini* file.
5. Restart Access from the Windows Program Manager.

Changing Permissions for the System Objects

Before you can use the database analyzer, you need to grant yourself permission to read the MSysObjects file:

1. In Access, open the database you want to analyze.
2. Choose View ➤ Options, and change the Show System Objects option to *Yes* in the General category. Then choose OK.
3. In the database window, click on the Table object button, then click on the *MSysObjects* table name.

4. Choose Security ➤ Permissions and choose the Read Data permission.

5. Choose the Assign button, then Close.

Creating the Analyzer Macro

Next, you need to create a macro to run the database analyzer:

1. Choose File ➤ New ➤ Macro.

2. Choose *RunCode* as the action, and set the Function Name argument to *StartAnalyzer( )* as in Figure 18.2.

3. Choose File ➤ Close and choose *Yes* when asked about saving the macro. Assign the name **Analyzer** to the macro, then choose OK.

FIGURE 18.2

Macro to run the database analyzer

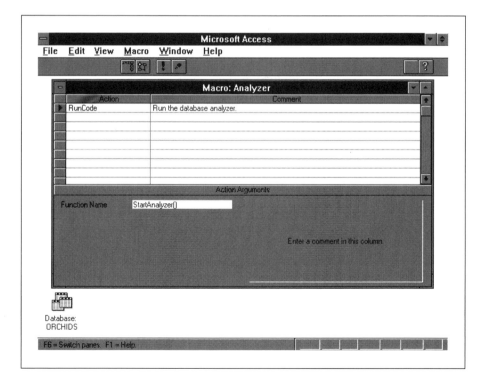

Running the Database Analyzer

To run the database analyzer:

1. Click on the Macro object button in the database window.

2. Double-click on the *Analyzer* macro name.

You'll be taken to the **Database Analyzer** window, which is shown in Figure 18.3.

Now you can choose the type of object you want to analyze, from the object buttons at the left side of the window (i.e., click on Table). Then select the name of the object that you want to analyze from the Items Available list, and use the → button to move that name to the Items Selected list. You can choose as many object names as you wish, from as many categories as you wish.

FIGURE 18.3

The Database Analyzer window, where you select objects to analyze

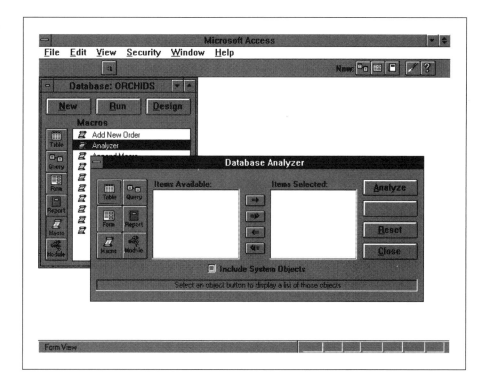

When you've finished selecting names, click on the Analyze button. You'll be prompted for a database name, where the analyzer will store its results. You can select the currently open database, if you wish. Then choose OK.

When the analyzer is done, you'll see a message indicating that the process is completed. Choose OK, then choose the Close button in the Database Analyzer window.

Next, click on the Table button in the database window to view table names. (If you opted to store the results of the analysis in another database, open that database.) The results of the analysis are stored in tables that start with an @ character. For example, @TableDetails stores the results of analyzing table structures. You can open any one of those tables to see its contents by double-clicking, or by using the Open button in the database window. Because the analysis data is displayed in a regular Access table, you can use File ➤ Print to print the information. For more information on the database analyzer, search the Access help system for *database analyzer*.

Summary

This chapter has covered a variety of techniques for managing Access databases and objects. In the next chapter, we'll look at general techniques for using Access with other applications on your system.

Using Access with
Other Applications

fast TRACK

An embedded OLE object is copied   803

to your Access database. Changing an embedded object updates a *copy* of the object, and has no effect on the original object. You can embed saved files, portions of saved files, or
objects that aren't saved permanently.

A linked OLE object remains attached   803

to the original application file. Changing a linked object through
Access or the source application updates the original object file.
You can link to saved files or portions of saved files only.

You can link and embed objects   804

in OLE Object fields of a table, or in an unbound control on
a form or report, using most of the standard Windows 3.1 object linking and embedding techniques.

To change, play, or run an OLE object   810

you can usually double-click on it. If that doesn't work, select
the object and choose Edit ➤ Object ➤ Edit, or Edit ➤ Object
➤ Play, or Edit ➤ Object ➤ Run, as appropriate for the type of
object you've selected.

To change OLE object's properties   819

select the object and choose options from the Edit ➤ Objects
menu. You can also use an object's properties sheet to change
properties of OLE objects in report or form designs.

TODAY'S computers are chock-full of data created by all kinds of applications—databases, spreadsheets, word processors, painting programs, and more. It's not at all unusual to project your annual budgets with the help of Microsoft Excel, write memos and print illustrated product catalogs through Microsoft Word for Windows, manage sales and customer data in an Access database, and maintain your product inventory in a SQL database on your network.

As you'll learn in this chapter, Microsoft Access truly lives up to its name when it comes to accessing data from many different applications. Like most applications, Access lets you import data from, and export data to, other applications. But Access also lets you *attach* data from other applications, which means that you can manipulate the data from another application *as though* it were an Access table.

Access also supports Windows OLE (Object Linking and Embedding), a powerful technique for placing objects, such as pictures, graphs, charts, spreadsheets, and text from other Windows applications, directly into an Access report, form, or even a table field. Once placed, a linked or embedded object can be updated simply by double-clicking on it. You never have to leave Access to make a change.

We'll start this chapter by looking at techniques for importing, attaching, and exporting data. Then we'll look at techniques for linking and embedding objects later in the chapter.

Importing or Attaching External Tables

You can import or attach data into the currently open Access database from any of the database formats listed below:

- Paradox version 3.x

- dBASE III Plus and dBASE IV

- FoxPro 2.0 (import only)

- Btrieve (with Xtrieve dictionary file)

- SQL databases, including Microsoft SQL Server or Oracle

- Access databases that aren't open at the moment

Once a table is imported or attached from another application, you can use it to retrieve and update data, create forms or queries, and print reports just like any other Access table.

Deciding Whether to Import or Attach a Table

Before bringing a table in from another database, you must decide whether to *import* the data or *attach* it. When you import data, the imported data is copied to an Access table, and is indistinguishable from any Access table that you create from scratch. By contrast, an attached table retains its original database format and location. However, you can manage that data as though it were stored in an Access table. That is, the data will appear to be stored in an Access table, and you can manage the data using most of the standard Access techniques. Any changes you make to the attached data, however, *will* carry over to the original data, and will be readily apparent when you use the original application to view that data.

NOTE When importing tables, Access will translate fields from other database files to its own field types automatically. No translation is needed when you attach a table.

Each time you import or attach a table, Access will add an appropriate table name and icon to the database window. Initially the imported or attached table name may appear in uppercase letters. You can use the File ➤ Rename option to rename the file if you wish. For example, in Figure 19.1 we attached dBASE IV tables named Areacode and Billed to our Orchids database, and imported a table named Courses. Notice how the icons next to the attached tables include an arrow symbol to indicate a *link* to the external tables, while the icon next to the Courses table looks like any other Access table icon.

FIGURE 19.1

Attached tables are indicated by special "link" icons

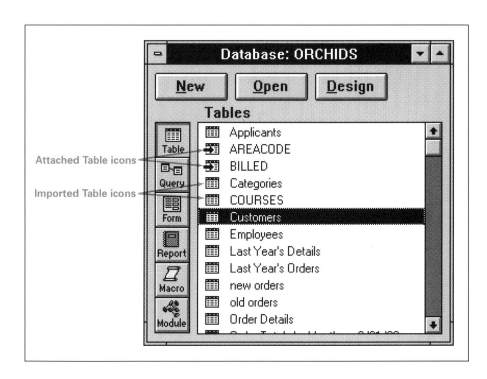

Deciding whether to import or attach a table boils down to these two decisions:

- If you'll never need to view or update the table with its original application, you should import it. Access generally works faster with its own tables, and because imported tables are just like any other Access table, you can freely customize their structure and properties.

- If you still need to use a table with its original application (or someone else in your company needs this capability), you should attach it instead; *do not* import it. After attaching the table, you can use Access to update it. You can also create queries, forms, and reports that use the table's data, just as you would for any "normal" Access table. However, you cannot change the table's structure.

Table 19.1 summarizes the most important differences between importing and attaching a table.

TABLE 19.1: Differences between imported and attached tables

IMPORTED TABLE	ATTACHED TABLE
Converted to Access format.	Retains its original database format.
Copied from the external table to your open database.	Linked to your open database. No copies are made.
Deleting the table deletes the copy from your open database.	Deleting the table deletes the link only, not the external table.
Use when you no longer need to have the original application update the table.	Use when you still need to have the original application update the table.
Access can work faster with imported tables.	Access may work more slowly with attached tables.
You can change any properties, including the structure, of an imported table.	You can cannot change the structure of an attached table.
Access translates certain data types of the original table to Access data types.	No translations are necessary.

Tips for Importing and Attaching Tables

In a moment, we'll explain how to import or attach each of the available database formats. But first, let's consider a few points about tables with passwords and tables on networks.

NOTE   See "Using Imported and Attached Tables" for information about working with imported and attached tables and changing their properties for optimal performance.

Importing and Attaching Tables That Have Passwords

When importing or attaching a table from Paradox, Btrieve, or a SQL database, you may need to supply a password. Keep in mind that this password is set in the external application, and is different from an Access user password.

Passwords of attached tables are stored in your database so that you can open the table later, simply by double-clicking on it in the Access database window. For this reason, you may wish to encrypt any database containing attached tables that have passwords. (Chapter 18 discusses data encryption.)

Attaching Tables on a Network

When attaching to a table that's stored on a network, you must connect to the network and have access to the database file. To have Access automatically connect to the correct file server each time you open an attached table, be sure to specify a fully qualified network path name (instead of just the drive, directory, and file name) as appropriate for your network.

Importing or Attaching Paradox Tables

Access can import or attach Paradox Version 3.0 and 3.5 tables, and can even open encrypted tables if you provide the correct password. After attaching a Paradox table to your Access database, you can view and update it even if others are using it in Paradox.

An attached Paradox table must have a primary key file (~.*px*) if you intend to update it through Access. Without a primary key, you'll only be able to view the attached table. Furthermore, if the Paradox table does have a primary key file, that file must be available or Access won't be able to attach the table. To import or attach a Paradox table:

1. Start from the Access database window and choose File ➤ Import (to import a table) or File ➤ Attach Table (to attach a table).

2. In the Data Source list box, select *Paradox 3.X* and choose OK.

3. Select the .*db* file you want, then click on Import or Attach.

4. If the Paradox table you chose is encrypted, you'll be prompted for a password. Type the exact password that was assigned to the table in Paradox, then choose OK.

5. When Access displays the dialog box telling you the operation is complete, choose OK.

6. If you want to import or attach another table, repeat Steps 3 through 5. When you're finished, click Close.

Table 19.2 summarizes how Access translates data when you import a Paradox table.

TABLE 19.2:   How Access translates data when you import a Paradox table

PARADOX DATA TYPE	ACCESS DATA TYPE
Alphanumeric	Text
Number or Currency	Number, with FieldSize property set to Double
Short Number	Number, with FieldSize property set to Integer
Date	Date/Time

Importing or Attaching dBASE Files

You can import or attach dBASE III and dBASE IV data files (*.dbf*), and can also import FoxPro 2.0 *.dbf* files. When attaching a dBASE file, you can have Access use one or more dBASE index files (*.ndx* or *.mdx*), which will improve performance later when you use the attached table. Access will update the index files automatically when you update the table. Access keeps track of the index files in a special information file (*.inf*).

CAUTION

Do not move or remove any *.ndx*, *.mdx*, or *.inf* files that Access is using. Also be aware that Access can't use an attached table if the indexes you specified aren't current. Therefore, if you use dBASE to update data you've attached to Access, be sure to update any associated indexes as well.

To import or attach a dBASE file:

1. Start from the Access database window and choose File ➤ Import (to import a table) or File ➤ Attach Table (to attach a table).

2. In the Data Source list box, select *dBASE III*, *dBASE IV*, or FoxPro 2.0 as appropriate and choose OK.

3. Select the *.dbf* file you want, then click on Import or Attach. If you're importing a file, skip to Step 5. If you're attaching a file, a **Select Index Files** dialog box appears, as in Figure 19.2; continue with Step 4.

4. Select a dBASE index (*.ndx* or *.mdx*) file, then click on Select. Repeat this step until you've selected all the indexes you want, then click on Close.

5. When Access displays the dialog box telling you the operation is complete, choose OK.

6. If you want to import or attach another table, repeat Steps 3 through 5. When you're finished, click on Close.

FIGURE 19.2

The Select Index Files
dialog box allows you
to associate one or
more dBASE indexes
with the attached table.

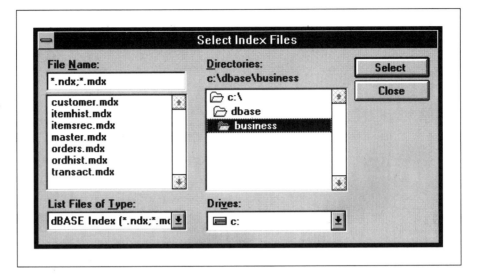

Table 19.3 summarizes how dBASE and FoxPro fields are converted to
Access data types when you import a table.

TABLE 19.3:   How Access translates data when you import a dBASE file

DBASE DATA TYPE	ACCESS DATA TYPE
Character	Text
Numeric	Number, with FieldSize property set to Double
Logical	Yes/No
Date	Date/Time
Memo	Memo

Importing or Attaching
Btrieve Tables

Instead of specifying an actual table file when you import or attach a
Btrieve table, you must tell Access where to find the Xtrieve dictionary file
(*file.ddf*) that contains information about your database. Access cannot
import or attach Btrieve files unless *file.ddf* is present.

To import or attach Btrieve tables:

1. Start from the database window where you want the table to appear, then choose File ➤ Import (to import a table) or File ➤ Attach Table (to attach a table).

2. In the Data Source list box, select *Btrieve* and choose OK.

3. Select the dictionary file you want (*file.ddf*), then choose OK.

4. Select the table you want from the Tables list box, then click on Import or Attach.

5. If the Btrieve table you chose requires a password, you'll be prompted for a password. Type the exact password that was assigned to the table in Btrieve, then choose OK.

6. When Access displays the dialog box telling you the operation is complete, choose OK.

7. If you want to import or attach another table, repeat Steps 4 through 6. When you're finished, click on Close.

Table 19.4 shows how Btrieve fields are converted to Access data types when you import a table.

TABLE 19.4: How Access translates data when you import a Btrieve table

BTRIEVE DATA TYPE	ACCESS DATA TYPE
String, Lstring, Zstring	Text
Integer (1-, 2-, or 4-byte)	Number, with FieldSize property set to Byte, Ingeter, or Long Integer
Float or Bfloat (4-byte)	Number, with FieldSize property set to Single
Float or Bfloat (8-byte), Decimal, Numeric	Number, with FieldSize property set to Double
Money	Currency
Logical	Yes/No
Date, Time	Date/Time
Note	Memo
Lvar	OLE Object

Importing or Attaching SQL Database Tables

You can use Access and *Open Database Connectivity* (*ODBC*) drivers to open tables on Microsoft SQL servers and other SQL database servers on a network.

NOTE Before connecting to a SQL database, you must use the Setup program on the ODBC disk provided with Access to install the proper ODBC driver for your network and SQL database.

To import or attach SQL database tables:

1. Starting from the Access database window, choose File ➤ Import (to import a table) or File ➤ Attach Table (to attach a table).

2. In the Data Source list box, select <*SQL Database*> and choose OK. The **SQL Data Sources** dialog box appears, as shown below:

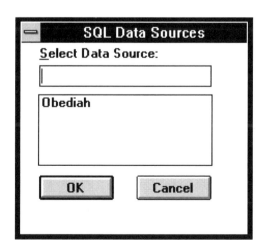

3. Select the SQL data source you want to import or attach, then choose OK.

4. Fill in the **SQL Server Login** dialog box shown in Figure 19.3 with your login ID, password, and any other options required on the SQL database server, then choose OK. Access will connect to the SQL database and display the list of SQL tables you can import or attach.

5. Select the table you want from the Objects list box, then click on Import or Attach.

6. When Access displays the dialog box telling you the operation is complete, choose OK.

7. If you want to import or attach another table, repeat Steps 5 and 6. When you're finished, click on Close.

N O T E

If an error occurs while you're importing, attaching, or using a SQL table, there may be a problem with your account on the SQL database server or the database itself. Please contact your SQL database administrator for assistance.

FIGURE 19.3

The SQL Server Login dialog box

Importing or Attaching Objects from Access Databases

Normally you'll want to store all the tables, forms, reports, and other objects that make up a given application in a single Access database. But in a large company, different departments might create their own separate Access databases. You can import and attach data from a separate, unopened Access database in the same way you import or attach data from a different application. You can attach as many Access files as memory allows. For example, you can attach to other Access tables on a network and use them just as if they were part of your currently open Access database.

You can also import objects (tables, queries, forms, reports, macros, and modules) from another database into your open database. This is much easier than using copy and paste to copy several related objects at once.

NOTE

When importing tables, you can import just the structure or both the structure and the data. If you intend to import objects (forms, reports, queries, and so forth) for use with tables in the open database, the name and structure of the tables in the open database must match the name and structure of the tables originally used to create the objects you're importing.

To import objects or attach tables from another Access database:

1. Open your Access database with the usual File ➤ Open Database commands. Then, starting from its database window, choose File ➤ Import (to import a table) or File ➤ Attach Table (to attach a table).

2. In the Data Source list box, select *Microsoft Access* and choose OK.

3. Select the Access database (*.mdb*) file you want, then choose OK.

4. If you're attaching a table, you'll see the **Attach Tables** dialog box shown in Figure 19.4; skip then to Step 6. If you're importing

objects, you'll see the **Import Objects** dialog box shown in Figure 19.5; continue then with Step 5.

5. If you're importing objects, choose the type of object you want to import from the Object Type dialog box. Your options are *Tables*, *Queries*, *Forms*, *Reports*, *Macros*, and *Modules*. If you chose *Tables*, specify whether you want to import just the table's structure (click on Structure Only) or both the structure and the data (click on Structure And Data).

6. Select the table or object you want, then click on Import or Attach.

FIGURE 19.4

The Attach Tables dialog box

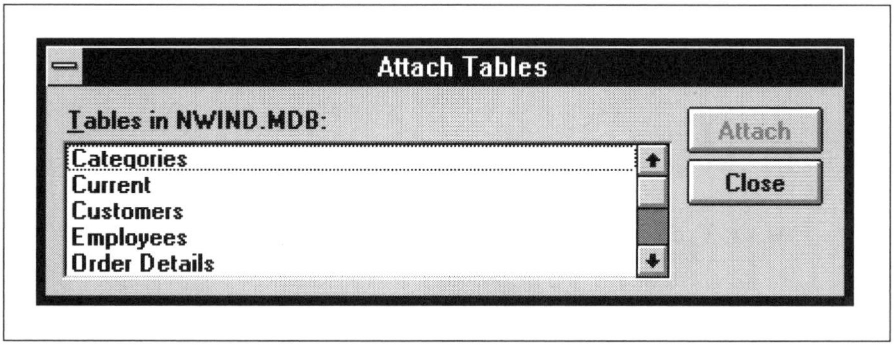

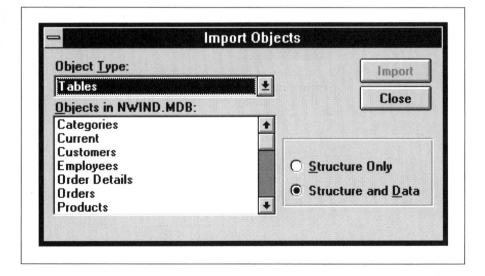

FIGURE 19.5

The Import Objects dialog box

7. When Access displays the dialog box telling you the operation is complete, choose OK.

8. If you want to import or attach another table or object, repeat Steps 5 through 7. When you're finished, click on Close.

Remember that when you *attach* a table, that table is still stored in the original database. Any changes you make to the attached table are actually made in that original database. When you *import* an object, the copy that's in your database is separate from the copy in the original database. Any changes you make to the imported object are *not* reflected in the original database.

Using Attached Tables

After attaching a table from another database, you can use it much like any other Access table. You can enter and update data, use existing queries, forms, and reports, or develop new ones. So even if the data resides in separate applications on separate computers, Access can use the external table almost as if you had created it from scratch in your open database. The only real restriction is that you cannot change the structure of an attached table.

Setting Properties of Attached Tables

Although you cannot add, delete, or rearrange fields of an attached table, you can set many table properties, including the Format, Decimal Places, Caption, Default Value, Validation Rule, and Validation Text. As discussed in Chapter 6, you can change these properties in the table design view.

NOTE   Actually, Access will allow you to add fields to an attached table. But you'll lose those fields as soon as you close the database.

Renaming Attached or Imported Tables

Because most applications store various database objects as separate files, the names of those objects will be their original DOS file names (eight characters.) When you've imported or attached such a file, however, you can give it a more descriptive Access name in your database window. For instance, you could rename a dBASE file named *PlntFood* to *Plant Foods and Supplements (from dBASE)*.

To rename an imported or attached table, select its name in the Access database window. Then choose File ➤ Rename, type in a new name, then choose OK.

Optimizing the Performance of Attached Tables

Keep in mind that although attached tables behave a lot like Access tables, they aren't actually in your Access database. Each time you view attached data, Access must retrieve records from another file that may be on another computer in the network or in a SQL database. Not surprisingly, this can take time.

Here are some guidelines for speeding up performance when using an attached table on a network or SQL database:

- View only the data you absolutely need, and don't scroll up and down unnecessarily. Avoid jumping to the last record of a large table unless you need to add new records.

- Use queries to limit the number of records that you view in a form or datasheet.

- Avoid using functions, especially domain aggregate functions such as DSum( ), anywhere in your queries. These require Access to process all the data in the attached table.

- If you frequently add new records to an attached table, create a form that has the Default Editing property set to *Data Entry*. That way, Access won't bother to display any existing records from the table when you enter data.

Viewing Link Information for an Attached Table

Access stores information about the link to an attached table in the table's Description property. To view the information, open the table in design view, click on the Properties button on the tool bar, or choose View ➤ Table Properties from the menu. Figure 19.6 shows the result of opening the **Table Properties** dialog box for an attached dBASE IV table named *areacode.dbf* that's stored on the directory *c:\dbase\giftco* of our local hard disk.

FIGURE 19.6

The Table Properties dialog box for an attached dBASE IV table

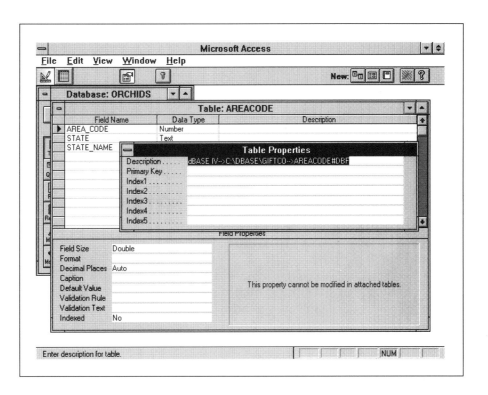

NOTE   You cannot change the Description property of the table.

Deleting a Link to an Attached Table

When you no longer need to use an attached table, you can simply delete the link. To do this, open the database window containing the attached table, select the icon for the table you want to delete, and press the Delete key (or choose Edit ➤ Delete). When asked if you're sure you want to delete the table, choose OK.

Remember that deleting a link deletes the information used to access the attached table, but has absolutely no effect on the table itself. You can reattach the table at any time.

NOTE   If the attached table is moved or its password is changed, you won't be able to access it. To solve the problem, delete the link, then reattach the table.

Importing Spreadsheets and Text Files

So far, we've talked only about importing and attaching data from other database management systems. However, you can also import any of the following spreadsheet and text formats into Access tables:

- Microsoft Excel (versions 2.x, 3.0, and 4.0)

- Lotus 1-2-3 or 1-2-3 for Windows (*.wks*, *.wk1*, and *.wk3* files)
- Delimited text where values are separated by commas, tabs, or other characters
- Fixed-width text where each field value is a certain width

When importing from a spreadsheet or text file, you can choose to create a new table, or append the data to an existing table. If your spreadsheet or text file contains field names in the first row, Access can use them as field names in the table.

TIP   As discussed in Chapter 5, you can also cut and paste data from a spreadsheet into an Access table.

Access looks at the first row of actual data and does its best to assign the most appropriate data type for each field you import. For example, importing cells A2 through C11 from the spreadsheet at the top of Figure 19.7 creates the Access table at the bottom of the figure. Here we told Access to use the first row of the range as field labels. Values in row 3 (the first actual row of data) were then used to determine the data types for each field.

In Figure 19.8, we imported a delimited text file, where each field is separated by a comma and text fields are enclosed in quotes. In this case we again asked Access to use the first row as field labels. The second row was used to determine each field's data type.

The example in Figure 19.9 shows the results of importing a fixed-width text file into an Access table. As usual, we asked Access to use the first row as field labels; it then used the second row to determine the data types of each field.

When you import
cells A2 through
C11 of this Excel
spreadsheet...

...Access creates this table

FIGURE 19.8

Importing from a
delimited text file into
an Access table

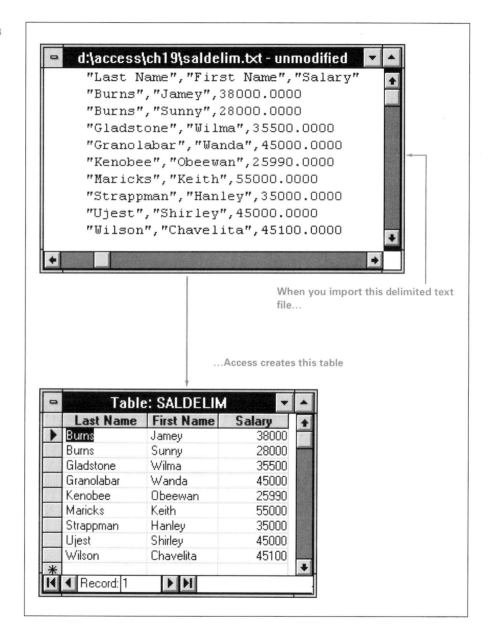

When you import this delimited text
file...

...Access creates this table

FIGURE 19.9

Importing from a
fixed-width text file
into an Access table

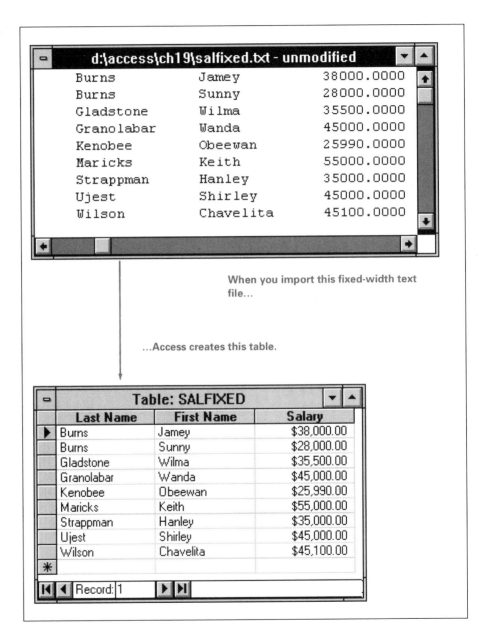

When you import this fixed-width text file…

…Access creates this table.

Importing Spreadsheets

Data that you import from spreadsheets must be arranged so that each field contains the same type of data and each row contains the same fields. If the portion of the spreadsheet you intend to import doesn't fit this specification, you'll need to modify it. To import a spreadsheet:

1. Start from the Access database window, and choose File ➤ Import.

2. Select the spreadsheet format you want to import, then choose OK. Your choices are *Microsoft Excel, Lotus (WKS), Lotus (WK1),* and *Lotus (WK3)*.

3. Select the spreadsheet file you want to import, then click on Import. You'll see the **Import Spreadsheet Options** dialog box shown in Figure 19.10.

4. Select the import options you want, as described in the following sections, then choose OK.

5. When Access displays the dialog box telling you that the operation is complete, choose OK.

6. If you want to import another spreadsheet, repeat Steps 3 through 5. When you're finished, click on Close.

FIGURE 19.10

The Import Spreadsheet Options dialog box

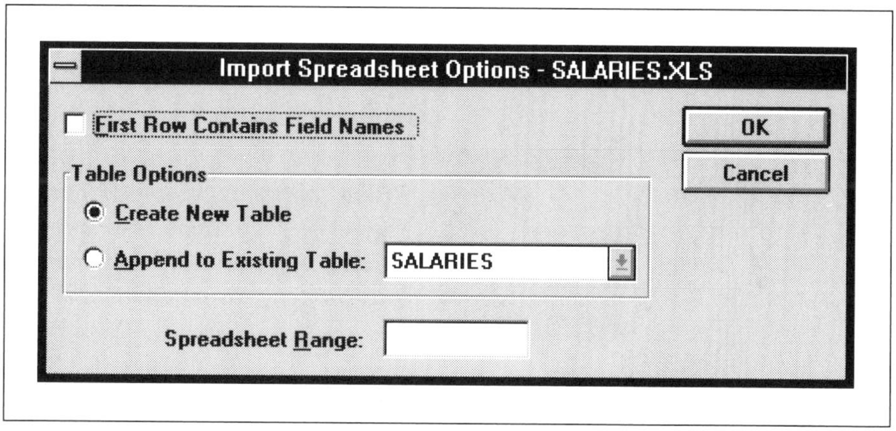

Using the First Row as Field Names

If the first row of the range you're importing contains labels that you want to use as field names for the table, select the First Row Contains Field Names check box. If you don't check this box, Access will import data beginning with the first row of the range, and will assign sequential numbers as the field names. You can change the field names after importing the table.

Appending Data to an Existing Table

Access normally creates a new table for imported data. If you prefer to append records to an existing table, select Append To Existing Table, then select the table you want from the drop-down list. When appending records to an existing table, remember that the records must be compatible. Each field in the spreadsheet must have the same data type as the corresponding field in the destination table, and each field must be in the same order. What's more, if you're using the first row as field names, the field names in your spreadsheet must exactly match the names of your table fields.

Specifying a Spreadsheet Range

Access imports the entire spreadsheet if you leave the Spreadsheet Range box empty. Sometimes, however, you'll want to import just a portion of the spreadsheet. For example, suppose you need only a few records from the spreadsheet, or maybe you need to exclude part of the spreadsheet (such as the title) because it breaks the arrangement of even columns and rows that Access requires.

NOTE   When importing the spreadsheet shown in Figure 19.7, I excluded the spreadsheet title ("Salaries"), so Access could import data that was properly arranged in table format.

To import just a portion of your spreadsheet, specify the range of cells you want in the Spreadsheet Range box. For example, if you want to import cells in the range A2 through C11, type **A2:C11** or **A2..C11** into the Spreadsheet Range text box. If you've told Access that the first row contains field names, be sure to include the labels in the first row of the range. If the data you want to import is in a named range in the spreadsheet, you can type that range name into the Spreadsheet Range box.

Importing Delimited Text Files

A delimited file is one in which fields are separated by a special character such as a comma or a tab, and each record ends with a carriage-return/linefeed combination. Typically, character data are enclosed in quotation marks, as in the example presented at the top of Figure 19.8.

Before importing a delimited text file, make sure it's arranged so that each field contains the same type of data and the same fields appear in every row. The first row can contain the field names you want Access to use when creating the table. To import a delimited text file:

1. Start from the database window where you want the table to appear, then choose File ➤ Import.

2. Select *Text (Delimited)*, then choose OK.

3. Select the delimited text file you want to import, then click on Import. You'll see the **Import Text Options** dialog box shown in Figure 19.11.

4. Select the import options you want, as described in the following sections, then choose OK.

5. When Access displays the dialog box telling you the operation is complete, choose OK.

6. If you want to import another delimited text file, repeat Steps 3 through 5. When you're finished, click on Close.

FIGURE 19.11

The Import Text
Options dialog box

Using the First Row as Field Names

If you want to use the first row of the import file as labels for the table that Access creates, select the First Row Contains Field Names check box. If you don't check this box, Access will import data beginning with the first row, and will assign sequential numbers as the field names. You can change the field names after importing the file.

Appending Data to an Existing Table

Access normally creates a new table for imported data. If you prefer to append records to an existing table, select Append To Existing Table, then select the table you want from the drop-down list. When appending records to an existing table, remember that the records must be compatible. Each field in the text file must have the same data type as the corresponding field in the destination table, and each field must be in the same order. Moreover, if you're using the first row as field names, the field names in your text file must exactly match the names of your table fields.

Specifying Import Text Options

As mentioned earlier, Access expects delimited text files to have commas between fields, and character data surrounded by double quotes ("). But suppose your text file has tabs or spaces instead of commas between fields, or character data are surrounded by single quotes (') instead of double quotes. Perhaps dates aren't in the standard month/day/year order used in the United States. Or maybe the text file was created with an MS-DOS or OS/2 application instead of a Windows application. In situations like these, you must specify the format of your file. You can either load in a previously saved specification or define a new one by clicking on the Options button in the **Import Text Options** dialog box (see Figure 19.11). An expanded Import Text Options dialog box will appear, as shown in Figure 19.12.

The option First Row Contains Field Names and the area Table Options in this expanded dialog box are the same as described above. You can also define the following specifications:

- **Specification Name** If you want to use a previously saved set of specifications with this text file, open the drop-down list and

FIGURE 19.12

The Import Text
Options dialog box
after you click on the
Options button in
the dialog box shown
in Figure 19.11

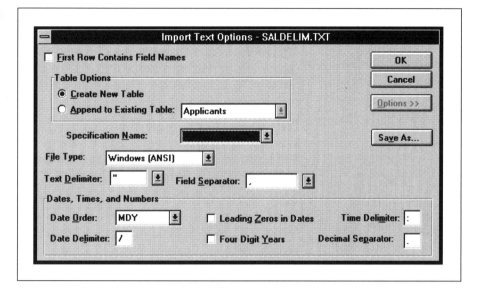

choose the specification name you want. You can then make additional changes as needed, or click on the OK button to begin importing the text file.

- **File Type**   The way Access interprets extended characters (those with ASCII codes higher than 128) depends on the origin of the text file you're importing. If the text file was created with a Windows application, you should choose *Windows (ANSI)* from the File Type drop-down list (this is the default setting). If the file was created with a DOS or OS/2 application, choose *DOS or OS/2 (PC-8)* from the list.

- **Text Delimiter**   If the file you're importing uses a delimiter other than double quotation marks (") to surround text fields, type in the correct character, or open the drop-down list and select a character. Select *{none}* if your file doesn't use a text delimiter.

- **Field Separator**   If the file you're importing uses a character other than a comma to separate fields, type in the correct character, or open the drop-down list and select a character. The drop-down list includes *{tab}*, *{space}*, and , (comma) options.

- **Date Order**   Access expects dates in the MDY (for month, day, year) order commonly used in the United States. However, foreign dates often appear in a different order, such as DMY (day, month, year) in France or YMD (year, month, day) in Sweden. You can use the Date Order drop-down list to specify the order you want.

- **Date Delimiter**   In the United States, each portion of the date is normally separated by a slash (/), as in 11/9/53 for November 9, 1953. Other countries use different delimiters, such as the period in France (09.11.53) and the hyphen in Sweden (53-11-09). If necessary, specify the date delimiter in the Date Delimiter text box.

- **Leading Zeros in Dates**   United States dates normally appear without leading zeros. If the dates in your text file include leading zeros, select the Leading Zeros in Dates check box.

- **Four Digit Years**   If years in your text file include all four digits, as in 11/9/1953, select the Four Digit Years check box.

- **Time Delimiter**   If times are delimited by a character other than a colon (:), specify the correct character in the Time Delimiter text box.

- **Decimal Separator**   If a character other than a period is used for the decimal point in numbers with fractions, specify the correct character in the Decimal Separator text box.

You can save your specifications for reuse later when importing or exporting similar text files. To save your specifications, click on Save As, type a descriptive name for your specification, then choose OK. Access will save your specifications and return you to the Import Text Options dialog box.

When you're ready to begin importing the file, choose OK in the Import Text Options dialog box.

NOTE   Please see the next section for more information on defining and changing import/export specifications.

Defining Import/Export Specifications for Text Files

If you're importing or exporting a standard delimited text file with commas between fields and double quotes surrounding text data, you needn't bother setting up a specification. However, if you're importing a delimited text file that doesn't follow the standard format, or if you're importing *any* fixed-width file, you must define a specification to describe the exact format of your data. Once created, the specification can be reused with any text file that matches its format.

N O T E

You can use the methods discussed previously under "Specifying Import Text Options" or the methods described below to define and save specifications for *delimited* text files. For *fixed-width* text files, however, only the methods discussed below will do.

Creating or Editing an Import/Export Specification

The specification for a *delimited text file* includes the file type, text delimiter, field separator, and options for dates, times, and numbers described in the previous section. However, a *fixed-width text file* specification includes all these, plus information about the field name, data type, starting position, and width for every field in the file. To create or edit an import/export specification:

1. Start from the database window and choose File ➤ Imp/Exp Setup. The **Import/Export Setup** dialog box appears, as shown in Figure 19.13.

2. If you want to edit an existing specification, select the specification you want from the Specification Name drop-down list.

3. If you're creating or editing a fixed-width text file specification, fill out the four columns in the Field Information section for *each* field in the table (see Figure 19.15 for an example).

FIGURE 19.13

The Import/Export
Setup dialog box

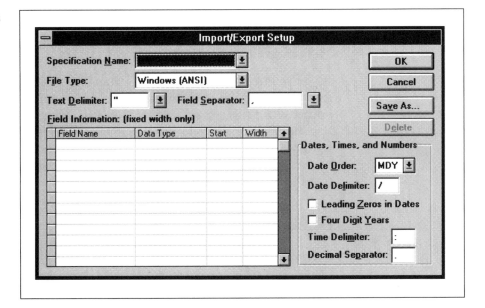

- *Field Name* is the field's name in the Access table.
- *Data Type* is the field's data type. You can either type in the data type or click on the Data Type column, then click on the drop-down arrow that appears and select the data type you want.
- *Start* is the field's starting position (column) in the text file.
- *Width* is the field's width (number of characters) in the text file.

4. Specify other attributes for the text file, such as File Type, Text Delimiter, and Field Separator, and Dates, Times, and Numbers as described in the previous section.

5. To save your specification, click on Save As, type a specification name, then choose OK.

6. When you're finished, choose OK. Access will return to the database window.

Figure 19.14 shows the Import/Export Setup dialog box after we opened an existing specification for the fixed-width text file shown at the top of Figure 19.9.

FIGURE 19.14

A specification for the fixed-width text file shown in Figure 19.9.

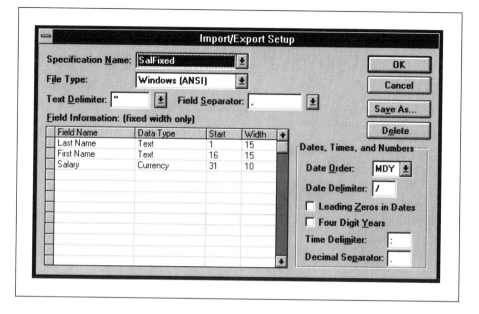

Deleting an Import/Export Specification

If you no longer need an import/export specification, you can delete it. To do so, open or switch to the database window and choose File ➤ Imp/Exp Setup. Select the specification you want to delete from the Specification Name drop-down list, and then click on Delete. You can delete as many specifications as you wish. When you're finished, choose Cancel.

Importing Fixed-Width Text Files

After defining a fixed-width text file specification, you can import it by following these steps:

1. Start from the database window where you want the table to appear, then choose File ➤ Import.

2. Select *Text (Fixed Width)*, then choose OK.

3. Select the fixed-width text file you want to import, then click on Import. You'll see the **Import Text Options** dialog box shown in Figure 19.15.

4. If you want to append records to an existing table instead of creating a new table, select Append To Existing Table and then select the table you want from the drop-down list box.

NOTE

As for spreadsheets and delimited text files, the format of your fixed-width text file records must be compatible with the table you're appending to.

5. Select a fixed-width specification from the Specification Name drop-down list, then choose OK.

6. When Access displays the dialog box telling you the operation is complete, choose OK.

7. If you want to import another text file, repeat Steps 3 through 6. When you're finished, click on Close.

Refining an Imported Table's Design

After importing a table, you can improve its design in several ways. To get started, open the table and switch to design view. Then...

FIGURE 19.15

The Import Text Options dialog box for a fixed-width text file

```
┌─────────────────────────────────────────────────────────┐
│ ▬  Import Text Options - SALFIXED.TXT                     │
│ ┌─Table Options──────────────────────────┐   ┌────────┐  │
│ │ ● Create New Table                      │   │   OK   │  │
│ │                                         │   └────────┘  │
│ │ ○ Append to Existing Table: │SALFIXED  ▼│   ┌────────┐  │
│ │                                         │   │ Cancel │  │
│ │      Specification Name:  │SalFixed    ▼│   └────────┘  │
│ └─────────────────────────────────────────┘               │
└─────────────────────────────────────────────────────────┘
```

- Add field names or descriptions if necessary. This is especially helpful if you didn't import field names along with the data.

- Change data types if necessary. Access does its best to guess the correct data type for each field, based on the data you imported. However, you may need to refine these guesses.

- Set field properties, such as Field Size, Format, and so forth, as best suits your needs.

- Set a primary key to uniquely identify each record in the table and improve performance. If your table doesn't have a primary key, Access can create one for you.

NOTE   See Chapter 6 for more information on changing and customizing tables.

Troubleshooting Import Problems

If Access encounters problems when importing records into your table, it will report the number of errors found, as shown below:

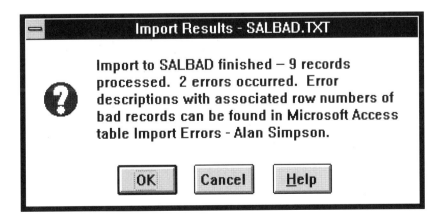

> **Import Results - SALBAD.TXT**
>
> Import to SALBAD finished — 9 records processed. 2 errors occurred. Error descriptions with associated row numbers of bad records can be found in Microsoft Access table Import Errors - Alan Simpson.
>
> OK   Cancel   Help

For each record that causes an error, Access adds a row to a table named **Import Errors** in your database. You can open that table from the database window to view the error descriptions. For example, Figure 19.16 shows the Import Errors table created when we tried to import the delimited text file at the top of the figure. Notice that the second line contains a tilde (~) instead of a comma as the field delimiter, while the sixth line has an exclamation point (!) where the decimal point belongs. The SalBad table at the bottom of the figure contains the records Access successfully imported from the text file.

When importing records to a *new* table, Access may encounter these problems:

* Access chose an erroneous data type for a field because the first row of data didn't properly reflect the type of data you were importing. This can happen if you forget to check the First Row Contains Field Names option, or if a field that contains mostly text values has a number in the first row.

* One or more rows in the file contain more fields than the first row contains.

* The data in the field doesn't match the data type Access chose for the field. For example, a number may contain an erroneous character (as in the example of Figure 19.16), or a row may contain extraneous characters or summary information.

When importing records to an *existing* table, Access may be tripped up if:

* The data in a numeric field is too large for the field size of a table field. For example, Access can't import a number greater than 255 into a field that has the number data type and a Field Size property of *Byte*.

* One or more records in the data contain duplicate values for a primary key field in the table, or for any field that has an Indexed property set to *Yes-No Duplicates*.

* One or more rows in the file contain more fields than the table.

* The data in a text file or spreadsheet field is the wrong type for the corresponding table field. For instance, the table field may be a date/time type, but the data contains a person's name.

FIGURE 19.16

The delimited text file at the top of this figure caused errors shown in the Import Errors table. The valid records from the text file were stored in the SalBad table.

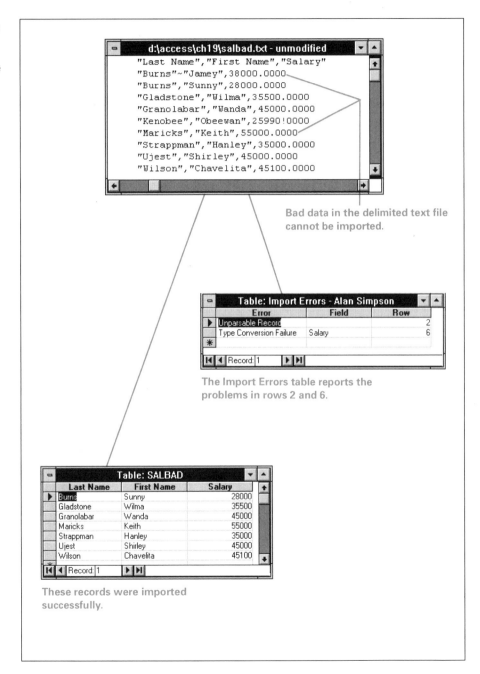

```
d:\access\ch19\salbad.txt - unmodified
"Last Name","First Name","Salary"
"Burns"~"Jamey",38000.0000
"Burns","Sunny",28000.0000
"Gladstone","Wilma",35500.0000
"Granolabar","Wanda",45000.0000
"Kenobee","Obeewan",25990!0000
"Maricks","Keith",55000.0000
"Strappman","Hanley",35000.0000
"Ujest","Shirley",45000.0000
"Wilson","Chavelita",45100.0000
```

Bad data in the delimited text file cannot be imported.

Table: Import Errors - Alan Simpson

Error	Field	Row
Unparsable Record		2
Type Conversion Failure	Salary	6

Record: 1

The Import Errors table reports the problems in rows 2 and 6.

Table: SALBAD

Last Name	First Name	Salary
Burns	Sunny	28000
Gladstone	Wilma	35500
Granolabar	Wanda	45000
Maricks	Keith	55000
Strappman	Hanley	35000
Ujest	Shirley	45000
Wilson	Chavelita	45100

Record: 1

These records were imported successfully.

If Access reports errors, open the Import Errors table and try to figure out what went wrong. You may need to correct your data file, or you may need to change the structure of an existing table. After solving the problems, you can import the data again. Be careful to avoid adding duplicate records when importing the data the next time. One way to prevent duplicate records would be to make a copy of your original data file and delete from the copy all records that made it successfully into the table. Make any necessary corrections to your data or table, then use the Append To Existing Table option when importing your data.

Exporting Data from Access

You can export data from your Access tables to any of the text file, spreadsheet, or database formats we've already discussed. You can also export Access database objects to other Access databases. As for the sections on importing and attaching data, feel free to skip to the section describing the type of file you want to export to.

NOTE Many database applications do not allow table and field names to contain spaces or have up to 64 characters as Access does. When you export a table, Access will automatically adjust names that aren't allowed in another application.

Exporting Access Tables to Text Files

If you're using a Windows word processor such as Microsoft Word for Windows or WordPerfect for Windows, you can simply copy records from your Access table to the Windows Clipboard, then switch to your word processing application and paste the contents of the Clipboard into your document. However, when using an MS-DOS–based word processor such as Microsoft Word for DOS or WordPerfect for DOS, you must first export your records to a *text file*. Most MS-DOS word processors will happily read delimited text files.

TIP   Delimited text files are particularly handy for supplying data for form letters or mail-merge files. Please see your word processing documentation for specific details on using delimited text files.

To export an Access table to a text file:

1. Start from the database window containing the table you want to export and choose File ➤ Export.

2. Select either *Text (Delimited)* or *Text (Fixed Width)*, then choose OK.

3. Select the table you want to export, then choose OK.

4. Enter a file name for the exported table, then choose OK. The **Export Text Options** dialog box appears. Figures 19.17 and 19.18 show this dialog box for a fixed-width text file and delimited text file, respectively.

NOTE   If the text file already exists, you'll be asked if you want to replace it; choose Yes if you want to replace the file or No to return to the Export To File dialog box.

5. If you're exporting a fixed-width text file, select the name of a previously saved specification and choose OK. If you're exporting a delimited text file, select any options you wish (click on the Options button if necessary), then choose OK. Access will create the text file containing all the data from your table.

FIGURE 19.17

The Export Text
Options dialog box
for a fixed-width
text file

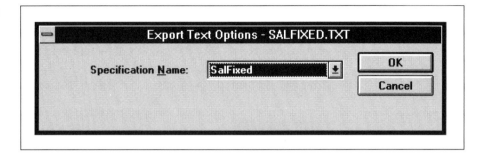

FIGURE 19.18

The Export Text
Options dialog box
for a delimited text file

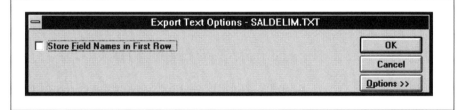

Exporting an Access Table to Spreadsheets, Paradox, or dBASE

You can use the following procedure to export Access tables to Microsoft Excel, Lotus 1-2-3, Paradox, or dBASE files. Later sections explain how to export to other database formats.

1. Starting from the database window containing the table you want to export, choose File ➤ Export.

2. Select the spreadsheet or database format you want, then choose OK.

3. Select the table you want to export, then choose OK.

4. Enter a file name for the exported table, then choose OK. Access will create the database or spreadsheet file containing all the data from your table. For spreadsheets, the first row will contain the

field names from the table. (If the spreadsheet or database file already exists, you'll be asked if you want to replace it; choose Yes if you want to replace the file or No to return to the Export To File dialog box.)

Exporting an Access Table to a Btrieve Table

When exporting to a Btrieve table, you must already have an Xtrieve dictionary file (*file.ddf*), which keeps track of your Btrieve tables. Here are the steps to follow:

1. Start from the database window containing the table you want to export, then choose File ➤ Export.

2. Select *Btrieve*, then choose OK.

3. Select the table you want to export, then choose OK.

4. Select the dictionary file (*file.ddf*), then choose OK.

5. Enter a name for the new table, then choose OK. Access will create the new Btrieve table and update the Xtrieve dictionary file. (If the Btrieve table already exists, you'll be asked if you want to replace it. Choose Yes if you want to replace the file or No to return to the Export To File dialog box.)

Exporting an Access Table to a SQL Database

You can follow these steps to export an Access table to a SQL database:

1. Start from the database window containing the table you want to export, then choose File ➤ Export.

2. Select *<SQL Database>*, then choose OK.

3. Select the table you want to export, then choose OK.

4. Enter a name for the SQL table and choose OK.

5. Select the SQL data source you want to export to, then choose OK. A sample **SQL Data Sources** dialog box appears below.

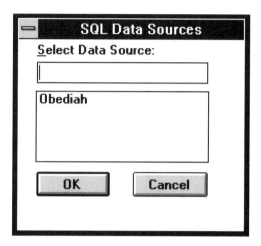

6. Fill in the **SQL Server Login** dialog box (shown in Figure 19.19) with your login ID, password, and any required options. Access will connect to the SQL database and create the new table. (If the SQL database table already exists, you'll be asked if you want to replace it; choose Yes if you want to replace the file or No to return to the Export To File dialog box.)

FIGURE 19.19

The SQL Server Login dialog box

Exporting an Access Object to Another Access Database

Earlier in this chapter, you learned how to import or attach objects from another Access database to the open database. You can also perform the inverse operation: copy a table, query, form, report, macro, or module from your open database to another existing Access database. Here are the steps to follow:

1. Start from the database window containing the table you want to export, then choose File ➤ Export.

2. Select *Microsoft Access*, then choose OK. The **Select Microsoft Access Object** dialog box shown in Figure 19.20 appears.

3. Select the type of object you want to export from the Object Type drop-down list. If you're exporting a table, specify whether you want to export the structure only (select Structure Only) or both the structure and data (select Structure And Data).

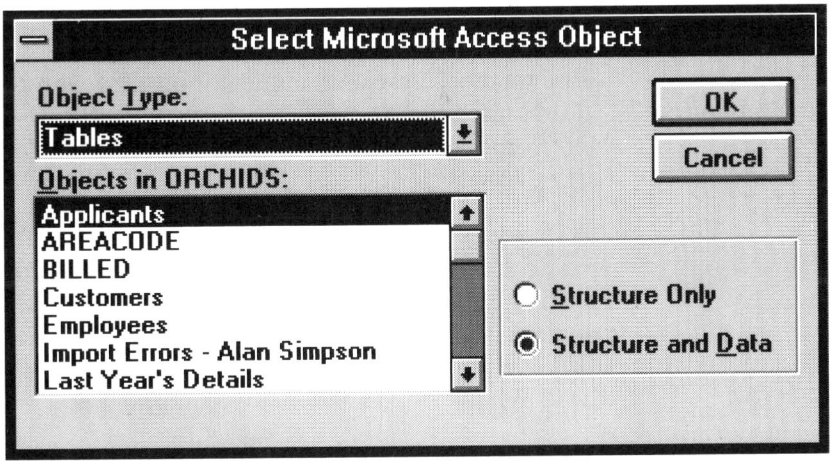

FIGURE 19.20

The Select Microsoft Access Object dialog box

4. Select the object you want to export from the list of objects, then choose OK.

5. Select the Access database (.*mdb*) file you want to export to, then choose OK.

6. Enter a name for the exported object, then choose OK. Access will copy the object to the other database. (If the Access object already exists, you'll be asked if you want to replace it; choose Yes if you want to replace the file or Cancel to return to the database window.)

Importing and Exporting from Non-Supported Applications

If you want to import data from, or export data to, an application other than those that Access supports directly, you can use a format that Access *does* support as an intermediary format.

For instance, almost all applications allow you to import and export data in delimited text format. Thus, you could export data to a delimited text file from one application, then import that delimited text file into the other application.

Techniques for importing and exporting delimited text files in Access were described earlier in this chapter. For information on importing or exporting delimited text files in other applications, check that application's documentation. Be aware that delimited files often go by the name *ASCII delimited file*, *ASCII text file*, or simply *DOS text file*.

Using Object Linking and Embedding to Share Objects

All of the importing, exporting, and attaching techniques described so far in this chapter center around *data* stored in the row and column format of an Access table. But Access also supports Object Linking and Embedded (OLE), which lets multiple applications share *objects*. A couple of important differences between OLE and data sharing are summarized below:

- *Data* that you import or attach is stored in rows and columns.

- An *object* is stored in an OLE Object field of an Access table or in an unbound object frame of an Access form or report.

It's important to keep in mind that OLE is a feature of *Windows* (versions 3.1 and later), and *not* just a feature of Access. While we'll be looking at OLE from an Access perspective here, you may want to learn more about OLE in general from your Windows documentation.

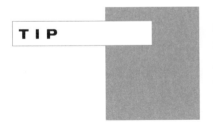

TIP

Chapter 5 presents specific instructions for using OLE to store objects in an OLE Object field in an Access table. Chapter 10 shows how to display an OLE Object (a picture) on a form, using the Unbound Object frame tool.

Linking Objects vs. Embedding Objects

As the name implies, Object Linking and Embedding provides two ways of sharing objects among applications: linking and embedding. When you *embed* an object in Access, you store a separate, independent copy of the original object in your Access database. When you *link* an object, you store a reference to the original object in your Access database. Here are some guidelines for deciding whether to link or embed an object:

- If you want to keep your changes "in sync," whether you edit the object in the original application or in Access, use linking.

- If you want the same object to appear in multiple tables, forms, or reports and to always have the same content everywhere it appears, use linking.

- If you want to make changes to an OLE object through Access *without* affecting the original object, use embedding.

Using OLE in a Form or Report Design

Linked and embedded objects can add real sizzle to your forms and reports. For example, Figure 19.21 shows a fancy employee-update form containing several linked and embedded objects. The form header includes a sound file, a drawing, a spreadsheet, and the results of adding up all the annual salaries contained in the spreadsheet ($352,500). The detail area of the form includes two OLE fields from the Employee table—Signature and Photo.

After placing an embedded or linked field, you can usually edit (or play or run) the object by double-clicking on the object. We'll discuss some exceptions to this "double-click rule" later in this chapter.

Using Unbound and Bound Object Frames

When designing a form or report, you can place OLE objects in bound or unbound object frames. *Unbound* object frames store OLE objects that aren't bound to any field of the table. Thus, unbound objects are never stored in the table itself; instead they're used to repeat the same information in every record of a form or every page header, footer, or detail area of a report.

FIGURE 19.21

An employee update
form containing
several OLE objects

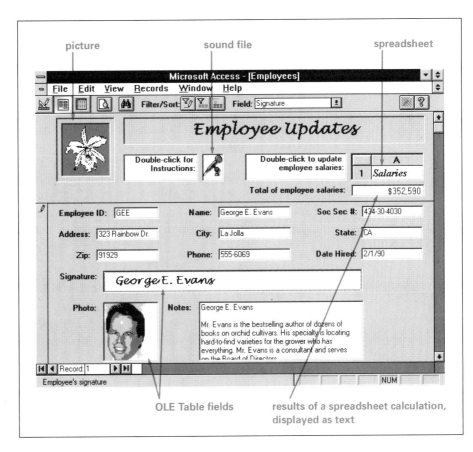

In Figure 19.21, we used unbound object frames to store embedded and
linked objects in the form header (though they can be placed anywhere
on the form). The sound object, in this example, contains voice instructions that the user can play back by double-clicking on the microphone
icon. The spreadsheet contains salary information, which the user can
display or change as needed, again by double-clicking. The "Total of
employee salaries" object is a special *DDE link* (explained later in this
chapter) to a single spreadsheet cell that totals the employees' annual
salaries. The link is stored in a text box that cannot be edited from the
form, but will be updated if the individual salaries in the spreadsheet
change. The orchid graphic is just for decoration, and cannot be edited
from the form.

NOTE Later in this chapter we'll outline the techniques used to place each unbound object into the form shown in Figure 19.21.

Bound object frames, by contrast, display the contents of an OLE Object field from the underlying table or query. For example, the Photo and Signature in the form shown in Figure 19.21 are relevant to that particular employee, and are stored in the underlying Employees table. The person using that form could double-click on the appropriate field to activate the source application. You can also embed or link data from the Clipboard into those OLE Object fields.

NOTE In OLE, the term *source application* refers to the application that was originally used to create the object, or can be used to edit the object. For instance, the source application for a picture or photo might be Paintbrush.

If you used the FormWizards or ReportWizards to create your initial form or report design, your table's OLE Object fields will already appear in bound object frames. However, if you started with a blank form or report, or deleted the OLE fields from your design, you can use the Bound Object frame tool in the form or report design screen to add a control to display the contents of an OLE Object field.

So When Do I Link or Embed?

Before we get into the various different techniques that you can use to link and embed objects, let's take a moment to describe *when* you can do it:

- To link or embed an object into an OLE Object field, or a bound control that represents an OLE object field on a form, you want to be in *datasheet* view or *form* view (as in the examples presented under "Storing Data in OLE Object Fields" in Chapter 5).

- To link or embed an object into an unbound OLE Object frame in a form or report, that form or report must be open in *design* view (as in the example presented under "Adding a Picture to a Form" presented in Chapter 10).

Now, let's take a look the various ways that you can use OLE to link or embed.

Using Copy-and-Paste to Link or Embed an Object

The copy-and-paste technique is probably the easiest way to update OLE fields in a table and to embed or link objects into a report or form design. Here are the steps to follow:

NOTE It's *not* necessary to create the unbound object frame in a report or form design first when using the copy-and-paste technique to link or embed.

1. Start or switch to the OLE server (source) application, such as Microsoft Paintbrush or Microsoft Excel.

2. Choose File ➤ Open (or equivalent options) to open a saved object, or create a new object from scratch. (Remember that you can link only to *saved* objects.)

3. Select the part of the object you want to embed or link (or select the entire file).

4. Choose Edit ➤ Copy or press Ctrl+Ins to copy your selection to the Clipboard.

5. Switch back to Access without closing the application, by using the Task List (Ctrl+Esc) or Alt+Tab.

6. Click on the field in the record you want to update in datasheet or form view, or open a form or report in design view, and move the pointer to wherever you want to place the object.

- If you want to embed the object, choose Edit ➤ Paste or press Shift+Ins.
- If you want to link the object, choose Edit ➤ Paste Link, then choose OK (and also see "Using Manual and Automatic Links" below).

TIP

If you want to create the same link between several objects, create one link as usual. Then copy and paste the link as needed.

If you linked or embedded to a form or report design, Access automatically creates an unbound object frame for the object.

Using Manual and Automatic Links

When you *link* an object to an unbound object frame in a form or report design, you can choose to have Access update the link automatically or manually.

NOTE

When linking or embedding to an OLE Object field in a table, Auto Update is dimmed and unavailable.

A *manual link* requires you to take a special action if you want to see changes to the linked object after the data in the source document changes. An *automatic link* is updated automatically whenever the information in the source document changes, providing that you establish a link to that object when you first open the form or report. (See "Updating a Link" later in this chapter).

Embedding an OLE Object

The copy-and-paste procedures described in the previous section require you to start the embedding process from the source application. Alternatively, you can use Edit ➤ Insert Object to embed an OLE object without switching to the source application first. Here's how:

1. Click on the field in the record you want to update in datasheet or form view, or click in the section of a form or report in design view where you want to embed the object.

2. Choose Edit ➤ Insert Object. You'll see the **Insert Object** dialog box shown below:

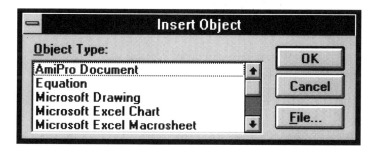

3. Select an object type from the dialog box. Then...

   • If the object isn't saved yet, choose OK, then create the object in the source application. When you're finished, choose File ➤ Update (if it's available), then File ➤ Exit (or a similar Exit option). If asked whether you want to close the connection and update the object, choose Yes.

   • If the object is saved, click on the File button. In the **Insert Object from File** dialog box that appears, choose the drive and directory location of the object you want to embed, then choose the file name of the object from the list under File Name. Choose OK.

 If you're designing a form or report, you can use the Unbound Object tool (shown at left) in the left-hand column of the tool bar instead of choosing Edit ➤ Insert Object in Step 2. Select the tool from the tool bar, then click on and drag to outline the frame. When you release the mouse button, the Insert Object dialog box will appear and you can continue with Step 3.

TIP Although you can use the above technique to embed a graph from Microsoft Excel or Microsoft Chart, it's much easier to use the Graph tool on the tool bar. That tool has a friendly GraphWizard to help you through the design process (see Chapter 12).

Using Embedded or Linked OLE Objects

When you select an unbound OLE object in a form or report's design view, or select a bound OLE object in a table's datasheet or form view, the Edit menu will include an Object option as its last entry. For example, the Edit menu shown in Figure 19.22 includes Paintbrush Picture Object at the bottom. The name of the Object command changes to reflect the type of object you've selected, though the underlined "hot key" letter is always O for Object.

In the sections below, we'll explain how to make various changes to embedded and linked OLE objects. For convenience, we'll just use the word "Object" when referring to the last option on the Edit menu.

Playing or Running an OLE Object

The easiest way to play or run an OLE object such as a sound or media file is to double-click on it. However, if double-clicking doesn't work, you can select the object you want to play or run, then choose Edit ➤ Object ➤ Play or Edit ➤ Object ➤ Run.

NOTE You cannot play or run the object if the Enabled property is set to *No*.

FIGURE 19.22

After you select
an OLE object, the
bottom of the Edit
menu will include
an Object option.

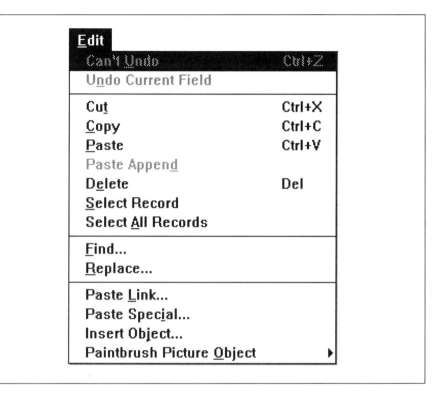

Editing an Embedded or Linked OLE Object

You can edit most linked or embedded objects simply by double-clicking on the object. If double-clicking doesn't do the job, select the object you want to edit, then choose Edit ➤ Object ➤ Edit. Your embedded or linked object will be opened in the source application.

After making your changes, choose File ➤ Update or File ➤ Save (if those options are available). Then choose File ➤ Exit (or a similar Exit option). If asked whether you want to close the connection and update the object, choose Yes.

 You cannot edit an object if the Enabled property is
set to *No*.

Updating a Link

If a form or report contains any linked objects, you'll always see the dialog
box below when you first open that form or report:

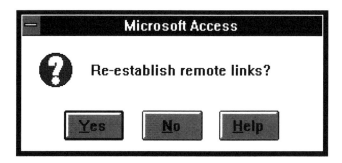

If you choose Yes, Access opens the source application that the object is
linked to, and immediately updates the link. If you choose No, Access
doesn't open the source application, and does not update the link.

So now, how does this relate to the difference between automatic and
manual links described earlier? Well, *if* you created an automatic link, *and*
you choose Yes when asked about reestablishing the remote links, then Access will automatically update the linked object on your screen as other
users make changes to that object.

However, if you choose No when asked about reestablishing the remote
links, Access won't reflect current changes to the linked object, until you
manually update the link. To do so, select the object you want to update,
then choose Edit ➤ Object ➤ Update Now. After a short delay, the OLE
object will reflect any changes made in the source application.

Relinking an Object

Renaming or moving the file an object is linked to breaks the link, because
the OLE object is no longer connected to the original file name. To fix a

broken link, or link to a different OLE object, select the object, then choose Edit ➤ Object ➤ Change Link. When the **Change Link** dialog box appears, choose the drive and directory location of the object you want to link to, then choose the file name of the object from the list under File Name. Now choose OK to reestablish the link.

TIP You can also delete a linked object, then link it again, because deleting a linked object only makes it vanish from the current window—it doesn't delete the object file on disk.

Preventing Edits to Linked or Embedded Objects

You can prevent any more changes to a linked or embedded object in its source application by changing the object to a picture. To do this, select the object and choose Edit ➤ Object ➤ Change To Picture. If the object was linked, changing the object to a picture also breaks the link to the source application.

Keep in mind that changing an object to a picture is a one-way step: you won't be able to update the object in its source application again. A gentler alternative involves setting the Enabled property to *No*, as described later. This method preserves the link to the source application and still allows you to make changes if necessary (after resetting Enabled back to *Yes*).

Deleting a Linked or Embedded Object

If you want to remove a linked or embedded object from a field in the datasheet or form view, or from your form or report design, simply select the object and press the Delete key.

Keep in mind that deleting an OLE object is different from breaking a link. When you break a link, the object still exists but it's no longer tied to the original application. When you delete an *embedded* object, it disappears from the window you're viewing at the moment. When you delete a *linked* object, it disappears from the window, but the original document is still saved as a disk file.

Using Special OLE Techniques (Paste Special)

When you copy information to the Clipboard, the information is actually sent in more than one format. You can select the format used, which in turn determines whether the copied information can be linked, embedded, or connected through a Dynamic Data Exchange (DDE) "conversation." The format also determines whether you can edit the object from a form or report.

NOTE　DDE initiates a special conversation with another Windows application and requests an item of information from that application. It's especially handy for displaying a spreadsheet calculation result in a text box.

If you're happy with the way Windows is linking and embedding your objects, you can skip the rest of this section. However, if you'd like to embed objects in a different format than the default chosen by Windows, or you'd like to use DDE links, please read on.

Using Paste Special

Here are the steps for using the Paste Special option:

1. Switch to or start the source application for the object you want to link or embed.

2. Open an existing file (if you want to embed, link, or use DDE), or create a new document (if you only need to embed).

3. Select the data you want to link or embed.

TIP

If you're designing a form or report and want to create a DDE text box link showing the results of a spreadsheet calculation, select the cell in your spreadsheet that performs the calculation you want.

4. Choose Edit ➤ Copy.

5. Switch back to Access without closing the application.

6. Click on the field in the record you want to update in datasheet or form view, or open a form or report in design view.

7. Choose Edit ➤ Paste Special to open the **Paste Special** dialog box shown below:

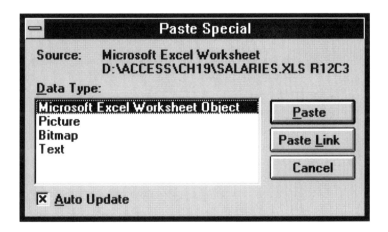

NOTE

The Source area of the Paste Special dialog box identifies the application, directory, and file you're pasting from (if the information is available). The formats shown in the Data Type list depend on the type of information you selected. If your file wasn't previously saved, the Auto Update check box and Paste Link button are unavailable.

8. In the Data Type box, select the format you want. The available formats are summarized in Table 19.5.

9. If the Auto Update check box is available and you want to choose manual or automatic linking, select or clear the option as desired.

10. Click on Paste to embed the object or Paste Link to link the object. If you chose a text data type along with Paste Link, you'll create a special *DDE link* to the object. (See the next section for more information.)

NOTE

Using the Edit ➤ Paste Special command and choosing a Picture format has the same effect as changing an object to a picture, as described earlier.

TABLE 19.5: "Paste Special" formats available in the Data Type list of the Paste Special dialog box

SELECT THIS FORMAT...	WHEN YOU WANT TO...
Object	Edit the object (for example, a Microsoft Excel worksheet object) by opening its source application from a form, report, or datasheet. Object formats can be embedded or linked.
Picture or Bitmap	Display the object and minimize the space it occupies in your database. Use Picture format if you plan to change the size of the object in a form or report. Picture and Bitmap formats can be embedded only and you won't be able to edit the resulting object.
Text	Display the text from an object in a text box. Text objects can be embedded or linked. If you choose Text and then Paste Link in a form or report design, you'll create a DDE Link and the text box will contain an expression that uses a DDE function to show where the object came from. When you switch to form view or print preview, you'll see the actual linked text.

A Short Course in DDE

When you create a DDE link in a form or report design, the linked object is placed in a text box. In some ways, DDE links are like "normal" links. For example, when the source object changes, the changes are reflected in form view or print preview. However, unlike normal linked objects, DDE linked objects contain an expression, called a *DDE function*, that shows where the text came from. In the design view, you see the expression in the text box; however, when you switch to form view or print preview, the text box displays the actual data, as illustrated below:

design view   form view

Another important difference is that DDE links cannot be edited by double-clicking on them. If you need to update the contents displayed by the DDE linked object, you must switch back to the source application and make your changes there.

N O T E   DDE links are most often used to display the results of spreadsheet calculations in a report or form. You cannot place DDE links in table fields.

To create a DDE link to a spreadsheet cell, switch to your spreadsheet application and open the spreadsheet. Select the cell containing the calculation you want to display, as shown in Figure 19.23. Now switch back to your Access form or report design and choose Edit ➤ Paste Special. Choose *Text* in the Data Type list, then click on Paste Link. Access will create a DDE link to the spreadsheet cell and add a text box to your form or report design. This text box contains a DDE function showing where the object came from. For example, the DDE function that references the object selected in Figure 19.23 is:

```
=DDE("Excel","D:\ACCESS\CH19\SALARIES.XLS","R12C3")
```

FIGURE 19.23

After selecting cell C12 in a saved Microsoft Excel spreadsheet, we created a DDE link to the cell by switching back to the Access form design, choosing Edit ➤ Paste Special, selecting the Text data type, then clicking on Paste Link.

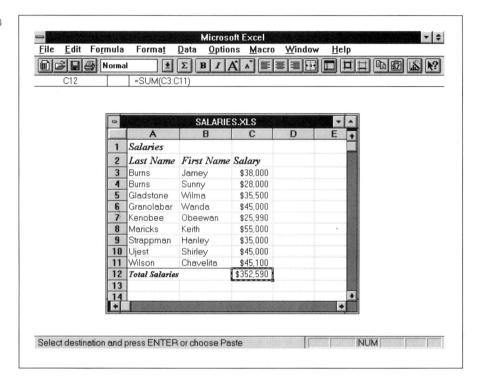

A DDE function consists of three parts: the application, the topic, and the item. The *application* names the application this object is linked to, and is usually the name of an *.exe* file for a Windows application (but without the *.exe* extension). For example, *Excel* is the application in the above DDE function. The *topic* is often the name of the data file used by the application (for example, *D:\ACCESS\CH19\SALARIES.XLS*). Finally, the *item* is the name of the data item returned by the application. For Microsoft Excel, *item* is a row or column identifier, such as *R12C13*, or the name of a range of cells.

When you create a DDE link, the control becomes read-only in form view. Hence, you cannot edit the contents of the text box from Access. Instead, you must return to the original application (such as Excel) to make your changes.

TIP

The DDE function is placed in the object's Control Source property. You can change the application, topic, or item by *carefully* editing the Control Source property for the text box, as described later. Alternatively, you can just delete the object in Design view and repeat the Paste Special steps again.

Using OLE Properties

Whenever you create a control, Access automatically sets some of its properties to default settings. The settings for a control are listed in its properties sheet, and you can change many of them.

NOTE

A *control* is any graphic object such as a text box, unbound object frame, or bound object frame that you place on a form or report design.

 To change a control's properties, switch to design view, then click on the Properties button in the tool bar (shown at left), or choose View ➤ Properties. The properties sheet window will appear. Select a control to see the properties sheet for that object (for example, click on the unbound object frame for a linked or embedded object or on the bound object frame for an OLE table field), then click on the property you want to change in the properties sheet. Use normal editing techniques to change the setting, or click on the drop-down arrow next to the property setting, then select the property you want.

Figure 19.24 shows the properties sheet that appears after we clicked on the embedded orchid graphic in our employee form design. Notice that we also clicked on the drop-down arrow next to the Scaling property.

Several property settings are particularly relevant to OLE objects, as discussed in the following sections.

FIGURE 19.24

The properties sheet
for an embedded
graphic, with the
Scaling property's
drop-down list opened
to reveal available
scaling options

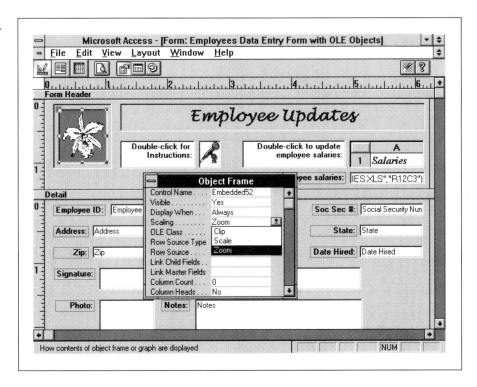

Adjusting the Size and Proportions of Objects

After adding an object to a form or report, you can resize its frame with the usual clicking and dragging techniques. However, after doing this, the image may no longer fit properly in its frame. But that's no problem, because you can easily adjust the size and proportions of the object in a form or report design. First drag the object's frame to the size you want it, then open the properties sheet as outlined above and select the object frame you want to modify. Click on the *Scaling* property, then click on the drop-down arrow to reveal the available options. Your choices are:

- **Clip**   Displays as much of the object as possible, without changing the size of the object.

- **Scale**   Grows or shrinks the object to fit the size of the frame. This may distort the proportions of the picture.

* **Zoom** Grows or shrinks the object to fit the frame, but keeps the proportions the same.

Figure 19.25 shows the effects of applying each scaling property to our now-familiar orchid graphic. The scaling properties are useful for adjusting the proportions of graphics, spreadsheets, and other graphical images. Scaling is available for both bound and unbound object frames.

FIGURE 19.25

Three different ways to scale the same graphic

Locating and Changing Linked Data

Several other properties affect the location and behavior of linked OLE objects. For example, Figure 19.26 shows the properties for the Salaries spreadsheet we linked to the employee form, and Figure 19.27 shows the properties for the DDE text box DDE-linked to cell C12 of the Salaries spreadsheet.

N O T E

Links created via Edit ➤ Paste Link have the OLE Class, Source Object, Item, and Enabled properties. DDE-links created via Edit ➤ Paste Special have the Control Source and Enabled properties.

FIGURE 19.26

The properties for a linked Microsoft Excel spreadsheet

The most important property settings for linked and DDE-linked OLE objects are listed below:

- **Control Source**   Contains the DDE function described earlier. You can edit the application, topic, or item of the DDE function, if you know the correct entries to make. If you're not sure, it's best to delete the DDE-linked object and repeat the Paste Link procedure to make any needed corrections.

- **Update Method**   Determines whether the linked object is refreshed automatically or manually. You can change the update method to Automatic or Manual, as needed. This is faster than deleting the object and linking it again.

- **OLE Class**   Describes the kind of OLE object in the frame. The only way to change this setting is to delete the object and link it again.

FIGURE 19.27

The properties for a
DDE-linked cell in
a Microsoft Excel
spreadsheet

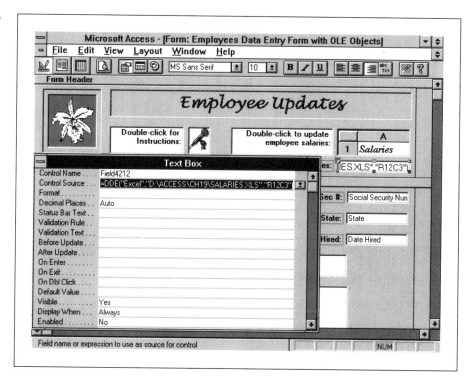

- **Source Object**   Identifies the complete name of the file containing the linked data. You must use the Edit ➤ Object ➤ Change Link command to change the source object.

- **Item**   Describes the data displayed in a linked object frame. You cannot change this setting.

- **Enabled**   Determines whether or not you can double-click on the linked object to open its source application. When set to Yes, you can open the object by double-clicking on it; when set to No, you can't open the source application, and the object will appear dimmed in form view. Note that DDE-linked objects can never be double-clicked to open them, regardless of the Enabled setting.

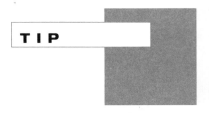

T I P

The most reliable way to change the properties of a linked object is to delete the object from your design, then link it again, or to use the Edit ➤ Object options described earlier.

Multi-User Considerations for OLE

If you're designing forms and reports that will be used by other users on a network, you'll need to know what software is installed on their computers when you use linking and embedding. Table 19.6 provides guidelines to help you decide when or whether to use embedded and linked objects.

TABLE 19.6:   Guidelines for using linked or embedded objects on a network

TO INCLUDE	USERS MUST HAVE
Embedded objects that can be edited (Enabled = Yes)	The same application you used to create the embedded objects
Embedded objects that cannot be edited	No other applications required
Linked objects	The same application you used to create the linked objects, and the file that contains the linked object

Summary

Access allows you to import or attach tables from other database applications (including Access on other computers), and to import spreadsheets and text into Access tables. You can also convert Access tables into spreadsheets, text, and database files that other applications can use. Imported or attached tables can be used just like "native" Access tables (although there are some restrictions with attached tables). When you export a table to another application, the exported data behaves exactly as if you had originally created it in the other application.

Object linking and embedding (OLE) provides a powerful method for sharing objects with *any* Windows application that also supports OLE. You can link or embed spreadsheets and pictures, sound files, word processing documents, and other OLE objects into forms, reports, and OLE fields in your Access tables. To launch the source application for an OLE object, simply double-click on that object. You can then make and save any changes you wish in the source application, without ever having to leave Access.

Using Access on
a Network

f a s t **TRACK**

To add a user to a group 842

Choose Security ➤ Users, select the user from the Name field, highlight the group in the Available Groups field, and click on Add.

To change permissions for a user or group 846

Choose Security ➤ Permissions, select the object type, object name, and user or group name. Check or uncheck the appropriate permissions from the list.

MANAGING and using a database in a multiuser networked environment requires quite a bit more effort than a database on your workstation alone. It's important to understand how multiple users can use the same database at the same time without causing problems. It is also important to know how to manage the database to ensure that different users can or cannot perform certain functions based on their security level.

Using Access with Multiple Users

In the multiuser environment, you need to be concerned with how your actions will affect others in the same database. In Access, as in many other multiuser systems, certain actions can be performed without affecting other users, but other actions can seriously disrupt users who are in the database at the same time.

Avoiding Conflicts

Access has a few safeguards built in to keep you from accidentally messing up another user's data or overwriting another user's changes to an object:

- Whenever someone opens an object (table, query, form, report, or macro) that you have been working on, they will be given the latest version that you've saved.

- If someone else has a table open or is running a query, form, or report, you can't make any design changes to these objects.

* If you have made changes to an object and try to save it, and another user has also made changes to the object since you first opened it, Access will give you the option to overwrite the other changes or save your object under a different name.

However, as a general rule, whenever you need to make fairly major revisions to any commonly used objects in a database, you should check the Exclusive box in the **Open Database** box.

Opening Databases in Exclusive Mode

You will notice in the figure below that each time you open a database in Access, you are given the option to open a database in *Read Only mode* or *Exclusive mode*.

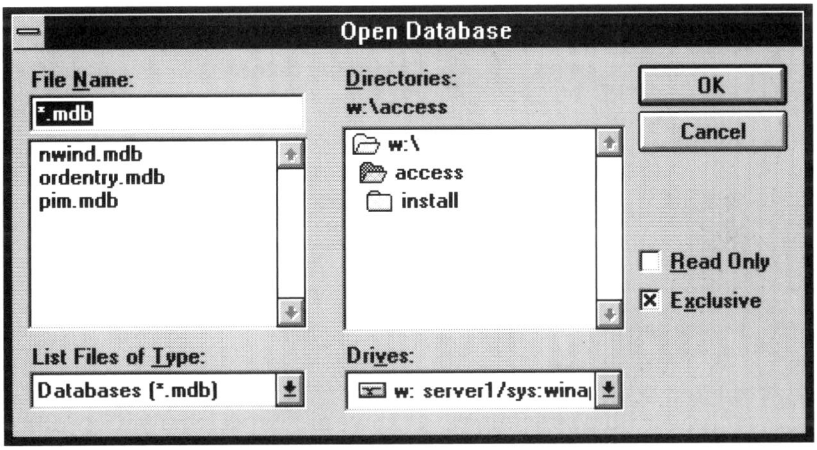

With the database open in Read Only mode, you can look at data—but you are prevented from changing it. With the database open in Exclusive mode, any other users who try to open the database will see the warning below:

Similarly, if you try to open a database in Exclusive mode while someone else is using it, you will see the same warning message.

CAUTION   Once you have made your changes, be sure to close the database and reopen it with the Exclusive box unchecked so that others can again use the database.

Sharing Data

In the same way that we are concerned with multiple users working on the same objects, we must also be concerned with the data shared between users. Of primary concern here is the *record locking* strategy. Record locking refers to the way that Access controls who can do what to the data while someone else is editing it.

There are three ways that Access can handle record locking:

- **No Locks** Even if you are editing a record in a table or query, another user can edit that record as well. If both try to edit the same record, the first user can save the changes. The second user, however, will be given the following choice:

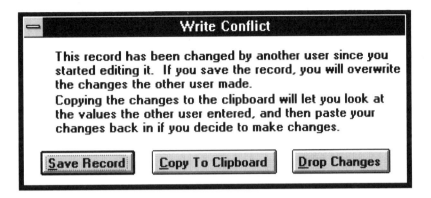

The No Locks strategy is the least secure but the most flexible, because it allows full access to data at all times. This is the default setting.

- **Edited Record** Locks the record being edited (and possibly a few records on either side). Any users attempting to edit this record will see a locked symbol beside the record. The Edited Record strategy guarantees that the changes the first user makes will be saved.

- **All Records** Locks all records in the table and any associated tables (a form may reference multiple tables) for the entire time a user has them open. No other users will be able to edit these tables, although they may read from them. This is a very restrictive setting, and you should choose it only if you can be sure that only one user at a time will need to edit the data.

While editing records in Access, you'll notice the following symbols next to the current record:

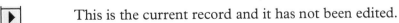

This is the current record and it has not been edited.

You are editing the record and have not yet saved your changes.

The record is locked by another user, so you can't edit it.

Each user should set his or her record-locking strategy to be the same. We'll look at how to do this and how to set other multiuser options in the next section.

Setting MultiUser Options

To set the multiuser options for your login:

1. Choose View ➤ Options.

2. From the Category list, select *Multiuser*.

The default settings are shown below:

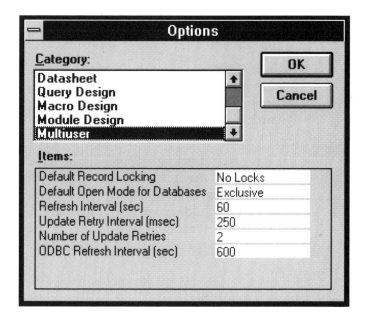

The various multiuser settings are:

- **Default Record Locking**   The choices for this option are *No Locks*, *Edited Record*, or *All Records*. Choose based on your strategy.

- **Default Open Mode for Databases**   The choices for this option are *Shared* and *Exclusive*. (If you set this default to *Shared*, you can still manually check *Exclusive* in the **Open Database** dialog box on those occasions when exclusive access is needed.)

- **Refresh Interval (sec)**   This is the interval, in seconds, in which Access will update records in the current form or table.

- **Update Retry Interval (msec)**   This is the interval, in milliseconds, in which Access tries to save a changed record that's locked by another user.

- **Number of Update Retries**   This is the number of times that Access will try to save a changed record that's locked by another user.

- **OBDC Refresh Interval (sec)**   This determines how often Access will refresh records from databases accessed via ODBC (Open Database Connectivity) drivers.

Updating Your View of Data

As you can see, Access tries to give you updated data as quickly and automatically as possible. However, there may be times when you want to update your views of the data manually. Access provides manual refresh and requery options. *Refresh* simply redisplays the records that were previously displayed while reflecting any changes or deletions that may have occurred in the meantime. *Requery* actually reissues the query to show new records and remove any deleted records, and reorders the records if necessary.

- To refresh your data: choose Records ➤ Refresh.

- To requery your data: press Shift+F9.

Using Access Security

Security is always an important issue in a multiuser environment. The underlying network operating system has security built in to keep people from viewing, running, or altering files they shouldn't.

A multiuser database needs even more security than the network itself. The database administrator needs to make sure that people in the Marketing department, for example, can view but not alter financial reports. Accounting users, however, need to view this data, enter new data, and edit existing data.

Microsoft Access security is based on two elements: the *user* and the *group*. Each user has a login name, a PIN (personal identification number), and a password. Each group has a name, a PIN, and one or more user members.

Security *permissions*, or *rights*, are based on the user and the group. For example, members of the Accounting group may be able to read and modify forms and records, while an individual user (e.g., MATT) can only run specific reports.

Activating Security

The first step in securing your multiuser Access system is to activate security. When Access is first installed, all users are automatically logged in under the *Admin* account, the account with overall supervisory privileges for all databases. This is obviously not a secure setup, so you'll want to add a password to the *Admin* account:

1. Start Access by double-clicking its icon.

2. Open a database using File ➤ Open Database.

CAUTION

Once you begin this procedure, you will need to enter a password every time you start Access in the future. Passwords can be up to 14 characters long, and *are* case-sensitive. So be sure to remember or jot down the exact upper/lowercase letters or your password.

3. Choose Security ➤ Change Password.

4. Leave the Old Password field blank.

5. Enter a new password in the New Password field.

6. Retype your password in the Verify field.

7. Choose OK or press Enter.

As you can see below, only asterisks will appear in password fields, so that no one can look over your shoulder and see a password.

```
┌─────────────────────────────────────────────────┐
│ ▬              Change Password                    │
├─────────────────────────────────────────────────┤
│  User Name:    Admin            ┌──────────────┐  │
│                                 │      OK      │  │
│  Old Password: [              ] └──────────────┘  │
│                                 ┌──────────────┐  │
│                                 │    Cancel    │  │
│                                 └──────────────┘  │
│  New Password: [*****         ]                   │
│                                                   │
│  Verify:       [*****         ]                   │
└─────────────────────────────────────────────────┘
```

Creating a New System Administrator

At this point, you should create another account that is the equivalent of *Admin*. For example, if you are the person who will be responsible for system administration of Access, you can add your login name and PIN and make yourself the equivalent of the Admin.

To add yourself as a user:

1. Choose Security ➤ Users.

2. Click on the New button.

3. Enter your login name and choose a PIN, as shown below:

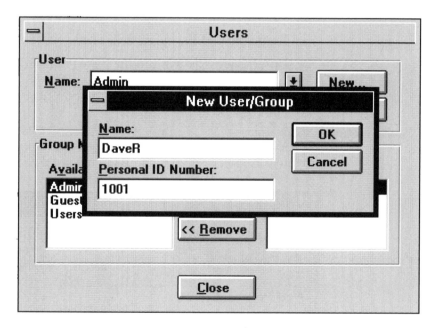

NOTE   Access only uses the combination of the name and the PIN internally, to identify the account.

4. Choose OK.

5. In the Available Groups field, choose *Admins*.

6. Click on Add.

7. Choose Close.

We will come back and explore this Users box in detail in a later section.

Logging In as the Administrator

At this point, you should log out of Access and log in as yourself.

1. Close Access by double-clicking the Control Menu box or pressing Alt+F4.

2. Restart Access by double-clicking its icon.

This time, you will be prompted for your username and password (your password is blank at this point, but we will change it as soon as you re-enter Access).

1. Enter your Username.

2. Leave the Password field blank.

3. Choose OK or press Enter.

Changing Your Password

Now that you have re-entered Access as yourself, use File ➤ Open Database to reopen your database. At this point, your account doesn't have a password. Since you are an administrator, your account needs a password to keep users from logging in as the administrator and getting full access to all databases.

To change your password:

1. Choose Security ➤ Change Password.

2. Leave the Old Password field blank.

3. Enter a new password in the New Password field.

4. Retype your password in the Verify field.

5. Choose OK or press Enter.

CAUTION

Don't forget your password. If you are the only administrator for the system and you don't have your password, you can't change it or clear it and you will be locked out of the system.

Deleting the Admin Account

Access is now almost secure. You have made yourself or another user the administrator, so the generic *Admin* account is no longer needed. In fact, if multiple Access systems are connected, a user logged in as Admin on another system may be able to get into your databases.

To delete the Admin account:

1. Choose Security ➤ Users.

2. Select *Admin* from the Name list.

3. Click on Delete.

4. Choose OK to confirm.

5. Choose Close to close the **Users** box.

TIP

To make your system extra secure, log in as the *Guest* account (and assign it a password, since it doesn't have one by default).

At this point, your system is totally secure. Only you (and anyone else who knows your password) can get into Access. Your next step will be to start defining groups of other users who can log in to Access.

Users and Groups

Groups are essential to the management of any multiuser system. To best see the benefits of using groups, let's look at a system without them. To add a user to a large system, you may have to manually assign permissions for 10 or 12 tables, 15 or 20 forms, 7 or 8 reports, and so on. To add 5 more users is at least 5 times the work! To take the time once to add those users to a group is obviously a worksaver.

Creating a Group

To create a group:

1. Choose Security ➤ Groups.

2. Click on New.

3. Enter a Name for the group.

4. Enter a PIN (your screen should look similar to the one shown below).

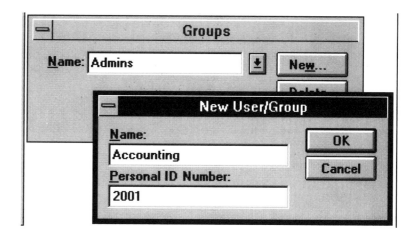

5. Choose OK to close the **New User/Group** box.

6. Choose Close to close the **Groups** box.

Deleting a Group

With the exception of the *Admins*, *Users*, and *Guests* groups, groups can also be *deleted* from the system.

To delete a group:

1. Choose Security ➤ Groups.

2. Select the group name.

3. Click on Delete.

4. Choose OK to confirm.

5. Choose Close to close the **Groups** box.

Adding Users

Now that we have a group to play with, let's add some Users.

1. Choose Security ➤ Users.

2. Click on New.

3. Enter a Name and PIN for a new user.

4. Choose OK.

Notice that in the figure below the new user is automatically added to Access's **Users** group.

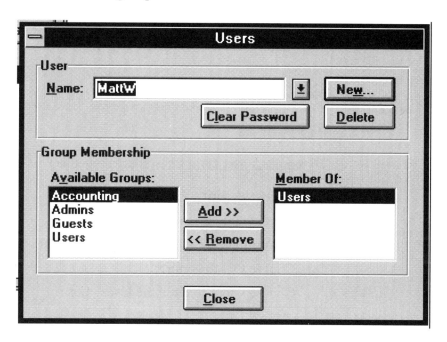

To add the user to another group:

1. Select the desired group (*Accounting*, for example) from the Available Groups field.

2. Click on Add.

3. Choose Close to close the **Users** box.

Removing Users

In the **Users** dialog box, users can also be removed from groups or deleted altogether.

To remove a user from a group:

1. Choose Security ➤ Users.

2. Select the user name from the Name list.

3. In the Member Of field, highlight the group to be removed.

4. Click on Remove.

5. Choose Close to close the **Users** box.

NOTE   You can't remove a user from Access's *Users* group.

To remove a user from the system altogether:

1. Choose Security ➤ Users.

2. Select the user name from the Name list.

3. Click on Delete.

4. Choose OK to confirm.

5. Choose Close to close the **Users** box.

Clearing a Password

If an Access user has forgotten his or her password, the administrator can clear the password for that account. This allows the user to reenter the system without having to use a password.

To clear a user's password:

1. Choose Security ➤ Users.

2. Select the user name from the Name list.

3. Click on Clear Password.

4. Choose Close to close the **Users** box.

CAUTION

After clearing a user's password, make sure that the user immediately uses Security ➤ Change Password so that the account is again secure.

Securing Objects

Every object in Access—table, query, form, report, macro, and module—can be secured. These objects are associated with users and groups by means of *permissions*. A permission is simply that—it allows a user or a group to perform a certain action on an object or data. Each object has a set of permissions associated with it.

The permissions that Access uses are:

PERMISSION	ALLOWS USER(S) TO
Read Definitions	View objects
Modify Definitions	View, change, or delete objects
Read Data	View data
Modify Data	View, change, or delete data
Execute	Run an object
Full Permissions	All of the above

Not every object in Access uses every permission. For example, it is not logical to execute a table, nor does it make sense to modify data with a report.

Table 20.1 shows the set of objects and their associated permissions.

TABLE 20.1: Objects and Permissions

	READ DEFINITIONS	MODIFY DEFINITIONS	READ DATA	MODIFY DATA	EXECUTE
TABLE	X	X	X	X	
QUERY	X	X	X	X	
FORM	X	X			X
REPORT	X	X			X
MACRO	X	X			X
MODULE	X	X			

Effective permissions for a user are determined by combining user and group rights. For example, if a user has Read permissions for an object, but is also a member of a group with Modify permissions for the same object, both permissions apply.

Changing Permissions for Users and Groups

To view or change permissions:

- Choose Security ➤ Permissions.

The **Permissions** dialog box from the Northwind sample database is shown below. It shows that the user account Admin is a member of the *Admins* and *Users* groups and has full permissions for the table called Categories.

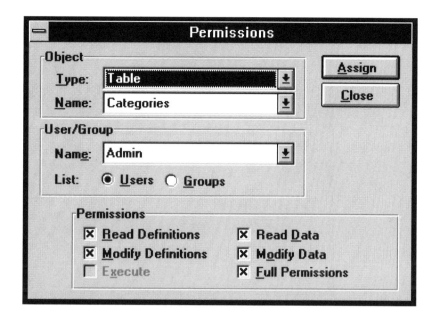

By selecting *Groups* instead of *Users* from the List field, you can view or change the permissions associated with groups. In the next figure, for example, we have changed the permissions for the Query object entitled "Category Sales for 1991" to only allow reading of the definitions and data for the group *Users*. You will see how to do this in the next section.

Securing Database Objects

All viewing and changing of permissions for users, groups, and objects is done through the Permissions dialog box.

To add or change permissions for a user or group:

1. Select the Object Type.
2. Select the Object Name.
3. In the List field, choose *Users* or *Groups*.
4. Choose the User or Group name.
5. Check or uncheck the desired Permissions.

Checking the Full Permissions box automatically checks all other applicable permissions, but unchecking Full Permissions does not uncheck all others.

6. Click on the Assign button to save the changes.

7. Choose Close to close the Permissions box.

If you do not have Modify Definitions permissions for the object, you can't change your, or anyone else's, permissions for that object.

Securing New Database Objects

By default, whenever a new database is created, all users have full permissions for its objects. To secure new database objects, you must remove some of these permissions from objects that don't warrant full access by all users.

Fortunately, Access does not automatically give full access to each individual user account—it does it through the *Users* group. Therefore, you will probably find it easier to take away unnecessary permissions through the *Users* group than through each of the individual users.

Using Queries and Permissions

There is a clever way in Access to allow users to view only certain fields of certain tables. If a user has no rights to a customer table, for example, but needs to run a report of only names and addresses, you can build a query to view only those fields:

1. Create the query displaying only the necessary data.
2. Choose View ➤ Options.
3. Select *Query Design* from the Category list.
4. Make sure the Run With Owner's Permissions propery is set to *Yes*.
5. Choose Security ➤ Permissions.
6. Remove all permissions from the table for the user or group.
7. Assign at least the Execute permission to the query for the user or group.
8. Choose OK.

The user or group will now be able to execute the query without any permissions to the underlying tables.

Summary

In this chapter you've learned about using Access in a multiuser environment. You also now have an understanding of how you can (and why you should) secure Access databases for groups and individual users. In the next chapter, we'll look at techniques that you can use to create database applications.

PART SIX

Developing Applications

Using Macros to Design Applications

fast TRACK

After creating macros for each drop-down menu   **877**

you need to create a macro that uses AddMenu actions to add your macro groups to the custom menu bar. Then attach this macro to the On Menu property of the form that you want to display the menu.

To create custom help screens for your Access application   **879**

you need to purchase a copy of the **Windows Help Compiler,** and a text editor that supports rich text format (RTF), such as **Microsoft Word for Windows,** version 2.0. After creating your custom help screens, you can attach them to the Help File and Help Context Id properties of forms, or open the help screen using a RunApp action in a macro.

To have Access automatically run a macro   **880**

as soon as you open the database, name that macro *AutoExec.*

To define shortcuts keys for running macros   **882**

create a macro group where each macro name is the shortcut key that runs it. Save the macro group with the name *AutoKeys.*

A N APPLICATION is a collection of all the objects you've created—tables, queries, forms, reports, and macros—in your database. When you've finished creating all those objects, you may find that you need to simplify the use of that application for personnel who have little or no computer experience.

There are several items that you can add to your application to simplify its use, including:

- Switchboards
- Dialog boxes
- Custom menus
- Custom toolbars
- Custom help
- AutoExecute macros
- Shortcut keys

In this chapter, we'll look at techniques for creating all of these items.

Creating a Main Switchboard

One way to simplify the use of your application is by creating forms that act as *switchboards*. Each switchboard uses command buttons to provide instant access to various objects within the database. For example, Figure 21.1 shows how you might design a switchboard for our example Orchids database to provide easy access to various components of the overall database.

NOTE

The Northwind database (*nwind.mdb*) includes a similar switchboard, named *Main Switchboard*, that's listed with other forms in the database window.

FIGURE 21.1

Our Orchids main switchboard provides easy access to various parts of the overall database.

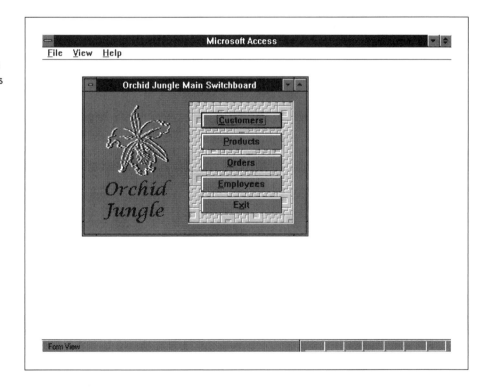

To create a switchboard, you first create a form that isn't attached to a table. That is,

1. Starting from the database window, choose File ➤ New Form (or use the New Form button) to get to the **New Form** dialog box.

2. Make sure the Select A Table/Query option is empty.

3. Choose the Blank Form button.

Once you get to the design window for the blank form, you can use all the basic skills, tools, and techniques described back in Chapters 9 and 10 to create the form. For instance, to create the form shown in Figure 21.1:

- I used the Unbound OLE Object Frame tool to add the *Orchid Logo* picture and the button background pattern. (The pattern is the *chitz.bmp* wallpaper from Windows 3.1.)

- I used the Label tool for text (*Orchid Jungle*).

- I used the Command Button tool to create one command button. Then I sized that button, and used Edit ➤ Duplicate to create several equal-size buttons. To underline a letter in the command button, precede the letter with an ampersand (**&**) when defining the button caption. For instance, the Caption property for the Exit button in Figure 21.1 is **E&xit**.

- I used the Color Palette to color the form and design object borders.

You might also want to change some of the form's properties to control its appearance (choose Edit ➤ Select Form, and open the Properties sheet). The properties I changed in the example shown in Figure 21.1 are:

PROPERTY	SETTING
Caption:	Orchid Jungle Main Switchboard
Default View:	Single Form
Allow Editing:	Unavailable
Scroll Bars:	Neither
Record Selectors:	No

Creating Macros for the Switchboard

To get your switchboard to actually *do* something, you create macros that respond to events on the form. You can attach a macro to the On Push property of each button on the form, as well as attach one to the form as a whole (i.e., On Open, On Close). Figure 21.2 shows some macros designed for use with the main switchboard shown in Figure 21.1.

Let's take a look at some of the macros presented in the figure.

Hiding the Database Window

You can create a macro that hides the database window as soon as your switchboard opens. The *Hide db Window* macro in the Orchids Main

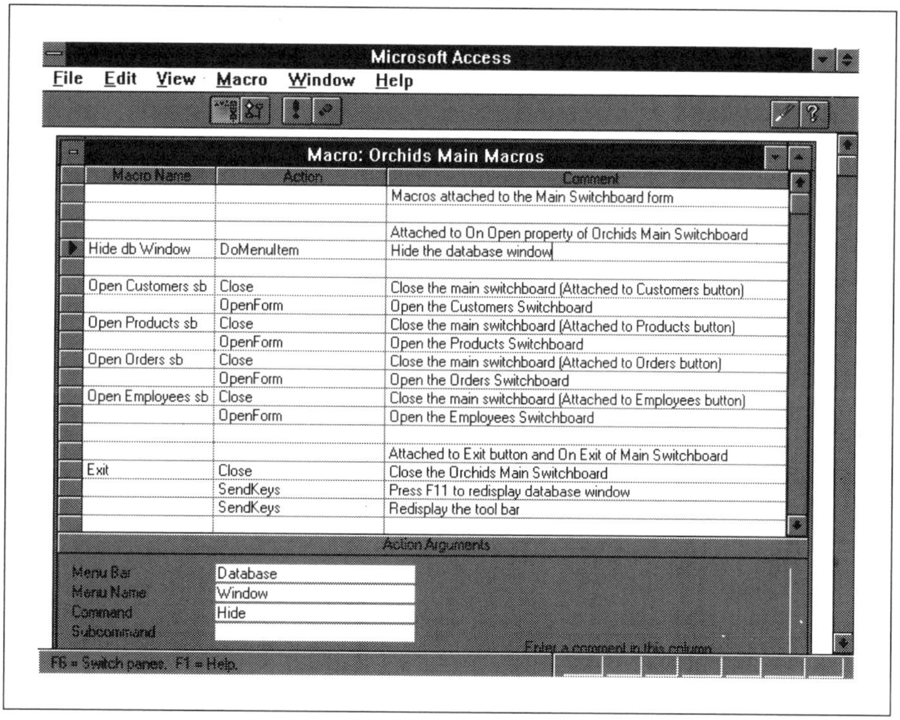

FIGURE 21.2

Macros attached to the Orchid Jungle Main Switchboard form

Macro group does just that, using the action and arguments listed in Table 21.1.

TABLE 21.1: Arguments for the DoMenuItem action in the Hide db Window macro of the Orchids Main Macros group

ARGUMENT	SET TO
Menu Bar	Database
Menu Name	Window
Command	Hide

Attaching the *Orchids Main Macros.Hide db Window* macro to the On Open property of the Main Switchboard form ensures that the database window disappears as soon as the form is opened.

Redisplaying the Database Window

You can also create a macro to redisplay the database window as soon as the person using the switchboard exits the form. The *Exit* macro in the Orchids Main Macros group is attached to the On Push property of the Exit button in the main switchboard. When the user clicks that button on the form, the macro is executed.

TIP You can bring the database window out of hiding at any time by pressing F11.

Table 21.2 lists the actions and arguments used in the *Exit* macro. You can attach the *Orchids Main Macros.Exit* macro to the On Push property of the Exit button, as well as to the On Close property of the Main Switchboard form. (This macro displays the tool bar. I'll talk about how you hide the tool bar a little later in the chapter.)

TABLE 21.2: Actions and arguments in the Exit macro of the Orchids Main Macros group

ACTION	ARGUMENT	SET TO
Close	Object Type	Form
	Object Name	Orchids Main Switchboard
Sendkeys	Keystrokes	{F11}
	Wait	Yes
Sendkeys	Keystrokes	%vo{Tab 3} Yes{Enter}
	Wait	Yes

Displaying Another Switchboard

You can use as many switchboards as you wish in your application design. For instance, I designed my application in such a way that choosing the Customers button on the Orchids Main Switchboard opens another form, named *Customers Switchboard* (Figure 21.3).

The macro to open the Customers Switchboard is named *Open Customers sb* in the Orchids Main Macro group. That macro is attached to the On Push Property of the Customers button in the Main Switchboard. The actions and arguments in that macro are listed in Table 21.3.

The other macros in my sample Orchids Main Macros group are also attached to the On Push property command buttons in the Main Switchboard form: Products, Orders, and Employees. Each one of those macros also opens another switchboard, similar to the Customer Switchboard.

FIGURE 21.3

The Customers Switchboard provides easy access to data about customers.

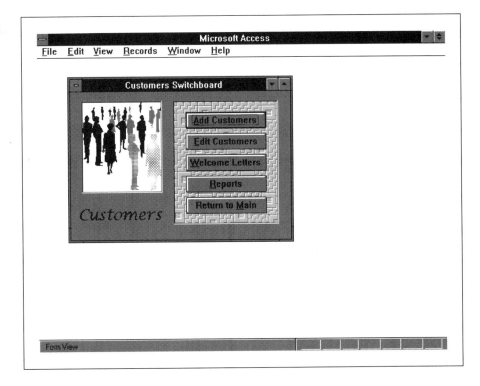

TABLE 21.3: Actions and action arguments in the Open Customers sb macro of the Orchids Main Macro group

ACTION	ARGUMENT	SET TO
Close	Object Type	Form
	Object Name	Orchids Main Switchboard
OpenForm	Form Name	Customers Switchboard
	View	Form

Managing Multiple Switchboards

When your application uses multiple switchboards, you need to create a separate macro group for each switchboard. For example, Figure 21.4 shows a macro group, named *Customers Switchboard Macros*, that's attached to command buttons and form properties of the Customers Switchboard form.

The macros in the Customers Switchboard Macros group are summarized below:

- **Add**   Opens the Customer Data Entry form, in the Add Data mode. Attached to the On Push property of the Add Customers command button in the Customers Switchboard form.

FIGURE 21.4

A group of macros, named Customers Switchboard Macros, attached to buttons and properties in the Customers Switchboard form

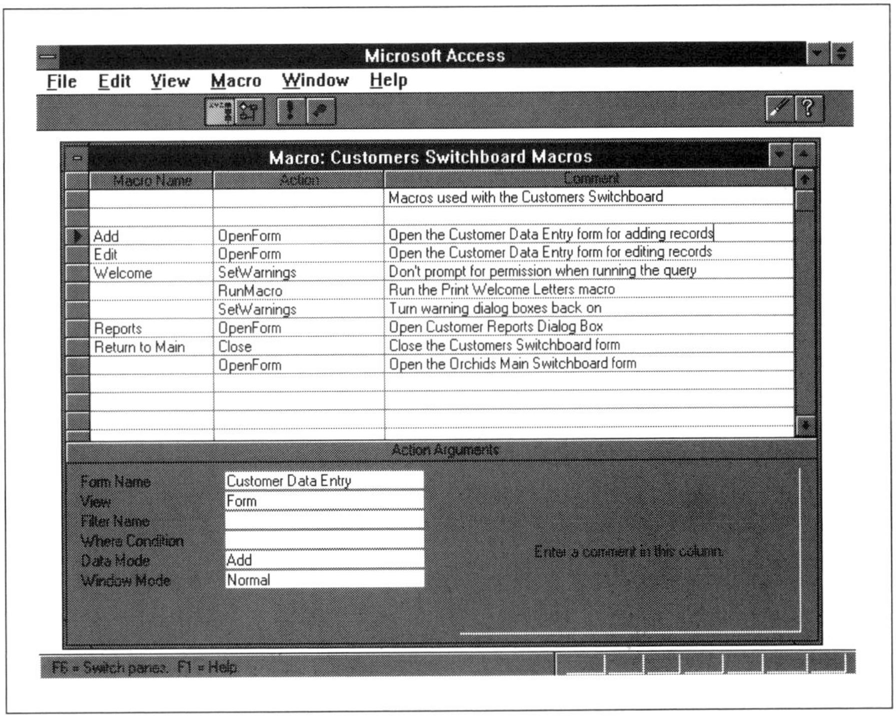

* **Edit** Opens the Customer Data Entry form, in the Edit data mode. Attached to the On Push property of the Edit Customers command button in the Customers Switchboard form.

* **Welcome** Turns off the warning messages, runs the *Print Welcome Letters* macro described in Chapter 16, then turns the warning messages back on. Attached to the On Push property of the Welcome Letters button in the Customers switchboard.

* **Reports** Opens the **Customer Reports** dialog box, described below. Attached to the On Push property of the Reports button in the Customers Switchboard form.

* **Return to Main** Closes the Customers Switchboard form, and opens the main form. Attached to the Return To Main button, and On Close property, of the Customers Switchboard form.

You can create similar switchboards, with their own sets of macros for other parts of the application. For instance, you could create a switchboard that makes it easy to add, edit, print, and post new orders, and switchboards for managing products and employees as well.

Creating Custom Dialog Boxes

You can also create your own dialog boxes to collect information from the user of your application. For example, in my sample application, clicking the Reports button in the Customers switchboard presents a dialog box giving the user a choice of reports and the option to print all records or all records within a range of dates, as shown in Figure 21.5.

Two properties in the form design window allow you to convert a form to a dialog box:

* **Modal** When set to *Yes*, the all other forms on the screen are disabled until the form is closed. When set to *No* (the default), you can switch to another form without closing the current form.

FIGURE 21.5

A custom dialog box appears when the user clicks the Reports button in the Customers Switchboard.

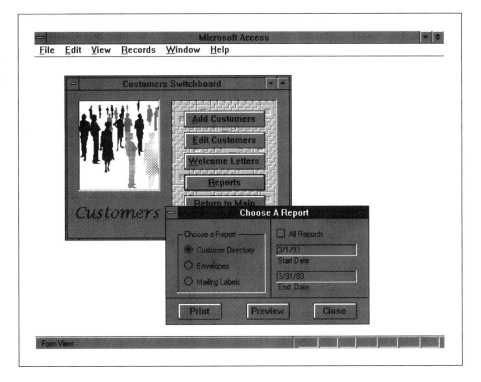

- **Pop-Up**   When set to *Yes*, the form's window has thin borders (it cannot be resized), and floats above all other windows. When set to *No* (the default) the window has thicker borders, can be resized, and can be covered by other windows.

Remember, to set form properties in the form design window, open the Properties sheet and choose Edit ➤ Select Form, or just double-click the form background.

To create a custom dialog box, create a form that's not based on a table or query (as when you're creating a switchboard). In the form design screen, open the Properties sheet for the form, and set both the Modal and Pop-Up properties both to *Yes*, and Record Selectors to *No*.

N O T E

When you switch from design view to form view, the form still looks like a regular window. It only takes on the appearance of a dialog box when you open it from the database window or a macro.

Add command buttons, text boxes, and other controls using the standard techniques. Remember to set the Control Name property for each control that you create to a name that will be easy to remember later. You'll use that name in macros to refer to information in the dialog box.

Figure 21.6 shows the sample dialog box from Figure 21.5 in design view. Here's some information about the form:

- **Choose a Report**   This is an option group, with the Control Name set to *Report Choice*. The first option button in the group

FIGURE 21.6

Sample dialog box, named Customer Report Dialog, in design view

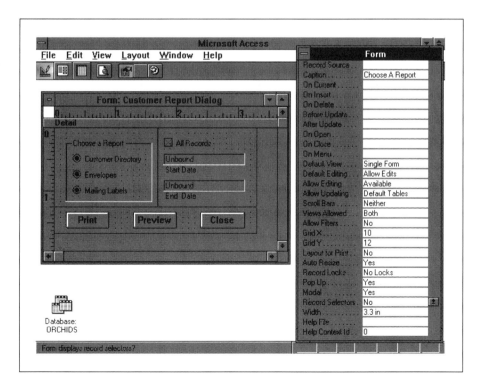

has an Option Value property of *1*. The second option button has an Option Value property of *2*, the third button an Option Value of *3*. A macro can test for the user's choice by checking the contents of the Report Choice control name.

- **All Records** A check box, with the Control Name property set to *All Records*.

- **Start Date** A text box with the Control Name property set to *Start Date*.

- **End Date** A text box with the Control Name property set to *End Date*.

- **Command Buttons** The command buttons at the bottom of the dialog box were created with the Command Button tool. Macros in the Customer Report Dialog Macros group are attached to the On Push properties of these command buttons.

Macros for the Dialog Box

Like any other form, your custom dialog box can have its own set of macros that respond to events that occur within the dialog box. For example, if your dialog box has any command buttons, you'll need to attach macros to the On Push properties of those buttons.

You'll probably also want to create macros that can use the information in the dialog box to make decisions. For example, you might want to create macros that print reports and filter records based on information in the dialog box. The macros can also hide the dialog box, by setting its Visible property to *No*. That way, the dialog box won't obscure any new windows (such as Print Preview) that appear on the screen, but the controls within the dialog box will still be accessible to the macro. Let's look at an example.

Figure 21.7 shows the macros for my **Customer Reports** dialog box. The Print macro, which is attached to the Print command button in the dialog box, contains the actions and action arguments listed in Table 21.4.

FIGURE 21.7

Macros in the
Customer Report
Dialog Macros group.
These are attached to
buttons and events in
the Customer Report
Dialog form.

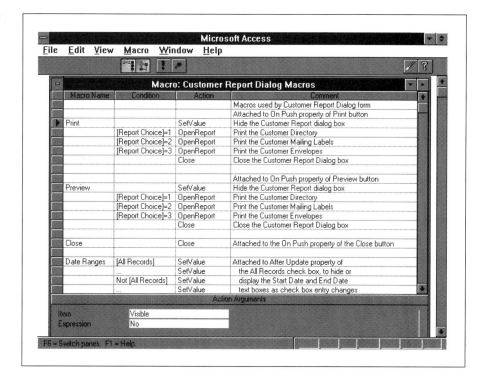

TABLE 21.4: Conditions, actions, and action arguments in the Print macro of the Customer Report Dialog
Macros group

CONDITION	ACTION	ACTION ARGUMENT	SET TO
	SetValue	Item	Visible
		Expression	No
[Report Choice]=1	**OpenReport**	Report Name	Customer Directory
		View	Print
		Where Condition	=IIF(Forms![Customer Report Dialog]![All Records]," ",[Date Entered] Between Forms![Customer Report Dialog]![Start Date] And Forms![Customer Report Dialog]![End Date])

TABLE 21.4: Conditions, actions, and action arguments in the Print macro of the Customer Report Dialog Macros group (continued)

CONDITION	ACTION	ACTION ARGUMENT	SET TO
[Report Choice]=2	**OpenReport**	Report Name	Customer Mailing Labels
		View	Print
		Where Condition	=IIF(Forms![Customer Report Dialog]![All Records]," ",[Date Entered] Between Forms![Customer Report Dialog]![Start Date] And Forms![Customer Report Dialog]![End Date])
[Report Choice]=3	**OpenReport**	Report Name	Customer Envelopes
		View	Print
		Where Condition	=IIF(Forms![Customer Report Dialog]![All Records]," ",[Date Entered] Between Forms![Customer Report Dialog]![Start Date] And Forms![Customer Report Dialog]![End Date])
	Close	Object Type	Form
		Object Name	Customer Report Dialog

The rather hefty **IIF( )** expression is the same in each action. That expression checks to see if the All Records check box in the dialog box is checked. If so, it makes the **Where** condition into a null string (" "), which ensures that all records in the table are printed in the report. If the All Records check box *isn't* checked, then the IIF expression evaluates to the expression:

[Date Entered] Between [Start Date] And [End Date]

The expression, however, uses the identifiers Forms![Customer Reports Dialog]! to get the Start Date and End Date values from the dialog box. It needs to do so because once the report is opened the dialog box is hidden and is no longer the current form.

The *Preview* macro in the Customer Report Dialog Macros group is identical to the *Print* macro, except that the View argument in each Open-Report action is set to Print Preview rather than Print. The *Close* macro uses the Close action, with both arguments left blank, to close the dialog box.

The *Print, Preview,* and *Close* macros are attached to the On Push properties of the Print, Preview, and Close command buttons in the dialog box.

The *Date Ranges* macro is a tricky one that hides the Start Date and End Date text boxes when the All Records check box is selected, and displays those text boxes when the All Records check box is cleared. That macro is attached to the After Update property of the All Records check box, and contains the conditions and actions listed in Table 21.5.

TABLE 21.5: Conditions, actions, and action arguments in the Date Ranges macro, attached to the After Update property of the All Records check box in the Customer Report Dialog form

CONDITION	ACTION	ACTION ARGUMENT	SET TO
[All Records]	**SetValue**	Item	[Start Date].Visible
		Expression	No
...	**SetValue**	Item	[End Date].Visible
		Expression	No
Not [All Records]	**SetValue**	Item	[Start Date].Visible
		Expression	Yes
...	**SetValue**	Item	[End Date].Visible
		Expression	Yes

Activating the Dialog Box

Activate the dialog box (and its macros) by opening it with an OpenForm action in a macro, or from the database window. In this example, the Reports button on the Customers Switchboard opens the dialog box, via the Reports macro in the Customer Switchboard Macros group (Figure 21.4 above). The action and action arguments for that macro are:

```
OpenForm
    Form Name:   Customer Report Dialog
    View:   Form
    Data Mode:   Edit
    Window Mode:   Normal
```

The Easy Way to Query Records for a Report

I should mention here that dialog boxes are not the only way to request data for querying reports before you print them. If you always want a particular report to prompt for criteria before you print that report, you can create a parameter query (see Chapter 8) that asks for values. Then base the report on that parameter query.

If you've already created a report, and want to base it on a parameter query, go ahead and create and save the parameter query. Then open the report in design view, choose Edit ➤ Select Report, open the Properties sheet, and change the Record Source property to the name of your parameter query.

Creating a Dialog Box That Pauses a Macro

Normally when a macro opens a dialog box (or any other type of object), the macro keeps running and responds to events on the form. In some situations, you might want the macro to stop running while the dialog box is open—for example, when you want the macro to make decisions based on the user's entries in the dialog box.

TIP

If you're a programmer, it might help to think of controls in a dialog box as variables. But remember, those controls are only available while the form is open. And, once the macro opens some other window, you need to use identifiers to refer to controls on the dialog box.

If you do want the macro to stop executing while the dialog box is open, use the OpenForm action in the macro, as usual, to open the dialog box. However, set the Window Mode action argument to *Dialog*, rather than *Normal*, as in the example below. Commands beneath the OpenForm action are not executed until the dialog box is closed.

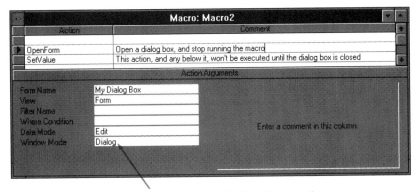

Mode setting for the OpenForm action

Northwind Dialog Box Examples

If you want to explore some existing dialog box examples, open the **Northwind** database, and then open the Main Switchboard form. Click the Print Reports button to get to the **Print Reports** dialog box.

To explore the underlying design of the dialog box, open the Northwind *Print Reports Dialog* form, in design view, from the database window. Or, to explore the macros, open the *Print Reports* macro, in design view, from the database window.

There are several other switchboards and dialog box examples in Northwind as well. In the database window, take a look at forms that have the words *Switchboard* and *Dialog* in them to see more examples.

Creating Custom Tool Bars

You can create your own tool bars using a pop-up form that contains only command buttons. Set the Modal property for the form to *No*, and the Pop-Up property to *Yes*. That way, your tool bar will always be in view, even as you switch among windows on your screen.

Here's an example where the first button opens the database window, and the next three buttons open the Windows Calculator, Character Map, and Calendar applets.

Figure 21.8 shows the design screen for the Tools form, with the Properties sheet for the form open. Notice the Pop-Up and Modal property settings.

I created each button in the form with the Command Button tool in the toolbox. Then I assigned a separate macro to each command button's On Push property. For example, the On Push property for the File Cabinet button is set to *Tools.File Cabinet*.

In case you're wondering where I got the pictures for the buttons, I got the *File Cabinet* icon from **Visual Basic**'s icon collection. The next three icons come straight from the Accessories window in the **Windows Program Manager**. The "exit door" icon comes from *progman.exe*, via the **Windows 3.1 Object Packager** application. To convert each icon to a

FIGURE 21.8

The custom tool bar, and the Tools macro, displayed in design view

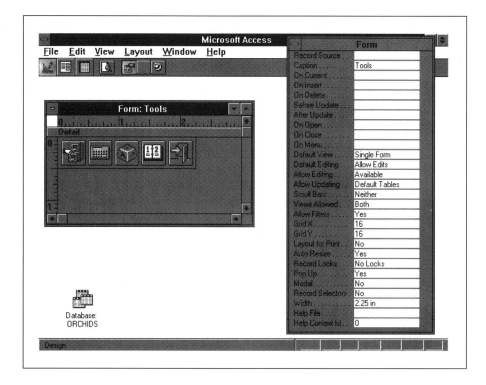

bitmap file, I first displayed the icon on the screen, then used Alt+Print-Screen to capture that screen to the Clipboard. Then I pasted that captured screen image into **PaintBrush**, where I colored the background to a light gray using the Paint Roller tool. Then I used the Pick tool and Edit ➤ Copy To in Paintbrush to copy each icon to a separate bitmap file. After creating the small bitmap files, I attached them to the command buttons in the form using the Picture property, as discussed in Chapter 10.

TIP

You can purchase collections of icons from most computer dealers, and create your own icons with Paintbrush. There are also programs that are specifically designed for creating icons.

Figure 21.9 shows the macro group for the custom Tools form. Each macro in that group is attached to the On Push property of one of the buttons in the customer tool bar. The actions and action arguments in the *Tools* macro are listed in Table 21.6.

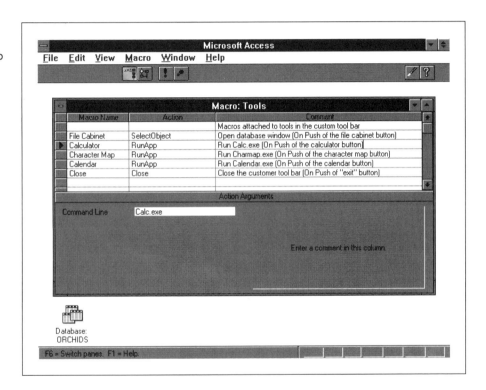

You can open a custom tool bar from the database window just as you would any other form—by double-clicking its name in the database window, or by executing an OpenForm action (with the Window Mode action argument set to *Normal*) in a macro.

TABLE 21.6: Actions and arguments in the Tools macro. Each macro is attached to the On Push property of a command button in the custom tool bar form.

MACRO NAME	ACTION	ACTION ARGUMENT	SET TO
File Cabinet	**SelectObject**	Object Type	Table
		In Database Window	Yes
Calculator	**RunApp**	Command Line	Calc.exe
Character Map	**RunApp**	Command Line	Charmap.exe
Calendar	**RunApp**	Command Line	Calendar.exe
Close	**Close**	Object Type	Form
		Object Name	Tools

Creating Custom Menus

You can spruce up an application by creating custom menus that replace the standard Access menus. The menu bar you create will be attached to a form, and will only be visible when that form is open in form view. Once open, the menu replaces the standard Access menus, and acts like the menus in any other Windows application.

For instance the custom menu bar below contains three menus, named File, View, and Help. Currently, the Help drop-down menu is open.

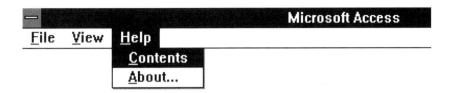

Creating the menus is a three-step process:

1. Create a macro group for each drop-down menu. The name you give to each macro will be the command that appears in the drop-down menu. If you want an underlined letter in the menu command, precede the underlined letter with an ampersand (**&**).

2. Create a macro that defines each menu across the menu bar. Use the AddMenu action to define each drop-down menu name.

3. Attach the menu bar macro to the On Menu property of the form that you want to display the menu.

The macro groups for the File, View, and Help drop-down menus are shown in Figure 21.10. The Macro Name column in each macro group defines the commands that will appear in each drop-down menu. Each macro also includes the actions that will be performed when the user chooses the command from the custom menu.

Next, you need to create the macro that defines the menu bar. This macro can only contain AddMenu actions. For each drop-down menu in the menu bar, create an AddMenu action that defines:

- The Menu Name as it is to appear in the menu bar (e.g., *&Help* in the currently selected action below).

- The Menu Macro Name, which is the name of the macro group you created earlier to define the menu commands (e.g., *Help Menu* in the example below).

- The Status Bar Text that's to appear in the status bar when the menu name is selected in the menu bar (e.g., *Help Options* in the example below).

FIGURE 21.10

Three macro groups,
named File Menu,
View Menu, and Help
Menu. Each contains
macros that appear as
commands on a
drop-down menu.

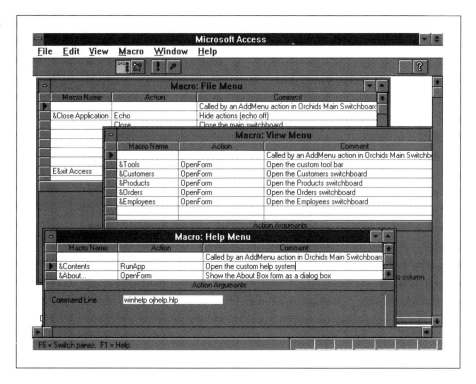

In the example below, I've created a macro, named *Main Menu*, with three
AddMenu actions. Each of those AddMenu actions adds one of the
macro groups described earlier—File Menu, View Menu, and Help Menu
(you can see the action arguments for the last AddMenu action in the figure).

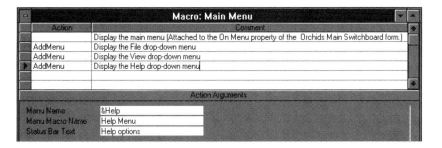

Finally, after creating, closing, and saving all the macros, you need to attach the macro that contains the AddMenu actions to the On Menu property of the form that you want to display the menu. That is, open the form in design view, choose Edit ➤ Select Form, then open the Properties sheet. Below, you can see where I've assigned the macro name *Main Menu* to the On Menu property of the *Orchids Main Switchboard* form.

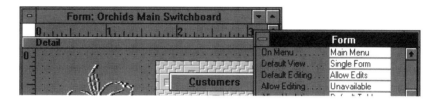

Custom Menu Examples

The **Personal Information Manager** database that came with your Access package presents a great example of a custom menu. Use File ➤ Open Database to open *pim.mdb*, and log in as *John Doe* with the password **John**. To view the underlying macros, press F11 to get to the database window, and click the Macros object tool. The macros that contain menu commands all have the word *Menu* in their names (e.g., *FileMenu*, *HelpMenu*.) The macro that contains the AddMenu commands for the first menu you see is named *DailyMenu*.

Creating Custom Help Screens

If you want to create custom help screens for your application, you'll need to get a copy of the **Windows Help Compiler** (available from Microsoft). You'll also need a word processor that supports rich text format (RTF), such as **Microsoft Word for Windows** version 2.

Once you've created the custom help file, there are several ways that you can make it accessible to the user of your application:

- In form design, use the Help File property in the Form Properties sheet to identify the name of your custom help file. And, use the Help Context ID property to identify the subject within the custom help file that you want to access from the form.

- Select individual controls within the form, then use the Help Context Id property to identify the help topic that's appropriate for that particular control.

- To open your custom help screen from a macro, use the RunApp action, with the Command Line argument set to *winhelp* followed by the name of your custom help file, e.g. *winhelp myapp.hlp*.

Creating AutoExecute Macros

You can create a macro that's executed as soon as a user opens your database. That macro can then hide the tool bar, open a particular form, request login information, ... whatever. All you need to do is create the macro and save it with the name *AutoExec*.

Figure 21.11 shows a sample *AutoExec* macro for the Orchids database. Here's what the actions in the macro do:

- The first Echo action has its Echo On argument set to *No* to hide the screen activity in the macro actions that follow.

- The SendKeys action hides the tool bar (see below).

- The OpenForm action opens the Orchids Main Switchboard form. (As you may recall, that form automatically hides the database window, so there's no need to do that within the *AutoExec* macro in this example.)

• The last Echo action turns screen activity back on (its Echo On argument is set to *Yes*).

If you want to start your application without the *AutoExec* macro, hold down the Shift key while using File ➤ Open Database to open the database.

Hiding the Toolbar

There are two techniques that you can use to have a macro hide the toolbar. The first is to use a Sendkeys action with the following arguments, as shown in Figure 21.11.

```
Sendkeys
    Keystrokes: %vo{tab 3}No{Enter}
    Wait:    Yes
```

FIGURE 21.11

A sample AutoExec macro to hide the tool bar and open a form as soon as the database is opened

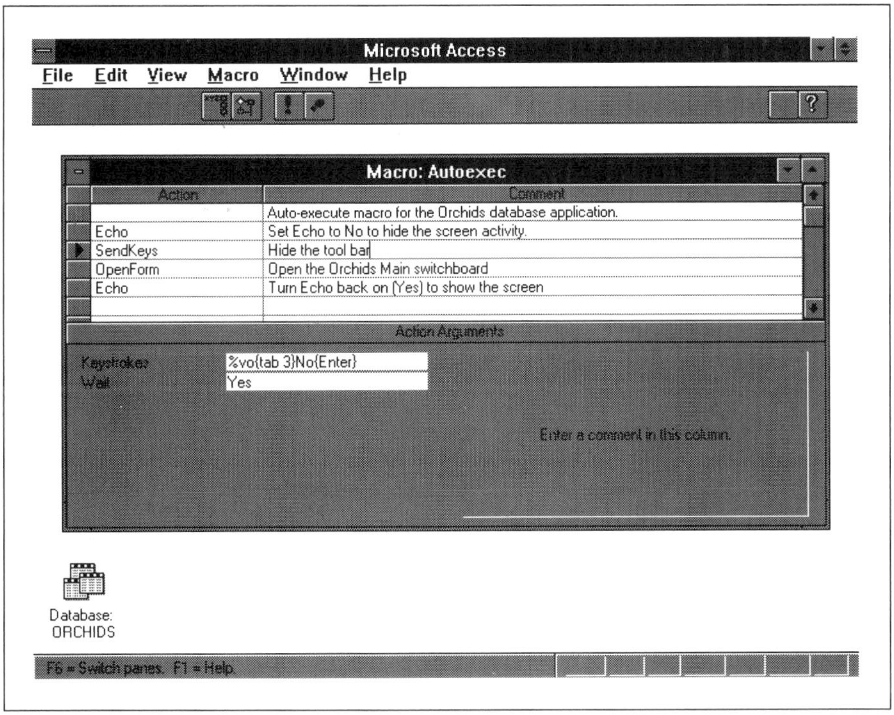

The %vo presses Alt+V to open the View menu and choose *Options*. The {tab 3} tabs down to the *Show Tool Bar* option in the Items menu, and changes its setting to *No*. Then {Enter} chooses OK to close the dialog box.

NOTE Search the help system for *Sendkeys* (one word) for more information on how to define keystrokes in a SendKeys action argument.

To redisplay the tool bar, create a macro that includes this action:

```
Sendkeys
    Keystrokes: %vo{tab 3}Yes{Enter}
    Wait:    Yes
```

The *Exit* macro in the Orchids Main Switchboard macros group (Figure 21.2 earlier in this chapter) includes this action.

NOTE The *OrdEntry* and *Pim* databases that came with your Access package uses an Access Basic module, named *HideToolbar( )*, to hide the tool bar.

Using Shortcut Keys to Run Macros

You can also simplify the use of your application by creating shortcut keys for common tasks. For instance, you might want to create a macro that you can run by pressing Ctrl+P, to print the current record on a form. Or you might want to create a Shift+Ctrl+X macro that closes the current form.

To create shortcut keys, you first need to tell Access the name of the macro that will contain the shortcut key definitions. To do so:

1. Starting at the database window, choose View ➤ Options.

2. Choose the Keyboard category.

3. Check the Key Assignment Macro setting, as shown below. By default, the name of the macro is *Autokeys*, but you can provide a different name if you wish.

4. Choose OK.

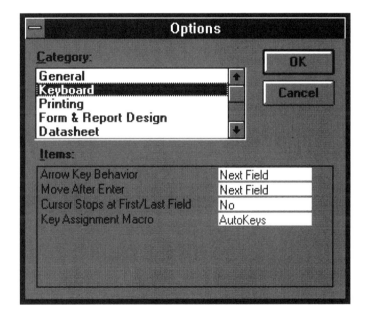

Next, create a macro group where the name of each macro is the shortcut key that you want to run the macro. To define combination keystrokes, use the SendKeys symbols for Ctrl, **+** for Shift, and **%** for Alt. For example, use **^p** for Ctrl+p, and **+^X** for Shift+Ctrl+X. Enclose function key names in curly braces—for instance, **+{F11}** for Shift+F11. For more information, search the help system for *Sendkeys*.

Be aware that if you assign an existing shortcut key to a macro, the macro shortcut key will override the normal role played by that key. To prevent confusion, avoid using

- Alt+*key* combinations—These are used throughout Windows for menus and dialog boxes.

- F11—This is your shortcut to the database window.

- Ctrl+C, Ctrl+X, and Ctrl+V—These are used for cut-and-paste.

Figure 21.12 shows an example of a macro, named *Autokeys*, that contains two macros—one named ^{p} (Ctrl+P) to print the current record on a form, and another named $+^X$ (Shift+Ctrl+X) to close the current form. Table 21.7 lists the actions and arguments in each of the macros.

FIGURE 21.12

An Autokeys macro that defines two shortcut keys: ^p (Ctrl+P) and +^x (Shift+Ctrl+X)

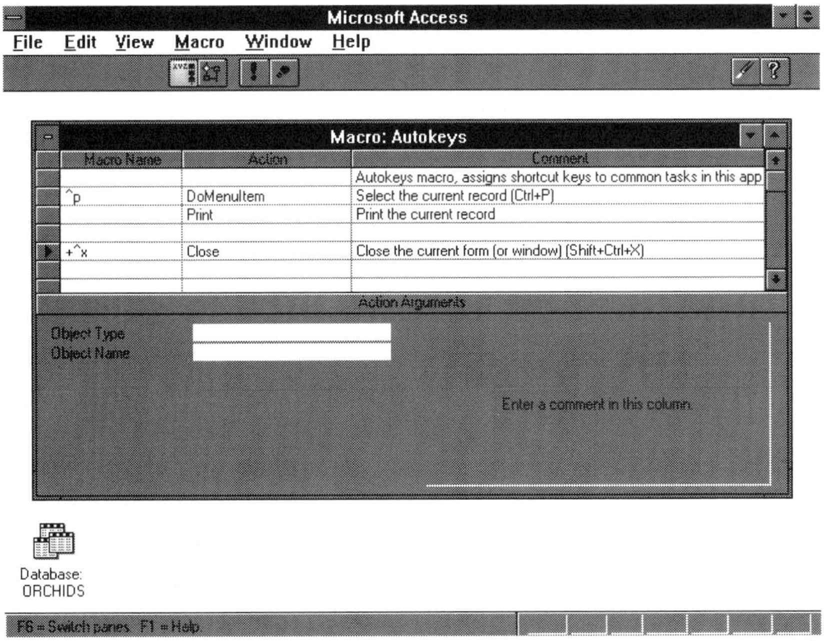

TABLE 21.7: Actions and action arguments for macros in the Autokeys macro group

MACRO NAME	ACTION	ACTION ARGUMENT	SET TO
^x	**DoMenuItem**	Menu Bar	Form
		Menu Name	Edit
		Command	Select Record
+^x	**Close**		

Be sure to save the macro group with whatever name you specified in the Macro Key Assignment option earlier (*Autokeys* in this example). Access activates the keys as soon as you save the macro, so you can test the keys immediately. Also, each time you open the database in the future, Access will automatically read the *Key Assignment* macro, so your shortcut keys will be available as soon as you start using the database.

Summary

In this chapter we've looked at many ways to simplify and spruce up an application with custom switchboards, dialog boxes, menus, help screens, autoexec macros, and more. Chances are, you'll be able to create a complete, easy-to-use application using techniques we've described in this chapter. But for those times when you need more precise control over how your application behaves, you do have the option of using **Access Basic**, which is the topic of our next chapter.

CHAPTER

22

Introduction to Access Basic

fast TRACK

**To create an Access Basic module in your
own database**   **896**

> open your database and click the Module object button. Then
> click the New button.

To close and save a module   **897**

> choose File ➤ Close, as usual, and provide a name when
> prompted.

**To copy an existing procedure into your
own database**   **898**

> open the database that contains the procedure you want to
> copy, then open the module and select the procedure. Choose
> Edit ➤ Copy. Then open the database and procedure that you
> want to copy to, and choose Edit ➤ Paste.

Before you can use a procedure   **899**

> you need to compile its module, by choosing Run ➤ Compile
> All from the menu bar in the procedure window.

**To use a procedure that's been defined
as a function**   **899**

> use the function in expressions, just as you would use a built-
> in Access function.

I N THIS chapter, we'll take a look at the last of the object types that are available in the database window: the *modules.* As you'll learn, you use modules to create custom procedures written in Access Basic.

Before you begin this chapter, it's important to understand that, for the most part, the modules are entirely optional. Chances are, you'll be able to use Access, and even create sophisticated applications, without ever creating or using Access modules. Nonetheless, if you're an experienced programmer and want to try your hand at writing Access Basic routines, the module object is the place to do it.

What Is Access Basic?

Access Basic is a programming language, patterned after other BASIC languages that Microsoft offers, such as WordBasic and Visual Basic. However, Access Basic is specifically designed for use within Microsoft Access. In fact, you need a thorough understanding of all the other objects that Access offers—tables, queries, forms, reports, and macros—before you can use Access Basic effectively.

Why Use Access Basic?

As you've seen in previous chapters, you can create sophisticated applications with automatic updating, switchboards, custom menus, and so forth using update queries, forms, and macros. So, chances are, you won't even need to use Access Basic to build a database application.

Nonetheless, if you're a seasoned programmer, you might want to build more advanced capabilities into your application. In particular, you might want to create your own user-defined functions, to add to the collection of functions that are already included in Access.

How Access Code Is Organized

All Access Basic code (i.e., the Basic commands and routines that you write) is organized into procedures. There are two types of procedures that you can create:

Functions: Procedures that can accept values and return values, and can be used in Access expressions just like the built-in functions.

Subs: Procedures that perform some action when executed, but don't return any values. You cannot use subs in an Access expression.

You can organize your Access Basic procedures into separate groups, called *modules*. You might want to put all the procedures for a single application into one module. Or, you can divide procedures into separate modules based on the types of jobs the procedures do. For instance, you might group general-purpose procedures into a module named *Utilities*, and group procedures that handle user log-in into a module named *Login*.

Viewing an Existing Module

A good starting point for getting a feel for how procedures are organized into modules is to open up an existing module and go exploring. For example, to explore the procedures in the Northwind database:

1. Starting at the database window, choose File ➤ Open Database, and choose *nwind.mdb* as the database to open.

2. In the database window, click the Module object button to view the names of existing modules. The Introduction To Programming module name should appear in the list.

3. Click the Design button.

You'll be taken to the module window, as shown in Figure 22.1. The window shows one procedure at a time. Initially, this will be the "declarations" portion of the module, which defines certain options about how

FIGURE 22.1

The module window, showing the declarations portion of the module named Introduction To Programming in the Northwind database

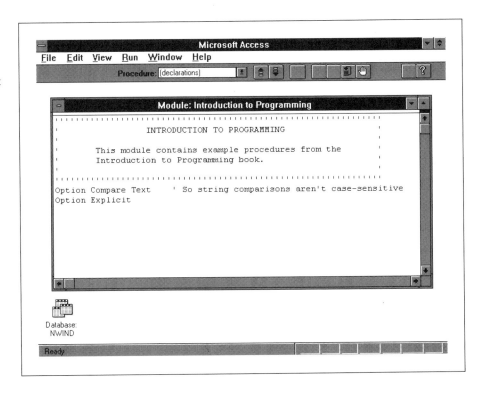

data is defined in the module. For example, the statement Option Compare Text prevents case-sensitivity in text comparisons.

TIP You can get information about any command in an Access Basic module by moving the insertion point to that command and pressing F1.

Viewing a Procedure

You can use any of the following techniques to view a procedure within the current module:

- Choose a procedure name from the Procedure drop-down list in the tool bar (see below).

- Use the Next Procedure and Previous Procedure buttons to scroll up and down through procedures.

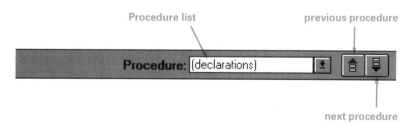

Procedure list   previous procedure

Procedure: [declarations]

next procedure

- Choose View ➤ Procedures, and choose a procedure from the View Procedures dialog box that appears.

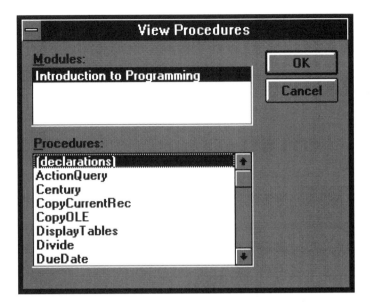

If you use one of those techniques to take a look at the NullToZero procedure in the Northwind database, you'll get an idea of how Access Basic code looks when written (see below).

```
Module: Introduction to Programming

Function NullToZero (anyValue As Variant) As Variant
' Accepts: a variant value
' Purpose: converts null values to zeros
' Returns: a zero or non-null value
' From: Chapter 10, User's Guide

    If IsNull(anyValue) Then
        NullToZero = 0
    Else
        NullToZero = anyValue
    End If

End Function
```

Here's what the commands in the procedure do:

- The first command, Function, defines the procedure as a function named NullToZero, which accepts one value, named *anyValue* within the procedure, as the Variant data type. (The Variant data type is used only in Access Basic and can accept data of any data type.)

- The lines that start with apostrophes (') are programmer comments.

- The If...Else...End If clause checks to see if the data passed to the procedure, in *anyValue,* is a null. If so, the procedure sets Null-ToZero to the number zero. If the data passed to the function was not a null, the function sets NullToZero to the value as it was passed.

- End Function marks the end of the NullToZero function.

Using a Procedure

Because the NullToZero procedure is defined as a function, it can be used anywhere within the Northwind database where you could use a built-in function. For example, if you open the Quarterly Orders Subform in Northwind in design view, open the properties sheet, and then select one of the calculated controls for a quarterly total, you'll see that the control uses the NullToZero function, as below:

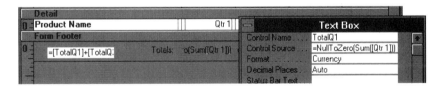

It's important to keep in mind that an Access Basic procedure is available only within the database in which it resides. You can create your own modules and procedures in your own database, and also copy procedures from some other database into your own database. Your first step, however, would be to create a module in your own database, as described next.

TIP   You can easily copy an entire Access Basic module from one database to another using the standard copy-and-paste or File ➤ Export techniques described in Chapter 19.

Creating a Module

To create a module in your own database:

1. Open your database, and click the Module object button in the database window.

2. Click the New button in the database window.

3. The module window appears, with the Option Compare declaration set to Database.

At this point, you can change the declaration to Text (to compare text without regard to upper/lowercase) or Binary (to compare text with regard to upper/lowercase). For the sake of example, let's suppose that you want all text comparisons in the current module to be made without regard to upper/lowercase. In that case, you'd just use standard text-editing techniques to change Database to Text, and perhaps change the comment next to the command as well, as shown below:

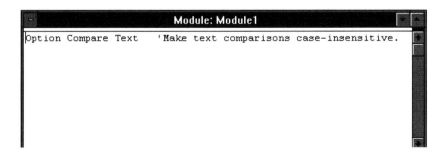

```
Option Compare Text    'Make text comparisons case-insensitive.
```

Now, let's assume that for starters, you just want to copy one or more procedures from the examples that came with your Access package into your module. In that case, you can just close the module you created, and give it a name of your choosing:

1. Choose File ➤ Close.

2. When prompted, choose Yes to save the module.

3. Enter an Access name (up to 64 characters) for the module. (I'll refer to this module as Orchid Jungle Procedures as we progress through the chapter.)

The name of your module appears in the database window, as below:

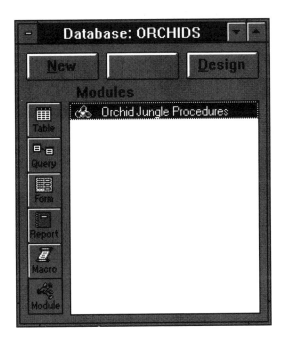

Copying a Procedure to Your Database

Now let's say you want to use NullToZero, or some other procedure, from one of the existing Access databases. You can simply copy the procedure from its source database into your own:

1. Use File ➤ Open Database to open the database that contains the procedure you want to copy (*nwind.mdb* in this example).

2. Click the Module object button in the database window, click the name of the module that contains the procedure you want to copy, then click the Design button.

3. Use the Procedures drop-down list, or View ➤ Procedures, to view the procedure you want to copy.

4. Select the entire procedure by dragging the mouse pointer through it, as below:

```
Module: Introduction to Programming
Function NullToZero (anyValue As Variant) As Variant
' Accepts: a variant value
' Purpose: converts null values to zeros
' Returns: a zero or non-null value
' From: Chapter 10, User's Guide

    If IsNull(anyValue) Then
        NullToZero = 0
    Else
        NullToZero = anyValue
    End If

End Function
```

5. Choose Edit ➤ Copy to copy the procedure to the Clipboard.

Now you can open your own database and copy the procedure into your module:

1. Choose File ➤ Close to close the module.
2. Choose File ➤ Open Database, and open the database that you want to copy the procedure to.
3. Click the Module object button, click the name of your module, then click the Design button.
4. Choose Edit ➤ Paste.

Access copies the procedure into the module and displays it on the screen.

Compiling a Module

Before you can use a procedure, it needs to be *compiled,* a task that copies the English-like Basic commands in a module to instructions that the computer can execute quickly. To compile a module:

- Choose Run ➤ Compile All (this option will be dimmed and unavailable if the module does not need to be compiled).

Now you can close the module and save your changes.

Using the Copied Procedure

Now you can use the NullToZero function to convert any null values to zeroes, so that those nulls won't propagate. For example, let's suppose your Orders table includes a Sales Tax Rate field and a Shipping Charge field. If either of these fields is blank, you want Access to treat them as zeroes.

In your order entry form and invoices reports, you can use NullToZero to convert the contents of those fields to zeroes, in case they're blank.

Here's an example using some calculated controls from the order entry form described in Chapter 11:

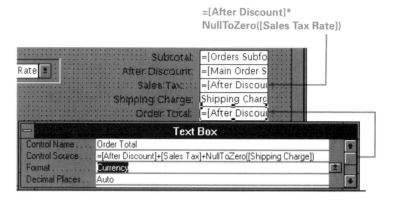

Creating Your Own Access Basic Procedures

Creating your own Access Basic procedures is a task that requires programming, a huge topic that extends well beyond the scope of this book. But do keep in mind that you rarely *need* to create your own procedures in Access, since you can create very sophisticated applications using macros and forms.

Nonetheless, if you do want to learn more about Access basic, you can refer to the *Introduction to Programming* and *Language Reference* manuals that came with your Access package. You can also use the Help screens within the module window to get context-sensitive help. If you're an experienced programmer and want a quick overview of the commands and functions available to you, search help for *access basic*. Choose Show Topics, then choose Programming Topics from the topics list.

Summary

Access Basic is a programming language that you can use to create custom procedures for your database. You use the module object to create the procedures. For more information on creating and using procedures, refer to the *Introduction to Programming* manual that came with your Access package.

APPENDIX

A

Installing Microsoft Access

BEFORE you can use Microsoft Access for Windows, it must be installed on your computer. You need only install Access once, not each time you plan to use it.

Hardware and Software Requirements

Before you install Access, make sure your hardware and software meet the following minimum requirements:

- An IBM or compatible PC with an 80386 or higher processor
- A hard disk with at least 10MB of free space
- At least 2MB of memory (RAM), preferably 4MB
- A mouse or similar pointing device
- An EGA or a VGA display (preferably VGA)
- DOS version 3.1 or later
- Windows version 3.0 or later

If you are installing the Version 1.1 upgrade to Access, be sure to refer to Appendix B for additional installation information.

Answering Prompts and Swapping Disks during Installation

During the installation, you may be asked to make some decisions about what to install. For a standard installation, just press ↵ to accept the default choices.

 **NOTE** The examples and lessons in this book assume that you have installed the entire Access program and chosen all the default answers.

The installation program will also tell you when to swap disks and exactly which disk to place in drive A (or drive B). Swap the disks as instructed, then press ↵ to proceed with the installation. If you accidentally put the wrong disk in the drive, the program will beep and ask you to insert the correct one.

You can cancel the installation program at any time simply by clicking the Cancel Setup button whenever it appears on your screen.

Installing Access for the First Time

The following steps will install Access in a single-user environment. To install Access on a network, refer to the section "Installing Access on a Network" later in this Appendix.

1. Start your computer and get to the Windows Program Manager.

2. Insert *Microsoft Access Disk 1: Setup* in drive A or B, and close the drive door (if any).

3. From the Program Manager menu bar, choose File ➤ Run.

4. Type **a:setup** if the setup disk is in drive A, or **b:setup** if the disk is in drive B, then press ⏎.

5. After a few moments you will see the initial Microsoft Access Setup screen, followed by the User Information screen. Type your full name in the Name box and press Tab. Type your company's name in the Company box and press ⏎. After verifying that the information you entered is correct, press ⏎ or choose Yes.

6. Setup asks you to specify the directory in which Access should be installed on your system. To accept the default, *c:\access*, press ⏎ or choose Continue. Setup checks for available disk space, existing copies of Access files, and required space for Access options.

NOTE   If there is not enough available space to install Access, Setup will display a message specifying the number of additional bytes needed to complete the installation.

7. Next, the Installation Options screen appears, as shown in Figure A.1. Choose option 1 for a complete installation.

8. Follow the instructions on the screen for replacing the disk in drive A or B. After replacing the disk, press ⏎ so the Setup program can continue copying files to your hard disk.

The main menu for
installing Access

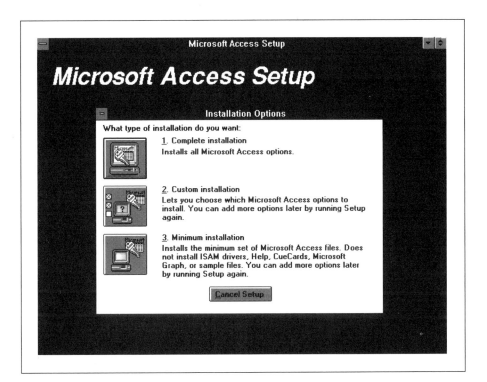

NOTE   You'll see a message about the ODBC disk, though you won't be prompted to insert it during a normal single-user installation. ODBC installation is optional and is explained in "Setting Up ODBC" later in this Appendix.

9. When copying is complete, you may see a prompt asking for permission to modify your *autoexec.bat* file so that it loads the DOS SHARE program. Press ↵ or choose Modify to change *autoexec.bat* and save the original as *autoexec.bak*.

10. When the installation is complete, you'll see a screen indicating that Setup is done. If you allowed Setup to change your

autoexec.bat file, remove any floppy disks from the drives and reboot by clicking the Reboot button or by pressing Ctrl+Alt+Del.

See Chapter 2 of this book for complete information on starting Access.

Performing a Custom Installation

You can use the custom installation to choose specific Access options to install, which can help conserve disk space. You can use the Custom Installation option at any time, to add any options that you may have previously decided not to install. To perform a custom installation:

1. Follow steps 1–6 listed in the previous section.

2. At the Installation Options dialog box, shown previously in Figure A.1, choose option 2, Custom Installation.

NOTE   Selecting option 3, Minimum Installation, installs the minimum set of Access files.

3. The Microsoft Access Setup Options dialog box appears, as shown in Figure A.2. Click the check box next to the options you want to install.

4. Optionally, click the Select button next to the dBASE, Paradox, Btrieve Drivers option if you want to install ISAM drivers.

Here is a brief description of each Access option:

Microsoft Access   Installs the Access program (required, the first time you install Access).

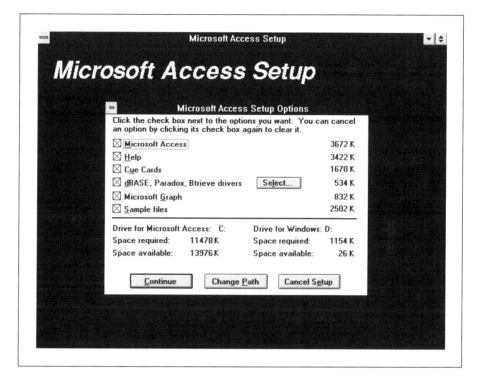

Help   Lets you access an online information system. It provides help on everything from creating databases, forms, tables, and queries to explanations of error messages.

Cue Cards   Installs the Cue Cards, Access's online coach, which helps you create a database as you learn.

dBASE, Paradox, Btrieve drivers   Lets you import and export existing data to and from other database applications, such as FoxPro, dBASE, and Paradox.

Microsoft Graph   Installs the Microsoft Graph application, for graphic data from your database on business charts.

Sample files   Installs sample files that come with Access, including the Personal Information Manager (*pim.mdb*) and Order

Entry (*ordentry.mdb*). You can use them as a learning tool or for creating your own applications.

After you choose options, you'll see instructions for completing the installation, like the instructions presented during the single-user installation.

Installing Access on a Network

You use a special setup routine to install Access on a local area network (LAN). The network operating systems that Access currently supports are

- Novell NetWare
- Microsoft LAN Manager
- Artisoft LANtastic
- Banyan VINES

You can install Access in any one of the following network configurations:

- Full copy of Access on each workstation from floppy disks. This configuration requires 5MB to 15MB of hard-disk space on each workstation.
- Full copy of Access on each workstation from the shared directory on the server. This configuration requires 5MB to 15MB of hard-disk space on each workstation and 15MB on the server.
- Copy only the individual configuration files of Access on each workstation and use the shared directory on the server. This configuration requires 1MB of hard-disk space on each workstation and 15MB on the server.

Choosing a Network Configuration

There are pros and cons for each configuration; however, the main issues are available disk space, network speed, and ease of upgrading.

Perform the full workstation installation from floppy disks if you have a few users with large hard disks. Installing a few users from floppies is not time-consuming, and you won't need 15MB on the file server.

If you have many users with large hard disks or your network is relatively slow, perform the full workstation installation from the server. Access will run from each user's hard disk, avoiding heavy network traffic and the hassle of installing from floppies.

If you have many users with small hard disks or your network is fast, perform the shared copy on the file server installation. Only the necessary configuration files will be copied to each user's workstation, and upgrading Access is easier because you only need to upgrade the copy on the file server.

Installing Access in a Shared Directory

If you choose one of the network-based configuration options, you must copy all the files on the Access disks to a shared directory on the file server. To install Access in a shared directory:

1. Start your computer and get to the Windows Program Manager.

2. Insert *Disk 1: Setup* in drive A or B.

3. From the Program Manager menu bar, choose File ➤ Run.

4. Type **a:\setup /a** or **b:\setup /a** and press ↵.

Once the Setup program is running, you need to locate the files on the server, shown in Figure A.3. Specifically, you must choose the location for the program files, Microsoft Graph, and the databases you create.

CAUTION

Before you can install the files, you must have read/write permissions to the network drive.

Figure A.4 is an example of the tree structure created during installation on drive W.

FIGURE A.3

The Specify Directories dialog box, for choosing the location of the files on the server

Microsoft Access Server Setup

Microsoft Access Setup

Specify Directories

If they don't already exist, Setup will create the directories shown below and install files in them. If you want to install the files in a different directory, type the drive and directory you want.

Microsoft Access **P**rogram Files
Install in: `W:\ACCESS`

Microsoft Graph
Install in: `W:\MSAPPS\MSGRAPH`

Note: If you already have Microsoft Graph installed, type the drive and directory where it's currently located.

System **D**atabase
Install in: `W:\MDB`

Note: Databases you create will also be stored in this directory. Users must have read/write access to this directory.

[**C**ontinue]   [Cancel S**e**tup]

Example of a network
tree structure

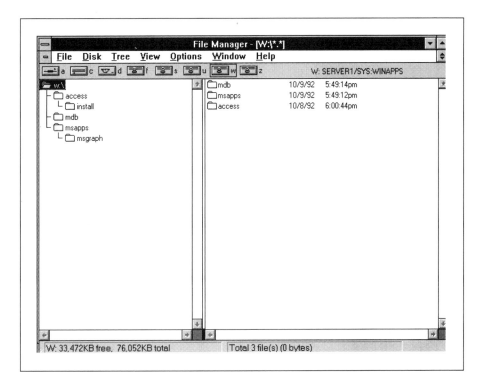

Network Rights

To run Access and use databases, each user must have the appropriate access rights to the following directories. The actual rights required may vary across network operating systems. The minimum required rights are

\ACCESS   Read. The executable files are located in this directory. Users don't need rights to alter these files.

TIP

Because the sample databases are also installed in this directory, users who want to change data or objects in the sample databases must copy the databases to a personal directory.

\MDB Full rights. Newly created databases should be placed in this directory for access by all users. The *system.mda* file (the control file for all user and security accounts) is also located in this directory.

\MSAPPS Read. Users do not need to alter the Microsoft Graph utility or its Help files that are installed in this directory.

CAUTION

Back up the *system.mda* file each time you make a security-related change. Because it is the master security file, you will not be able to run Access if the file is lost or damaged.

On most networks, rights "flow down" through subdirectories. For example, if you are assigned Read rights for *w:\access,* the Read rights also apply to the *w:\access\install* subdirectory.

Installing Access on a Workstation

After you have installed the full copy of Access on the server, you are ready to install Access on a workstation. Follow these steps from the workstation:

1. Start your workstation and get to the Windows Program Manager.

2. From the Program Manager menu bar, choose File ➤ Run.

3. Type the path to the INSTALL directory, for example, **w:access\install** followed by **\setup.exe /n**, as in the example below:

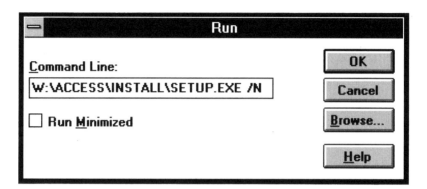

 Use the Browse button to navigate the network drive files, and select the file with the mouse.

4. Next, decide between a full hard-disk installation and a network installation, as shown below:

5. Choose Yes for a full hard-disk installation or No for a network installation.

6. Press ↵ to install the Access files for either type of installation in the *c:\access* directory on your hard drive, as shown below:

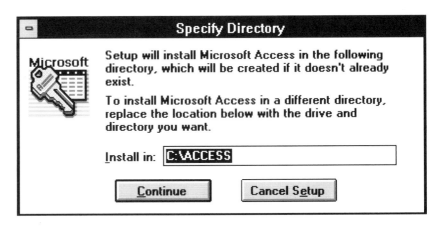

7. Next, if you don't want to join an existing workgroup in order to use existing multiuser databases, choose the Single User option. If you want to join an existing workgroup, you must specify the path to the *system.mda* file, as shown below:

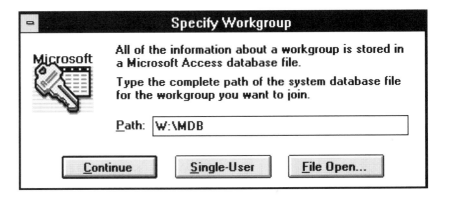

There are two ways to specify the path to the *system.mda* file:

- Enter the path directly, for example, *w:\mdb*.
- Use the File ➤ Open button to browse through the network, and select the file *w:\mdb\system.mda*.

8. For the next few minutes, the Setup program will copy all the Access files to the directory you specified. When copying is complete, you'll see a screen asking for permission to install *share.exe* in your *autoexec.bat* file. Press ↵ or choose Modify to change *autoexec.bat* and save the original as *autoexec.bak*.

Finally, you'll see a message indicating Microsoft Access Setup is complete. See Chapter 20 of this book for complete information on getting started with Access on a network.

Setting Up ODBC

If you have installed Microsoft's SQL Server, and you want to connect to SQL database servers from Access, you can install the Open Database Connectivity interface (ODBC) application. ODBC is optional and is shipped on its own disk in the Access package.

Installing ODBC

To install the ODBC drivers on your workstation:

1. Insert the ODBC disk in drive A.
2. From the Program Manager menu bar, choose File ➤ Run.
3. Type a:**setup.**
4. Press ↵.

INSTALLING MICROSOFT ACCESS

As shown in the illustration below, the Setup program lets you

* Select the ODBC drivers for the databases you need access to.
* Install the ODBC Administration utility, which lets you configure drivers to work with your particular databases. This is the utility that you'll use to configure database access once the installation program is completed.

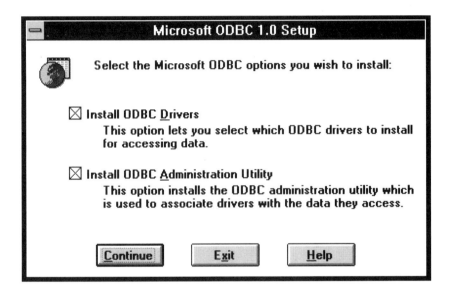

Because you need to install and configure database drivers, you should

1. Leave both boxes checked.
2. Choose Continue.

The next screen lets you choose where to install the Administration program and Help file. The necessary drivers and configuration files will automatically be copied to your *windows* and *windows\system* directories, so you don't need to worry about choosing their locations.

1. Enter the path for the Administration program. The default is *c:\odbc*.

2. If the directory does not exist, the program will offer to create it for you.

3. Choose Continue.

Choosing a Database

At this point in the installation, you must choose the database you wish to connect to. In version 1.0 of Access, your only choice is Microsoft SQL Server, as seen in the illustration below:

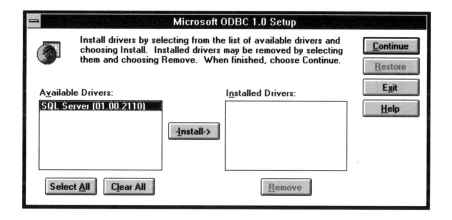

To install the SQL Server ODBC drivers:

1. Select SQL Server from the Available Drivers field.

2. Click Install.

3. Choose Continue.

Configuring a Database Driver

Now that you have the SQL Server drivers on your system, you can define which database servers on the network you want to connect to. To set up a connection to a SQL Server:

1. Select SQL Server from Installed Drivers.

2. Click Add New Name.

3. Enter a name for the SQL Server (for example, the finance department may have a database server called FINANCE). If you have previously entered any names, you can also choose one from the list.

4. Click Add.

NOTE   The next steps may require information from the administrator of the SQL Server database system.

ODBC SQL Server Setup

Enter the data source name, network address, and description, then choose OK. Contact the SQL/Server administrator if you have questions regarding the network address or library.

Data Source **N**ame: `Finance`

Description: `SQL Server on server Finance`

Network **A**ddress: `\\Finance\PIPE\SQL\QUERY`

Network **L**ibrary: `dbnmp3`

☐ **C**onvert OEM to ANSI characters

Additionally, run the SQL/Server script INSTCAT.SQL (on the ODBC setup disks) to prepare the ODBC host environment.

[**OK**]   [**Cancel**]   [**H**elp]

---

5. You may use the Description field to add a more helpful description of the database, as shown above.

6. The Network Address should be provided to you by the SQL Server administrator.

7. The file name in the Network Library should be *dbnmp3*.

8. If neither you nor the database server are using ANSI-standard character sets (a rare occurrence), you should check the Convert OEM To ANSI Characters box.

9. Choose OK.

NOTE Your SQL Server administrator, or another user with full privileges on that server, should execute the *instcat.sql* script from the ODBC disk to prepare the SQL Server for use with Access.

Completing the Setup

To complete the installation of ODBC:

1. Choose Continue.

TIP The installation program creates a Microsoft ODBC group in Program Manager and places the Microsoft ODBC Administrator icon in it. You may want to move this icon to your Microsoft Access group and delete the empty ODBC group.

2. Exit Windows.

3. Restart Windows.

You're now ready to use Access with Microsoft SQL Server.

Standardizing ODBC for Multiple Users

The ODBC Setup program gives an administrator a powerful routine to standardize database driver configurations across multiple users. You can set up and test one workstation and then use its configuration for all your other users.

Creating the Automatic Setup Disk or Directory

To create the "master" configuration:

1. Follow all the steps outlined in the section "Setting Up ODBC" for one workstation.

2. Add and configure all the database drivers that you need.

3. If you want to set up subsequent workstations from the network, create an ODBC directory on the file server and copy all the files from the ODBC disk to that directory.

4. Copy the *odbc.ini* and *odbcinst.ini* files from the workstation's *windows* directory to the file server directory (or to the ODBC disk, if you're not using a network directory).

Setting Up ODBC Automatically

From the next workstation you want to set up, follow these steps:

1. Insert the disk in drive A, or connect to the ODBC directory on the file server.

2. From Program Manager, choose File ➤ Run.

3. Type **a:setup/auto** (or **f:setup /auto**, where *f* is the letter of the network drive).

4. Press ↵.

This will automatically set up the workstation's ODBC drivers exactly as they are on the first. For more information on ODBC, see Chapter 20.

What's New and Different in Access 1.1

VERSION 1.1 of Access offers some new features that users have been requesting, as well as fixes to some early bugs that occurred in multiuser environments. Here, in a nutshell, is what's new and improved, and discussed in more detail in this appendix:

- ODBC offers Oracle and SQL Connectivity.

- You can import and attach FoxPro 2.5 files.

- The maximum size of a database increased from 128 megabytes to 1 gigabyte.

- Nordic sort orders have been corrected.

- There is a new Microsoft Word for Windows mail-merge export.

- There is a Microsoft Excel Database Range Import/Export feature.

- You can access dBASE and FoxPro data on a CD-ROM.

- Btrieve support has improved—it no longer requires INDEX.DDF.

Hardware Requirements for 1.1

The hardware requirements for installing Version 1.1 of Access are the same as those indicated on page 904, except that you need at least *four* megabytes of memory, and *six* is recommended.

Installing the 1.1 Upgrade

Installing the 1.1 upgrade is a simple procedure. Put the Access 1.1 Setup Disk (Disk 1) in drive A or B. Start Windows, and choose File ➤ Run from the Program Manager menus. Type **a:setup** or **b:setup** and choose OK. Then follow the instructions that appear on the screen.

Files that contained 100 in their file names in Version 1.1 will now have 110 in their file names. For instance, msabc100.dll becomes msabc110.dll. Version 1.0 files that are no longer used will be deleted.

Installing ODBC 1.1 to Access SQL Databases

You can use the 1.1 ODBC driver to access SQL database servers, such as Microsoft SQL Server Version 1.1 or later, as well as Oracle Server. For specific instructions, see "Setting Up Microsoft Access to Use SQL Databases" in Appendix D of the *User's Guide* that came with the Access package.

Converting 1.0 Access Databases to 1.1 Format

Access 1.1 uses a new database format that increases the maximum size of a database from the original 128 megabytes to one gigabyte. Access 1.1 can read and write to Access databases created in either 1.0 or 1.1 format. However, if you think an existing 1.0 database will exceed 128 megabytes, you should convert it to the new 1.1 format. All you need to do is compact the existing database, choosing 1.1 as the new file type.

CAUTION   The compaction procedure creates an extra copy of the database on disk. Make sure you have enough disk space available before you start compacting.

To compact an existing database, start Access 1.1. If you have any databases open, close them. (On a network, make sure all users close the database.) Then choose File ➤ Compact Database, and the name of the database you want to convert, and choose OK. In the next dialog box to appear, choose make sure Access V1.1 is selected under List Files of Type:.

Then, enter a file name for the converted file, and choose OK. After testing the new copy of the database, you can delete the original copy, then rename the new copy if desired. For more information on compacting a database, see Chapter 18.

New and Improved Features

The rest of this appendix lists new, improved, and changed features of Access 1.1. As you'll see, most of these changes and improvements involve installation and configuration. Of course, you can skip any sections that aren't relevant to your system configuration.

Banyan Vines: Notes on Servers

Large Access operations often require many locks. Earlier versions of Banyan Vines limit the number of locks to anywhere from 100 to 500. Banyan Vines 5.5, however, allows at least 10,000 locks.

Btrieve Notes

When you install Access 1.1, it stores a file named BTRIEVE.TXT on your hard disk. If you want to access Btrieve data, you should print and read that file. It contains information on using Btrieve in a multiuser environment, using compressed Btrieve files, configuring Novell NetWare Loadable Modules (NLM), and more.

You'll need the Btrieve for Windows dynamic link library, named WBTRCALL.DLL, which is provided with Novell Btrieve for Windows, Novell NetWare SQL, and other products. That DLL, however, is not included with Access.

Access no longer requires the INDEX.DDF file to access Btrieve data.

CD-ROM: Reading and Writing dBASE/FoxPro Data

To attach to dBASE or FoxPro files on a CD-ROM, or any other read-only drive, add this line to the [dBASE ISAM] section of the MSAC-CESS.INI file:

```
INFPath=c:\access
```

The command tells Access where to store the .INF file when you open a dBASE or FoxPro file on a read-only drive. If you don't have a directory named Access on your C drive, replace *c:\access* with a valid read/write drive and directory path.

Excel Database Ranges: Import/Export

When importing or exporting Excel data using File ➤ Import and File ➤ Export, you'll be given the opportunity to specify the special range named *Database*. For additional information about this range, refer to your Excel documentation.

FoxPro 2.5: Reading and Writing Data

You can now import from, and attach to FoxPro 2.5 files, using the same general technique you'd use with dBASE files. See Chapter 19 in this book for more information about importing and attaching.

Nordic Sort Orders

The Nordic sort orders for Swedish/Finnish, Norwegian/Danish, and Icelandic languages have been changed in Version 1.1. To update to the new sort orders, first install Access 1.1 in its entirety. Open the database that's currently using a Nordic sort order, and choose a *New Database Sort Order* option from the General category. Then close the database, and compact it, as discussed in Chapter 18.

Novell NetWare: Notes on Servers

If you're attempting to use large Access databases on a Novell Netware server, you must set the number of locks on the server to MAX. Otherwise, the server may run out of LOCK connections, causing the server to crash.

Oracle: Reading and Writing Data

When you install Version 1.1 of ODBC, it installs a file named ORACLE.TXT to your Windows\System directory. If you want to use Access with ORACLE, you must read that file for configuration instructions. See also: "ODBC: More Help Files" below.

Paradox: Attaching to Shared Tables

To attach to a shared Paradox table on a network server, you must set the ParadoxNetPath option in the [Paradox ISAMs] section of MSAC-CESS.INI to the path of the Paradox.Net file (e.g., **ParadoxNet-Path=A:\WRKGRP**).

ODBC: More Help Files

If you install ODBC, you should read the appropriate help files for more information. After you've installed ODBC, the files will be on your Windows\System directory, named as follows:

FILE NAME	DESCRIPTION
ODBCINST.HLP	ODBC Control Panel help
DRVSSRVER.HLP	SQL Server driver help
DRVORACL.HLP	ORACLE driver help

Sybase Connectivity

ODBC now offers Sybase connectivity. For information on installing ODBC, see "Setting Up Microsoft Access to Use SQL Databases" in Appendix D and Chapter 4 of the *User's Guide* that came with your Access package.

Word for Windows Mail-Merge Files: Export Data

Version 1.1 of Access lets you export data to Microsoft Word for Windows mail-merge files without going through an intermediate file format. To use data from an Access table as the *data source* for a Word for Windows mail merge:

1. Start Access 1.1 and open the database that contains the table you want to export.

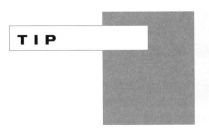

TIP

If you only want to export certain records from your Access table, first create and run a Make Table query. Then export the data from the resulting table. See "Creating a New Table from a Query" in Chapter 8 for more information.

2. Choose File ➤ Export.

3. Choose *Word for Windows Merge*, then OK.

4. Choose the table that contains the data that you want to export, then choose OK.

5. In the Export to File dialog box that appears next, choose the drive, directory, and a name for the exported file. Choose OK.

6. As necessary, choose formats for dates and times from the next dialog box. (If you need help with these options, press F1 or see page 788.) Choose OK.

Access creates the data source file and then returns you to the database window. The table's field names become the data source's header row, as discussed in your Word for Windows documentation. If necessary, Access also makes the following changes to exported field names:

• If the field name is more than 20 characters in length, Access truncates it at the twentieth character.

• Any spaces or illegal characters are converted to underlines.

• If the field name doesn't start with a letter, Access precedes the field name with *m_*.

These changes might cause two fields to have the same name.

Furthermore, it's important that the fields in the Word for Windows *main document* exactly match the field names in the exported data source file. It's recommended that you inspect the exported data source file, and make any changes, before merging it with your Word for Windows main document. Remember, the exported data source file might have a .txt extension, rather than the usual .doc extension that Word provides by default.

Using 1.1 to Create a 1.0 Database

Access version 1.1 is downwardly compatible with version 1.0. That is, version 1.1 of Access can read and write to Version 1.0 databases but not vice-versa. To create a new 1.0 database using Access 1.1, choose File ➤ New Database, as usual. Under the List Files of Type: option, choose *Access V1.0 (*.mdb)*. Then create your database normally.

Decompressing 1.1 Files without Setup

If you need to decompress any files from the 1.1 disks, without using Setup, use the Decomp.exe file that comes on the 1.1 Setup disk, using the syntax:

```
decomp [/A /F /Q] source [dest]
```

where *source* is the file(s) to be decompressed, and *[dest]* is the name of the drive or directory to decompress to (the current drive\directory if omitted). Optional switches are **/A** (appends the decompressed version of the source file to the specified destination file), **/F** (forces overwriting of the destination file), and **/Q** (calculates the size of the decompressed file without actually decompressing it).

GLOSSARY

THIS glossary contains common terms that you're likely to run up against when you work with Access. Here you'll find short definitions, along with references to specific pages or chapters where you can learn more about the topic.

Obviously, the definitions and this book offer *printed* information about Access. Keep in mind, though, that lots of *on-line* information about Access is just a few mouse clicks and menu selections away:

- The **Access Glossary** offers pop-up definitions of many terms. To view the on-line glossary, choose **Help ➤ Contents**, then click *Glossary* in the Help Table of Contents. Next, click the button that shows the first letter of the term you're interested in. For instance, if you want to find out what the term *select query* means, click the *S* button at the top of the Glossary screen. Then click the term to view its definition. You can click the mouse again or press any key to remove the definition from the screen.

  You can also click the *Glossary* button on any Access Help screen to open a window of terms. Scroll through the window that appears and click on the term you're interested in.

- The various on-line help facilities—the standard on-line help, the **"What Is…?"** help, and **Cue Cards**—provide more detailed information on just about any Access feature or action you can imagine. See pages 115–117 for details on using these handy tools.

Access Basic The programming language that you use to write custom procedures called modules. Access Basic resembles other BASIC languages that Microsoft offers. See Chapter 22.

Action The basic building block of a macro. An action is a task the macro performs, such as opening a table or sounding a beep. You can assign actions to a macro by dragging and dropping an object from the database window to the macro window's Action column. Or, you can click in the Action column and choose an action from the drop-down list. See pages 624–631.

Action Query A type of query that takes an action on your data. This category includes append, delete, make-table, and update queries. Delete and update queries change existing data; append and make-table queries move existing data. See pages 334–358; see also *Select Query*.

ANSI An acronym for "American National Standards Institute." The ANSI character set uses 8 bits to represent up to 256 characters that you can type on your keyboard. Microsoft Windows uses the ANSI character set. The ASCII character set consists of the first 128 ANSI characters. See also *ASCII* and *Special Characters*.

Append Query A query that copies all or some records from one table to the bottom of another table. Append queries help you add data from one table to another table that has a similar structure, without retyping. See pages 339–347.

 Apply Filter/Sort Button Click this button on the tool bar to apply the current filter. The filter displays a subset of records or sorts the records according to criteria you specify. See page 400–402.

Argument You use an argument to pass information to an Access macro or Access Basic procedure. An argument can be a constant, variable, or expression. You can also add arguments to the command line that starts Access from the Windows Program Manager or File Manager. See pages 627–629.

ASCII An acronym for "American Standard Code for Information Interchange." The ASCII character set uses 7 bits to represent the letters and symbols on a standard U.S. keyboard. The standard ASCII set of characters is the same as the first 128 characters in the ANSI character set. See also *ANSI* and *Special Characters*.

Attach (Table) You can attach tables from other database applications (Paradox, dBASE, FoxPro, Btrieve, and SQL) or from closed Access databases. The attached tables will appear in your open database window. After attaching tables, you can add, delete, and change their records, just as if you were using "native" Access tables. See pages 763–778.

Automatic Link A type of link in which Access updates the destination document automatically whenever the linked information in the source document changes. See pages 808, 812 and the glossary entry for *Manual Link*.

Bitmap A graphic image composed of pixels (dots) on the screen and stored as individual bits. You can scan in bitmap images, create them in painting programs such as Windows Paintbrush, or purchase them as "clip art" files. Bitmap image files often have the file extension *.BMP*. See pages 89, 168–175, and 814–816.

 Blank Form A form that has no preset formats. You can use the Blank Form button in the New Form dialog box to create a new form from scratch. Or, you can use the FormWizards button to set up attractive formats with just a few clicks of your mouse. Chapters 9, 10, and 11 explain how to design forms.

 Blank Report A report that has no preset formats. You can use the Blank Report button in the New Report dialog box to create a new report from scratch. Or, you can use the ReportWizards button to set up attractive report formats automatically. Chapter 12 explains how to design reports.

BMP The filename extension of a bitmap graphic file.

Bookmark A way to mark your place so that you can return to it later. You can use bookmarks in the online Help to return to a topic after you move somewhere else in Help. You can also use bookmarks in Access Basic to mark a record that you want to return to later.

Bound Control A control on a form or report that's tied to a field in the underlying table or query. In an employee update form, the text box that shows an employee's name is a bound control because it's tied to the Name field in the underlying Employees table. See page 380.

 Bound Object Frame A control on a form or report that displays OLE objects in the underlying table or query. A bound object frame is a type of *bound control*. See pages 464 and 806.

Calculated Control A control on a form or report that computes a value based on data in the table and displays the results. Access will refresh the value in a calculated control automatically, whenever you change values of fields used in the control. You could use a calculated control such as [Qty]*[Unit Price] to show the extended price of a product on an invoice. See pages 380 and 434–438.

Calculated Field A field in a query that computes a value based on data in the table. Access will refresh the value in a calculated field automatically, whenever you change values of fields used in the calculated field. You could, for example, define a query field with the expression [Qty]*[Unit Price] to calculate the extended price of an item. See pages 267–270.

Case-Sensitive In a case-sensitive search, text must match uppercase and lowercase letters exactly. A *case-insensitive* search, by contrast, matches any combination of uppercase and lowercase text. When you ask Access to find or replace text values in a table, you can search with case-sensitive matching on or off. See pages 155–158 and 207.

Cell The intersection of a row and column in a datasheet or grid. Each cell in the datasheet stores a single piece of data.

Character Any symbol, digit, letter, or punctuation mark that you can type on your keyboard or choose from the Windows Character Map. See pages 129–130; see also *ANSI* and *ASCII*.

 Check Box A control that shows whether you've selected or cleared an option. An × appears in the box when you've selected it. Check boxes on forms make it easy to assign a Yes or No value to Yes/No fields in a table.

Some Windows dialog boxes also use check boxes to let you turn an option on or off. See pages 438–441.

Clipboard A temporary storage area that Windows uses to hold text, graphics, and other data to help you share data between Windows applications. You can use options on the Edit menu to copy data to and paste data from the Clipboard. See pages 159–173.

Column The visual presentation of a field in a datasheet, query, or filter window. A relational database stores data in tables that are arranged into horizontal rows (records) and vertical columns (fields). See pages 6–7.

Combo Box A control that works like a combined text box and list box. Combo boxes on forms make it easier to enter values into fields, because you can either type in the value or select it from a drop-down list. Some Windows dialog boxes also use combo boxes to let you choose options. See pages 444–458.

Command Button A control that runs a macro or calls an Access Basic function. You simply click a command button on a form to start the macro or function. Command buttons work like the pushbuttons in many Windows dialog boxes and applications. See pages 464–467 and Chapter 14.

Command Prompt The characters (usually **C>** or **C:\>**) shown at the beginning of the MS-DOS command line to tell you that DOS is ready for your next command. To enter commands in MS-DOS, type the command name and press ↵ at the command prompt.

Comment Text that you add to a table or macro to describe your work. You can also use comments in Access Basic programs to explain how something works (precede the comment text with an apostrophe or the word **Rem**). Access Basic ignores comments. See pages 99, 624–627, and 895.

Comparison Operator An operator that you can use to compare two values or expressions. You can use comparison operators throughout Access. For instance, you can define a range of acceptable values for a field as **>=Date()**. This will disallow entries prior to today's date. See pages 203–208 and 721–722.

Condition Expression An expression that Access evaluates and compares to a specific value. If the expression is true, Access takes one set of actions; if it is false, Access carries out another set. For instance, you could use a condition expression in a macro to find out if the Zip Code field is empty. If it is empty, you could display an error message. If it isn't, you wouldn't display any message. See pages 633–634.

 Conditions Button Click this button to show or hide the Condition column in the Macro window. You can use this column to write condition expressions in a macro. See pages 633–634.

Constant A numeric or text value that doesn't change. Access provides five system-defined constants—Yes, No, On, Off, and Null. You can use constants to define default field values in forms or tables and to test conditions in macros. See pages 719–720.

Control Any object that displays data, takes an action, or shows a decoration on a form or report. The three main types of controls are *bound controls*, *unbound controls*, and *calculated controls*. You use the toolbox (shown on the back inside cover of this book) to create controls on a form or report. See Chapters 9, 10, and 12.

 **Control Menu** A menu of commands that restore, move, resize, minimize, maximize, or close a window or application. To open the Control menu, click the Control-menu box at the upper-left corner of the application or window that you want to work with. Then select the option you want.

Control-Menu Box The short horizontal line at the upper-left corner of an application or window. You can click the Control-Menu box to reveal the control menu. To close a window, simply double-click its Control-menu box.

Counter Data Type A type of field that stores unique, sequential numbers. Access assigns a numeric value to a counter field automatically as you add new records. The records are numbered sequentially (1, 2, 3, 4, 5, and so on). You cannot change the contents of a counter field. See pages 89 and 90–93. Pages 744–745 explain how to start a counter at a number other than 1.

Counter Field A field that has the Counter data type.

Criteria Conditions in a query or filter that specify which records you want to display. For example, you could set up query criteria to find customers in Cucamonga, California who haven't ordered left-handed widgets within the last six months. See pages 247–273.

Crosstab A query that computes summary totals based on values for each row and column. Crosstab queries answer questions like "What are my monthly sales by region?" "Who has ordered each of my products, and how many items of each product did they order?" See pages 325–332.

Cue Cards Cue Cards offer step-by-step coaching help to guide you through common tasks in Access. To display the Cue Cards main menu, choose **Help** ➤ **Cue** Cards from the menus or click the Cue Cards icon on the Help Table of Contents screen. See pages 116–117 and the inside front cover of this book.

Currency Data Type A type of field that stores numeric data representing dollar amounts. Access rounds values in currency fields to two decimal places and encloses negative values in parentheses automatically. See pages 89, 127, 194–197, 248, and 732.

Current Record The record you're using now.

Data Type The attribute of a field (or Access Basic variable) that determines what kind of data it can hold. Access supports the following data types: text, memo, number, currency, counter, date/time, yes/no, and OLE object. See pages 88–93.

Database A file that holds all the data and other things (objects) that suit a particular purpose. You could, for example, use one database to manage a mail-order flower business, another to manage your CD collection, and yet another to manage your personal investments. Database objects can include tables, queries, forms, reports, macros, and modules. See Chapter 3 and pages 97–98.

Database Window The window that appears when you open an Access database (**File ➤ O**pen Database). You can click the Table, Query, Form, Report, Macro, and Module buttons in the window to create and use objects in the database. See pages 29–30 and 56–57.

 Datasheet View The window that displays data in a row-and-column (tabular) format. The datasheet shows as many records and fields as will fit on the screen. You can use the scroll bars and options from the menu bar to scroll through and locate records. To return to Datasheet view from another view of your table, click the Datasheet button in the tool bar or choose **View ➤** Datasheet. See pages 125–126.

DBMS An acronym for "Database Management System." A DBMS is an application (or program) that you use to organize and analyze data that you've stored in a computer. Microsoft Access is an example of a DBMS. See Chapter 1.

DDE An acronym for "Dynamic Data Exchange." DDE sets up A "conversation" or link between two Microsoft Windows applications and provides a way to display one application's data in another application. In Access, DDE is useful for displaying results of spreadsheet calculations in a form or report. See pages 814–819; see also *OLE*.

Declarations Section The topmost level of an Access Basic module that appears before any Sub or Function procedures. The declarations section contains definitions for user-defined data types, global constants, and global variables. See pages 892–893.

Default A preset choice. That is, "what you get if you don't choose something else." You can change default settings if you wish. For example, "MS Sans Serif" is the default font for forms. But you can change this to any font that's available on your computer. Likewise, you can change the default size (pages 189–192), appearance (pages 193–201), and value for a field (pages 201–203) when you define or change the table structure.

Delete Query An action query that deletes whatever rows match criteria that you specify. Delete queries provide a fast, automatic way to delete a certain set of records from a table without disturbing other records that don't match the criteria. See pages 347–351.

Delimited Text File A text file that contains values separated by commas, tabs, semicolons, or other characters. You can import delimited text files into new or existing Access tables. See pages 785–791.

 Design View The window that allows you to design tables, queries, forms, and reports. You can click the Design View button in the tool bar or choose View ➤ Design to return to Design View from another view of your table. See pages 126 and 186–187.

Destination Document A document that contains a DDE link to an object in a source document. If you've linked a spreadsheet cell to an Access form, the form would be the *destination document*. The spreadsheet would be the *source document*, and the cell would be the *object* in the source document. See pages 814–819.

Detail Section The part of a form or report that displays records from your table or query. Also called the *detail band*. See pages 379 and 420–426.

Dialog Box A window that lets you select options or provide more information so that Access can carry out a command. Many dialog boxes include an OK button (that continues the command) and a Cancel button (that cancels the command).

DLL An acronym for "Dynamic-Link Library." A DLL contains routines (programs) that extend the abilities of Microsoft Access. For example, the file CUECARDS.DLL contains programs that display Access Cue Card help.

Domain A set of records. A table, query, or SQL statement can define the domain. You can use functions (called *domain aggregate functions*) to return statistical information about a specific domain. See pages 730–731.

Domain Aggregate Function A function that gathers (aggregates) statistical information about a set of records (a domain). Domain aggregate functions can calculate averages, counts, largest/smallest value, sums, standard deviations, variances, and so forth. See pages 730–731.

Double Data Type A type of number field that stores double-precision floating point numbers. Double-precision numbers range from -1.797×10^{308} to 1.797×10^{308}, can have up to 15 decimal places, and occupy 8 bytes of storage. This is the default for numbers. See pages 191–197 and 732.

Duplicate Key A value that already exists in the table's primary key field or in an index field that doesn't allow duplicates. Access won't allow you to enter duplicate key values into the table. See pages 175–176, 210–212.

Dynamic Data Exchange See *DDE*.

Dynaset An Access term for the set of records produced when you run a query or apply a filter. The dynaset looks like a table's datasheet view, but contains only the information you've requested. When you change records in a dynaset, Access updates the underlying tables automatically. See pages 239–240.

Embed What you do when you insert an object into a form or report. You can embed objects in these ways:

* Use the **Edit** ➤ Insert Object command (pages 173–174).
* Use copy and paste options on the Edit menu (see pages 168–173 and 803–819).
* Use the Graph tool to embed a graph in a form or report (see pages 594–603).

Equi-join A join that combines records from two tables that have matching values in a common field. Suppose two tables—Customers and Orders—each have a Customer ID field. An equi-join of these tables would match customers and the orders they placed. No information would appear about customers who haven't placed orders. See pages 275 and 285–287.

Event An action, such as a mouse click or key press, that Access can recognize and respond to. On a form, for instance, you can add a command button that runs a macro when you click the button. See Chapter 15.

Expression A calculation that results in a single value. An expression can contain any combination of Access operators, object names (identifiers), literal values, and constants. You can use expressions to set properties and action arguments, to set criteria or define calculated fields in queries, and to set conditions in macros. You can also use expressions in Access Basic. See Chapter 17.

Field A category of information that you store in a table. You could, for example, create Last Name, First Name, Address, City, State, and Phone fields in a Customer table. Fields appear as columns in a datasheet, and controls in a form. See pages 7–10, and Chapters 4–6.

Field List A small window or drop-down list that shows all the fields in an underlying table or query. You can display field lists in tables, forms, reports, and queries. See pages 126, 235–236, and 394–396.

Field Name The name that you assign to a field. A field name can have up to 64 characters (including letters, numbers, spaces, and some punctuation characters), and must be unique within the table. See pages 86–88.

Field Properties Attributes that affect a field's appearance or behavior. The properties for a field appear whenever you click that field name in a table's Design view. See pages 187–214.

Filter A temporary, instant query that you can use in form view to select and sort records. You can save a filter as a query, or use a query as a filter. See pages 400–402.

Font The typeface, point size, and weight used to display or print numbers, symbols, and alphabetic characters. For instance, "Lucida Handwriting, 12-point, Bold" describes a font. People often use the terms *font* and *typeface* interchangeably. See pages 145–146 and 391–392.

Footer Text and graphics shown at the bottom of each page, at the end of a form or report, or after a group of records. You can define page footers, form and report footers, and group footers. See pages 377, 379–380, 420–426, and 534–552.

Foreign Key A field or fields in one table that refer to the primary key field or fields in another table. The foreign key is the common field on the "many side" of a one-to-many relationship between two tables. See page 225.

Form A customized, on-screen document that makes it easy to enter, display, and edit fields in a table. You can design Access forms to resemble the paper forms you currently use in your business. See pages 10–13 and Chapters 9–11.

 Form Properties The appearance and behavior of the form as a whole. Examples of form properties include the form's caption and whether you can edit data in the form. To change form properties, choose **Edit** ➤ Select Form and then select options on the properties sheet in Design view. See pages 412–419.

 Form View A window that shows data on a form, one record at a time. Most people use Form view to add and change data in a table. See pages 147–151.

 FormWizard A tool that makes designing custom forms a snap. The FormWizards ask you questions and create the form based on your answers. You can further customize the completed form later, if you wish. See pages 48–51, 373–376, and 478–481.

Function An Access Basic procedure that returns a value. The *Date* function, for example, returns the current date, and the *FV* function returns the future value of an annuity. Access provides the following types of functions: financial, math, date/time, string, logical, aggregate (or summary), domain aggregate, and data type conversion. You can use functions in Access expressions or Access Basic programs. See pages 727–732.

GraphWizard A tool that simplifies the job of creating graphs in forms or reports. The GraphWizards ask you questions and create the graph based on your answers. You can further customize the completed graph later, if you wish. See Chapter 13.

Group *In a secure network system,* you can use groups to identify a collection of user accounts, each with its own group name and personal identification number (PIN). Permissions assigned to a group apply to all users in that group. See pages 841–842.

In a report, you can sort records and organize them into groups based on field values or ranges of values. Moreover, you can display introductory and summary data for each group. See pages 541–552.

In a query, you can use groups to categorize data and perform summary calculations. See pages 302–331.

 Group/Total ReportWizard A ReportWizard that lets you organize report data into groups. The report appears in tabular format with labels above each data column. The Wizard creates subtotals for each group and a grand total for all groups automatically. See pages 543–545.

Header Text and graphics shown at the top of each page, the beginning of a form or report, or before a group of records. You can define page headers, form and report headers, and group headers. See pages 377, 379–380, 420–426, and 534–552.

I-Beam The mouse pointer appears as an I-Beam when you move it through text. The word "I-beam" refers to the pointer's shape, which resembles the capital letter "I." You can move the I-Beam to a specific character and then click the mouse to position the insertion point.

Icon A miniature picture representing an object, concept, or tool. In Windows, icons often represent minimized applications or closed windows. Access uses icons to represent objects in the database (tables, queries, forms, etc.), to show the purpose of a tool on the tool bar, to show the source application for a linked or embedded object, and so forth. See pages 57, 764, and 873–874.

Index A feature that speeds up sorting and searching for data in a table. Access maintains each index in sorted order and keeps it in memory for quick retrieval. Primary key fields are indexed automatically. You can define additional index fields in the table's Design view. See pages 208–216.

Insertion Point The blinking vertical line that shows where Access will insert the next character you type. See pages 134–135 and the glossary entry for *I-Beam*.

Integer Data Type A type of number field that stores whole numbers. Integers range from –32,768 to 32,767, cannot include a decimal point, and occupy 2 bytes of storage. See pages 191–197 and 732.

Join A query operation that combines some or all records from multiple tables. Access supports three types of joins: *equi-join*, *outer join*, and *self-join*. See pages 273–293.

Key A general name for *key field*, *primary key*, or *foreign key*.

Key Field A common field that links two tables. For example, you can define a Customer ID field for both the Customers and Orders tables. Later, you can use this key field to match customers with their orders. See pages 65–67, 107, 225; see also *Foreign Key* and *Primary Key*.

Label A control on a form or report that displays descriptive text such as a title, caption, or instructions. See pages 426–428 and 432–433.

Left Join See *Outer Join*.

Link A connection between a source document and destination document. A link inserts a copy of the object from the source document into the destination document, and the two documents remain connected. Thus, changes to the linked object in the source document are also reflected in the destination document. Links provide a powerful and convenient way to share objects among Windows applications. See pages 168–173, 594–612, and 803–824.

List Box A control on a form that presents a list of possible choices. The list box, which is always open, consists of a list and an optional label. See pages 444–453.

Literal A value that's used exactly as you see it or type it. Examples of literals are the number *47*, the text *You want it when?*, the date *#11-09-53#*, and the constant *No*. You can use literals in expressions, and can assign literals to Access Basic constants or variables. See pages 718–720.

Macro A series of actions that you can play back. Macros make it easy to do time-consuming tasks quickly and automatically, often with just a mouse click or two. Chapter 14 explains how to create and use macros. Chapter 15 explains how to use macros with forms and reports.

Main/Subform FormWizard A FormWizard that makes it easy to create a multitable form. The main form is based on the table that's on the "one side" of a one-to-many relationship. The subform is based on the table on the "many side" of the relationship. The Main/Subform Wizard will ask you questions and create the main form and subform based on your answers. You can further customize the completed form later. See pages 478–481.

Make-Table Query A query that creates a new table from the results (the dynaset) of a previous query. Make-table queries provide a handy way to create "snapshots" of tables that you want to edit, print, graph, or cross-tabulate. They're also helpful when you need to export data to a non-relational application such as a spreadsheet. See pages 334 and 351–355.

Manual Link A type of *link* which requires that you tell Access to show changes in the destination document after the source document changes. See pages 808, 812, and the glossary entry for *Automatic Link*.

Many-to-Many A relationship where many records in one table might refer to many records in another, and vice versa. A classic example is a Customers and Products relationship, in which a customer can order many products, and each product can be ordered by many customers. Often we set up a third table as a go-between, so that we end up with two one-to-many relationships. For instance, we could use an Orders table as the go-between: here, Customers would have a one-to-many relationship with Orders and Orders would have a one-to-many relationship with Products. See pages 69–70.

Memo Data Type A type of field that stores large amounts of text (up to 32,000 characters). Memo fields are useful for storing job descriptions, product descriptions, journal abstracts, and other information that's too long to fit into a Text Data Type field. See pages 88, 91.

Menu A list of commands that you can select by clicking a menu name on the menu bar atop a form or window. See pages 656–657 for an explanation of how to have a macro select options from menus. See pages 876–879 to see how to create custom menus in an application.

Modal A type of form that prevents you from switching to another form until you close it. Most modal forms are dialog boxes, warnings, or pop-up forms. See pages 864 and 873.

Module A set of related Access Basic procedures. Each module can contain declarations, statements, and procedures that you store as a group and assign a module name. For instance, you could group general-purpose procedures into a module named *Utility*, or create a module named *Reservations* to handle reservations for a travel agency. See pages 891–900.

Mouse Pointer The mouse pointer shows what your mouse is pointing to and moves across the screen as you slide your mouse. The shape of the mouse pointer changes in various parts of the screen to let you know what the mouse will do if you click or drag it at that point. See page 384.

Move Handle A square that appears at the top left edge of a control when you draw or select it in Design view. You can drag a move handle to move the control. See pages 381, 383–384; see also *Sizing Handle*.

Network A group of connected computers that can share data, programs, printers, and other devices. Users on networks can often communicate with one another via electronic mail. Access provides many safeguards to protect data from being clobbered or viewed by unauthorized users in a multiuser environment. See Chapter 20 and pages 910–923.

Normalize The steps you take to avoid storing redundant information in related tables of a database. In a normalized database, every field describes a uniquely defined record, non-key fields do not depend on other non-key fields, and you repeat only the key fields that link related tables. See page 79; see also *Foreign Key*, *Key Field*, *Primary Key*.

Null Field A blank (empty) field that contains no data. You can use the Null constant to test for null fields. Note that a zero value is different from a null value. See pages 511, 513, and 719–720.

Null Propagation What happens when any part of an arithmetic expression is null: the null values carry over (propagate) to other expressions that use those values. Thus, if any part of an arithmetic expression is null, the result will be null. Likewise, other calculations that refer to the null result will also be blank. See page 511.

Number Data Type A type of field that stores numbers that you can use in mathematical calculations. See pages 88–89, 127, 191–197, 718, and 731–732. See also pages 744–745 for an explanation of converting number fields to counter fields.

Object Any element of a database system. Access recognizes the following types of objects:

- controls and database components, including tables, queries, forms, reports, macros, and modules
- special system objects used in Access Basic programming
- linked or embedded objects such as a graph, drawing, spreadsheet cell, table, and so forth

See pages 56–57, 742–743, 773–778, 803–824, and 845–849.

Object Linking and Embedding See *OLE*.

ODBC An acronym for "Open Database Connectivity." ODBC is an optional set of Microsoft drivers that lets you connect to and use data from SQL database servers, such as Oracle and SQL Server. See pages 771 and 917–923.

  OLE An acronym for "Object Linking and Embedding." You can use OLE to link or embed an object (such as a graph or spreadsheet) from its source document to a destination document. OLE lets Windows applications share objects with one another. To update (or play or run) an OLE object, you can usually double-click it—either in the source document or the destination document. See pages 168–175, 462–463, 599–603, 610–612, and 803–824.

OLE Client An application that can accept embedded or linked objects. Access, Write, and Cardfile are client applications. See *OLE*.

OLE Object An object that can be linked with or embedded into another application document. See *OLE*.

OLE Server An application that can create objects that you link or embed into other documents. Paintbrush, Sound Recorder, and Microsoft Excel are examples of OLE servers. See *OLE*.

One-to-Many A relationship between two tables in which each record in the first table can be associated with many records in the second table. Customers and Orders illustrate a common example of a one-to-many relationship: each customer can place many orders. See pages 64–68.

One-to-One A relationship between two tables in which each record in the first table can be associated with exactly one record in the second table. A one-to-one relationship usually suggests a poor database design. See pages 71–72.

Operator A symbol or word that shows the type of operation you want to perform on a value. For example, in the expression **>5000**

(greater than 5000), the operator is **>**. In the expression **Hot OR Cold** (either "Hot" or "Cold"), the operator is **OR**. See pages 249–252 and 720–723.

 Option Button A control on a form that works like a station selector button on a radio. (For this reason, it is also known as a "radio button.") When selected, an option button contains a dot and inserts the value Yes (or −1) into the underlying table field. When cleared, the option button is empty and inserts No (or 0) into the field. See pages 438–441.

Option Group A control on a form that frames a set of check boxes, option buttons, or toggle buttons. You can use option groups to provide a limited set of alternative values to choose (e.g., Cash, Check, or Credit Card). The selected option will store a number in the underlying table field. Therefore, if you select the first button in an option group, Access will store the number 1 in the field; if you select the second button, Access stores 2; and so forth. See pages 440–444.

Outer Join A join that shows all records from one table, and only those records in the second table that have matching key field values. In a Left (Outer) Join, the left-hand table contributes all the records. In a Right (Outer) Join, the right-hand table contributes all the records. See pages 287–290.

Page 1. The portion of the database (.MDB file) where Access stores record data. Each page may contain more than one record, depending on the size of the records.

2. A screenful of data in a form or a page in a report. See pages 467–468 and 554–555.

 Page Break A place in your form or report where you've used the Page Break tool to start a new screenful of data or a new page. In reports, you can also force a new page to print before a section, after a section, or both. See pages 467–468 and 535–537.

 Palette A dialog box that lets you choose the color, special effects (raised or sunken), border, and width for a control on a form or report. See page 393.

Parameter Query A flexible type of query that prompts for criteria when you run it. Instead of specifying actual values when you create a parameter query, you use placeholders called parameters. Later, when you run the query, you'll be prompted to type in the values you want to display. See pages 358–363, and 871.

Paste Errors Table A table that Access creates when it can't paste in one or more records from the Clipboard. The Paste Errors table will appear in the database window and will include all the records that Access couldn't paste. See page 168.

Permissions What users can and cannot do with a database table, query, form, report, macro, or module. Permissions are most useful in network environments where you must restrict access to some users but not to others. See pages 845–850.

PIN An acronym for "Personal Identification Number." Like the PIN assigned to your automatic teller banking card, an Access PIN secures data against unauthorized use. On a secure network database, each user has a login name, four-digit PIN, and password that grant access to a database. Each Access group also has a name and a PIN. See pages 836–844.

Pixel An abbreviation for "picture element." A pixel is a dot that represents the smallest graphic unit your screen can display.

Point The unit typically used to measure font sizes. There are 72 points in one inch. See page 391.

 Pointer The arrow-shaped tool at the top of the report and form design toolbox. You use the pointer to select a control in the form or report Design view. See pages 426–427.

Also, an indicator (such as an arrow) that shows what your mouse is pointing at. The shape of the pointer changes in different parts of the screen to reflect the task you can perform at that moment. See page 384.

Pop-Up Form A window, dialog box, or submenu that stays on top of other windows. The tool bar and Palette are examples of pop-up forms.

You can create custom pop-up dialog boxes and tool bars when you design an Access form. See pages 865 and 873.

Preview See *Print Preview*.

Primary Key A field or fields whose values uniquely identify each record in a table. The primary key can help Access manage data more efficiently because:

- It prevents duplicate entries in primary key fields.
- It sorts records based on values in primary key fields.
- It speeds up sorting and searching.

See pages 95–97, 102–105, and 215–216.

Print Preview A "look before you print" feature that lets you preview a report on screen before you print it. Both the database window and report Design view provide Print Preview buttons. See pages 526 and 533–534.

Procedure A command or routine that you write in Access Basic. You can create two types of procedures:

- *functions*, which accept and return values;
- *subs* (subroutines), which perform actions but do not return values.

See pages 891–900.

Property A characteristic of a control, field, or database object that affects its appearance or behavior. Typical properties include size, color, screen location, whether you can update a control, and whether a control is visible. See pages 187–214, 412–419, 428–430, 468–469, 487, 535–539, 603–605, and 819–823.

Property Sheet The window that lets you view or change properties of the selected object. You can click the Properties button to display the window. See *Property*.

QBE An acronym for "Query by Example." QBE is a graphical technique that lets you design a query. With QBE, you create an *example* of the fields to show, calculations to perform, and sort order to use. See Chapters 7 and 8.

QBE Grid The grid that appears in the lower part of the Query window. You use the QBE grid to define a query. See Chapters 7 and 8.

Query A question that you ask about data or an action you perform on data. You can create four types of queries:

1. *select queries*, which display a set of records (called a dynaset), that answer questions about your data;

2. *action queries*, which change, delete, or move data;

3. *crosstab queries*, which compute summary totals based on table values;

4. *parameter queries*, which prompt you to type in criteria when you run the query.

See Chapters 7 and 8.

Query by Example See *QBE*.

RDBMS An acronym for "Relational Database Management System." An RDBMS manages information that's organized into one or more tables. You can "connect" or "relate" the tables by common fields, such as a Customer ID or Product Number. See pages 6–7.

Read-Only A property of a field, record, or database that allows you to view data but not change it. See pages 417, 419, 468–471, and 831–832.

Reboot To restart your computer, often by pressing Ctrl+Alt+Del or a reset button. (Caution: Information that isn't saved yet or that's stored on a RAM disk is lost when you reboot the computer.)

Record A collection of related data (fields) that describes a single item (row) in a table. A customer record, for example, might consist of the customer's first and last name, address, city, state, zip code, telephone number, and FAX number. See pages 7–9 and Chapter 5.

Record Number Box A small box that shows the word "Record" followed by the current record number. The box appears at the lower left corner of the datasheet, query, or form window. To move to a specific record, type the record number in the box and press ↵. See pages 132–133.

Referential Integrity The rules that ensure data integrity by preserving relationships between tables when you enter, change, or delete records. For example, referential integrity rules will not let you add records to an Orders table unless corresponding records already exist in the Customers table. See pages 217–225.

Refresh To update your screen with the latest changes made by other users on the network. Access will automatically refresh your view of the data at regular intervals. You can also force Access to refresh your screen manually, so that you're sure to see the most up to date information. See pages 834–835.

Relational Database A database that stores data in one or more tables (rows and columns). Relational databases provide an efficient and non-redundant way to store and manage data. See pages 6–7, 14–18, and the glossary entry for *RDBMS*.

Relationship The connection between common fields (columns) in two tables. You can define a one-to-one, one-to-many, or many-to-many relationship between tables. See Chapter 3.

Report A formatted presentation of data that's meant to be printed. Generally, reports show data from multiple records in an attractively arranged format. See pages 53–56 and Chapters 12 and 15.

ReportWizard A tool that simplifies the job of designing custom reports. The ReportWizards ask you questions and create the report based on your answers. You can further customize the completed report later. See pages 53–55, 525–526, and 806.

Right (Outer) Join See *Outer Join*.

Row The visual presentation of a record in a datasheet, query, or filter window. A relational database stores data in tables, which are arranged into horizontal rows (records) and vertical columns (fields). See pages 6–7.

Row Selector A small box or bar that you can click to select an entire row when you design a table or macro. (Also called a *field selector*.) See pages 100–101 and 630.

Rulers You can use on-screen rulers to align controls horizontally or vertically when you design a form or report. To hide or display rulers, choose View ➤ Ruler. See pages 377–378.

Search A way to find data without having to scroll around for it. You can also search for and change (replace) data globally. Search and replace are available in the datasheet and form view windows and when you run queries. See pages 152–158, 256–267, and 747.

Search Help You can click the Search button in Help to find topics that pertain to a word or phrase you specify. See pages 115–117.

Section Part of a form or report, such as the header, footer, or detail section. See pages 377, 379–380, 420–426, and 534–552.

Secure System An Access database that requires you to type in a correct user name and password before you can use it. Secure systems are most useful on networks where people need to share data and protect it from prying eyes. See Chapter 20.

Select Query A query that asks a question about your data and returns a *dynaset* (result) without changing the data. See Chapter 7; see also *Dynaset* and *Action Query*.

Self-Join A table that's joined to itself in a query. For example, if a part consists of other parts, you could identify the "parts of a part" using a self-join on a Parts table. See pages 291–293.

Shortcut Key A function key or key combination that you can use instead of choosing a sequence of options from menus. For instance, Ctrl+X is a shortcut key for the menu sequence **E**dit ➤ Cut. See pages 28 and 882–885.

 Show All Records The Show All Records button (or **R**ecords ➤ **S**how All Records) displays all records in the underlying table or query. This feature removes any filter that you applied previously in form view. See page 400.

 Single Step A way to run through a macro (or Access Basic procedure) one step at a time so that you can find out exactly what's happening at each stage. Click the Single Step button or choose **M**acro ➤ **S**ingle Step, then run the macro as usual. See pages 642–644.

Sizing Handle A small square that appears on the edge of a control when you draw or select it in Design view. You can drag a sizing handle to resize the control. See pages 381 and 386; see also *Move Handle*.

Sort A process that rearranges records into a new order. You can sort records using queries, using filters in form view, or using group headers and footers in a report design. See pages 44, 243–247, 400, 541–552, and 747.

Special Character A foreign-language or other special character that you can type into any text or memo field. Because these odd characters don't appear on your keyboard, you'll need to use special typing techniques or the Windows Character Map to enter them. See pages 128–130.

SQL An acronym for "Structured Query Language" (pronounced *sequel*). A high-level language to create, update, and manage relational databases. You can choose View ➤ SQL in the query window to view or write Access queries as SQL statements. You can use SQL within Access, and to import and export data between Access and SQL servers. See pages 363–364, 456–458, 609, 771–772, 799–800, and 917–923.

Standard Deviation A statistical measurement equal to the square root of the variance. You can use the standard deviation operator (StDev) in a query to perform a summary calculation on a group of records. See pages 303, 729, and 731.

Status Bar The horizontal bar at the bottom of the screen that shows information about commands, buttons, and other options. Look here for useful information about what you're doing at the moment. See pages 38 and 746.

String A collection of numbers and text characters. For example, the characters "CRE8 a string" form a string. See pages 252, 269–270, 555–556, 728, and 732.

 Subform A form that's inside another form or report. You can use subforms to combine data from multiple related tables onto a form or report. See Chapter 11 and page 726.

 Subreport A report that's inside another report. You can use subreports to combine data from multiple related tables onto a report. See Chapter 11.

Syntax The rules (or "grammar") you must follow when entering a statement or expression. You get a *syntax error* if you break a syntax rule.

System Object An internal object that Access defines. System objects, which usually are invisible, begin with the letters *MSys* (as in *MSys-Indexes*). See pages 746–747 and 753–754.

Tab Order The order in which you move from one field or button to another when you press the Tab or Shift+Tab key. To control the tab order, switch to form design view and choose **Edit** ➤ **Tab** Order. See pages 403–404.

Table A collection of information that's neatly organized into rows (records) and columns (fields). See pages 7–9 and Chapters 4, 5, and 6.

 Text Box A control in a form or report that lets you view or enter text. See pages 426–427 and 434–438.

Text Data Type A type of field that stores any combination of letters, numbers, spaces, and other symbols, up to 255 characters. See pages 88, 91, and the glossary entry for *Memo Data Type*.

Title Bar The bar at the top of a window that displays the window's name.

 Toggle Button A control in a form or report that acts as an on/off (or Yes/No) button. When the button is sunken (depressed), the underlying table field has the value Yes or −1. When it is raised, the field's value is No or 0. See pages 438–441.

Tool Bar A horizontal bar of buttons at the top of an Access window (the buttons vary from one window to the next). You can click a button instead of choosing the equivalent options from the window's menus. You also can create custom tool bars. See pages 126, 747, 873–876, and the inside back cover of this book.

Toolbox A floating vertical bar of tools that you can use to create or select controls in a form or report. To find out how to use a tool, click on it in the toolbox and press F1. See pages 426–468 and the inside back cover of this book.

 Totals A totals query displays totals or summary calculations for data in one or more tables. You can also calculate totals and subtotals in forms and reports. See pages 234, 302–325, and 556–566.

Twip A unit of measure used by Access to very precisely address locations on the screen. A twip is equal to $\frac{1}{20}$ of a pixel.

Unbound Control A control that isn't bound (tied to) the underlying table. You can use unbound controls to display titles, pictures, graphs, shapes, and other items that decorate your form or report but aren't tied to the table's data. See pages 380 and 804–824.

 Unbound Object Frame A control in a form or report that stores objects that aren't in the underlying table. Unbound objects do not change from record to record. You can use them to display the same pictures, sounds, spreadsheet cells, graphs, and other objects throughout a form or report. See pages 803–824.

Uniqueness Access usually shows all records that match your query criteria, even if the results would include duplicate values. To avoid repeating the duplicates, you can choose **View** ➤ Query Properties and check Unique Values Only. See pages 271-273.

Update (Automatic) You can use queries, macros, and other objects to update tables automatically and streamline your day-to-day management tasks. For instance, you can update inventory automatically when new items arrive at the warehouse. Or you can automatically generate dunning letters to deadbeat customers who owe you money. See Chapter 16.

Validation Rule A rule that restricts the values you can enter into a field. Access will display an appropriate error message if you enter data that violates the validation rule. You can specify validation rules when you design a table or form. See pages 177, 189, 203–207, 414–415.

Value The contents of a field. For instance, "Smythe-Browne" is a possible value for the Last Name field in a table.

Variable A placeholder used in Access Basic to store data that can change as the code runs. See pages 893–895.

Variance A statistical calculation defined as the square of the standard deviation. You can use the variance operator Var in a query to perform a summary calculation on a group of records. See pages 303 and 730–731.

Variant A catch-all data type used in Access Basic. Variant variables can accept data of any data type. See pages 732 and 894–895.

View A window that presents your Access object(s) in a special way in order to make certain types of tasks easier. You can:

- Design objects in *Design view.*
- Change and view data in table format in *Datasheet view.*

- Change and view data in a form in *Form view.*
- Preview data as it will appear when printed in *Print Preview.*

See pages 56–57.

WHERE Clause Part of a SQL statement that specifies which records to retrieve. WHERE clauses reflect criteria that you define in your query. See pages 363–364.

Wildcard Character You can use wildcard characters—**? * # [ ] -** and **!**—to broaden a search for text in a find, replace, or query operation. For instance, the wildcard pattern **9### Oak** would match any address between *9000 Oak* and *9999 Oak.* See pages 155–156, 249, 251, 253–255.

Yes/No Data Type A type of field that can store only one of two possible values, such as Yes or No, True or False, On or Off, −1 or 0. See pages 89, 127, 150, 200, 211, and 438.

Zoom An expanded text box that lets you enter expressions or text more conveniently. You can press Shift+F2 to open a zoom box in property sheets and in the grid in various Access windows. See pages 204, 258, and 437–438.

You can "zoom" in Print Preview to switch between a close-up and full-page view of the report page (pages 533–534).

Finally, OLE objects have a Scaling property called "Zoom" that grows or shrinks the object to fit its frame, but keeps the proportions the same (page 821).

INDEX

Note to the Reader: **Boldface** page numbers indicate chapter sections in which the item is the main topic of discussion. *Italic* page numbers indicate illustrations.

Symbols

M

Help Yourself with
Another Quality Sybex Book

Windows Magic Tricks
Judd Robbins

This book/disk combination brings you over 60 engaging, amusing, mesmerizing, and useful Windows programs, gleaned from dozens of shareware and freeware sources. Install the programs, then flip through the book to learn how to get the most fun out of each one.

200pp; 7 1/2" x 9"
ISBN: 0-7821-1119-X

Available at Better Bookstores Everywhere

Sybex Inc.
2021 Challenger Drive
Alameda, CA 94501
Telephone (800) 227-2346
Fax (510) 523-2373

Sybex. Help Yourself.

SYBEX

FREE BROCHURE!

Complete this form today, and we'll send you a full-color brochure of Sybex bestsellers.

Please supply the name of the Sybex book purchased.

_____

How would you rate it?

_____ Excellent   _____ Very Good   _____ Average   _____ Poor

Why did you select this particular book?

_____ Recommended to me by a friend

_____ Recommended to me by store personnel

_____ Saw an advertisement in _____

_____ Author's reputation

_____ Saw in Sybex catalog

_____ Required textbook

_____ Sybex reputation

_____ Read book review in _____

_____ In-store display

_____ Other _____

Where did you buy it?

_____ Bookstore

_____ Computer Store or Software Store

_____ Catalog (name: _____)

_____ Direct from Sybex

_____ Other: _____

Did you buy this book with your personal funds?

_____ Yes   _____ No

About how many computer books do you buy each year?

_____ 1-3   _____ 3-5   _____ 5-7   _____ 7-9   _____ 10+

About how many Sybex books do you own?

_____ 1-3   _____ 3-5   _____ 5-7   _____ 7-9   _____ 10+

Please indicate your level of experience with the software covered in this book:

_____ Beginner   _____ Intermediate   _____ Advanced

Which types of software packages do you use regularly?

_____ Accounting	_____ Databases	_____ Networks
_____ Amiga	_____ Desktop Publishing	_____ Operating Systems
_____ Apple/Mac	_____ File Utilities	_____ Spreadsheets
_____ CAD	_____ Money Management	_____ Word Processing
_____ Communications	_____ Languages	_____ Other _____ (please specify)

Which of the following best describes your job title?

_____ Administrative/Secretarial _____ President/CEO

_____ Director _____ Manager/Supervisor

_____ Engineer/Technician _____ Other _____
(please specify)

Comments on the weaknesses/strengths of this book: _____

_____

_____

_____

_____

Name _____

Street _____

City/State/Zip _____

Phone _____

PLEASE FOLD, SEAL, AND MAIL TO SYBEX

SYBEX, INC.
Department M
2021 CHALLENGER DR.
ALAMEDA, CALIFORNIA USA
94501

SYBEX

SEAL

Tools for Designing Forms and Reports

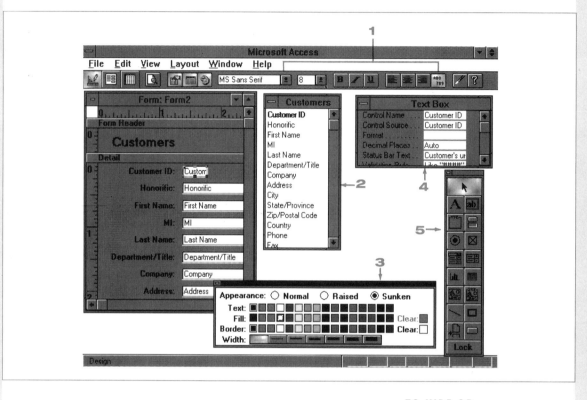

	DESCRIPTION	**TO HIDE OR DISPLAY TOOL**
1	Font, appearance, alignment	Select control(s)
2	*Field list:* Drag field names to the form/report	
3	*Color palette:* Choose colors, borders, special appearance effects	
4	*Properties sheet:* Define control names, expressions, formats, other properties	
5	*Toolbox:* Create pictures, labels, calculated controls, graphical controls	View ► Toolbox